ISLAM IN PAKISTAN

PRINCETON STUDIES IN MUSLIM POLITICS

DALE F. EICKELMAN AND AUGUSTUS RICHARD NORTON,
SERIES EDITORS

A list of titles in this series can be found at the back of the book

Islam in Pakistan

A HISTORY

Muhammad Qasim Zaman

PRINCETON UNIVERSITY PRESS
PRINCETON & OXFORD

Published by Princeton University Press,
41 William Street, Princeton, New Jersey 08540

In the United Kingdom: Princeton University Press,
6 Oxford Street, Woodstock, Oxfordshire OX20 1TR

press.princeton.edu

Jacket photograph: Ed Kashi, 1997 / National Geographic Creative

Library of Congress Cataloging-in-Publication Data

Names: Zaman, Muhammad Qasim, author.
Title: Islam in Pakistan : a history / Muhammad Qasim Zaman.
Description: Princeton, N.J. : Princeton University Press, [2018] | Series: Princeton studies
    in Muslim politics | Includes bibliographical references and index.
Identifiers: LCCN 2017039100 | ISBN 9780691149226 (hardcover : alk. paper)
Subjects: LCSH: Islam—Pakistan—History. | Islam and state—Pakistan.
Classification: LCC BP63.P2 Z36 2018 | DDC 297.095491—dc23 LC record available at
    https://lccn.loc.gov/2017039100

British Library Cataloging-in-Publication Data is available

This book has been composed in Miller

Printed on acid-free paper. ∞

Printed in the United States of America

10 9 8 7 6 5 4 3 2 1

For Shaista

CONTENTS

ACKNOWLEDGMENTS

MANY PEOPLE AND INSTITUTIONS have assisted me in the course of my work on this book. I am grateful above all to Shaista Azizalam and to our children, Zaynab and Mustafa, for continuing to enrich my life with their love and companionship. I owe a great debt as well to my sister and brother-in-law, Rabia Umar Ali and Umar Ali Khan, for hosting my visits to Islamabad with their unmatched hospitality and for facilitating my research in Pakistan. I would not have been able to carry out my work without their help. My nephews and nieces, too—Valeed and Moosa, Ayesha, and Rahem and Samah—have been the source of much joy and hope, for which I am grateful.

I would like to thank Megan Brankley Abbas, Sarah Ansari, the late Zafar Ishaq Ansari, Michael Cook, Eric Gregory, M. Şükrü Hanioğlu, Robert W. Hefner, Husain Kaisrani, Muhammad Saeed Khurram, Sajid Mehmood, Steve Millier, Hossein Modarressi, Gyan Prakash, Ali Usman Qasmi, and Qamar-uz-Zaman for their help with accessing research materials and, in several cases, for answering my queries and providing valuable feedback. The writing of this book has been made possible by a grant from the Guggenheim Foundation as well as research leave and other support from Princeton University. I am much indebted to these institutions. I wish also to thank the library staff at the various places in Pakistan, India, the United Kingdom, and the United States where I have carried out my research. In particular, I wish to thank David Magier, other members of the staff of the Firestone Library at Princeton University, and all those working behind the scenes at its interlibrary loan and Borrow Direct offices for attending to my requests with great courtesy and efficiency. My students, undergraduate as well as graduate, have been instrumental in helping me try new approaches, deepen my knowledge, and explain things better. For this I am very grateful.

Some of the material on which this book is based was presented as lectures at Boston University; the Davis Center for Historical Studies at Princeton University; Northwestern University; the School of Oriental and African Studies, University of London; the University of Chicago; and the Yale Law School. I thank the organizers of those events for their invitations—in particular, Owen Fiss, Robert Gleave, Brannon Ingram, Anthony Kronman, Philip Nord, Tina Purohit, Mariam Shaibani, Zayn Siddique, SherAli Tareen, and Amir Toft—and their audiences for their comments and questions. I also thank Indiana University Press and Cambridge University Press for permission to use, in revised form, some of the material I have previously published as the following articles: "Islamic Modernism, Ethics, and the Shari`a in Pakistan," in Robert W. Hefner, ed., *Shari`a Law and Modern Muslim Ethics* (Bloomington: Indiana University Press, 2016); "Pakistan: Shari`a and the State," in Robert W. Hefner, ed., *Shari`a Politics: Islamic Law and Society in the Muslim World* (Bloomington: Indiana University Press, 2011); and "The Sovereignty of God in Modern Islamic Thought," *Journal of the Royal Asiatic Society*, 3rd ser., 25 (2015).

Over the course of many years, Fred Appel, my editor at Princeton University Press, has offered support, encouragement, and much astute advice. It has been a privilege and a pleasure to work on this and other projects with an editor of such remarkable abilities. Feedback from the outside readers has helped improve this book in some important ways; I am deeply appreciative of their careful and sensitive reading and their counsel. I would like to also thank Sara Lerner, who has shepherded this book through production with her characteristic thoughtfulness, skill, and efficiency. I am especially glad to have had the opportunity to work with her a second time. I wish as well to acknowledge Thalia Leaf, Theresa Liu, and many others at Princeton University Press for their assistance with various matters related to this book. I owe a special debt to Jennifer Harris, whose keen eye and expert advice in copyediting the manuscript have helped turn it into a much better book.

Shaista has long been my mainstay. She has patiently fostered the conditions that have allowed me to bring this work to fruition. As a small token of my gratitude for this and for much else, I dedicate this book to her.

A NOTE ON TRANSLITERATION, SPELLING, ABBREVIATIONS, AND OTHER CONVENTIONS

THIS BOOK USES a system of transliteration that often reflects Urdu pronunciation of Arabic and Persian words and names. In cases where a proper name is spelled by the person concerned in a particular way in English, that spelling has usually been retained—hence, Liaquat Ali Khan rather than Liyaqat `Ali Khan; Abdul Hakim rather than `Abd al-Hakim; Ayub Khan rather than Ayyub Khan, and so forth. In some cases, however, the English and the Arabic spellings of a name have had to be distinguished from each other: thus Mawdudi when referring to the Urdu titles of his books and Maududi when citing the English translations.

With the exception of the ` to signify the Arabic letter `ayn (as in `Umar or shari`a) and ' to represent the *hamza* (as in Qur'an), diacritics are not used in this book. The hamza itself is used when it occurs within a word (as in Qur'an) but not when it occurs at the end (thus `ulama rather than `ulama'). With the notable exception of the term `ulama (singular: `alim), the plural forms are usually indicated by adding an "s" to the word in the singular, as in madrasas (rather than madaris) or fatwas (rather than fatawa). Certain terms that occur repeatedly in the book, such as shari`a and `ulama, are not italicized. Other Arabic and Urdu words are italicized at their first occurrence, but usually not afterward. When the fuller version of an Arab name is not being used, I also dispense with the Arabic definite article "al-" (for example, Fakhr al-din al-Razi but subsequently Razi).

Unless otherwise noted, translated passages from the Qur'an follow M.A.S. Abdel Haleem, *The Qur'an: A New Translation* (Oxford, UK: Oxford University Press, 2004), and, less often, A. J. Arberry, *The Koran Interpreted*, 2 vols. (New York: Simon & Schuster, 1996), with occasional modifications.

The following abbreviations are used in this book:

AFM	Archives of the Freedom Movement
AISC	All India Shi`a Conference
BL	British Library
BPC	Basic Principles Committee
CAPD	*Constituent Assembly of Pakistan Debates*
CF	Cabinet Files
CRO	Commonwealth Relations Office
GAPP	Ghulam Ahmad Parwez Papers
JP	*Jinnah Papers*
JUI	Jam`iyyat al-`Ulama-i Islam

MMA   Muttahida Majlis-i `Amal
NAP   National Archives of Pakistan
NAPD   *National Assembly of Pakistan Debates*
NDC   National Documentation Center, Cabinet Division, Islamabad
NWFP   North-West Frontier Province
PMS   Prime Minister's Secretariat
PPP   Pakistan People's Party
Q   Qur'an
RAC   Rockefeller Archives Center, Sleepy Hollow, New York
TNA   The National Archives, Kew
UP   United Provinces

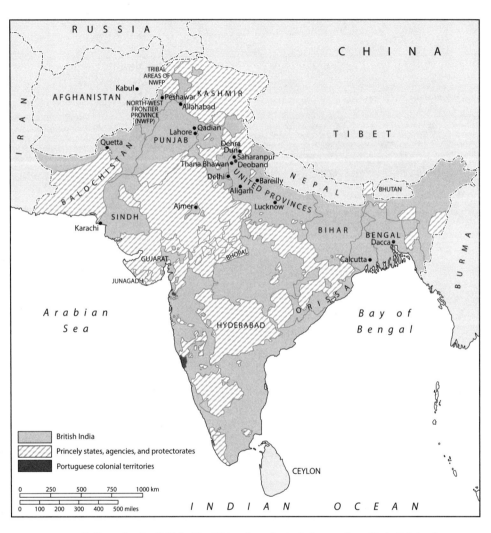

MAP 1. India under the British, identifying the principal places referred to in this book.

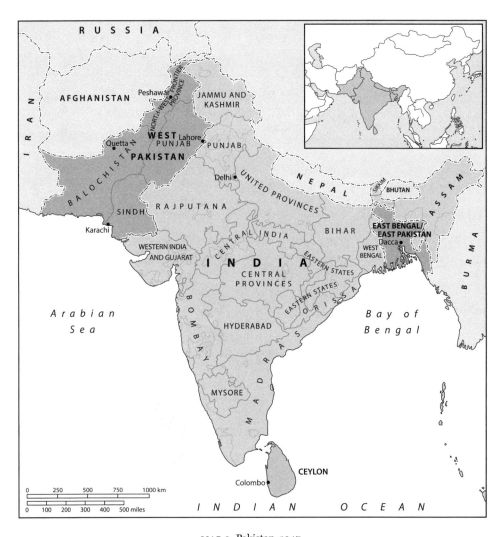

MAP 2. Pakistan, 1947.

MAP 3. Pakistan today, identifying the principal places mentioned in this book.

ISLAM IN PAKISTAN

Introduction

THIS BOOK IS CONCERNED with the history of, and the contestations on, Islam in colonial India and Pakistan. The first modern Muslim state to be established in the name of Islam, Pakistan was the largest Muslim country in the world at the time of its foundation; today, it is the second most populous, after Indonesia. All the key facets of modern Islam worldwide were well represented in colonial India and they have continued to be so in Pakistan: Sufism; traditionalist scholars, the `ulama, and their institutions of learning, the madrasas; Islamism; and Islamic modernism. Several of them received their earliest and what proved to be highly influential articulations in this vast region. It was in colonial India, for instance, that some of the first modernist Muslim intellectuals had emerged, and their work soon came to resonate well beyond South Asia.[1] Sayyid Abul-A`la Mawdudi (d. 1979), whose career straddled British India and the first three decades of Pakistan, was, for his part, one of the most influential Islamist ideologues of the twentieth century. South Asia did not pioneer madrasas, but few countries match the growth that this institution and those associated with it have witnessed over the course of Pakistan's history. It is in Pakistan, too, that the movement of the Taliban emerged in the years following the withdrawal of Soviet troops from Afghanistan. And in the aftermath of the terrorist attacks of September 11, 2001, Pakistan has been not only a major front in the global War on Terror but also the site of an Islamist radicalism that has had important implications for contemporary Islam, and not just in South Asia.

As one might expect, there is a significant body of literature on different facets of Islam in colonial South Asia and in Pakistan. What is lacking is a work that brings them together within the confines of a single study.[2] Such studies have seldom been attempted for other regions of the Muslim world either. This is hardly surprising, given that the examination of any particular facet, whether Islamism or the Islam of the `ulama, already poses enough challenges to allow a venture very far beyond it. Yet, the sum of more specialized studies can fall considerably short of meeting the need for a broader view of the religious landscape. This book is an effort in that direction. How have various facets of Islam interacted with one another and with a state created in the name of Islam? How are the different Islamic orientations to be distinguished from one another? What sort of constraints have the differences among them placed on the ability of their adherents to join hands at particular moments in history? How significantly and to what effect had the various religious orientations that occupied the South Asian Islamic landscape at the beginning of the twentieth century changed in relation to one another by the early twenty-first century? What is the context, both immediate and long term, in which Islamist militancy has emerged in Pakistan? What has hampered the ability of the governing elite to effectively combat it? And why has Islamic modernism undergone a decline in the course of Pakistan's history, as I would argue it has? These are among the questions I address in this book.

Though the scope of this study is necessarily broad, certain facets of Muslim religious life have had to remain largely unattended here. How Islamic beliefs and practices are reflected in and shaped by poetry and fictional literature, art, media, and film falls, with some exceptions, outside the scope of this book. So does the lived practice of Islam. It would take extensive ethnographic work, not attempted for this study, to shed light, for instance, on the nature and meaning of devotional practices at Sufi shrines or how such shrines participate in the political economy of the region in which they are located. The question of how madrasas are viewed in or sustained by the local communities among which they operate likewise requires the kind of work that lies beyond the ambition and scope of this study. By the same token, questions relating to the religious beliefs of ordinary women and men and the changes their understandings of the faith have undergone would have to depend not only on microlevel studies but also on large-scale surveys, neither of which exist in abundance for Pakistan.

This is not intellectual history in the narrow sense of being concerned only with a history of ideas; it is keenly interested in the political and other contexts in which particular ideas developed and why certain understandings of Islam found themselves disadvantaged vis-à-vis others. Nor does it posit any sharp distinction between belief and practice, between normative and lived Islam.[3] Yet, it does rely more often than not on written expressions of Islam, of debate and contestation on it, of the development and change it has continued to undergo. It is therefore more attentive to the discourses and the initiatives of those aspiring to shape people's religious and political life than it is to those whose lives were presumably being informed or shaped by such discourses. Once again, however, the barriers between these two sides look firmer in outward appearance than they may be in reality. Official archives, too, can shed much light on life, thought, and agency at the grassroots, after all. For instance, the extensive records of the Court of Inquiry that the government of the Punjab had established in the aftermath of a religio-political agitation directed against the Ahmadis, a heterodox community, in 1953 is an unusually rich resource for an understanding not only of the views of the modernist elite governing the new state but also of the perspectives of the religio-political groups that had been involved in the agitation. We also get occasional glimpses in these records of small-time mosque-preachers, local leaders, and ordinary people caught up in it. An archive such as this, despite its focus on one particular set of events, has much to say about varied facets of Islam in Pakistan and that is how I have utilized it here.[4] When it comes to state legislation, to take another example, we may not always know very well how particular initiatives relating to Islam actually shaped people's lives. But even here, what we can try to understand is not only what vision animated those legislative initiatives but also what responses they evoked from members of particular religious groups and how the initiatives and the responses in question have shaped a contested religious sphere in colonial India and in Pakistan.

If not all facets of Islam can be accommodated into this study, not all even among those represented here can obviously occupy center stage. That belongs to Islamic modernism, which I understand as a complex of religious, intellectual, and political initiatives aimed at adapting Islam—its beliefs, practices, laws, and institutions—to the challenges of life in the modern world. Such challenges were felt most forcefully under European colonial rule. Late nineteenth- and early twentieth-century modernists—and not just the Muslims among them, though it is on them that I focus here—had internalized to various degrees colonial assessments of the societies under European governance. These were seen, in contrast with the European world, as tradition-bound, stagnant, priest-ridden, and superstitious; their laws as antiquated, capricious, and barbaric; their precolonial rulers as corrupt and despotic; their intellectual cultures as decadent, and their systems of education as devoid of useful knowledge.[5] Defeat at the hands of the European powers had exposed the hollowness of traditional norms, practices, and structures, showing them all to be unsustainable. While colonial officials saw such contrasts as a justification for their rule, the early modernists viewed them as necessitating a thoroughgoing reform of Muslim thought and practice.

Modernist reformers tended also to differ from colonial, and Orientalist, analyses of Muslim societies in their conviction that Islam could, in fact, be adapted to the needs of the modern world without ceasing to be Islam. Writing in the early twentieth century, Lord Cromer, the consul-general of Egypt (1883–1907), had cautioned: "let no practical politician think that they have a plan capable of resuscitating a body which is not, indeed, dead, and which may yet linger on for centuries, but which is nevertheless politically and socially moribund, and whose gradual decay cannot be arrested by any modern palliatives however skillfully they may be applied."[6] The modernist enterprise was, however, predicated precisely on the conviction that the decline of Muslim societies could indeed be remedied and that it did not require relinquishing Islam itself. What it did require was that Islam be restored to its original purity, and its core values combined with what European science and other forms of modern knowledge had to offer. Only then would the adherents of this religion be capable of scientific, moral, and material progress in the modern world. Yet, the acquisition of Western knowledge, a key facet of modernist reform, carried significant costs, some of which threatened only to substantiate predictions about the irreconcilability of Islam and the modern world. As Sayyid Ahmad Khan (d. 1898), the pioneering modernist of Muslim South Asia observed in 1884, "May the English-educated young men ... forgive me, but I have not seen a person ... with an inclination for the English sciences who still has complete faith in the Islamic matters as they are current in our time."[7] The silver lining to this sobering assessment was, of course, that the "Islamic matters ... current in our time" were not the authentic teachings of Islam. Yet, it did underscore the herculean nature of the project of giving Islam an expression that was true to its original teachings, at home in the modern world, and capable of being seen by the community at large as authentic. Nearly nine decades later, Fazlur Rahman (d. 1988), an influential scholar who will figure prominently in this book, found that a robust combination of properly Islamic norms and modernizing reform was still elusive among the governing elite of countries like Pakistan: "many of the bureaucrats in these countries are not Muslim modernists but simple modernists, i.e., Westernizers, while quite a few are simple conservatives and the instances of Muslim modernists are very few indeed. But it is my belief that Islamic modernism has good chances of eventual success, although ... the final outcome is uncertain."[8] That belief and that uncertainty have continued to characterize Islamic modernism.

The modernists have never become anything akin to a school of law or theology, let alone a sect.[9] They have had significant differences among themselves and their positions have continued to evolve, as one might expect. Even so, as the foregoing would already suggest, some core convictions are recognizable as having frequently guided modernist thought and policy: that the true "spirit" of Islam resides in the Qur'an and in the teachings of the Prophet Muhammad rather than in how Muslims have either lived or thought about their religion for much of their history; that self-professed loci of Islamic authority, such as the `ulama and the Sufis, have distorted the teachings of Islam, illegitimately assumed the role of intermediaries between God and the believers, fragmented the unity of the faith and, in concert with unenlightened despots, been at the heart of Muslim decline; that the fundamental teachings of Islam are not merely in accord with but superior to, and no less universal than, the best of what modern, liberal, values have had to offer to the world.[10] As Liaquat Ali Khan, the first prime minister of Pakistan, had put it in the constituent assembly in March 1949, in moving what has come to be known as the Objectives Resolution, the goal in establishing the new state was "to give the Muslims the opportunity that they have been seeking, throughout these long decades of decadence and subjection, of finding freedom to set up a polity which may prove to be a laboratory for the purpose of demonstrating to the world that Islam is not only a progressive force in the world, but it also provides remedies for many of the ills from which humanity has been suffering."[11]

Easy to caricature today for their idealism and bombast, such convictions have had great purchase in Muslim circles seeking to find a way of simultaneously being good Muslims and leading successful lives in the colonial—and postcolonial—dispensations. Those holding them have often sought much more than that, however. Enjoying positions of considerable influence as intellectuals, makers of public opinion, political leaders, and the governing elite, they have sought to transform the entire religious landscape in accordance with their conceptions of Islam and of how its interests, and those of ordinary believers, are best served. Insomuch as the sweep and audacity of their aspirations relate to all facets of Islam, it does seem worthwhile to study Islam in conditions of modernity with reference to them.[12]

Some scholars have seen Islamic modernism as a particular phase in the intellectual and political history of the modern Muslim world, one largely limited to the era of European colonialism. Later generations, according to this view, would go in other directions, among them secular nationalism, Marxism, and Islamism.[13] I take a rather different view in this study. Secular nationalism and Marxism have not had much purchase in Pakistan, and while Islamism has always been an important part of the religio-political landscape, it has never come close—despite warnings from different quarters—to governing the country, either through electoral or other means. For its part, modernism has continued to guide official policy on matters relating to Islam, its institutions, and its practices. Modernism has indeed been in gradual decline in Pakistan. But it took several decades after the establishment of the state for that decline to set in. Among my concerns in the following chapters is not only to illustrate and account for this decline but also to shed some light on how, both in its aspirations *and* in its decline, modernism has shaped, even as it has been shaped by, other facets of Islam.

To speak of decline in this case is not, moreover, to posit that modernism has exited the scene or is about to do so. The fact that it remains ensconced in the corridors of power is enough to suggest otherwise. In the wider Muslim world and beyond, too, modernist intellectuals have continued to make their presence felt.[14] Though couched in a rather different language, the key concerns of such intellectuals in the contemporary world reveal broad continuities with their acknowledged and unacknowledged predecessors. Such continuities are to be observed in discourses on the Qur'an's "universals," which alone are held to encompass the shari`a's principal concerns and the religion's true spirit, as opposed to the specifics of a medieval consensus on this or that matter. They are equally in evidence in the purported concordance between Islam and liberal values. Speaking in terms of any clearly recognizable end to the phenomenon of Islamic modernism misses such continuities. Some scholars would posit the transformation of an earlier modernism into what is sometimes referred to as today's Islamic liberalism, with the latter consisting in constitutionalism, the rule of law, the universality of human rights, the empowerment of women, and social justice, all justified in terms of a critique of traditionalist Islam by way of a rereading of the foundational texts—the Qur'an and hadith, the reported teachings of the Prophet Muhammad.[15] Given, however, that there are major similarities of approach between the modernists and the Islamic liberals in question, with the same figures sometimes characterized in the scholarly literature as modernists and at others as liberals, the analytical value of a sharp distinction between the two remains unclear. [16] It can also obscure the fact that, for all its stress on constitutionalism, Islamic liberalism, like statist liberalism elsewhere, has tended to have an authoritarian streak.[17] As will be seen, such authoritarianism has long been a marker of Islamic modernism, too.

Though it is modernism that this study foregrounds, a different choice could arguably have been made as a way of studying broader religio-political trends in colonial India and Pakistan. The audacity of modernist aspirations is matched by that of the Islamists, who in fact share much with them in their social and educational backgrounds as well as in their dim view of how Islam has been lived in history.[18] If anything, the Islamists go further in seeking to harness the state to the project of implementing their scripturally anchored vision of Islam. As Mawdudi, the preeminent Islamist ideologue of South Asia, had it in an early work:

> The state that the Qur'an envisions has not just a negative but also a positive goal. It does not seek merely to prevent people from oppressing one another, to guard their liberties, and to defend itself against foreign aggression. It strives also to implement that balanced system of social justice that the Book of God has presented. Its aim is to erase all those forms of evil and to establish all those facets of the good that God has elucidated with His clear guidelines. To accomplish these goals, political power, persuasion and proselytism, means of education and upbringing, societal influence and the pressure of public opinion will all be used, as necessitated by the circumstances.... This is an all-encompassing state. The sphere of its operation extends to the entirety of human life. It seeks to mold all areas of culture in accordance with its particular moral conceptions, its reformist program.[19]

In the case of the Islamists, this vision is predicated, of course, on the very opposite of a self-conscious accord with Western, liberal values.[20] It is based, rather, on the aspiration to make the shari`a the law of the land, to order all aspects of Muslim life in accordance with its presumed dictates, to have everyone submit altogether to the implications of the sovereignty of God. One could, in principle, write about various dimensions of Islam by showing how the Islamists have sought to shape, even as they have been influenced by, those *other* dimensions, diverging from or converging with them and illuminating in the process some major Islamic developments in the region as well as their social and political contexts.

One could likewise write about Islam with the `ulama as a key point of reference. After all, a good deal of the intellectual, religious, and social history of medieval Islam is intertwined with that of the `ulama, not only because of their claims to religious leadership but also because their intellectual concerns straddled a variety of disciplines and because they were well-represented among the local notables across Muslim societies.[21] The transformations their institutions and practices have undergone since colonial times are a useful index of many broader changes that have shaped Islam and Muslim societies in the modern world. At the same time, the `ulama's identity and authority are defined, more than anything else, by their grounding in a long-standing religious and scholarly tradition, and it is with reference to this tradition that they typically articulate their understanding of Islam, answer questions of belief and practice, and draw boundaries between themselves and others. This fact can open revealing vistas on the transformations in question. Tensions between resistance to perceived encroachment on their hallowed tradition and their acknowledged and unacknowledged adaptations to change provide fertile means for understanding not just the thought and politics of the `ulama but also the larger world they inhabit.[22]

Despite such competing and potentially fruitful possibilities, I have chosen to give center stage to modernism in this study of Islam in colonial India and Pakistan. Besides their intrinsic interest, this is largely because the modernists were some of the most influential intellectual and political elite under the British, and, as noted, it is they who have controlled the levers of power since the inception of Pakistan.[23] While the Islamists have *aspired* to the public implementation of Islamic norms through the state as, indeed, have the `ulama, they have not come to power, as they did in Iran after the revolution of 1979, in Afghanistan with the Taliban, and, more recently, under the so-called Islamic State of Iraq and Syria (ISIS). Instead, it is the modernists who have actually defined, if with mixed results, what position Islam would have in the Pakistani constitution, how and on what terms the madrasas would be reformed or Sufi shrines brought under state regulation, what shari`a-based laws would be enacted and within what boundaries they would have effect, and so forth. The justification, scope, and limits of such measures have been matters of intense contestation. It is in the context of such contestation that competing conceptions of Islam are cast in sharp relief and rival claims to religious authority have continued to be articulated.

Four methodological points are worth noting before proceeding further. First, that the modernists—the intellectuals among them as well as members of the political and the governing elite—loom large in this study and yet the book is not exclusively devoted to them has required choices of its own. I have tried to delineate major aspects of competing religio-political trends in British India and in Pakistan in such a way that they are not reduced to how the modernists have viewed them, or vice versa. Nor have I limited my account of those other facets to points of direct contact with modernism. The fact that modernism does occupy center stage in my account has nonetheless allowed me to highlight some particular dimensions rather than others of the wider landscape. For instance, the career of Sufism in twentieth-century South Asia could be described from a variety of different angles: the history of particular Sufi orders; reformist discourses among the Sufis; Sufism, politics, and the colonial and the postcolonial state; South Asian Sufi trends in their interaction with those in the wider Muslim world, and so forth. My account is especially attentive to how Islamic modernism has figured in some of the contestations on Sufism, but the ways in which the `ulama and the Islamists have viewed Sufism and how they have been variously shaped by aspects of Sufi thought and practice is part of my discussion, too. The concern throughout is to offer a broadly illustrative view of Islam in some of its key dimensions and the complex ways in which these dimensions have interacted with and been shaped by one another. This approach would, I hope, allow for a fuller account of the changing Islamic landscape in British India and Pakistan than has usually been attempted while helping avoid a reification of any of the Islamic orientations under discussion here.

Second, a focus on Islam, as is the case here, admittedly poses some interpretive danger: of assuming that it plays a greater role in people's lives than does anything else and of making it the key explanatory factor in accounting for their thought and practice; conversely, of setting it apart from the rest of their lives. Without engaging in a detailed methodological discussion of such matters, suffice it to say here that I have tried to remain mindful of these pitfalls in what follows. I have done so primarily by placing my discussion of varied facets of Islam in the relevant historical, social, and political contexts, without reference to which it is impossible to make sense of the developments in question. We ought to be equally mindful of the fact that treating putatively religious matters as merely incidental to the study of a society, polity, or economy poses at least as many interpretive problems as does an examination that takes Islam seriously. Indeed, such neglect can be quite misleading in studying a society and state where contestations on Islam have indeed occupied center stage.

Third, a discussion of Islam in the modern world often made it tempting for scholars of an earlier generation and still does for many observers and policy analysts today to posit an age-old "tradition" in conflict with "modernity," with the former visualized as either in the process of being swept away by the latter or as thwarting it from ushering in an era of enlightened progress.[24] Tradition in such narratives is the very opposite of change—it is blindly imitative of the past, inflexible, anachronistic, sterile; modernity is the sum of values one ought to aspire to. The language of such binaries poses special problems in the study of Muslim societies since the nineteenth century because this is precisely the language that the Muslim modernists have themselves used to characterize their rivals;[25] the latter, for their part, have often been equally enamored of this language, with the difference that the *pejorative* implications of what the modernists call traditionalism are abandoned and the modernist concern with reform, innovation, and change is invested in turn with the darkest, most foreboding colors.[26] Yet, as will be seen in the following chapters, traditionalist scholars could be flexible and pragmatic in accommodating themselves to new circumstances; to the extent that their critics have recognized this, they have attributed it to their opportunism. We need not rule out political opportunism in all instances, of course, but it hardly accounts for the variety of positions the `ulama and the Islamists have been capable of taking on particular issues. Likewise, it is important to recognize that they have often had good strategic and rhetorical reasons to be *in*flexible when they have chosen to be so. Conversely, the modernists have not necessarily been more open to rethinking *their* certainties than have many `ulama and Islamists, and over the course of their history, they too—without becoming a school of law or theology—have evolved a tradition of their own. In what follows, I will need to occasionally speak in terms of the modernists versus the traditionalists, of the conservative opposition to modernism, and so forth. On such occasions, it should be kept in mind that this language is intended principally to evoke certain contrasts in the religio-political landscape, usually as seen by those inhabiting it, not to give it any normative value. Nor is it to prejudge the outcome of the contests, of which we will observe many instances in this book, among feuding but not always clearly delineated sides.

Finally, the use of the term "modernism" for the kind of thought and practices that I examine in this book might be seen by some as problematic. In the context of early twentieth-century European and American art and literature, modernism has other connotations, among them, "the recurrent act of fragmenting unities (unities of character or plot or pictorial space or lyric form), the use of mythic paradigms, the refusal of norms of beauty, the willingness to make radical linguistic experiment, all often inspired by the resolve (in [T. S.] Eliot's phrase) to startle and disturb the public."[27] There *could* be overlaps between the philosophical underpinnings of that modernism and the aspirations of particular figures among Muslim modernists, but it is not my concern to explore them in this book.[28] Though commonly used by earlier scholars and observers of Islam, modernism has come to be replaced by categories such as liberalism and reformism. As used by the critics of the modernists, the term can also carry pejorative suggestions about a new-fangled and inauthentic Islam.

Yet, its usage in the context of Western art and literature does not, by itself, render the term unserviceable for other purposes. As Nils Gilman has argued, American modernization theorists of the 1950s and the 1960s, too, can be characterized as modernists. In their case, "modernism was not just an aesthetic phenomenon but also a form of social and political practice in which history, society, economy, culture, and nature itself were all to be the object of technical transformation. Modernism was a polysemous code word for all that was good and desirable."[29] Something similar could be said of the Muslim modernists who will figure in this book. Further, there is no clear dividing line between modernism and liberalism, as has been observed, and a category like "reformism" would not allow us to distinguish the approaches of many among the `ulama and the Islamists from those characterized as modernists here. As for its pejorative connotations, it is worth bearing in mind that the modernists have used this characterization for the likes of themselves.[30]

Needless to say, terms used to describe other religious and political trends can have their own difficulties. Islamists, for instance, do not usually characterize themselves as such, preferring to be seen simply as good Muslims. Islamism tends, moreover, to be conflated by many observers with militancy, yet violence is not a defining feature of this phenomenon. And even as many scholars and political leaders have been keen to insist that Islamists are not representative of Islam as a religious tradition, the term *Islam*ist could be taken to posit precisely that conflation between the phenomenon and the wider tradition. Such difficulties do not make Islamism unusable as category of analysis, but they do suggest the need for some careful handling. Much the same is true of modernism.

The Structure of This Book

This book on the whole is organized in thematic rather than chronological terms. The first two chapters are designed, however, not only to highlight certain facets of Islam but also to provide a broad historical overview of developments in colonial India and in Pakistan, roughly from the mid-nineteenth century to the present. In focusing on particular groups or themes, subsequent chapters fill in historical detail as needed, but their primary goal is to illustrate evolving trends as they relate to the group or theme in question and, of course, to show how the various facets of Islam have interacted with one another. Consequently, these chapters will often range freely over the entire period covered by this book, though the primary focus continues to be on developments since the birth of the state of Pakistan.

Chapter 1 introduces many of the groups that will form the subject of this book and charts their emergence and development in conditions of British colonial rule. As will be seen, the traditionalist orientations that enjoy great prominence in the South Asian landscape had begun to take a recognizable shape only in the late nineteenth century, though they drew, of course, on older styles of thought and practice. The early modernists, for their part, were rooted in a culture that was not significantly different from the 'ulama's. Among the concerns of this chapter is to trace their gradual distancing from each other. The processes involved in it would never be so complete, in either British India or in Pakistan, as to preclude the cooperation of the modernists and their conservative critics at critical moments. Nor, however, were the results of this distancing so superficial as to ever be transcended for good.

Chapter 2 provides an overview of modernism in Pakistan, from the country's inception to the present. It draws attention to the salience of ethical commitments in modernist conceptions of Islam—commitments that were often meant as a counterweight to traditionalist understandings of Islamic law and as justifications for its reform, but which also stood in some tension with the authoritarianism that has often characterized Islamic modernism. Much of this authoritarianism came from the fact that it was the modernists who populated the ranks of the governing elite, that this elite has remained in power for long periods of time without much accountability to the people, and that the best chance that many modernist intellectuals have had of seeing their ideas implemented has been through unsavory alliances with unrepresentative rulers. But some of the authoritarianism has been endemic to modernist conceptions of Islam itself, a fact far more apparent to those at their receiving end than to the modernists themselves.

The 'ulama are the focus of chapter 3, which seeks to bring out some of the ambiguities of the relationship in Pakistan between them and the modernists. The traditionalist 'ulama have had some very particular ideas about an Islamic state, ideas at considerable variance with those of the modernist governing elite. Yet, even as the 'ulama have bitterly resisted modernist legislation on matters seen as encroaching upon their understandings of Islam, they have often been willing to accommodate themselves to constitutional and political developments in the country as spearheaded by the modernists, and they have continued to benefit from the patronage extended to them by successive governments. The modernists, for their part, have seldom been able to develop a significant constituency among the 'ulama, and this despite the existence in Pakistan's early decades of some 'ulama with a modernist orientation. Besides drawing attention to the latter, and thereby to fractures within the ranks of the 'ulama, this chapter seeks also to shed some light on how the `ulama associated with particular doctrinal orientations have fared in relation to one another and how one of these, represented by the Deobandis, has overtaken others in the religio-political sphere.

In turning to Islamism, chapter 4 provides an account of one of the most central of all Islamist ideas, in Pakistan and in the wider Muslim world—the idea that sovereignty belongs to God alone. As Mawdudi and other Islamists have articulated it, the implication is that all legal and political authority derives from God and His injunctions, as enunciated in the Qur'an and in the normative example of the Prophet Muhammad. One could not be a Muslim without accepting this idea, nor could a state be Islamic without recognizing it. As will be seen, however, the Islamists are not the only people who have espoused the sovereignty of God. It has figured prominently in non-Islamist, including modernist, circles, too. For instance, the previously mentioned Objectives Resolution endorses it as well. Part of the concern of this chapter is to examine what it has meant in different circles. We would seek also to explore the provenance and history of this idea. Though it is usually taken for granted that Mawdudi had put this idea into circulation, the question of how he may have come upon it has never been asked. Then there is the question, which we will also examine in this chapter, of why *his* formulation, rather than any other, has been the most influential among competing conceptualizations of the idea.

Any study of Islam in a predominantly Muslim state and of aspirations to give it a prominent place in the state necessarily raises questions about religious minorities. Though I touch briefly in this book on non-Muslim minorities, the focus of chapter 5 is on two *Muslim* minorities, the Ahmadis and the Shi`a, and some of the contestations around their position in the state. How these communities have fared in Pakistan is part of the story here, with the Ahmadis being declared a non-Muslim minority in 1974 and significant Shi`i-Sunni sectarian violence in the country since the 1980s. The principal concern of the chapter is, however, to explore the anxieties that the existence and activities of these minority communities have generated among the `ulama and the Islamists. In case of the Ahmadis, it will be seen that the anxieties in question have had to do not merely with the peculiarities of Ahmadi beliefs about the Prophet Muhammad, but with Islamic modernism itself. Though most South Asian modernists are not Ahmadis, Ahmadi discourses have tended to echo ideas similar to those of many modernists, and this has served to aggravate conservative opposition to the Ahmadis. The anxieties generated by the Shi`a, much exacerbated by the impact and rhetoric of the Iranian revolution of 1979, have a different locus, and they, too, go beyond Sunni discomfort with particular Shi`i beliefs and practices. Much more than the Ahmadis, the Shi`a have raised difficult questions about what, if any, kind of Islamic law can be given public force in Pakistan, laying bare in the process nagging uncertainties about whether Pakistan can ever fully claim to be an Islamic state.

Chapter 6 moves to some other expressions of contestation in the religious sphere, taking place in this instance on the once expansive terrain of Sufism. Long a core part of Muslim identity, in South Asia and elsewhere in the Muslim world, Sufi practices, doctrines, and institutions have continued into modern times to exercise considerable influence not only on common people but also on the religious and political leaders of the community. Though many among the `ulama, including the reformists in their ranks, have often had a relatively seamless relationship with Sufism, the Islamists, too, and even the modernists have been receptive to the appeal of Sufism. It is not difficult, for instance, to detect ideas of a Sufi provenance in some core modernist commitments. Yet, the conditions of modernity, the claims of the modern state, and modernist and Islamist efforts to radically reshape Islam in a particular image, with some recent help from militant Islamist groups, have hit institutional Sufism hard. Sufism has had some other vulnerabilities, too, which have also contributed to a certain shrinking of the space it has traditionally occupied in this part of the world.

Chapter 7 focuses on religio-political violence, whose widespread incidence, after Pakistan's realignment in the US-led War on Terror in the aftermath of September 11, 2001, and the subsequent rise of a new, *Pakistani*, Taliban, has threatened the very fabric of state and society. Like the rest of the book, this chapter takes a long historical view, one that goes well beyond the post-2001 developments and their immediate context. I examine the violence in question from two broad and intertwined perspectives, one relating to the state and the other to Islam and those speaking in its terms. Part of my concern in this chapter is to contribute to an understanding of how the governing elite and the military have often fostered the conditions in which the resort to religiously inflected violence has been justified. But I also suggest that the non-state actors—ideologues and militants—have had an agency of their own, which is not reducible to the machinations of the state, and that their resort to relevant facets of the Islamic tradition also needs to be taken seriously in order to properly understand their view of the world and such appeal as they have had in particular circles. By the same token, even as it has helped cultivate a certain narrative of jihad, the Pakistani ruling establishment has often labored under severe constraints in trying to control that narrative, and some understanding of such constraints, too, can shed useful light not only on religio-political violence but also on the career of Islam in Pakistan.

The epilogue ends this book with some reflections on the changes Islam has undergone in Pakistan, over the course of the country's history but also in comparison with where the relevant religious trends stood in the early twentieth century.

CHAPTER ONE

Islamic Identities in Colonial India

An Islamic Mosaic

South Asia has been home for centuries to rich traditions of learning in the Islamic foundational texts as well as law, theology, and philosophy. Yet, it is a remarkable fact that the doctrinal orientations that now dominate Sunni Islam in South Asia all took their distinctive shape only during colonial rule in the late nineteenth century. Shi`ism, too, underwent significant change during this period. How did members of these rival orientations interact with one another? How do these orientations relate to facets of Islam in earlier times? In what ways were Islam and Muslim politics in colonial India shaped by political and other developments in the wider Muslim world? And how, in late colonial India, did the movement for a separate Muslim homeland both develop and navigate its way through this fraught religio-political landscape? In addressing such questions, it is important to avoid a teleological view that would have this landscape necessarily result in the religio-political contestations that are the subject of the following chapters. At the same time, as will be observed, subsequent developments in Pakistan cannot be adequately understood without reference to it.

I begin with the orientations that might broadly be characterized as traditionalist, in that they are premised on a self-conscious continuity with a scholarly tradition that extends back into the formative period of Islam. This is a tradition represented by the `ulama, the religious scholars who have long seen their vocation as the preservation and transmission of religious knowledge and the concomitant guidance of lay people in its light. The first of these orientations in South Asia's Sunni Islam came to be associated with a madrasa established in 1866 in the north Indian town of Deoband. Inaugurated less than a decade after the formal establishment of British colonial rule over India, the madrasa represented the idea that the Muslim community's beliefs and practices had to be reordered in light of the foundational texts and rooted in unswerving fidelity to Islamic legal norms. What was perhaps most notable about this vision was not the appeal to the need for reform, of which there had been many earlier expressions in and outside India, but rather the underlying view that a reinvigorated Islamic identity offered the most effective means of coping with the radically changed world in which the Muslims of India had come to find themselves. It was by learning to be true to their Islamic commitments that Muslims could survive the adversity and the dislocations of life under colonial rule, and it was the calling of those associated with the madrasa at Deoband to inculcate proper Islamic norms among people while continuing long-standing traditions of Islamic scholarship.

What were these dislocations? Centuries of Muslim rule had come to an end with the abortive Mutiny of 1857. Although many among the `ulama had long maintained a certain distance from the royal court, the existence of Muslim rulers had been taken for granted and deemed necessary for the implementation of the shari`a. Even rulers whose policies and lifestyles did not conform much to Islamic prescriptions appointed Muslim judges—*qadis*—as well as other judicial and religious functionaries, and even those among the scholars and the Sufis who did not frequent royal courts could indirectly benefit from the largesse of the rich and powerful. Two of India's Muslim neighbors, Iran and Afghanistan, escaped colonial rule. Several other Muslim countries— for instance, Egypt and Morocco—managed to retain at least the formal trappings of Muslim rule even when they came to be governed by European powers. India, on the other hand, was subjected to the full force and effects of colonialism, the only exception being pockets of Indian regions that were left by the British to the governance of hereditary indigenous rulers, some of whom happened to be Muslim. The onset of colonial rule meant, among other things, the establishment of a new legal system, one that was administered according to the norms of English common law even when it allowed facets of the shari`a to govern matters of personal status—notably, marriage, divorce, and inheritance. It also required that those dependent on the patronage of the erstwhile Muslim ruling elite had to fend for themselves in other ways. An entire culture and way of life were in peril.

Deoband was a response to the establishment of colonial rule, but it was not a revolt against it. The madrasa in the town of that name and numerous others all over India that soon began to be patterned on it were more indebted to the model of English public schools—classrooms, an academic calendar, a fixed curriculum, annual examinations—than they were to the institutions that had previously existed in India or elsewhere.[1] Some of those associated with the management and support of these madrasas were themselves lower-ranking officials in the colonial bureaucracy. British officials did have their suspicions of such institutions, and there inevitably were those within them, as well as doctrinal rivals outside, whose words and actions could give substance to such suspicions. Many Deobandis were nonetheless keen to affirm loyalty to the British,[2] and it was not before the second decade of the twentieth century that the Deobandis became active in colonial politics.

Loyal or not, there could be no mistaking that Deoband sought to represent an alternative to the conditions in which Muslims of colonial India found themselves. It was an alternative articulated in religious terms, but it had other dimensions too, and these included not just the political, to which we will come later, but also the socioeconomic. The Deobandis did not refuse such patronage as came their way, from an Afghan king or the rulers of the Muslim princely states of Hyderabad and Bhopal—the sort of patronage that would have sustained madrasas in earlier times as well.[3] However, they depended primarily on the support of ordinary members of the community. Even meager donations by large numbers of people could go far toward generating the funds that were necessary for the upkeep of these relatively modest institutions. In turn, such fundraising helped foster networks of supporters and gave them a stake that they had not had before in the continuance of these institutions. This model of support has helped sustain madrasas in South Asia since colonial times and not just those of the Deobandis. It has undergirded their growth even as it has made it difficult for governments to regulate their financial and other affairs, much more so than would have been the case if they were tied, say, to landed endowments or other clearly identifiable sources of funding.

The second orientation that has come, since colonial times, to occupy a large space in modern South Asian Sunnism is associated with Ahmad Riza Khan (d. 1921) of Bareilly, a town in north India. The Barelawis, as they are commonly characterized, stand in marked contrast to the Deobandis. They have had their own madrasas, where hadith, Islamic law, and other religious sciences are studied. But they are best known not for scholarship in these areas but rather for Sufi and other devotional practices centered on the shrines and persons of holy men. Though the Deobandis have also had considerable space for Sufi piety in their doctrinal orientation, the world of the Barelawis was and remains a significantly more enchanted one. The Prophet is deemed not merely to be a source of normative teachings, but a living presence, and supplication to the saints is a regular feature of Barelawi practice. This style of religiosity has deep roots in South Asian Islam. Ahmad Riza Khan had tried to give it a new respectability both by preaching against particular practices that he viewed as blurring the boundaries between Islam and Hinduism *and* by defending particular practices against Deobandi and other critics. It was his followers who continued in the proper ways of earlier Muslims, he said, and *they* were the true Sunnis, not those others whose puritanical attitudes amounted to a break with the past and a profound disrespect toward some of Islam's holiest personages.[4]

The Barelawis are in some ways the most traditionalist of the Sunni orientations to emerge in colonial India. Indeed, despite their association with a colonial-era figure, their emergence had more to do with their doctrinal rivals and the desire to stand their ground against them than it did with their own beliefs and practices, which had a long history in Indian Islam. It also had to do of course with the conditions of colonial rule. As will be observed, print and other technologies allowed Ahmad Riza Khan, no less than his rivals, to reach new audiences, and the ever-growing number of madrasas enabled the Barelawis to train new generations of `ulama on a larger scale and with a greater measure of standardization than could have been possible earlier. The increasing awareness—fostered in part by ubiquitous colonial practices of enumeration and classification—of the existence of a large Hindu majority in India also necessitated that a distinctive Muslim identity be articulated in opposition to it, the more so in a milieu in which the rivals of the Barelawis alleged that their practices were insufficiently distinguishable from those of the polytheists. For all that, there are important substantive and rhetorical continuities between the devotionalism of the colonial Barelawis and earlier traditions of Sufi-inflected piety. Indeed, it would be difficult to account for the prominence of the Barelawi orientation in colonial India without recognizing that what it represented in many cases was a new name for a complex of long-standing devotional and customary practices.

Deoband, by contrast, was often self-conscious in distinguishing itself from existing practice. Its reform consisted precisely in such distinction. Yet, the success of the Deobandis in colonial India owed itself not merely to a new organizational model but also to the fact that they, too, could make credible claims to a sense of continuity with the past. The learning their madrasas imparted was aligned with a long-standing tradition. Deobandi reformism gave pride of place to the study of hadith, which had a venerable history in India. A key figure in the Deobandi genealogy was the great eighteenth-century north Indian hadith scholar Shah Wali Allah (d. 1762), whose significance has rested not only on his magisterial writings or the scholarly networks his distinguished family spawned but also on the fact that he has come to be seen as a crucial link in the onward transmission of religious learning from earlier times. This last point is best appreciated by noting that, despite a thriving book culture, the authenticity and authority of hadith texts has continued well into modern times to depend on a chain of identifiable human links going back all the way to Muhammad. In early modern South Asia, Wali Allah was the most prestigious of them.[5] The Deobandis have been important in extending Wali Allah's intellectual influence to new circles; in turn, Wali Allah's image as one of the most important of precolonial India's religious scholars and reformers has served to give credibility and historical depth to the Deobandi enterprise.

The least traditionalist of the conservative Sunni orientations to emerge in colonial South Asia is that of the Ahl-i Hadith. In marked contrast with the Deobandis and the Barelawis, both of whom adhere to the Hanafi school of Sunni law, the Ahl-i Hadith reject the authority of *all* such schools (*madhhabs*) and therefore of a legal tradition that has guided Muslim societies since the ninth century. To the Deobandis and the Barelawis, a Hanafi identity has meant working within the framework of the rules, norms, and methods associated with past scholars of this school of law—of submitting to their over-arching authority (*taqlid*). The Ahl-i Hadith, by contrast, view taqlid as investing fallible humans with an authority that belongs only to God and the Prophet Muhammad. To them, this is not very different from the abhorrent "saint-worshipping" practices of the *pirs*—claimants to Sufi authority—and their ignorant followers. Instead, they insist on a purity of belief that replicates that of Islam's first generations, the *salaf* (hence their common designation as the Salafis), and on direct recourse to the Islamic foundational texts, as opposed to approaching those texts through the distorting lenses of a long-standing legal tradition.

This is not to say, however, that the Ahl-i Hadith lack their own authoritative figures from the past. In the eighteenth century, Wali Allah had argued against the rigidity of the boundaries between the Sunni schools of law and in favor of *ijtihad*—that is, the derivation of new legal rulings, as needed, in light of the foundational texts. Although he had not gone quite so far as the Ahl-i Hadith, the latter, too, see him as an important figure in their own genealogy. Given the centrality of the Prophet's teachings to their doctrinal orientation, earlier scholars and commentators of hadith are also crucial links in the Ahl-i Hadith understanding of their scholarly tradition. Indeed, Siddiq Hasan Khan (d. 1890), a leading Ahl-i Hadith scholar of the late nineteenth century whose career had taken an unexpected turn with his marriage to the ruler of the princely state of Bhopal, had utilized some of the resources that had thereby come his way to sponsor the printing and dissemination of classical and early modern commentaries on hadith. He had also written commentaries of his own on the Qur'an and hadith, as did some other Ahl-i Hadith scholars of the colonial era.[6] Theirs is a far less colorful tradition than that of the Barelawis, but it is a tradition nonetheless.

The Shi`a of colonial India reveal notable similarities with their Sunni rivals, though these need to be seen against the background of some obvious differences. By far the most numerous of the Shi`a were, and are, the Imamis or Ithna `asharis ("Twelvers"), who, unlike the Sunnis as well as other Shi`i orientations, believe in twelve divinely appointed imams. The last of these imams is believed to have gone into occultation in the late ninth century and is awaited as the promised *mahdi* or messiah. Several ruling dynasties in pre-colonial India were Shi`i, but the Shi`a as a whole comprised a minority of the total Muslim population in South Asia. Since the eighteenth century, the region of Awadh in what under the British became part of the United Provinces (UP) was ruled by a wealthy Shi`i dynasty, with its patronage of Shi`i causes extending to the revered Shi`i shrine cities of southern Iraq. Lucknow, the capital of this princely state, would remain the center of Shi`i learning and culture in colonial times even as it emerged as a theater of growing conflict with the Sunnis.

Within decades of the formal establishment of British rule, Shi`i madrasas had begun to be established in UP and elsewhere with organizational features similar to those of Deobandi and other Sunni institutions. Cadres of `ulama trained at these madrasas built on centuries-old traditions of Shi`i learning all while benefiting from the opportunities provided to them by colonial rule. Much like the Sunni madrasas, Shi`i institutions came to impart learning in ways that were more standardized than had been the case earlier, and they too showed a greater awareness than before of the need to distinguish themselves from other Muslims.[7] An All India Shi`a Conference began as well to hold annual meetings from 1907, with attendees drawn from across the Indian subcontinent. Though riven from its first years by tensions between the Shi`i `ulama and their critics, this institution, along with many others, had a role in shaping a distinct Shi`i identity in colonial India. For instance, its delegates were regularly tasked during its early years with visiting different parts of the country to report on the state of the Shi`a living there—the number of mosques and centers of devotional practice (*imambargahs*) in particular locales, the degree to which Shi`i rituals were observed by people, the economic condition of the community, and so forth.[8] The conditions in question were frequently stated to be grim. As the honorary secretary of the conference observed in 1911, basing himself on his travels in India over the previous two years, "in some places there is no one to lead the funeral prayer, marriages do not take place in accordance with the prescriptions of the sinless imams, and people are not acquainted with basic matters relating to prayer and fasting."[9] Such assessments could be emotionally powerful, and they helped undergird unceasing appeals for Shi`i self-awareness, organization, networking, and fundraising. None of this was unique to the Shi`a.

For all the deeply unsettling effects that colonial rule had had on Muslims of South Asia, it had also served to kindle a new intellectual and religious vitality in traditionalist circles. A good deal of it came from the need to respond to questions on which the very future of Islam seemed to many people to hinge. How were the interests of Islam and Muslims best served under foreign, non-Muslim rule? Was it by reforming putatively inauthentic customary norms under the searing light of the Islamic foundational texts and with a renewed commitment to the Hanafi legal tradition or, as the case may be, to textually anchored Shi`i norms? Was Islam best served through a reinvigorated Sufi piety? Did the most appropriate path to a good Muslim life lie instead in a rejection of Sufi practices and of the medieval schools of law, which tended to obstruct rather than facilitate an anchoring of Islamic norms in the foundational texts? Muslim traditionalists might lament that Islam was under siege in British India, that the British were out to destroy their law and their culture, but the very challenge of responding to this threat had also given a new vigor, a new sense of agency, to the traditionalists. Even the All India Shi`a Conference, though it came to be dominated by the modernists, had begun as an `ulama-led platform.[10]

Some of this agency came, as observed, from the framework and the tools that the conditions of colonial rule had provided. Though all foreign rule is, by definition, exploitative, it has not been seen as equally oppressive. Muhammad Rashid Rida (d. 1935), an influential Syrian scholar and pan-Islamist of the early twentieth century, thought, for instance, that British colonial rule allowed people greater freedom than did any other colonial powers.[11] Shi`i, Deobandi, Barelawi, and Ahmadi scholars took turns praising British rule in early twentieth-century India.[12] Much of this was guided by an instinct of self-preservation in a milieu in which the hostility of a well-entrenched colonial power carried heavy costs. For all that, it is worth noting that the British in India had sought to leave the arena of religion outside their formal purview, and this may be part of what Rida and others had had in mind. The avoidance of direct intervention in the religious sphere does not mean, of course, that it had escaped the effects of colonial regulation. The very definition of a sphere as "religious" shaped it in distinctive, and often coercive, ways. By decreeing, for instance, that the shari`a in the context of the colonial judicial administration meant only the laws of personal status and that the shari`a rules even in those areas would be guided by the principles of English common law and administered by judges trained in that legal tradition rather than specifically by Muslim judges, the British reshaped Islamic law to its very core. Nevertheless, there *was* an arena that colonial rule made available to the `ulama of different doctrinal orientations, one in which they were relatively free to establish as many madrasas as they could, and issue as many *fatwas* and publish as many books as they wanted to.

This sort of freedom was not quite new to India. Already in the time of the Mughal emperor Akbar (r. 1556–1605), his courtier Badayuni (d. 1615) had remarked in an acerbic history he was then secretly writing that India "is a wide place, where there is an open field for all licentiousness, and no one interferes with another's business."[13] Such freedom would, however, become institutionalized in British India. The traditionalists did not necessarily appreciate it any more than had Badayuni, for it meant that their rivals, and all kind of heretics, had as open a playing field as they did themselves. Other Muslim voices could be equally suspicious of it. So Akbar Ilahabadi (d. 1921), an Urdu poet noted for his sarcasm, evoking the memory of Hallaj, the mystic who was executed in early tenth-century Baghdad for what his opponents had deemed blasphemous statements: "Friends, celebrate our government ... , [under which] you can say, 'I am the Truth [that is, God]' but not be hanged for it."[14] The modernist poet and philosopher Muhammad Iqbal (d. 1938), too, had attributed the emergence of the heterodox Ahmadis—many of whom viewed Mirza Ghulam Ahmad (d. 1908) as a prophet and were seen by other Muslims as contravening the doctrine that Muhammad was the last of God's prophets—to the British policy of laissez faire in religious matters. We will examine the controversy surrounding the Ahmadis in Pakistan at some length in chapter 5. Iqbal's misgivings about British religious policy in India are, however, worth highlighting in the present context: "In so far as Islam is concerned," Iqbal wrote, "it is no exaggeration to say that the solidarity of the Muslim community in India is less safe than the solidarity of the Jewish community was in the days of Jesus under the Romans. Any religious adventurer in India can set up any claim and carve out a new community for his own exploitation. This liberal state of ours does not care a fig for the integrity of a parent community, provided the adventurer assures it of his loyalty and his followers are regular in the payment of taxes due to the state."[15]

It is in this colonial framework that we should see the significance of technologies facilitating as never before the travel of people, goods, and ideas. The Indian railway system, for instance, was a major feat of colonial engineering and bureaucracy. Between 1861 and 1946–47, railway tracks had grown from 1,587 to 40,524 route miles; already by 1902, India was "the world's fourth-largest railway system measured by route length."[16] The number of passengers traveling by trains had grown from 19,283,000 in 1871 to 1,189,428,000 in 1946–47.[17] This obviously created unprecedented opportunities in the economic, social, and political arenas, but it did so in matters relating to people's religious life as well. Two examples are instructive here. Jama`at `Ali Shah (ca. 1841–1951), a Sufi master belonging to the Naqshbandi order, had taken to traveling by rail from his base in the Punjab for months on end to visit groups of disciples all across the Indian subcontinent. It was not unusual for Sufi *shaykh*s to be mobile, but the degree of his itinerancy was striking.[18] By contrast, the Deobandi Sufi and scholar Ashraf `Ali Thanawi (1863–1943) spent much of the first four decades of the twentieth century at his Sufi lodge in Thana Bhawan, a small town not far from Deoband, and it was there that throngs of visitors came to him, thanks again to the small railway station that connected his lodge to the rest of the subcontinent. Thanawi, it is worth noting, also carried on an extensive correspondence with those seeking his guidance. He would reply to the letters almost as soon as he had received them, often responding point by point to the queries posed to him and frequently on the original letter itself. It was then put back in the mail, but not before the relevant portions had been copied for the record. Colonial postal service was as crucial to the dissemination of the master's teaching as was the railway system to bringing people (and the mail—twice a day) to him. So, of course, was the technology of print, which extended the reach and influence of such figures beyond anything an earlier age could offer. Many of the fatwas that Thanawi later published had originated in his letters to particular correspondents.[19] One of his most important Sufi works, the *Training of the Wayfarer* (*Tarbiyat al-salik*), is likewise based on letters to those seeking the master's spiritual and ethical guidance.[20]

Though Thanawi was an unusually prolific author, his writings as well as those produced by associates under his supervision give us an idea of the range of publications by the ʿulama and the Sufis in colonial India. Besides numerous fatwas, he published an Urdu translation of and commentary on the Qur'an, a number of books—to some of which we will return later—on matters relating to Sufi thought and practice, a work on norms of comportment for women that has come to enjoy the status of a veritable classic in the genre, and much else. Deobandi ʿulama were not unique in the production of such works. Nor were the pursuit of learning and the edification of fellow scholars the only functions of these writings. They served also to stake out new claims to authority—within a particular doctrinal orientation vis-à-vis other scholars of that orientation and, within the crowded field of colonial Islam, vis-à-vis doctrinal and other rivals. Ahl-i Hadith commentaries on the reported teachings of the Prophet Muhammad tended, among other things, to show how the Hanafi legal norms had only a tenuous basis in them. Such challenges could hardly be allowed to go unanswered, of course, and there was much ink, ingenuity, and money that was spent on the production of impressive Deobandi commentaries on hadith. The technology of print also meant that autodidacts could challenge the ʿulama's understanding of the foundational and other texts in unprecedented ways, which in turn required the traditionalists to articulate and defend their authority and to try to broaden the reach of their own discourses in new ways.

The challenges and the opportunities brought forth by colonial rule would not, however, have produced a traditionalist revival without the prior existence of a vibrant religious and scholarly tradition. Rashid Rida had commented on the vitality of traditionalist scholarship in India in late medieval times and contrasted it unfavorably with the state of affairs elsewhere: "Were it not for the meticulous attention to the study of hadith on the part of our brothers, the ʿulama of India, it would have become extinct in the eastern lands. For it has been debilitated in Egypt, Syria, Iraq, and the Hijaz since the tenth century of the hijra [sixteenth century CE], reaching its nadir towards the beginning of the fourteenth century [the late nineteenth century CE]."[21] Rida had scores to settle against the representatives of what he saw as the moribund scholarly culture of the famed al-Azhar in Cairo, yet his claim was not unfounded. It was on this scholarly tradition that the Deobandis and the Ahl-i Hadith had built, and even Shiʿi madrasas, long known for a focus on philosophy and theology, had come to give a prominent place to the study of hadith in their colonial-era institutions of learning.[22] The study of law, so important a feature of Deobandi scholarship since the late nineteenth century, likewise drew on a core area of Indian Islamic scholarship in precolonial times. The Islamic "rationalist" sciences, too—notably logic and philosophy—had continued in colonial India, and their association with particular clusters of scholars would persist into the early twentieth century. For their part, a number of Sufi orders had seen a certain revival in parts of eighteenth-century South Asia.[23] Quite apart from the fact that the ʿulama did not agree on how to address the challenges posed to them by the onset of colonial rule, the very depth and breadth of their intellectual heritage would, by itself, have precluded a shared answer. This, incidentally, is a significant part of what may account not simply for the vigor of the traditionalist response to colonialism but also for its fragmented character.

It is easy to see the Muslim modernists as breaking decisively with the sort of tradition the ʿulama represented in colonial India. There is more than a little truth to this, as will be observed. Yet, it is important to recognize that the early modernists, who occupied a growing space in the Islamic mosaic of colonial India, were part of the same broad culture that their contemporary ʿulama inhabited. Sayyid Ahmad Khan (d. 1898), the pioneering modernist of the late nineteenth century, had established his Muhammadan Anglo-Oriental College in Aligarh (hereafter, often Aligarh College), in the UP, in the conviction that the only way in which Muslims could cope with the adversities of colonial rule was through an English schooling. This position was premised on a dim view of traditional madrasas and those associated with them. Sayyid Ahmad's social background and his norms of cultural comportment were nonetheless hardly different from his contemporary ʿulama's and of those supporting their institutions. He belonged to a family that was devoted to some leading Islamic figures of the time: the descendants of Shah Wali Allah, on the one hand, and the circle of Shah Ghulam ʿAli, a revered Sufi master of Delhi, on the other.[24] In the early 1850s, he had commenced a translation of the *Alchemy of Happiness* (*Kimiya-i saʿadat*), a famous Persian work on ethics by the great Sufi and jurist al-Ghazali (d. 1111). The idea of the translation had come from Hajji Imdad Allah (d. 1899), a Sufi of the Chishti order who figures prominently in the genealogy of the founders of the madrasa at Deoband.[25] Incidentally, it was at the lodge previously occupied by Imdad Allah that Ashraf ʿAli Thanawi would later establish himself in Thana Bhawan. Some of Sayyid Ahmad's own writings before the formal establishment of British rule in 1858 could have come from one of his Sufi contemporaries. Then there is the fact that, even as a modernist reformer breaking with the tradition of the ʿulama, Sayyid Ahmad expressed at least some of his views through the traditional medium of the commentary on the Qur'an. Further, as his biographer Altaf Husayn Hali (d. 1914) argued, a number of the theological and exegetical positions that Sayyid Ahmad's critics had found objectionable could be shown to have some basis in medieval Islamic thought itself.[26]

Much the same is true of Sayyid Ahmad's leading allies and of other early modernists. Mahdi `Ali Khan (d. 1907), better known as Muhsin al-Mulk, was born a Shi`i but had later become a Sunni and, early in his career, had written a hard-hitting polemic against Shi`ism.[27] He had translated a small portion of Ghazali's magnum opus, *The Revival of the Religious Sciences* (*Ihya `ulum al-din*), while drawing extensively on the great Persian mystical poet Rumi (d. 1273) to elucidate and enliven the work.[28] Despite what he shared of Sayyid Ahmad's modernist outlook, the two men had significant disagreements on particular theological and exegetical matters, and Muhsin al-Mulk had enough traditional learning to be able to invoke it in defense of his own arguments.[29] Hali was likewise rooted in a traditional intellectual culture. He is most famous for his biography of Sayyid Ahmad, which, in its robust support of his protagonist's religious views, showed considerable grounding in classical and modern Islamic theology. But the biography that earned him greater respect from his peers was not Sayyid Ahmad's but rather that of the Persian poet and moralist Sa`di (d. 1291).[30] The early modernists were often altogether fluent in the world of medieval Persian ethics.

Another figure in Sayyid Ahmad's circle, who also served as a trustee of Aligarh College, was Nazir Ahmad (d. 1912). In the history of Urdu literature, he is best remembered as the author of early didactic novels that sought to instruct Muslims in how to navigate their lives in the colonial milieu. But he also published an Urdu translation of the Qur'an as well as a major work called *Rights and Duties* (*al-Huquq wal-fara'iz*). Published in three substantial volumes, this was a systematic treatment of what the author took to be the full spectrum of proper Islamic beliefs and practices, with the final volume devoted to matters of morality and ethics. Each section in the book, discussing a particular belief, ritual, or other practice, a virtue or a vice, is structured in the form of passages from the Qur'an, citations from the traditions of the Prophet, an effort to resolve disagreements between and among the relevant hadith reports, and the author's own comments on the topic in light of those texts. The resulting work, impressive simultaneously for its erudition and its accessibility, was meant to be a "code of conduct" (*dustur al-`amal*) for all. As he put it in the preface to this largely forgotten book, every Muslim able to read the Urdu language ought to have a copy of this code of conduct—at the very least, each family should.[31]

Though both Hali and Nazir Ahmad had significant traditional learning, it was Shibli Nu`mani (d. 1914), who served for many years as a professor of Persian and of Arabic at Aligarh College, who had perhaps the strongest claim to being a member of the `ulama.[32] Shibli, as he was commonly known, had been educated by `ulama well known for their expertise in the Islamic rationalist tradition. On Sayyid Ahmad's encouragement, he would later write two important books on Islamic theology—one a historical overview of major theological orientations, the other a normative work toward a reformulation of some key theological tenets. In addition, he wrote full length biographies of `Umar (r. 634–44), the second successor of the Prophet Muhammad, and of the `Abbasid caliph al-Ma'mun (r. 813–33) as well as of several major figures, including Abu Hanifa (d. 767), the eponymous founder of the Hanafi school of law; Ghazali; Rumi; and the medieval Persian poet and astronomer `Umar Khayyam (d. 1131). Toward the end of his life, he also embarked on a biography of the Prophet Muhammad, a monumental work that was completed many years after Shibli's death by his star pupil, Sayyid Sulayman Nadwi (d. 1953).

Shibli was a key figure in the founding of the Nadwat al-`Ulama ("the conclave of religious scholars") in Lucknow in 1894, a forum that sought to mobilize the `ulama in support of the reform of traditional religious education and to bring some order to the institutions imparting it. A decade later, it established an educational institution, a *dar al-`ulum*, of its own, which has also come to be popularly known as the Nadwat al-`Ulama. With people like Shibli as its guiding lights, the Nadwa—both the movement and the school—had been meant as well to bridge some of the distance between traditionalist institutions and modernist colleges, though it would come to be significantly closer to the Deobandi orientation than to Aligarh. The Nadwa has produced many distinguished scholars, all bearing the suffix "Nadwi" as a mark of their association with its Dar al-`Ulum. Shibli's biographer, Sulayman Nadwi, was one of them. By the time of his death, he had become a disciple of the traditionalist Sufi Ashraf `Ali Thanawi. Some of the other graduates of the Nadwa we will meet later would be truer to Shibli's modernist inclinations.

My final example of the intellectual culture of the early modernists is Mirza Muhammad Hadi (d. 1931), a Shi`i contemporary and acquaintance of Shibli from Lucknow. A graduate of the University of the Punjab, Hadi is best known in the history of Urdu literature for a novel, written under the pen name Ruswa ("the disgraced"), that depicts the life of a courtesan of Lucknow. He spent considerable time as a translator, too, rendering works by Plato and Aristotle into Urdu (via their available English translations), as well as writings on psychology by some of his English contemporaries. He also wrote on medieval Islamic thought, and one of his works in this area is an abridged Urdu translation of an Arabic commentary on al-Suhrawardi, a twelfth-century thinker controversial even by the standards of the premodern Muslim philosophers.[33]

That the early modernists were well acquainted with, and in several instances, deeply immersed in, a traditional intellectual culture is not surprising, of course, for that is the only culture they had really known while growing up. This should not, however, obscure their critique of that culture and tradition, or the sometimes strident responses their writings and activities provoked in turn from those who saw themselves as the guardians of that tradition. For instance, at the inaugural session of the All India Shi`a Conference in 1907, Mirza Hadi had strongly opposed a resolution that wanted nothing to be done under the conference's auspices that was opposed to the shari`a. His point was not, of course, that this forum ought to be able to contravene the shari`a, but only that there was no clear mechanism for deciding whether something was or was not in consonance with the sacred law.[34] This made no allowance for the Shi`i `ulama, who considered themselves to be precisely that mechanism. He had also proposed a resolution of his own asking that the conference dissociate itself from polemical and other "inflammatory" writings against sectarian rivals. This gesture toward Islamic ecumenism provoked sharp rebukes from the Shi`i `ulama and their associates, who took it to be a thinly veiled attack on their scholarly concerns and, indeed, an affront to their efforts to give their community a distinct identity.[35] This initiative, too, was defeated, but it was an unpropitious beginning for the conference. More challenges to their authority awaited the `ulama in subsequent sessions of this annual conference, and they decided some years later to withdraw their support for it.

Critics of Sayyid Ahmad Khan alleged, for their part, that he wanted the Muslims to become English in all but their religion.[36] Some thought that even the religion of those studying at Aligarh would not be safe.[37] Such fears were exaggerated, but it is not difficult to see why they would have resonated with many people. Sayyid Ahmad was not only an educational entrepreneur; he was also a theologian. In a series of ambitious works, including a biography of the Prophet Muhammad and unfinished commentaries on the Bible and the Qur'an, he sought to defend Islam against Orientalist criticisms and to argue that the theological doctrines and legal institutions that tended to attract the most adverse comment either had no basis in scripture or could be explained in modern, rational terms. Thus, he denied that the Qur'an really spoke of any supernatural or miraculous occurrences. And he argued that, far from allowing slavery and polygyny, the Qur'an had in effect prohibited them. Nor did he think that the Qur'an's strictures against usury were to be understood as a prohibition of all financial interest; the monetary assets of his college were kept in interest-bearing accounts.[38] Underlying these and other positions was his fierce opposition to taqlid. He blamed it, as would generations of modernists, for the intellectual stagnation of Muslims, but an attack on it also meant a challenge to the authority of the `ulama that was anchored precisely in firm adherence to the norms and methods of their earlier masters. His rejection of taqlid had obvious affinities with the Ahl-i Hadith. The latter did not, however, share his advocacy of a wholehearted embrace of European modernity.

As Sayyid Ahmad and some of his associates viewed it, his ventures in Islamic theology were intended to produce an antidote to the sort of doubts about Islam that he knew an exposure to Western learning would create in the Muslim youth.[39] The task of producing a new theology could hardly be left to a people—the `ulama—who refused to see that the *old* theology was no longer adequate to responding to the religious challenges Muslims faced and who, in any case, had only a faint understanding of the social, intellectual, and political developments in the contemporary world to which a new theology had to be a response. From the `ulama's perspective, however, any such theology was meant only to turn people away from core Islamic beliefs. Despite a broadly shared culture, these were not small disagreements between the early modernists and the `ulama. They remained unresolved. That the study of Islam did not acquire more than a token place at what purported to be the *Muhammadan* Anglo-*Oriental* College had much to do with the fact that the purpose for which the college was founded was the imparting of an English, not an Islamic, education. So far as the study of Islam was concerned, the most significant intellectual presence on campus during the last decade and a half of Sayyid Ahmad's life was Shibli's. Yet, his was an uncomfortable presence. According to Shibli's biographer, part of what had led to his departure soon after the death of Sayyid Ahmad in 1898 was the concern of the administration that his lectures on Islam had become a little too popular with the students and were leading them to neglect their other subjects.[40] But the `ulama's opposition to Sayyid Ahmad the theologian had also helped marginalize the study of Islam at Aligarh, with the modernist reformer concluding in effect that salvaging his educational venture was much more important than courting ceaseless religious controversy. This meant excluding not just his own theological views from the curriculum, but, with some exceptions, much of Islam itself. The exceptions included collective ritual prayers, which even the English administrators of the college saw as good for a sense of discipline among the students. [41]

Indian Politics and the Wider Muslim World

How did colonial politics shape the key orientations that formed the Islamic mosaic of the late nineteenth and the early twentieth centuries? How was the political landscape itself shaped by them? And how did developments in the wider Islamic world impact on, and were themselves impacted by, Islam in colonial India? The early modernists, to begin with them, were largely docile in political terms. Their calls upon Muslims to acquire an English education and to rethink the ways they understood their religious tradition were predicated, after all, on the conviction that the British Empire was there to stay and that the best the Muslims could hope for was a position of respectability within the framework of that empire. Given moreover that Aligarh College was modeled on English institutions of learning, it made sense for Sayyid Ahmad Khan and his associates to look to colonial authorities for moral, financial, and political support. As conservative Muslim opposition to Aligarh grew, with a concomitant weakening in its fundraising efforts, so did its dependence on the patronage of the British.[42]

This indebtedness meant that political causes that were unpopular with colonial authorities were distasteful to Sayyid Ahmad as well. The British were suspicious of the Indian National Congress, founded in 1885, and of its effort to mobilize Indian political opinion in pressing for greater indigenous representation in the governance of the colony. Sayyid Ahmad, too, opposed this organization and urged Muslims to stay away from it. But it was not just a fear of antagonizing the British that underlay this opposition. Sayyid Ahmad could take daring positions when he deemed it necessary to do so. Against the counsel of some of his associates, he had embarked on his biography of the Prophet Muhammad to refute that of Sir William Muir (d. 1905), despite the fact that Muir was one of the most powerful men in northern India at the time.[43] Sayyid Ahmad's misgivings about the Congress also rested on larger concerns. Among these was the worry that Muslims would be at a disadvantage vis-à-vis the Hindu majority in a system of representative government. There was also the fear that the better-educated and politically more conscious Bengalis—by whom he primarily meant Hindu Bengalis—would lord it over everyone else in any such dispensation. And at the heart of his discomfort with the Congress was the conviction that India was home to many diverse nations, and that Muslims would be ill-served if they labored under the illusion that they and the Hindus were members of a single nation with shared interests.[44]

Less than a decade after Sayyid Ahmad's death, similar concerns had begun to find expression in the All India Muslim League. Limited forms of representative government were on the horizon in British India, and the question was no longer whether but *how* Muslims should participate in the emerging political system. The founders of the Muslim League, many of whom had strong ties to Aligarh College, believed that Muslims had their own interests to protect and that they were best represented as a distinct religious and political community. This meant, among other things, that Muslims ought to have the right to separate electorates, whereby only Muslims could vote for Muslim candidates standing for elected office. A number of Muslims did participate in the annual meetings of the Congress from its first years, and it was a Muslim from Bombay, Badr-ud-din Tyabji (d. 1906), who presided over the third annual session of the organization in 1888. Some even at Aligarh had pro-Congress leanings. Shibli was one of them.[45] Conversely, there would be occasions in the course of its early career when the Muslim League would join hands with the Congress in pursuit of particular causes. Nonetheless, the idea of a separate Muslim identity was a powerful one, and no organization would embody it more fully than the Muslim League.

Like the modernists, the `ulama, too, were generally docile during the half century or so following the Mutiny of 1857. That was a lesson learnt from the Mutiny itself. The two founding fathers of the Deoband madrasa, Muhammad Qasim Nanotawi (d. 1877) and Rashid Ahmad Gangohi (d. 1905), were remembered to have participated briefly in this last great challenge to the onset of colonial rule, and the decision of their mentor, Hajji Imdad Allah, to leave India for good and take up residence in Mecca may have had to do with those events as well. Even as their religious activities were a response to the challenges of colonial rule and, in this sense at least, had a political dimension to them, the early Deobandis were keen to steer clear of overt political activism. Colonial authorities, too, tended to leave them alone.

By the early years of the twentieth century, however, Deoband was undergoing change in its politics.[46] Some at the madrasa were keen to establish a network of their own, perhaps along the lines of an old boys' association that already existed for Aligarh's graduates.[47] To this end, Mahmud Hasan (d. 1920), a much respected professor of hadith at Deoband, had summoned `Ubayd Allah Sindhi (d. 1944), a Sikh convert to Islam who had once been a student at the madrasa, to establish an association of Deoband's alumni now scattered all over the country. Though the thinking behind this association, the Jam`iyyat al-Ansar, remains opaque, it caused enough nervousness among the loyalist administrators of Deoband to expel Sindhi from the madrasa. That was in 1913. Indians, including many Muslims, were by then increasingly awake to the possibilities of political action to resist colonial rule. With a vigorous Indian Muslim press, there also was a new awareness in many circles of the dismal plight Muslims of India shared with their coreligionists abroad. Morocco was brought under French colonial rule in 1912 and Italy soon came to rule Libya. Greece, Bulgaria, Serbia, and Montenegro had joined hands against the Ottoman Empire, which fared poorly in these Balkan wars. There was much to unsettle such accommodation as many Muslims had made over the past half century to life under colonial rule.

With Mahmud Hasan's blessings, if not at his instigation, Sindhi sought to find ways of bridging some of the gulf between the products of institutions like Deoband and those of Aligarh. This was a cause to which he would remain committed all his life. Another commitment of his at this time was pan-Islam. Indeed, the effort to bring together Muslims of varied intellectual formations was part of the larger venture to forge an anti-colonial alliance among Muslims of different lands. The latter effort soon overtook the former. Shortly after the beginning of World War I, Sindhi left for Kabul to explore the possibilities of a grand coalition that would include Muslim and non-Muslim revolutionaries from India, the king of Afghanistan, the Ottomans, and the Germans. The plot—remembered by the British colonial authorities as the Silk Letter Conspiracy—came to nothing. Mahmud Hasan, who had traveled from

Deoband to Mecca to assist Sindhi with the plan from the holy city, was arrested by the pro-British Sharif of Mecca and handed over to the British. They interned him and some of his associates on the island of Malta for the duration of the war. Sindhi, for his part, would spend the next quarter century in exile in Afghanistan, Soviet Russia, and Turkey, but mostly the Hijaz, which, by the time he arrived there, had become part of the Saudi kingdom. It was not until 1939 that he was allowed to return to India.

Though Sindhi's efforts to galvanize a pan-Islamic movement against British colonial rule, to bring English-educated and madrasa-trained Muslims together on a shared platform, and to enlist Muslims and non-Muslims in a joint anti-colonial venture had borne little fruit, all three found powerful expression in the Khilafat movement that was launched in India at the conclusion of World War I. The Muslims of India were already perturbed during the course of the war at the prospect of having to fight against the Ottomans on behalf of Britain and its allies; with the Ottoman defeat, the caliphate teetered on the brink of collapse and the security of the Muslim holy places in the Hijaz, which had long been under Ottoman oversight, seemed itself to be in peril. It was in defense of the Ottoman Empire and especially of the Islamic holy lands that the Muslims of India came together as they never had before.

Ottoman claims to the caliphate were not secure. Most glaringly, perhaps, they lacked lineal descent from the Prophet's tribe of Quraysh, which much of medieval constitutional theory had required as a condition for the caliph's legitimacy. Nonetheless, in nineteenth- and early twentieth-century India, the Ottoman Empire had come to be viewed by many as a veritable center of the Muslim world, the symbol of such unity as Muslims still possessed; any threat to it was a threat to Islam itself. Even Sayyid Ahmad Khan had been an avid supporter of the empire, and he had changed this stance only after the British and the Ottoman empires found themselves on opposite sides.[48] Shibli, for his part, had received a medal of honor from the Ottoman government in the course of his travels through Istanbul and Egypt in the early 1890s,[49] and it was at his initiative that the Syrian pan-Islamist Rashid Rida had been invited to preside over the annual session of the Nadwat al-`Ulama in 1912.[50] Shibli, however, had died in 1914, and new leaders were on the scene by that time.

One of them was Abul-Kalam Azad (d. 1958), a traditionally educated religious scholar who had become a firebrand Urdu journalist. At the conclusion of World War I, Azad came to play a key role in mobilizing Muslim sentiment around the idea that the defense of the Ottoman caliphate was a religious obligation upon all believers. In a book, *The Problem of the Caliphate*, published in 1920, he castigated the British for allowing freedom to its Muslim subjects on "small" matters, such as prayer and fasting, while attacking the institution of the caliphate, which stood at the very foundation of their religion.[51] Turning on their head the modernist apologetics that had sought to push jihad to the margins of Islamic doctrine and practice, Azad argued that it became a binding obligation upon every single Muslim (*fard `ayn*) when a Muslim land was under attack and that this obligation was plainly stated in the very same Islamic legal texts to which the British themselves had given official recognition, for purposes of judicial administration, in their courts in India.[52] In a withering swipe at Deoband, whose administrative head had recently been honored by the government for his loyalism, Azad stated: "The spectacle of those claimants to religious knowledge and veneration who have received [such] titles ... is striking. ... They profess to be religious leaders of the Muslims and they control large institutions of learning—institutions in which the very books are studied day and night that enumerate [the aforementioned] rules [on jihad]. Even stranger is the fact that many Muslims whole-heartedly accept their claims to leadership."[53] The Muslims clearly needed new religious leadership, and Azad was eager to present himself as a candidate for it.

Others were on call, too. The aforementioned Mahmud Hasan had great stature even before he became publicly associated with pan-Islamic causes. His aura of piety was such that 600 of the 750 or so people on board the ship that was taking him from India to Arabia had become his disciples en route.[54] But Mahmud Hasan was gravely ill when released from internment on Malta after World War I. He died in 1920, though not before he had publicly given his blessings to the Khilafat movement and to the alliance between Hindus and Muslims in their anti-colonial struggle. Another key figure from among the `ulama on the political scene at this time was `Abd al-Bari Farangi Mahalli (d. 1926), the scion of a distinguished family of religious scholars from Lucknow. He was also a Sufi pir, his wide circle including some English-educated Muslims as well.

By far the most prominent leader of the Khilafat movement was the journalist Muhammad `Ali, a graduate of Aligarh who had subsequently obtained a BA from Oxford. Though he had benefited from Shibli's presence at Aligarh and would later become a disciple of `Abd al-Bari, Muhammad `Ali was the product of a very different milieu than the one to which the early modernists had belonged. His education reflected Sayyid Ahmad's decision to exclude any substantial study of Islam from Aligarh's curriculum, and it would be later in his life, under British internment, that Muhammad `Ali would "discover" the Qur'an.[55] The significance of that discovery will be discussed in chapter 4. What bears mentioning here is that his lack of religious credentials did not prevent him from a full embrace of a religious idiom in defense of the Ottoman caliphate or the forging of an alliance with the traditionally educated religious scholars.

Even as he had urged Muslims to end all dealings with the British, Azad, like Mahmud Hasan, had provided them with a religious justification for cooperation with the Hindus. Adducing Qur'an 60.10, Azad had argued that Islam did not forbid friendship with non-Muslims qua non-Muslims but only with those among them who were hostile to Muslim interests.[56] `Abd al-Bari and the `ulama-led Jam`iyyat al-`Ulama-i Hind, founded at the end of World War I, took a similar view. It was at the hands of Muhammad `Ali that the potential for bringing Muslims and Hindus together on a shared platform was to be realized, however. His key partner on the Hindu side was M. K. Gandhi (d. 1948), a lawyer who had recently returned from South Africa and had come to establish himself as one of the most important leaders of the Congress.

That Gandhi should have joined hands with the Khilafatists and the `ulama in defense of a resolutely Islamic institution might sound surprising. After all, pan-Islam conjured anxieties about a grand transnational alliance against non-Muslims not just among the British but also in many Hindu circles. For Gandhi, however, this was an opportunity to establish closer ties with the Muslim leadership and to mobilize popular sentiment against colonial rule. For their part, Muhammad `Ali, his Aligarh-educated elder brother Shaukat `Ali (d. 1938), Azad, and other Khilafat leaders did not need to make neat distinctions between Indian and Islamic interests, for the British were a threat to both sets of them. And so the alliance was forged. But it did not last long. In his struggle against apartheid in South Africa, Gandhi had been developing a politics of peaceful noncooperation and of civil disobedience, and it is these political strategies that he wanted to bring to the Khilafat movement. By contrast, some Hindu and Muslim leaders—including Muhammad Ali Jinnah (d. 1948) and Jawaharlal Nehru (d. 1964)—preferred negotiation with the colonial regime; there were those, on the other hand, who wanted a fuller confrontation with the government. The anticolonial sentiment that the Khilafat and noncooperation movements had generated proved difficult for their leaders to contain, and challenges to colonial authority inevitably came to acquire violent dimensions. In one notable incident, twenty policemen were burned alive in a UP village, leading Gandhi to indefinitely suspend the noncooperation movement and to call off the impending civil disobedience movement. That dealt a blow to the Khilafat movement, but it was not the only one. The leaders of the movement had spent a good deal of their energy raising funds for the Ottomans, and a portion of the proceeds would play a not insignificant role in the Turkish war of independence.[57] But there also were instances in which the Khilafat funds had been misappropriated, and the much publicized financial scandals contributed their part to weakening the movement. The greatest psychological setback to the movement was administered, however, by the Turks themselves. In late 1922, the Turkish Grand National Assembly decided that the religious institution of the caliphate and its putatively political arm, the sultanate, were to be separated and the latter abolished. In early 1924, the caliphate itself was terminated. The following years would see much discussion of the possibilities of resurrecting the caliphate, and there were many competing candidates for it. The movement in India no longer had its raison d'être, however.

Despite its failure, the Khilafat movement was momentous in significance. Confirming the worst fears of colonial authorities, it had demonstrated the power of pan-Islam in mobilizing Muslim sentiment. It had shown that the pan-Islamic sentiment could be effectively combined with Indian politics and that Muslims and Hindus could come together in pursuit of at least partially shared goals. It had also highlighted the authority and influence of the `ulama. Many Muslims had been willing to give up their jobs when the `ulama told them, in a famous "collective fatwa," that they could not work for or under a government that was hostile to Islam.[58] More dramatically, Azad and some fellow `ulama had issued a fatwa in 1920 stating that it was no longer permissible for people to live in what, under British rule, had become a "land of war"—an infidel territory.[59] Tens of thousands of people heeded the call to begin what would soon turn out to be a disastrous trek to Afghanistan. Even apart from such demonstrations of the `ulama's influence on the lives and thinking of ordinary believers, the Khilafat movement would have been inconceivable without the religious justification prominent religious scholars had provided for it. It is a mark of the prominence of the `ulama in the movement that even the English-educated Muhammad `Ali and his brother Shaukat would come to be known, in the course of their participation in it, by epithets typically reserved for the `ulama; they had become *Mawlana* Muhammad `Ali and *Mawlana* Shaukat `Ali, and they retained these titles till the end of their lives. The movement had also shown that it was possible for the English-educated—the "men of the 'New Light,'" as Muhammad `Ali and others referred to them—and the `ulama to come together on a shared platform. The `Ali brothers had Mawlana `Abd al-Bari of Farangi Mahall as their pir, their spiritual guide, and those associated with Aligarh and with Deoband worked hand in hand. No less remarkable was the spectacle of `ulama belonging to varied doctrinal orientations working together in defense of the Ottoman caliphate and the Islamic holy lands.

But the limits of such cooperation were equally telling, and no less significant for future developments. Even as many among the `ulama had joined hands with the English-educated, the `ulama were not a united bloc. Ahmad Riza Khan, the leader of the Barelawis, had been appalled at Hindu leaders being invited into mosques in the euphoria of the Khilafat movement.[60] Some prominent Deobandis shared those misgivings. Unlike Mahmud Hasan and Husayn Ahmad Madani, a fellow internee on the island of Malta who would soon rise to greater prominence in Indian politics, Ashraf `Ali Thanawi was opposed to the movement. He, too, found it intolerable that Gandhi—for whom he liked to use the Qur'an term *taghut*, "idol"—and other Hindu leaders should have been invited into mosques to address Muslims.[61] The suggestion on the part of some Khilafat leaders, notably the fellow scholar `Abd al-Bari, that Muslims refrain from the consumption of cow meat was equally unpalatable to Thanawi.[62] It was not that consuming it was obligatory; it was rather, Thanawi said, that no one had the authority to forbid what Islamic law had permitted, and doing so in deference to the polytheists was the more reprehensible. Thanawi also believed that Muslims were party to an implicit "contract" with the British colonial authorities, and the Khilafat agitation was not only a breach of that contract, the failure of the movement also threatened to make life less tolerable for Muslims.[63]

Though in the case of some Muslim leaders—Azad and Madani, in particular—the Khilafat movement helped forge lifelong alliances with the Hindu political leadership, communal harmony had begun to fray while the movement was still in progress. The concord of the modernist leadership and the `ulama did not endure either. Here, too, those paying some attention would have noticed signs of vulnerability at the very moment that this alliance was being forged. The basis on which the authors of the "collective fatwa" of 1920 had called upon Muslims to boycott government-supported Westernized educational institutions is telling in this regard. "The prevailing education and training lead to ... evils such as the predominance of the love of worldly affairs, love for honour, worship of lust, negligence of and carelessness towards religion, etc., and all these things are 'haram' [forbidden]. Therefore, on the basis of 'the means of sin are sin' it is obligatory to refrain from getting and giving such education."[64] Though the modernist and the `ulama leadership of the movement was as one in arguing for this boycott, justifications such as these leave little ambiguity about what the `ulama really thought about the "men of the new light." The latter's own misgivings, as expressed by Muhammad `Ali in an autobiographical fragment, are not difficult to detect even in what profess to be words of praise for the `ulama who had joined hands with the modernist leaders of the movement; for the other `ulama, his contempt was unrelieved. "Be it said to the credit of the `Ulama," Muhammad `Ali wrote, "that they did not hesitate ... to *pocket their pride* and in a way even accept the lead of men whom they had but a generation ago finally consigned to perdition.... Only those of the Ulama whose concern seemed to be the retention of their own quasi-priestly authority more than the maintenance of orthodoxy still kept aloof, and these for the most part exhibited a deplorable pusillanimity when faced with some unpleasant consequences of religious zeal."[65] Not long after the end of the Khilafat movement, Muhammad `Ali and his brother Shaukat had parted company even with their own pir, `Abd al-Bari.[66]

Finally, the Khilafat movement had raised the question, more forcefully than it had been posed before, of what the relationship was between pan-Islam and national belonging. Was it the case, as Iqbal had asserted in a speech that was quoted in the 1911 census of India, that the "idea of Islam is ... our eternal home or country wherein we live, move, and have our being"? That would mean, as he thought it did, that "it is above everything else as England is above all else to the Englishman and 'Deutschland über alles' to the Germans."[67] At the other end of the spectrum on this question, the Kemalists of the nascent Turkish Republic had decided that no reconciliation between pan-Islam and nationalist aspirations was possible. Some among the Indian leaders, too, would come to renounce their pan-Islamic past. `Ubayd Allah Sindhi, one of the most zealous in the pursuit of a grand pan-Islamic alliance, was later also among the most vocal in criticizing such ambitions, counseling his coreligionists and others to focus instead on building an intercommunal platform geared toward Indian independence and socioeconomic justice.[68] Less vocally, Azad, too, moved away from pan-Islamism and in the direction of secular nationalism as the best framework in which to promote the interests of the people of India. Others seemed to want it both ways. As Muhammad `Ali put it just weeks before his death in 1931: "I have a culture, a polity, an outlook on life—a complete synthesis which is Islam. Where God commands, I am a Muslim first, a Muslim second, and a Muslim last, and nothing but a Muslim.... But where India is concerned, where the welfare of India is concerned, I am an Indian first, an Indian second, an Indian last, and nothing but an Indian.... I belong to two circles of equal size, but which are not concentric. One is India, and the other is the Muslim world."[69]

Islam, Law, and Politics in the 1930s

Many of the religious and political trends we have encountered so far are mirrored, in some of their complexity and the ambiguities of their interrelationship, in the career of Muhammad Iqbal, the single most important modernist intellectual of late colonial India. Iqbal was a product not of Aligarh but instead of another institution of English learning, the Government College of Lahore, and he later studied philosophy at Cambridge and Munich, from where he received a PhD in 1908. While in England, he had been called to the bar, and practicing law was to be his principal means of livelihood. Yet unlike many other modernists of his generation but like those of a generation earlier, Iqbal was anchored in some key areas of the Islamic intellectual and religious tradition. His doctoral dissertation was a study of Islamic metaphysics in the medieval Persian world, and it was in the Persian language that he wrote some of his most eloquent verse.

Iqbal's early poetry reveals a marked attachment to the "soil of the homeland" of which, he said, he considered "every speck to be a deity."[70] Though he never became a firebrand in the manner of Azad and Muhammad `Ali, the expanding reach of European colonialism and the increasingly obvious weaknesses of the Ottoman Empire in the early years of the twentieth century came nonetheless to shape his thinking in other directions. Before long, as noted, Iqbal had begun to speak of Islam as the "eternal home" of Muslims, and he would develop this theme during the remainder of his prolific career. A famous passage in a long Persian poem Iqbal published in 1917 reads:

> Our essence is not bound by any place
> The vigour of our wine is not contained
> In any bowl. Chinese and Indian
> Alike the sherd that constitutes our jar
> Turkish and Syrian alike the clay
> Forming our body. Neither is our heart
> Of India, or Syria, or Rum
> Nor any fatherland do we profess
> Except Islam . . .[71]

Iqbal's Persian epic, *Javid nama* (1932), has Jamal al-din "al-Afghani" (d. 1897), the quintessential pan-Islamist of the late nineteenth century, admonish fellow Muslims in rousing words such as the following:

> The Lord of the West, cunning from head to toe
> Taught the people of religion the concept of country
> He thinks of the centre, while you are at discord—
> Give up talk of Syria, Palestine, Iraq!
> If you can discriminate between good and evil
> You will not bind your hearts to clods, stones, bricks.
> What is religion? To rise up from the face of the dust
> So that the pure soul may become aware of itself![72]

Similar ideas informed his presidential address to the All India Muslim League in Allahabad in 1930. There he argued that "Islam, regarded as an ethical ideal plus a certain kind of polity—[that is,] . . . a social structure regulated by a legal system and animated by a specific ethical ideal—has been the chief formative factor in the life-history of the Muslims of India."[73] Thanks to this "free gift" of Islam to them, they alone among the peoples of India were "a nation in the modern sense of the word."[74] Insomuch as it was *Islam's* gift, this sense of nationhood transcended particularistic boundaries. However, it could not exist as a mere idea; it had to find concrete realization. Not unlike "the Lord of the West," Muslims, too, needed a sociopolitical center, which nonetheless would not bind their hearts to mere clods, stones, and bricks. For all the pan-Islamic drift of Iqbal's thought, there is a palpable tension here between what Muhammad `Ali had described almost contemporaneously as his two nonconcentric circles.

The ambivalent relationship between Islamic universalism and territorial centralization is illustrated further by Iqbal's response to the Kemalist termination of the Ottoman caliphate. One might have assumed that the unceremonious demise of a key pan-Islamic symbol would evoke deep anguish from the poet. However, though he had briefly served on the Punjab Khilafat Committee, his participation in the movement was at best listless, and he had been opposed to the noncooperation movement and what it entailed in terms of the boycott of educational institutions.[75] Remarkably, in 1922, at a time when many other Indians were renouncing the titles they had received from colonial authorities, Iqbal had received knighthood. And once the Kemalists had made their fateful move, it was not with the emotion of a poet but with the cool-headed analysis of a philosopher that he commented on it. In a lecture on ijtihad, in which he had spoken in a characteristic modernist vein of the need for a radical rethinking of the Islamic legal tradition, Iqbal adduced the Turkish Grand National Assembly's decision to abolish the caliphate as an instance of precisely such rethinking: "Turkey's Ijtihad is that according to the spirit of Islam the Caliphate or Imamate can be vested in a body of persons, or an elected Assembly."[76] He considered this to be a "perfectly sound" position.[77] More importantly, he saw Republican Turkey as charting the path to an intellectual awakening of momentous proportions:

> It is, I think, the English thinker Hobbes who makes this acute observation that to have a succession of identical thoughts and feelings is to have no thoughts and feelings at all. Such is the lot of most Muslim countries today. They are mechanically repeating old values, whereas the Turk is on the way to creating new values. He has passed through great experiences which have revealed his deeper self to him. In him life has begun to move, change, and amplify, giving birth to new desires, bringing new difficulties and suggesting new interpretations. The question which confronts him today, and which is likely to confront other Muslim countries in the near future, is whether the Law of Islam is capable of evolution—a question which will require great intellectual effort, and is sure to be answered in the affirmative.[78]

Though Iqbal was not always quite so laudatory in his comments on the Kemalists,[79] his misgivings about nationalism took a back seat in this instance to his excitement about new possibilities of ijtihad. Those misgivings never went away, however. They would find a striking expression in the poet's last days, conjoined in that instance with all that the modernists disliked about the `ulama.

In a speech in late 1937, the aforementioned Husayn Ahmad Madani, a leading figure in the Jam`iyyat al-`Ulama-i Hind and a close ally of the Congress, had made the remark that nations were defined by territory, so that the Muslims living in the subcontinent were part of the Indian nation (qawm). There was some misreporting of this observation in the Indian press and Iqbal took Madani to be asserting that a religious community (millat) was defined in territorial terms. He reacted sharply, insisting, as he had in his writings for many years, that the bonds of Islam transcended the limits imposed by territory, race, and language.[80] But the controversy involved issues that were much

larger than the precise connotations of particular terms—qawm and millat—
or even the universal claims of Islam, on which Madani's view was not different from Iqbal's.[81] Iqbal believed that to see a nation as defined in territorial
terms was, in case of Muslims, to sunder the unity of their global religious
community. Madani, for his part, thought that his way of making an accommodation with Indian nationalism was in fact truer to the spirit of Islamic
universalism. Differences of religion, Madani argued, were immaterial to the
constitution of a nation, though they were central, of course, to a community
of faith—the millat. Conversely, the unity of that faith-community was not
undermined by the existence of territorially based composite nations. In subsequent years, he would develop this point further to assert, in articulating
his opposition to the demand for a separate Muslim homeland, that what
contravened global Muslim unity was the existence of territorially based *Muslim* polities such as the one being demanded in the name of Pakistan. The
assumption was, of course, that a secular state comprising members of different religious communities would not demand religious allegiance from its citizens; a Muslim state, on the other hand, would demand such allegiance from
the Muslims living within its territories, thereby serving in effect to cut them
off from the wider Muslim world.

From Iqbal's vantage, Madani was the very prototype of the `ulama who
did not understand modern ideas, in this case, nationalism, and were thus
providing dangerously bad counsel to their followers. If, Iqbal wrote in refuting Madani, "a nation comprises different religions and communities, the
communities generally die away and the only common factor that remains in
the individuals of that nation is irreligiousness."[82] At the very least, in such a
nation, "Islam will be reduced to an ethical ideal with indifference to its social
order as an inevitable consequence."[83] But men like Madani did not understand the Qur'an either: "Circumstances have forced the present-day ulama to
say things and interpret the Quran in a way which could never have been the
intention of the Prophet and the Quran."[84] In an extraordinary move, he concluded the rejoinder to Madani by comparing the latter's position to that of
the Ahmadis, against whom the Deobandis had been leading the charge for
many years: adopting the modern ideology of nationalism was tantamount to
admitting, Iqbal said, that Islam was imperfect and needed something new,
much like the Ahmadis thought that Islam had needed a new prophet.[85] The
modernists have often castigated the `ulama for failing to change with the
times. There is some irony here in Iqbal's upbraiding Madani and his likes for
being rather too willing to change, thereby losing sight of what were meant to
be timeless Islamic teachings.

By the time of Iqbal's death in April 1938, at least some elements in the Islamic mosaic of colonial India had come to acquire a sharper delineation than
had been the case a half century or so earlier. Many others remained fluid,

however, as they do to this day. Thanks to Ahmad Riza Khan, who had died in 1921, the Barelawis had an identity that went beyond an amorphous devotionalism; they were a distinct doctrinal orientation in late colonial India. In at least some cases, the differences between the Imami Shi`a and the Sunnis had also become sharper. Sunnis of Lucknow, like those of many other places, had long participated in Muharram processions commemorating the martyrdom of Husayn, a grandson of the Prophet Muhammad and the third Shi`i imam. Yet, such processions could also be flashpoints for sectarian tension because they provided occasions for ritual Shi`i execration of leading companions (*sahaba*) of Muhammad. The Shi`a hold these companions—including Abu Bakr and `Umar, the first two successors of Muhammad—responsible for thwarting the legitimate claims of `Ali to the community's headship; the Sunnis, for their part, revere these companions as second only to the Prophet in virtue and authority. Nothing underscored the growing tensions between the Sunnis and the Shi`a in late colonial Lucknow more than the demand by some Sunnis to publicly praise the Prophet's companions (*madh-i sahaba*) as a counterpoint to Shi`i execration of them. Husayn Ahmad Madani was one of the key leaders of this campaign.

Madani's role in this controversy suggests that the Deobandis, too, had come to articulate a distinct identity for themselves, indeed well before the Barelawis did, and their influence would continue to grow in late colonial times. Their ever-increasing madrasas were key to this identity and to their visibility in the colonial religious sphere. The official history of Deoband, written to commemorate its centenary, counted nearly 9,000 madrasas providing religious education at various levels throughout South Asia.[86] It is worth noting by way of comparison that the aforementioned `Abd al-Bari of Farangi Mahall had founded a madrasa in Lucknow in 1905, but, for all his family's prestige and networks, the madrasa spawned no other institutions and its own doors would close in 1969.[87] The Barelawis, the Ahl-i Hadith, and the Shi`a had their madrasas as well, but they did not compete in numbers with those of the Deobandis.

The Deobandis had other assets, too. Though they were not necessarily more prolific than their doctrinal rivals, at least two of their works had acquired the status of classics already in colonial times, unlike anything produced by their rivals. One was a translation of the Qur'an by Mahmud Hasan, the revered scholar involved in the Silk Letter Conspiracy. Even before that involvement turned him into a figure of national importance, the administrators of Deoband expected his translation to become a source of revenue for the madrasa's publishing house.[88] It is based on an early Urdu translation of the Qur'an by a son of Shah Wali Allah, and it has, in turn, remained perhaps the most influential Urdu rendering of the Qur'an.[89] The other book was the *Heavenly Ornaments* (*Bihishti zewar*) of Ashraf `Ali Thanawi. As noted, Thanawi was a much sought after Sufi master and a seemingly limitless source of fatwas, all of which helped cement not just his own status in late colonial India but also that of his doctrinal orientation. That influence, in marked contrast with that of most other scholars of his age, had reached the central legislative assembly itself by the mid-1930s. This merits a brief detour here.

Though the British had given recognition to Islamic law in matters relating to personal status, their judicial administration was based on the assumption that any judge schooled in English common law and ruling according to what were taken to be the Muslim community's authoritative norms could decide on the matter at hand. To many `ulama, however, none but a Muslim judge could implement the religious law. Thus, it was impermissible to them for a woman to have recourse to colonial courts to have her marriage dissolved in the event, say, of the disappearance of her husband. Instead, that woman had to wait for the duration of a natural lifespan before being able to presume the death of her husband. The hardship that the `ulama's insistence on following the relevant Hanafi norms created in such instances was sufficiently severe for an apparently substantial number of women to renounce Islam itself. There is nothing to suggest that this was a protest against Islam; it sought rather to exploit a loophole in Hanafi law. Medieval jurists had stipulated that apostasy served to dissolve a marriage. In earlier times, an apostate woman would presumably have been forced to reconvert and been punished for her infraction, but, with its commitment to religious freedom, apostasy carried no such consequences in British India.

The `ulama were compelled to respond, with Thanawi taking the lead. He conferred with prominent scholars in India, most of them Deobandi, wrote to scholars in the Hijaz, and then published a juridical treatise—*The Consummate Stratagem for the Helpless Wife* (al-Hila al-najiza lil-halila al-`ajiza)— in 1933.[90] The book argued that a woman whose husband had gone missing could have her marriage dissolved *four* years after his disappearance, as the somewhat more accommodating Maliki law stipulated, though it still required the decision of a Muslim judge before such dissolution could take place. It also argued that the woman's apostasy had no effect on the marriage. When the Dissolution of Muslim Marriages Bill was introduced in the central legislative assembly in December 1935, it was this treatise that provided the intellectual basis for it.

The debate on the bill and its outcome are illuminating not only as an illustration of a growing Deobandi influence,[91] but also for what it tells us about the ambiguities of the `ulama's relationship with the modernists. When the bill was enacted into law in 1939, the key `ulama demand that the dissolution of marriage take place at the hands of a Muslim official had been pointedly left out. Significantly, many modern-educated Muslims had themselves opposed that demand. As the representative of the Muslim Ladies Association of Karachi had observed, "Though the spirit of Muslim law requires that

... [it] should be administered by Muslim kazis [judges], my Association is not aware that the Tribunal in a country which has a non-Muslim government must necessarily be Muslim."[92] Many others had concurred, not all for the same reasons.[93] In his concluding remarks on the bill, Sir Muhammad Zafrulla Khan of the All India Muslim League had argued that the requirement relating to Muslim judges was "not at all practicable" and, in any case, that a non-Muslim judge might well be more knowledgeable than one who was Muslim. He had also observed that to give legislative effect to this demand after nearly a century or so during which non-Muslim judges had annulled Muslim marriages and permitted women plaintiffs to remarry would be tantamount to "casting the stigma of illegitimacy upon innocent people and ... laying the foundation of widespread and complicated litigation."[94]

Zafrulla Khan was an Ahmadi. In 1953, as Pakistan's first foreign minister, he would be at the center of an anti-Ahmadi agitation in Pakistan, though that story belongs to chapter 5. In view of the history of Deobandi hostility toward the Ahmadis, it is ironic that he found himself on the same side as Ashraf ʿAli Thanawi on many core aspects of the Dissolution of Muslim Marriages Bill. Yet, Zafrulla Khan was also a modernist, and as suggested by his opposition to the demand for Muslim judges, there were significant differences between him and the ʿulama. His reasoning, moreover, was his own even when he seemed to *agree* with the ʿulama. Whereas Thanawi had made a painstaking case to show that certain strands of the Hanafi tradition allowed a marriage to stand even in case of a spouse's apostasy, Zafrulla Khan's position was far more radical:

> as the result of such study as I have been able to devote to this question over a number of years, I venture to submit that in Islam as interpreted in the time of the Holy Prophet and in the time of the first four caliphs, for mere change of faith unaccompanied by anything else which might constitute an offense against the State, there is prescribed no penalty whatsoever.... [T]his doctrine of the automatic dissolution of marriage in case of a woman who renounces Islam is a legacy from the doctrine of capital punishment for traitors, which was misapplied to apostates, and the attempt is being made by means of this ... [legislation] to abolish one of the consequences of that penalty.[95]

In its break with the classical scholastic tradition in favor of a direct recourse to the foundational texts and in its liberal commitments, this was vintage modernism. The modernists had helped the ʿulama get some of what they wanted, but not without leaving a distinctly sour taste in their mouths.

Two years earlier, in 1937, the outcome of another legislative initiative had turned out even less happily for the ʿulama. In that instance, it was the Bombay-based lawyer and president of the Muslim League, Mohammad Ali

Jinnah, who had taken the lead in shepherding the Muslim Personal Law (Shariat) Application Bill through the central legislative assembly. The initiative had had the support of the Deoband-dominated Jam'iyyat al-'Ulama-i Hind—"the greatest Moslem religious body," as the bill's statement of objects and reasons had characterized it in again underscoring the growing prominence of the Deobandi orientation in the Indian religious landscape.[96] A key rationale for the bill, which sought to replace customary norms with the shari'a in matters of personal status, was to restore to Muslim women the rights that were often denied to them in practice.[97] The situation that the bill sought to rectify prevailed largely in the Punjab, where the British colonial administration was tied to the support of the landed magnates. The landholdings there had needed to be protected from fragmentation not just at the hands of rural, often Hindu, creditors but also from the workings of the Islamic law of inheritance, which granted women shares that were unequal to those of men but substantial enough to threaten the viability of agricultural estates. In a milieu in which the 'ulama had been preaching and writing for decades against un-Islamic, including local customary, practices, it had come to look increasingly scandalous to many Muslims that they should be prevented from living according to their sacred law. This bill was a symbolically resonant effort to remedy just that.

The symbolism of the bill soon came to get the better of its substance, however. Under pressure from colonial officials, as well from the estate holders themselves, the inheritance of *agricultural* land—which is where the most egregious contravention of the shari'a law tended to occur—was removed from the bill's purview from the start. Ironically, therefore, the very women whose "disgraceful" status[98] had prompted this legislation in the first place were largely left out of it. Yet, this did not divest the bill of all its appeal, which rested after all on the claim that the shari'a, however truncated it had come to be in colonial India, was being brought back to life. As David Gilmartin has argued, Jinnah, fully alert to this appeal, was willing to make all necessary compromises on the bill's content as long as its shari'a-laden symbolism was retained.[99]

Given those compromises, the 'ulama's response was mixed. Husayn Ahmad Madani clearly viewed it as a failure.[100] To scholars of his ilk, too much had been conceded on the path to this legislation, which meant that it could no longer be viewed as an expression of the shari'a, properly speaking. More ominously, the modernists' willingness to see the shari'a tailored as necessary suggested that Islam was merely a plaything in their hands, that they would stop at nothing in pursuit of their interests. Yet, there *were* 'ulama, of decidedly lesser stature but influential perhaps in their local contexts, who took a different view. It was that view that Justice Din Muhammad, a respected modernist jurist from the Punjab, had adduced in opposing the shari'at application bill in the first place. He claimed that "none" of the ʿulama of the Punjab, when consulted earlier about such legislation had been

> prepared to say that from a purely Muslim point of view it was essential that a Bill on the lines proposed should be introduced. In fact they expressed their willingness to support any measure which provided for mandatory compensation to be given to the daughters in lieu of their share in their fathers' inheritance.... This by itself would show that the doctors of Islamic law in the Punjab realized the delicacies of the situation here and did not favour any measure which may go to the length visualized in the present Bill.[101]

Though Madani and some modernists would have dismissed such unnamed ʿulama as either insufficiently knowledgeable about their legal tradition or as too beholden to the beneficence of their landholding patrons, such views do show that the ʿulama could take unpredictable and *varied* positions even on important shariʿa-related questions. For his part, Justice Din Muhammad was unusual in recognizing greater interpretive flexibility among the ʿulama than did most of his peers. Iqbal had recognized no such thing in his aforementioned exchange with Madani.

The Movement for Pakistan

For all the criticism directed at it, the Shariʿat Application Act of 1937 was a success for Jinnah. Yet, this was a difficult time for him. The Muslim League had done poorly in the provincial elections held under the Government of India Act of 1935. The Congress, for its part, had won many impressive victories in the elections and had proceeded to form ministries in eight provinces. There were gleams of hope even in those dark days, however. An ʿalim and Sufi of Thanawi's stature had come out in support of the League and, prior to the elections, even the normally pro-Congress Jamʿiyyat al-ʿUlama-i Hind had entered into an alliance with the League. The elections had also shown that the victorious Congress had vulnerabilities of its own when it came to the Muslim vote. It had not won a single seat from among those reserved for Muslims in UP; the League had won twenty-nine of those, out of a total of sixty-six.[102] Choosing to ignore such warning signs, the Congress leadership showed itself unwilling to share power with the League and instead launched a Muslim mass contact campaign—a thinly veiled effort at a hostile takeover of the Muslim constituency. The conduct of the Congress ministries, in UP and elsewhere, was not designed to reassure Muslim skeptics either. There had long been some disconnect between the inclusive, noncommunalist, and secular positions that were the trademark of the Congress high command and an aggressive Hindu-inflected politics at local levels, and this became more noticeable under Congress rule.[103] The Muslim League did everything to play up such instances, to paint them as a preview of an impending Hindu raj, and to present itself as the exclusive representative and guardian of Muslim interests. When the Congress ministries resigned at the outbreak of World War II, in protest against Britain's inducting India into the war without consultation with the Indian political leadership, the League celebrated a "day of deliverance." It was against the backdrop of this experience with the Congress ministries and of the insistence by the Congress leadership that Indian support in the war effort was contingent on a British promise of full independence for India that the Muslim League first articulated its demand for Pakistan.

Speaking in Lahore on March 22, 1940, as the president of the Muslim League, a decade after Iqbal's famous address to the party, Jinnah made the clearest case thus far that the Muslims of India were no mere minority but rather a distinct nation and were accordingly entitled to a political future of their own:

> The problem in India is not of an inter-communal but manifestly of an international character, and it must be treated as such. So long as this basic and fundamental truth is not realized, any constitution that may be built will result in disaster and will prove destructive and harmful not only to the Musalmans, but also to the British and Hindus. If the British Government are really in earnest and sincere to secure the peace and happiness of the people of this Subcontinent, the only course open to us all is to allow the major nations separate homelands, by dividing India into "autonomous national States".... It is extremely difficult to appreciate why our Hindu friends fail to understand the real nature of Islam and Hinduism. They are not religions in the strict sense of the word, but are, in fact, different and distinct social orders. It is a dream that the Hindus and Muslims can ever evolve a common nationality.[104]

The following day, the League adopted a momentous resolution:

> no constitutional plan would be workable in this country or acceptable to the Muslims unless it is designed on the following basic principles, viz, that geographically contiguous units are demarcated into regions which should be so constituted, with such territorial adjustments as may be necessary, that the areas in which the Muslims are numerically in a majority, as in the North-Western and Eastern zones of India, should be grouped to constitute Independent States in which the constituent units shall be autonomous and sovereign.[105]

This had echoes of what Iqbal had said in 1930, and Iqbal had in fact come to be informally associated in his last years with the demand for "Pakistan." A delegation from Egypt's al-Azhar that had visited India in 1936 and met Iqbal had reported that he "speaks of the necessity of the state of Pakistan (*mamlakat Bakistan*), one that will comprise Punjab, Kashmir, the [North-West] Frontier, and Baluchistan in order to return Islam's glory to it in this region. He speaks as well of the exchange of inhabitants between the state of Pakistan and the rest of the Indian states."[106] The word "Pakistan" came not from Iqbal, however, but rather, in 1933, from Rahmat Ali, an imaginative Indian Muslim studying at Cambridge.[107] It was not long after the Muslim League's Lahore Resolution that many friends and foes alike came to associate it with the demand for Pakistan.

Precisely when Jinnah himself adopted the idea of Pakistan, as a state that would be self-governing and separate from the rest of the Indian subcontinent, is a matter of considerable disagreement. Pakistani historiography tends to see the Lahore Resolution of 1940 as marking the decisive moment at which the demand for a separate state was finally articulated, and it was thenceforward only a matter of having it accepted by the British and the Congress. A very different view, which has found wide acceptance among historians of late colonial India, posits that even after Jinnah had come to speak regularly of Pakistan, it was a tactic to secure concessions from the British and the Congress for the Muslim-majority provinces *within* a loosely confederated Indian union.[108] On this view, it was ironically the Congress leadership that, for all its identification with a united India, had eventually concluded that the division of the country was preferable to what would otherwise be a cripplingly weak and ineffective union. If the official Pakistani perspective is too teleological, however, and allows little by way of change since 1940 in the League's thinking on Pakistan, the interpretation that posits Pakistan as essentially a "bargaining counter" until almost the eve of India's partition makes the idea of a Muslim homeland much too vacuous;[109] and it does not adequately account for Jinnah's ability to rally people around it. Mobilizing support for a Muslim center, a homeland, required the conception to have some content, with more substance accruing to it over the years. Conversely, the idea need not be fully worked out, let alone nonnegotiable in its implications, for it to develop a growing appeal. What it did need was for Jinnah to stake out a credible claim that the Muslims of India were a distinct nation and that the Muslim League was their sole representative.

The first of these claims was not a particularly hard sell. After all, the British had long based their administration on the idea that India was inhabited by different religious communities. Much as the Congress resented it, the system of separate electorates had enshrined that idea in the evolving political system of colonial India. The Muslim League's insistence in the 1940s on being a distinct nation represented an extension of that same position. Significantly, even those Muslims who were allied with the Congress did not deny that Muslims were, indeed, a community set apart from the others that inhabited India. In his exchange with Iqbal, as would be recalled, Madani had argued that the Indian Muslims were part of the same nation as the others living in this country, but he had had no doubt, any more than the British or the Muslim League did, that they were a separate religious community. Islamic ties trumped all others, he had said.[110] And he did not even rule out the establishment of an Islamic state in India at some indeterminate point in the future, once the generality of India's inhabitants had converted to Islam.[111] The leaders of the Jam`iyyat al-`Ulama-i Hind did not see in such formulations any slippery slope to the Muslim League view. But some at least of their followers could be excused if they discerned no sharp distinction between a separate community and a separate nation. [112] Even so literate a person as Iqbal had failed to see that distinction in any neat terms.[113]

The second claim, that the Muslim League was the exclusive representative of the Muslim community, was obviously extremely contentious. The Congress wanted to be seen as representing the people of India as a whole, including its Muslims. In striking illustration of that claim, it had elected Abul-Kalam Azad to preside over the party's annual session in March 1940, just days before the Muslim League session at which Jinnah would make his historic speech. Muslim Congressmen like Azad were a standing argument against the Muslim League's raison d'être, just as they were against the very idea of a separate Muslim nationhood. Jinnah had no illusions about that challenge. His Lahore address in March 1940 can be read in part as a point by point refutation of Azad's argument—far more clearly enunciated than anything Madani would ever say—that Muslims had nothing to fear in a united India, for the country belonged as much to them as it did to the Hindus: "Our eleven centuries of shared history has filled all corners of our Indian life with its building blocks," Azad said. "Our languages, our poetry, our literature, our culture, our tastes, our dress, our norms and customs, and numerous facets of our daily lives—there is no area that does not bear the stamp of this shared existence."[114] Jinnah could not have had it more differently: "The Hindus and Muslims belong to two different religious philosophies, social customs, and literature. They neither intermarry nor interdine together, and indeed they belong to two different civilizations which are based mainly on conflicting ideas and conceptions."[115] Jinnah was not above personal rebukes either, which only underscored the gravity of the threat he perceived Muslims like Azad to represent to the League's claims. In July 1940, Jinnah stated in a telegram to Azad: "you have completely forfeited the confidence of Muslim India. Can't you realize you are made a Muslim 'show-boy' Congress President to give it colour that it is national and deceive foreign countries. You represent neither Muslims nor Hindus. The Congress is a Hindu body. If you have self-respect, resign at once."[116] Azad, however, would remain the president of the Congress for the next six years, to the Muslim League leader's great discomfort.

Though Jinnah had to occasionally remind enthusiasts that the Muslim League was "mainly a political organization,"[117] the fact that it was tied to a

particular religious community meant that invocations of Islam were anything but uncommon from its platform. Iqbal's presidential address in 1930 is
a prominent example of this. Jinnah's own statements came to be laced with
references to Islam from around the time of the 1937 elections.[118] Pakistan,
Jinnah told Aligarh students in 1941, was the only way "to save Islam from
complete annihilation in this country."[119] He urged the Muslim League delegates from the Punjab, whose province had been slow in warming to him, to
"substitute love for Islam and your Nation . . . for sectional interests."[120] Islam
and the Qur'an, he told his audience in Karachi in December 1943, were "the
sheet-anchor of Muslim India. I am sure that as we go on and on there will
be more and more of oneness—one God, one Book, one Prophet, and one
Nation."[121] An especially effusive message he delivered on the occasion of Eid,
marking the end of Ramadan in September 1945, deserves to be quoted more
fully:

> Every Musalman knows that the injunctions of the Quran are not con-
> fined to religious and moral duties. "From the Atlantic to the Ganges,"
> says Gibbon, "the Quran is acknowledged as the fundamental code,
> not only of theology, but of civil and criminal Jurisprudence, and the
> laws which regulate the actions and the property of mankind are gov-
> erned by the immutable sanctions of the will of God." Everyone, except
> those who are ignorant, knows the Quran is the general code of the
> Muslims. A religious, social, civil, commercial, military, judicial, crimi-
> nal, penal code, it regulates everything from the ceremonies of religion
> to those of daily life; from the salvation of the soul to the health of the
> body; from the rights of all to those of each individual; from morality
> to crime, from punishment here to that in the life to come, and our
> Prophet has enjoined on us that every Musalman should possess a
> copy of the Quran and be his own priest. Therefore, Islam is not merely
> confined to the spiritual tenets and doctrines or rituals and ceremo-
> nies. It is a complete code regulating the whole Muslim society, every
> department of life, collectively and individually.[122]

Any `alim worth his salt would have looked askance—and for more than
one reason—at the recommendation that every Muslim ought to be his own
"priest."[123] Even so, the broad spirit of such appeals to Islam had significant
purchase among the `ulama, and the League was keen to enhance it. Not long
after the Lahore Resolution, the UP branch of the Muslim League set up a
committee to formulate a vision of what an Islamic state would look like. Its
members, not limited to supporters of the League, included Sayyid Sulayman Nadwi, Azad Subhani, `Abd al-Majid Daryabadi, and Sayyid Abul-A`la
Mawdudi. They had all participated in different capacities in the Khilafat
movement. Two of them, Sulayman Nadwi and Daryabadi, were close to
Thanawi. Sulayman Nadwi and Subhani were both `ulama; Mawdudi had

enough traditional religious learning to pass for one when it suited him to do so, but it was as journalists that he and Daryabadi had made their names. We will return to facets of Mawdudi's thought in chapter 4. What is worth noting here is that it was around this time, in 1941, that Mawdudi had founded his Jama`at-i Islami, which has been a major contributor ever since to public debates on Islam. Such was the composition of the committee. The actual task of delineating the characteristics of an Islamic state fell to another religious scholar, Muhammad Ishaq Siddiqi Sandelawi Nadwi. A product of the Nadwat al-`Ulama and later a professor there, he soon produced a substantial manuscript titled "The Political System of Islam." More peculiarly, perhaps, the committee was never able to meet to discuss its contents, and it took many years for it to be published as a book.[124] This might suggest that the Muslim League leadership was rather more interested in being seen as taking the religious scholars seriously than it was in what they had to say. What they did have to say in this instance deserves notice, however.

Although the treatise did not call explicitly for reviving the caliphate, the contours of the Islamic state it delineated were suffused with the idea and the memory of the caliphate. Ishaq Nadwi argued that the cornerstone of the "system of the caliphate" was the doctrine of God's oneness and the concomitant necessity of human servitude to God.[125] God alone is sovereign and the exclusive source of all law,[126] and it was a recognition of this fact that made the Islamic system of government different from, and superior to, all others of a human devising.[127] The Qur'an reports God's promise "to those ... who believe and do good deeds ... to make them successors [the Arabic term here is a cognate of 'caliphs'] to the land, as He did those who came before them" (Q 24.55). But, Ishaq Nadwi cautioned, this promise did not simply depend on sound belief and good deeds. It required actively striving for the establishment of an Islamic political order.[128] Indeed, such struggle was a religious obligation, which some people had to undertake on behalf of the community as a whole or else the community at large would be remiss.[129]

One more feature of this work is worth mentioning, and that relates to the central role it gave to the `ulama in the running of the state. Medieval Sunni political theory requires that the caliph be elected and his actions regulated by "those who loosen and bind." Many jurists thought that this group consisted of leading `ulama, others argued that it comprised the military and political elite, and yet others wanted both sort of notables to be counted among this select group. Ishaq Nadwi leaned toward the third view, but he made it clear that it was the `ulama who really were to be in charge and that other notable figures were to be called in only as needed and always under the careful oversight of the `ulama.[130] The `ulama were to occupy a central position in the legislative assembly—a key site of binding and loosening the public affairs of the community—for it made no sense for Islamic legal matters to be overseen by those not knowledgeable in them, let alone by non-Muslims or

Muslims of wayward beliefs (he mentioned the Shi`a and the Ahmadis in this regard).[131] The ruler himself was to be well-grounded in religious and juridical matters, much as many medieval jurists required of the caliph, but if not, he would need to be all the more dependent on the `ulama's guidance.[132] This utopian vision of government leaves little room for the sort of modernizing elite that was at the forefront of the movement for Pakistan; it seems also to leave uncertain space for autodidact intellectuals like Mawdudi. It is not clear how Mawdudi would have responded to this imagining of an Islamic polity if he, as a member of the committee, had been able to debate it with its author.[133]

Quite apart from the League leadership's failure to take such discourses seriously, there were good reasons for the Islamists and the Sunni `ulama to resist coming over to Jinnah's side. Mawdudi, for one, spent the last years of colonial rule bitterly opposing the League on grounds that its Westernized leadership was unsuited to the task of establishing an Islamic state. For their part, the Sunni `ulama feared that they and their conceptions of Islam would come in for some rough treatment in a state governed by the modernists.[134] The *internal* partition that Muslim India would undergo with the establishment of Pakistan also represented a frightening prospect, though not to them alone. Many of their centuries-old centers of religious life, the final resting places of their revered teachers and Sufi masters, would have to be left to the mercy of non-Muslims. The Muslim community itself would be sundered. Jinnah could talk cavalierly about the "sacrifice" the Muslims of the minority provinces needed to make for the good of the Muslim-majority provinces, on occasion arrogating to himself the authority *to* sacrifice them. In a speech in Kanpur in March 1941, he was reported to have said that "in order to liberate 7 crores [70 million] of Muslims where they were in a majority he was willing to perform the last ceremony of martyrdom if necessary and let two crores [20 million] of Muslims be smashed."[135] Such language raised questions about whether Jinnah could be entrusted with guarding the interests of the community at large; and it could not but be anathema to the representatives of a religious tradition that saw the protection of life as one of its cardinal values.[136] All stakeholders in the future of the Indian subcontinent could perhaps agree, these `ulama thought, to grant Hindus and Muslims parity in the central legislature of a free, united India and on its Supreme Court. This, indeed, is what the Jam`iyyat al-`Ulama-i Hind had proposed in a constitutional formula in 1945 as a way of keeping India undivided and securing Muslim interests within it.[137]

The religious arguments for *supporting* the Muslim League were no less weighty, however. The demand for a separate Muslim homeland had created the prospect of establishing an Islamic state with a central role in it for the `ulama, and there was no telling when, if ever, any such opportunity would arise again. The League leadership was not known for its piety, but that was scarcely different from the generality of earlier Muslim leaders. The `ulama could try to reform these leaders' waywardness and to reorient them toward proper Islam. They could also mobilize Muslim public opinion in such a way that anyone who did not adhere to the `ulama's guidelines in religious matters would be ousted from the League itself.[138] Ultimately, then, the `ulama had to decide whether to trust the Muslim League or the Congress, and some notable figures had convinced themselves, as Thanawi had earlier, that the Muslim League was the preferable option. In late 1945, long-simmering tensions within the ranks of the Deobandi `ulama took an institutional form with the establishment of the Jam`iyyat al-`Ulama-i Islam (JUI), a pro-Muslim League breakaway faction of the Jam`iyyat al-Ulama-i Hind. Shabbir Ahmad `Usmani (d. 1949), a Deobandi stalwart, was its president. Like the Deobandis, the Barelawis, too, were divided on the question of Pakistan, with some notable figures among them opposing the demand for Pakistan while the All India Sunni Conference, a Barelawi organization, supported it.[139] The Shi`a were no different. Though Jinnah himself was a Shi`i and Shi`i modernists tended to preach sectarian harmony far more frequently than any exclusionary message, there were significant misgivings in various Shi`i circles about what it would mean for them to live in a state dominated by the Sunnis.[140]

The Muslim League put the influence of `ulama like Shabbir `Usmani to good use as the movement for Pakistan gained momentum. For all of Jinnah's insistence that his party alone represented the Muslims of India, the claim was still untested. The elections to the central and provincial legislative assemblies in 1945–46 provided him the opportunity, indeed the imperative, to vindicate it. The party labored against significant odds. Much of the League's leadership, like Jinnah himself, came from provinces in which Muslims were a minority, rather than from the Muslim-majority provinces that needed to be won over to comprise the new Muslim homeland. The League had never developed anything comparable to the Congress's grassroots organization in those provinces, which meant that bringing them over would have to be a matter of opportunistic alliances at elite levels—and of intense religious propaganda.[141] In the Punjab, for instance, where politics was dominated by rural magnates associated with a ruling party—the Unionists—that did not identify itself with Islam, Muslim League propagandists put much imagination and energy into articulating their religious appeal. Though no less attentive than others to considerations of kinship and other local ties, it was the transcendent appeal of Islamic solidarity that the League showed itself to represent, while its rivals were portrayed as a throwback to dissension, intrigue, and moral chaos—all captured by the resonant Qur'anic term *fitna*.[142] The specter of fitna had always haunted Muslims; the fitna par excellence of Islamic history was the civil war less than a quarter century after the death of the Prophet Muhammad, which had sowed the seeds of sectarian groups for all times to come. In late colonial India, the demand for Pakistan was a promise to reunite disparate Muslims in a homeland of their own. So far as League propagandists were concerned, this unity had in fact already been achieved in the person of Jinnah and it was now only a matter of putting it on display. It is telling that Husayn Ahmad Madani had to go out of his way to argue in 1945 that Jinnah did not in fact represent a binding legal consensus—*ijma`*—of Muslims, which would make it sinful for people to oppose him.[143]

Those associated with hereditary shrines also played an important role in helping with the propaganda effort. They included not just the keepers of shrines in the Punjab, a province rich in them, but also influential people from much further afield. The shrine of Mu`in al-din Chishti (d. 1236) in Ajmer is among the most hallowed Sufi precincts in all of India. Its *sajjada nishin*—"the occupier of [the ancestors'] prayer rug" there—was a supporter of the Muslim League, though Rajasthan, where the shrine is located, had no prospect of becoming a part of Pakistan. He also helped the party leadership identify other `ulama and Sufis who could be invited to a conference the League was planning to highlight its Islamic commitments in the fall of 1946.[144] Jama`at `Ali Shah, another League supporter mentioned earlier with reference to his train trips, went so far as to characterize Jinnah as a saint (*wali Allah*).[145] Coming from saintly figures, such endorsements could be powerful.

Compared to the elections of 1937, the Muslim League was spectacularly successful in its campaign in 1945–46: it emerged as the biggest winner in the two largest Muslim-majority provinces of the Punjab and Bengal, and it had a majority in Sindh as well. The League's victory had much to do with its simultaneous embrace of Islam in its varied forms—modernist, `ulama-led, Sufi, and Shi`i, among others. It had to do as well with Jinnah's success in reorganizing the party at the all-India level and in persuading Muslim politicians at local levels, in the Punjab, Bengal, Sindh, and elsewhere, to switch to the Muslim League at little or no cost to their political habits or their inherited privileges.[146]

There were vulnerabilities, however. The specter of "sectionalism" haunted the Muslim League then, as it had Iqbal in 1930,[147] and it would continue to inform the deep misgivings with which the central government, already from the time of Jinnah's governor-generalship, viewed provincial elites in Pakistan. The `ulama's support, too, carried costs, though the League's leadership may not have noticed the full price just yet. Pressing leading `ulama into service in support of the Muslim League meant an endorsement of their influence; this at least is how *they* tended to see it. For his part, Shabbir Ahmad `Usmani had left little doubt that his support—and that of the other `ulama— was a partnership in equal terms with the Muslim League: "One section possesses religious knowledge (`*ilm*) and the other represents the nation's power and authority (*qawmi qudrat o iqtidar*). In the realm of politics, knowledge and power have to work together. Knowledge without power is helpless and impoverished. And power without knowledge leads to oppression and imbalance. Political authority and religion are twins."[148] He had also tied the `ulama's support to how the Muslim League conducted itself in the new homeland. What the `ulama had agreed to help legitimize they could also divest of its legitimacy. The same was true of the pirs. Less than six years after the establishment of Pakistan, an anti-Ahmadi agitation would severely test government authority in the Punjab and bring life in the provincial capital and other major cities to a standstill. It had the support not just of leading `ulama but also of prominent pirs, and the precincts of major shrines were used then to denounce the Muslim League government just as they had once been used to bring people under the party's banner.[149]

As the religious rhetoric accompanying the demand for Pakistan became ever more extravagant, the League leadership had less control than it would have admitted of the forces that were being unleashed. Jinnah may have remained willing to negotiate the precise form Pakistan would take almost till the eve of the partition of India, but it was not clear if those most galvanized by the promise of a Muslim homeland would see such negotiations as anything but a betrayal. The following report from a campaign worker on religious sentiment in rural Punjab in the run-up to the 1945–46 elections is instructive both about the popular mood and about the apprehensions it was creating in some party circles:

> One thing which we have particularly noticed is that the message of the League has reached even the remotest villages. We saw people who knew Pakistan, League and Quaid-i-Azam [Jinnah's title, "the Great Leader"]. They think that the League wants to establish a Muslim State, and about Quaid-i-Azam they think that he is some big Moulvi who has a long beard and is very religious. Villagers are very anxious to see him. . . . The most touching scene we noticed was in a village where we went with a green flag; the villagers followed us and then an old man of eighty years came forward and kissed the flag and burst into tears. . . . At certain places young villagers questioned us when jihad would be declared. They were anxious to make sacrifices. I feel that the League should take some steps after elections, otherwise it would have terrible effect on the masses who were awakened now.[150]

Some of the ferocity with which government authority was challenged in 1953 was not unrelated to the perception in many circles that the promise of Pakistan, and of Islam in Pakistan, had not been realized.

The decades between the formal establishment of British colonial rule in India and the birth of Pakistan were a time of extraordinary ferment in the history of Muslim South Asia. By the end of this period, a number of Muslim orientations with a more or less distinct identity existed that had not been on the scene at its beginning. There were the Deobandis, the Barelawis, the Ahl-i Hadith, the Ahmadis. The Shi`a had had a long prior existence, but they, too, had undergone significant changes akin to those of their Sunni rivals in conditions of colonial rule. The Islamists were beginning to make their presence felt, though they had yet to come into their own. Perhaps most visible of all were the modernists, whose thought and careers exhibited more concretely than others the impact of colonial rule and who provided a good deal of the Muslim political leadership.

Some quite specific visions of Islam, of what it meant to lead a good Muslim life—what was good and what was Muslim about it—were in competition in colonial India, as indeed they were in other Muslim societies. The Shi`a, the Sufis, the `ulama, and the modernists had conflicting ideas on these matters. But the ideas also crisscrossed and converged across these communities just as they could be and often were in conflict within them. Sunni and Shi`i `ulama shared much in their vision of their place, as `ulama, in society, though this did not alleviate the competition and conflict *between* `ulama of various doctrinal orientations. The `ulama and the modernists could be at greater or lesser distance from one another as well; that distance was at its smallest in case of the first modernists of the nineteenth century, but it grew as a new generation, schooled in Westernized institutions of learning, came of age.

The modernists did not have a sectarian identity in the way the `ulama, with their increasingly articulate doctrinal orientations, did. Indeed, a criticism of such divisive orientations and the polemics and boundary drawing that accompanied them was a staple of modernist polemics against the `ulama. As Iqbal had put it early in the twentieth century, "I condemn this accursed religious and social sectarianism.... Islam is one and indivisible; it brooks no distinctions in it. There are no Wahabies [Ahl-i Hadith or Salafis], Shias, Mirzais [Ahmadis] or Sunnies in Islam. Fight not for the interpretations of the truth, when the truth itself is in danger."[151] Yet, the modernists, too, had some very particular ideas about Islam, and despite caricatures suggesting that they followed wherever their English masters led them, they were no less committed to *their* religious beliefs, to shaping everything around them in their light. This had made for a difficult and unstable relationship with the `ulama and others, but it had not precluded instances of concerted action, most notably during the Khilafat movement and even more so during the movement for Pakistan. The establishment of a state the modernists had envisioned and one they were poised to govern after successfully leading the movement for it created unprecedented new opportunities to put their vision of Islam into place. It also came to reveal great gaps in that vision, and many yet unanswered questions about what it would take to put some such vision into practice in a fledgling polity and a fractured religious landscape.

CHAPTER TWO

Modernism and Its Ethical Commitments

IN HINDSIGHT, blurred as it is by the state's chronic political instability and eventually its dismemberment in 1971, it is easy to miss the excitement that the creation of Pakistan had produced among many of its citizens. This excitement did nothing to alleviate the severe problems that the country faced in its early and subsequent years. But it would be difficult to make sense of some of the grandiose modernist rhetoric that we will encounter in the following pages without recalling the euphoria that had accompanied the birth of this Muslim homeland. An overview of the major phases in the political history of Pakistan and of how modernism has fared in it is the principal concern of this chapter. I take modernist political ethics—conceptions of the good as they relate to the public and political spheres—as a key point of reference in this overview.[1] This chapter seeks equally to bring out some of the ambiguities and contradictions that have both accompanied and enervated modernist thought. Many of these have had to do with the fact that, while modernist intellectuals have frequently spoken of justice, liberty, equality, and tolerance, they have often been allied with authoritarian regimes. Such alliances are partly explicable by the desire to bring about change in a hurry, from the top down, partly by the belief that traditionalist and Islamist authoritarianism cannot be combated in any other way, and partly by the fact that the governing elite have often had modernist commitments of their own.[2] However, quite apart from questions of strategy, there is also an authoritarian streak in at least some of the modernist intellectuals' own discourses, the implications of which have sometimes been clearer to their opponents than they have to the modernists themselves.

The First Years

In an uncomplimentary piece on the guerilla warfare then taking place in Kashmir, the influential American magazine *Life* had observed in January 1948 that "Jinnah still had no real national program for Pakistan except the incitation of fanatic Moslem zeal."[3] Despite the prominence of Islam in his prepartition discourse, "fanaticism," however, was far from Jinnah's temperament. When necessary, he tried to reassure his audiences on that score. In a speech addressed to the American people in February 1948, he noted that "Pakistan is not going to be a theocratic State, that is, rule of or by priests with divine mission. We have many non-Muslims such as Hindus, Christians, Parsis. But they are all Pakistanis and equal citizens with equal rights and privileges and every right to play their part in the affairs of Pakistan national state."[4] In his very first speech as the president of the constituent assembly of Pakistan, he had offered similar assurances, indeed in a language that sits uncomfortably with the idiom in which he had frequently made the case for Pakistan:

> If you will work in co-operation, forgetting the past, burying the hatchet, you are bound to succeed. If you change your past and work together in a spirit that every one of you, no matter to what community he belongs, no matter what relations he had with you in the past, no matter what is his colour, caste or creed, is first, second and last a citizen of this State with equal rights, privileges and obligations, there will be no end to the progress you will make.... We should begin to work in that spirit and in course of time all these angularities of the majority and minority communities, the Hindu community and the Muslim community—because even as regards Muslims you have Pathans, Punjabis, Shias, Sunnis and so on and among the Hindus you have Brahmins, Vashnavas, Khatris, also Bengalese [*sic*], Madrasis, and so on—will vanish.... You are free; you are free to go to your temples, you are free to go to your mosques or to any other places of worship in this State of Pakistan. You may belong to any religion or caste or creed—that has nothing to do with the business of the State.[5]

At a moment of wild communal frenzy—with several hundred thousand killed and nearly twelve million displaced[6]—these sober words may have been Jinnah's way of urging calm and of underlining the state's commitment to the welfare of all its inhabitants, including religious minorities. Yet, he did not cease to refer to Islam. "If we take our inspiration from the holy Qur'an, the final victory ... will be ours," he said in Lahore in October 1947.[7] A few months later, addressing the Karachi Bar Association, he castigated those "who deliberately wanted to create mischief and made propaganda that the Constitution of Pakistan would not be made on the basis of Shari`at."[8] What Jinnah seems to have meant by the shari`a was what the British in India had meant by it, viz, the Muslim laws of personal status governing matters such as marriage, divorce, and inheritance. What he seems *not* to have meant was that the state should commit itself to Islamic law in its fullness, as Mawdudi and the `ulama had it. The religious vocabulary the modernists often shared with the Islamists and the `ulama would cause many problems, but Jinnah died well before they came to a head.

Many of Jinnah's modernist successors would continue to articulate their Islamic sensibilities with some fervor. One of the most striking expressions of these was a resolution, moved in March 1949 by Liaquat Ali Khan, the prime minister, outlining the objectives of the constitution that was then being framed. The Objectives Resolution began by declaring that "sovereignty over the entire universe belongs to God Almighty alone and the authority which He has delegated to the State of Pakistan through its people for being exercised within the limit prescribed by Him is a sacred trust." It then went on to affirm the "principles of democracy, freedom, equality, tolerance and social justice, as enunciated by Islam," and assured fundamental rights to all its citizens, including the minorities. At the same time, Muslims were to "be enabled to order their lives in the individual and collective spheres in accord with the teachings and requirements of Islam as set out in the Holy Quran and the Sunna [the normative example of the Prophet]."[9]

There is much ambiguity in the Objectives Resolution. God and the state of Pakistan are both sovereign and, though the people of Pakistan are to exercise it as a trust from Him, it is left unspecified how God's sovereignty finds expression in the rest of the world.[10] There is a commitment to liberal values, but precisely how they are to be guided by Islam and what that would mean for non-Muslims remains unstated. Yet, modernist supporters of this resolution were not much troubled by such ambiguities. A recognition of the sovereignty of God, the subject of chapter 4, was to them not a matter of setting up dueling claims to ultimate authority but rather of underscoring the state's democratic aspirations—since this sovereignty was to be exercised by the people—and of underlining that even the people could not overturn certain fundamental commitments. To these modernist politicians, far from there being any conflict between Islam and liberal values, Islam was their very embodiment.[11] Tethering them to Islam was not to dilute them but instead to affirm the sincerity of modernist convictions: it was not just that such values were good in themselves, adhering to them meant nothing less than being true to Islam itself. For its part, the "enabling clause" of the Objectives Resolution, as it came to be known in Pakistan's constitutional history, was simply what one would expect of a state that had been created in order to allow Muslims to preserve their particular way of life and their religion. But again, insomuch as Islam embodied ethical values that the entire world could relate to, en-

abling the country's citizens to live in accordance with them held great promise for everyone.

Exhilarating as it was to many people, this vision of an Islamic polity created unease in other circles. The `ulama did not want to see the modernists
conduct their experiments unsupervised in what Liaquat Ali Khan had referred to as a laboratory,[12] and there were secular Muslim voices in and outside the constituent assembly that warned against a constitution based on
religious ideas. Some of the most vocal opposition came from representatives
of the non-Muslim minority in the house. According to the 1951 census, Hindus comprised about 13 percent of the country's population and 22 percent
of the population of East Bengal (later East Pakistan).[13] Despite assurances
to the contrary by Muslim modernists in and outside the assembly, leaders of
the Hindu minority found it impossible to shed the fear that they would be
relegated to the status of second-class citizens in the new polity. One leader of
the Congress, the opposition party in the constituent assembly, had discussed
the matter with some `ulama from the Punjab, and they had underlined to
him their standard view that a non-Muslim could not be the head of a Muslim state.[14] Indeed, so close was the association in people's minds between
being Muslim and being a Pakistani that this Hindu member, Sris Chandra
Chattopadhyaya, had been asked, when traveling in Europe, how he could
consider himself a Pakistani at all.[15]

The Hindu members of the assembly would continue to voice significant
objections as the seemingly never ending constitution-making process continued. During the debate in 1953 on the report of the Basic Principles Committee (BPC), they offered some especially uncomfortable criticism of the
Islamic provisions of the proposed constitution. For instance, to require that
the head of the state be a Muslim, as the BPC had recommended,[16] begged
the question of what the definition of a Muslim was that the head of the state
had to fit.[17] The BPC had also recommended that no legislation was to be "repugnant" to the Qur'an and the *sunna*.[18] In response, a Hindu member, Raj
Kumar Chakraverty, had asked "how far the principles of the Quran may be
enforceable or practicable or suitable in our public life and public relations in
the modern context of things."[19] Though they would not have warmed to the
parallel, Muslim modernists themselves were known to ask this question in
deriding *traditionalist* understandings of the shari`a. The BPC had sug-
gested, furthermore, that "an organization should be set up for making the
teachings of Islam known to the people."[20] In being seen as a barely disguised
attempt to enlist the resources of the state in the cause of proselytism, this
had provoked an especially sharp reaction from the Hindu opposition. Indeed,
some went beyond a rejection of state-sponsored proselytism to question the
superiority of Islam over other religions. As one Hindu member bitingly observed, "every milkman calls his curd the best." In language that would be

unthinkable for a non-Muslim member of the Pakistani parliament to use today, he continued, "We Hindus do believe that our religion is superior to the primitive religion of Muslims."[21]

For the modernist members of the assembly and others in the government, such observations were as unwelcome as they were troubling. They also raised suspicions about the allegiance of the Hindu parliamentarians to the new Muslim state. Some of these non-Muslim legislators were found to maintain residence across the border, in West Bengal, and the governor of East Bengal was keen to have their membership of the assembly revoked on this and other grounds.[22] The questions that such members raised could not, however, be resolved by such threats. For they went to the heart of what it meant to claim, as Jinnah had, that the Qur'an was a code of law.[23] Their observations also cast some disconcerting light on the gap between Islamic ideals and the far from edifying realities of contemporary Muslim life. A common modernist response to this last point was to acknowledge this distance but to turn it into a reassurance to the minorities: since Pakistan would be guided by true Islam, which was very different from how Muslims had actually lived their faith, non-Muslims had nothing to fear from Islam. This left unanswered the question of why Muslims would be able to follow proper Islam now if they had failed to do so for much of their history. One suggestion in this regard, which came from the modernist philosopher Khalifa Abdul Hakim (d. 1958) and seemed more indebted to the Hegelian march of history than to a study of the Muslim past, was that only in modern times had the world become sufficiently mature to properly handle and implement Islamic values in their true spirit.[24] But such formulations could not have satisfied the critics either. Then there was the question, perhaps the most uncomfortable of all, of *whose* understanding of Islam was to take precedence over that of others. The interpretations put forth by the `ulama and the Islamists were very different from the picture of Islam that many modernists of the constituent assembly wanted the world to see. Yet, representatives of the conservative camp had high hopes for a prominent voice in the state, not least because of all that had been said in the run up to the establishment of Pakistan. In acknowledgement of such hopes, the BPC report had envisioned a board of five people "well versed in Islamic laws" to advise the president and the provincial governors on whether any new legislation contravened the Qur'an and the sunna.[25] Not everyone agreed that this was a "mullah board"—a characterization that used a familiar modernist pejorative for the `ulama—but it did raise unsettling questions about precisely who would guide parliamentary legislation when it came to Islam.[26] Here the modernists' discomfort with the prospect of having to defer to the `ulama matched that of the non-Muslims.

Modernist misgivings on this score are on full display in a bitterly polemical tract, "Iqbal and the Mulla," that Khalifa Abdul Hakim published in Urdu in 1952. Originally from the Punjab, Abdul Hakim had obtained a DPhil from

Heidelberg University in 1925, with a dissertation on the metaphysics of Rumi, and he had taught philosophy for many years at the Osmania University in the princely state of Hyderabad.[27] Very unusually for the modernists, his writings included a translation of the Bhagavad Gita in Urdu verse.[28] Shortly after his arrival in Pakistan, he had established the Institute of Islamic Culture in Lahore and he served as its first director. Abdul Hakim moved in the highest government circles in the early years of Pakistan. In 1952, he had been dispatched by the governor-general, Ghulam Muhammad, to East Bengal to report on the mood in that province.[29] Earlier that year, the governor of that province had written to the governor-general with the suggestion that he "distribute free copies [of Abdul Hakim's *Islamic Ideology*] to [the] Ulema Conference now being held in Karachi."[30] Evoking Iqbal, that book represented a sustained engagement with "[t]he inescapable fact ... that Muslim life in all its aspects has to be thoroughly reconstructed if Muslims have to occupy an honourable place in the life of contemporaneous and future humanity. The question is whether Islam is a worn-out creed and is to be discarded as a hindrance to progress or whether we have to reinterpret it in the light of material and intellectual advance of humanity."[31] The worn-out Islam was, of course, that of the *mulla*s; it needed to be replaced with something else. As Iqbal had put it in his *Reconstruction*, quoting an unnamed author, "The verdict of history ... is that worn-out ideas have never risen to power among a people who have worn them out."[32]

Abdul Hakim's tract, "Iqbal and the Mulla," a sustained effort to document the extremely poor opinion Iqbal had of the traditionally educated religious scholars, was clearly produced at official bidding. It is a mark of modernist self-confidence at the time that Abdul Hakim showed no interest in *defending* Iqbal against any misgivings that this caricature of the `ulama might have given rise to. Instead, it was deemed sufficient to expose the mullas by drawing on Iqbal's verse and—given Abdul Hakim's personal acquaintance with the poet—some anecdotes from him. The author did not desist from adding his own reflections to this already colorful material. The `ulama come across as opportunistic, covetous for material gain, wedded to an anachronistic tradition, indifferent to matters of social welfare and, above all, intent upon creating and perpetuating sectarian divides in the community. They were a threat to both state and religion and to give them a formal role in legislative matters would jeopardize both.[33] From the perspective of many modernists in and outside the constituent assembly, the proper response to the threat of the mulla was not, however, to divest the proposed constitution of its Islamic moorings, as the non-Muslims demanded; it was to disentangle Islam from the mulla.

The debate on the basic principles of the yet unframed constitution was taking place under the shadow of riots that had rocked the Punjab province in early 1953. A long-simmering movement led by the Majlis-i Ahrar-i Islam, an organization that had often been allied with the Indian National Congress in prepartition India but had managed to align itself with the Muslim League in Pakistan's early years, sought to have the Ahmadis declared non-Muslims and those among them occupying important government positions removed from office. The most notable of such figures was Pakistan's first foreign minister, Sir Muhammad Zafrulla Khan, and it was around the calls for his dismissal that the agitation came to a head in February and March 1953. Aspects of this agitation will be examined in later chapters. Here, it would suffice to observe that this Punjab-based agitation had laid bare what the modernists saw as the menacingly raw power of religious zealotry. As the Punjab chief minister, Mian Mumtaz Daultana, understood things, two distinct orientations faced each other in the country. There was, on the one hand, "the scourge of Mullaism which has threatened our state from the first day." On the other, there was the proper "Islam [that] does not stand for any nonsense which resembles priesthood or Brahmanism.... It advocates a society where there is no dictation from sanctified Mullas and wherein every adult Mussalman is as good and as much responsible follower of the faith as the other."[34]

What the agitation had also revealed was that the governing elite's stock in political legitimacy had already plummeted by this time. The implications of this were less openly acknowledged by the elite than was the threat of the mulla, but the inspector-general of the Punjab police did not mince words in his own confidential assessment of the situation:

> In Pakistan everyone says that leaders are most chary of giving up their positions and continue in office by undemocratic methods.... Severe criticism is made against the Central Government as in spite of more than five years having passed even the constitutions [*sic*] has not so far been drawn up.... [T]he Government ... has no mass contact. The Muslim League leaders cannot give an intelligent lead and in fact cannot face the electorate. In India the situation is probably equally difficult, but Pandit Nehru is still the popular leader. No Government can run today without the goodwill of the common man.... The bridge between the common man and the leaders is widening.[35]

Such invitations to soul searching did not go anywhere, however. Martial law had briefly had to be imposed in Lahore to quell the agitation, giving the province, and the country, its first taste of military rule. Though boding ill for the future of civilian authority, it had served to reassure the modernists that, when it really mattered, conservative forces could be kept at bay. The true locus of Islam did not, in any case, lie with such forces. As Sardar Abdur Rab Nishtar (d. 1958), sometime governor of Punjab, observed during the debate on the basic principles of the constitution in October 1953, "my friends [the Hindu members of the house] should not have any misapprehension on the basis of a saying of a Mullah here or a Maulvi there; such type of people you find everywhere. They are mostly people who are not learned in the real sense of the term."[36] Yet, as a member of the Hindu opposition noted, one could not ignore the views of the `ulama at will. And even some very learned religious scholars had expressed themselves in ways that did not fit modernist reassurances about what the state's Islamic identity would mean for those who did not subscribe to it.[37]

Muslim modernists have seldom spoken in a single voice. Nonetheless, as has been seen, theirs is an Islam that professes to be democratic, though not necessarily according to Western specifications; it affirms pluralism, though with a high premium on unity; and rather than being legalistic, it is anchored in ethical norms, which are best derived from the Islamic foundational texts. If it is not the Islam of the secularists, with their putatively separate religious and political spheres, it is even less that of the `ulama. For all the barely concealed disagreements of their own, the `ulama had wanted to reserve a role for themselves in determining that no legislation was repugnant to the teachings of the Islamic foundational texts. The constitution that was finally put into force in March 1956 gave them no such role. It had significant Islamic content, but it was almost entirely in accord with modernist sensibilities.

The Objectives Resolution, with its declaration that sovereignty belongs to God and that the people of Pakistan exercise it as a sacred trust, served as the preamble to the constitution. In its "directive principles of state policy," the constitution envisioned that the state—now named the Islamic Republic of Pakistan—would take various measures "to enable the Muslims ... individually and collectively to order their lives in accordance with the Holy Quran and Sunnah."[38] A federal and parliamentary system of government was outlined, with the proviso that the office of the president, the titular head of the state, could only be occupied by a Muslim.[39] In keeping with the recommendations of the Basic Principles Committee, the constitution reiterated the provision that no law would be repugnant to the Qur'an and the sunna and that laws already on the books would be brought into accord with the foundational texts. To this end, a commission was to be appointed to advise the government on matters of repugnancy to Islam.[40] This, incidentally, was the modernist answer to the `ulama's demand that they be able to determine whether the laws of the land conformed to Islamic norms. Nothing was said about the composition of the commission. The constitution also envisioned an institution "for Islamic research and instruction in advanced studies to assist in the reconstruction of Muslim society on a truly Islamic basis."[41] What this would mean in practice was also left undefined.

Ironically, though it had taken the country nearly nine years to get its constitution, the final product was drafted in some hurry. In 1954, the governor-general, Ghulam Muhammad (d. 1956), had decided that the house had lost the confidence of the people, whereupon he had proceeded to dissolve the assembly. There had been growing distrust between East Bengal and the western provinces of the country and especially between Bengali and Punjabi politicians. In East Bengal, the Muslim League had been routed in the 1954 provincial elections, and this had created anxieties among the military and bureaucratic elite, preponderantly from the western provinces, about the impending domination not just by the Bengalis but especially by left-leaning politicians among them. Military and bureaucratic officials had already come to exercise an authority well beyond their normal job descriptions and this, they felt, had to be guarded in the greater national interest against corrupt, incompetent, squabbling, even subversive politicians. Delicate negotiations had been taking place with the United States on Pakistan's joining security alliances against the Soviet Union in return for much needed military and economic aid and these, too, had had to be insulated from the harsh glare that some politicians wanted to cast on them.[42]

Political instability did not, however, end after the last governor-general, Iskandar Mirza (d. 1969), had become the first president of the republic under the new constitution, drafted by the second constituent assembly. There was a succession of prime ministers, all serving at the pleasure of the president, himself a former bureaucrat, and of an increasingly visible commander-in-chief, General Ayub Khan. In the end, the bureaucratic and military elite, unhappy with the politicians they saw around them, unsure about what the forthcoming general elections would mean for them and for their vision for the country but confident that they had the support of Western powers and especially of the United States, decided to bring Pakistan's first experiment with parliamentary democracy to an end. In early October 1958, Iskandar Mirza declared martial law in the country and abrogated the constitution. By the end of that month, General Ayub Khan, the chief martial law administrator, had pushed Mirza out of office to himself become the president. He would remain in office over the next decade.

Modernism in the Ayub Khan Era

In his view of Islam, Ayub Khan shared much with the modernist politicians he had replaced. As he told the `ulama in May 1959 in a speech at a Deobandi madrasa, the Dar al-`Ulum Islamiyya at Tando Allahyar in Sindh, Islam was a "progressive religion" but a great distance had come to separate religion and life.[43] He chastised them for reducing Islam to a set of dogmatic beliefs and practices, of presenting it as the enemy of progress, of "impos[ing] on twentieth century man the condition that he must go back several centuries in order to prove his bona fides as a true Muslim."[44] Rather than remaining mired in their sectarian squabbles, the `ulama needed to help bring people together on the basis of shared beliefs while learning to speak to them across educational and occupational divides. He also alerted them to the threat of communism then facing the world. This was best combated not through Western materialism but rather through Islam, which, he said in echoing Liaquat Ali Khan's speech on the Objectives Resolution, "alone provides a natural ideology that can save the soul of humanity from destruction."[45]

Though Ayub Khan had called for the `ulama's assistance in the task of national development, the latter would have seen it more as harangue than an olive branch.[46] In any case, he seems never to have expected much of them. It was on military, bureaucratic, and judicial officers that he relied for ideas and governance, and even the functioning of the "basic democracy" that he envisioned for Pakistan depended on them. The president wanted a complete overhaul of the country. To this end, no less than thirty-three commissions were appointed to make recommendations to him about various facets of national life, most of them during his first years in office.[47] Among these was the constitution commission, whose recommendations became the basis of Pakistan's second constitution, which came into effect in 1962.

THE NEW CONSTITUTION

In contrast with the 1956 constitution, Pakistan was to have a presidential form of government and the political system was based on Ayub Khan's view that the interests of the country were best served by a "controlled form of democracy."[48] The key political unit was the union council/committee, with its members elected by people at local levels. As laid down in the Basic Democracies Order promulgated in October 1959, these councils comprised the machinery of the government at local, district, and divisional levels—in each instance, working together with and under the guidance of bureaucratic officials.[49] Drawn equally from East and West Pakistan and numbering eighty thousand in all, the basic democrats were to serve as an electoral college for the election of the president, the federal legislature, and the two provincial assemblies.[50] (The four provinces of West Pakistan had been amalgamated into "one unit," on par with East Pakistan, in 1955.) Ayub Khan's emphasis was on development, unity of purpose, and efficiency. A powerful president who sat at the helm of the administrative pyramid and was able to exercise effective control over the legislature was the means to these ends. As Ayub Khan put it in an autobiography published while he was still in office, this "type of executive and legislature ... approximated ... those that existed at the time of the early Caliphs."[51]

The new constitution had its share of explicit Islamic provisions, too, and several of these were in line with the previous constitution. The president was required to be a Muslim and a version of the Objectives Resolution again formed the preamble to the constitution. No law was to be "repugnant to Islam"[52] and Muslims were to be "enabled ... to order their lives in accordance with the fundamental principles and basic concepts of Islam."[53] The constitution provided for an Advisory Council of Islamic Ideology to help the government do so while also advising the executive and the legislature on the principles that were to guide law-making.[54] It also mandated the establishment of the Islamic Research Institute, much as had the previous constitution.[55]

There also were significant contrasts with the previous constitution on matters Islamic. Where the Objectives Resolution and the 1956 constitution had spoken of sovereignty as a sacred trust from God to be exercised by people "within the limits prescribed by Him," the preamble to the 1962 constitution made no reference to any such limits. It had also omitted to mention that the Islam that the government was to enable people to live by was the one "set out in the Holy Quran and Sunnah."[56] Even the official name of the state was the Republic of Pakistan and not the *Islamic* Republic.[57]

Such changes to the 1956 constitution were too much for the `ulama and the Islamists. Though the constitution commission had affirmed that Pakistan was "an ideological, and not a secular, State,"[58] conservative critics of the constitution feared that the country was being set precisely on the path to secularism. In those circles, secularism did not simply mean that public policy would be independent of religion (which the constitution said it would not be); it also conjured the image of moral anarchy. The omission of any reference to the divine "limits" within which people were to exercise the sovereignty delegated to them by God likewise suggested that the government was intent upon flouting those limits. This impression was reinforced by the lack of reference in the constitution to the Qur'an and the sunna as the foundational sources in which the government's understanding of Islam was to be anchored. Although these foundational texts can and have been understood by Muslims in a variety of different ways, the notion that the modernists were now trying to free their interpretations of Islam from *any* textual restraint conjured sinister images in religious circles.

It did not help that a religious movement known as the Ahl al-Qur'an and much maligned in `ulama circles was thought to have influenced the constitution's pointed omission of the Qur'an and sunna as sources of Islamic guidance.[59] The movement, best known for rejecting the authority of hadith, had arisen in British India and, for several decades after the establishment of Pakistan, it was led by Ghulam Ahmad Parwez (d. 1985), an autodidact Punjabi religious intellectual and, for many years, a government bureaucrat.[60] From his early years in office, the president was in touch with Parwez, as the latter's private papers make clear. Parwez would later also serve as a member of the Committee on Fundamental Conflict, constituted by the government of Pakistan in 1967 to suggest ways of dealing with "the conflict between the Mullah and the intelligentsia," which meant, in effect, devising ways of countering the influence of the `ulama and the Islamists in society.[61] Yet, perceptions aside, the degree to which Parwez may have been able to put his stamp on public policy on Islam is far from clear.[62] The simplicity of reference to "Islam" in the

1962 constitution probably reflects the president's own desire to streamline things rather than Parwez's influence, which one would expect to have taken the form of affirming an exclusive reliance on the Qur'an,[63] not of omitting any reference to the sunna *and* the Qur'an. And though Parwez's understanding of the Qur'an was often at considerable remove from the mainstream,[64] the president's went further in some respects. In a letter to Parwez in July 1960, Ayub Khan had observed that "even in the Quran[,] while respecting the principles, matters that relate to rules and regulations should be subject to adjustment in accordance with the circumstances of the time. Unless this happens, I do not foresee any future for Muslims in this new world."[65] An Islam unencumbered by the specifics of the foundational texts was obviously better suited to this vision. In response, Parwez had refused to believe that the president could really have meant that "the Quran should partly be taken as immutable, partly as redundant and partly as alterable."[66] Despite such disagreements, and irrespective of how far the regime wanted to heed him, Parwez would have recommended himself to Ayub Khan for such help as he could offer in combating the influence of the `ulama and of Mawdudi's Jama`at-i Islami. Lacking a social base for his movement and with limited appeal in the public sphere, there was little he was able to do.[67] But he did provide considerable aggravation to the `ulama, who went so far as to formally rebuke his views in a 1962 fatwa that bore over a thousand signatures.[68]

Taking on the `ulama was not easy, however. Even as the regime occasionally thought of a decisive confrontation with them, its ongoing struggle with the `ulama had mixed results and no clear victors. Ayub Khan did not relent on some of his key modernist initiatives, notably the Muslim Family Laws Ordinance of 1961.[69] But all the Islamic provisions of the 1956 constitution that the 1962 constitution had initially lacked were brought back into it with the first amendment, enacted less than two years after its promulgation. The country's name, too, was the Islamic Republic of Pakistan once again.[70] The president's retreat on the more expansive Islamic provisions was not merely a recognition of the `ulama's influence, however. It was also good politics. With the new constitution in effect, Ayub Khan had decided to enter the political arena. He had already been elected president by the basic democrats in February 1960; in a time-honored authoritarian tradition, 95.6 percent of the electorate had voted for him.[71] But he would need to be reelected in due course and it was to this end that he became a member of the venerable Muslim League. Indeed, he was elected president of the party the very day the parliament passed the first amendment to the constitution.[72] As a card-carrying politician, Ayub Khan needed to allow greater space to people's religious sensibilities, as the `ulama claimed to understand and define them, than he had wanted.[73] For all that, modernism was still in its element. And no one represented it better during the 1960s than the Oxford-educated Fazlur Rahman (d. 1988).

FAZLUR RAHMAN

Although he was the son of an early graduate of the Deoband madrasa, much of Fazlur Rahman's own education took place in Westernized or Western institutions of learning. He completed his master's in Arabic at the Punjab University in Lahore and earned a DPhil from Oxford in 1949, with a dissertation that provided a critical edition of a work on psychology by the great Muslim philosopher Avicenna (d. 1037). Rahman taught for some years at the University of Durham in England and then at the Institute of Islamic Studies at McGill University before returning to Pakistan. After a year as a visiting professor at the Institute of Islamic Research, he became its director in 1962. He would continue in this position until 1968.[74]

Envisioned by the constitution of 1956 as a key instrument in the "reconstruction of Muslim society on a truly Islamic basis," the institute was founded *after* the abrogation of that constitution but before the enactment of the second. Its own constitution was understandably more expansive in stating what was expected of it: "to define Islam in terms of its fundamentals in a rational and liberal manner and to emphasize, among others, the basic Islamic ideals of universal brotherhood, tolerance and social justice," all while keeping the religion's "dynamic character" in view.[75] With his credentials as an internationally respected scholar of Islamic thought and his modernist inclinations, Fazlur Rahman was the right person for the job. The inaugural issue of the institute's journal contained the first installment of a series of essays by him that sought nothing less than to reconfigure the relationship among what Muslims have long recognized as the fundamental sources of Islamic law while also offering a radical reinterpretation of the nature and authority of the sunna, the normative example of the Prophet.[76]

It has been widely accepted by Sunnis since the third century of Islam— the ninth of the common era—that the Qur'an, the sunna, consensus (ijma`) and human reason exercised within particular limits are the four sources of the law. The sunna is seen as enshrined in hadith, statements attributed to the Prophet Muhammad or purporting to describe some aspect of his conduct. Human reason could take the form of ijtihad to arrive at new legal rulings in light of the foundational texts. But, in the interest of preserving the coherence and integrity of their legal tradition, Sunni scholars came to gradually restrict it largely to *analogical* reasoning, whereby existing rulings could be extended by way of analogy to new cases. The very positioning of reason at the bottom of the scale suggested its subordinate role in the articulation of norms, for it was constrained not only by what the Qur'an and the sunna had already delineated but also by the consensus of the earlier scholars; matters already agreed upon by those scholars could usually not be reopened for debate. As Rahman saw it, this way of conceptualizing the relationship among the sources of the law had led to a deep-seated aversion to change and a concomitant intellectual sterility. For someone committed to the view, as he was, that God could not have wanted this outcome for His religion any more than He could have intended that human beings take leave of their reason, Islamic orthodoxy was a deviation from the original spirit of Islam. This was a familiar modernist view. Unlike many others, Rahman had the intellectual tools to demonstrate how the results of a medieval scholarly consensus contrasted unfavorably with the dynamism of Islam's first generations.

In line with contemporary Western scholarship, Rahman argued that much of what is attributed to the Prophet in the form of hadith does not go back to him but reflects instead the evolving views of the early community. Early Muslim scholars recognized that numerous hadith reports were unreliable, and they developed sophisticated methods for trying to sift what they saw as "weak" or outright forged traditions from the "sound" ones. The latter came to comprise major collections of hadith, recognized as the most authoritative guides to the Prophet's normative example. Rahman was unwilling to treat even the contents of these authoritative collections as an exception to his view of hadith. Yet, unlike many Western scholars, he did not see hadith merely as pious forgery—statements attributed to the Prophet by subsequent generations of Muslims in pursuit of their particular ends. Instead, he argued that the early community had come to model itself on the practice of the Prophet while continuing to elaborate on and to develop that model in light of their changing circumstances. Hadith gave concrete form to this lived tradition, which could be glimpsed through it.[77] Yet, the idea, one that became the defining feature of Sunni orthodoxy, that the sunna could only be found in the form of hadith reports—fixed statements attributed to the Prophet—meant that it ceased to be a living and evolving tradition, henceforth to be found in hallowed texts, with their gatekeepers, rather than in the community's lived practice. Reclaiming Islam's original dynamism required that Muslims today liberate themselves from servitude to those texts and instead seek guidance in the principles still discernible behind the Prophet's sunna.[78] Unlike Parwez and the Ahl al-Qur'an, Fazlur Rahman did not want to jettison hadith as a source of norms, for it was an indispensable bridge to understanding the Prophet's thought and practice and to the Qur'an itself;[79] but it was as this bridge that it was to be used, rather than as a fixed source of unalterable rulings.[80]

Even the Qur'an, for all its preeminent authority, was not necessarily binding in all its particulars. This was partly because the teachings of the Qur'an were meant to be interpreted by people in light of their changing circumstances, which required something other than a literalist submission to those teachings. But it was also because Muhammad himself had given expression to divine revelation in terms of how he had understood it in *his* milieu, which could hardly be transposed seamlessly onto other times and places. No wonder that "the early generations were not bound by what later came to be called '*nass*' or the letter of the text."[81]

In view of this understanding of the sunna and of the Qur'an, it made sense that the relationship between the foundational texts, consensus, and ijtihad needed to be reconfigured, again in light of how Rahman understood it to have worked in early Islam. The consensus of the community had then functioned as a means of legitimizing the results of juridical reflection—ijtihad—on how best to follow the Qur'an and the normative example of the Prophet. That is, ijtihad was logically prior to ijma` and was continuously evaluated by it. The sunna, for its part, was essentially what the community had come to agree upon, its consensus.[82] As Rahman put it in concluding his *Islamic Methodology in History*, "our earliest generations looked upon the teaching of the Qur'an and the *Sunnah* of the Holy Prophet not as something static but essentially as something that moves through different social forms and moves creatively. Islam is the name of certain norms and ideals which are to be progressively realized through different social phenomena and set-ups."[83]

With this historically informed theoretical framework, one would think that Rahman did not need to engage in any elaborate demonstration of how the `ulama had gotten things wrong on particular matters. He could have contented himself simply with articulating what a "progressive" interpretation of the foundational texts would entail. But he did engage in a sustained critique of some long established norms, and he did so with relish. An article on financial interest published in his institute's Urdu journal in 1963 and in its English journal some months later offers a useful illustration.[84]

The Qur'an categorically forbids *riba* (Q 2.278–79; 3.130), and this prohibition has generally been understood by Muslim scholars to extend to all transactions that involve financial interest. Such blanket prohibition would obviously impede the working of any complex economy, and medieval Muslim societies knew of many strategies through which to circumvent it. For their part, Muslim modernists have sought to explain it away by arguing that while some Qur'anic teachings are universal in scope and application, others—including polygyny and the severe punishments prescribed by the Qur'an for particular infractions (*hudud*)—are best seen as specific to their time and place. They have also argued that what riba really means is exorbitant forms of usury rather than financial interest as such. Rahman adhered to these modernist views on all scores, but it is his mode of argumentation that merits attention here.

Rahman began by adducing the various forms in which the Arabic root "r-b-w" occurs in the Qur'an in order to determine the original connotations of the term riba, and he then proceeded to establish how the Qur'anic verses on the matter relate to one another. He acknowledged that the Qur'anic prohibition had, in fact, typically been understood to apply to all interest-based transactions, including seemingly nonoppressive ones, but he argued that it had intended to target only the sort of practices that involved a "redoubling" of interest. This expansive application was to be explained by the fact that "all these individual cases were part of one riba-system in whose nature it was to be so exorbitantly usurious. Therefore, what had to be banned was the system as a whole, and hence no exceptions could be made in individual cases. When the entire system was banned, the milder cases within that system were also naturally abolished since the system itself was tyrannical. It cannot, therefore, be argued that since the Qur'an abolished even the milder cases ... the bank-interest of today also stands condemned."[85] Rahman went on to examine the hadith-reports on riba, noting their ample contradictions and demonstrating how an increasingly rigid view had come to overtake chronologically earlier indications that certain forms of interest may have been permitted and practiced in the time of the Prophet and his companions.[86] Throughout the discussion, he critiqued not just premodern juristic understandings of riba but also the stringent views of modern Islamists and `ulama. He argued, for instance, that a common definition of riba as "every loan from which some profit accrues" may have originated in tenth-century lexicographical attempts at offering comprehensive definitions and that it was only in the eleventh century that it found its way into hadith collections.[87] Modern `ulama and Islamists refused to recognize the late origins and therefore the unreliability of this sort of hadith-reports; nor did they acknowledge the *variety* of ways in which riba had been understood by the medieval lexicographers and exegetes.[88]

It should be clear from the foregoing that Fazlur Rahman posed a serious challenge to the `ulama. Not content simply to call for ijtihad, which was odious enough to many `ulama of the time, especially when coming from the wrong circles, he wanted to unsettle the very foundations of their legal theory. His detailed critique of their views, as in case of riba, showed not only that he could speak their scholarly language but also that he could highlight embarrassing inconsistencies in the revered tradition from which they derived their authority. It would have been surprising if the `ulama had ignored him. They did not.

Already in 1963, Ihtisham al-Haqq Thanawi, a prominent Deobandi `alim and public intellectual at whose madrasa Ayub Khan had spoken some years earlier, had taken issue with Rahman's views on financial interest, denying that the Qur'an had intended to prohibit it only in its excessive forms.[89] In a press conference, he went on to also castigate Rahman for unorthodox views on the nature of prophethood. While still teaching at Durham in the UK, Rahman had published a book in which he had analyzed medieval Islamic discourses on this subject and shown how the Sunni theologians differed in their understanding of prophecy from the Muslim philosophers who wrote in the Hellenistic tradition. In his comments to the press, Thanawi gave the impression that Rahman saw a prophet merely as a superior intellect rather than one receiving revelations from God, as the standard Islamic view would have it. This would have been damning in the Pakistani context, though Rahman was on firm ground in pointing out in his rejoinder that what he had been describing were Avicenna's views rather than his own.[90] Thanawi had also acquired a copy of a letter that Rahman had written in August 1962 to Wilfred Cantwell Smith (d. 2000), the founder of the Institute of Islamic Studies at McGill, where Rahman had taught before coming to Pakistan. In this letter, Rahman had observed that "this country suffers from extremes, the most dangerous being the politics-mongering conservatives." He had also mentioned his plan to invite Western scholars of Islam who could "constructively participate in training researchers here."[91]

Responding to the questions put to him by the national daily *Dawn* in light of Thanawi's allegations, Rahman questioned the ethics of "utilizing a stolen personal letter," though he did acknowledge that he had written to Smith in this vein. He made a distinction, however, between scholarly methods, which is what he wanted to cultivate with the aid of Western scholars, and interpretive Islamic work, which only Muslims could undertake. He also noted that it was not just Western scholars of Islam but also those from the Muslim world that he wanted to associate with the work of the institute.[92]

Such assurances would not have assuaged the ʿulama any more than did Rahman's reminder that his father, a Deobandi scholar, had contributed to his intellectual formation. As Thanawi caustically observed, if Rahman had thought like his father, his book on the idea of prophecy would have been dedicated to him or to some other Deobandi, "rather than to the Jew[ish] Orientalist" Simon van den Bergh.[93] The roster of early contributors to the institute's journal, *Islamic Studies*, would not have reassured the ʿulama either. During its first three years, to limit ourselves to this small sample, the list is a veritable who's who of Western scholarship on Islam: A. J. Arberry, Bernard Lewis, Marshall Hodgson, G. E. von Grunebaum, Henri Laoust, Claude Cahen, C. E. Bosworth, Louis Gardet, Annemarie Schimmel, Henri Corbin, S. D. Goitein, and E.I.J. Rosenthal. There were Muslim contributors, too, but few were of the stature of these European scholars. The fact that these scholars were willing to contribute articles to this journal reflected their estimation of its promise and their respect for Rahman's own scholarly standing. But none of this cut any ice with leading figures among the ʿulama. Instead, they would have seen the very respect for Rahman in Western scholarly circles as confirmation of his wayward views. What made these views positively dangerous from the perspective of these ʿulama was, of course, the fact that their author had access to the highest echelons of power.

Rahman was not squeamish about the close alignment between his scholarly positions and government policies. The article on financial interest had been occasioned by questions in the parliament about whether a budget that took financial interest for granted could be Islamic.[94] Rahman had expressed himself in support of birth control as well. This was a high-priority issue for the government, but it was opposed by the Islamists and the `ulama.[95] Together with Ghulam Ahmad Parwez, Rahman was also a member of the Committee on Fundamental Conflict, discussed in more detail later. One of the tasks this committee had been assigned by the government in 1967 was "to provide a definition of the ideology of Islam."[96] Rahman began publishing a series of articles on this subject in his institute's journal the same year.[97]

There was much in these articles that would have pleased Ayub Khan, who had read the first of them.[98] They contained a strong endorsement of the system of basic democracies, which was presented as a check on "the vested interests of various educated classes ... to conceal the mind of the dumb masses from being correctly expressed."[99] They offered suggestions to the effect that local imams and preachers should be recruited to provide "moral backing" to the local administration[100] and that the religious sphere should be made subject to government regulation.[101] Though Ayub Khan had reluctantly come round to allowing political parties to operate and himself led the Muslim League, Rahman argued that a multiparty system was undesirable on Islamic grounds.[102] A statist vision was on full display in these articles: "Islam is a charter for interference in society and this charter gives to the collective institution of society, i.e., the Government, the right and duty to constantly watch, give direction to, and actually mould the social fabric."[103] A Qur'anic justification was offered even for press and media censorship: "The Qur'an ... asks the Government to disallow the public broadcast of news which is not in the public interest, and denounced such practices as a mischievous license calculated to demoralise the people and disunite them."[104] In 1960, Ayub Khan had promulgated his notorious Press and Publications Ordinance, which had drastically curtailed the freedom of the press. If the government needed a belated endorsement of it from the Qur'an, Fazlur Rahman thought he could provide it.

In keeping with the statist view, it is no surprise that Rahman underlined the need for a strong man at the helm of the affairs. But some of the language is extraordinary, for instance when elucidating how the Qur'an presents God: "God's concept is functional, i.e., God is needed not for what He is or may be but for what He does. It is exactly in this spirit that Aristotle compares God to a general of the army. For the general (in Aristotle's concept) is not a soldier among other soldiers—just as God is not an extra-fact among facts—but represents 'order,' i.e., the fundamental function of holding the army together."[105] In a later work, Rahman was markedly more restrained in speaking of the strong man: "The Qur'an will tolerate strongman rule only as a temporary arrangement if a people is immature, for how can a society whose people remain immature produce mature leaders? The efforts of several Muslims in the nineteenth and twentieth centuries to justify and propagate the idea of a strongman rule, therefore, run in the very teeth of the Qur'an."[106] But that was a decade *after* the fall of Ayub Khan.

Not everything in the articles from the 1960s fit government policy very well. For instance, there was a strong emphasis in them on social justice, and though the constitution spoke of it as well, it would have been discordant in Ayub Khan's Pakistan. As the country's chief economist had observed in 1967, a mere twenty-two families had come to be in control of 66 percent of the country's industrial resources and of 80 percent of its banking industry.[107] On the other hand, common people had seen the price of basic food commodities sky rocket: the price of fish, the staple food in East Pakistan, had increased 140 percent between late 1964 and early 1967 and that of wheat, the staple in West Pakistan, had risen by 78 percent during the same period.[108] Nonetheless, Rahman's was a largely unflinching effort to provide an Islamic justification for the policies of the government and the "moral backing" it needed to reshape the religious sphere.

In early 1967, the year Rahman began publishing these articles, there was talk in government circles of a "showdown" with the religious scholars.[109] It was in this regard that the governors of West and East Pakistan had met in February to establish the Committee on Fundamental Conflict, characterized by its chairman, the minister for information and broadcasting, as "the most important Committee that has ever been set up in the country."[110] This was apparently precipitated by a particularly noisy controversy in January that year over the sighting of the Eid al-Fitr moon. The official "moon sighting committee" was headed by the defense minister, a naval official,[111] and it included only one member of the `ulama. The committee had declared Thursday, January 12, to be the day of Eid, but many leading religious figures refused to accept this, instead urging their followers to celebrate it on Friday. There was a whispering campaign that the regime saw a Friday Eid as auguring ill for its future and that this was the reason it had wanted it on Thursday.[112] At issue for the government, leaving aside the alleged superstition, was its claim to authority—to decide when the country would celebrate its most important religious festival. To the `ulama and Islamists like Mawdudi, the issue was instead the government's tampering with even the most basic of Islamic rituals. It is a mark of the government's impatience with such challenges that five leading religious figures, including Mawdudi and the aforementioned Ihtisham al-Haqq Thanawi, were imprisoned and the press was secretly warned not to carry any news stories in that connection. Meanwhile, the government prepared to "crush the Mullahs, first by taking on all the Mullahs who speak against the Government."[113]

That showdown never took place, however. Though Rahman could still flatter Ayub Khan by invoking Aristotle and, in another analogy from ancient

Greece, the Harvard political scientist Samuel Huntington could describe the Pakistani president as coming closer than anyone else in the developing world to "a Solon or Lycurgus,"[114] the government had begun by then to look increasingly vulnerable on a variety of fronts. The self-confidence with which Ayub Khan himself had assured Ghulam Ahmad Parwez in 1960 that political systems "unsuited to our genius" would not be allowed back into the country and that "[t]hese are issues over which right-minded people with convictions have accepted even civil wars" would have been misplaced in 1967.[115] A real rather than merely hypothetical civil war was then brewing in East Pakistan. There was discontent, too, on the outcome of the India-Pakistan war of 1965, which the regime had intended to be limited to the disputed Kashmir region but which had become an all-out military engagement between the two countries and in which Pakistan had fared less well than the government propaganda had it. The Tashkent agreement that the Soviet Union had brokered in early 1966 between India and Pakistan had embarrassed the government further by leaving the Kashmir question unresolved. Food prices were soaring. Islamists and the `ulama did not have enough street power to take on the regime on their own, and they seem not to have wanted to do so. But they could, and did, continue to contribute to a sense of its illegitimacy. The controversy over the correct Eid day was a sign of their growing disaffection. Another took the form of their increasingly vocal opposition to Fazlur Rahman.

In 1966, Rahman had published a new book, *Islam*—a broad-ranging survey of key facets of the religious tradition from a distinctly modernist perspective. Chapters of the book began to appear in Urdu translation in the institute's journal the following year. Before long, the book became part of public debate in Pakistan, and the chapter on the Qur'an gave to the `ulama what they had been looking for. Here Rahman had argued for the agency of the Prophet in the making of the Qur'an, a view that goes against the orthodox insistence that Muhammad was simply the deliverer of a divine revelation that was altogether external to him. As he had put it, "orthodoxy (indeed, all medieval thought) lacked the necessary intellectual tools to combine in its formulation of the dogma the otherness and verbal character of the Revelation on the one hand, and its intimate connection with the work and the religious personality of the Prophet on the other, i.e., it lacked the intellectual capacity to say both that the Qur'an is entirely the Word of God and, in an ordinary sense, also entirely the word of Muhammad."[116] This meant that the Qur'an would have looked rather different, in its idiom and its teachings, if it had taken shape in circumstances other than Muhammad's. The implication was, of course, that its teachings needed to continue being tailored to changing times and places. In the wake of the controversy over this position, Rahman argued that the eighteenth-century jurist and Sufi Shah Wali Allah had held similar views, and so had Muhammad Iqbal.[117] But the `ulama, despite professions of great reverence for Wali Allah, have never been altogether comfortable with many of his views,[118] and Iqbal, though often quoted for rhetorical effect, carries little weight in their circles. Irrespective of its cogency as a psychological interpretation of prophethood or of its genealogy, Rahman's critics saw it as an attack on the timeless universality of the Qur'an and the nonnegotiable authority of its norms. The controversy that his 1958 book on the idea of prophecy had generated was as nothing compared to the public outcry on *Islam*. Rahman's position as the director of the Institute of Islamic Research was no longer tenable. The government was too weak to try to defend him with any vigor, as the minutes of the cabinet meeting a day before his resignation on September 5, 1968, make clear:

> True that the masses were steeped in ignorance about the correct nature of our religion but the time was not ripe now for the Government to start the propagation of reformed ideas. With our current rate of literacy it was difficult to put across rational views in religious matters. It would serve no useful purpose if Government took upon itself the responsibility to expound and defend the views of Dr. Fazlur Rahman. He should defend himself and Government should only provide him the necessary assistance and backing. The relevant portions of his book which was being misinterpreted should be translated into Urdu and Bengali and widely publicized. He should volunteer to appear in the discussion meetings and Government should only make it possible for the parties to meet.[119]

The president noted helplessly in his diary on September 5: "[I]t is quite clear that any form of research on Islam which inevitably leads to new interpretations has no chance of acceptance in this priest ridden and ignorant society. What will be the future of such an Islam in the age of reason and science is not difficult to predict."[120]

In tendering his resignation, Rahman had stated that he had not written this book at the bidding of the government and, in fact, that it was written *before* he had taken up his position at the institute.[121] Ironically, the book that he *was* then writing at the behest of the president, on the ideological underpinnings of Pakistan, may have made his views on the nature of revelation more odious to the religious groups than they may have been otherwise.

THE END OF AN ERA

As dark clouds hung over the country—with talk even of its breakup—the Ayub Khan regime finally gave way after a decade in power. The people of East Pakistan had long nursed grievances against the decision, going back to Jinnah,[122] to make a culturally alien Urdu the national language of the country. Those grievances contributed to an increasingly strident Bengali nationalism that was in full bloom by the last years of Ayub Khan. There were economic disparities between the two wings, too, and these had been exacerbated to East Pakistan's disadvantage by the much touted industrial development of the Ayub Khan era. The substantial Hindu population of the region was viewed with suspicion even by high-ranking government officials, and Muslim Bengalis, too, were treated by West Pakistani officials with some derision. I will return to these points later. The Awami League, the most influential political party of East Pakistan, came to formally demand in 1966 a reconfiguring of the country into a loose confederation that would leave only defense and foreign affairs to the center, have the provinces collect all taxes, and even give East Pakistan its own military. These were among the famous "six points" of the party. For obvious reasons, this was not acceptable to the rest of the country, least of all to the Punjab-dominated military. In early 1968, the government claimed to have discovered a Bengali conspiracy to secede from the union through an armed insurrection supported by India. There was skepticism in some circles about the gravity of this conspiracy, though the government took serious note of it and Sheikh Mujibur Rahman (d. 1975), the leader of the more radical wing of the Awami League, was incarcerated. The effort to bring him to trial proved abortive, but not before it had contributed to turning the sentiment in East Pakistan from anti-government to more resolutely anti-state.

Many leading figures had been allowed back into the political arena in early 1967. They wasted little time in forming an alliance against the government. Later that year, Zulfikar Ali Bhutto (d. 1979), who had long served in Ayub Khan's cabinet, established his own political organization, the Pakistan People's Party (PPP).[123] Ayub Khan's last days in office also saw much student and labor unrest. There was growing student radicalism in East Pakistan, and labor strikes throughout the province. Many of these took place under the leadership of the Deoband-educated Mawlana Abdul Hamid Khan Bhashani (d. 1976), who was known as much for his socialism as for developing a new and fearsome tactic of having mobs "encircle" government offices and other targets of choice.[124] West Pakistan, too, saw its share of unrest. On one occasion, in March 1969, nearly 2.5 million laborers participated in a strike in the western wing.[125] By that time, the military was no longer willing to continue to bolster the regime. Once that was clear, Ayub Khan resigned from office, handing over the reins of government to the commander-in-chief, General Yahya Khan, who proceeded to declare martial law and abrogate the constitution of 1962.

General elections were held in December 1970—the very first by way of adult franchise in Pakistan's history.[126] About two dozen parties participated in them, including a number of religio-political organizations. It was widely expected that Mujibur Rahman's left-leaning Awami League, campaigning on its six-points platform, would do well, but almost no one had anticipated the scale of its victory. The campaign had taken place in the immediate aftermath of unprecedentedly destructive cyclones in East Pakistan that killed around 500,000 people and left many more seething at what they saw as the government's indifferent relief operations.[127] The Awami League won every single seat earmarked for East Pakistan in the National Assembly—162 out of a total of 300—and not a single seat from anywhere in western Pakistan, where it had contested for a mere eleven seats. (The West Pakistan One Unit had been dissolved in July 1970, prior to the elections, resurrecting the four provinces of Punjab, Sindh, North-West Frontier Province [NWFP], and Balochistan there.) The other leading organization was Bhutto's People's Party. Campaigning on a platform of "Islamic socialism," it secured 81 seats in the National Assembly, all from the western provinces; it had not even bothered to put up candidates in East Pakistan.[128]

Despite the Awami League's electoral triumph, the military had qualms about handing over power—and the task of framing the new constitution—to a party that harbored secessionist aspirations. Mujibur Rahman was not willing to share power with the People's Party, and Bhutto, unlike smaller parties from West Pakistan, was strongly opposed to any political arrangement that meant his party's exclusion from the government. For its part, the Awami League feared a West Pakistani conspiracy to prevent it from coming to power; its leadership was also under pressure from those of its supporters who would brook no compromise on the party's platform. Amidst a political deadlock and escalating violence in East Pakistan, a military operation was launched in the province in late March 1971. East Pakistan was now in open revolt, with an increasingly organized militia, the Mukti Bahini, leading the resistance with Indian military and logistical support. The following months saw many massacres, by Pakistani troops and militia attached to it and by the Mukti Bahini. Several million people fled to India,[129] which eventually precipitated a short war between the two countries. By the time the war ended, with the surrender of 93,000 Pakistani soldiers in Dhaka on December 16, 1971, a new Muslim country had emerged in South Asia. The Pakistani military estimated that about 26,000 people had been killed in East Pakistan in the course of its operations. According to Bangladesh sources, the figure was closer to three million.[130] Neither estimate is credible, though it remains clear that a very heavy cost had been incurred in terms of human suffering. The provinces of West Pakistan were now all that remained of the country that had been founded a quarter century earlier. Zulfikar Ali Bhutto took office as its president and subsequently, after the new constitution had been promulgated in 1973, as the prime minister.

The Bhutto and Zia al-Haqq Years

It is extraordinary how little public discussion there has been in Pakistan about the events leading to the secession of East Pakistan.[131] In any case, Bhutto's image was clearly tarnished by those events; he had been instrumen-

tal in preventing the transfer of power to the Awami League and many therefore thought that he shared the blame for the country's breakup. There were
other vulnerabilities, too. In particular, Bhutto's Islamic socialism did not sit
well with conservative religious groups. A much publicized fatwa issued in
1970 and condemning socialism of all kinds had carried more than one hundred signatures by the `ulama, some of them prominent figures in the religious
sphere.[132] Bhutto strove hard to bolster his Islamic credentials. The 1973 constitution was well-stocked in its Islamic provisions, though these were largely
in line with those of the two previous constitutions. In March 1974, the summit meeting of the Organization of the Islamic Conference, a pan-Islamic
body with its headquarters in Jeddah, Saudi Arabia, was held in Lahore. Luminaries including King Faysal of Saudi Arabia, Zayed bin Sultan al-Nahyan
of the United Arab Emirates, Anwar Sadat of Egypt, Hafiz al-Asad of Syria,
Mu`ammar Qaddafi of Libya, and Yasir `Arafat of the Palestinian Liberation
Organization were in attendance at this gathering, which took place in the
wake of the Arab-Israeli war of 1973 and the Arab oil embargo against several
Western countries for their support of Israel. In hosting this conference, Pakistan had signaled that it still retained the aspiration to play a prominent role
in the Muslim world, though it was also motivated by Bhutto's desire to gain a
measure of religious legitimacy within Pakistan.[133] As Syeda Abida Hussain,
a Punjabi politician belonging to the People's Party, told Bhutto's wife in offering her assessment of the event, "Prime Minister Bhutto has emerged as the
undisputed leader of the Muslim World.... Pakistanis feel proud that we are
led by a modernist who can hold his own against any world leader and effectively advocate all just causes of Muslims."[134] The summit meeting also gave
Bhutto the political cover to officially recognize Bangladesh as a sovereign
state; Sheikh Mujibur Rahman was among those who attended the summit.

Later that year, the Bhutto regime gave in to growing `ulama pressure to
have the Ahmadis declared a non-Muslim minority. A constitutional amendment now defined a "Muslim" in such a way that the Ahmadis were explicitly
excluded. On other fronts, even as he sought to improve the lot of industrial
labor, Bhutto had taken on the more radical leftist elements in the labor movement almost from the beginning of his tenure.[135] He also came to distance
himself from hardline leftist elements in his own party, again in an effort to
reassure conservative critics. To similar effect, in October 1974, a Ministry of
Religious Affairs was established. In December that year, in a smaller yet symbolically meaningful gesture, the Bhutto government had a gold-plated door
installed at the shrine of the Sufi saint Shaykh `Ali Hujwiri in Lahore.[136]

Fazlur Rahman, by then professor of Islamic thought at the University of
Chicago, was among the people whose advice the government again sought
on Islamic matters. Rahman was keen to offer it, sometimes taking the initiative himself. In December 1974, he wrote to Bhutto, commenting on the prime
minister's statement on the occasion of the National Assembly's declaring the

Ahmadis to be non-Muslims. Bhutto had stated that this was "a secular decision because we live in modern times, have a secular constitution and believe in the citizens of the country having equal rights." "But surely," Rahman wrote to Bhutto,

> living in modern times and belief in the equal rights of all citizens are not *secular* <u>for Muslims</u> but Islamic; nor do we have a secular constitution but an Islamic one—and self-professedly so! And this Islamic Constitution has *Islamically* granted Fundamental Rights to all citizens.... It is commonly said that "Islam comprehends both religious and secular matters," or that "Islam is at the same time a religion, a polity, a law etc." Such clichés are always misleading since they insinuate the dichotomy of the religious and the secular all over again into Islam which is seen as something composite of the two. The truth seems to be rather that Islam, as such, is concerned with all moral values—whether these are in the social, economic or political fields.[137]

To this, Bhutto had replied that the statement in question

> related not to the *content* of the decision of the National Assembly but to the *process* by which it was taken. What I wanted to convey was that this process was entirely democratic and, therefore, quite within the comprehension of people who have a secular orientation. A decision of this kind has to be understood not only by Muslims but also by others.... As you know, we cannot afford to let a misunderstanding arise that we are running a theocratic state.[138]

Together with Leonard Binder, a political scientist also at the University of Chicago, Rahman was then directing an ambitious, multicountry project called Islam and Social Change funded by the Ford Foundation, and he was keen to have the assistance of the bureaucracy in facilitating the research in Pakistan. More importantly, however, he would have seen in his contacts with the Pakistani government an opportunity to pursue some of the goals that had been interrupted with the fall of the Ayub Khan regime. Despite his aforementioned misgivings about "the dichotomy of the religious and the secular," Rahman did not hesitate to offer specific suggestions on the goals the newly created ministry concerned specifically with religious affairs ought to set for itself. In part, he said in this regard, it was necessary "to present Islam in socio-moral terms and to link these socio-moral principles positively with the broad ideals of rational, liberal and humanitarian progress." This had been done "for the first time" under Ayub Khan. But it had been done to the neglect of "religious emotion." "[T]he regime had hoped that this religious emotion will, in course of time, be largely channeled towards the socio-moral side, which did not happen on any large scale."[139] The new ministry of religious affairs needed, therefore, to systematically address this side of Pakistani religious life, for instance, by turning devotional practices such as those relating to the Prophet's birthday into "opportunities to effectively communicate to the masses the positive virtues of Islam like good neighbourliness, mutual help, sacrifice for others and for social progress, cleanliness, honesty, etc. The vast emotional fund must be turned towards *positive moral and social* virtues of nation building and national integration. Otherwise, this emotionalism will become riotous and end up as a negative and destructive force."[140] In line with his statist views of the Ayub Khan era, and in the interest of shaping the religious sensibilities of the people, he suggested that the ministry set up a "directorate of public preaching" to train and employ mosque-imams. He also proposed the establishment of an Islamic university to train ʿulama and to help reduce some of the distance between traditional Islamic and the modern sciences. He floated as well the idea of a Dar al-ifta, an official body that would issue authoritative rulings on religious matters.[141]

Rahman expressed some similar ideas in a note he wrote in 1975 at the request of the government, in which he made recommendations on what the People's Party should say on Islam in its manifesto for the next general elections. Leaving the specific recommendations aside, his introductory comment is worth quoting here:

> It is commonly believed that Islam is not just a "religion" in the narrow sense regulating an individual's relationship with God but "a comprehensive way of life" regulating mutual human relationships in the family and in the public life.... Whereas this view of Islam is essentially correct ... [m]any groups, like the Jamaʿat-e-Islami, have sought, through this formula, to perpetuate and impose on Muslims a whole medieval structure of law and institutions which they call "the Islamic System," thereby obstructing healthy and necessary socio-economic development. The only sense in which this formula is tenable and practicable is that Islam be viewed as a set of *values* and social *objectives* to be gradually realized in a given society rather than any fixed system of law deduced at any given period of time, past and future. Any system of law and institutions that, in the public sector, will seek to realize these eternal values at a particular time will be the *Islamic system for that time.*[142]

As would be noticed, these ideas are very similar to what Rahman had said in his *Islamic Methodology in History*, published in 1965. He may have felt that a democratically elected government, such as Bhutto's, might have better success than an authoritarian regime in fostering an understanding of Islam based on "values and social objectives" rather than on an anachronistic religious law. He was to be disappointed in any such hope. The Bhutto regime was nervous about the challenge the religious parties posed to its legitimacy, and the manifesto that the People's Party unveiled in launching its election campaign showed little interest in any Islamic experimentation.[143] Instead, it was content to affirm its Islamic credentials by designating Friday the weekly holiday rather than Sunday.[144] Such measures did not satisfy the religious parties, who formed a powerful electoral alliance against it. The official results pointed to a victory for the People's Party, but the opposition alleged widespread rigging and proceeded to launch a country-wide agitation to dislodge Bhutto and install "the system of the Prophet" (*nizam-i Mustafa*). The unrest in the country led, in July 1977, to the imposition of martial law by General Muhammad Zia al-Haqq. Bhutto was hanged two years later. Zia al-Haqq stayed in power till 1988, overseeing during those years the most extensive effort the country had yet experienced to "Islamize" the society and economy.

It is tempting to see the Zia al-Haqq years as marking a sharp decline in the fortunes of Islamic modernism in Pakistan. In broad terms, that would be a fair assessment, but with two caveats. First, though the `ulama and the Islamists received a good deal of state patronage in the Zia al-Haqq era, the civil and judicial bureaucracy continued to be staffed by many of the same Western-educated people who had manned these offices in earlier decades. And despite its rhetoric of Islamization, the regime itself took measures to carefully delimit its scope. Banks continued to deal in financial interest, though they now had "interest-free" sections as well. And Ayub Khan's Muslim Personal Laws Ordinance of 1961, another bête noire of the Islamists and the `ulama, was protected against judicial review. It fell outside the jurisdiction of the Federal Shari`at Court, whose mandate, ironically, was to see if new and existing laws were in contravention of the shari`a. But, second, it is important to recognize that modernism was already in retreat under Bhutto.[145] There was some mention of Islamic social justice and related themes in the pages of *Islamic Studies*, the journal of the Islamic Research Institute, during the Bhutto years, but there was little, in that journal or anywhere else, to parallel the sort of modernist discourse witnessed in the Ayub Khan era. Bhutto was keen to avoid taking positions that could be controversial in Islamic terms. Further, as Fazlur Rahman had noted in reporting on his trip to Pakistan in 1975, "the government [was] ... anxious to keep on the right side of Saudi Arabia both for reasons of economics and of a political Islamic solidarity."[146]

Some of those who might have been important contributors to modernist discourse had left that camp well before Bhutto came to power. There is perhaps no better illustration of this than the career of Muhammad Hasan `Askari (d. 1978), a much respected Urdu literary critic. `Askari had acquired some prominence in literary circles already before the partition of the Indian subcontinent, and he consolidated that reputation in the years following the establishment of Pakistan. He was fiercely patriotic, a stance that led him to castigate those associated with the left-leaning Progressive Writers Association for putting their class-based ideological commitments above loyalty to the new state. Yet, `Askari himself had leftist leanings. Before partition, he had defended the demand for Pakistan on grounds that "it would be the first populist and socialist state in the Indian subcontinent. As such, it would serve the interests not just of the Muslims but also of the Hindu masses, since it would assist in uprooting capitalism ... and in the establishment of a permanent peace and security."[147] In the 1950s, he remained highly critical of Pakistan's alignment with the United States in the Cold War in ways that accorded with left-leaning sensibilities.

But things changed during the Ayub Khan era. Newspaper columns and writings in literary magazines had been the main vehicles of `Askari's expression, but the Ayub Khan regime imposed severe restrictions on the press. By the time of Ayub Khan's fall, as Aftab Ahmad, a close associate of `Askari, has recounted it, the literary critic was a changed man. Some leftist leanings remained, making him a staunch Bhutto loyalist. But, in other respects, `Askari had gravitated irrevocably to the camp of the `ulama. Ashraf `Ali Thanawi was the yardstick of the orthodox tradition for him, and he spent his last years translating into English a major Urdu commentary on the Qur'an by Mufti Muhammad Shafi`, a disciple of Thanawi and the founder of what today is the largest Deobandi madrasa in Pakistan.[148]

`Askari's traditionalism was never quite that of Deoband. It was at least as indebted to the Perennialist philosophy of Rene Guénon[149] as it was to Thanawi, and his critique of modernism had its roots in his dissatisfaction with literary modernism in Europe.[150] It is significant nonetheless that his conflation of European anti-modernist and Islamic trends took him all the way to Deobandi traditionalism in Pakistan. Around the time of the fall of the Ayub Khan regime, he had written a short book titled *Modernism*, specifically for the benefit of madrasa students.[151] Here, he sought to introduce those training to become `ulama to key moments in the history of Western thought, laying much of the blame for the deleterious effects of unrestrained individualism and the breakdown of religious authority on the rise of Protestantism.[152] His concern was not, of course, to defend Catholic structures of authority but rather to urge the `ulama to be cautious in their criticism of Catholic Christianity, for what they said about Catholic priests was echoed in what Westernized Muslims had come to say about the `ulama themselves.[153] His larger purpose in this treatise was to make Western thought and its specialized terminology intelligible to his madrasa audience so that they could better defend themselves and others against the subtle challenges it posed. By extension, the goal was to enable the `ulama to be on their guard against certain Muslim modernist proclivities. For instance, `Askari argued that eighteenth- and nineteenth-century European thinkers had tended to separate morality from religion, basing the former not on revealed truth but rather on human nature and reason. Instead of thinking of morality and ethics as a facet of religion, religion itself had come to be reduced to them. This way of thinking had had a significant impact on Sayyid Ahmad Khan, the pioneering Muslim modernist in South Asia, and on subsequent generations, he said, and he went on to offer this warning: "The ʿulama should be on their guard when English-educated people praise the ethical principles of Islam. For these people tend to think of [all Islam,] even Sufism, as mere ethics."[154]

The case of Muhammad Hasan ʿAskari helps draw our attention to weaknesses in the appeal of modernism well before the advent of Zia al-Haqq, and indeed even of Bhutto. It also points to some other things, however. Even as the ʿulama have faced sharp polemics from the modernist camp, they have been able to make some prized inroads within that camp. What this example also shows is that the ʿulama have received some unexpected help from the modernist governing elite in making such incursions. At the very time when Islamic modernism was practically a matter of state policy, Ayub Khan's draconian curbs on the freedom of expression may have done more than the ʿulama could on their own to draw the likes of ʿAskari in their direction.[155] Yet, the opposition to modernism, and to modernist ethics, has also inhibited the ʿulama from venturing beyond their long-standing concern with the ethical formation of the individual toward any sustained engagement with social and political ethics.[156] If anything, such engagement within the ranks of the ʿulama has declined in recent decades.

Telling as they are in some ways, the implications of ʿAskari's example should not, however, be exaggerated. For even under authoritarian rule, there could be significant cultural vibrancy and experimentation. An instance relating to the wider cultural arena in the 1970s and the 1980s, rather than specifically to Islam, is worth considering here. The widely read poet Parvin Shakir (d. 1994), who published four collections of verse between 1977 and 1990, is noted for bringing a self-confident feminine voice to her work and for exploring themes relating to female desire.[157] As the literary critic C. M. Naim observed in 1993 with reference to Shakir and some other contemporary women poets, "What often comes as the greatest surprise to an unaccustomed Urdu reader is the palpable sensuality in some of their poems; it is of a different order from that attempted by any male poet in Urdu." Naim continued: "the new women poets, including Shakir, have written on a range of experiences within marital love which no male poet ever wrote about in Urdu. Sexual intimacy, pregnancy, childbirth, infidelity, separation and divorce—these are topics that one would look for in vain in the books of contemporary male poets, not to mention their predecessors."[158]

Shakir was not engaged in any overt subversion of religious, social, or gender norms. Instead, as an officer in the civil service of Pakistan, she was a member of the bureaucratic establishment. The fact that three of her collections of poetry were published in the Zia al-Haqq years and that two of them won important prizes suggests that she was not seen as a threat to that or any other establishment. Some of her sharper social criticism was published, moreover, *after* the Zia al-Haqq era.[159] That does not necessarily mean that she was complicit in the regime's authoritarianism. To explore female sensuality in suggestive if guarded verse at a time when conservative gender norms were a matter of state policy was not a conformist move. Shakir's position as a member of the higher bureaucracy probably gave her protections not available to many of the more strident left-leaning opponents of Zia al-Haqq. Her case indicates nonetheless that the cultural sphere even under authoritarian rule was more varied than `Askari's trajectory might suggest. Even so, traditionalist and Islamist forces were continuing to gain ground.

The rise to power of the Harvard- and Oxford-educated Benazir Bhutto on Zia al-Haqq's death in 1988 appeared to create new openings for Islamic modernism.[160] Yet, despite the popular mandate that she carried, she was always vulnerable to charges of being too Westernized, too little committed to the implementation of Islamic norms. It was a matter of great pride for her, and for her admirers in Pakistan and abroad, that she was the first Muslim woman ever to be elected to the office of the prime minister anywhere in the Muslim world. Her conservative opponents insisted on making it a liability, however, arguing that Islam did not allow a woman to serve as the head of a government.[161] This argument had clearly not been influential enough to prevent Benazir Bhutto's election. That leaders of religio-political opinion could themselves adopt unexpected positions on precisely this issue had already been demonstrated in early 1965 when Mawdudi had decided to support the candidacy of Fatima Jinnah, the sister of the nation's founder, in her contest with Ayub Khan for the country's presidency.[162] Another illustration would be furnished by Mawlana Fazlur Rahman's alliance with Bhutto during her second term in office—an alliance significant because he was the leader of one of the most conservative of religio-political parties, the Jam`iyyat `Ulama-i Islam.[163] For all such pragmatism on the conservative side, it is significant that there was no serious effort on the part of the modernists to make an Islamic case for a woman's political leadership.

Benazir Bhutto's religious critics found much other ammunition against her as well. During what proved to be his last months in office, Zia al-Haqq had promulgated the Implementation of Shariah Ordinance.[164] It served to highlight his religious aspirations at a time of greatly depleted support for the regime even in religious circles. Questions about whether particular laws were repugnant to the shari`a were to be referred under this ordinance to the Federal Shari`at Court. Yet, in a measure of the continuing modernist hold on public policy, certain core areas remained outside the Shari`at Court's jurisdiction: "[I]f the question relates to Muslim personal law, any fiscal law or any law relating to the levy and collection of taxes and fees or banking or insurance practice and procedure, the Court shall refer the question to the High

Court which shall decide the question."[165] With such exclusions and given the fact that the high courts did not have any `ulama presence on them, there was no immediate danger to the country's modernist laws or its interest-based economy. The ordinance did, however, have symbolic power, and Bhutto's opponents castigated her bitterly when she allowed it to lapse. To make things more difficult for her government, the conservative and center-right parties dominating the parliament's upper house adopted a "shari`at bill" of their own, though the president had dismissed the government on charges of corruption before the bill could be debated in the more powerful lower house, the National Assembly.[166]

The next government was led by Nawaz Sharif (1990–93), whose party had helped with the passage of the shari`at bill in the Senate. Keen to highlight his Islamic commitments and to contrast them with Bhutto's deficit in that respect, Sharif quickly maneuvered the passage of the Enforcement of Shari`ah Bill and put it into effect in May 1991. Though the measure was hailed as "one of the most significant events in Islamic history,"[167] it did little to change how the country was governed or how Islamic law was given effect, let alone improve the lives of ordinary people. It did serve, however, to fuel further expectations as regards Islamization. But this government, too, proved short-lived, to be succeeded a second time by that of Benazir Bhutto (1993–96).

By far the most important development of these years had to do with neighboring Afghanistan. The Soviet occupation of that country had come to an end in 1989 and the Soviet Union itself collapsed shortly thereafter. Though the Afghan struggle against the occupying forces had been supported by the United States, underwritten by rich Arab regimes, and coordinated in good measure by Pakistan's military intelligence, it was as a jihad that it had been carried out. How and with whose backing the war had been waged was ultimately less important than the fact that a seemingly mighty superpower had been brought low by bedraggled *mujahidin*. This was profoundly empowering for religio-political groups, in Pakistan and in the wider Muslim world. The mujahidin, however, had never succeeded in sorting out their mutual disagreements, and the end of the Soviet occupation led to a civil war among factions dominated by the Afghan warlords. It would continue for several years, to the great misery of ordinary Afghans. A seemingly surprising response to this situation came in late 1994, while Benazir Bhutto was the prime minister, in the form of a movement emerging from the Afghan refugee camps of Pakistan. Its leaders and many of those comprising it were associated with Deobandi madrasas of Pakistan, hence their designation as the Taliban—"students." They had risen to end the atrocities of the warlords, to restore order, to bring proper shari`a norms to Afghanistan.

There was much murky intrigue and politics behind the rise of the Taliban. The Pakistani military, working through its Inter-Services Intelligence (ISI), wanted an alternative to the fractious mujahidin. It also sought "strategic depth" in Afghanistan, a place to fall back on in the dire straits of an Indian penetration across Pakistan's eastern front. There were also close connections between guerilla warfare in Afghanistan and the insurgency in Kashmir, as will be observed in chapter 7. Peace in Afghanistan was coveted, too, by the US petroleum conglomerate, Unocal, which sought to build a pipeline through Afghanistan to oil-rich Central Asia. Once again, however, such unsavory calculations were largely irrelevant to religio-political groups in Pakistan. What mattered to them was the fact that a movement uncompromisingly committed to the implementation of Islamic norms had emerged on the scene. There was no stopping it. By September 1996, the Taliban were in control of the Afghan capital, Kabul.[168] Already before entering it, they had begun to implement some of the most stringent punishments that could be found in Islamic law. As a Pakistani newspaper reported in March 1995, "The first ever amputation of hands and feet of three Afghans convicted of theft was recently carried out in Helmand province in southwestern Afghanistan on the orders of the Islamic courts established by the Taliban."[169]

It is hard to imagine Benazir Bhutto not being profoundly embarrassed by the Taliban. On occasion, she tried to make light of their excesses: "I believe the Taliban lock up their women behind closed doors, but as a woman leader we have come into power [*sic*] through votes," she said in late February 1995.[170] In a posthumous work, published shortly after her death in December 2007, she would try to elide the question of her government's role in the rise of the Taliban, arguing instead that her *removal* from power had served to make the Taliban more extreme.[171] Leaving aside the merits of that claim, it is true that officials elected even to Pakistan's highest offices have often had a rather limited say in the policies pursued by the military vis-à-vis Afghanistan and India.[172] Yet, Bhutto's own interior minister had been a key figure in facilitating the rise of the Taliban, and the aforementioned Mawlana Fazlur Rahman, whose Jam`iyyat al-`Ulama-i Islam was among the strongest of Taliban supporters in Pakistan, was an ally of the government at the time.[173] The point is not, of course, that Bhutto shared the Taliban's sensibilities. It is rather that aggressively conservative voices had become far more prominent in the Pakistan of the 1990s, sometimes in alliance with the government, than had been the case earlier. Nawaz Sharif's second stint as prime minister (1997–99), following Bhutto's dismissal in 1996, would continue that trend. A notable feature of his time in office in that instance was a vigorous effort to amend the constitution so that it would be possible to bring about further amendments with a simple majority in the two houses of the parliament rather than a two-thirds majority in each house. The initiative was billed as a move toward "the removal of any impediment in the enforcement of any matter relating to the Shariah and the implementation of the injunctions of Islam."[174] Critics, some within Sharif's own party, saw it however as a power grab by a perennially insecure prime minister seeking to capitalize on what was then a large parliamentary majority. Sharif's worries were not unfounded. Before the constitutional amendment had cleared both houses, his government, too, had fallen to a military takeover in 1999.

For much of the 1990s, as this brief survey shows, the winds were clearly not blowing in any direction conducive to modernist initiatives. Yet, given that modernism has usually been sponsored from the top down, a change of government could always create quick opportunities for a reversal of trends. The military coup of 1999 created just such opportunities. There would be concerted efforts to imbue Islamic modernism with new life in the years when General Pervez Musharraf was in power in Pakistan (1999–2008), especially in the aftermath of September 11, 2001.

The Years of "Enlightened Moderation"

The terrorist attacks in New York and Washington, DC, and subsequent developments have exacted an enormous price from Pakistan. In being forced to abruptly change course from being a sponsor and key supporter of Afghanistan's Taliban regime to an ally of the United States in the War on Terror, the Musharraf government faced the wrath of the country's Islamist and other religio-political groups. The years following 2001 saw the emergence of a neo-Taliban insurgency not just in Afghanistan but also in Khyber Pakhtunkhwa, the former North-West Frontier Province of Pakistan (hereafter, frequently, the Frontier). The militant groups associated with this insurgency would long resist the military operations periodically launched against them while carrying out scores of suicide bombings and other terrorist acts that have not ceased to put severe strains on the economy and society and to imperil the country's stability.[175]

Ironically, the 2001 terrorist attacks also gave the regime of General Musharraf an opportunity to recharge a dormant modernism. As the new government tried, with uncertain vigor, to confront militant Islamists and allied groups, it also took it upon itself to pursue a larger modernist program. Thus, in 2002, the government was able to secure a new ruling on the vexed question of financial interest from a reconstituted Shariʿat Appellate Bench of the Supreme Court—the highest judicial body established in the Zia al-Haqq era to rule on questions relating to Islamic law. In 1991, the Federal Shariʿat Court had determined that all forms of financial interest constituted the riba prohibited by the Qurʾan. The Shariʿat Appellate Bench had upheld that judgment in 1999, requiring the government to end all interest-based transactions by July 2002. Days before the deadline, the latter court set aside those rulings, sending the case back to languish with the Federal Shariʿat Court.[176] The Musharraf regime also took some steps toward regulating the affairs of the country's numerous madrasas. And in late 2006, it set aside some of the more draconian provisions of shariʿa-based penal laws, the Hudood (hudud)

Ordinances, that General Zia al-Haqq had promulgated in 1979. Passed by the parliament as the Protection of Women Act, 2006, this law made it more difficult than had been the case earlier to use the Hudood laws as an instrument of social control, for instance, by bringing accusations of sexual impropriety to court. It will be discussed in chapter 3.

The regime had coined a term for its modernist initiatives. Musharraf liked to speak of "enlightened moderation." "It is a two-pronged strategy," he wrote in a programmatic article in the *Washington Post* in June 2004. "The first part is for the Muslim world to shun militancy and extremism and adopt the path of socioeconomic uplift. The second is for the West, and the United States in particular, to seek to resolve all political disputes with justice and to aid in the socioeconomic betterment of the deprived Muslim world."[177] Musharraf presented this vision to the Organization of the Islamic Conference and received an endorsement from it.[178] Not for the first time in the history of Islamic modernism, Pakistan appeared to have a role to play both within the Muslim world and in facilitating better relations between the Muslim world and the West. There was some talk as well as of making enlightened moderation a part of the social studies curriculum in the country's public schools.[179] None of this would survive the fall of the Musharraf regime in 2008.

Some of the ambiguities of this phase in Pakistani modernism may be brought out with reference to Javed Ahmad Ghamidi (b. 1951), an ally of sorts that Musharraf had found during his years in power. Ghamidi, then a Lahore-based commentator on the Qur'an, had once been a member of the Islamist Jama`at-i Islami but had left that organization on account of disagreements with Mawdudi. He was an informal but lifelong student of Amin Ahsan Islahi (d. 1997), a prominent Qur'an exegete who, in his early career, had himself been a leading figure in the Jama`at-i Islami. Ghamidi had been writing well before the advent of General Musharraf, and some of his ideas came to be seen as well-suited to the regime's interests.[180]

Ghamidi has argued, for instance, that Muslim religious scholars, the `ulama, should not meddle in politics but ought, rather, to concentrate on the religious guidance of the people as well as of the ruling elite.[181] In marked contrast with Mawdudi, he holds that the establishment of an Islamic state is not a religious obligation.[182] And unlike the expansive view that the Islamists tend to take of the powers of the state, Ghamidi believes that, in religious terms, the state cannot require its Muslim citizens to do anything more than believe in God and the Prophet, perform their ritual prayers, and pay the *zakat* tax. It cannot, for instance, obligate them to undertake the pilgrimage to Mecca or to fast, or conscript them for jihad.[183] Nor does he believe that jihad can be prosecuted by any but an established government, thus ruling it out on the part of militant groups and other nonstate actors. It is worth noting, finally, that Ghamidi was highly critical of Zia al-Haqq's Hudood Ordinances, which he saw as contravening the shari`a on a number of grounds. Views such as these could and did lend useful support to the Musharraf regime as it battled

Islamist militants and worked to revise the Hudood Ordinances. Ghamidi was appointed as a member of the Council of Islamic Ideology. Since 2002, a significant number of new television channels have made their debut in Pakistan, and this, too, helped give Ghamidi a new prominence in the country and, by extension, greater usefulness from the viewpoint of the government.[184]

Yet, the alignment between Ghamidi's positions and the concerns of the government was far from perfect. For instance, to Ghamidi, all forms of financial interest are covered by the Qur'anic prohibition of riba,[185] which was hardly a convenient view from the perspective of the Musharraf regime. That a Muslim government can impose only a very small number of religious obligations on its citizens may have been welcomed by the government as an antidote to Islamist conceptions of the state, but the idea in question is opposed to the expansive power of *any* government, not just an Islamist one. Ghamidi's view on this score is based, moreover, on a narrow textualism, his justification being that the relevant Qur'anic verses and hadith reports require only the aforementioned three things of those submitting to the authority of the state.[186] This is a very different approach from, say, Fazlur Rahman's, with its often detailed engagement with the Islamic religious tradition in defending or critiquing particular positions. On the question of hudud, to be discussed more fully in the next chapter, Ghamidi leaves the imposition of the penalties to the discretion of the state and his formulations serve to considerably restrict the application of the severest punishments.[187] Yet, it is significant that he does not question the *principle* of the continued applicability of hudud laws.[188] Once again, there is a significant contrast to be noted here with Fazlur Rahman's effort in the Ayub Khan era to offer an ethical reinterpretation of hudud by arguing that it is not the content and the authority of hudud laws that should be seen as invariant—as the traditionalist jurists have tended to do—but rather their goal of deterring people from committing certain crimes and of reforming the criminals.[189] It is telling that there was no discussion of Rahman's work when the Musharraf regime took it upon itself to rectify some of the excesses of the Hudood Ordinances. And Rahman, who in the 1960s had written an extensive rebuttal of the traditionalist views on the prohibition of financial interest, was passed over in almost complete silence as the judges of the Shari`at Appellate Bench went about their task of reversing the earlier, anti-interest, verdict.

Though Ghamidi's television appearances were presumably watched by many urban, middle-class Pakistanis, he lacked any meaningful social base in the country. And even the government of General Musharraf had no compunctions about ignoring him when so doing seemed politic. On the other hand, Ghamidi's conservative views on many Islamic matters did little to shield him from the wrath of the militants. The editor of his journal was injured in an attack, and one of Ghamidi's close associates was later assassinated. Ghamidi himself was forced to flee to Malaysia in 2010.[190]

Two other intellectuals also merit a brief discussion to further highlight the ambiguities as well as the constraints of contemporary modernism. The first is Muhammad Shakil Auj, who, at the time of his assassination in 2014, was professor and dean of the faculty of Islamic Studies at the University of Karachi. Auj's approach to Islam, outlined in numerous articles on a wide variety of exegetical, social, and legal issues, was guided by the conviction that the Qur'an alone was the source of authoritative norms and that the positions enshrined in the Islamic scholastic tradition ought to be evaluated in its light and not vice versa.[191] In principle, few Muslims would dispute this proposition, except that, in practice, the foundational texts have tended to be refracted through the lenses of the later juristic and other traditions. This approach led Auj to move away from the positions espoused by mainstream Hanafi `ulama in Pakistan and toward some distinctly modernist views. He argued, for instance, that a "philosophical ijtihad" aimed at reorienting the entire juridical tradition had become necessary in modern times, and that this needed to precede the "legal ijtihad" that sought only to address specific needs.[192] He insisted, as have other modernists, that the shari`a was intended by God to create ease rather than hardship for people.[193] Adducing the relevant Qur'anic passages, he tried to show that many non-Muslims could be considered believers, even "Muslims" in their particular contexts, and that such Qur'anic teachings could serve as the basis of mutual "coexistence" in today's world.[194] In a series of essays on matters relating specifically to women, Auj critiqued the practice of underage marriage, whose validity is recognized by most premodern jurists and which continues to be accepted by many `ulama today.[195] He made a case for the permissibility of a Muslim woman's marriage to a Jewish or Christian man, disallowed by most jurists.[196] And he argued that a woman was not prohibited from going outside her home and traveling alone, without her face covered, even going on the pilgrimage to Mecca without a male guardian.[197] He explained why the testimony of a woman should be considered equal to a man's, except in the specific case of certain financial transactions where the Qur'an says that they are unequal (Q 2.282) as well as in matters of inheritance, on which, too, the Qur'an is explicit (Q 4.11–12).[198]

Yet, rather like Ghamidi, there were severe limits to Auj's professed desire to rethink traditional norms. The most striking instance of this is his spirited defense of polygyny.[199] Arguing against the familiar modernist tack of seeing it as tied to the need to provide for orphan girls—a context the Qur'an itself invokes (Q 4.3)—Auj observed that this logic would require also limiting numerous other Qur'anic passages according to the specificities of *their* contexts: "What would be left of the Qur'an, for purposes of general [that is, non-context-bound] application if we continued to proceed in this way?"[200] Auj also rejected any extension in a woman's right to initiate a divorce beyond the limited recourse Islamic law has traditionally allowed to them.[201]

In the treatise that became the basis of the Dissolution of Muslim Marriages Act of 1939, Ashraf ʿAli Thanawi had helped institutionalize the practice of inserting a clause in the marriage contract whereby the groom "delegated" his authority to divorce his wife *to* her, to be used by her when necessary. Auj insisted that this, too, was not a right that the shariʿa allowed to women.[202] He also argued against the payment of alimony beyond the three-month "waiting period" following the divorce, as stipulated in the Qur'an.[203]

Auj's positions on polygyny, divorce, and alimony show how traditionalist views—sometimes significantly more conservative than a Thanawi's—can stand unsteadily alongside progressive ones. His reliance on the Qur'an to the exclusion of the legal (*fiqh*) tradition allowed him to challenge established social and legal norms, but this was accompanied by a refusal, in marked contrast with many earlier modernists, to systematically rethink the scope and implications of particular Qur'anic injunctions. The progressive positions were nonetheless enough to fuel opposition to him. The circumstances of his assassination remain murky. He was shot and killed while being driven to a social event organized by the Iranian Cultural Center in Karachi in honor of a "medal of distinction" he had received from the government of Pakistan for his scholarly work.[204] He was not a Shiʿi, but any perception of cultural patronage from Iran would have been unwelcome to Sunni militants. University politics may also have played a role: he had been investigating the complicity of some of his colleagues in the granting of fake degrees,[205] and there were petitions from students against his anti-Islamic views.[206] There were allegations, too, that he had blasphemed Islam at a lecture while visiting the United States.[207] And the head of a leading Deobandi madrasa in Karachi was said to have characterized some of his views as amounting to apostasy, though the *mufti* later claimed that his fatwa to this effect was itself fake.[208] Whatever the actual cause of his assassination, his religious views seem to have played some role in it. The government's conferring an award on him for writings that some thought blasphemous may have made him even more of a target in a city, Karachi, where target killings are unremarkable events.[209]

My second example relates to Muhammad Khalid Masud (b. 1939), an internationally respected scholar of Islamic law, who served for several years under General Musharraf as the chairperson of the Council of Islamic Ideology. Masud received his PhD from the Institute of Islamic Studies at McGill with a dissertation on the Andalusian jurist Abu Ishaq al-Shatibi (d. 1388). The idea that the shariʿa is meant to serve certain overarching purposes (*maqasid*) and that legal rulings should be enacted or evaluated in light of those purposes—the protection and promotion of life, religion, property, progeny, and intellect—has had significant purchase in reformist circles in modern Islam. Shatibi was among the jurists most closely associated with this idea, and his work has therefore received much admiring attention from scholars in modern times. Masud is a notable figure among such scholars.[210]

To Shatibi, the shari`a's broad concern with the good (*maslaha*) of the believers was classifiable into three categories: necessities (*daruriyyat*); needs (*hajiyyat*); and things conducive to promoting general human welfare (*tahsiniyyat*). Viewed another way, the necessities comprised the nonnegotiable core of the shari`a, the needs were lower on the scale, and matters merely conducive to public interest were to be understood as "embellishments" rather than as core values. Such categorizations, too, have helped the modernists make the case for a rethinking of particular legal norms in light of how they address human necessities and how changing needs might be accommodated by the shari`a.[211] Masud has argued, for instance, that the rulings that belong to the second and third of these categories are best seen as sociocultural norms, which are therefore not central to the shari`a and ought to remain open to change.[212] Thus, while many jurists have insisted that a woman needed a male guardian to authorize and validate her marriage, Masud observes, following Shatibi, that "[g]uardianship is not an essential requirement, as its absence does not damage the essential objectives of the law, but it imbues those laws with a cultural and aesthetic value.... [In the past, the position of] the guardian created a balance to protect the vulnerable gender.... Modern concepts of equality before law and justice based on individual rights ... require a redefinition of the rights of parents, who would not need the authority [of guardianship] ... to keep that social balance."[213]

Masud has also argued that there is no Qur'anic injunction that prevents a woman from having full rights of divorce. During his tenure as its chair, the Council of Islamic Ideology did, in fact, recommend a change in the law to that effect. [214] Shakil Auj's understanding of the Qur'an had brought him to the opposite conclusion on this question, as has been seen. Arguably, both Auj and Masud had a point: the Qur'anic language does take it for granted that it is men who divorce their wives, as Auj had observed,[215] but it is also true that the Qur'an does not explicitly reject a woman's right to initiate a divorce, as Masud has it. Incidentally, this example goes some way toward illustrating the limits of a legal approach that is anchored, as it is in Auj's case, exclusively in the Qur'an.

Masud, too, has been the object of conservative ire. A national newspaper had quoted him as saying in November 2007 that "Islam is not a complete code of life. This was Mawlana Mawdudi's idea. Rather, Islam is only a complete [that is, perfect] religion. And Islam does not require [women] to cover their face and head; this is only a cultural norm." In a strident response, the editor of *Bayyinat*, the journal of a prominent Deobandi madrasa in Karachi, accused Masud of insulting Islam, the Prophet, and God:

> If Islam is not a complete code of life, then the question is whether or not God has in fact given to people a code of life according to which to order their lives in keeping with His will. If the answer is in the

affirmative, then that code ought to be identified so that one can gain God's favor by living accordingly. If, however, the answer is in the negative, then is this not insulting God and is it not tantamount to denying His divinity (*uluhiyya*) and His [attribute of] being the nurturer (*rububiyya*)? ... Following [Masud's] logic, would we not have to concede—God preserve us from it!—that Muslims are misguided, wayward, and ignorant? If so, would this be true only of Muslims today or would this foul judgment also extend to the early Muslims—the legal authorities (*mujtahid imams*), the companions [of the Prophet] and their followers, even the Prophet himself?[216]

The words carried an unmistakable threat, and though no one seems to have tried to act on them, it would not have been surprising if someone had. What is more remarkable perhaps is the government's choice for Masud's successor as chair of the Council of Islamic Ideology. In 2010, President Asif Ali Zardari of the People's Party appointed Mawlana Muhammad Khan Shirani, a Balochistan-based leader of the government's coalition partner, the Jam`iyyat al-`Ulama-i Islam, to head the council. It would have been hard to find someone representing a sharper contrast with Masud or, by the same token, more in accord with the sentiment behind the *Bayyinat* editorial. As chairman, Shirani has declared, inter alia, that a husband may discipline his wife with "light beatings," that a wife has no legal right to divorce in the event of her husband taking an additional wife, and that the existing laws against underage marriages are not in conformity with the shari`a.[217] Among the Council's ten members at the time, there was only one woman, the daughter of a previous head of the Jama`at-i Islami.[218]

Islam, as imagined by the Pakistani modernists, has had strong ethical sensibilities. This foregrounding of ethics—in the Objectives Resolution, among other places—was alluring enough for the literary critic Muhammad Hasan `Askari to have had to warn even the `ulama against its appeal. Such concerns have continued to guide the modernists even in exile. They are, for example, at the heart of Fazlur Rahman's influential book, *Major Themes of the Qur'an*, first published in 1980 and incorporating, incidentally, some of the ideas first adumbrated in the articles he had written on the ideology of Islam for Ayub Khan.[219] When Rahman was awarded the Giorgio Levi Della Vida Medal by the Center for Near Eastern Studies at the University of California, Los Angeles (UCLA), in 1983 in recognition of his contributions to the study of Islam, the theme of the conference in his honor was none other than "ethics in Islam."[220] Ghamidi, too, has continued to develop his ideas in exile—for instance, on the matter of Pakistan's blasphemy laws. Within Pakistan, Shakil Auj was given as well to highlighting the ethical dimensions of Islam. He had dedicated one of his books to his late father, "who taught me to love all human beings irrespective of religion or doctrinal orientation—indeed, to love not just humans but also animals, which I consider to be the final lesson of religion and the pinnacle of humanity."[221] For its part, Masud's approach to legal reform has continued to be informed by the shari`a's overarching ethical purposes.

Although some of the decline of Pakistani modernism can surely be imputed to the Islamization policies of the late 1970s and the 1980s, which themselves were part of global Islamic "revivalist" trends of those decades, the story, as recounted so far, is considerably more complex. The fact that modernist initiatives have emanated from a governing elite with a tenuous political legitimacy or from the intellectuals allied with them has also contributed much toward weakening those initiatives. Khalifa Abdul Hakim was a friend and confidant of Ghulam Muhammad, the bureaucrat turned governor-general who is remembered for unrelenting political intrigue and for the dismissal of the country's first constituent assembly.[222] Some of the vehemence with which Fazlur Rahman's *religious* views were opposed by the `ulama surely had to do with his very visible association with an authoritarian regime.[223] Nearly four decades later, similar misgivings presumably led Qazi Husayn Ahmad, the leader of the Islamist Jama`at-i Islami, to characterize Musharraf's "so-called enlightened moderation as a threat to the identity of Pakistan and Islamic values."[224]

But it is not just the embrace of the governing elite that has threatened to undermine Pakistani modernism. Authoritarianism has also tended to narrow the space in which modernist intellectuals may have been able to articulate their views, as the case of Muhammad Hasan `Askari illustrates. Another example relates to the declining fortunes of the ideal of social justice. It was in modernist circles rather than among the `ulama or even among the Islamists that this ideal had once resonated most widely. An especially strong commitment to it is in evidence in Abdul Hakim's work. The first edition of his *Islamic Ideology*, published in 1951, had even contained a chapter titled "Muhammad and Marx."[225] Yet, fears of communism, heightened by Pakistan's alignment with the United States during the Cold War, meant a significant weakening of the discourse on social justice.[226] The suspicion on the part of authoritarian and even quasi-democratic governments of all forms of organized opposition likewise found expression in their efforts to curtail the trade unions. Ironically, a good deal of the weakening of the labor movement in Pakistan is attributable already to the policies of the democratically elected Islamic socialist Zulfikar Ali Bhutto.[227] The Zia al-Haqq regime contributed its own considerable share to it. And since the early 1990s, the increasing privatization of the economy has tended to weaken the trade unions still further. A mere one percent of labor was unionized in 2014.[228] This is not a conducive climate for modernist disquisitions on social justice and related ethical ideas.

Finally, the modernists have often been less than eager to reassure those skeptical of their intentions. Their discourses on non-Muslim minorities, for instance, have not comforted them, as has been seen. The commission established by Ayub Khan to make recommendations for a new constitution for the country was not unrepresentative of modernist sentiment—and its attendant blind spots—when commenting on a Hindu parliamentarian's complaints that young Pakistani Hindus were being forced to seek employment in neighboring India:

> As a matter of fact, it appears to us that these "brilliant young men" are not anxious to work for Pakistan. There have been, we understand, cases of persons, of the Hindu community, who had been abroad on scholarships earned in Pakistan, going away to India after being fully qualified. This indicates that these young men are not seen in employment in our country not because they are unable to secure it, but because they are not desirous of serving this country. They apparently do not feel happy here, which indicates that they are not reconciled to the idea of Pakistan.[229]

For a country that then had a substantial Hindu minority, this was an extraordinary statement to come from the highest levels of government.[230] The Islamists and the `ulama could hardly have expressed their misgivings toward the minorities more bluntly.

All too frequently, modernist attitudes toward the `ulama as well have been marked by a thinly disguised contempt. Given the `ulama's influence in society, this has not served the modernists well. Khalifa Abdul Hakim's "Iqbal and the Mulla," for instance, seemed almost designed to offend them. Ironically, Abdul Hakim did more than many other modernists to cultivate a site for `ulama with a modernist orientation.[231] We will meet some of them in the following chapter. But this, too, was an initiative toward supplanting the traditionalists more than it was of building bridges to them. The `ulama, even the traditionalists among them, are a diverse lot, with considerable flexibility in their ranks and substantial ability to adapt to change. An insufficient recognition of this fact has often prevented the modernists from finding or cultivating long-term allies in the conservative camp, with significant attendant costs.

CHAPTER THREE

The `Ulama and the State

IF THE MODERNISTS have tended to see the `ulama as deadening the true spirit of Islam and of impeding the realization of Islamic ideals in society and polity, it is worth asking what the `ulama have found wanting in some key modernist initiatives in Pakistan. I address this question by taking matters relating to constitution-making, Islamic legislation, and madrasa reform as my key points of reference. Another concern of this chapter is to bring out some not insignificant differences within the ranks of the `ulama when it comes to attitudes toward the modernists. Pakistan's early decades saw `ulama who might even be characterized as modernist in some of their approach and attitudes. But, as in colonial India, even those decidedly opposed to modernist legislation and other initiatives have often maintained relations with the modernists that are far from being uniformly adversarial. How have the `ulama benefited from the patronage of the governing elite and what has it meant for how their doctrinal orientations have fared in the Pakistani religio-political sphere? Without reducing a changing religious landscape to its political context, an evocation of the contours of this landscape, too, is among the concerns of this chapter. Other dimensions of this evolving scene will become clearer in the following chapters.

The Traditionalist `Ulama: A Negotiable Maximalism

Though he died just over two years after the establishment of Pakistan, no religious scholar has enjoyed the stature Shabbir Ahmad `Usmani did in the new state. He was known to be close to the prime minister, Liaquat Ali Khan, and he had come to be informally designated as the *shaykh al-Islam*, a title that was clearly meant to evoke the head of the sprawling religious establishment under the Ottomans. The day following his death on December 13, 1949, was declared a national holiday in Pakistan.[1] To many among the modernists, `Usmani was a standing argument against those who had questions about their understanding of Islam or about the sincerity of their convictions. Further, as the prime minister had observed during the debate on the Objectives Resolution in March 1949, if people with misgivings about the public role of Islam genuinely wanted to be reassured on that score, they should listen not to the "so-called Ulemas [who] ... have come with [the] particular mission of creating doubts in your mind regarding the bona fides of the Mussalmans of Pakistan" but rather to "what we and men like Maulana Shabbir Ahmad Osmani have been telling [them] ... about Islam."[2] Yet, `Usmani's vision of an Islamic polity was not quite the prime minister's.

Like Liaquat Ali Khan, `Usmani had delivered what became a famous speech on the Objectives Resolution.[3] It had several important commonalities with that of the prime minister, briefly discussed in the previous chapter. Like Liaquat Ali Khan, `Usmani spoke of Islam's ability to serve as a panacea for the ills afflicting humanity, and he contrasted Muslim achievements in the past with the historical record of other nations and communities. Like the prime minister, he stressed Islam's democratic nature and sought to assuage minority anxieties about life in a state guided by Islamic norms. Yet, there were some striking differences between the two statements. While Liaquat Ali Khan had spoken of the justification for Pakistan in terms of safeguarding the Muslim way of life, he had made no reference to the implementation of Islamic law.[4] `Usmani, on the other hand, saw an "Islamic system" (*Islami nizam*), by which he evidently meant a system anchored in Islamic law, as the goal of the state,[5] and he quoted Jinnah several times in support of this point. Unlike the prime minister, `Usmani underscored the centrality of the model of the Prophet Muhammad's first four successors, the Rashidun, to the new state.[6] The more discerning listeners would also have noted that the prime minister and the shaykh al-Islam were not quite on the same page so far as the role of the religious scholars in the new polity was concerned. "Islam does not recognize either priesthood or any sacerdotal authority," Liaquat Ali Khan had said; "therefore, the question of a theocracy simply does not arise in Islam. If there are any who still use the word theocracy in the same breath as the polity of Pakistan, they are either labouring under a grave misapprehension, or indulging in mischievous propaganda."[7] `Usmani, too, had noted that, "in Islam, a religious government does not mean papacy or church government. Having broken an idol with its statement, 'they [that is, the Jews and the Christians] take their rabbis and their monks as lords beside God' [Q 9.31], can the Qur'an conceivably allow its worship?"[8] Yet, while the prime minister would have clearly counted the `ulama as part of the "priesthood" that he wished to spurn,[9] `Usmani, as the new state's preeminent `alim, could hardly be expected to go along with this. And it is telling that in quoting Jinnah's Eid message of 1945, which had "our Prophet enjoin ... on us that every Musalman should possess a copy of the Quran and be his own priest,"[10] `Usmani had quietly omitted this line about the priesthood of all believers.[11]

Much like the blueprint prepared by Ishaq Nadwi in the wake of the Lahore Resolution of 1940 had it, `Usmani and his `ulama associates saw themselves as the people whose views the governing elite needed to recognize as
authoritative in all matters concerning Islam. In appointing a subcommittee
of the `ulama to advise it on how Islamic norms ought to inform the much
awaited constitution, the Basic Principles Committee went some way toward
precisely such recognition. `Usmani had died by the time this subcommittee,
the Board of Ta`limat-i Islamia ("Islamic Teachings"), was established, and the
board's designated chair, Sayyid Sulayman Nadwi, took some time to arrive
from India. In any case, the board's recommendations provide a useful win-
dow on the `ulama's vision of Pakistan as an Islamic state, as well as their
view of the modernist elite.[12]

The board envisioned the functions of the Islamic state in ambitious, albeit vague, terms:

> Such a state is required to work for the consolidation and glory of
> Islam, implementation of its scheme of life in all its fullness, eradica-
> tion of vices, propagation of virtues, creation and maintenance of
> healthy moral atmosphere, ensuring procurement of necessaries of life
> and dispensation of full justice to all the people inhabiting the terri-
> tory irrespective of their religion, race or colour, etc., preservation of
> human dignity as enunciated by Islam, diffusion of knowledge and
> learning, maintenance of peace and order inside the territory, enforce-
> ment of punishments and penalties prescribed by Shariat, control and
> disbursement of public money in an equitable manner as laid down by
> Islam, maintenance and consolidation of armed forces to avoid and
> meet all possible danger from any quarter whatsoever, protection, as a
> Divine trust, of the legitimate interests of Non-Muslims living within
> the territory and the general well-being and prosperity of the masses.[13]

This was a utopian view of how the state should act and, in being guided by
medieval constitutional theory, also a very traditional one. The traditionalism
is underscored, besides much else, by the idea that a pious ruler, elected for
life on the model of the Rashidun caliphs, was most suited to convert Islamic
political theory to practice. Given, furthermore, that Pakistan was to be an
ideological state,[14] only those committed to its Islamic ideology could be entrusted with the highest offices. This meant obviously that non-Muslims could
not hold such offices.[15] And should the country adopt a parliamentary rather
than a presidential form of government, the real powers were to rest exclusively with the parliament's *Muslim* members.[16] As for women, the board
saw their proper sphere of activity as the household rather than the public or
political arena. But if they must become part of the parliament, only those
beyond menopause ought to serve.[17] The assumption was, of course, that post-
menopausal women would no longer pose the same degree of threat to the

moral order that was represented by younger women. The office of the president was, in any case, to remain a male preserve. And the person occupying that office had to be not merely a Muslim but also "virtuous in ... terms of the Shariat, ... not guilty of major sins, ... not habitually indulgent in the commitment of minor sins and ... not openly profligate in the observance of the Rules of Shariat."[18]

On the question of ensuring that no laws were repugnant to the teachings of Islam, as the Objectives Resolution had already laid it down, the board envisioned a body such as itself—a "Committee of Experts on Shariat"—to advise the president and the parliament.[19] This, of course, was a rechristened version of what the medieval jurists would have called the people "who loosen and bind" the public affairs of the community. Its critics called it the mulla board. Any parliamentary disagreement on interpreting Islamic matters was to be referred to this body.[20]

Like the Objectives Resolution, it is easy to caricature the recommendations of the Ta`limat-i Islamia board—in this case, for its traditionalist romanticism.[21] They seem wedded to the memory of the Rashidun, without seriously examining whether there was any historical basis to that memory or how the putative ways of Islam's first caliphs could be replicated in mid-twentieth-century Pakistan. Yet, caricatures apart, the `ulama were open to considerable flexibility. Even as they staked out what clearly was a maximalist position, they repeatedly showed themselves willing to compromise. Though the board thought that a pious ruler need not have any term limits, they were not opposed to having them.[22] Though they recommended a presidential system of government as being more in line with Islamic political traditions, they found a parliamentary system acceptable.[23] Though they did not approve of the non-Muslim minorities playing any significant role in the parliament, they were willing to accept their membership in the legislative assemblies.[24] Though they believed that women were best suited to domestic life, they did not disallow their presence in the parliament. Perhaps most importantly, though they saw the Islamic state as mandated to implement God's law, they recognized the legitimacy of parliamentary legislation on matters not already regulated by the shari`a. This did not quite mean, as Leonard Binder has it, that "legislation ... was limited by the Shari`a, but outside of it."[25] In the board's words, it meant rather that new laws "are not only not [to be] in conflict with the requirements of Shariat but are also devised in light of its broad and basic principles, go well with the spirit of Islam and are conducive to the accomplishment of the aims and objects of an Islamic state."[26] Insomuch as such legislation was guided by shari`a norms, it scarcely needed to be *outside* it.

In the interim (and quickly withdrawn) report it submitted to the constituent assembly in September 1950, the Basic Principles Committee had rejected almost all the recommendations of the Board of Ta`limat-i Islamia.[27]

The `ulama lamented this in a famous statement issued in 1951 on the princi-
ples that they thought should guide an Islamic state.[28] The final BPC report,
submitted in late 1952, was significantly more favorable to the `ulama, though
the constitution of 1956 again scaled back what the modernists were willing
to offer them. A number of Islamic provisions aside, the constitution was a far
cry from any maximalist vision of the Islamic state. Yet, it is again a measure
of their flexibility and pragmatism that the `ulama and the Islamists came
almost immediately to endorse it.[29]

If recommendations such as those of the Ta`limat-i Islamia board, as well
as other pronouncements to similar effect, had more flexibility about them
than stereotypes of hidebound `ulama might have suggested, their rhetorical
and moral force should not be missed either. Among other things, they were
meant to put the modernist elite on the defensive in what was billed on all
sides to be an Islamic state. In prepartition India, Shabbir Ahmad `Usmani
had brushed aside the fears of some prominent `ulama that the modernists
were out to destroy the religious scholars.[30] `Usmani's speech to the constitu-
ent assembly, the Ta`limat-i Islamia board's recommendations, and the `ulama
resolution of 1951 were all vigorous if not aggressive appeals, in the court of
public opinion, to what the modernists needed to live up to if they were to be
true to their professed Islamic commitments. The board's recommendations
were also a thinly veiled critique of prevailing conditions. While many `ulama
subscribed, as they still do, to the ideal of a ruler "virtuous in terms of the
Shariat," positing that ideal was clearly also meant as an indictment of a governing elite whose lifestyles diverged markedly from it. The modernists were
sensitive to such charges. Consider the testy exchange between justices Muhammad Munir and M. R. Kayani—the two judges comprising the Court of
Inquiry looking into the Punjab anti-Ahmadi disturbances of 1953—and Amin
Ahsan Islahi, a noted religious scholar and exegete who was then associated
with Mawdudi's Jama`at-i Islami:

Q: Have you been making speeches and publicly saying that leaders in
   Pakistan have been leading a notoriously un-Islamic life?
A. I do believe that they are leading an un-Islamic life and I must have
   expressed this opinion.
Q. When you denounce a man that he is leading an un-Islamic life,
   do you know his inner character; and can you, without knowing
   anything about his character, consider it right to proclaim that he
   is leading a notoriously un-Islamic life?
A. Whatever his character may be, if he does not observe outwardly
   all the apparent injunctions of Islam, I claim for myself the right
   publicly to accuse him of leading an un-Islamic life. Such criticism
   of public leaders is fully justified by all standards.

Q. Do you give to your own critic the right that despite your compliance with the outward forms of Islam, he considers you, according to modern ethical standards, a debased and depraved man?

A. Yes.[31]

The Modernist `Ulama

As discussed in the previous chapter, the `ulama have been able on occasion to turn some members of the modernist camp into their allies. The modernists, too, have had some significant allies within the ranks of the `ulama. Despite impeccable scholarly credentials, such people have fared poorly at the hands of the more traditionalist `ulama, however, and though some noted modernists had served as their patrons, they have not had much visibility in accounts of Islamic modernism either. Yet, no study of Islamic modernism or of the `ulama, for that matter, would be complete without some attention to their discourses. In this section, I consider two examples of such `ulama, Muhammad Hanif Nadwi and Muhammad Ja`far Phulwarwi, both of whom were members of the team of scholars assembled by Khalifa Abdul Hakim at his Institute of Islamic Culture in Lahore in the 1950s.

A native of Gujranwala in the Punjab, Hanif Nadwi (d. 1978) was educated, as his name suggests, at the Nadwat al-`Ulama in Lucknow. He later served for many years as a prayer leader at a mosque in Lahore, where he came to be well-known for his lectures on the Qur'an. Over the course of a prolific career, he published a number of books on hadith—he was an adherent of the Ahl-i Hadith or Salafi orientation—and on the Qur'an, works on Islamic law, and studies on such medieval luminaries as Ghazali (d. 1111), Ibn Taymiyya (d. 1328), and Ibn Khaldun (d. 1406). Though his scholarly career had begun well before the partition of the Indian subcontinent, a good deal of his published work belongs to his decades-long association with the Institute of Islamic Culture. He had joined this organization shortly after its inception in 1951. It gave him financial security and it provided a direction to his writings. Late in his life, he also served as a member of the Council of Islamic Ideology.[32]

Books published under the auspices of the institute were typically addressed to a modern-educated audience. They were meant to instruct such readers in Islam while buttressing particular modernist positions. But they also sought to speak to the traditionally educated, especially when written in Urdu rather than in English, and by `ulama like Hanif Nadwi rather than by intellectuals like Khalifa Abdul Hakim. Not all those who had studied in madrasas were learned scholars, of course, which meant that they, too, could be educated further in Islamic matters and perhaps steered away from an inherited conservatism. There may have been the hope that even distinguished traditionalists would join in a conversation that the institute was trying to sponsor through its researchers. A good example of a work that strove to address these varied audiences is Hanif Nadwi's *Problem of Ijtihad* (*Mas'ala-i ijtihad*).[33]

Published in 1952, just a year after the institute's foundation, the book is much broader in its scope than its title suggests. Echoing Shah Wali Allah, Hanif Nadwi posited that Islamic prescriptions were not merely a matter of mindlessly obeying God but were based rather on the pursuit of human interests (*masalih*), and that these interests were discernible through human reason.[34] This was an argument against literalist readings of the sacred law but also, by the same token, for the adaptation of that law to changing circumstances and needs. Not everything in the sacred law was amenable to change, and Hanif Nadwi distinguished, as others had before him, between divinely mandated ritual practices (`*ibadat*), which must remain immutable, and laws governing human interaction (*mu`amalat*), which were subject to modification in changing circumstances. In the latter case, particular rulings could be set aside in light of the general principles embedded in the foundational texts, he said, even when the rulings in question were specifically present in those texts. For this would be a case not of ignoring the teachings of the foundational texts in favor of something else, but rather of reinterpreting some legal rulings in those texts with reference to others of a broader import.[35] This was precisely where ijtihad came into play, which he defined, following the thirteenth-century jurist Sayf al-din al-Amidi (d. 1233) via the nineteenth-century Yemeni scholar Shawkani (d. 1834), as "the exertion of one's utmost effort, beyond which no further effort seems possible, to arrive at the most plausible view in legal matters."[36] To this, Hanif Nadwi juxtaposed the following "nontechnical" definition of his own:

> Given that Islam is a sagacious (*hakīmana*) system of thought and practice, there are subtle strengths (*ustuwariyan*) in the form of [legal] rationales and [human] benefits that are built into its structure. Delicate meanings and interconnections lie behind its rulings; and a vibrant and comprehensive philosophy underlies its laws. A mujtahid is one whose gaze is fixed on the totality of its intellectual system, one who is able to discern the strengths that are concealed within it, one who discovers the meaning and connections that are hidden yet present in it.... He is then able to find the solution to new problems in light of the rationales behind the rulings, their meaning and their interconnections, and to apply the results to new circumstances.[37]

That Islam was a "complete religion" meant only, Hanif Nadwi said, that "it provides guidance on all facets of life, not that it takes society itself to be static ... or that it does not envision society's progression beyond the levels at which it found itself in the time of the Prophet."[38] The task of Islam was to provide guidance to its adherents as they moved through changing times,[39] and the mujtahid was at the forefront of those who did so. The Prophet himself was a mujtahid, Hanif Nadwi said, and he made clear that more was at stake in this assertion than to elevate the later mujtahids' pedigree and the significance of their intellectual endeavor. What it meant was that the Prophet was not merely the deliverer of the divine message but also its interpreter, one continuously engaged in applying it to particular circumstances and deriving broad principles from it.[40] Not to see the Prophet as actively engaged with the divine message in some such way was, Hanif Nadwi said, to take a "mechanical view of prophethood." A skilled physician was one, he said, who did not merely apply received knowledge to the ailments he treated; rather, he possessed an ability and an understanding that went beyond the sum of his acquired knowledge. The same was true of a musician or an architect. But if we were willing to take this view for such practices, he rhetorically asked, "why should we take a mechanical view of prophethood, viz, that it does not produce the insight of a mujtahid, or that the prophet only remembers the text of the Qur'an and is appointed to disseminate it rather than also reflecting upon it and undertaking ijtihad in its light."[41]

This extraordinary position fell well short of Fazlur Rahman's view of the Prophet's role in the making of revelation, though it did go considerably beyond that of the traditionalists in how it visualized the Prophet's active interaction with the text of the revelation. Hanif Nadwi was at pains to emphasize the authority of the Prophet's teachings, against Orientalist skepticism about their authenticity and the arguments of the (unnamed) Ahl al-Qur'an, and this included the authority of his ijtihad as well.[42] Yet, in seeing some of the Prophet's teachings as his ijtihadic extrapolations from revelation, he did leave the distinct impression that they were not necessarily any more binding on succeeding generations than was the ijtihad of a distinguished scholar. For someone with Salafi leanings, this was a quite remarkable stance.

The modernists have always had strong aspirations toward implementing their vision of Islam in Pakistan and of reforming Islamic law to that end. Hanif Nadwi's work sought to facilitate the path to such reform or, as he put it, toward "the codification of a new fiqh."[43] The book exuded a clear sense not only that a rethinking of the law was imperative in modern conditions of radical change but also that the newly established state had the opportunity to lead the charge in that direction.[44] Two examples of what such rethinking might look like are worth mentioning. First, in a discussion of the qualifications for ijtihad, Hanif Nadwi noted the view of the aforementioned Shatibi (d. 1388) that, provided he met other conditions, a non-Muslim, too, could undertake ijtihad. This went against the common juristic view that being a Muslim was a necessary condition for ijtihad. With some agility, Hanif Nadwi argued that there was no contradiction between Shatibi's view and that of the generality of other jurists. For while only a Muslim could be a mujtahid, properly speaking, a non-Muslim could *participate* in a more inclusive activity of ijtihad. Consequently, non-Muslims, too, could be part of a modern legislative assembly engaged in ijtihad. This was to say that such an assembly could be the site of ijtihad without having to lose its democratic credentials, which it would if the state's non-Muslim inhabitants were given no representation in it.[45]

A second example, which occurs near the very end of the book, relates to the question of private property.[46] Developing his earlier argument that norms relating to matters of human interaction were subject to change while those concerning worship were not, Hanif Nadwi observed that property owner-ship fell into the former category and "the shari`a has no interest in whether it is permitted or disallowed—this is a purely worldly matter."[47] This, again, was a significant departure from the received tradition. From the perspective of the traditionalist `ulama, just because particular norms fall into the cate-gory of human relations rather than that of worship did not necessarily mean that they could be reordered at will, and, as historians of Islamic law have often noted, the right to property is among the most sacrosanct in the world of the medieval jurists.[48] Why those jurists had protected the right to private property is, Hanif Nadwi said in an uncharacteristically romanticized vein, because the sort of evils that now attend upon it did not yet exist: "Today pri-vate property does not mean what it did then. There was no complexity about it earlier. The life and rights of any group or class were not affected by it to the degree they are now. It was not the case then that a group had the right, on the basis of feudal practices, to monopolize all luxuries while ceaselessly en-larging the circles of poverty and deprivation for others. Nor was the current uneven system of elections and representation prevalent then, one that en-trusts the reins of government and the control over all sources of power to those who are already in possession of unlimited amounts of it."[49] This view was in accord with the socialist-leaning writings of Khalifa Abdul Hakim, the institute's founding director. It was very far from the views of many Deoban-dis, though scarcely from all of them.[50]

Ideas similar to those of Hanif Nadwi were articulated by Muhammad Ja`far Nadwi Phulwarwi (d. 1982), who was also associated with the Institute of Islamic Culture from the time of its inception until 1973. He, too, had been educated at the Nadwat al-`Ulama and was, in fact, the son of one of the Nadwa's founders—a locally influential pir from Bihar in eastern India. In a book aptly titled *The Religion Is Easy (al-Din yusr)*, first published in 1955, Phulwarwi argued at length that Islam promoted human welfare in all con-ceivable forms but that the `ulama had imposed unwarranted constraints on things permitted to people by God and His Prophet. The most effective way of reclaiming this easy-to-live religion was for Muslims to return to their foundational texts.[51] But even within those texts, a distinction was to be made between universal, eternal norms and those that were of a "provisional" na-ture. The teachings of the Qur'an regarding the fair treatment of slaves were not to be taken to mean, Phulwarwi said, that it envisaged the existence of this institution for all time. Qur'anic injunctions on the welfare of the poor did not presuppose that conditions of poverty should be preserved in order to then apply those injunctions. The same was true of the rules governing warfare. "There is so much on jihad and the preparation for it in the Book [of God] and in the sunna, and our intellectuals have so idealized it as a goal, that all Islam appears to have been encompassed by it. There is no denying the importance of warfare, yet this, too, is a provisional matter, a means toward a higher end. The true purpose [of such teachings ultimately] is to eliminate warfare from the world, to establish such peace and security that no trace of fighting remains."[52]

Phulwarwi proposed a further, and related, distinction between what he called shari`a and *din*. The latter, he said, was an abstraction comprising "eternal values" (he used the English words here). Shari`a, on the other hand, was a specific embodiment of those values, and it was not unalterable. For example, he said, God has repeatedly enjoined ritual prayer (*namaz*). "The essence of this injunction is to express [human] servitude" to God. The actual practices that constituted ritual prayer were, on the other hand, a facet of the shari`a. While servitude to God was an unchangeable value, the particular manner in which it had been given expression was not. Thus, the ritual prayer is performed not only while standing upright but also, in case of the infirm, while sitting or even lying down; sometimes it has four cycles, sometimes two or even just one; sometimes one faces the Ka`ba while performing it, and at other times it can be undertaken irrespective of direction, and so forth. Yet, such variation had no bearing on the fundamental value it was meant to articulate.[53] Phulwarwi was aware of the significance of his chosen illustration: "We have adduced the most important element of religion (din) as our example here. It should not be difficult to extend this [idea] to all of religion."[54] But there was more to it than he stated. As seen with Hanif Nadwi, even those who eagerly endorsed the adaptability of religious and legal norms often tended to exclude matters of ritual worship from that purview. To Phulwarwi, on the other hand, it was not such rituals but certain universal values that lay at the core of religion, and they alone were eternal.

To say that particular religious and legal norms ought to remain receptive to change was not, however, to make them dispensable at will. Rather, `ulama like Hanif Nadwi and Phulwarwi were considerably more cautious in how they understood the dialectic of continuity and change than was true of many a Western-educated modernist. A useful example relates to the hudud, which Phulwarwi discussed toward the end of his book and to which I will return in another context later in this chapter. In juristic parlance, the hudud refer to punishments—for such infractions as theft, brigandage, drinking, and unlawful sex—that are specifically mandated in the Islamic foundational texts and, unlike many other punishments, are considered to be nonnegotiable. They are also draconian, and authoritarian regimes have sometimes advertised their

Islamic zeal by embracing them, as did General Zia al-Haqq with his Hudood Ordinances. The punishment for theft under hudud laws is the cutting off of a hand; one of the punishments for brigandage is the cutting off of a hand and a foot; for unlawful sex between an unmarried man and woman it is a hundred lashes; and for those who are (or have previously been) married it is stoning to death. Phulwarwi could conceivably have taken the tack of arguing that such punishments no longer had a place in the modern world. That, however, is not what he said. Rather, he argued that even the hudud could be interpreted in a way that revealed Islam's concern with facilitating things for people. "Hudud absolutely do not mean that you go out of your way to find excuses for imposing punishments and be on the lookout for ways to impose the severest penalties. The spirit behind the hudud is just the opposite of this—it is finding reasons to ignore [wrongdoing] and forgive it, giving preference to erring on the side of forgiveness than to erring on that of penalty."[55] The Prophet, he said adducing the relevant traditions, was often reluctant to impose the hudud punishments, and so were the first caliphs.[56] He argued further that the Qur'anic injunction to cut off the thief's hand could be interpreted metaphorically, too, in the sense of cutting off all that induces or compels people to steal. And, he suggested, if the Qur'an notes several alternative punishments for the more serious crime of brigandage, including capital punishment but also exile, it stood to reason that the lesser crime of theft be also amenable to less severe punishments, such as exile or imprisonment.[57] What the Qur'an referred to as brigandage was itself to be understood as a crime whereby someone tries to "sabotage" the social order, he said, and it was this feature of such crimes, rather than a fixed and specific act, that called forth the severest penalties in particular circumstances.[58]

The consumption of alcohol, though part of the hudud crimes, was also to be evaluated according to the specificities of circumstances, Phulwarwi said. He cited a telling anecdote from Ibn Taymiyya in this regard. Passing by a company of Tatars who were drinking, a companion of Ibn Taymiyya's condemned them for it. But Ibn Taymiyya reprimanded him for this censoriousness. God had forbidden alcohol because it obstructed people from prayer and the remembrance of God, Ibn Taymiyya said. But, in case of the Tatars, their drinking distracted them *from* killing, enslaving, and looting people.[59] Phulwarwi also adduced a hadith in which the Prophet asks his companions not to curse a man who had been repeatedly caught drinking for, as the Prophet put it, "he loves God and His messenger." What this hadith suggested, Phulwarwi said, was that "such criminals might do [great] things that pious and sinless people cannot. You have surely seen scores of instances in which a dissolute (*fasiq*) man has endangered his life for the sake of a wronged person, whereas the pious man sits aloof; a sinful man gives away his savings for some noble cause whereas the devout person sits like a serpent on his wealth. An ignorant person preserves his integrity (*khudi*) at all costs while the scholar is bought

off by the unbelievers. Hence a man defines his place through his overall character, not by the externals of some of his actions."[60] No names were named,
but it is tempting to see these last sentences of the book as something more
than an argument for a flexible and differentiated view of the hudud. It was
also a defense of the Pakistani modernists, frequently maligned by the ʿulama
and the Islamists for their Westernized lifestyles.

Just as it is not hard to buy into modernist stereotypes of traditionalist
ʿulama, it is easy to dismiss ʿulama like Phulwarwi and Hanif Nadwi as simply toeing the modernist lines of argument—the more so, of course, because
they were employed at a modernist research institute.[61] Yet, their views represent serious arguments, arrived at through careful engagement with the Islamic scholarly tradition. Implicitly and sometimes explicitly, their positions
sought to remind their readers that the Islamic tradition was more varied
than the traditionalists would have them believe, that important voices from
the hallowed past could be mustered in support of *departures* from the conservative mainstream as well. At the same time, for all their very substantive
differences with the traditionalists, there were limits to how far even Phulwarwi and Hanif Nadwi would go in backing the modernists. One example
of this deserves notice here. In discussing the qualifications for ijtihad, Hanif
Nadwi made it clear that anyone who did not have a mastery of the Arabic
language had no business engaging in ijtihad: "People who dabble in ijtihad
as a pastime (*mashghala-i ijtihad*) without being able to read Arabic should,
for God's sake, take stock of their limitations. They need to see if they possess
enough knowledge to move forward in its light. [Ijtihad] is not a trivial task
such that everyone can undertake it. Rather, it is the final station of knowledge and understanding/gnosis (*maʿrifat*), one whose frontiers intersect
with those of prophethood."[62] With some notable exceptions such as Fazlur
Rahman and Javed Ahmad Ghamidi, English-educated Pakistani modernists
are not well-known for their knowledge of the Arabic language. Persian was a
different matter. Muhammad Iqbal was a distinguished poet in that language,
and Khalifa Abdul Hakim had written his doctoral dissertation on the metaphysics of Rumi. But a knowledge of Persian, though central to the Sufi tradition in the eastern Islamic lands and to Islamic ethics, cut no ice with the
ʿulama when it came to demonstrating expertise in Islamic law. Elsewhere in
his book on ijtihad, Hanif Nadwi referred derisively to "ignorant mujtahids,"[63]
which again was plainly meant to deflate the modernist hubris on matters of
ijtihad.

Legal Reform: Transgressing God's Limits?

Given that such criticism as a Jaʿfar Phulwarwi or a Hanif Nadwi had of the
English-educated modernists would be dismissed as toothless by the traditionalist ʿulama, it is now worth asking how the latter have sought to take on

modernist initiatives. Their responses to state-sponsored legal reform provide some useful illustrations of their misgivings toward its authors and backers but also of the ambiguities that characterize all sides of a fraught relationship.

In 1956, shortly after the promulgation of Pakistan's first constitution, the Commission on Marriage and Family Laws had submitted its recommendations to the government for reform in this core area of Islamic law. The commission was headed by Mian Abdul Rashid, a retired chief justice of the Supreme Court; Khalifa Abdul Hakim served as its secretary and the moving spirit behind it. The sole representative of the `ulama on the commission was Ihtisham al-Haqq Thanawi (d. 1981), whose polemics against Fazlur Rahman were noted in the previous chapter. The commission's report and Ihtisham al-Haqq Thanawi's note of dissent are both documents of considerable interest for our purposes here.[64]

The report exuded great assuredness in the modernist enterprise. It quoted Iqbal's famous lecture on ijtihad and implicitly staked out a claim to the only kind of new legal thinking that Iqbal had been interested in discussing, viz, "ijtihad as complete authority in legislation."[65] Like Iqbal, the report lamented the tendency of the religious scholars to rigidly adhere to the views of earlier jurists and it attributed the decline of Islam to such rigidity.[66] True Islam, on the other hand, was anything but opposed to progress:

> No Muslim can believe that Islam is an outworn creed incapable of meeting the challenge of evolutionary forces. Its basic principles of justice and equity, its urge for universal knowledge, its acceptance of life in all its aspects, its world-view, its view of human relations and human destiny, and its demand for an all-round and harmonious development, stand firmly like a rock in the tempestuous sea of life.[67]

It was not just the medieval jurists and their latter-day followers who had made the shari`a unresponsive to people's needs, however. The colonial courts and the Anglo-Muhammadan law of British India had also contributed to making the law both cumbersome and static. It was now for the new state to embark upon the project of legal reform in light of Islam,[68] and remedying problems in the laws of personal status was just the beginning of this larger project: "If the reforms proposed by the Commission are welcomed by the liberal and enlightened section of the public and receive legislative sanction they will form an important contribution to the scheme of reconstruction demanded by all who are not fossilized by tradition or blinded by sheer authoritarianism."[69]

Among other things, the commission recommended that all new marriages should be recorded on standardized marriage certificates and registered with local representatives of the government.[70] It proposed the legal age for marriage as sixteen years for women and eighteen for men. Where all major schools of Sunni law recognized that a couple was irrevocably divorced if the husband had pronounced certain words to that effect three times, even if he did so in a single sitting, the commission recommended that a divorce become final only after the husband had declared his intention of ending the marriage three times over the course of three months. While there are few constraints in Sunni law on a husband's authority to repudiate his wife, the commission required a matrimonial court to be part of the divorce proceedings. It also recommended severe restrictions on polygyny: a matrimonial court had to approve the request, on grounds of "an inescapable necessity,"[71] for a second marriage, and the court had to be convinced that the husband could equitably provide for his wives.

Ihtisham al-Haqq Thanawi was unsparing in his response to these recommendations. In a note of dissent that was longer than the report itself, Thanawi ridiculed the commission's pretensions to ijtihad and bitingly observed that its members lacked even the most elementary acquaintance with the Islamic juridical tradition.[72] This was far more derisive than anything Hanif Nadwi had said on the matter of unqualified mujtahids. Thanawi was especially bitter in complaining that a long introductory note spelling out the need for legal reform had been included with the recommendations but that there had been no consultation on its contents.[73] He then proceeded to show how all of the major recommendations of the commission were in contravention of Islamic law. The shari`a stipulated no minimum age for marriage, and `A'isha, one of the Prophet Muhammad's wives, was six or seven at the time of her marriage.[74] While recognizing that child marriage was an undesirable custom, he insisted that to impose a minimum age for marriage constituted "interference in religion."[75] The British, too, had tried to legislate against it, but they had faced severe opposition. Indeed, he insinuated that the modernist Muslims may have been behind that colonial initiative as well.[76] Thanawi was equally opposed to the proposal that the utterance of the divorce formula three times in a single sitting should be counted as only one of the three times a husband needed to say the relevant words, that the divorce could take effect only over the course of three months, and that a matrimonial court had to officiate over the process. This went against the consensus of the scholars, he said, and it again meant interfering in religious matters.[77] So did the proposed restrictions on polygyny, which he saw simply as an expression of the modernist desire to conform to Western expectations. It was a mark of "blind imitation" of the West that the report recommended legislation against polygyny but said nothing against extramarital sex. To Thanawi, such legislation would only make society more promiscuous.[78]

The commission's report had claimed that it "proposed no new rights for women which the Qur'an and Sunnah had not already granted them."[79] Thanawi disputed this, arguing that the commission had illegitimately taken upon itself to "make the shari`a."[80] Repeatedly, he also accused the commission of having distorted (*tahrif*) the Qur'an in trying to find a warrant for its recommendations.[81] In Islamic theology, tahrif is often viewed as one of the more grievous sins of the Jews and the Christians, viz, their distorting of scriptural texts in order to make them conform to their own whims. Besides constituting a tampering with God's law, such distortions had made them averse to accepting the truth of Islam; without them, they would have seen that their scriptures already testified to Islam's truth. From Thanawi's vantage, the modernists were guilty of the same kind of distortions as had earned God's displeasure toward the recipients of the earlier scriptures.

It would have been difficult to come up with a stronger public indictment of the work of the modernists.[82] Yet, two things are worth noting. First, objections such as Thanawi's could be answered and many of them were by none other than Ja`far Phulwarwi, indeed *before* Thanawi had articulated them. In a short tract on the question of reform in Islamic family law, published under the auspices of the Institute of Islamic Culture in 1955, Phulwarwi invoked his aforementioned distinction between shari`a and din to challenge the idea that shari`a norms were necessarily immutable or that a modification in them constituted an interference in religion.[83] On the sensitive question of the precedent from `A'isha's age at the time of her wedding, Phulwarwi denied that she was in fact quite as young as some reports asserted. But he also made the larger point that "the permissibility or impermissibility [of marriage at a very young age] rests on social conditions at any given time rather than on mere precedent. Adhering to the sunna does not consist in literally accepting something that had taken place in the Prophet's time. Rather, true adherence to the sunna means adopting a rule in light of the common good (masalih) and the rationales behind particular rulings (*hikam*)."[84] Phulwarwi had also taken a swipe at the `ulama's frequent invocation of the binding authority of consensus. Responding to the traditionalist view that the permissibility of polygyny could not be set aside since it was a matter of the Muslim community's continuous practice, he denied that this was a compelling argument:

> Is there any reprehensible innovation (*bid`a*) which is not a matter of continuous inherited practice (*mutawaris*) in this community? Monarchy, lineal succession, the existence of harems, slavery and concubinage, the selling of captives, despotism—which of these things accords with an Islamic temperament? And yet, because of some misunderstanding [of Islamic teachings], they have continued to be practiced widely and without interruption (*tawatur o ta`amul ke sath*) by the community. How bad can it be if polygyny, too, is included in this list [of falsely justified practices]?[85]

Such arguments were meant to bolster modernist positions though they were not necessarily identical, in either tone or substance, with those of the English-educated modernists. Ironically, and this is the second point to note about Ihtisham al-Haqq Thanawi's rejoinder to the marriage commission report, the modernists themselves seem to have given greater credibility to such strident views than they did to their own allies among the `ulama. Yet, not all even among the traditionalists took stringent positions in conformity with modernist expectations. There are instructive illustrations of this in the testimony of witnesses called before the Court of Inquiry investigating the anti-Ahmadi disturbances of 1953. In one instance, the court wanted a religious scholar, `Abd al-Halim Qasimi, the founder and head of a Deobandi madrasa in Lahore and an active participant in the anti-Ahmadi agitation, to concede that any effort to implement Islamic law in Pakistan would entail severe restrictions on non-Muslims. The scholar, who taught the medieval compendium *Hidaya*—among the most authoritative expressions of Hanafi law not only to the `ulama but also in British colonial courts—would have none of it, however:

> Q. Will you allow the Christians and the Jews to construct new
> churches and synagogues?
> A. Undoubtedly yes.
> Q. [...] What do you say to the view expressed at page 219 of the
> second volume of Hedaya that in an Islamic state Christians and
> Jews cannot be permitted to build new places of worship?
> A. Hedaya is merely a book of jurisprudence, and it is open to one to
> have different views on the subject, unless the exposition of law in
> the Hedaya is based either on Qur'an or true Traditions.[86]

It has often been remarked that Thanawi was the only member of the `ulama to have been appointed to the marriage commission.[87] What is equally significant is that *he* was the `alim appointed to it, though he was hardly the most eminent of the Pakistani `ulama. As Fazlur Rahman had sarcastically noted in 1963, in responding to Thanawi's charge that he was trying "to 'modernise' Islam by exploiting the Central Institute of Islamic Research in collaboration with foreign Christian missionaries": "I only wish that a dignitary like Maulana Ehtashamul Haq would produce some academic works of a standard comparable to some produced by non-Muslims on our problems."[88] If Thanawi's choice as the *sole* `ulama-representative on the marriage commission suggests an effort on the part of the governing elite to hold traditionalist voices at bay, it equally points to a modernist recognition that some among such `ulama needed to be heard, even cultivated. Thanawi's views had the merit of fitting modernist stereotypes better than those of many others, which may be at least part of what recommended him to a governing elite otherwise as hostile to him as he was to them. Not long after the imposition of martial law, it was the madrasa Thanawi had founded in Tando Allahyar, Sindh, that Ayub Khan visited to harangue the `ulama along modernist lines. And in 1960, when the Ayub Khan regime formed the board of governors for the then recently established Central Institute of Islamic Research, Thanawi was the one member from among the `ulama appointed to it.[89] It was the recognition that the government had bestowed on Thanawi that had enabled him to later go on to publicly challenge Fazlur Rahman on his wayward views.

Thanawi's career may have owed something to the ambiguous embrace[90] of the governing elite, but his critique of the marriage commission's majority report did nothing to sway the commission's recommendations. If anything, it would have confirmed the modernists in their dim view of the `ulama. In March 1961, Ayub Khan, considerably less hesitant to take on conservative sentiment than the parliamentarians of the mid-1950s had been, promulgated the Muslim Family Laws Ordinance. In almost all respects, it followed the recommendations of the marriage commission while specifying penalties for the violation of particular provisions.[91] The `ulama and the Islamists opposed the ordinance vociferously, as they still do. The modernists knew this very well, but, already by 1961, they seemed to be having trouble recalling the specifics of what the traditionalists had said about it. In an editorial in March 1961 praising the ordinance, Pakistan's national daily *Dawn* posed a challenge to the `ulama that would have left many among them incredulous: "Is a single one of these provisions contrary to any *explicit and unambiguous* injunction of the Quran? If so, they are welcome to point it out. . . . If our Ulema can find no such fault with the new Law they will be well advised to support it or, at any rate, to accept it as the inevitable fulfillment of the demands of the contemporary age in which mere dogma and blind orthodoxy can no longer hope to sway the minds of men."[92]

Around the same time, Mufti Muhammad Shafi`, the founder and head of the Dar al-`Ulum madrasa of Karachi and an important voice among the `ulama in the early constitutional debates in Pakistan, had written a letter to President Ayub Khan, pointing out the several ways in which the ordinance contravened express injunctions of the Qur'an and the sunna as well as the agreed-upon views of the early jurists.[93] The jurists in question, he said, were not just those of the Hanafi school, to which most Sunnis of South Asia adhered. That would be bad enough; what was worse was that no jurists of *any* of the recognized schools of Sunni law held the positions that the ordinance had come to implement.[94] This, of course, was an argument that Phulwarwi had anticipated and refuted, but it remained a weighty argument.

Shafi`'s tone was more restrained than Thanawi's. Even so, he too noted the damning irony that even the British had left the marriage and family laws untouched, since they were "purely religious laws," and the post-partition government of India had likewise left them alone. Yet, such core Islamic laws were now in peril in an Islamic country.[95] Coming from a figure who had played an active role in giving religious legitimacy to the Muslim League's case for Pakistan, Shafi`'s letter conveyed a palpable sense of betrayal. In an understated yet ominous manner, he also warned the government that such infractions of the shari`a would not be tolerated by the people, who would "find themselves utterly oppressed in their own Islamic country. In these circumstances, even if they are silenced through some legal pressure, their religious sentiments would have been very badly bruised. Always seeing themselves as oppressed, they would lead restive lives, which could pose a danger to the country at any time."[96] Rather than make a public statement in response to the numerous queries he was receiving on the provisions of this ordinance, he said, he had written privately to the president precisely to avoid adding to popular anxiety on this matter.[97] He concluded his letter by outlining three options for the government: cancel the ordinance and appoint a new commission comprising 'ulama trusted by the people as well as those capable of translating shari'a norms into the language of modern legislation; cancel the ordinance and defer the matter until the parliament was convened (under the yet to be promulgated constitution); or, to save face, neither implement nor cancel this ordinance but instead put it in cold storage.[98]

This was a powerful indictment of the government's modernism. What lent it greater force was Shafi''s scholarly stature. In contrast with Ihtisham al-Haqq Thanawi, Shafi' was a major figure in the traditionalist Deobandi camp and he had served as the head mufti of the Dar al-'Ulum madrasa in Deoband for many years in prepartition India before immigrating to Pakistan to found an identically named madrasa in Karachi. Yet, Shafi', too, was far from being irreconcilable to the government or averse to receiving its patronage. He had been a key member of the Ta'limat-i Islamia board and he went on to serve on many other government committees. His madrasa had begun its life on "evacuee property" [99]—left behind by those fleeing the country at the time of the partition and often requiring political connections to be allotted to new claimants. Though a good deal of the support for the madrasa came from private donations, including the sprawling 56 acres on which it has stood since 1957, those associated with its early administration were influential people. Among them, around 1960, was Hakim Muhammad Sa'id (d. 1998), the owner of a business empire in traditional—"Greek"—medicine and a prominent philanthropist; he was the madrasa's treasurer. A former military accountant-general was also on its board of administrators.[100] One of Shafi''s best known works, a large commentary on the Qur'an in Urdu, was itself the product of a governmental initiative. The making of this commentary merits a brief digression before proceeding further.

Taking its inspiration from the efforts of the Nasser regime in Egypt to regulate mosques in that country as well as the content of sermons that were delivered on the occasion of the Friday congregational prayers, the government of Pakistan, too, had contemplated in the early 1950s the preparation of a volume of standardized sermons to be distributed to mosques around the country. That effort did not go very far. Echoing the *Report of the Court of Inquiry* on the anti-Ahmadi disturbances in the Punjab in 1953, bureaucrats at the Ministry of Information and Broadcasting took the view that "no two

Ulema would agree to the reproduction of their khutbas [sermons] in one volume, nor would they hold one opinion on a given subject." Even if a volume of sermons were somehow produced, "the mullas cannot be expected to adopt them for their sermons, and very few persons will read this publication.... [A]ny attempt at prescribing a standard book of khutbas is more likely to raise religious controversies and release forces of dissension than to promote national unity."[101] Instead, the ministry proposed airing select sermons on the radio each week, and this is what was soon put into effect in the form of "a special programme called 'Maarif-ul-Quran' broadcast every Friday. This programme is based on the Holy Quran and Hadith, the special aim being to impress the need for national unity."[102] Shafi` was the `alim chosen for this task. He would continue to deliver his talks each Friday for the next twelve years. The commentary on the Qur'an that he began publishing from the early 1960s was based on these talks and it carried the same title—*Ma`arif al-Qur'an* ("Knowledge of the Qur'an")—as his program on Radio Pakistan. Upon completion, it comprised more than 5,500 pages in eight volumes.[103] This is the commentary that the literary critic Muhammad Hasan `Askari would begin translating into English toward the end of his life.[104]

Shafi`'s standing as a scholar and his willingness to work with the government may well have made it difficult for the ruling elite to ignore him. Yet, they did ignore him, for the most part. The letter Shafi` had sent the president was forwarded for a response to Ghulam Ahmad Parwez, the government's modernist ally.[105] Parwez wrote a spirited defense of the family laws ordinance, arguing that it was not the ordinance but rather the `ulama's view of Islam that was in conflict with the teachings of the Qur'an.[106] Nothing in that tract would have convinced Shafi` or Ihtisham al-Haqq Thanawi, however, and Shafi` complained afterward that his objections to the ordinance had remained unanswered. He also complained of bad faith on the part of the government, which had proceeded to publish Shafi`'s letter to the president but not the content of the substantive objections to the law that Shafi` had appended to it.[107] The family laws ordinance remained in effect, as it does to this day. There was no popular unrest either. It would continue, however, to be a bête noire of the `ulama and the Islamists. And it is not the only one.

My second illustration of the fraught relationship between the `ulama and the state relates to legislation under the Musharraf regime to reform the Hudood Ordinances of General Zia al-Haqq. Though the implementation of the ordinances had always lagged far behind their rhetoric, many people, men and women, had nonetheless been charged over the years with hudud offenses, especially in matters relating to fornication, adultery, and rape. Indeed, much of the attention that Zia al-Haqq's Hudood Ordinances has received from scholars and civil rights activists has had to do with sexual crimes, and it is on this aspect that I, too, will focus here.

`Ulama and religio-political leaders belonging to different doctrinal persuasions had welcomed the Hudood Ordinances warmly.[108] Critics of these laws frequently pointed out, however, that they were unsuited to a modern state, that they caused great hardship to women, and, indeed, that they misconstrued Islamic criminal law itself. For instance, the ordinance relating to *zina* did not make a clear distinction between the legal consequences of unlawful but consensual sexual intercourse (zina) and rape, with the result that a woman alleging sexual assault could find herself charged with sexual impropriety if she failed to produce the requisite witnesses testifying to the assault. The fact that women (and men) were often acquitted in court, especially on appeal to the Federal Shari`at Court (FSC) and the Shari`at Appellate Bench of the Supreme Court, did not prevent people from being brought to court on zina-related charges. According to the noted human rights lawyer Asma Jahangir, "Between 1980 and 1987, the FSC heard 3,399 appeals in zina cases. Statistics collected in 1988 showed that around 46% of all female prisoners were accused of zina."[109] The ordinances had tended also to become an instrument of social control. As political scientist Charles Kennedy observed in 1988, there was "seemingly widespread use of the Zina Ordinance to file nuisance or harassment suits against disobedient daughters or estranged wives."[110]

Benazir Bhutto, who became prime minister shortly after the death of Zia al-Haqq in 1988, was well-known for her opposition to the Hudood Ordinances. Yet, during her two terms in office (1988–90, 1993–96), she had remained under intense pressure from the religious and center-right parties to demonstrate her Islamic commitments. This obviously meant that any effort to amend, let alone to repeal, the ordinances was deemed impolitic. Nawaz Sharif, who twice succeeded Benazir Bhutto as prime minister (1990–93, 1997–99), did not do much more to implement the laws than she had, but they firmly remained part of the criminal justice system. It was only in the final years of General Pervez Musharraf that the laws relating to sexual crimes were amended through parliamentary legislation in the form of the Protection of Women Act of 2006.

Some years earlier, in 2002, a particularly shocking case had helped galvanize women and human rights groups against the Hudood Ordinances. Ruling under those laws, a district court judge in Kohat in the Frontier province had sentenced a twenty-six-year-old illiterate woman to death. The woman, Zafran Bibi, had been repeatedly raped by her brother-in-law while her husband was in jail. The resulting pregnancy was viewed by the court as proof that she had engaged in unlawful sex; the brother-in-law was released for lack of evidence. As she awaited her punishment—stoning to death—in solitary confinement, there were protests by women's groups and extensive bad press within and outside the country. The Federal Shari`at Court eventually overturned the decision in light of the new facts presented to it. Zafran Bibi's husband had come forward to say that his wife had visited him in jail and that he was the newborn's father; Zafran Bibi had been persuaded to concur with that statement and to deny the rape. This had given the Shari`at Court enough grounds to set aside the lower court verdict, though not without a distinct sourness:

> This is an unfortunate case, which received much publicity in the national/international press. It also gave rise to several controversies. On account of disinformation, misunderstanding, lack of knowledge of the facts and circumstances of the case, some organisations resorted even to take out [sic] processions and demand repeal of the Hudood laws itself without realizing that it was not the laws of Hudood ... but its misapplication that resulted in miscarriage of justice.[111]

Already before the Shari`at Court decision, the government had referred the Hudood Ordinances to the National Commission on the Status of Women, which President Musharraf had established not long after coming to power. It was then headed by Majida Rizvi, a retired judge of the Sindh high court. Under Justice Rizvi's leadership, the commission issued a report in late summer 2003 calling for the repeal of, rather than merely an amending of, the ordinances.[112] As Justice Rizvi observed, writing for the special committee that her commission had established to examine the ordinances, their "enforcement has brought about injustice rather than justice, which should be the main purpose of the enforcement of Islamic law."[113] The government would content itself with their amendment, however. And it would be some years before it had mustered the political will to do so.[114]

The `ulama and the Islamists were generally hostile to any significant change in the Hudood Ordinances, which they rhetorically equated with God's own law. The opposition alliance in the parliament, the Muttahida Majlis-i `Amal (MMA; United Action Front), which included many `ulama and was led by the Taliban ally Mawlana Fazlur Rahman, repeatedly threatened that it would resign en masse if the government embarked upon legislation that contravened the Qur'an and the normative example of the Prophet. Rectifying the excesses of the ordinances was important to the government's self-image, however, and even as frequent public assurances were offered that "nothing would be done contrary to the Holy Quran and Sunnah,"[115] efforts continued apace to persuade the conservative camp to support the initiative. To this end, a group of prominent `ulama from outside parliament was mustered to help negotiate with the MMA. Mufti Muhammad Taqi `Usmani, the vice president of Karachi's Dar al-`Ulum madrasa, was the most prominent among them.[116]

Like his father, Mufti Muhammad Shafi`, Taqi `Usmani, too, had a long history of association with the government. For more than a decade and a half, until 2002, he had served as a judge on the Shari`at Appellate Bench of the Supreme Court of Pakistan. It was in that capacity that he had written a detailed legal opinion in support of banning all interest-based transactions in the country.[117] His elevation to this judicial position, and to the Federal Shari`at Court prior to that, had much to do with his impressive scholarly productivity and his ability to speak and write in a manner that people of a Western intellectual formation were able to understand, including judges trained in the common law tradition. Such appointments served, in turn, to consolidate his standing, in Pakistan and abroad, as an `alim who could masterfully draw on his scholastic tradition to address the legal and economic problems of the contemporary world. All this had also earned him lucrative positions on the "shari`a boards" of several international financial institutions in the Middle East and the West, including the Abu Dhabi Islamic Bank, the Saudi American Bank, IISBC, the Dow Jones Islamic Markct Indcx, and the Robert Fleming Oasis Fund in Luxembourg.[118] Taqi `Usmani's position on the question of financial interest meant, however, that the Musharraf regime could not rely on him to help *overturn* the Shari`at Appellate Bench's earlier verdict against it. In order to get this done, he was removed from the bench in 2002, with the government citing his membership on the corporate boards as the reason: "the fact that he had financial interest in holding that 'all interest-based banking is un-Islamic' disqualified him from sitting on the bench."[119] Four years later, the same government found itself turning to Taqi `Usmani for help with the Protection of Women Bill.

Members of the "government's `ulama team"—as Taqi `Usmani and others on the committee were often characterized in the national media[120]—had many misgivings about the proposed bill. While the Hudood Ordinances mandated the punishment of stoning to death for those convicted of rape, the proposed bill made this crime punishable only under the somewhat less stringent provisions of the Pakistan Penal Code. The `ulama on the government team were strongly opposed to moving rape out of the list of hudud crimes. These `ulama also insisted that, in case the requisite four witnesses were not available to testify to an act of adultery or fornication, the act in question should still be subject to some form of what Muslim jurists call "discretionary" punishment (*ta`zir*)—that is, something less than the *hadd*-punishment but sufficiently severe to deter such acts. For its part, the proposed bill made it difficult to punish anyone for consensual premarital or extramarital sex. Nonetheless, for reasons that are not altogether clear, the `ulama had come away with the impression that their demands for modifications in the bill were acceptable to the government. Taqi `Usmani was quoted as saying at one point that "all issues had been settled unanimously and there was delay in preparing the revised draft [only] because every clause was considered in light of Quran and Sunnah."[121] Leaders of the MMA had had significant reservations about the proposed bill, but the provisional endorsement of the government-appointed `ulama seemed to ease many of their concerns, too.

The bill that was actually passed by the National Assembly and the Senate and ratified by President Musharraf in late 2006 was, however, significantly different from the version the government-appointed ʿulama had apparently consented to. Rape was no longer a hadd-crime, that is, not subject to the penalty of stoning to death. Consensual sex remained a punishable offense but accusations in this regard now had to be lodged in the relevant court rather than with the police, thereby making it more difficult to file such complaints, and it was left to the court's discretion whether or not to admit the complaint. Perhaps the most important achievement of this new law was to ensure that women victims of sexual assault could not themselves be accused of sexual misconduct and punished for it.[122] The ʿulama did not object to this last-mentioned aspect of the new legislation. They did, however, vociferously denounce other key provisions of the Protection of Women Act. As Mawlana Fazlur Rahman, the leader of the opposition MMA in the National Assembly put it, this law was intended to turn "Pakistan into a free-sex zone."[123] And Musharraf's appeal to the nation, in the wake of the passage of the bill by the National Assembly, to support the "progressive elements" against the "extremists"[124] was interpreted by the MMA leadership as "a declaration of war against Islamic culture and civilization."[125]

Ironically, it was Taqi ʿUsmani, a key member of the team of ʿulama the government had appointed to help win over the MMA leadership, who emerged as by far the most articulate critic of the Protection of Women Act. He had been writing on the proposed legislation in leading Pakistani newspapers while the bill was being considered by parliament, and he was scathing in his criticism after it became law.[126] Offering a detailed, point by point analysis of the bill, Taqi ʿUsmani argued that it clearly contravened the teachings of the Qur'an and the hadith, and he cited many examples to illustrate this point. But he also built his case against this legislation on other grounds:

> I myself have been directly hearing cases registered under Hudood Ordinance, first as a Judge of Federal Shariah Court and then for 17 years as a member of Shariah Appellate Bench of the Supreme Court. In this long tenure, not once did I come across a case in which a rape victim was awarded punishment because she was unable to present four witnesses.[127]

That criminal charges could be filed and verdicts given against women under these laws—as in the case of Zafran Bibi—was largely ignored in this unforgiving commentary, except by way of a brief acknowledgment of the laws' abuse at the hands of the police. If men could misuse the Hudood Ordinances against hapless women, as has frequently been argued, Taqi ʿUsmani claimed that women, too, had used them for their own interest. In a move calculated to address the English-educated members of his audience, Taqi ʿUsmani cited the work of the aforementioned Charles Kennedy to suggest that some women entering adulterous relationships had alleged in court that they had been raped by their sexual partner—in such instances, the courts had tended to convict the man but to exonerate the woman.[128] The point of this testimony from "an unbiased non-Muslim scholar who has got no sympathies toward the Hudood ordinance" was to demonstrate Taqi 'Usmani's own familiarity with Western scholarship. It sought to show as well that women's oppression under the Hudood Ordinances was largely a matter of malicious propaganda. But Taqi 'Usmani's point was also that if some women could already use the ordinances to avoid being punished for consensual extramarital sex, the new law would provide men and women greater opportunity to do so. At the same time, he argued, the *protections* that the ordinances had provided to women— for example, by prescribing a draconian punishment for rape—had been weakened. As the title of one of his online articles on the subject had it, the new law amounted to "making Pakistan safe for rapists."[129]

The language some of the 'ulama used to denounce the Protection of Women Act of 2006—turning Pakistan into a "free-sex zone," making the country "safe for rapists"—plainly illustrates the degree of their hostility to this measure and, more broadly, to what they see as the Westernizing policies of the ruling elite. Yet, once again, such stridency did not necessarily translate into a complete break with the government pursuing such policies. Though the MMA had repeatedly threatened to resign from the National Assembly in the event the Hudood Ordinances were amended along the lines they eventually were, they did not resign. There was a serious rift within the MMA on this issue: the Islamist Jama'at-i Islami, the party that Mawdudi had once led, was in favor of resigning, while Mawlana Fazlur Rahman, the MMA general-secretary and the leader of the 'ulama-led Jam'iyyat al-'Ulama-i Islam, was opposed to this. Mawlana Fazlur Rahman seems to have believed that staying in the National Assembly gave the religious parties greater influence than leaving it, though the elected 'ulama have often also been insecure about whether they would be reelected. By the time of the next general elections, in early 2008, there no longer was an alliance of the religious parties. The Jama'at-i Islami boycotted those elections, and the other religious parties won few seats in the National Assembly. It was the mainstream political parties— the Pakistan People's Party of the recently assassinated Benazir Bhutto and the Pakistan Muslim League faction led by Nawaz Sharif—that were the big winners in those elections.

If, in practice, the 'ulama and the religious parties have often been considerably more pragmatic than their rhetoric would suggest, the effects of their rhetoric can scarcely be discounted. This rhetoric has arguably contributed toward delegitimizing Pakistani governments on Islamic grounds. Much like Ihtisham al-Haqq Thanawi and Mufti Muhammad Shafi' a generation earlier, Taqi 'Usmani did not mince words in asserting that the bill which later became the Protection of Women Act "blatantly violate[d] the injunctions of the Quran and Sunnah."[130] This would be a serious charge in any Muslim society, but it was especially grave in the Islamic Republic of Pakistan, where the government is constitutionally mandated to ensure that no legislation is repugnant to the Islamic foundational texts.

The `ulama's arguments did not remain altogether unchallenged. Already in 2003, as has been seen, the National Commission on the Status of Women had issued a report calling for a repeal of the Hudood Ordinances, helping pave the way for the 2006 legislation. As Justice Rizvi put it later, "I myself studied the Quran and Sunnah to analyze how far these [Hudood] laws are derived from these sources.... [The 2003] report ... made people realize that these laws were man-made. We made people think."[131] Religious intellectuals like Javed Ahmad Ghamidi tried as well to educate public opinion on the many inadequacies of the ordinances, and the Council of Islamic Ideology—of which Ghamidi was a member—did the same in a detailed report on them.[132] Such challenges had serious limits, however. Justice Rizvi was not a religious scholar, and her committee was an eclectic group of lawyers and retired higher court judges, bureaucrats, members of non-Muslim minorities, civil society activists, and a few scholars of Islam. Taqi `Usmani, too, had been appointed to it, but he had declined to participate in the proceedings.[133] He did not go out of his way to discredit the work of the committee, as he would in the case of the Protection of Women Act of 2006. Yet, in refusing to take any part in the committee's work, he had made clear what he thought of it. For their part, as observed earlier, Ghamidi's views on hudud are not devoid of equivocation, and his appeal in some circles scarcely matches the national and international standing that Taqi `Usmani has come to enjoy as an authority on Islamic law. Ironically, in calling upon a team of conservative `ulama to help make the case in 2006 for reforming the Hudood Ordinances, the government had itself lent further credibility to those who soon emerged as the severest critics of this initiative. Ghamidi, for one, saw the government's overtures toward these `ulama as a slight to the Council of Islamic Ideology, whose raison d'être, after all, was to advise the government on precisely such issues. In protest, he had tendered his resignation from the council, though he, too, was soon induced to resume his membership of it.[134]

Madrasa Reform: Challenge and Opportunity

Apart from the specter of modernist tampering with Islamic law, few issues have tended to arouse greater misgivings among the `ulama than the question of madrasa reform. The need to modernize these institutions, to bring them closer to the educational mainstream, to better regulate them, and to make their products useful to society and the state are familiar motifs in modernist discourses on Islam in Pakistan. For their part, many `ulama have seen governmental initiatives not as reforming madrasas but as seeking rather to undermine these last bastions of authoritative Islamic learning, diluting the "purely religious" instruction offered in them and thereby undercutting the `ulama's ability to reproduce and replenish their ranks.[135] This extravagant rhetoric does not illuminate very much, however, either about what the governmental reforms have actually sought to accomplish or about the impact they have had on the madrasas. Both issues merit a brief examination.

Major governmental initiatives aimed at reforming madrasas have taken place in the early 1960s, in the late 1970s, and in the aftermath of September 11, 2001. On the first occasion, in 1962, a government-appointed committee (with a number of prominent `ulama, including Mufti Muhammad Shafi`, but dominated by government officials) had called for the teaching of English, mathematics, general science, and social studies in the madrasa.[136] In order to create space for these disciplines without excessively overburdening the curriculum, the report had recommended a drastic reduction in the "unnecessary and out of date ... nonreligious" materials, by which it primarily meant not only medieval Islamic discussions of natural science, but also of philosophy and logic.[137] The "strictly religious subject matter" was, for its part, to be emphasized,[138] and this entailed "an increased emphasis" on the Qur'an and hadith.[139] Ironically, the very effort to find space in the madrasa for modern forms of knowledge was premised on a sharp divide between the religious and the nonreligious. In another irony, by locating religious authority and authenticity not in an evolving tradition but squarely in the Islamic foundational texts, the committee had found itself in inadvertent agreement with a defining tenet of the much disliked Islamists. The larger goal of this reorientation simultaneously toward the foundational texts *and* modern knowledge was to enable the `ulama to "address modern educated masses in a convincing manner," to "present Islam in a rational manner so that it can be really understood and devotionally practiced."[140]

The second major set of recommendations on reform, put forward in 1979, was the work of a committee constituted for the purpose by General Zia al-Haqq. Although produced under a regime distinctly more friendly to the `ulama than Ayub Khan's had been in the 1960s, the 1979 report was no less concerned than its predecessor with the unstated aspiration of bringing madrasas under government supervision. But it went further in the effort to integrate the public school or "general" curriculum into the madrasas, and it offered a new and important incentive for the `ulama's consent in this regard: the degrees awarded by madrasas were to be recognized as the equivalent of university diplomas provided particular portions of the general curriculum were also taught in madrasas. Thus, madrasas were to teach the entire general curriculum at the five-year-long primary-school level; they were to devote one-third of the time to this curriculum during the next five years, culminating in matriculation; and they were to have English, politics, and economics as electives during the following four years, whereupon the successful student would receive the madrasa's equivalent of a bachelor's degree. This was to be followed by two years of further study, amounting to work at the master's level. Completion of studies at the latter two stages was to be recognized by Pakistani universities, as well as prospective employers, as the equivalent, respectively, of a bachelor's and a master's in Arabic or Islamic studies from a public university. In turn, the universities' own master's curriculum in Arabic and Islamic studies was to be the same as that of the madrasas.[141] Since the late 1950s, madrasas belonging to different sectarian orientations have had their own boards to coordinate their educational activities throughout the country. The 1979 report sought to build on that development by recommending the establishment of a single national organization to oversee those boards, thereby to further facilitate the standardization of madrasa education and its equivalence with mainstream public education.

That many of the recommendations of the 1979 report for the introduction of the modern disciplines into the madrasa curriculum were similar to those of the 1962 committee suggests not merely a shared bureaucratic understanding of what needed to be done with the madrasas but also the limits on the government's ability to implement its reforms. Two decades after the 1979 report, the government of General Pervez Musharraf continued—in the third major initiative toward madrasa reform—to urge the introduction of modern, secular, disciplines into the madrasa. But in the aftermath of September 11, 2001, this initiative was much more directly focused than its predecessors on bringing the madrasas under government monitoring.[142] Having a madrasa officially registered with the government was now required not merely to have its advanced degrees recognized by the public universities but as the very condition of the madrasa's legitimate functioning.[143] Even in this changed atmosphere, however, the government was not notably successful in implementing its stated policy—that is, in shutting down madrasas that failed to register with it. The new initiative also envisaged establishing certain government-supported "model" madrasas where secular learning could be fully integrated with the religious sciences.[144] But given that all registered madrasas were supposed to be imparting a religious education together with elements of the public school curriculum, precisely what would set these model institutions apart from other madrasas remained uncertain. The resolve toward the "registration and regulation" of madrasas was reaffirmed as part of the National Action Plan adopted by the government in the immediate aftermath of the horrific massacre of more than 130 children at a school in Peshawar in December 2014. That resolve, too, has yielded uncertain results so far.[145]

As might be expected, the `ulama have offered much public commentary, sometimes at considerable length, on government-sponsored initiatives to reform and regulate their institutions. One brief illustration will have to stand for many others here. This was in response to the reforms proposed in 1979, and it came from the Deobandi scholar Muhammad Yusuf Ludhianawi (d. 2000), a professor of hadith at the Jami`at al-`Ulum madrasa in Karachi.

Ludhianawi argued that to integrate madrasas into the educational mainstream, as the 1979 report had proposed, meant nothing less than destroying Islam itself. The government of an Islamic state would thereby achieve, he said echoing a familiar motif, what the British never could.[146] Madrasas were the "defenders of the religious sciences" in society; their integration into the state-sponsored system of education would signify nothing but to "prevent them from their purely religious services and to subordinate them to the modern [Western] sciences."[147] Further, a "mixed" curriculum, with something from both the religious and the modern sciences, would not produce men who "combine the medieval and the modern.... [Rather], the products of such a system would be useless equally for religion and the world."[148] What the reform sought to create was not `ulama, Ludhianawi concluded, but "only loyal government servants."[149]

Contrary to what one would expect from such broadsides, madrasas have, in fact, adapted themselves to governmental initiatives at reform. Leading madrasas of Pakistan have come to provide for instruction precisely along the lines proposed by the 1979 report. For instance, in addition to departments for the memorization of the Qur'an, Taqi `Usmani's Dar al-`Ulum in Karachi has long had a primary and a secondary school, thus serving both to prepare students for the traditional Dars-i Nizami curriculum and to offer instruction in the public school curriculum. In July 2016, it was announced that the boards overseeing the madrasas belonging to different doctrinal orientations had agreed to teach the same high school curriculum as that followed by the Islamabad-based board of public education.[150] This seems merely to have ratified a development that had already been materializing for some time.[151]

The results of such adaptation have not been detrimental to the `ulama's interests. For instance, the equivalence between the degrees awarded by madrasas and those of the public universities has created new possibilities for them, notably in terms of employment. It has allowed madrasa graduates to teach Arabic and Islamic studies in public schools and colleges. Not content simply with mere equivalence, some `ulama have gone on to receive academic degrees directly from the universities. Taqi `Usmani has bachelor's degrees in the humanities and in law from the University of Karachi and a master's in Arabic from the University of the Punjab in Lahore, though he had earned these degrees long before the 1979 proposals. Mukhtar Allah Haqqani, the compiler of a six-volume collection of fatwas issued during the second half or so of the twentieth century by the Dar al-`Ulum Haqqaniyya—the madrasa best known in the West for the fact that several members of the Afghan Taliban leadership had once studied in it—has a master's degree in Islamic studies from the University of Peshawar.[152] Some `ulama have also been able to proceed to doctoral programs by virtue of the formal recognition of their prior degrees. For instance, Nizam al-din Shamzai, the chief jurisconsult and professor of hadith at the Jami`at al-`Ulum al-Islamiyya madrasa in Karachi at the time of his death in 2004, had a PhD in Islamic studies from the University of Sindh.[153] Mas`ud Baig, who headed the girls' section of the Jami`a Bannuria al-`Alamiyya in Karachi and was assassinated by sectarian rivals in 2014, also had a doctorate from Karachi University and he taught there as well.[154] Both a son and a nephew of Taqi `Usmani have earned PhDs from Pakistani universities, in addition to degrees from the Dar al-`Ulum madrasa. Their dissertations, now published, are concerned with showing how modern economic problems are to be addressed from the standpoint of Islamic law.[155]

Even when the `ulama lack degrees from colleges and universities, as most still do, the rhetoric and, as the case may be, the practice of their openness to public education facilitates their interaction with those schooled in them. It is worth noting, for instance, that the desire of segments of the population for a deeper grounding in Islam than is provided to them by the mandatory public school courses in Islamic studies has sometimes brought them to madrasas for part-time religious instruction. As Matthew Nelson has observed with reference to attitudes toward Islamic education in contemporary Pakistan, "the overwhelming majority do not approach their educational options (for example, religious versus non-religious education) as a zero-sum game. Instead . . . most families are inclined to construct a careful balance of sorts, including both types of education at the same time."[156]

Though I speak in this book in terms of particular facets of Islam, ordinary believers are not classifiable, of course, as `ulama, Islamists, modernists, Sufis. They do tend to follow various orientations—Sunni or Shi`i; Deobandi, Barelawi, Ahl-i Hadith, among the Sunnis—but it has often taken much work by interested parties to make their contours sufficiently distinct for those who are supposed to belong to them. The receptivity of ordinary believers to particular ideas and claims to authority is the prize for which the leaders of the various religio-political facets and orientations compete. However, even when they incline toward some claimants to authority rather than others, many ordinary believers have tended to combine ideas of varied provenance, just as they would combine religious with a worldly education. To take one example, the `ulama often lament divisiveness in the Muslim community, yet they have tended to take the existence of rival doctrinal orientations more or less for granted.[157] On the other hand, the Islam of the modernists professes to brook no sectarianism. To Iqbal, as would be recalled, "[t]here are no Wahabies, Shias, Mirzas or Sunnies in Islam."[158] In explaining his approach in *Islamic Ideology*, Khalifa Abdul Hakim had observed likewise that "[a]ll sectarian controversial matter has been eschewed [in the book] and Islam is presented in its broad basic principles."[159] In positing a single, true Islam that transcends sectarian and other commitments, many—perhaps most—ordinary educated believers are closer to the modernist view than they are to the `ulama's.[160] But this has not stopped them from also recognizing the `ulama's authority in particular areas of their lives or from turning to them for guidance and to their madrasas for some of their education.

The `ulama's madrasas are not, however, the only institutions providing Islamic education. The influential Islamist organization, the Jama`at-i Islami, has long had its own madrasas, though they have functioned on a much more limited scale than the Deobandi or the Barelawi madrasas.[161] Since the early 1980s, an educational and religious movement called the Minhaj al-Qur'an— "the path of the Qur'an"—has come to spawn a substantial number of schools across the country, with aspirations to bridge the gap between traditional Islamic and modern, Western education and to bring to people "a [human] nature- and Sufi-based approach to individual reform."[162] This is an educational movement led by a university-educated Sufi of Barelawi leanings, Muhammad Tahir al-Qadiri, whom we will meet again in chapter 6. Since the mid-1990s, a movement called al-Huda ("Guidance"), has also organized highly structured study groups focused on the Qur'an for middle- and upper-middle-class urban women. Founded by Farhat Hashmi, who has a PhD in Islamic studies from the University of Glasgow and was once associated with the Jama`at-i Islami, al-Huda study groups have sought to cultivate a pious personhood among college- and university-educated women in light of Qur'anic teachings. Though it is very conservative social norms that are inculcated among them in the process, Islam is presented as a "rational" religion well suited to the lives of well-educated, often English-speaking people.[163] This Islam is also billed as resolutely nonsectarian.[164]

It is not lost on the traditionalist `ulama that the likes of Farhat Hashmi are a challenge to their authority.[165] Yet, insomuch as they can be characterized as representing an "innovative traditionalism,"[166] movements such as hers serve paradoxically to also foster a kind of religiosity that other traditionalists can build on—once, that is, they have made some necessary adjustments in how to package their own wares. Openness to modern forms of education is a crucial part of that adjustment. That, however, is not the only or even perhaps the most important reason why madrasas have continued to grow in Pakistan.

The Madrasa: Growing Numbers

Although the bureaucrats leading madrasa reform in the early 1960s had envisioned new generations of imams with whom "true religious values would flourish" in the country,[167] they would have been hard pressed to see why the institutions producing such people would need to multiply. After all, any unregulated, parasitical growth could not but add to a poor nation's burdens. An exasperated General Pervez Musharraf put it this way almost a half century later: "I ask these seminaries how many mosques ... there [are] in the country to accommodate all these 1 million students as imams."[168] Unforeseen or not, madrasas have in fact steadily grown in number throughout much of the history of Pakistan, at times at an extraordinary pace. In this final section of this chapter, I propose to briefly examine this development and the conditions in which it has taken place.

A significant part of the context in which madrasas have continued to exist and to grow has to do with their ability to meet needs that the Pakistani state often does not. The state's promise to provide education to all its citizens has remained unrealized. In 2013–14, nearly 29 percent of primary-school-age children were receiving no schooling.[169] Of those who did, about 10 percent, or around 1.8 million, studied in madrasas (which here includes institutions of primary education as well).[170] The actual figures may be higher because many madrasas remain unregistered and many others uncounted. In contrast with madrasas, the growth of public schools has often remained stagnant. For instance, the student population in public primary schools hardly grew between 2011–12 and 2013–14 and that in high schools declined during those years.[171] Aggravating matters further in recent years, the Pakistani Taliban and allied insurgents have targeted public schools—a key symbol of government authority—in the tribal areas of the Khyber Pakhtunkhwa province, while madrasas have continued to stand and to grow. According to a 2014 report, in one such tribal area, the Khyber Agency, "where militants have destroyed 85 schools since 2005, disrupting the education of 50,000 children, over 56 percent of six- to sixteen-year-olds attended private schools or madrasas in 2013."[172] It is also worth noting that, unlike many other schools, a madrasa typically provides an education that is free of charge and students receive free food and lodging. Ironically, by equipping their students with the knowledge that allows them to act as prayer leaders and preachers, to officiate over a variety of other religious functions, and in many cases to establish their own mosques and madrasas, these institutions might offer more secure prospects of a job to their graduates than do many public schools and colleges to their students. Some of the larger madrasas have come to impart new skills to their students. The national organization coordinating the madrasa boards claimed in 2009 that "dozens of seminaries registered with its five boards are offering courses on banking, journalism, computer science and other modern subjects which appeal greatly to students."[173]

The failure of successive governments to provide basic amenities to the citizens of the state is not the whole context, of course, in which the growth of madrasas is to be understood. Directly or indirectly, government policies have sometimes also paved the ground for their growth in other ways. The most notable instances of this belong to the Zia al-Haqq era. As part of its Islamization campaign, the government had begun in 1980 to collect the religiously mandated zakat tax from the people, and a portion of these funds was made available to the `ulama. This was important financial inducement to support

the military regime. It would have helped relieve some of the financial burdens on existing madrasas, but it also provided an incentive to establish new
madrasas to *receive* the promised funds.[174] The Soviet occupation of Afghanistan and the resulting influx of Afghan refugees into Pakistan also contributed to the growth of madrasas during those years. Many madrasas in the
North-West Frontier and in Baluchistan were established, and others grew
in size, specifically to cater to the Afghan refugees. Some became part of
the war effort, with students regularly participating in the Afghan jihad, madrasas adjusting their calendar to accommodate them, and the government
and the military helping, presumably, with both finances and logistics.[175] It
was from madrasas in Pakistan that the Taliban, too, would emerge, with one
of the largest of the Frontier madrasas—the aforementioned Dar al-ʿUlum
Haqqaniyya—providing several of those who came to comprise the movement's leadership.[176] Decades earlier, too, and for all their suspicion of the
ʿulama, government officials had seen traditionalist religious institutions as
a potential barrier against regional separatism and leftist subversion. Already
in December 1947, just months after the establishment of Pakistan, the finance minister had submitted a memorandum to the prime minister on the
"Bengali–Non-Bengali Question in East Bengal." "Rural areas of East Bengal
are saturated," the memorandum had stated, "with Ulemas, Madrasah educated people who look up to Deoband, Saharanpur, Jaunpur, Rampur as their
spiritual home. But the contagion has undoubtedly spread among a considerable section of the English educated intelligentsia who thinks that morsel [*sic*]
is being taken out of their mouth by outsiders. Politicians, Muslim communists, fifth columnists are all exploiting the situation for their own purpose.
There is potential danger of disruption of the solidarity of Pakistan State."[177]
Among possible remedies, the memorandum had suggested that "Ulemas,
public men and propagandists should be mobilized to propagate the message
of Muslim solidarity throughout the urban and rural areas of East Bengal."[178]
In 1949, the interior minister thought likewise that the ʿulama could be help-
ful against Communism, "the most serious threat to the peace and internal
security of Pakistan."[179] Although specific evidence is usually lacking, it seems
reasonable to assume that the government saw the establishment of madrasas and related institutions not merely as an acceptable price to pay for the
support of the religious conservatives but also as a bulwark against the leftist
intelligentsia. A religious menace tended, moreover, to be seen, and not just
in Pakistan, as more amenable to eventual control than one represented by
secular activists. In the Egypt of the 1970s, for instance, the government of
President Anwar Sadat had not merely tolerated but actively cultivated Islamist groups as a way of taking on the leftists.[180] In the 1980s, a similar logic
would help underwrite the alliance between the Afghan mujahidin, the Pakistani military, and the CIA.

Socioeconomic change in Pakistan has also contributed to the growth of madrasas over the decades. Though poverty is frequently seen today, even by the madrasa leadership, as fueling this growth,[181] it is arguably a relative *affluence* in society that had helped increase their numbers during the 1970s and the 1980s.

Pakistani labor had unprecedented opportunities to work in the Gulf states of the Arab Middle East between the mid-1970s and the mid-1980s. The revenues of the petroleum-producing Arab states had skyrocketed in the wake of the Arab oil embargo and so did their development projects in subsequent years: Saudi Arabia's petroleum revenues rose from $4.3 billion in 1973 to $22.6 billion a year later and to $102.2 billion in 1980; those of Kuwait from $1.7 billion in 1973 to $6.5 billion in 1974 to $17.9 billion in 1980; and those of the United Arab Emirates from $0.9 billion in 1973 to $5.5 billion in 1974 to $19.5 billion in 1980.[182] As seen in the previous chapter, Bhutto was keen to cultivate ties with the Arab and Islamic world and, indeed, to position Pakistan as an intermediary between the West and the Arab states.[183] Pakistan was a beneficiary of the effort by Saudi and other oil-rich Arab states to extend their influence in the Muslim world, and calculations about Saudi patronage could not but be a factor in moving Bhutto away from some of his party's hardline socialist ideologues. This was small price to pay for what the economic possibilities in the Gulf region could mean for Pakistan. According to political economist Omar Noman, "[a]pproximately 10 million people or 11 percent of the total population (a figure that includes dependents) ... benefited directly from the exodus to the Middle East. The vast majority of the beneficiaries came from low-income households. On average, their salaries increased between 600 and 800 percent."[184] Unsurprisingly, this dramatic upward mobility brought about a significant growth in the ranks of the lower middle and middle classes in urban Pakistan, especially in the Punjab, which had contributed nearly 70 percent of the expatriate labor.[185] Already in 1953, a good deal of the support for the anti-Ahmadi agitation had come from the petit bourgeois.[186] By the 1980s, thanks to the labor influx, there was a new depth and breadth in their ranks. As many returning migrants and their families moved from ancestral villages to small towns and cities, they often sought new, more self-conscious and heightened expressions of religious identity, a sharper sense of what separated their putatively universalistic Islam from what would now have looked like the muddled beliefs and practices of village life. Support for up and coming mosques and madrasas, and for sectarian organizations ready at hand to teach them what their piety must consist in if it was to be credible, were important markers not just of religious but also of socioeconomic change in the 1980s and beyond.[187] Though these militant organizations began to emerge in the mid-1980s, the madrasas had already begun to grow at a dramatic pace in the Bhutto years. Table 1 makes this clear.

Table 1. Madrasas in Pakistan, 1960–79

Orientation	Madrasas in 1960	Madrasas in 1971	Madrasas in 1979
Deobandi	233	291	354
Barelawi	98	124	267
Ahl-i Hadith	55	47	126
Shi`a	18	15	41
Other/unaffiliated/ affiliation unknown	68	86	957
Total	472	563	1,745

Sources: Nazr Ahmad, *Ja'iza-i madaris-i `arabiyya-i Maghribi Pakistan* (Lyallpur: Jami`a Chishtiyya Trust, 1960), 797–811; Nazr Ahmad, *Ja'iza-i madaris-i `arabiyya-i Maghribi Pakistan* (Lahore: Muslim Academy, 1972), 688; *Report qawmi committee bara'i dini madaris-i Pakistan* (Islamabad: Ministry of Religious Affairs, 1979), 210–13.

Note: The figures for the years prior to 1971 refer to West Pakistan only. For the madrasa figures, also see Jamal Malik, *Colonialization of Islam: Dissolution of Traditional Institutions in Pakistan* (Delhi: Manohar, 1996), 198.

As table 1 suggests, while they had increased 19 percent (from 472 to 563) between 1960 and 1971, madrasas had grown about 210 percent over the course of the 1970s (from 563 in 1971 to 1,745 in 1979). Much of this growth had clearly preceded the advent of Zia al-Haqq's martial law regime and its Islamization campaign.[188] It is unlikely that the Bhutto government was actively encouraging the establishment of madrasas. Rather, some of the aforementioned socioeconomic processes were presumably at work in paving the way toward their growth during those years. The anti-Ahmadi agitation of 1974 had also mobilized conservative religious sentiment across the country, and that, too, is likely to have had some effect on the growth of the `ulama's influence and of their institutions. Despite the government's efforts to highlight its religious commitments, the religio-political parties tended to be highly suspicious of it, which probably also impelled them both to resist perceived government encroachments on their turf and to pursue their activities more aggressively. An example is worth noting here. Denials by the Bhutto regime notwithstanding, many `ulama feared that the government intended to take over their madrasas. It did attempt to do so in some instances—notably, in case of the Deobandi Nusrat al-`Ulum madrasa in Gujranwala in 1976, though that had to do not with a broader policy regarding madrasas but rather with the local administration's wish to punish political opponents associated with the institution in question. The manner in which the latter resisted this move is instructive in showing something of the relationship between political opposition and religious action. Realizing that leaving the madrasa vacant during the summer holidays in the Islamic months of Sha`ban and Ramadan would allow the local administration to occupy it for good, the madrasa's president, Mawlana Sarfaraz Khan Safdar (d. 2009), began a series of lectures on the Qur'an during those months. These would continue for the next *twenty-five* years.[189] An opportunity soon arose for such localized acts of resistance against the government to become part of a country-wide agitation. The religious and center-right parties had formed an electoral alliance in 1977, and they subsequently launched a massive movement to protest what were widely seen as rigged elections. The movement, which eventuated in the martial law of General Zia al-Haqq, was launched in the name of establishing "the Prophet's system" (*nizam-i Mustafa*) in the country, to replace corrupt, godless regimes like Bhutto's. Such powerful shows of force in the name of Islam, the patronage the new military regime was all too keen to offer, and the effects of the Afghan war could only facilitate the growth in subsequent years of institutions the ʿulama viewed as bastions of a beleaguered Islam. Table 2 provides some indication of the growth of madrasas in Pakistan's most populous province.

The available figures on the growth of madrasas also shed some light on a related question, viz, how the various doctrinal orientations have fared in relation to one another. The data in tables 3 and 4 are again limited only to the Punjab, and the figures reported by different sources often show considerable and often hard to reconcile divergence among them. Despite these caveats, the data are suggestive of some broad trends.

Table 1 suggests that the Deobandis have come to dominate the religious landscape in Pakistan. However, as it also shows, Barelawi madrasas grew at a considerably faster rate in the 1960s and the 1970s than did those of the Deobandis. The latter grew 24.89 percent from 1960 to 1971 and 21.64 percent from 1971 to 1979. Over the entire period, 1960–79, they grew nearly 52 percent. By contrast, Barelawi madrasas grew by 26.5 percent from 1960 to 1971 but an extraordinary 115.3 percent from 1971 to 1979; over the entire time

Table 2. Growth of Madrasas in the Punjab, 1975–2001

Administrative division	1975	1980	1985	1990	1994	2001
Bahawalpur	278	417	598	795	883	971
Dera Ghazi Khan	153	217	297	363	411	397
Multan	45	102	179	212	325	363
Lahore	75	120	170	219	323	356
Rawalpindi	58	85	119	157	169	186
Sargodha	75	98	130	148	149	164
Gujranwala	52	66	96	131	140	154
Faisalabad	?	?	?	?	112	124
Total					2,512	2,715

Sources: Zindagi, February 17, 1995; *News*, March 7, 1995; *News*, May 26, 1997; *Dawn*, January 22, 2002.

Note: Figures for the Faisalabad division were not available prior to 1994.

Table 3. Madrasas in the Punjab, 1994 (Estimated Number of Students in Parentheses)

Administrative division	Madrasas	Deobandi	Barelawi	Ahl-i Hadith	Shi`a
Lahore	328	143 (17,892)	136 (18,336)	? (5,524)	4 (373)
Rawalpindi	164	83 (8,367)	64 (8,307)	6 (417)	16 (442)
Gujranwala	140	36 (3,632)	87 (4,700)	13 (1,712)	4 (373)
Faisalabad	112	47 (11,631)	39 (5,027)	18 (3,141)	8 (70)
Sargodha	149	68 (6,158)	64 (6,427)	9 (1,318)	8 (341)
Multan	325	127 (11,888)	159 (10,798)	27 (2,620)	12 (660)
Dera Ghazi Khan	411	133 (8,816)	174 (9,593)	24 (1,829)	30 (669)
Bahawalpur	883	335 (32,204)	493 (29,308)	36 (2,319)	19 (746)
Total	2,512	972 (100,588)	1,216 (92,496)	(18,880)	101 (3,674)

Source: Zindagi, February 17–23, 1995.

Table 4. Madrasas in the Punjab, 2001 (Estimated Number of Students in Parentheses)

Division	Madrasas	Deobandi	Barelawi	Ahl-i Hadith	Shi`a
Lahore	356	157 (19,781)	149 (20,169)	45 (7,074)	5 (610)
Rawalpindi	186	91 (9,203)	70 (9,137)	7 (459)	18 (559)
Gujranwala	154	40 (3,995)	95 (10,140)	14 (2,883)	5 (419)
Faisalabad	124	52 (3,578)	43 (7,527)	20 (3,445)	9 (770)
Sargodha	164	75 (6,973)	70 (9,277)	10 (2,548)	9 (475)
Multan	363	140 (6,076)	175 (12,878)	30 (3,880)	13 (726)
Dera Ghazi Khan	397	146 (10,897)	191 (13,565)	27 (4,109)	33 (940)
Bahawalpur	971	368 (38,404)	540 (35,238)	39 (5,549)	21 (841)
Total	2,715 (252,125)	1,069 (98,907)	1,333 (117,931)	192 (29,947)	113 (5,340)

Source: Asif Shahzad, "Over 250,000 Students in Punjab Seminaries," *Dawn*, January 22, 2002.
Note: These figures, which do not always add up, are based on police reports.

span covered by table 1, they grew about 172 percent. The Ahl-i Hadith madrasas grew 168 percent between 1971 and 1979 and 129 percent over the entire time period shown in table 1. Shi`i madrasas, for their part, grew 173 percent from 1971 to 1979 and nearly 128 percent over the entire period. This means obviously that *all* madrasas benefited from the socioeconomic processes outlined earlier. The Ahl-i Hadith madrasas may have benefited also from being able to garner a larger proportion of international Salafi patronage—emanating primarily from Saudi Arabia—though that often came to the Deobandis as well. What table 1 suggests about the growth of the Shi`i madrasas is especially impressive because it precedes the impact of the Iranian revolution of 1979. As will be observed in chapter 5, the revolution galvanized the Pakistani Shi`a and contributed to the rise of sectarian militancy in the country. Yet,

Table 5. Madrasa Students in the Punjab, 2005

Deobandi	Barelawi	Ahl-i Hadith	Shi`a	Total
200,246	199,733	34,253	7,333	441,565

Source: Sajjad Shafiq Butt, "441,565 Students Are Enrolled in Punjab Madaris," *News*, January 2, 2006.

Note: These figures are based on a report by the Punjab Police.

that sectarian radicalism may itself have been fueled by the growing numbers of madrasas during the 1970s.

So far as the Barelawi madrasas are concerned, two additional factors may account for their growth. First, most of the labor migrants to the Middle East in the mid-1970s had a rural background,[190] where Sufi-inflected beliefs and devotional practices broadly identifiable as Barelawi have long been at their strongest. This means that the mosques and madrasas such migrants would have supported were more likely to be those of a Barelawi than of a Deobandi orientation. Second, the growth in question may well be the effect of how particular madrasas were reporting their affiliations. Of all the doctrinal orientations not just in Pakistan but in South Asia more broadly, the Barelawis have tended to be the most loosely organized. They had formed their madrasa board in 1960, but it had remained largely inactive until revived in January 1974.[191] The increase in Barelawi madrasas that table 1 shows between 1971 and 1979 may well reflect not only a growth in absolute numbers but also the listing of previously unaffiliated, even undocumented, madrasas on the Barelawi roster. The fact remains, in any case, that the Barelawis and the Deobandis have had the lion's share of madrasas and of their students in the Punjab, as tables 3, 4, and 5 indicate. And according to some estimates, the Barelawis had maintained an edge until recently. In the country as a whole, however, Deobandi madrasas outstrip Barelawi ones, and probably do so now by wide margins. The Deobandi madrasa board claimed in 2016 to have approximately 18,600 affiliate madrasas, with a student body of over 2,000,000. By contrast, the Barelawi board put the number of affiliate madrasas at about 9,000, with around 1,300,000 students.[192] While allowing for the possibility of inflated numbers, the difference between the two estimates is nonetheless worth noting. In more general terms, too, that is, apart from the sheer number of madrasas, the Deobandis have cast a much larger shadow over religious and political life in Pakistan than have any of their doctrinal rivals.

In some measure, the prominence of the Deobandis vis-à-vis others continues a trend already in evidence in late colonial India. Pakistani governments have contributed in turn to a further consolidation of that trend. Given the crucial support Shabbir Ahmad `Usmani had given toward bolstering the Muslim League's Islamic credentials in the run-up to the partition of India, it is not surprising that he became the most influential of the `ulama after the state's inception. His associates had even wanted him buried next to Jinnah, though that request was denied by the government.[193] Significantly, many of the other `ulama who played an influential role in Pakistani politics and society in subsequent decades were also Deobandi. These include Mufti Muhammad Shafi` as well as Ihtisham al-Haqq Thanawi and Taqi `Usmani. Sayyid Sulayman Nadwi, the head of the Ta`limat-i Islamia board, though not a Deobandi by training, had become a disciple of Ashraf `Ali Thanawi by the end of the latter's life. Mawdudi was closer in doctrinal orientation to the Deobandis than he was to any of their rivals. Even the modernist Fazlur Rahman was the son of a Deobandi `alim.

Deobandi influence in Pakistan cannot be reduced, however, to government patronage and there is more to it than even the fact that its textualism— blending scripturalism and the legal tradition as it does—appeals to people drawn to the idea of an authentic Islam cleansed of its accretions. The Deobandi orientation is also buttressed by the Tablighi Jama`at, a proselytizing movement that had originated in colonial India and has come to have a global presence. Though people associated with this movement are not known for their intellectual pursuits, being focused instead on inculcating pious living at the grassroots, the upper echelons of the Deobandi `ulama do remain notable for their often vibrant intellectual concerns. Indeed, this is much more the case with the Deobandis than it is with the contemporary Barelawis, and the intellectual output of prominent Deobandis has inevitably helped further their influence, in Pakistan and abroad. Even a casual visit to the Urdu Bazar of Lahore, which houses many publishers and sellers of books on Islamic topics, should suffice to show the Deobandi dominance in this area. The works of Ashraf `Ali Thanawi have continued to be reprinted in Pakistan. Mahmud Hasan's translation of the Qur'an has remained influential in South Asia since its publication in 1925. Significantly, it was this rather than some other competing translation that the Saudis chose to publish in a new edition in 1993 as part of their program to disseminate the Qur'an in reliable local translations throughout the world.[194] Mahmud Hasan's translation comes with a brief commentary by Shabbir Ahmad `Usmani, whose separate commentary on the Qur'an has also been published.[195] Mufti Muhammad Shafi`'s exegetical work has already been discussed earlier. And Taqi `Usmani is among the most prolific of `ulama anywhere in the Muslim world today.

Although Islam in postindependence India falls outside the purview of this book, Taqi `Usmani's account of a visit to India in 2010 sheds useful light on some of the things touched upon in this chapter, and it is with that account that I conclude. Taqi `Usmani was invited for a lecture tour by a Muslim businessman from Chennai and he addressed people in that city, in Bangalore, Deoband, and elsewhere.[196] He notes with satisfaction that "the economic conditions of Muslims are much better than before,"[197] an assessment that may reflect the privileged company he kept on this visit more than the actual state of the Indian Muslim community at large. Foremost among his audience were Muslim businessmen and members of the intelligentsia, after all, who wanted their questions about banking and other economic matters answered in relation to Islam.[198] Yet, he also drew large crowds in Deoband, the bookish but economically depressed town that houses the original Dar al-'Ulum after which Taqi 'Usmani's own madrasa in Karachi is named.[199] In this town, in particular, but also at the other madrasas he visited, he was seen as someone who had brought distinction to the Deobandis by his religious learning and his many books but also by his ability to bridge traditional and modern learning, his recognition in both the Arab world *and* in the West.[200] Far from conjuring up stereotypes of mullas at a loss in their changing environs, he represented the forward-looking yet authentic face of contemporary Islam. As someone introducing him on one occasion had put it, he was "the interpreter of the Dar al-'Ulum of Deoband throughout the world."[201] The fact that he is the son of Mufti Muhammad Shafi', the original Deoband madrasa's leading jurisconsult prior to the partition of India, and that he was born in the town of Deoband itself, had made for an even stronger basis on which to claim Taqi 'Uthmani's distinction as Deoband's own.

What this account allows us to see is the continuing appeal of the 'ulama's traditionalism in the contemporary world, including among circles of Western-educated and upwardly mobile people. The latter, too, are part of the support base, in Pakistan, India, and in the South Asian diaspora, that has helped sustain madrasas. Taqi 'Usmani has been able to address their questions with considerable skill; and it was to cater to similar kinds of people in Western societies that several financial institutions had wanted him to serve on their corporate boards.[202] But traditionalism—in this case, a demonstrated mastery of Islamic law and a facility with age-old juridical and exegetical approaches to seemingly arcane texts—needs to be translated into a language that an audience lacking those assets could readily understand. Taqi 'Usmani is skilled in that language, too. The dividends of the 'ulama's accommodation to modern forms of knowledge are in full evidence in his case. This accommodation is nonetheless very much in the service of a traditionalist understanding: his Islam is closer to that of his father Mufti Muhammad Shafi', whom he invoked at every conceivable opportunity during this Indian tour,[203] than it is to the modernist 'ulama's—the likes of Hanif Nadwi and Ja'far Phulwarwi. This arguably is precisely what gives it a sense of authenticity among many Muslims of a modern upbringing.

Traditionalism is also a matter, of course, of being able to show that one's understanding of Islam is not merely one's own, that revered figures from the recent and remote past have held similar views.[204] During his visit to India, he took time to argue against those who claim that "the Book of God is enough for us. We need nothing [or no one] else. We will study the Book ourselves, understand it on our own, and follow the path that this study and understanding point to us."[205] Such views are as characteristic of the modernists as they are of the Islamists. To Taqi `Usmani, though, they betray "a lack of understanding of the Qur'an. In its very first chapter, al-Fatiha, God has clearly stated that the straight path is not the one that you will arrive at through your intellectual effort and your reading of the Qur'an. Rather, the 'straight path' is that which has been adopted by those whom God has blessed."[206] Drawing ideas straight from the Book of God has an appeal, however, that is not easily countered. The Islamists have been masterful at it, but others are not immune to it either.

CHAPTER FOUR

Islamism and the Sovereignty of God

THOUGH WE WILL OFTEN SEE the ʿulama and the Islamists sharing many goals, rhetorical motifs, and practices when it comes to undermining the modernists as well as in other respects, the Islamists need to be viewed in their own right, too. The present chapter is an effort in that direction. I take a somewhat unusual approach in this instance, however. Rather than providing a broad overview of some major trends in relation to a particular facet of Islam, as in much of this book, my focus here is on one very particular idea— the sovereignty of God. More, perhaps, than most other ideas, the assertion that sovereignty belongs exclusively to God has come to be associated with Islamism everywhere, in South Asia and the wider Muslim world. Yet, this idea has had a purchase well beyond Islamist circles, and it is not among the Islamists that its origins lie. An exploration of this idea, of its ramifications, and of the contestations over it allow us a unique vantage from which to observe Islamist thought and practice in colonial India and in Pakistan, their relationship with the medieval tradition, with Islamist trends in the wider world, and, not least, with representatives of other facets of Islam.

The Qur'an speaks repeatedly of the power, the authority, and the majesty of God. As the Qur'anic Joseph reminds his fellow inmates, "Authority (*al-hukm*) belongs to God alone" (Q 12.40), and we are told elsewhere that it is God's prerogative to give authority (*al-mulk*) to whom He will and to take it away at His pleasure (cf. Q 3.26).[1] From passages to this effect, it is not a big leap to the idea of the sovereignty of God. Some translators have, indeed, rendered the Qur'anic mulk as sovereignty. A notable example of this is Marmaduke Pickthall (d. 1936), the English convert to Islam who published his translation of the Qur'an while in the service of the Nizam of Hyderabad, one of the many Indian princes recognized as quasi-independent by the British colonial regime.[2] Yet, it is no mere quibbling to observe that the idea of sovereignty has a very particular history in European political thought and that it emerged in tandem with the rise of the modern state. Whatever terms like al-hukm and al-mulk had meant to medieval commentators of the Qur'an, they could not have meant what "sovereignty" meant to, say, Jean Bodin (d. 1596) or Thomas Hobbes (d. 1679).[3] To many Muslims of the twentieth century, writing under the threat or the promise of the modern state, the idea of sovereignty does, however, evoke precisely the sort of things that a Bodin or a Hobbes had theorized about, and the question for them has often been whether such sovereignty can belong to a mere human being, a collectivity of people, the "artificial person" of the state, or whether it properly belongs only to God.[4] In influential formulations, twentieth-century Islamist ideologues like Mawdudi and Sayyid Qutb (d. 1966) of Egypt have argued that anything less than exclusive submission to God's law and all that it entails in religious and political terms is idolatry—the most heinous of sins in a monotheist's universe. Before examining how this idea became such a crucial part of Islamist discourses, we need to take a quick measure of the sort of things premodern commentators discussed when they explained passages that Islamist ideologues take as central to the idea of the sovereignty of God.[5]

The Medieval Tradition

As might be expected, medieval exegetes understood the mulk of Q 3.26 and other such passages in a variety of ways. It refers, according to some, to God's response to the Prophet Muhammad's prayer that dominion over Persia and Byzantium be given to his people.[6] Others glossed it as the faith and the ability to submit to God (al-islam) that He grants to whom He wills, or as prophetical authority,[7] whereby God honors those who follow the prophet and debases those who do not.[8] Some commentators reported, in discussing Q 3.26, that the `Abbasid caliph Ma'mun (r. 813–33) had seen an inscription in a Byzantine palace which read, in Arabic translation: "In the name of God: With the alternation of the day and night and the rotation of the celestial bodies in the heavenly sphere, felicity (al-na`im) passes from a king whose rule has ended to another king. But the king possessing the [real] throne is everlasting; He does not die and has no partner."[9] As the hadith scholar and Qur'an commentator Baghawi (d. 1122) noted in explicating Q 3.26: "God has said in one of His books: 'I am God, the king of kings and the master of kings. The hearts of kings and their forelocks are in my hand. If my servants obey me, I make the kings a mercy for them; and if they disobey me, I make the kings a punishment for them. So do not concern yourself with reviling the kings but turn instead towards me and I will dispose them favorably towards you.'"[10] Though God's granting of political authority might be foregrounded, as it was in these instances, al-mulk, at its broadest, could be construed to mean possession and control of all kinds of desirable things that God bestows upon select people: "the endowment of prophethood, the possession of knowledge, intellect, health and praiseworthy dispositions, power and the ability to implement [things], the power of love, and the possession of wealth."[11] Yet other things could be and were often added to this already expansive list, for instance, the mystical powers that God grants to His saintly "friends."[12]

As will be seen, the Qur'an's affirmation that "authority (al-hukm) belongs to God alone" (Q 12.40) receives keen attention from modern Islamists, but the medieval exegetes are not equally excited by the idea. The influential tenth-century historian and Qur'an commentator Tabari (d. 923) interpreted it to mean simply that God alone is to be worshipped;[13] and the noted Andalusian exegete Qurtubi (d. 1273) offered a gloss—God "is the creator of everything"—and quickly moved on.[14] The phrase reappears in the same chapter (Q 12.67), and this time Tabari glossed al-hukm as "judgment" and Qurtubi likewise explained it as "command and judgment" (al-amr wal-qada) but neither took more interest in it than he did earlier.[15] The historian and Qur'an commentator Ibn Kathir (d. 1373), for his part, explained al-hukm as "the power of disposal, will, and authority (al-tasarruf wal-mashi'a wal-mulk), all of which belongs to God."[16]

For some exegetes, Qur'anic passages such as the foregoing also raised important theological questions. The aforementioned Baghawi has already shown us a glimpse of this. The theologian Fakhr al-din al-Razi (d. 1210) understood the Qur'an's affirmation that "authority belongs to God alone" to argue against the idea of free will and to affirm that all possibilities are determined exclusively by God rather than by human agency.[17] He held likewise that it was not because of a person's merit that God granted him royal authority but rather that all authority came from God, irrespective of the virtue of the one holding it.[18]

Theological issues are also foregrounded in medieval juridical discussions of the idea that "there is no authority (al-hakim) other than God, the exalted, and that there is no command other than what God has commanded." To the jurist Amidi (d. 1232), this entails that "the intellect cannot characterize anything as good or bad nor does [the intellect suffice to] demonstrate the necessity of showing gratitude towards a benefactor. There is no command prior to the advent of the divine law."[19] The eighteenth-century Indian scholar Muhibb Allah Bihari (d. 1708) brought out more clearly the theological stakes of the idea that "there is no command (al-hukm) except from God." He wrote:

> There is no disagreement on whether an act is rationally good or bad in the sense of its having perfection or deficiency or of its being suited or unsuited to a worldly matter. The disagreement is only on whether [the intellect itself can tell us if] the act deserves God's praise and reward or, conversely, His condemnation and punishment. According to the Ash'aris, it is only through the divine law ... [that one knows

this]. What God commands is good, what He forbids is bad. If the situation were reversed, so would the values in question. To us [Maturidis] and to the Mu`tazila, this can be known through the intellect, that is, it does not depend on the divine law. However [in contrast with the Mu`tazila and some others], we do not believe that God must command the humans in accordance with what the intellect suggests; rather we believe that what the intellect prefers is what deserves to be commanded by the wise God, for He does not prefer the less desirable. Yet there is no command unless God commands it.[20]

In short, God's authority and power, as the medieval and early modern exegetes, jurists, and theologians understood them, could mean a whole range of things. As should be clear from the foregoing illustrations, the point is not that kings and rulers were outside the purview of this authority, but rather that God was seen to be the source of everything and, by that token, of political power as well. This range continues to be well-represented in the work of many traditionally educated scholars of modern times. For instance, the early twentieth-century Urdu commentary of the Indian scholar Amir `Ali Malihabadi (d. 1919) gave pride of place to Sufi understandings of Q 3.26 without, however, neglecting varied other ways of understanding this passage, including God's statement "in one of His books" that he is "the king of kings and the master of kings."[21]

Yet, there were signs of change, too, and this was illustrated by the aforementioned Rashid Rida in his unfinished but influential commentary on the Qur'an. Rida interpreted Q 3.26 in a manner that foregrounded the political in speaking of God, "the wielder of supreme and unrestricted power" (*sahib al-sultan al-a`la wal-tasarruf al-mutlaq*).[22] God gives power to people as He wishes—by way of descent from a prophetical lineage, as in case of the descendants of Abraham, or, Rida said in evoking Ibn Khaldun, through the working of sociological laws. And God takes it away from people when they begin to violate the principles of good rulership.[23] Like many of his predecessors, Rida noted that al-mulk could also refer to prophetical authority, and he added that, when it did, the authority in question was superior to others since it involved power not merely over bodies but also over souls.[24] In a biting swipe at the many Muslim rulers propped up in his time by their colonial masters, Rida noted furthermore that there was no necessary correlation between authority and glory (*al-`izz*), for it was possible for one to pretend to be a king while being at the mercy of others—rather like those assuming such roles in a theatrical performance.[25] All this could be rephrased to say that real sovereignty and mere pretensions to power were very different things and that true sovereignty belonged only to God. Rida did not, however, use that language, which indeed is "completely absent in [his] *Tafsir al-Manar*."[26] But it was not long before the Islamists began to use it, and to spell out the implications of God's authority and what was entailed by the imperative to submit to it.[27]

Islamist Discourses

With Sayyid Qutb, it is indeed possible to speak of God's power and authority in terms of sovereignty, and Qutb did so with great rhetorical effect. Commenting on Q 12.40, which he took to be of key significance in elucidating the Qur'anic conception of God, Qutb wrote:

> Authority belongs to the exalted God exclusively by virtue of His divinity. For sovereignty (*al-hakimiyya*) is among the characteristic features of divinity. Whoever lays a claim to sovereignty—whether it is an individual, a class, a party, an institution, a community or humanity at large in the form of an international organization—disputes the primary characteristic of His divinity. And whoever does so is guilty of unbelief in the most blatant manner.... Laying claim to this right [to sovereignty] does not necessarily take a particular form, which alone might be deemed to remove the claimant from the fold of 'the true faith' (*al-din al-qayyim* [Q 12.40])…. Rather, one lays claim to it … simply by … deriving laws from a source other than [God].... In the Islamic system, it is the community that chooses the ruler, thereby giving it the legal right to exercise authority according to God's law. But [this community] is not the source of sovereignty which gives the law its legality. God alone is the source of sovereignty. Many people, including Muslim scholars, tend to confuse the exercise of power and the source of power. Even the aggregate of humanity does not have the right to sovereignty, which God alone possesses. People only [have the right to] implement what God has laid down with His authority. As for what He has not laid down, it has neither authority nor legality.[28]

This is a decidedly modern view of God's supreme power and authority. For one thing, the very term Qutb used for sovereignty—al-hakimiyya—is a neologism, though it is derived from the aforementioned Qur'anic term al-hukm, which is usually rendered as authority or judgment.[29] Second, as the passage just quoted makes clear, Qutb really did have sovereignty as a political concept in mind when he spoke of God as the exclusive locus and source of all power. This idea of the sovereignty of God lies at the heart of Islamist conceptions of the state, of the law, and of Islam itself. Thus an Islamic state is one that is based on a recognition of God's sovereignty; this recognition entails that no law other than God's is to have any claim on people, that any failure to submit to this conception of the sovereignty of God is unbelief. The

Qur'an does say that "those who do not judge according to what God has revealed are unbelievers" (Q 5.44), "wrongdoers" (Q 5.45) and "ungodly" (Q 5.47). But medieval scholars had been far from clear on precisely what it meant not to judge or rule according to God's law. And in the first years of the twentieth century, Rashid Rida had been of the view that it was legitimate for a Muslim judge to rule according to *British* colonial laws. In other words, even if Rida had some hazy notion of the sovereignty of God, he did not think that it entailed the illegitimacy of all "man-made laws." The query to which Rida was responding in this instance had come from India. In his answer, Rida had invoked the idea of the common good (maslaha) to argue that a Muslim judge could advance the interests of his coreligionists better by serving under the British than by refusing to do so, and that working in this capacity was not covered by the Qur'anic prohibition in the aforementioned verses.[30] Sayyid Qutb and other Islamists clearly had a very different view of the matter.[31]

It has often been observed that Qutb's ideas on the sovereignty of God are much indebted to those of Mawdudi.[32] Mawdudi had begun his career as a journalist and religious intellectual in colonial India, and he had started speaking of the sovereignty of God from the late 1930s. In a work on "the political concept of Islam" first published in 1939, Mawdudi adduced passages like Q 12.40 and Q 5.44 to argue that "sovereignty (*hakimiyyat*) rests only with God. God alone is the law-giver. No human being, not even a prophet, has the right to command and prohibit on his own."[33] To leave no doubt about exactly what he meant, but also perhaps to flaunt his familiarity with Western political thought, Mawdudi here gave the words "sovereignty" and "law-giver" in the original English. In a work published two years later, Mawdudi developed the idea of the sovereignty of God further. He argued that "power (*iqtidar*) is the true spirit of divinity,"[34] that this power is indivisible,[35] that its "indivisibility entails that all forms of sovereignty and rule (*hakimiyyat wa farmanrawa'i*) should be concentrated in one supreme being,"[36] and that no one can have any say in His "kingdom's organization" (*intizam-i sultanat*).[37] Mawdudi continued:

> If a person considers anyone's command to be binding without its carrying the support of God's command, then that person is guilty of associating partners with God in the very same manner as does someone who directs his prayers to other than God. If anyone claims in a political sense to be "the holder of all control" [(*malik al-mulk*) Q 3.26], the sovereign (*muqtadir-i a`la*) and the absolute ruler (*hakim `alal-itlaq*), then his is a claim to divinity in just the same manner as the claim of someone, in metaphysical terms, that he is that person's [ultimate] master, deity (*karsaz*), support, and protector.[38]

This was well before Qutb had begun speaking in this vein. How Mawdudi's ideas were transmitted to the Arab world is a point I will take up later.

First, however, it is worth examining how *Mawdudi* may have come upon this idea of the sovereignty of God. This is a question that seems not to have been asked either by scholars of Islamism or by those who have studied Mawdudi's thought. Most scholars have taken it for granted that the idea had originated with Mawdudi himself. In posing this question, my concern here is not with trying to determine who may have been the very first to begin speaking of the sovereignty of God in modern Islam. Rida, as has been seen, comes close to it. A case could also be made that the Young Ottoman `Ali Suavi (d. 1878), who had had a traditional Islamic education but also substantial exposure to Western ideas, was among the first to invoke this idea. In an article in the *Ulum Gazetesi* published in 1869, he had sought to refute the idea of the sovereignty of the people, a view popular with the Young Ottomans, and argued that God was the true sovereign.[39] Suavi was in exile in Paris at the time, and this short-lived journal was itself published from Paris. The traditional resources he had drawn upon in trying to refute his opponents had little to do with the sovereignty of either God or the people. Instead, the jurists and theologians he had fleetingly referred to spoke of God as the ruler, by which they meant that God was the source of the commands that human beings had to submit to.[40] Suavi's innovation, if that is what it was, consisted in placing this idea in a political context, to deny that human beings could be considered to possess sovereign power.

Leaving Suavi and Rida aside, my concern before proceeding further is to draw attention to some overlapping ways in which ideas related to the sovereignty of God had come to find expression in early twentieth-century India, at a time when Mawdudi (b. 1903) was coming of age. A new awareness that the Muslim population in India, despite its large size, was nonetheless an increasingly disadvantaged minority in relation to the Hindus, memories of centuries of Muslim rule, and deep anxieties about the future of Islam not just at home but in the world at large had combined to make colonial India a particularly fertile soil for reflections on the sovereignty of God.

The Indian Background

A key figure to articulate this idea in the early twentieth century was Abul-Kalam Azad, whom we met in chapter 1. A firebrand journalist before he gained national prominence as a politician, Azad was the editor of the Urdu weekly *al-Hilal*, which had begun publication from Calcutta in mid-1912. It brought him a wide readership, but its uncompromising hostility to colonial rule and its stridently pan-Islamic tone and content also spelled its end within less than three years. Those were years of great turmoil, and the Muslims of India, with help from the likes of Azad, were keenly attuned to events in the wider world. Indeed, Azad had taken it upon himself to not only report on the crises that faced Muslims everywhere but also to put them into a very particular interpretive framework. An article titled "Authority Belongs to God Alone," published in *al-Hilal* in July 1913, made the clearest case for the irreconcilable claims upon Muslims of British rule, on the one hand, and of "God's government," on the other. Azad wrote:

> Today, an intense war is taking place between the government of God (*khuda ki hukumat*) and human kingdoms (*insani padshahaten*). Satan's throne has been placed over the largest portion of the earth. The inheritance of Satan's household has been distributed among his worshippers and the army of the "great deceiver" (*dajjal*) has spread everywhere. These satanic kingdoms seek to utterly destroy God's government. On their right side is the bewitching paradise of worldly pleasure and honor, and on their left rages the clearly visible hell of hardship and corporeal punishment. These unbelieving and dark deceivers open the doors of their sorcerous paradise for any son of Adam who denies the kingdom of God (*khuda ki padshahat*) ... and they push anyone who affirms God's kingdom into the hell of their satanic torments and corporeal punishments.[41]

Azad's government or kingdom of God is not yet the sovereignty of God that we find in Mawdudi, though it is hardly a big leap from the one to the other. It is significant, too, that Azad naturalized the idea of God's government by reading it directly into the Qur'an. For instance, in the same article, he translated the Qur'an's reference to the Day of Judgment (Q 82.17–18) as "the day of God's kingdom" (*khuda ki padshahat*).[42]

Such renditions were not peculiar to him. For instance, Shah `Abd al-Qadir (d. 1813), a son of Shah Wali Allah and one of the first translators of the Qur'an into Urdu, had rendered the key portion of Q 12.40 to mean that "*hukumat* does not belong to anyone but God."[43] In the early years of the twentieth century, the ethicist Nazir Ahmad had likewise translated the passage in question as "*hukumat* belongs only to the one God."[44] Significantly, *hukumat*, the standard term for government in Urdu and commonly also in Persian, had been rendered, inter alia, as "sovereignty" in John Richardson's influential *Dictionary of Persian, Arabic and English*, which had been prepared for the benefit of overseas British officials and merchants of the late eighteenth and the early nineteenth centuries.[45] Readers of `Abd al-Qadir and later of Azad and Nazir Ahmad could have understood *hukumat* as authority or government, but they could also have begun to understand it as sovereignty in the modern sense of the term.[46] Unlike Azad, Nazir Ahmad was no rebel, however. He was an official in the colonial bureaucracy, had translated an English work on the law of evidence into Urdu, and, in 1902, was awarded an honorary DLitt by the University of Edinburgh, of which Sir William Muir was then the principal.[47]

One of the readers of Nazir Ahmad's translation of the Qur'an was Azad's contemporary and fellow journalist, Muhammad 'Ali (d. 1931), who would emerge as the single most prominent leader of the Indian Khilafat movement. Already during World War I, the government had seen him and his brother, Shaukat 'Ali, to be enough of a threat to limit their movements to a small town, Chhindwara, in the Central Provinces (now Madhya Pradesh). Unlike Azad, who had native fluency in Arabic (his mother was an Arab woman and he was born in Mecca) and had received a traditional religious education, neither Muhammad 'Ali nor Shaukat had had much exposure to Islamic learning, and it was during their confinement that they "discovered" the Qur'an. It was in the translation of Nazir Ahmad that they did so.[48]

As Muhammad 'Ali came to see it, "the main theme of the Qur'an and . . . of the sayings of the Prophet as perceived in authentic Traditions is the Kinghood of God and the Service of Man as His Agent and vicegerent."[49] He may have been aided in this understanding by some of the language used in an English translation of the Qur'an that had been published in 1917 and that Muhammad 'Ali had also been reading while in confinement. This was the work of his namesake Maulana Muhammad 'Ali (d. 1951), a Lahore-based scholar who was a prominent figure in the Ahmadi community. (Though both are often referred to as "Maulana" Muhammad 'Ali, I will use the honorific only for the Qur'an translator in order to distinguish him from the Khilafat leader.) As will be seen further in the next chapter, the Ahmadis came to be formally excluded from the fold of the Muslim community through an amendment to the Pakistani constitution in 1974. Attitudes toward the Ahmadis were not so stringent in the early decades of the twentieth century, however, especially in the case of the Lahore-based group, who viewed Mirza Ghulam Ahmad as a reformer rather than a prophet. The future leader of the Khilafat movement would not have had to make any apology for consulting Maulana Muhammad 'Ali's translation.

The Ahmadis have always been keen proselytes for Islam, and a good deal of that effort has long been aimed at Western societies. To this end, but also to refute Western Orientalist and missionary criticisms of Islam, Maulana Muhammad 'Ali had been especially attentive to explaining the Qur'an in light of Christian scriptures. For instance, he translated Q 3.26–27 as follows: "Say: O Allah, Owner of the Kingdom, Thou givest the kingdom to whom Thou pleasest, and takest away the kingdom from whom Thou pleasest. . . . Thou makest the night to pass into the day and Thou makest the day to pass into the night; and Thou bringest forth the living from the dead and Thou bringest forth the dead from the living." More illustrative for our purposes is the explanatory note he added to this passage. These verses, he wrote, "apparently refer to the fact that kingdom and honour shall be given now to another nation, whose night shall be made to pass into a day of triumph. . . . The Jews had already been warned by Jesus that 'the kingdom of God shall be taken from you, and given to a nation bringing forth the fruits thereof' (Matt. 21: 43). A living nation of Muslims was brought forth from among the dead Arabs, and the living nation of Israelites was represented now by a people who were spiritually dead."[50] Echoes of the New Testament are even more explicit in his rendering of Q 67, whose title, al-Mulk, he translated as "The Kingdom" and to whose first batch of verses he gave the subtitle "The Kingdom of God."[51]

By his own acknowledgment, the poetry of the modernist philosopher Muhammad Iqbal also exercised some influence on Muhammad `Ali during his confinement in Chhindwara.[52] He read two of Iqbal's long Persian poems, *The Secrets of the Self* (1915) and the *Mysteries of Selflessness* (1918) during this time and found Iqbal to be confirming what he, Muhammad Ali, had begun to discover about Islam: "it was a commonplace of Muslim religious literature that Islam meant submission to God's Will and that He was Supreme Ruler of the Universe, but this truth had been allowed by the theologians to sink into the insignificance of a truism, so that we all passed it by, thinking we were fully familiar with it, when in fact, we were entirely ignorant of its true valuation." Much to Muhammad Ali's satisfaction, Iqbal was once again making people aware of the implications of this truth.[53]

A more surprising influence on Muhammad Ali came from the English novelist H. G. Wells (d. 1946). He had met Wells some years before, and he read Wells's wartime novel, *Mr. Britling Sees It Through*, while in confinement. First published in 1916, this novel is an extended meditation on the senseless death and destruction that the war had brought to all sides. Mr. Britling lost a son to the war, but he was also pained by the death of a young German whom he and his family had come to know before the war and to whose father he addresses some of his reflections near the end of the book. The novel concludes with the discovery by Mr. Britling of the presence of God in and around himself, which helps him deal with his anguish even as it points toward the emergence of a "world republic":

> God was with him indeed, and he was with God. The King was coming to his own. Amidst the darkness and confusions, the nightmare cruelties and the hideous stupidities of the great war, God, the Captain of the World Republic, fought his way to empire.... "[God] is the only King.... And before the coming of the true King, the inevitable King, the King who is present whenever just men foregather, this bloodstained rubbish of the ancient world, these puny kings and tawdry emperors, these wily politicians and artful lawyers, these men who claim and grab and trick and compel, these war makers and oppressors, will presently shrivel and pass—like paper thrust into a flame."[54]

The God that Mr. Britling finds, and of whom Wells also spoke in some of his other writings, is very much a personal and immanent God rather than one who is absolute and "comprehensive."[55] Commenting on Wells's *God the Invisible King*, Muhammad `Ali observed later that "there is much in ... [it that one] would have to outgrow before he could become a Muslim." Yet, he felt that there was a basic affinity between what Wells was describing and what he, Muhammad `Ali, understood to be true Islam.[56]

Some of what Muhammad `Ali had imbibed during his confinement in Chhindwara, from the translations of the Qur'an available to him and from Wells, would find powerful articulation at his trial in the port city of Karachi. The `Ali brothers had been released from Chhindwara in June 1919, but they were arrested once again in September 1921 and charged this time with inciting Muslim soldiers against serving in the colonial military. Greece, supported by the British, was then at war with Turkey and, anticipating the possibility that Indian Muslim troops might be called upon to participate in the war, a fatwa had been issued that prohibited Muslims from fighting fellow believers. Muhammad `Ali and other Khilafat leaders had made their own statements to similar effect, and this is what had led to the new charges against them.[57] At the hearings in Karachi, first in the court of the city magistrate and then in that of the judicial commissioner of the province of Sindh, Muhammad `Ali expounded at great length on what he took to be the teachings of Islam that had required him to take the position he had.[58]

Much like Azad, Muhammad `Ali argued that the king's law and God's law were in manifest conflict. The colonial administration expected its Muslim soldiers to serve wherever they were needed, but Islam forbade them from fighting other Muslims. They could obey their worldly rulers, but only if such obedience did not conflict with obedience to God. As Muhammad `Ali, speaking in English, told the city magistrate, "Islam recognizes one sovereignty alone, the sovereignty of God, which is supreme and unconditional, indivisible and inalienable." He then proceeded to quote the famous passage, Q 12.40, in which Joseph tells his fellow inmates that "there is no Government but God's."[59] The English translation is presumably his own, though he drew on Nazir Ahmad's Urdu rendering ("*hukumat* belongs only to the one God").[60] Addressing the jury in the court of the judicial commissioner of Sindh, he also invoked *Mr. Britling* to make the point that one's "only allegiance—his only duty—is to God."[61]

In the aftermath of the Mutiny of 1857, Queen Victoria had proclaimed that her Indian subjects would enjoy complete freedom of religion. The British, Muhammad `Ali said, now had a choice to make. They could either allow Muslims to follow the dictates of their faith, which meant the refusal by Muslim soldiers to fight fellow Muslims, or they could admit that there was, in fact, no freedom of religion in India and, indeed, declare that people serving in the military should be ready to violate the most basic dictates of their faith.[62] The British could not have it both ways. He concluded, sounding very much like Mr. Britling: "You pray now 'Thy Kingdom come.' But gentlemen,

His Kingdom *has* come. God's Kingdom has come. God's Kingdom is here even today. It is not the kingdom of king George, but God's and you must decide on that basis and I must act on that assumption. That is why I say I will follow the law of king George so long as he does not force me to go against the law of God."[63]

Muhammad ʿAli and his coaccused were sentenced to a two-year imprisonment at the conclusion of this trial. In prison, he embarked upon writing a book that was to introduce Islam to a Western readership. Unsurprisingly, perhaps, the book was to be called "Islam: Kingdom of God." It was never completed.[64]

Mawdudi had participated in the Khilafat movement and had apparently come to know Muhammad ʿAli.[65] He had even written a biography of Gandhi, a rather remarkable fact in view of Mawdudi's later politics. According to Mawdudi's own account, this biography was confiscated by the police prior to publication.[66] It was around the time of the Khilafat movement that Mawdudi also learned English,[67] which may have given him access, in the original English, to Muhammad ʿAli's powerful rhetoric on the occasion of his trial. There is good reason to think that Mawdudi's idea of the sovereignty of God was at least influenced by Muhammad ʿAli's. Mawdudi never acknowledged this for, to him, this idea had come to be the most natural way in which to think about God. Anyone who did not think in those terms could scarcely be a believer.[68]

Even Jesus, Mawdudi later wrote, was committed to the idea of the sovereignty of God, and in this and other respects, there was no difference between his "mission" and that of Moses, Muhammad, and the other prophets. That Jesus had affirmed the sovereignty of God would have come as no surprise to John Calvin—for all that he never used the phrase himself[69]—and to generations of Christian theologians. Mawdudi's point was, however, that this was no mere religious or spiritual sovereignty but one that governed all aspects of life. The present versions of the Gospels, having been corrupted by later Christians, were less clear on this score than was the Qur'an, but various indications to this effect could still be retrieved from them. Quoting, among others, Matthew 6.10 ("Your kingdom come. Your will be done, on earth as it is in heaven"), as Muhammad Ali had done at his trial, Mawdudi observed: "The Messiah has made his goal very clear in [this] last verse. It contradicts the widespread misconception that, by the Kingdom of God, he had meant merely a spiritual kingdom. His goal clearly was that the law of God, His legal decrees (*hukm-i sharʿi*), be implemented in the world just as God's laws of nature (*qanun-i tabiʿi*) are in effect in the universe."[70] The idea of the sovereignty of God comes full circle here: from its putative New Testament origins to the leading Islamist ideologue of the twentieth century via an anti-colonial agitator, and then back not merely to the Qur'an but to what the Gospels themselves preserve of the teachings of Jesus on this crucial matter.

The sovereignty of God is not the only idea that may have carried over from Muhammad `Ali to Mawdudi. Mawdudi's stark contrast between God's law and man-made law is also reminiscent of the Khilafat leader's discourse,[71] though the vivid image of worshipping God rather than mere slaves of God has deep roots in the tradition.[72] And even Muhammad `Ali's challenge to the British to make a choice between either allowing Muslims to live by the commands of their faith or acknowledging that they had no freedom of religion in India is echoed in Mawdudi's powerful challenge to the Muslim modernists of Pakistan's first years. They needed to decide, Mawdudi had told them, what their "moral values" were. If they wanted to live by Islamic values, then they had to follow all that Islamic law demanded of them. But if it was Western values that were to continue guiding them, then they ought to stop calling themselves Muslims.[73]

I have focused principally here on the likely and hitherto neglected influence of Muhammad `Ali on Mawdudi, but the latter had encountered other influential voices as well in the crowded public sphere of colonial India. I have already mentioned Iqbal in connection with Muhammad `Ali, but his influence on Mawdudi is also worth considering. The two men knew each other, and Iqbal was associated with a plan to set up an educational institution in Pathankot, in eastern Punjab, which is what had brought Mawdudi to the Punjab shortly before Iqbal's death. The extent of their relationship is a matter of disagreement among people who have written on it; given Iqbal's subsequent stature in Pakistan, the Jama`at-i Islami has had an interest in magnifying the poet-philosopher's high regard for Mawdudi.[74] In any case, Iqbal does seem to have left a mark on Mawdudi. One illustration of this is relevant to our discussion here.

In a significant departure from conventional Muslim discourses on the caliphate, Mawdudi argued that the caliphate the Qur'an speaks of belonged to all believers. It is, he said in also supplying the English terms, "popular vicegerency" (`umumi khilafat). "Every believer is a caliph of God in his particular place. As caliph, he is individually answerable to God."[75] To Mawdudi, since the Qur'an reserved sovereignty exclusively for God, it could only speak of vicegerency when it came to human beings.[76]

Iqbal, too, had spoken of the vicegerency of God (niyabat-i Ilahi) in some of his verse.[77] This does not sound promising at first, for Iqbal seemed to evoke the Nietzschean Superman in describing this vicegerent. Yet, he had also suggested elsewhere that the sort of qualities he had in mind were potentially available to everyone: "The Democracy of Islam ... is a spiritual principle based on the assumption that every human being is a centre of latent power, the possibilities of which can be developed by cultivating a certain type of character. Out of the plebian material Islam has formed men of the noblest type of life and power. Is not, then, the Democracy of early Islam an experimental refutation of the ideas of Nietzsche?"[78] Though Iqbal did not specifically speak of the sovereignty of God, so far as I am aware, Mawdudi's conception of popular vicegerency is closer to Iqbal's than either is to medieval discussions of the caliphate.[79] And for Mawdudi, at least, this popular vicegerency was inextricably tied to divine sovereignty.

An additional source of likely influence on Mawdudi's early political thought, so far as the question of sovereignty is concerned, also merits attention before proceeding further. This takes us back to the princely state of Hyderabad, where he was born and raised. The largest and richest of such principalities, Hyderabad was viewed by its rulers to be a "sovereign" entity, except in matters of foreign affairs, which were to be handled by the government of British India. The British, however, disputed this understanding, and saw the Nizam of Hyderabad, like the rulers of other such states, as subservient to their government. The matter had come to a head in the early 1920s, with the Nizam insisting on being treated as a sovereign power *on par* with the British in negotiating the return of a part of his territory that had previously been leased to the British. The viceroy of India, however, had quickly disabused the Hyderabad government of any such pretensions. In 1928, no longer living in Hyderabad but still thinking like a loyal subject of the Nizam, Mawdudi published a treatise in which he catalogued instances of British ingratitude for the financial and moral assistance the Nizam had given to them at various critical moments while making a case for Hyderabad's sovereignty vis-à-vis the British empire.[80] The issue of sovereignty was very much in the air in the political climate of Hyderabad at the time; its swansong would come soon after Indian independence, when the Nizam's government lodged what proved to be an ineffectual protest with the United Nations against the "police action" that had extinguished any remaining pretense to sovereignty by forcibly bringing the state into the Indian union.[81]

While the question of sovereignty occupied center stage in Mawdudi's treatise on the relations between the British and the Nizam's polity, Islam was strikingly absent from that discussion. When he used terms similar to those he would in his later writings, such as "complete and absolute sovereignty" (*kamil hakimiyyat-i mutlaqa*), it was with reference to the Nizam, not to God, that he did so.[82] The debate on sovereignty seems nonetheless to have provided him fertile ground on which to think about its *true* locus. Soon, it was no longer a matter of Hyderabad's sovereignty in relation to the British crown, but God's in relation to humankind.

Debating the Implications of the Sovereignty of God

How did the sovereignty of God and related ideas figure in the discourses of some of Mawdudi's contemporaries other than those we have met so far? In addressing this question, my concern is not to trace a genealogy of this idea in each of the instances I discuss here, but to show rather that it was very much in the air in late colonial India *and* that it could mean quite different things in different quarters. I begin with a posthumous and incomplete work, *Divine Government (Hukumat-i Ilahi)*, by Abul-Mahasin Muhammad Sajjad (d. 1940), a traditionally educated religious scholar from Bihar in eastern India.

Sajjad, a founding member of the Jam`iyyat al-`Ulama-i Hind, is best known for spearheading an initiative toward establishing nongovernmental courts that would rule according to the shari`a in colonial India. These courts, a response to the same crisis to which Ashraf `Ali Thanawi had responded with his treatise on the dissolution of marriage, were envisioned as comprising a network presided over by an *amir*, a head, to whom all would defer on questions relating to Islamic law. This idea of "shari`a governance" (*imarat-i shar`iyya*) was a response as well to the impending demise of the Ottoman caliphate, to which the Muslims of India had looked as the religious and political symbol of Islam and of the global Muslim community. At least at the level of India, the imarat-i shar`iyya was meant to stand in for the caliphate, and there was more than one Muslim leader—the aforementioned Azad among them—who had entertained hopes of being recognized as the head of some such institution.

Sajjad's *Divine Government* sought to offer an intellectual justification for this structure of judicial and religious authority. He argued that the proper fulfillment of basic human needs—material welfare and the safeguarding of life, progeny, and honor—required the existence of an institutionalized and collective system (*jama`ati nizam*).[83] Muslims exposed to Western education did not dispute the need for such a system, but, he said, they looked exclusively to the West for its prototypes. It was such people that Sajjad sought primarily to convince that the teachings of Islam provided the only system for collective human existence that was truly workable. The fundamental reason why other systems were inadequate was that they were based on man-made laws. People had to be bribed or coerced to obey laws that were made by their fellow humans and even then they broke such laws at the first opportunity. And precisely because some people made them for others, the laws in question could not be said to uniformly secure everyone's interests; some would always be at the losing end of this bargain. God, however, is a disinterested party, so that everyone could be on the same plane vis-à-vis His law. He is also omniscient, which meant that the law would genuinely cater to people's interests in a way that no mere human laws could. It was through a prophet that God's law came to be known, and the institutional structure Sajjad envisioned was meant to continue what the Prophet had instituted.[84]

Sajjad did not speak explicitly of the sovereignty of God, though the idea of divine government seems to come close to it. The provenance of this idea is difficult to determine in his case, though Muhammad `Ali's rhetoric may have had some role here, too. Sajjad's argument also rested on the strong contrast between God's law and human laws, which likewise was well-represented in Muhammad `Ali's rhetoric. The latter had little interest in affirming the authority of the `ulama, however.[85] Sajjad's project, on the other hand, was nothing if not an initiative toward giving institutional shape to the `ulama's authority. Irrespective of whether Mawdudi may have been influenced by Sajjad and Sajjad by Muhammad `Ali, the sovereignty of God and related ideas were being harnessed in each case to quite different ends.

The preface to the first edition of *Divine Government*, published in 1941, is further illustrative of the different purposes to which such ideas could be put in late colonial India. It was written by Hifz al-Rahman Seoharwi (d. 1962), a leader of the Jam`iyyat al-`Ulama-i Hind. In keeping with Sajjad's views, Seoharwi underlined the inadequacy of man-made political systems, but he then went on to make the distinctive point that the universal values of peace and equality could only flourish when they came from a divine rather than a merely human source.[86] This is what "divine government" seems to mean to him. Writing during World War II, Seoharwi did not need to call up all his rhetorical powers to highlight the inadequacies, the vacuous moral authority, and the interminable conflicts of man-made systems. But that was only part of the context. Another part surely was his support for the secular Indian National Congress, which claimed, unlike the communalist Muslim League, to represent the interests of all Indian people. He acknowledged that some leaders of the Khilafat movement had retained the goal of establishing "Islamic sovereignty or divine government" (*Islami iqtidar-i a `la [hukumat-i Ilahiyya]*), but, he said, they had amended that goal to first focus on bringing together different Indian communities on the shared platform of anti-colonial struggle.[87] It was on this platform that much of Seoharwi's own political career would play out. Though he wrote, like Sajjad, in an unabashedly Islamic idiom, his larger point was not about the political supremacy of Islam but rather about the universally applicable moral foundations that religion, and specifically Islam, provided to politics.

To Seoharwi, Islam also had some very specific teachings on economic matters, and one of his earliest books, first published in 1939, was devoted to a detailed explication of those matters. That book falls outside our purview here, except on one crucial point. In its second edition, published in 1942, Seoharwi invoked Q 12.40 ("authority belongs to God alone") to observe that God is not only the creator of the universe but also its ruler and that no individual or community could lay claim to sovereignty (*hakimiyyat*). A caliph or an amir was merely a deputy of this divine government on earth; accordingly, it was not for him or the community to legislate, for that prerogative belonged only to God. This much would seem to be in line with Sajjad. In an explanatory note, Seoharwi clarified, however, that for legislative authority to belong to God did not mean that the caliph and his associates—those who loosen and bind the public affairs of Muslims, in the language of medieval constitutional theory—could not adapt the law to changing needs. For otherwise, he said, the door to the articulation of new legal norms (ijtihad) would be barred, which could hardly be the case if the law was to remain receptive to changing needs. But the laws that were to be devised by human beings, he said, were to be framed in light of the fundamentals of God's law and of their underlying principles, which admitted of no change.[88]

The next edition of this book, published in 1946, repeated all this, but another note was added to avoid any possibility of misunderstanding the implications of Q 12.40. Here Seoharwi wrote: "This does not mean that the amir or caliph is not a ruler (*hakim*) and that his command (hukm) is not a command. That is a false doctrine, a product of the Kharijis. What it means is [only] that the basic and fundamental devising of the laws is in the hands only of God,"[89] which is to say, as the next note again clarified, that human beings can continue to adapt God's law to evolving circumstances. Though Mawdudi was nowhere mentioned in this book, it is not unreasonable to suppose that it was some of the implications Mawdudi was then busy deriving from the sovereignty of God that Seoharwi sought to correct. Mawdudi was, moreover, a fierce opponent of the Jam`iyyat al-`Ulama-i Hind, savaging Husayn Ahmad Madani for a very imperfect grasp of the implications of a united nationalism that he was recommending to the Muslims of India as an alternative to Pakistan. This could not have endeared his ideas to Seoharwi any more than it did to Madani.[90]

Mawdudi had founded his Jama`at-i Islami in 1941 and the party's constitution has remained explicit ever since in its affirmation of the sovereignty of God. According to the Jama`at's creedal statement, one is to "accept no one other than God as the king, the holder of all authority (*malik al-mulk*) and the supreme power (*muqtadir-i a`la*), nor see anyone as capable of commanding, forbidding, and legislating on his own, independent authority.... For no one except God has the right to ownership and sovereignty (*malikiyyat awr hakimiyyat*)."[91] Unsurprisingly, the first goal of the party is to strive for "the instituting of religion" which, we are told, is synonymous with "divine government" (*hukumat-i Ilahiyya*) and "the Islamic system of life."[92]

By the 1940s, many more voices were appealing to the sovereignty of God in South Asia. In a letter to Jinnah, who was about to embark upon his campaign for Pakistan, the Chishti Sufi master Sayyid Muhammad Zauqi Shah (d. 1951) wrote that "fundamentally, there can only be two conceptions about forms of government: 1) sovereignty of God, [and] 2) sovereignty of man." He went on to remark on the inadequacy of "man-made constitutions" and to assert that Muslims are "the only true exponents of the sovereignty of God and ... alone ... capable of giving to the world that peaceful atmosphere which [is] the crying need of the hour."[93] Though the language is similar to Mawdudi's, a more likely source of inspiration here is again the Khilafat leader Muhammad `Ali, with whom Zauqi Shah shared his modernist alma mater, Aligarh College.[94] Zauqi Shah wrote this letter just two months before Jinnah formally articulated the demand for a separate Muslim homeland at the annual session of the Muslim League in Lahore. The immediate context of this letter was, however, the conduct of the Congress-led ministries in a number of British Indian provinces, which had tended to exclude the Muslim League from a share in the government. In speaking of the dangers of man-made systems, including majoritarian democracy, Zauqi Shah's point was not to affirm Mawdudi's Islamist ideology—to which he was hostile[95]—but rather to sound the alarm against Hindu political domination of India.

Zauqi Shah's usage was also influenced by Marmaduke Pickthall, the English convert from Hyderabad. In letters to him in 1932–33, which were subsequently published under the title "Divine Sovereignty and Divine Messengership," Zauqi Shah had sought to correct Pickthall's understanding of Islam on some crucial issues.[96] Pickthall had argued elsewhere that one's salvation depended exclusively on belief in God and the Day of Judgment and, further, that religion meant "the full and glad submission to the will of Allah *as present in men's consciences*." Both claims seemed to Zauqi Shah to undercut the role of prophethood in guiding people aright and he was deeply disturbed at this prospect. "Everybody's conscience is not a safe guide," he wrote to Pickthall. "If it is a safe and reliable guide, why did God keep on sending messengers after messengers for the guidance of all sorts of people?"[97] Zauqi Shah could see no shades of gray between the two fundamental and mutually exclusive categories of the believer and the unbeliever.[98] Unbelievers were those who did not submit to Muhammad even though God had commanded them to do so. "How can you be consistent with yourself if you profess belief in Allah but refuse to obey Him? How can you be loyal to the King-Emperor if you reject his viceroy, governors and other petty officials? Defy a petty policeman in the street and you defy the king."[99] He continued in a similar vein in a subsequent letter to Pickthall: "There can be no surrender without obedience, and there can be no obedience without obeying, in a true Muslim spirit, all the commandments of Allah which have come to us through the 'proper official channel.'"[100] Leaving aside the language of the colonial bureaucracy that Zauqi Shah had imbibed, the implications of his argument went beyond an assertion of the authority of Muhammad. They included as well the mediatory role of the saints, as one might expect from a Sufi master. And they underlined the superiority of Islam over everything else. To properly affirm the sovereignty of God was to recognize this superiority. Unsurprisingly, as Zauqi Shah would put it to Jinnah in 1940, Muslims were "the only true exponents" of this idea.

Though there is nothing in Zauqi Shah's usage to suggest that the sovereignty of God was an unusual idea by the 1940s, it was only at the end of that decade that it would find its most important modernist articulation. This, of course, was in the Objectives Resolution adopted by the constituent assembly in March 1949, laying down that "sovereignty over the entire universe belongs to God Almighty alone and the authority which He has delegated to the State of Pakistan through its people for being exercised within the limits prescribed by Him is a sacred trust."[101] The modernist assumption clearly was that the *state* would determine the parameters of the sovereignty of God rather than the other way round. Though the `ulama have often tried to take credit for the Islamic sentiments enshrined in the Objectives Resolution,[102] as indeed did the Jama`at-i Islami,[103] the traditionalists among them could not have missed the implications of any such assumption, let alone consented to it. Despite the nod to the "limits" set down by God, it was not news to anyone that the modernists wanted a more or less free hand to legislate under the imprimatur of God's delegated sovereignty. As Khalifa Abdul Hakim had put it in his *Islamic Ideology*, not quite in line with the Objectives Resolution, "According to Islam sovereignty does not belong to any monarch or a class nor does it rest with the people in general. Sovereignty belongs to God.... To men of character and integrity that sovereignty is delegated."[104] And to the extent that the limits in question mattered to the modernists, they did so in ethical rather than strictly legal terms.[105] As seen earlier, Shabbir Ahmad `Usmani's endorsement of the Objectives Resolution was not quite the same as the prime minister's. Indeed, the `ulama had begun to express their concerns on this score already before the establishment of Pakistan.

In an essay published in 1946 and titled "The True Ruler Is God Alone," Sayyid Sulayman Nadwi, one of the most distinguished of his generation's `ulama, had affirmed once again that, as the ruler of the universe, God is the source of the law.[106] The real interest of the essay lies, however, in two "doubts" that Nadwi addressed in concluding this short piece. The first of these had to do with the question of how a law revealed a very long time ago could properly meet the needs of people at later times and places. This, of course, is a familiar modernist objection to `ulama and Islamist demands for the implementation of Islamic law in the modern world. Sulayman Nadwi argued in response that the fundamentals of God's law were timeless and that changing circumstances did not have any bearing on the applicability of these core fundamentals.[107] Elsewhere in the essay, he did however grant that while the core principles were eternal, legal scholars could continue to derive subsidiary rules from them in accordance with changing needs.[108] In other words, given that this law was from an omniscient God, its antiquity was irrelevant to the question of its applicability. And it was not enough to be guided by the ethical principles of Islam, as the modernists would have it; the law itself needed to be implemented.

The second doubt he addressed also related to the modernists, though he did not say so explicitly in this instance either. The question here was about the mujtahid, the master-jurist, articulating the law in changing conditions: should such activity not be seen as new legislation and, if so, what did that mean for the claim that God is the sole legislator? Sulayman Nadwi responded that ijtihad was not a matter of making new laws but rather of demonstrating how God's existing law can be extended to encompass new situations.[109] This again kept the law responsive to change while preserving its core principles intact. While modernist conceptions of ijtihad envisaged both setting aside older laws and making new ones, all in light of the putative spirit of the Qur'an, Nadwi's view of ijtihad was a decidedly constrained and conservative one. And his goal, unannounced but unmistakable, was not merely to set forth this view but to also caution the modernists against their legislative excesses. There could be no better framework in which to strike this cautionary note than that of the sovereignty of God. Sulayman Nadwi did not use this English phrase, though that is what the readers of his essay would have understood by it. And it is hardly surprising that the English translation of this essay, first published in 1948 and reprinted in 1953, is indeed titled "the sovereignty of Allah."[110]

For all their misgivings about the sovereignty of God being put to the wrong use, the idea had found its way into the discourses of the Pakistani `ulama. In January 1951, they had convened a conference to set forth the principles that should serve as the foundation of an Islamic state and they have always pointed to the statement produced on that occasion as a testament to the clarity of their thinking on this matter and to their ability—much doubted by their critics—to come to an agreement on key issues. The conference was presided over by Sulayman Nadwi, and the "ultimate sovereignty" of God "over all nature and all law" was the first of the twenty-two principles enunciated on this occasion.[111] Or so, at least, according to the English translation of this document—a point to which I will return. Two years later, in 1953, Mufti Muhammad Shafi` published *Qur'anic Constitution*, a tract setting out the teachings of the Islamic foundational text in the form of mock articles of the constitution. Article 2 stated that "the true ruler" (*hakim-i haqiqi*) is God, and the tract later affirmed that the "highest authority (*iqtidar-i a `la*) in the state belongs exclusively to God."[112]

For their part, the modernists would continue to use the language of the sovereignty of God, but with particular inflections that seemed calculated to challenge the `ulama and the Islamists. Two examples are worth noting, both from the 1960s. The first relates to Ghulam Ahmad Parwez, who had spent a great deal of time during that decade trying to cut Mawdudi and the `ulama down to size. Writing less than two years after Ayub Khan had brought Pakistan's first experiment with democratic governance to an end, Parwez argued that divine sovereignty consisted in the unified authority (*wahdat-i iqtidar*) that belonged only to God,[113] with the palpable though unstated implication that such authority was best exemplified in the real world by a strong government. One of the implications that Parwez did explicitly draw from it was that sovereign power did not belong to the people any more than it did to a king or a dictator.[114] (He obviously did not consider Ayub Khan to be an instance of the latter.) Taking his cue from the Qur'an's instruction to "return things entrusted to you to their rightful owners" (Q 4.58), he argued further that the affairs of government should be entrusted only to those who were *capable* of running them.[115] But if the sovereignty of God allowed no room for kings and dictators, or for an uncontrolled democracy, it did not have any space for a theocracy either, which is to say that "religious leaders can have no existence in such a dispensation."[116]

It is, Parwez said, through a recognition of God's sovereignty, and the ethical values articulated in the Qur'an, that all humanity could come together on a shared platform. The values in question—human dignity, justice, benevolence, individual responsibility, right to livelihood, and patriotism, among others[117]—were timeless, but the community enjoyed "complete freedom" to operate, and to enact laws, within the boundaries demarcated by them.[118] Pakistan, Parwez thought, could lead the way toward the goal of establishing this ethically grounded universal brotherhood. It would thereby put its own house in order but it would also help rescue the world from the destructive divisions that threatened its very existence. Among the `ulama, Seoharwi would have agreed with this foregrounding of Islam's ethical ideals. But leaving aside the fact that he had been a bitter opponent of Pakistan, he, no less than other `ulama, would have been deeply suspicious of anyone having a free hand within the playing field demarcated by the Qur'an's ethical signposts. [119]

The second example relates to Fazlur Rahman. Where Mawdudi had affirmed that God is not merely the object of worship (*ma`bud*) in a religious sense but also the sovereign in the legal and political sense,[120] Rahman saw it as "the greatest mischief ... to confuse the religio-moral and political issues." Taking issue explicitly with Mawdudi, Rahman continued: "Any student of political history knows that the term 'sovereign' as a political term is of a relatively recent coinage and denotes that definite and defined factor (or factors) in a society to which rightfully belongs *coercive force* in order to obtain obedience to its will. It is absolutely obvious that God is not sovereign in this sense and that only people can be and are sovereign, since only to them belongs ultimate coercive force, i.e., only their 'Word is law' in the politically ultimate sense."[121] Yet, even as he implicitly disagreed with the likes of Abdul Hakim and Parwez on the sovereignty of the people, Rahman did not dispute the idea of the sovereignty of God. But what it means, he said, is that the Qur'an's moral principles "are objective and do not depend on or even necessarily conform to the subjective wishes of a people."[122] Once this element of subjectivity was curtailed, through a proper understanding of the Qur'an and presumably under the tutelage of a resolute ruler like Ayub Khan, the community at large decided what expression to give to the Qur'an's moral norms: "the Muslim Legislature is the supreme body unencumbered by any limitations except such as are accepted by the Muslim community, viz, the principles of justice as enunciated in the Qur'an and as illustrated in the life of the Prophet. God neither acts as political Sovereign nor as a law-maker. The Muslim people themselves are the Sovereign and the law-maker."[123]

Although the modernists were not quite on the same page, it is nonetheless at points like these that the differences between them and Mawdudi stand in sharpest relief. As will be observed, Mawdudi too, unlike many other Islamists, had come to allow considerable scope for human legislation. But the idea that the Muslim community was itself the arbiter of what limitations to impose upon itself was, to him, the very negation of the sovereignty of God. It was tantamount to the cardinal sin of setting up partners with the one God.

The Sovereignty of God in Practice

While the importance of the idea of God's sovereignty as a theoretical principle should be clear so far as the ideology of Mawdudi and his Jama'at-i Islami are concerned, how has it worked in practice? What has it *enabled* the Jama'at to do in Pakistan's political life? And what has it *prevented* the party from doing?

What it has done for the Jama'at is, quite simply, to justify its participation in the political process. In late colonial India, Mawdudi had been bitterly opposed to Muslims standing for election and entering legislative assemblies. In arrogating to themselves the authority to make laws, such assemblies trespassed on a privilege that, he believed, belonged to God alone.[124] By the same logic, he could see the colonial judicial system as nothing but illegitimate on Islamic grounds. His response to a juridical query he had received sometime in the last years of colonial rule is instructive here. The questioner had asked whether the decision of a non-Muslim judge on matters of divorce had any religious validity if the judge had been following the prescriptions of Islamic law. Mawdudi argued in response that the question was poorly formulated, for the decision even of a *Muslim* judge acting under man-made laws had no Islamic legitimacy and that those serving in such courts were themselves criminals.[125] By way of context, it should be recalled that the colonial judicial system was based on the idea that any judge—Christian, Hindu, Zoroastrian, Muslim—trained in the English common law could rule according to the shari'a as encapsulated in a small number of Islamic legal texts that had come to be officially recognized. It was about the legitimacy of this judicial practice that Rashid Rida had been asked early in the twentieth century, and he had endorsed it with much enthusiasm. Mawdudi could have had no time for Rida's view. But he would also have been disdainful of Abul-Mahasin Sajjad's effort to create an informal sector of shari'a courts or of Thanawi's legal initiative regarding the dissolution of Muslim marriages, for the overall political system at whose pleasure such courts and laws existed was still one based on something other than a recognition of the sovereignty of God.

In his response to the aforementioned query to him, Mawdudi had also directed his readers' attention to the proceedings of a trial in 1945–46, in which three officers of the British Indian Army had been prosecuted for joining the anti-colonial Indian National Army during World War II. The officers had been serving in Burma when it fell to the Japanese forces, and it was under Japanese patronage that this nationalist army had been created. Upon being recaptured by the British, the Indian officers were charged, inter alia, with "waging war against the King"; they and their attorney argued to no avail that they were a legitimate force seeking to secure the freedom of their homeland and that they were acting under the authority of the Indian National Army Act that their government in exile had enacted. As the advocate general of India put it in his opening remarks, "[n]o authority purporting to be given under that Act can be recognized by this Court or indeed by any court of this county. The assumption of any such authority was illegal from the beginning. Any tribunal or authority purporting to be established under that Act would be in repudiation of the allegiance which is inherent in a court of the country. Those who instituted or took part in the proceedings were themselves liable to be punished for offences against the State." The advocate general's speech was "worth reading carefully," Mawdudi wrote, "for what it describes as the legal position of the Government of India vis-à-vis these so-called 'rebels' is exactly the position of the kingdom of the Lord of the universe vis-à-vis all genuine 'rebels.'"[126]

Westernized Muslims, too, might be rebels against God, but Mawdudi's position on the matter of legislation became considerably more nuanced once he had moved to the new state of Pakistan that was governed by such Muslims. Already in January 1948, he had told his law school audience in Lahore that Islamic law had its eternal rulings, as enunciated in the Qur'an and the sunna, and its unchangeable principles, but it also had mechanisms for interpreting this law, for adapting it to changing needs, and for devising subsidiary new laws.[127] The Jama`at had split into a Pakistani and an Indian organization upon the partition of the Indian subcontinent in 1947, and it would take the latter decades before its leadership agreed, under intense grassroots pressure, to enter electoral politics.[128] This, too, was in marked contrast with the case in Pakistan, where the Jama`at entered electoral politics, albeit indirectly at first, from the early 1950s.[129] As Mawdudi saw it, the Jama`at could not enter electoral politics so long as the people rather than God were recognized as sovereign. Perhaps more egregiously, Pakistan's dominion status as part of the British Commonwealth meant, as an official of the Ministry of Foreign Affairs and Commonwealth Relations explained to the country's high commissioner in the UK in 1948, that "King George VI is not only the King of England but is also the King of Pakistan."[130] King George was not usually referred to in Pakistan in this way, however, and Mawdudi does not appear to have made much of it. In any case, once the sovereignty of God was affirmed, as it was by the Objectives Resolution in 1949, it became possible for the party's members to live as full citizens of the state. The Jama`at's consultative assembly, which stands next to the party head (amir) in authority, put it this way:

> With Pakistan becoming an Islamic state in principle [with the passage of the Objectives Resolution], all forms of relationship with the state have become permissible, except those that involve acting in a manner that is opposed to the shari`a. Government employment is now open to the members of the Jama`at; they are permitted to go to court in pursuit of their legitimate rights; and they are allowed to participate in elections to [legislative] assemblies and in other democratic institutions.[131]

To turn to our second question, what has the idea of the sovereignty of God *prevented* the party from being able to do in Pakistani politics? Critics of the Jama`at as well as other observers have long pointed out that its political practice has tended to be far more pragmatic than its ideology would seem to allow. Thus the Objectives Resolution was embraced by the Jama`at even though the resolution had affirmed the sovereignty not only of God but also of the people of Pakistan. The Jam`at also accepted the constitution that was promulgated in 1956, applauding it for its recognition of the sovereignty of God.[132] The Objectives Resolution formed the preamble of this foundational document and it contained a number of provisions signaling the state's Islamic orientation. For the most part, however, it was a document that had built on the colonial-era Government of India Act of 1935 and it was guided by the example of Western, liberal constitutions.[133] After it was abrogated by the martial law regime in 1958, the Islamists would continue to refer to it as an Islamic constitution and to call for its restoration. When the country received new constitutions, in 1962 and then in 1973, these too were accepted by Mawdudi and his followers, though they were no closer to Mawdudi's vision of an Islamic state than had been the case with the first constitution.

Furthermore, for all of Mawdudi's strictures against the false assumptions underlying Western political systems, his organization has participated in most of the elections that have been held in Pakistan's checkered electoral history. This has meant entering into alliances with parties that are far from being godly, and accepting the legitimacy of a political system many of whose premises Mawdudi thought contravened core Islamic principles. The general-secretary of the Jama`at, Mian Tufail Muhammad, had even praised General Yahya Khan (r. 1969–71), while he was in power following the end of the Ayub Khan regime, as the "champion of Islam." This was presumably on account of hopes that the Jama`at would be a major winner once the military ruler had successfully combated the leftists represented by Zulfikar Ali Bhutto's People's Party and the separatists led by East Pakistan's Awami League.[134] But it made no allowance for the fact that Yahya Khan had a lifestyle that was fundamentally at odds with the sort of ideas that the Jama`at represented. As the official inquiry committee constituted to look into the causes of the fall of East Pakistan under Yahya Khan's watch would observe, "there is evidence to show that the General was addicted to heavy drinking, and was extremely friendly with a number of ladies of indifferent repute who took a lot of his time even during the critical days of the war [with India]."[135] The party would later enter into an alliance with the military regime of General Zia al-Haqq, who did have the merit of cultivating a devout persona and who, of course, oversaw the most vigorous campaign of Islamization that the country had seen thus far. Yet, the Jama`at would have had to be extremely indulgent toward Zia al-Haqq's policies to see them as a realization of divine sovereignty. Were the sovereignty of God and ideas anchored in it merely a strategic means, then, to maximize gains in the political marketplace, to find allies who had traveled at least some distance toward the positions the Islamists purport to represent?

As might be expected, the Jama`at has had its share of ideological conflicts within its ranks, and the question of ideological purity vs. political pragmatism has often simmered under the surface of such conflicts.[136] The most important of these took place in 1957. Some influential members of the organization were convinced that the time was not right for it to enter the political arena: this was a corrupt, and corrupting, field and the sort of work Mawdudi had initially envisioned to form cadres of righteous believers who would take the lead in bringing about a moral and political revolution had just begun. To become part of the political process in such circumstances was to legitimate the very structures the Jama`at had made it its mission to replace with a godly order. Mawdudi, however, took a strong position against that view. In a marathon six-hour address to party members in February 1957, he argued that there was no neat division of labor between moral formation and political participation, between ideas and practice:

> The virtues (*akhlaq*) needed for a particular task are only acquired by embarking upon that task. The virtues required for preaching are developed only *through* preaching; those needed in trade will only come about in the shop and the market. You can do [theoretical] exercises in your cells for a full decade, but the moment you actually enter the field of preaching or of trade, you would realize that, in moral (*akhlaqi*) terms, you are a mere novice in the face of the [real] challenges you face. The case of politics and of elections is similar. In view of their moral problems, their perils and their drawbacks, you may well decide that you should remove yourself from this field for ever. But to aspire to eventually return to this arena and yet move away from it now on grounds that you will train yourself for some years in the virtues that

are needed for proper participation in it is sheer immaturity.... The moral force that is needed in this arena cannot be brought to it upon being manufactured somewhere else. It can only develop within this field, through contestation with its satanic forces.[137]

Ideas were a necessary complement to political change, but this did not mean, as Mawdudi saw it, that an "intellectual revolution" needed to precede one in politics. The two could occur in tandem, as long as a committed body of people was at hand to work toward both. The career of the Prophet Muhammad showed this, but there were other illustrations of it, too. After attaining political power in Egypt, the prophet Joseph had used it in the service of his religious ends.[138] "In our own country, the British had first taken over power through purely political stratagems, and *then*, utilizing the country's own resources, they had transformed its thought, morality, customs, culture and civilization according to their own conceptions of life."[139]

Given that moral and political ideas were inextricably intertwined in Mawdudi's thought, as were ideology and political action, the question of what the sovereignty of God has meant in the Jama`at's political *practice* may not be the best one to ask. As a moral-political idea, at least some of the significance of divine sovereignty lies in its undergirding *all* action, which is to say that even the compromises that are routinely made in politics are made with the intention to change the political system in the desired direction. By this logic, though Mawdudi did not put it this way, until a righteous political order was in place, the practices of an organization like the Jama`at-i Islami could not be properly judged in terms of its guiding principles any more than the shari`a itself could be judged before it had had the opportunity to govern all facets of peoples' lives.[140] Needless to say, such a position leaves people dissatisfied on all sides. There are those who remain suspicious that the Islamists' willingness to work with the constituted political system is insincere and that their goal is ultimately to change it in accord with their long-standing ideological commitments. For their part, many among the Islamists would lament, as they did in 1957, that their organization was going too far in making compromises with an iniquitous world. Yet, others have argued that there is no compromise that one cannot try to justify with a religious veneer, and that Mawdudi had a masterful ability to do precisely that.[141] For all that, the sovereignty of God was not an ineffective way of claiming the moral high ground while putting others on the defensive for *their* failure to live up to its imperatives.[142]

Why Mawdudi?

Given that the sovereignty of God is not an idea that has been invoked exclusively by the Islamists and, indeed, that it did not even originate among them, why should it have become so intimately associated with the Islamists and specifically with Mawdudi? Two factors seem to have played a role in cementing this association. First, while many among the `ulama have adopted the language of the sovereignty of God, as observed, there has always been a certain awkwardness to their embrace of it. This has had much to do with the fact that it is not a concept indigenous to the Islamic tradition, though their adoption of it does provide an illustration of the `ulama's ability to work with concepts previously foreign to them. Seoharwi had used it in the 1942 edition of his book, and it was invoked in a work composed around the same time by a religious scholar tasked by the Muslim League with creating a blueprint for an Islamic government.[143] The contemporary `alim Taqi `Usmani also uses it in the lectures he delivered on comparative political theory for the benefit of madrasa students in 1995.[144] Yet, when Sulayman Nadwi had sought to offer some correctives to modernist views on legislation and its scope, the phrase he had used referred to God as "the true ruler" (*hakim-i haqiqi*). Similar phrases appear in the Urdu and Arabic texts of the 1951 resolution adopted by the `ulama on the principles of an Islamic state.[145] The official Urdu translation of the Objectives Resolution itself refers to God as "the absolute ruler of the universe, without any partner," which is not quite the sovereignty of God that the English version affirms.[146]

In contrast with the `ulama, Mawdudi's eclectic formation, which included a substantial amount of traditional Islamic education but also a knowledge of English—rare among the `ulama of his generation—and his readings in Western thought meant that this concept could be integrated into his thinking in a quite seamless manner.[147] There was little awkwardness or ambiguity to it when Mawdudi used it. When he referred to *hakimiyyat*, there is no mistaking that he meant sovereignty, and sometimes he even glossed the Urdu neologism with the English word.[148] This has made for a clearer identification of this idea with him than with anyone else.

Second, we can scarcely neglect the significance of Mawdudi's ability to introduce his ideas into the Arab world. In 1951, the Jama`at-i Islami had established an office to translate Mawdudi's writings and other party literature into Arabic and to disseminate this material in the Arab and the wider Muslim world.[149] Soon Mawdudi's books were being published in several Arab countries, notably Egypt, Syria, and Iraq, including early works in which he had expounded on the sovereignty of God and related ideas. Some of Mawdudi's works were also serialized in the Islamic press in the Middle East during those years; and associates of the Jama`at-i Islami such as Mas`ud `Alam Nadwi (d. 1954) were regular contributors to Arab periodicals. It was through such channels that Islamists like Sayyid Qutb were introduced to Mawdudi's thought.

Perhaps the most striking illustration of the relative newness of the idea of God's sovereignty in Qutb's thought is provided by the sixth and last edition of his *Social Justice in Islam* (1964). The idea is ubiquitous in this edition; the phrase was entirely absent in the previous five editions, published between 1949 and 1958.[150] It would have been self-defeating to acknowledge a specific debt to Mawdudi for this idea, but it is his influence that looms large here. And some of the Jama`at's literature itself credits Mawdudi with having introduced Qutb, and the Muslim Brotherhood of Egypt, to the sovereignty of God.[151] The writings of Qutb, and of Mawdudi, served in turn to popularize the idea in other circles. Its simplicity and power also helped it cross sectarian boundaries. Though Mawdudi and Qutb were both Sunnis, it has come to resonate in Shi`i circles, too, and it features, as articles 2 and 56, in the constitution framed in the aftermath of the Iranian revolution of 1979.

To return to Pakistan, it is worth noting that Mawdudi's recognition abroad served also to enhance his influence at home, rather like it would in case of Taqi `Usmani later. A grudging acknowledgement of this was provided by the modernist Ghulam Ahmad Parwez in a letter to President Ayub Khan in January 1968. Fazlur Rahman's Institute of Islamic Research was then busy organizing an international conference on the Qur'an to which Mawdudi had been invited. Parwez was worried that Mawdudi's ties with the `ulama—a term he used broadly, to refer to conservatives of different stripes— from abroad would enable him to dominate the proceedings and to shape them in directions detrimental to the government's interests. The same thing had happened, Parwez cautioned Ayub Khan, on the occasion of the international colloquium on Islam that the University of the Punjab had convened in 1957–58: "Maudoodi had full grip on this group [of religious intellectuals from abroad] and he made them all to express his own views on every subject. This gave him a good handle to propagate that all the Ulema of Islamic world supported him in his views. Maudoodi is sure to play the same game this time as well."[152] The paper Mawdudi had given at the 1957–58 colloquium was on the scope of legislation in Islam, and it had begun by affirming that God's sovereignty was not just a religious matter but extended equally to law and politics.[153] But he had allowed some room for human legislation as well.[154] Other Islamists had a much stricter view of the implications of God's sovereignty. Yet, such concessions may have made Mawdudi's position not less but even more influential. They served to reassure people that a recognition of God's legal sovereignty did not preclude adapting His law to changing circumstances, but they also made the point that this was to be a far more disciplined exercise in legal change than the sort of blanket mandate for legislation that the modernists seemed to want.[155]

That Mawdudi was not the originator of the idea of the sovereignty of God should not obscure the stamp that he was able to put on it. His formulation also had the virtues of simplicity and comprehensiveness: it made much better sense for an omnipotent God to have a sovereignty that extended to all areas of life, including the political; even Jesus had preached the same gospel.

Such ideas might be mischievous, as Fazlur Rahman saw it, but they did not lack appeal, as he acknowledged himself.[156] Rival conceptions of divine sovereignty—undergirding, as some Muslim modernists had it, a global community that would be united on a platform of shared ethical norms—were too idealistic and too abstract. They also seemed too closely tied to visions of an authoritarian state that was not above bending Islam to its Westernizing will. Once Mawdudi's formulation of the sovereignty of God had gained traction, inside and outside Pakistan, it was very difficult to argue against it. It is remarkable that few have even tried to do so. To many others, including Ahmadis, it has seemed the most natural thing to read it in the Qur'an. As Sir Muhammad Zafrulla Khan had put it in March 1949, in the course of a spirited defense of what the constituent assembly soon adopted as the Objectives Resolution: "To the ... statement ... that sovereignty over the entire Universe belongs to God Almighty alone, I do not conceive that any person believing in God could take exception."[157]

Zafrulla Khan was speaking on the occasion as a Muslim member of the assembly, and he was keen to reassure the non-Muslims, including the Hindus and the Christians, about an understanding of Islam in which religion and the state were not separate.[158] Ironically, his own status in the Muslim community and in a state that gave official recognition to Islam was anything but secure. Already in 1924, Shabbir Ahmad `Usmani, the most valuable of the government's `ulama-allies during Pakistan's first years and Zafrulla Khan's colleague in the constituent assembly, had published a tract in which he had sought to show that the Ahmadis were apostates and that they merited the death penalty that the Afghan government had meted out to one of them.[159] Though `Usmani had died by the end of 1949, a powerful movement was just beginning to take shape to have the Ahmadis declared non-Muslims in the new state. Zafrulla Khan's name would figure prominently in that movement. So would Mawdudi's, as one of its key ideologues.

CHAPTER FIVE

Religious Minorities and the Anxieties of an Islamic Identity

ONE WOULD HAVE THOUGHT that a country that came into being in order to enable the Muslim minority of South Asia to live in accordance with its religious norms would be especially sensitive to the insecurities of minorities. But majorities can have their own insecurities, perhaps never more so than on *becoming* a majority. In his very first speech as governor-general, Jinnah had gone out of his way to reassure religious minorities that they would be safe in Pakistan.[1] The country's first prime minister was likewise keen to affirm the government's liberal commitments, which he saw as compatible with his idea of an Islamic state. As the Indian prime minister, Jawaharlal Nehru, reported in 1950, after a series of meetings with his Pakistani counterpart, "Liaquat Ali was at pains to point out that all that was meant by the Islamic State was that Muslims should have their personal law etc. In no sense should they or could they have special privileges. His State was an ordinary democratic State like England. He was prepared to make this perfectly clear at any time.... But he could not denounce the Islamic State phrase for obvious reasons, as this would give a handle to the reactionary elements in Pakistan."[2] This chapter seeks to uncover and to understand some of the anxieties that the "reactionary elements" have had vis-à-vis the religious minorities in the country.

The population of Pakistan—207.77 million in 2017—is and has always been overwhelmingly Muslim. Though a substantial minority before the secession of East Pakistan, official estimates for 1998—the last complete census prior to the one conducted in the spring and summer of 2017—put the Hindus at less than 2 percent of the total population. The Christians, for their part, comprised a little over 1.5 percent of the country's population.[3] Though Jinnah had referred in his August 11, 1947, speech to minorities within the ranks of Muslims as well, it was non-Muslim minorities that he and Liaquat

Ali Khan had sought primarily to reassure. The "reactionary elements" have been particularly interested, however, in *Muslim* minorities, and it is on two of these—the Ahmadis and the Shi`a—that I will focus here.

A close-knit and well-educated community, the Ahmadis comprise a very small group—reckoned in 1953 to be only about 200,000 people in a country of 34 million, though subsequent Ahmadi estimates of their numerical size were considerably higher.[4] Mirza Ghulam Ahmad, the founder of the community, did not dispute Muhammad's prophethood, or the revelation to him that took the form of the Qur'an, or the authority of the religious law that Muhammad had brought forth. But his own claims—that though a "shadow" of Muhammad's more perfect prophethood and while belonging to the *umma* Muhammad had founded, he too was a prophet—are held by others to leave no room for the Ahmadis within the Muslim fold. The Punjab saw serious anti-Ahmadi riots in 1953, followed by the imposition of a martial law in the provincial capital. And there was a country-wide agitation in 1974 that culminated in a constitutional amendment declaring the Ahmadis to be non-Muslims.

There are those among the Sunnis who view the Shi`a with grave misgivings, too. And though there is a long history of Shi`i-Sunni hostility, in and outside South Asia, Pakistan has witnessed especially intense sectarian violence since the mid-1980s as well as concomitant calls upon the government to declare the Shi`a, like the Ahmadis, a non-Muslim minority.

This chapter does not seek to narrate the history of these Muslim minorities in Pakistan or even to document instances of their persecution. Nor is it my concern here to examine how members of these minority communities see themselves in relation to the Sunni majority. My purpose is instead to explore some of what may underlie the hostile attitudes of the `ulama as well as of Islamist ideologues and activists toward these minority communities. I will also touch upon instances of the conflicted ways in which Muslim modernists have viewed the Ahmadis. Needless to say, the point of exploring these attitudes and the anxieties that underlie them is not to try to explain away the manner in which these minorities have been treated in the country. It is instead to better understand some of the uncertainties, ambiguities, and conflicts that have continued to characterize definitions of an Islamic identity in Pakistan. What exactly is the nature of the challenge that a tiny community, the Ahmadis, has posed to conservative Sunnis, *apart from* what their doctrines represent? How did this Ahmadi challenge become implicated in wider contestations on Islam in the public sphere? What anxieties have the Shi`a— comprising around 15 percent of the country's population—provoked in particular Sunni circles, again apart from the perceived incompatibility of some of their doctrines with those of the Sunnis?[5] And how do the anxieties that each minority community generates compare with those produced by the other? These are among the questions I address in this chapter.

The Ahmadi Question

Though I argue in what follows that we need to go beyond doctrinal issues in order to understand the severity of the conservative Sunni response to the Ahmadis, it is important nonetheless to begin with some key doctrinal matters. For we would appreciate little of the scope and depth of the anti-Ahmadi sentiment in Pakistan or of the ability of the `ulama and the Islamists to harness it to particular goals if we do not recognize how Ahmadism unsettles the long-established ways in which Muslims have viewed the authority of their prophet and the theological edifice that rests upon that authority. To those who revere the person of Muhammad and seek to guard his honor more ardently than even God's, Ahmadi prophetology is an affront.[6] It is in defense of Muhammad's honor that the anti-Ahmadi sentiment has often been galvanized.

As it happens, there is in fact significant difference of opinion *within* the Ahmadis on how to view the claims of Mirza Ghulam Ahmad. The larger of the two groups among them is often referred to by opponents as Qadianis— with reference to Qadian, the birth place of the community's founder, now located in the Indian Punjab—and it is best known for the belief that Mirza Ghulam Ahmad was a prophet of some sort. In Pakistan, the members of this group founded a new town, Rabwah, in the Punjab, where the head of their community resided until relocating to London in the mid-1980s. The other group, called the Lahoris with reference to their base in Lahore, views Ghulam Ahmad as a reformer but not as a prophet. Though the Ahmadis themselves are keenly aware of the difference, their opponents have come to view both groups as almost equally unacceptable, the Lahore-based group being damned by association with a man venerated in putatively outrageous terms by his other followers. Both groups were declared non-Muslims in 1974.[7]

Although the idea of reform and of periodic "renewers" (*mujaddidun*) of the faith has a long history in Sunni Islam, Ghulam Ahmad's claims were larger and thus more difficult to accommodate within that genealogy. To those not well-disposed to them, these claims also implied that the Islam of Muhammad was not good for all times, that it needed to be continually retooled to new demands at the hands of figures like Ghulam Ahmad. This is a point that the modernist poet and philosopher Muhammad Iqbal had made in some hard-hitting polemics against the Ahmadis toward the end of his life.[8] The Ahmadis also question the obligatoriness of jihad, a position that the `ulama see as contravening explicit Islamic injunctions. There was the allegation, too, that such views were tailored to the interests of British colonial rule and, by extension, that the Ahmadi movement was little more than a child of the colonial effort to divide and weaken Islam. Then there was the nagging suspicion that the Ahmadis did not consider *other* Muslims as properly Muslim at all and wished to have nothing to do with them in religious and social matters. As Iqbal had put it, "Any religious society historically arising from the bosom of Islam, which claims a new prophethood for its basis, and declares all Muslims who do not recognize the truth of its alleged revelation as *kafirs* [unbelievers] must ... be regarded by every Muslim as a serious danger to the solidarity of Islam."[9] He had proposed that the colonial government "declare the Qadianis a separate community ... and the Indian Muslim will tolerate them just as he tolerates the other religions."[10]

The severity of the Ahmadi challenge would lead one to think that no one would ever consider them as fellow Muslims. Influential voices had, indeed, been raised against them, as in the case of Iqbal.[11] In 1932, Anwarshah Kashmiri, a Deobandi luminary, had testified, along with several other scholars, in favor of a woman plaintiff who wanted her marriage dissolved on grounds that her husband had become an Ahmadi. Kashmiri argued at length on this occasion to show that Ahmadi beliefs constituted apostasy from Islam, which entailed the dissolution of a marriage.[12]

Yet, part of the reason why the `ulama were so vehement in having the Ahmadis declared non-Muslims was precisely that not everyone viewed them as such. Early in his career, Iqbal himself had had "hopes of good results following from this movement," as he would acknowledge with some discomfort later.[13] And he had once referred to the founder of the Ahmadi community, while the latter was still alive, as "probably the profoundest theologian among modern Indian Muhammadans."[14] In a 1923 fatwa published in the Lahore newspaper *Zamindar*, Abul-Kalam Azad had characterized Ahmadi beliefs as severely misguided but had held that the Ahmadis could not be considered unbelievers, or excluded from the Muslim community, or subjected to a social boycott.[15] `Abd al-Majid Daryabadi, a devotee of none other than Ashraf `Ali Thanawi, likewise thought that the Ahmadis were best characterized as wayward Muslims rather than as outright infidels.[16]

In part at least, Iqbal had come to take a hostile view of the Ahmadis on account of the pressure exerted on him by the Majlis-i Ahrar-i Islam. The Ahrar did their best to make other modernists fall in line, too. In late colonial India, they wanted candidates standing for election to the Punjab legislative assembly on the ticket of the Muslim League to pledge that they would work toward excluding the Ahmadis from the Muslim fold. Though the parliamentary board of the Muslim League did make an announcement to that effect,[17] Jinnah continued to block any such move, which was obviously bad for his effort to forge a united Muslim front against the Congress.[18] In his famous 1940 address as the president of the Muslim League, Jinnah gave no inkling that his Muslim "nation" had any divisions within it or that anyone claiming to be a Muslim was in fact not so. Asked in 1944 by one of the Ahmadis if there was any impediment to their becoming members of the Muslim League, Jinnah, who had previously given an Ahmadi leader private assurances to this effect, responded with a lawyer's answer. He directed the questioner to the

League's constitution, according to which "every candidate for membership of a primary branch of the All India Muslim League must be a Musalman [Muslim]."[19] This left unresolved the question of whether the Ahmadis were Muslims. But it was enough to continue allowing the Ahmadis to associate with the League. Its most high profile Ahmadi was Sir Muhammad Zafrulla Khan, a member of the viceroy's executive council and subsequently Pakistan's first foreign minister. The demand for the removal of Zafrulla Khan from the latter position would be at the heart of the anti-Ahmadi agitation in the Punjab in 1953.

The Punjab disturbances had a political context, the relevant parts of which may be recalled from chapter 2 and briefly supplemented here.[20] In 1950, the Basic Principles Committee (BPC) appointed by the constituent assembly had submitted initial recommendations for how the provinces were to be represented at the center. It had proposed that the country would have two houses of parliament, with the upper house giving an equal number of seats to the five provinces—Punjab, Sindh, North-West Frontier, Baluchistan, and East Bengal; membership of the lower house was to be based on adult franchise. The two houses were envisioned as having equal powers. The Bengalis saw this as nullifying the numerical majority of their province and objected strenuously to it. The religious groups had their own grievances, seeing the interim report as inattentive to their vision of an Islamic state. Having been forced back soon afterward to the drawing board by the hostility that had greeted this report, the BPC submitted a revised set of recommendations toward the end of 1952. The report was now premised on the principle of parity between Pakistan's western and eastern wings. Each was to have an equal number of representatives in both the lower and the upper houses of the parliament, though the upper house lacked any effective power this time around. Within the western wing, however, the smaller provinces were to have greater representation than their population warranted, and a number of other small units were envisaged as well. All this was meant as a way of preventing the much-feared domination of the Punjab—the largest of the west Pakistani provinces—over the smaller units, but also over the country as a whole. The Punjabis, led by their chief minister, Mian Mumtaz Daultana, predictably saw it as denying their province its legitimate voice at the center. For their part, the religious groups resented the lack of attention to their increasingly aggressive demands regarding the Ahmadis.

With relations between the center and the Punjab becoming unhappier by the day over the shape of the future constitution, the Oxford-educated Daultana found in the Ahmadi issue a potent means of undermining the federal government. He encouraged the anti-Ahmadi camp to take their demands—of relieving high-ranking Ahmadis of their positions and declaring the community as outside the Islamic fold—to the center, for they bore on constitutional issues that only the federal government and the constituent assembly could resolve. The prime minister, Khawaja Nazimuddin (who had succeeded Li-aquat Ali Khan on his assassination in 1951), was known for personal piety and for good relations with the `ulama. But the demands of the Majlis-i `amal, the committee of action spearheading the anti-Ahmadi movement, were too extreme even for him, let alone for the Westernizing bureaucratic and political elite at the center. When the Majlis-i `amal presented him with an ultimatum, Nazimuddin refused to give in.[21] This was followed by widespread agitation in the Punjab in late February and March 1953. Lahore, the provincial capital was especially hard hit, with the city paralyzed by the protestors in the first days of March and lower-ranking government functionaries going on strike. Martial law was imposed in Lahore on March 6, though the agitation would continue for several more days elsewhere in the province. Some months later, Iskandar Mirza, the governor-general, dismissed the Nazimuddin government and appointed a new prime minister.

The 1953 disturbances also had an economic context. There were food shortages in parts of the country, with a corresponding rise in the price of wheat.[22] Unemployment was also a serious problem. In Sialkot, those who had previously been associated with the manufacture of sporting goods—an important local industry—were drawn to the agitation;[23] in Gujranwala, it was out of work metal and textile labor that had gravitated to it.[24] In Lahore, it was the support for the agitators in the public services—the railways, the electricity department, the telephone and telegraph department—that had caused some of the greatest nervousness in the higher echelons of government and may have precipitated the imposition of martial law in the city.[25] Communists, too, had become part of the agitation.[26] Conversely, some of those who stood on an explicitly Islamic platform had a history of activism in the socioeconomic realm as well. This was the case with the Ahrar, in particular, whose success in galvanizing the movement and trying in the process to rehabilitate themselves in Pakistani politics had something to do with their well-known advocacy of causes relating to social justice. It is telling, for instance, that the son of `Ata Allah Shah Bukhari (d. 1961), the most spellbinding of all Ahrar public speakers active in this agitation, was named Abu Zarr[27]—in honor of the companion of the Prophet Muhammad more closely associated than anyone in early Islam with protests against social inequalities. And the base of an influential preacher in Rawalpindi, who led the movement before eventually helping the government bring it under control, had once been memorialized as "the laborer's mosque" (*mazdur ki masjid*).[28] Unsurprisingly, it was not just symbols of government that were attacked during the agitation, but also those of affluence: the list of things damaged included an air-conditioned railroad coach, "one of the few that Pakistan had."[29] In Lahore, the "faces of people travelling in cars were blackened."[30]

There was more, however, to the Punjab disturbances than the machinations of the provincial government, the demagoguery of the Ahrar, or even the perceptible decline in people's standards of living. From the perspective of the `ulama and the Islamists, there was something deeply troubling about the fact that the government of what was meant to be an Islamic state had a non-Muslim for one of its most visible members. This was as clear an indication as any that the modernizing governing elite were not sincere about anchoring the state in proper Islamic norms or, what to them was the same thing, about following the `ulama's counsel in matters relating to Islam. That the foreign minister was held in high regard in Western capitals made matters worse, for it suggested that the government was more keen to cultivate its ties with the West than it was to fulfill its Islamic obligations.[31]

The challenge that Zafrulla Khan posed to the religio-political groups as an *Ahmadi* was more serious than he would if he had been a Hindu or a Christian. Pakistan's first law minister, Jogendra Nath Mandal, was in fact a Hindu from the scheduled castes, though that appointment had not ended well either.[32] The conservative camp knew that Zafrulla Khan was not a Muslim, but many others either did not know or did not care. As Mawdudi had observed in explaining the need for his tract on "the Qadiani problem" in March 1953, "a vast number" of the educated and even the ordinary believers did not understand the grounds for the demand that the Ahmadis be declared a non-Muslim minority.[33] It was bad enough that the person introducing Pakistan at international forums and highlighting its Islamic commitments should have been a non-Muslim. It was much worse that he was masquerading as a Muslim, thereby unsettling some of the boundaries that the new state was supposed to guard.

Then there was the fact that Zafrulla Khan did not merely happen to be an Ahmadi but was rather a committed and active member of that community. He sometimes delivered Friday sermons at Ahmadi congregations.[34] The 1953 agitation was itself precipitated by his decision to speak at a public gathering organized by the Ahmadi Association (Anjuman-i Ahmadiyya) in Karachi, Pakistan's capital at the time. The prime minister, Khawaja Nazimuddin, had advised him against attending that event, but he had refused and threatened to resign as foreign minister if he was prevented from speaking at it.[35] From its inception, the Ahmadi community had been keenly interested in proselytism. Zafrulla Khan would later claim, in fact, that it was "the most active missionary movement in Islam."[36] In his testimony before the Court of Inquiry regarding the Punjab agitation, Nazimuddin, for his part, had expressed the view that "the root cause of the trouble . . . [was] the proselytizing tendency of the Ahmadis."[37] To opponents of the Ahmadis, this proselytism has sought to promote the interests not of Islam but rather of the Ahmadi cause. Ahmadi proselytism served, on this view, to strengthen the heretical community at the expense of Islam; more insidiously, it brought unsuspecting people to Ahmadism under the façade of converting them to Islam.

Once again, the specter of a high-ranking government official advancing the cause of his wayward religious orientation was disquieting to his opponents.[38]

Three other things are worth noting in regard to Zafrulla Khan. First, to many `ulama and Islamists, he would have typified not just Ahmadism but also Muslim modernism, complete with its dim view of them. In his speech at the constituent assembly defending the Objectives Resolution, Zafrulla Khan was clearly thinking of the `ulama and the Islamists when he had cautioned against those who might "substitut[e] tinsel imitations and narrow bigotries" for Islam's higher ideals.[39] Pakistani modernists did not have to be Ahmadi to be contemptuous of conservative demands regarding this community. A. K. Brohi (d. 1987), the advocate-general of the province of Sindh, a prominent modernist intellectual, and later the country's law minister, had put it this way in 1952 in speaking of the still elusive Pakistani constitution, less than six months before the anti-Ahmadi agitation flared up in the Punjab:

> Lately we have brought before us a very unusual and *senseless question* of declaring the Ahmadis to be a minority community and it has been pressed by a section of our countrymen in Pakistan not only that we do declare this position but also to incorporate this declaration into the Constitution of Pakistan. I, for one, cannot see how anybody except a court of law can give a declaration of status. I cannot see the wisdom of the suggestion that such *a trivial matter* should be included in the future Constitution of Pakistan, which document ... ought only to deal with very important and fundamental questions.[40]

This was far from being a senseless question, a trivial matter, of course, for the `ulama, the Islamists, and those receptive to their discourses. But such words would surely have alerted them, if they needed a reminder, that Muslim modernists were themselves an impediment to the resolution of the Ahmadi issue.

Second, Zafrulla Khan was considerably better versed in Islam than many of his modernist peers. He could quote the Qur'an freely and in the original Arabic[41] and, over the course of his long life, he would write a number of books on Islam. The contrast with the more meager intellectual resources of many other contemporary modernists was probably not lost on the `ulama. Zafrulla Khan irked the `ulama and the Islamists not only because he was a heretic in power, but also because he was an articulate and very literate heretic. The fact that he was also a modernist made things worse, though, in the end, it was not *Ahmadi* modernism as such that provoked the conservative opposition so much as the manner in which the Ahmadi issue had become implicated in the conservatives' poor view of Islamic modernism as a whole.[42] We will observe instances of this point as we proceed.

The third thing to note here is the persistent allegation that Ahmadis like Zafrulla Khan were more loyal to the head of their own religious community than they were to the government or the country. It was often suggested that the Ahmadis had carved out a "state within a state," or that they wanted to do so,[43] and that orders received from Rabwah trumped all other commitments.[44] Such allegations are far from unusual when it comes to minorities anywhere. Yet, once again, there may have been more to it than the charge, with all its subversive implications, that the Ahmadis thought themselves accountable to an authority of their own. There are traces here of some resentment toward the modernists, too: whereas the modernist governing elite were busy forcing Islam upon the procrustean bed of Pakistani nationalism, the Ahmadis allegedly put their false religion above all else. Adherents of the *true* religion might have been expected to do at least as much.

The leaders of the anti-Ahmadi movement had considerable street power at their disposal and, in March 1953, they were able to create significant unrest in the Punjab. The military, however, put down the agitation with a heavy hand, with no concessions to the movement's demands. Mawdudi was condemned to death for his role in the agitation, though the verdict was soon commuted to a lesser sentence. The judicial report that was produced on the agitation by justices Muhammad Munir and M. R. Kayani of the Lahore High Court remains, for its part, unsurpassed as a modernist indictment of the wrong kinds of Islam. But the Ahmadi question had not gone away. It would reemerge just over two decades later, in 1974.

That year was a particularly bad one for the Bhutto government. Significant rifts had emerged by then within the ruling party. University teachers went on a country-wide strike in May 1974 to press their demands for a standardized system of salaries;[45] so did schoolteachers in Sindh,[46] and educational institutions in the Punjab had to be closed prematurely for the summer that year, with the examinations cancelled.[47] There were shortages of flour and cooking oil in the Punjab,[48] and 600,000 transit workers were threatening a strike.[49] On top of everything else, India undertook its first ever nuclear test on May 18, causing great anxiety in Pakistan, which now found itself staring at a new level of vulnerability vis-à-vis its arch rival.[50] There were also reports of Hindu-Muslim riots in Delhi around this time, which always made headline news in Pakistan. Then, on May 30, the newspapers reported that a group of medical college students returning to Multan, in the Punjab, from a vacation in the Frontier province had been severely beaten by a mob while their train was passing through the Ahmadi town of Rabwah.[51]

The students had apparently said derisive things about the Ahmadis while en route to the Frontier, and the Ahmadi mob was waiting for them on their return. The Ahmadis may have overreacted on this occasion, though hardly without reason. They had overreached before. In the mid-1930s, they had gone toe-to-toe in their conflict with the Ahrar and had tried, as some government officials saw it, "to goad the Ahrars into attacking them so that Government [would] have to defend the Ahmadis and so make the matter a war between the Ahrars and Government instead of between the Ahrars and Ahmadis."[52] Around the same time, they had provoked Sikh villagers by claiming that Guru Nanak, the founder of the Sikh community, had in fact been a Muslim.[53] The result, as a police report had put it in early 1935, was that "the increase of feeling against the Ahmadis has been very marked and is not confined to any one community."[54] In his testimony before the Court of Inquiry in 1953, Khawaja Nazimuddin, too, had noted that speeches at events organized by the Ahmadis could be as provocative as those of the Ahrar.[55] Nonetheless, few could have expected that the response to the Rabwah incident of 1974 would assume the proportions that it did. The incident acquired nationwide significance almost as soon as it had occurred, with much outpouring of public anger. There were well-coordinated general strikes in major cities, instances of arson directed at Ahmadi homes and businesses, and a number of deaths.[56] The government appointed a commission, headed by K.M.A. Samdani, a judge of the Lahore High Court, to investigate what had transpired at Rabwah. Though the testimony of those called before the commission received extensive coverage in the press, the murkiness of the events surrounding the "Rabwah incident" would remain unrelieved, not least because the commission's report to the Punjab government has never been made public.[57]

In view of the foregoing catalogue of troubles Bhutto was facing early in his administration, it is not unreasonable to think that he would have looked favorably upon something like the Rabwah incident to draw people's attention away from more pressing issues. Some did claim to see the ruling party's hand in staging the event, among them the head of the Ahmadi community.[58] Yet, it is unlikely that Bhutto had a direct role in it. Having the Ahmadis declared non-Muslims was an old demand of the `ulama, after all, and a recommendation to similar effect in April 1974 by the Muslim World League, a pan-Islamic body sponsored by Saudi Arabia, had given it added force.[59] Though the decision by the Pakistani parliament to follow suit and to classify the Ahmadis as a non-Muslim minority won some momentary praise for Bhutto from conservative circles, it was only under intense pressure from them that the government had acted. And the whole episode may have weakened Bhutto vis-à-vis the `ulama and the Islamists, who would spearhead a mass movement against him on charges of rigged elections less than three years later.

The Bhutto era had, in fact, begun auspiciously for the Ahmadis, and this returns us to some of the anxieties people have had about them. There were reports that the Ahmadis had contributed generously to Bhutto's political campaign in order to ensure his government's favorable disposition toward them. And as the British ambassador to Islamabad reported in a confidential note, "when Bhutto on coming to power sacked the chiefs of the three Armed Services and appointed two reputed Ahmadis to head the air force and navy, with Ahmadis in command of at least two of the five army corps, ... they seemed to be reaping their reward."[60]

In the wake of the Rabwah incident, the names of high-ranking military officials who were Ahmadis appeared in some magazines, reflecting and reinforcing concerns about an influential Ahmadi presence in the most powerful of Pakistan's institutions. There was much uncertainty and innuendo about who was or was not an Ahmadi; the days when the Pakistani foreign minister could embrace his Ahmadi identity at public gatherings were long gone. But the uncertainty created even more unease about how many of the "key positions" of the state—and not just in the military—were in fact occupied by members of this tiny community.[61] Even as the Ahmadis continued to be accused in 1974, as they were in 1953, of running a state within a state, it was easy to play upon fears that they could—might even be plotting to—take over Pakistan itself.[62] For a country that had lived for many years under martial law or other forms of authoritarian rule, it would not have taken much imagination to conjure up such fears. And those paying attention to international developments would have known that Hafiz al-Asad, the Syrian strongman who had risen to power just a few years ago in 1970, came not from that country's Sunni majority but rather from what was widely seen as a heretical minority.

As the anti-Ahmadi movement took shape in 1974, it was repeatedly mentioned that there was an "Ahmadi mission" working in Israel. The Ahmadis asked about it by the Samdani commission clarified that this Ahmadi presence in Haifa predated the partition of India[63] and that the proselytizing center in question was run by local Arabs.[64] Even so, in the immediate aftermath of the Arab-Israeli war of 1973, the mere suggestion that the Ahmadis had a presence in Israel would have sufficed for many to confirm their worst suspicions about an Ahmadi conspiracy against Islam and not just against Pakistan. There also were insinuations that Ahmadis were working for a reunited India, since their original center, Qadian, was now in India. Mawlana Yusuf Bannuri (d. 1977), a respected religious scholar of the Deobandi orientation and the convener of the anti-Ahmadi alliance, had little doubt that the Ahmadis were working in both Israeli and Indian interests.[65]

Questions about loyalty could, however, cut other ways, too, and some of the `ulama were themselves vulnerable on this score. In his testimony before the Samdani commission, Mawlana Ghulam Ghaus Hazarawi (d. 1981), a leader of the Deobandi Jam`iyyat al-`Ulama-i Islam, acknowledged, for instance, that he had been opposed to the establishment of Pakistan. But, he explained, once Pakistan had come into existence, he and like-minded `ulama had decided that working against its interests would be wrong.[66] Yusuf Bannuri had belonged to the same camp. He was a student of Anwarshah Kashmiri, and he had taught for many years at the madrasa Kashmiri had established in Gujarat, in western India, in the late 1920s. He was originally from the Frontier province, though it had taken him some years after the partition of India to come to Pakistan. This was not unusual in the early years of partition.[67] It had not been clear to everyone that the borders would eventually become virtually impassable or on which side one wanted to reside permanently. Things looked decidedly different a quarter century after partition, however. Even as Bannuri led the charge against the Ahmadis, front page advertisements were published in several national newspapers in early July 1974, questioning his credentials as a loyal citizen of Pakistan. Taking the form of queries addressed to him, these advertisements asked whether it was true that Bannuri had continued to live as an Indian citizen even after Pakistan had come into being, that he had once been the provincial president of the anti-Pakistan Jam`iyyat al-`Ulama-i Hind, that he had maintained ties with India even after coming to Pakistan. There were also rhetorical questions about whether his entry into politics on the Ahmadi issue was at India's bidding, in order to create chaos (*fitna*), even foment a civil war, in Pakistan and whether he was not getting a "purely religious issue" entangled with politics and thereby making it more difficult to resolve. The advertisements were sponsored by Members of the Association of Devotees of the Prophet [Muhammad], a hitherto unknown group.[68] That the Ahmadis were behind these advertisements might have been a natural inference, though the leading opposition lawyer involved in cross-examining those testifying before the Samdani commission thought that it was rather the government that had sponsored them, not least because they were published in newspapers then controlled by it.[69]

Whether or not the government was complicit in these advertisements, it would have benefited from this effort to discredit a politically influential religious scholar. In any case, it would not have been difficult for the `ulama to see things this way, or to interpret them as yet another instance of the governing elite's derailing of people's religious aspirations. Since coming to power, Bhutto government officials had made a number of statements showing that they were no friends of the `ulama. At almost exactly the time the Rabwah incident took place, a federal minister whose portfolios included the regulation of charitable endowments (*awqaf*) had stated that the government was planning to introduce legislation that would prohibit the use of mosques for political purposes.[70] To the `ulama, let alone the Islamists, there are no sharp distinctions to be made between "religious" and "political" purposes, so far as mosques go. What such statements meant to them was simply that the government expected them to endorse its policies or at least to stay clear of views critical of it. Some weeks later, the Punjab's minister of education had declared that the People's Party–controlled provincial government was preparing legislation to take over the madrasas.[71] So far as the `ulama are concerned, as has been observed, these are some of the last "bastions of Islam," and they have often equated their ability to resist governmental regulation of these institutions with the autonomy and integrity of their prized religious tradition. Khurshid Hasan Mir, a federal minister with strong leftist leanings, was among the most combative. "Now that the Ahmadi question is under consideration by the

National Assembly," he said in late August 1974, "the mullas need not make all this noise.... These so-called ʿulama are using mosques for political ends. If they don't put a stop to their charges and allegations [against the government], their tongues will be pulled out."[72] Even without such intemperate language, the government and many of its policies represented a serious challenge to the ʿulama.[73] From the latter's perspective, then, any backing down on the Ahmadi issue would be a victory not only for that community but also for a government intent on undermining the conservative camp. Such anxieties may not have triggered the anti-Ahmadi agitation, but they surely underlaid some of the ʿulama's determination to see it through to success.

One further node of possible anxiety is also worth considering, and this concerns the students of the medical college who had been beaten up at the Rabwah train station. Some of those testifying before the Samdani commission had vaguely suggested that the violence at the train station may have had something to do with bad behavior toward local women.[74] Ahmadi or not, rural and small town Punjabis are often quite conservative when it comes to gender norms, and matters of honor have long been important in people's sense of self-worth. It would not be surprising if some Punjabi Ahmadis had reacted violently in defense of their women. Some reports suggested that a student of the medical college had gone so far as to expose himself at the station.[75] If true, this could not but have provoked deep anger in the local community, indeed more than anti-Ahmadi slogans by themselves would. Members of the anti-Ahmadi campaign put their own spin on such embarrassing reports. Apart from denials that anyone had misbehaved with women,[76] it was alleged that the Ahmadi administration in Rabwah had "reared some girls" specifically for the purpose of being able to accuse unwanted people of harassment and to have them punished accordingly.[77] This may have sufficed for those who would put nothing past the Ahmadis. Yet, it is not hard to imagine that at least some among the ʿulama would have been deeply troubled by the alleged behavior of the medical college students.

The long history of suspicion, even hostility, between the products of modern education and those schooled in madrasas is worth briefly recalling here. A generation before the Rabwah incident, current and former college students had been at the helm of the movement for Pakistan, and the ʿulama opposing the demand for a separate Muslim homeland had come in for some vitriolic attacks by them. The words of one religious scholar bitterly lamenting to Shabbir Ahmad ʿUsmani the hooliganism he had witnessed at a pro-Congress rally led by Husayn Ahmad Madani in late 1945 are especially poignant in this regard:

> It felt like all the people [disrupting Madani's speech] had not just bid farewell to their religiosity and morals but had also turned from human beings into demons and animals.... They hurled filthy curses [at Madani] and shamelessly displayed a bestial and satanic behavior....

Then they resorted to mercilessly showering the gathering with rocks, which injured fifty or more people, some of whom remained unconscious all night.... Those engaging in such acts were no mere ignorant commoners. They were led by people educated at [English] colleges and universities who, at present, are the moving spirit and the life-blood of the Muslim League.[78]

As `ulama like Bannuri, the convener and head of the anti-Ahmadi coalition, faced embarrassing reminders about having been on the wrong side of the movement for Pakistan, they would have recalled as well the vitriol of those earlier years. For all its contribution toward bringing the Ahmadi issue to the very center of national attention, the alleged behavior of the medical students could scarcely have done much to put to rest the `ulama's caricatures of people of this ilk.

By early September 1974, a constitutional amendment had declared the Ahmadis a non-Muslim minority. This had followed an in-camera session of the National Assembly, the lower house of the Pakistani parliament, during much of August.[79] It would be another decade before the Ahmadis came back into the spotlight. On this occasion, the issue had to do with whether, being non-Muslims, the Ahmadis could refer to themselves *as* Muslims, their places of worship as mosques, their call to prayers as *azan*, and so forth. The answer was no, and in 1984, the president, General Zia al-Haqq, issued an ordinance amending the Pakistan penal code and making it an offense for the Ahmadis to "pose" as Muslims or to employ terms commonly used for the early caliphs and for the companions (*sahaba*) of the Prophet Muhammad to refer to associates or successors of Mirza Ghulam Ahmad. Such Ahmadi usage "outrage[d] the religious feelings of Muslims" and it was henceforth subject to criminal prosecution.[80] These regulations—sections 298-B and 298-C—of the penal code are part of what are commonly known as the blasphemy laws, which have been repeatedly invoked to target all perceived sacrilege, by Ahmadis as well as others. Other blasphemy laws include sections 295 (on defiling holy places), 295-A and 298 (insulting religious sensibilities), 295-B (desecrating the Qur'an), 298-A (insulting holy personages), and 295-C (insulting the Prophet Muhammad).[81] Already in 1952, the governor of Sindh had suggested to the prime minister that the government invoke the relevant provisions of the penal code in order to prevent the Ahmadis from propagating their belief in the prophethood of Mirza Ghulam Ahmad, "which necessarily wounds the religious feelings of the rest of the believers in Islam who constitute the bulk of the population." The governor's point was that freedom of conscience and expression was necessarily subservient to the law and to apply the legal provisions in question to the Ahmadis would therefore not jeopardize the government's liberal credentials.[82] In explaining the decision to declare the Ahmadis a non-Muslim minority, Bhutto, too, had been concerned to present it as an expression of the democratic will of the people.[83] Zia al-Haqq was perturbed by no such worries in 1984.

The draconian 1984 ordinance points to anxieties of its own, principally that the 1974 constitutional amendment had failed to effectively exclude the Ahmadis from the fold of the Muslim community, that in passing themselves off as Muslims they were continuing to undermine Islam from within while injuring Muslim sensibilities. However, no nationwide anti-Ahmadi movement had preceded the 1984 ordinance, as had been the case with the 1974 amendment. Instead, it was preceded by the recommendation of the Council of Islamic Ideology that the Ahmadis not be allowed to call their places of worship mosques or their calls to prayer azan, for these were "Muslim symbols."[84] Many among the `ulama seized on this recommendation and pressured the government to implement it.[85] To furnish the regime with Islamic symbols of its own, the council had also recommended that men not attending the Friday congregational prayers be fined, that women be required to cover themselves in public, and that women athletes not be allowed to participate in sporting events abroad.[86]

As with the 1953 agitation in the Punjab and the 1974 countrywide movement, the 1984 ordinance should also be seen against a wider political context, again without reducing it to that context. Things were not going well for General Zia al-Haqq. Since coming to power in 1977, he had promised several times to hold general elections and had put them off each time. Eleven political parties had come together in 1981 to organize the Movement for the Restoration of Democracy (MRD), a powerful challenge to the regime, and even some of the religio-political parties that had initially been excited by the military regime's program of Islamization had begun to grow weary of Zia al-Haqq's promises. The Jama`at-i Islami had lent valuable support to the regime in its early years, but not everyone in the party was happy about this. In 1983, the regime banned student organizations, of which the Jama`at-affiliated Islami Jam`iyyat-i Talaba was among the most powerful. This led to new, internal, pressure on the party's leadership to adopt a less accommodating course toward the government.[87] Though the `ulama had benefited much from the patronage that came with Zia al-Haqq's Islamization, they, too, had misgivings about what this Islamization entailed in terms of greater governmental regulation of the religious sphere. Many among them applauded the anti-Ahmadi ordinance. But it did little in the long run to shore up the regime's religious credentials, let alone its legitimacy. Nor did it put to rest anxieties about religious minorities.

The Shi`a

Shi`i imprecations against `A'isha, a wife of the Prophet Muhammad who had gone to war against `Ali, their first imam, or their hostility to `Umar, the second caliph, can be at least as offensive to Sunnis as the Ahmadi practice of referring to the head of their own community as a caliph, or *his* associates as companions, or his wife as the mother of the believers. In Pakistan, with a population that is overwhelmingly Sunni, the `ulama have often demanded restrictions on Shi`i Muharram rituals, when such imprecations tend to find formal expression. As a religious scholar observed at a national conference of the `ulama convened by Zia al-Haqq in August 1980, "if, today, anyone publishes insulting literature about the government, the president, or some other high official, he is immediately prosecuted for it. The only person who is not prosecuted is the one who insults God and His Prophet, the noble companions, the pure members of the [Prophet's] household, and the Rashidun caliphs. There is no provision in the law to bring such a person to court."[88]

That would change later the same year. Significantly, the first of General Zia al-Haqq's blasphemy laws was directed not against the Ahmadis but rather against the Shi`a. The legislation did not mention any group in particular, in marked contrast with the 1984 ordinance, which would single out the Ahmadis. Yet, there could be little doubt that, in making any insult to the companions and family of the Prophet a criminal offense (section 298-A of the Pakistan penal code), the intended target was Shi`i ritual revilement of figures venerated by the Sunnis.[89] It was also a way of settling scores with a community whose leadership had publicly challenged the regime earlier that year, as we will observe.

A deeper anxiety had to do, as it did in case of the Ahmadis, with the perceived outsized influence of the Shi`i minority in political life and the religio-cultural sphere. Jinnah was a Shi`i.[90] For the most part, he was keen to stay clear of sectarian entanglements. This was in line, of course, with the modernist view that true Islam had nothing to do with such things. But it was also good politics, since any sectarian trappings would have been fatal to his aspiration to be recognized, by the British, the Indian National Congress and, indeed, by the Muslims, as the exclusive voice of a unified Muslim community. His fleeting attendance in 1938 of the annual session of the All India Shi`a Conference was an exception.[91] As he put it a year later, the sectarian conflict in Lucknow was nothing less than "the surreptitious machinations of the enemies of the Musalmans [to] create and exploit the differences between them."[92] Accordingly, Jinnah kept his Muslim League firmly out of any engagement with the Madh-i sahaba conflict in Lucknow. Indeed, as the governor of the United Provinces reported to the viceroy in May 1939, "Jinnah had threatened excommunication to any Muslim Leaguer who should try to intervene."[93] Jinnah's critics among the Sunni `ulama thought nonetheless that if nothing else disqualified him from establishing a Muslim homeland, his Shi`ism sufficed to do so. His nemesis, Husayn Ahmad Madani, was most blunt on this score. He had been a key figure on the Sunni side in the Madh-i sahaba agitation in Lucknow, and he could never get past the fact that Jinnah was a Shi`i.[94] Using a derogatory term for the Shi`a in a letter written weeks after the establishment of Pakistan, Madani referred to Jinnah as a "self-described Rafidi" and observed that his new state was ruled by "heretics and apostates." One could hardly pray for such a state, though its Sunni inhabitants did merit one's sympathy.[95] The letter went on to quote Raja Muhammad Amir Ahmad Khan of Mahmudabad (d. 1973), a rich Shi`i philanthropist and politician, as telling a Shi`i gathering some years earlier: "Our great leader [Jinnah] is fortunately a true Shi`i. The history of Islam is undergoing change. Today, all the Sunnis of India have bowed their head in obedience to a descendant of the [first Shi`i] imam and they are willing to lay down their lives at his command."[96] It is taken for granted by Madani that any self-respecting Sunni would be disturbed by such words. The irony, however, which could not have been lost on the modernists, is that `ulama like Madani were far more open to living together with non-Muslims than they were with Muslims of the wrong kind.

Besides Jinnah, two Pakistani heads of the state—Iskandar Mirza (1955–58) and Yahya Khan (1969–71)—were Shi`is. Neither is remembered kindly in the country, though this has nothing to do with their Shi`ism. Iskandar Mirza, the last governor-general of the country and, with the adoption of the constitution in 1956, its first president, was the person who imposed martial law in 1958 before being forced to relinquish power to General Ayub Khan. It was to General Yahya Khan that Ayub Khan would, in turn, hand over the reins of the government. Yahya Khan declared another martial law, and it was under his watch that the province of East Pakistan seceded to become Bangladesh. General Muhammad Musa, Ayub Khan's commander-in-chief and subsequently his governor of West Pakistan, was also a Shi`i.[97] So was Nusrat, the wife of prime minister Zulfikar Ali Bhutto. More recently, Yusuf Reza Gilani, prime minister from 2008 to 2012, was a Shi`i.[98] Though most estimates put the Shi`a around 15 percent of the country's Muslim population, Nusrat and Benazir Bhutto were reported in 1980 to claim that the Shi`is accounted for as much as 40 percent of the armed forces. No one seems to have taken this claim seriously,[99] but it could be grounds for the sort of anxieties provoked by insinuations about Ahmadi influence on the government and *their* disproportionately large presence in the military. Worth noting, too, is the fact that Pakistan's highest military honor, the *Nishan-i Haydar*, evokes the gallantry in battle not of Abu Bakr, `Umar, or `Uthman, all revered companions of Muhammad, but rather of `Ali, the first Shi`i imam. Shi`i symbolism has also been prominent in the political rhetoric of the Muttahida Qaumi Movement (MQM), a Karachi-based party that draws its support from the migrants (*muhajir*s) who had relocated to Pakistan following its birth. Some of the regions from which the Urdu-speaking muhajirs had emigrated were centers of Shi`i culture in colonial India. Since its founding in the mid-1980s, the MQM's often violent struggle—against the native population of Sindh; against the Pashtuns who have come to settle in large numbers in a city, Karachi, that the MQM sees as its own; against a Punjabi-dominated state seen as indifferent to its claims—has often featured Shi`i motifs.[100]

In *local* contexts—for instance, in rural southern Punjab—the nexus of Shi`ism and political power has been most visible not in the person of an occasional president, prime minister, or a military official, but rather in that of the area's landlord. As the example of Yusuf Riza Gilani suggests, however, these are not mutually exclusive positions. A number of the "feudal" magnates in the Punjab—as they are sometimes referred to in the Pakistani political lexicon—have tended to be Shi`i. Syed Abid Hussain Shah (d. 1971), a politician and pir from Jhang in the Punjab, had owned 5,300 acres; his daughter, Abida Hussain, has owned somewhat less on account of sales as well as periodic land reforms, but still enough to make her one of the biggest landowners in the country.[101] In the decades following the establishment of Pakistan, much of the leadership of the Shi`a came from the Shi`i landowners, who also provided financial backing to the country's Shi`i organizations.[102] The peasantry, by contrast, remained largely Sunni—if, for a long time, rather unselfconsciously so. Besides being at the mercy of those wielding great political and economic power, the vulnerability of this putatively disenfranchised Sunni majority was exacerbated in local contexts by other factors, too. Like the Ahmadis, and by their own acknowledgment, Shi`i `ulama have often been active proselytes for their faith.[103] While in case of the Ahmadis, this often meant proselyting to non-Muslims, a good deal of the target audience of the Shi`i preachers comprised fellow Muslims. Many Shi`i preachers viewed this audience as people who really were Shi`is in some sense, and they sought accordingly to awaken among them a proper Shi`i identity anchored in authoritative beliefs and norms.[104] For their part, Sunni activists and preachers have been no less active in trying to win followers to their own orientations. From the latter's perspective, it was unsuspecting *Sunnis* that Shi`i preaching targeted and they needed help to be able to guard against such efforts. In this narrative, an oil-rich revolutionary Iran had come to pour unprecedented resources into this proselytism, which meant that the stakes had never been higher.

But it was not just local Shi`i preaching against which downtrodden Sunnis had to be protected. There was the lure of Shi`ism itself. For all the potential of the Muharram processions to become flashpoints of sectarian conflict, they have long attracted Sunni participation. Indeed, in Lucknow in the early twentieth century, the issue was not so much Sunni rejection of such processions as it was the demand to put Sunni devotion to the Prophet's companions on public display, as a counterpoint to Shi`i revilement of them.[105] The Ahrar had taken the lead in the Madh-i sahaba controversy, yet, in 1953, even they were recruiting Punjabi villagers to the anti-Ahmadi agitation by promising them that "*Imam Hussain* [the third imam in the Shi`i reckoning] would be waiting to receive those who sipped the cup of martyrdom in this crusade against infidelity."[106] Though accompanied by much public weeping and self-flagellation, the Muharram rituals can have a carnivalesque look to them, providing much colorful entertainment, besides food and drink, to participants and onlookers. The closest some Sunnis come to rivaling such events is when they commemorate the birthday of the Prophet Muhammad or the death anniversaries of some Sufi saints. But the Shi`is, too, celebrate the birthday of the Prophet and not a few of the Shi`i rural magnates double as hereditary guardians of major Sufi shrines in the Punjab. For their part, many Sunnis of the Salafi and, to a lesser extent, Deobandi orientations frown upon devotional practices associated with the Prophet's birthday or the saints' shrines, leaving their common fellow travelers exposed to the appeal of Shi`i commemorations.

Besides its local lure, Shi`ism—its iconic figures, its symbolic imagery—has had a strong hold on Indo-Islamic high culture as well. Many Shi`a of colonial India did not consider the early modernist Shibli Nu`mani to be a friend of their religious orientation, yet Shibli had written an important book comparing the literary merits of two major elegiac poets who had made their name writing about the tragedy of Husayn.[107] In his Urdu poetry, Mawlana Muhammad Ali of the Khilafat movement had summoned up Husayn's challenge to an iniquitous regime to frame his own anti-colonial struggle. The symbolic power of Husayn's martyrdom at Karbala is also palpable in Iqbal's Persian and Urdu verse, and Shi`i preachers in Pakistan have frequently laced their discourses with his poetry.[108] In the Pakistan of the 1960s, even the great leftist poet Faiz Ahmad Faiz (d. 1984) wrote an affecting elegy for Husayn.[109] In the 1980s, Parvin Shakir, too, regularly featured Shi`i motifs in her work, which were often intertwined with searing social criticism. The following poem, which must stand for others, evokes the tribulations of Husayn's sister, Zaynab, in the aftermath of the massacre at Karbala. The voice is Shakir's, with the suggestion that the afflictions are as much hers, or any harassed woman's, as they are Zaynab's:

> From the tent of innocence
> As soon as I proceeded towards the city of justice
> From their ambush
> My killers also emerged
> With ready-to-shoot bows, targeted arrows, loaded pistols . . .
> In the city square, the judge armed with a dagger
> Streets dotted with daggers hidden in sleeves
> Every resident of the city in waiting
> Listening to the sound of my solitary litter
> Weaving the web around me with spidery skill
> Someone seeking my banner
> Another wanting my head
> Yet another desirous of my cloak . . .
> My helplessness!

Covering the face with my hair
Hands folded
Head bowed
There was only one thing on my lips—
O Forgiver, O Merciful!
O Forgiver, O Merciful! [110]

At a time when the electronic media was largely controlled by the government, as it was in Pakistan till the early years of the twenty-first century, there were added anxieties about the state media becoming purveyors of an outsized Shi`i influence. Special programming was scheduled on radio and television in Muharram, and as the `Ashura—the tenth day of the month, on which Husayn was martyred—approached, the state television bore a strikingly somber look, complete with telecasts of Shi`i ritual gatherings (*majalis*) at which the travails of Husayn and his family were recounted to great emotional effect. While many Sunni viewers watched such programs with an interest that could verge on devotion, for they too venerate the memory of Husayn, some Sunni groups worried that the Shi`a were receiving an unjustified amount of airtime. A public appeal to the prime minister, Zulfikar Ali Bhutto, in January 1977 on behalf of a number of Sunni associations of Karachi reflects such sentiments:

In this democratic age, institutions of the media are people's institutions. They are supported through taxes by the entire populace, the majority and the minority. A particular way of thinking cannot therefore be foisted upon them.... Discussing historical events and religious beliefs without taking care to present them in their proper perspective has deleterious effects.... The month of Muharram is worthy of our respect in every way. Two great instances of martyrdom took place that month [the second being that of `Umar, the second successor of Muhammad]. In honoring the practice of Moses, the Prophet [Muhammad] fasted on the tenth day of this month.... Khadija, the mother of the believers, got married this month. Noah's ark came to rest at Mt. Judi this month and God chose Abraham as his "friend" this month. Jacob saw his beloved son Joseph after forty years this month, David was forgiven [by God], Solomon's kingdom was restored to him, Job's travails came to an end, Jonah emerged unharmed from the belly of the fish, the Pharaoh drowned in the Nile, and Jesus was born—all in this month. It was in this month that the [caliphate's] Islamic secretariat [*sic*, in Urdu transliteration] was inaugurated during the caliphate of `Umar, and [his successor] `Usman's great caliphate began this month. To ignore such momentous events in the media's programming is to forget one's historical heritage, which leads to the destruction of nations.[111]

The question of whether everything mentioned in this passage did indeed take place in the month of Muharram is best set aside here. What is relevant is rather the rhetorically powerful point that one single event—the martyrdom of Husayn—had come to completely overshadow the sacred history, and pre-history, of Islam and even that one event was being presented by the national media in inaccurate ways. In other words, a Shi`i view of history was being relayed through radio and television, and it was not just people in local neigh-borhoods that were exposed to the lure of Shi`i beliefs and practices but the nation at large.

Then there was the question of how to teach Islam in schools. The Shi`a had long demanded that their distinctive doctrines be presented separately in textbooks of Islamic studies (*Islamiyyat*)—a required subject in the public school system. The Ayub Khan regime had conceded this demand in princi-ple in late 1968, but it was not until 1975 that separate textbooks of Islamic studies were instituted for Shi`i students by the government of Zulfikar Ali Bhutto. [112] These textbooks, which were later discontinued,[113] had a shared section on the Qur'an, the life and teachings of the Prophet Muhammad, and ethics (*akhlaqiyyat*); but other sections were tailored to the separate needs of students, with Shi`i textbooks detailing matters of ritual according to Shi`i law and outlining the lives of the Shi`i imams. The Sunni `ulama had resisted this Shi`i demand bitterly. In August 1973, on the very day the new constitu-tion of Pakistan was promulgated, a number of `ulama had addressed an appeal to the prime minister, of which the first item was a call upon the gov-ernment to reject this Shi`i demand. The Shi`a could have their own syllabus in their denominational schools, the statement said, since the constitution guaranteed religious freedom to all people inhabiting the country. But to allow them a separate representation on the *public* school curriculum meant that "the minority Shi`i sect was being placed on par with the predominant Sunni majority." And if this was being done for the Shi`a, the signatories of the statement asked rhetorically, what was to prevent the teachings of the Ah-madis, the Christians, and the Hindus from also being included in the sylla-bus?[114] They went on to demand restrictions on Shi`i ritual practices and on Shi`i programming on radio and television and sought, as a preview of what was to come the following year, to have the Ahmadis declared a non-Muslim minority.

Worries that a minority was standing in the way of the majority's ability to realize its aspirations would arise most forcefully when General Zia al-Haqq began his campaign of Islamization in 1979. Among its highlights, as would be recalled, was the state's collection of zakat, which Muslims of means are required by the shari`a to pay annually on their wealth and property. Though zakat has sometimes been collected by the state—the first caliph, Abu Bakr, had gone to war against Arab tribes that had refused to send the proceeds of zakat to the central government following the death of the Prophet—Muslims, for the most part, have tended to informally disburse it among the needy in their local circles. Zia al-Haqq's implementation of zakat laws was a departure from that practice. It was also based on the norms of the Hanafi school of Sunni law, to which most Sunnis in South Asia have long adhered. The implementation of zakat laws in 1980 was an extension of state power in a new direction, presided over by a regime that had only recently executed the former prime minister. It immediately invited challenges. There were many among the Sunnis who complained bitterly about being deprived by state-owned banks of a portion of their hard-earned savings in the name of zakat. But it was from the Shi`i quarter that the most organized resistance to these laws came. Shi`i leaders argued that their religious law had its own specifications about zakat and they contested the government's right to collect it according to religious norms they did not recognize. Emboldened by the example of the street power that had helped topple the Iranian monarchy in early 1979, the Shi`a held massive sit-ins in the capital, Islamabad, in mid-1980 to press for their demands. The government—a martial law administration, no less—was taken aback by the determination of the protestors and forced to capitulate. The Shi`a were to be subject to their own laws, as administered by their religious authorities, when it came to zakat.

This was an embarrassing moment for the government, but it was also a deeply unhappy time for those Sunnis who had long had misgivings about unwanted Shi`i influence. Issues much larger than the immediate controversy over zakat were at stake here. To the extent that people believed that Zia al-Haqq was really trying to implement Islamic law in Pakistan rather than to justify and prolong his rule by invoking Islam, the Shi`i challenge to him revived the specter of a silent majority held hostage by a rowdy minority. But there was more. From the time of Pakistan's inception, `ulama and Islamists had been trying to counter modernist objections that a state whose inhabitants belonged to many different Islamic orientations could not possibly implement Islamic law in a way that would satisfy them all. Their usual response had been that, while people were free to follow their legal norms in matters of personal status (notably marriage, divorce, and inheritance), Islamic public law had to be guided by the school of law followed by the majority of the country's population.[115] It was to that idea that the Shi`a now represented a challenge.

The Shi`a wanted full recognition of their separate religious law in all respects. As Mufti Ja`far Husayn (d. 1983), the most influential leader of the Shi`i community at the time, put it in a defiant speech at an `ulama convention presided over by General Zia al-Haqq in 1980,

> No one can eliminate juridical disagreements. They are a reality and one should not shut one's eyes to them. Instead, we should acknowledge their existence and give people the liberty to act according to their

various juridical orientations. This is what justice demands and only in this way can we succeed in the implementation of Islamic law. If, on the other hand, the views of one school of thought are imposed upon others, success [in implementing Islamic law] would not be possible for us.[116]

Such statements hinted darkly at the Shi`a's ability to derail Islamization. In the late 1980s and the early 1990s, Shi`i groups would, indeed, be vocal opponents of the various "shari`at bills" that promised to bring Pakistan closer to its elusive Islamic ideals. Represented at the time by the Movement for the Implementation of Ja`fari (that is, Twelver Shi`i) Law (Tahrik-i nifaz-i fiqh-i Ja`fariyya, or TNFJ), the Shi`a were not alone in such opposition. Yet, the loud Shi`i challenge to such initiatives would have done nothing to assuage anxieties that it bore some responsibility for preventing the implementation of Islamic law in Pakistan. The TNFJ's very name created suspicion that the only law the Shi`a wanted to see implemented was their own.[117]

Though the Shi`a of Pakistan had been mobilizing with unusual intensity since the late 1960s,[118] the new ring of defiance in their collective voice had much to do with the success of the Iranian revolution. This was not lost on their Sunni rivals. As with the Ahmadis, there were anxieties that the Pakistani Shi`a were more loyal to their own religious guides—in this case, Ayatollah Khomeini—than they were to Pakistan. As it happened, neither the Shi`i leadership in Pakistan nor the revolutionaries in Iran did much to allay such fears. Shi`i leaders in Pakistan were sometimes caught saying that they would "take orders only from Ayatollah Khomeini."[119] And they urged their countrymen to see Khomeini as the leader and the "hero" not just of the Shi`a, but of all Muslims.[120] Iran, for its part, made no bones about its desire to see its revolution exported to other regions of the Muslim world. `Ali Khamene'i, the president of Iran, was quoted by Pakistani newspapers as saying in 1984 that "Iran's Islamic revolution had spread in every direction and no power could succeed in stopping it."[121] Such statements were not designed to bring comfort to Arab capitals or, for that matter, to Sunni religious circles in Pakistan. It was not uncommon for the Iranian embassy and cultural centers to also sponsor cultural and religious events in Pakistan, again creating considerable discontent in some Sunni circles.

There were at least two other ways in which the case of Iran raised uncomfortable questions in Pakistan. First, though there is a Sunni minority in Iran, it has never enjoyed the sort of recognition in terms of state law that the Shi`a of Pakistan were claiming for themselves from the Zia al-Haqq regime. This was brought home pointedly after the revolution of 1979, when the Iranian regime took it upon itself to implement Islamic law in its Twelver Shi`i form. Prominent Sunnis were not slow, sometimes tongue in cheek, to point to the example of Iran as something Pakistan ought to emulate. At the `ulama convention of 1980, Zafar Ahmad Ansari (d. 1991), who was associated with the Jama`at-i Islami and had played a key role in the parliamentary proceedings on the Ahmadi issue in the summer of 1974, referred to the recently ratified Iranian constitution as a beacon for other countries. The Iranians have decided, he said,

> that the state religion will be Islam and the [official] school of law is that of the Twelvers, which is the school adhered to by the vast majority of Iran's Muslims. The [majoritarian] argument on the basis of which they have made the Twelver school the official school [of the state] is just, reasonable, realistic and practical. Different sorts of dispute would have arisen if they had allowed any form of ambiguity here. With this decision, they have shut the door to any such conflict.... They have also provided that other schools of Islamic law—the Hanafi, the Shafi`i, ... the Maliki, the Hanbali, the Zaydi—will be entitled to full respect and that their adherents would be free to perform their [personal] religious rites according to their own laws.[122]

In other words, the Twelver Shi`is of Iran had made it clear to their non-Shi`i compatriots that, while enjoying their rights, they would have to live as a religious minority. The implication, left unstated by Zafar Ahmad Ansari but frequently enunciated by others, was that the Shi`a of Pakistan were overstepping acceptable limits in demanding more than Iran, to which they looked up for guidance, was willing to give to its own Muslim minorities. And Iran was guilty of double standards in implicitly supporting Pakistani Shi`i demands.

Second, in the years following the revolution, Iranian authorities did not flinch when it came to the implementation of Islamic criminal law, the hudud— the starkest marker, so far as the Islamists and many `ulama are concerned, of a state's Islamic identity. Hands were amputated for theft and people were stoned to death for unlawful sexual intercourse.[123] Though Saudi Arabia had long implemented such punishments, their incidence was considerably less frequent there than it was in Iran in the 1980s.[124] The real contrast was with Pakistan, however. As the headline of one national newspaper had giddily announced on the occasion of Zia al-Haqq's promulgation of the Hudood Ordinances in February 1979, "the thief's hand will be chopped off, the person committing adultery will be publicly stoned to death."[125] Yet, until the end of his rule in 1988, or in subsequent years for that matter, no thieves had their hands cut off and no adulterers were stoned to death. The Pakistani Taliban would later do such things, as will be seen, but they would do it as a challenge to the state's authority, not on its behalf. Flogging was the closest the state itself came to maintaining the symbolism of hudud, but even that was meant more to intimidate political opponents than to meet any traditional juridical specifications.

Idiosyncratic punishments in the name of hudud were already too much for human rights activists at home and abroad. They were too little for many Islamists and ʿulama, however, for they could hardly mistake them for the real thing. Here is what Ihsan Ilahi Zahir (d. 1987), a religious scholar of the Ahl-i Hadith orientation and a politician, had to say in 1980 about the non-implementation of the hudud, with General Zia al-Haqq in attendance:

> With apologies to those convinced of gradualism [in the implementation of Islamic law] ... this process of gradualism has remained unfinished for thirty-two years since the inception of Pakistan.... A [real] beginning does have to be made one day. When it is, it will have to be marked by the cutting off of the thief's hand and the stoning of the adulterer to death and the flogging of the person who drinks. Some people say that Islamic laws ought to be implemented only after the society has reformed itself [literally: become good]. But once the society has reformed itself, are we to flog [our fellow scholar] Mawlana ʿAbd al-Rahman! ... After all, it is *to* reform society that people are flogged. It is to eliminate people who rob others of virtue that they are stoned to death. It is the hands of those plundering the property of others that are cut off.... Mr. President, with respect, we do not doubt your intentions. But as one says [in such situations], there are things that are done with good intention but without enthusiasm. I do not want it to be said about the chief of the Pakistani military that he did something listlessly. We want [to be able] to say that the military chief has taken a step with the same determination that has always been characteristic of the Pakistani military and of which the nation is proud. There is nothing to be ashamed of here.[126]

In view of this mock deference of Zahir toward General Zia al-Haqq, it is not surprising that he eventually became one of the military ruler's more ardent critics, not only in the name of democracy but also in that of Islam, which he took the president to be cynically manipulating for his own ends.[127] Yet, the contrast with Iran would have perturbed even those less critical of Zia al-Haqq.

Pakistani Shiʿi ʿulama played up such contrasts. In an article written shortly after the Iranian revolution, Safdar Husayn Najafi (d. 1989) commented approvingly on the desire of many Pakistani ʿulama and intellectuals to revive the practice of ijtihad in readying Islamic law for implementation by the modern state. But since ijtihad had been defunct for centuries in the Sunni world, it would, he said, take a long time for the Sunnis to develop the requisite ability for it. The Shiʿa, on the other hand, had had a continuous tradition of ijtihad, and Pakistan ought to seek the guidance of scholars from Iran and Iraq. Najafi, the head of the Jamiʿat al-muntazir, a major Shiʿi madrasa in Lahore, and the translator into Urdu of some of Khomeini's key works, continued:

> If you really want to see the establishment of an Islamic system in Pakistan, you ought to request Grand Ayatollah Khomeini to send one or more mujtahids to Pakistan. All issues, individual or collective, political, economic or social, should be placed before them and they should look into them. Lawyers, judges, and `ulama should also benefit from these [mujtahids], so that a purely Islamic system can be established here. For otherwise, the laws that are enacted in the name of Islam by the non-mujtahids and by those who are not `ulama [of the requisite standard] will have nothing to do with Islam. For God's sake, consider this matter with a cool head! If you like this advice, then do not let sectarian prejudice or a false ego prevent you from acting upon it.[128]

Such swipes simultaneously at Pakistani nationalism—only by looking to the scholars of Iran and Iraq could Pakistan hope to establish a properly Islamic system at home—*and* at traditions of Sunni scholarship reveal much about Shi`i self-confidence during these years in Pakistan. They could not have endeared the Shi`i leadership to increasingly jittery Sunnis.

What made such remarks especially odious was the fact that the Sunnis, too, were going through a religious revival, which would have primed them to view the Shi`a as not only taunting them but as also standing in the way of realizing their own aspirations. As seen in chapter 3, socioeconomic changes from the mid-1970s had been fueling a new religiosity in the country, with a concomitant growth in mosques and madrasas. The articulation of sharp sectarian boundaries often accompanied this process. By the mid-1980s, with significant help from the effects of Zia al-Haqq's Islamization, militant sectarian groups had begun to emerge in the Punjab. The first of these to come to nation-wide attention was a Deobandi organization, the Sipah-i Sahaba. As its name announced, it was an "army" (*sipah*) mobilized to defend the besmirched companions (sahaba) of the Prophet. It also stood for defending the interests of the common man against the rapacious rural magnates. It is no accident that it was founded in Jhang, a town in an identically named district whose majority Sunnis had long been dominated by a Shi`i landed elite. The organization's founder, Haqq Nawaz Jhangawi, was a small-time mosque preacher with a reputation for spending long hours in local courts helping illiterate litigants. In 1988, he went on to challenge the aforementioned Syeda Abida Hussain, a Shi`i, in elections to the National Assembly. Hussain was never apologetic about her "feudal" power base. For, as she later put it in an autobiography, "[i]n my opinion, feudalism is a mindset: anybody powerful can come under the ambit of 'feudal.' … Feudal, in the context of rural Pakistan, only means flowing from a tradition, often upholding values of courtesy and kindliness, caring for those less privileged, sharing your bread, and nurturing relationships that are not always transactional."[129] Needless to say, Jhangawi and his supporters did not share that view. He lost the election, but his unusually strong showing at the polls was seen by his followers as a moral victory. After his assassination in 1990, his successors to the Sipah-i Sahaba leadership would win a series of elections, with substantial support not only from the rural peasantry but also from the urban Sunni bourgeoisie. The Shi`a responded with militant organizations of their own, with much bloodletting on all sides.[130]

Though the Sipah-i Sahaba did not put it this way, it was premised on the view that an Islamic state of the sort that General Zia al-Haqq was proposing—one in which all Islamic orientations could find a place by virtue of their shared allegiance to Islamic law—was unacceptable. Instead, in a mirror image of what post-revolution Iran had achieved, it wanted Pakistan to become a Sunni state, not just by way of its demographic weight, which made it one already, but by constitution and law. Not an undefined Islam but Sunni Islam was to be the religion of the state; the Shi`is, like the Ahmadis, were to live as a non-Muslim minority, and the Muharram commemorations were to be limited to their devotional centers as private affairs, if not proscribed altogether. The guiding examples in all matters of the state would be those of Muhammad's first successors, the Rashidun, and their death anniversaries were to be national holidays.[131] In an echo of the modernists' aspiration to bring the fruits of Islam to all humanity, but also as an alternative to the US-led global order, the Sipah-i Sahaba leadership sought to make the example of the Rashidun the basis of a "caliphal world order."[132] This would also be an antidote, of course, to Iranian aspirations to "export" their Shi`i revolution.

The Sipah-i Sahaba was banned by General Pervez Musharraf in January 2002, alongside a number of other militant organizations.[133] The core group has continued to exist under other names, however. Its most notorious splinter group, the Lashkar-i Jhangawi ("the battalion of [Haqq Nawaz] Jhangawi"), though also banned, has worked closely with groups affiliated with the Pakistani Taliban. Its members are sometimes also referred to as the Punjabi Taliban, to distinguish them from other, predominantly Pashtun, Taliban of the Frontier province.

The sort of anxieties the Ahmadis and the Shi`a have provoked in at least some Sunni circles have tended to revolve around rather different issues. In some ways, the difference is obvious, of course. Despite Ahmadi professions to the contrary, they are taken by the Sunnis to deny a fundamental tenet of the Muslim faith—the finality of Muhammad's prophethood—whereas the Shi`a are not, and it would be safe to say that far more Muslims have come to consider the Ahmadis as beyond the pale of Islam than have ever held a similar view as regards the Shi`a. Yet, the fact remains that many among the `ulama consider the Shi`a to be unbelievers, too. It was not clear even to Jawaharlal Nehru, as he had put it in commenting on a statement on the Ahmadis by Muhammad Iqbal, why the Ahmadis should have had greater trouble being accommodated into the community of Muslims than the Shi`a.[134] Nehru was referring to the *Isma`ili* Shi`a, who, as he saw it, "ascribe certain divine or semi-divine attributes"[135] to their imam, rather than to the more restrained Twelvers; but many Sunni scholars see even Twelver views of their imams as grievously trespassing on things that properly belong only to God and to His Prophet. In 1952, not long before the anti-Ahmadi agitation in the Punjab, the prominent Pakistani modernist Khalifa Abdul Hakim had warned darkly about what awaited the Shi`a at the hands of the Sunni religious leadership:

> The vice chancellor of a Pakistani university recently told me that he asked a leading religious scholar, who ... had migrated from India to Pakistan some time ago, about an Islamic sect. He gave the fatwa that the extremists (*ghali*) among them are liable to the death penalty and the non-extremists are subject to other punishments. Asked about another sect, whose members included many millionaires, he said that they were all liable to capital punishment.... Another prominent religious scholar remarked that for now we have declared jihad against one sect, but, God willing, we shall deal with the others after we have succeeded in this [venture].[136]

What then might be said to be different, apart from matters of doctrine, about the Ahmadi and the Shi`i challenges to conservative Sunni sensibilities in Pakistan?[137]

Misgivings about modernism have loomed especially large among the kinds of anxiety the Ahmadis have aroused in particular Sunni circles. This is not only because the Ahmadis themselves hold certain modernist positions, notably a derisive attitude toward the `ulama and the Islamists, an insistence on adapting Islam to changing conditions, and doubts about the state's implementation of Islamic law.[138] The Islamists and the `ulama have also seen the failure of successive Pakistani regimes to remove the Ahmadis from "key positions" in what professes to be an Islamic state as a stark illustration of the modernists' unwillingness to live up to their Islamic commitments. And the anti-Ahmadi agitation has tended to flare up in Pakistan at times of especially intense confrontation between the modernists, on the one hand, and the `ulama and the Islamists, on the other.[139] Some `ulama seem to have recognized as much, though not quite in these terms. In a conversation with the modernist Fazlur Rahman in the summer of 1974, Muhammad Yusuf Bannuri, who was leading the anti-Ahmadi agitation at the time, "admitted that the Ahmadi question was primarily socio-political rather than strictly religious (otherwise, he admitted, one would also have to declare several other sects, e.g., the Isma`ilis, as non-Muslims)."[140] In making this extraordinary remark,

Bannuri appears to have been thinking primarily of the Ahmadis running a "state within a state." But it also signals larger apprehensions about a modernist elite that was all too willing to sell the interests of Islam and of Pakistan to a people threatening them both. The Shi`a, too, have always been well-represented among the modernists, both in colonial India and after the establishment of Pakistan, but they have not called up the specter of modernism in anything like the way the Ahmadis did. Put differently, Shi`ism has never been intertwined with modernism the way Ahmadism has been, and in Pakistan—unlike the case of the All India Shi`a Conference in late colonial India—the leadership of the Shi`a has tended to be in the hands of traditionally educated religious scholars rather than of the modernists.

Yet, substantial though they were, the anxieties generated by the Ahmadis among the `ulama and the Islamists seem to be outweighed in the end by those provoked in particular circles by the Shi`a.[141] This is not particularly surprising since Ahmadi prophetology is so directly at odds with mainstream Islamic beliefs that it has been a relatively simpler matter to exclude the Ahmadis from the fold of the Muslim community. That they were not formally excluded for so long is, as the `ulama and the Islamists see it, an indictment of modernist insincerity in matters Islamic. The Shi`a are harder to exclude, and this makes for greater unease among their foes. The Shi`i belief in, inter alia, the sinlessness and the legitimist claims of their imams is anathema to many Sunni `ulama, but Sunnis, too, venerate Shi`i figures from early Islam. They decidedly do not revere Mirza Ghulam Ahmad and his successors. The devotional practices of the Barelawis, a major doctrinal orientation among South Asian Sunnis, echo Shi`i practices, and vice versa, leading many Deobandi reformists and Sunni sectarians to see Shi`ism as pervading the ranks of unsuspecting Sunnis. By contrast, and despite Ahmadi proselytism, there is little indication of Ahmadi beliefs ever having become pervasive among people. If anything, the Ahmadis have often been castigated, as they were by Iqbal, precisely for setting themselves apart from the larger Muslim community. There is likewise little to suggest any Ahmadi effort to use the national media to broadcast their own religious views. Though there were allegations, during the 1974 agitation, that influential Ahmadis in the Ministry of Information were trying to control how the agitation was being reported, this was a quite different matter than the anxiety that Shi`i norms were being actively disseminated through radio and television. Then there is the fact that the Shi`is are much more numerous than the Ahmadis and that they have been willing and able to respond in kind to violent Sunni attacks on them. In the late 1980s and the early 1990s, radical Shi`i organizations were no less active than those of the Sunnis, and it is not just leaders of militant Sunni groups but also some prominent Sunni scholars who were assassinated, often as a prelude to cycles of further violence on both sides.

Although individual Ahmadis and their places of worship continue occasionally to be targeted by militants and vigilantes, worries about Ahmadism appear largely to have receded into the past. Besides what has been said so far, this may be a function of the fact that there is little left to do to this harassed community. Modernism, much weakened as an intellectual force from what it was in the 1950s and the 1960s, continues to provoke conservative anxieties, but no longer in relation to the question of Ahmadism. Instead, apprehensions about modernism have migrated in recent decades to other issues, notably to blasphemy, which merits a brief comment here.

Blasphemy retains its link with the Ahmadis, of course, for it was against them that some of Zia al-Haqq's regulations were directed and they have not quite ceased to be victims of violence on grounds of blasphemy.[142] In 1993, in a majority decision upholding the 1984 ordinance, the Supreme Court had explicitly characterized some of the writings of Mirza Ghulam Ahmad on the Prophet Muhammad, and on Jesus, as blasphemous and had appeared even to condone vigilante action against the Ahmadis: "Mirza Sahib could have been convicted and punished, by an English Court, for the offence of blasphemy, under the Blasphemy Act, 1679 [sic], with a term of imprisonment.... Can then anyone blame a Muslim if he loses control of himself on hearing, reading or seeing such blasphemous material as has been produced by Mirza Sahib?"[143]

The net that accusations of blasphemy have come to cast since the 1990s is much wider, however. Besides Muslims, it has ensnared a disproportionate number of Pakistani Christians, mostly of an extremely humble background, who have found themselves accused of defiling pages from the Qur'an or of disparaging the Prophet.[144] Though petty disputes at local levels seem to lurk behind some at least of these accusations, they also have a broader context. Like the Ahmadis, Pakistani Christians are often seen in conservative Muslim circles as a reminder of colonialism's effort to undermine Islam, in this instance through proselytism with promises of material gain. The work of Western charitable organizations in contemporary Pakistan is viewed likewise as a thinly disguised means of seducing Muslims desperate for medical and educational assistance away from their religion.[145] When acts of violence against members of the Christian community make international headlines, as they often do, the media coverage tends in turn to be taken as proof of Western efforts to embarrass the Pakistani government and to pressure it to rein in the Islamists and the ʿulama. Needless to say, such perceptions are not a mark of solidarity with the government in question; they serve, rather, to reinforce the conviction that the government's own sympathies lie with the wrong side—with Western and Westernized liberals rather than the pious local Muslims. Members of the governing elite have sometime paid dearly for being seen as exemplifying this narrative. Around the time that the Taliban were coming to power in Afghanistan with the active support of her government, Benazir Bhutto was assailed by religio-political groups for criticizing a lower court's verdict of blasphemy against a fourteen-year-old Christian and for helping him find refuge in Germany.[146] In November 2010, Salman Taseer, the governor of the Punjab, was branded an apostate for his criticism of blasphemy laws and his efforts for the release of a Pakistani Christian woman who was in prison for alleged blasphemy. As the protestors put it on that occasion, such efforts represented "a West-sponsored movement against blasphemy laws through Western-funded NGOs and secular lobbies in Pakistan."[147] Less than six weeks later, the governor was assassinated by one of his own security guards.[148] The question of blasphemy is not reducible to anxieties about modernism, any more than is the Ahmadi question. Nonetheless, both have had a good deal to do with those anxieties.

The Shiʿa, for their part, though also implicated in the question of blasphemy, have tended to call in question the very project of an Islamic state. While the ʿulama and the Islamists routinely lay much of the blame for the failure to implement Islamic law at the doorstep of the modernizing governing elite, it is Shiʿi political agitation that had most conspicuously thwarted progress on that path at a time when, in the early years of Zia al-Haqq, the country had apparently come closer to it than it ever has. That wound has not healed. What makes it worse is the mostly unacknowledged but very real worry that, even without the Shiʿa, there would be no grand consensus on how to define or implement Islamic law. Such anxieties are deeper than those evoked by the Ahmadis, for they go to the very heart of unresolved issues of Islamic identity in Pakistan.[149]

CHAPTER SIX

The Contested Terrain of Sufism

SUFI THOUGHT AND PRACTICE have long pervaded life in South Asia, including that of the Muslim minorities discussed in the previous chapter. As observed, many rural magnates in the Punjab are not only Shi`i but also serve as the hereditary keepers of revered Sufi shrines. Devotional practices at local levels are, moreover, often inflected with norms of Sufi piety, and this has been as true of the Sunnis as it has of the Shi`a. It is such practices that Sunni and Shi`i reformers have sought to rein in, and sectarian organizations like the Sipah-i Sahaba and its successors have likewise militated against them in a quest for a more "authentic," textually anchored Islam. Yet, the symbolism of the Sipah-i Sahaba, too, had an aspect of Sufi devotionalism to it. The Rashidun caliphs were revered in a manner reminiscent not just of the Shi`i imams but also the Sufi masters of old, whom the leadership sometimes quoted alongside the Qur'an and the Prophet.[1] The Ahmadis, for their part, have tended to view the founder of their community in ways that can accord well with Sufi ways of communicating with God, and with Sufi claims to privileged knowledge and authority. Though we will return to some implications of this point later, the central concern of this chapter is different, viz, how Sufism itself has fared in Pakistan. Addressing this matter requires once again that we take a broad historical view that also encompasses colonial South Asia.

Three sets of questions will guide our discussion here. First, how have Muslim modernists critiqued Sufi thought and practice? How have the `ulama sought to curb what they see as the excesses of Sufism? And what challenges have the Islamists posed to Sufi devotionalism? My second set of questions concerns the ways in which Sufism has continued, for all the challenges it has faced, to exert its influence on rival trends. For instance, how has Sufism shaped modernist thought? In what ways have the governing elite drawn on Sufi symbolism in efforts to bolster their legitimacy? What place does Sufi thought and piety still occupy in the world of the Deobandis, who have often been keen to reform what they view as out of bounds Sufism? How have the Islamists, too, sought, as I will argue they have, to calibrate their attitude toward Sufi devotional piety in order to accommodate it into their worldview? My third set of questions has to do with whether one can speak of a certain decline of Sufism relative to other religious trends in Pakistan? What might be some indications of such decline and how are we to account for it?

Challenging Sufism

It is well-known that Iqbal's poetry is suffused with images, motifs, and ideas drawn from Persian Sufism and that the great Sufi poet Jalal al-din Rumi is, arguably, one of the strongest intellectual influences on his thought. Iqbal's philosophical writings in English also reveal significant engagement with the medieval Sufi tradition. Unlike many other modernists, who have tended to see the intellectual history of Islam as marked by a thoroughgoing sterility at least since the twelfth or the thirteenth century CE, Iqbal took a rather more nuanced view. He, too, saw the legal tradition as moribund since about that time, but Sufi thought remained, for him, a crucial site of intellectual creativity. He also believed, in what he surely saw as a way of highlighting Sufism's intellectual significance, that some prominent Sufis had hit upon ideas that had impressive parallels with those of modern, Western philosophers. Persian Sufism had, moreover, found the perfect balance between the action-orientation of monotheistic faiths and the proclivity of the Indian Vedantists toward pure thought: "the secret of the vitality of Sufism is the complete view of human nature upon which it is based. It has survived orthodox persecutions and political revolutions, because it appeals to human nature in its entirety; and, while it concentrates its interest chiefly in a *life* of self-denial, it allows free play to the speculative tendency as well."[2]

Yet, despite the present tense that he used in this instance, which comes from a work published in 1908, Iqbal believed that Sufism—and mysticism everywhere—had largely failed in his contemporary age to cater, as it once did, to varied needs. Instead, to the ordinary believer, it had romanticized a life of "false renunciation and made him perfectly contented with his ignorance and spiritual thralldom. No wonder then that the modern Muslim in Turkey, Egypt, and Persia is led to seek fresh sources of energy in the creation of new loyalties, such as patriotism and nationalism which Nietzsche described as a 'sickness and unreason' and 'the greatest force against culture.'"[3] Indeed, as Iqbal saw it, Sufism had long ago embarked on this path of otherworldliness and had set the "best minds in Islam" on that path. Without the moderating influence of this-worldly Sufism, Islamic law had become increasingly more rigid in its formulations, and the brain-drain caused by Sufism had resulted in the state being "left generally in the hands of intellectual mediocrities."[4] Iqbal also took aim at the custodians of Sufi shrines dotting the Indian landscape. Speaking in the voice of a rebellious disciple, Iqbal castigated the exploitative practices of these "Brahmins of the Ka`ba, who are worshiped like idols" and who deceive their followers on the basis of their inherited claims to religious authority.[5]

Iqbal's is at best a mixed view of Sufism, but it looks benign when compared with that of Fazlur Rahman. Rahman repeated the idea that medieval philosophical Sufism or Sufi theosophy had "sapped the energies and almost unreservedly claimed the minds of men of the greatest ability and creativity."[6] And he too lamented Sufism's otherworldliness.[7] But his indictment was harsher. On the one hand, Sufi theosophy posited a realm of knowledge that rested on a higher plane than the shari`a—the former being the preserve of a select few while the latter was meant only for those who were not sufficiently advanced on the mystic path. Having been battered by the traditionalists, the medieval philosophers themselves came to find refuge in Sufism, which allowed them not merely to survive but even to "avenge" themselves on Sunni traditionalism.[8] On the other hand, and despite the intellectual elitism of Sufi theosophy, Sufism came to converge with popular religion and to exercise an enormous influence on the Muslim masses. By the thirteenth century, "Islamic society underwent a metempsychosis. Instead of being a method of moral self-discipline and elevation and genuine spiritual enlightenment, Sufism was now transformed into veritable spiritual jugglery through auto-hypnotic transports and visions just as at the level of doctrine it was being transmuted into a half-delirious theosophy.... Ill-balanced majdhubs (i.e., those in perpetual trance), parasitic mendicants, exploiting dervishes proclaimed Muhammad's Faith [sic] in the heyday of Sufism. Islam was at the mercy of spiritual delinquents."[9]

Ghulam Ahmad Parwez, another modernist ally of Ayub Khan, was equally unsparing in his critique of Sufism. "*Tasawwuf*," he wrote, using the standard Arabic and Urdu word for it, "teaches escapism from life, so what relation can it have to the religion to God? In Iqbal's words, 'tasawwuf is an alien plant (*ajnabi pawda*) in the soil of Islam.' Religion causes the blood of life to run through the dead arteries of nations. Tasawwuf causes that blood to freeze in the living arteries. Religion is the spark that burns every false system down to ashes. Tasawwuf dampens the warmth of life to put nations to the sleep of death."[10]

Rahman and Perwez were almost as harsh in their indictment of the `ulama as they were of the Sufis, but that should not obscure the fact that many `ulama have themselves been sharply critical of Sufism. In turning to the traditionalist scholars, it is useful to see their views of Sufism along a broad spectrum, which ranges from outright denunciation to a full embrace. In its most unambiguous forms, the denunciation is exemplified by the Ahl-i Hadith, the South Asian Salafis, from whose perspective Sufi devotionalism has no basis in the foundational Islamic texts and it amounts practically to worshipping holy personages and therefore to the cardinal sin of setting up partners with the one God. The fullest embrace is represented, on the other hand, by the Barelawis, who see any impugning of the sanctity or the centrality of holy men and women as blasphemous. For their part, the Deobandis have traditionally stood somewhere around the middle of these two poles. Their doctrinal orientation is marked by a rejection of all practices for which, as they see it, no warrant can be found in the foundational texts. Yet, in colonial India, it would have been very unusual for a Deobandi scholar of any standing not to be affiliated with one or more Sufi orders. Unlike the criticism of many modernists and Islamists, Deobandi critiques of the excesses of Sufi devotionalism were not intended to undermine Sufism itself but rather, as internal criticism, to reform it from within. Such critique could have parallels with that of the modernists. As Ashraf ʿAli Thanawi saw it, many of his contemporary pirs were mere shopkeepers profiting from the gullibility of their ignorant followers.[11] Iqbal would have agreed, though Thanawi's point in offering this characterization was that people who came to *his* hospice should expect a strict moral regimen rather than just a pandering to their spiritual tastes, a mere doling out of amulets.

In other respects, there could be a wider gulf between the likes of Thanawi and the modernists. In 1909, Thanawi had published a commentary on the diwan of Hafiz (d. 1390), showing that the ubiquity of wine, the cup-bearer, and the beloved in the great Persian poet's verse was really his way of talking about the divine beloved and the mystical path.[12] This was not an uncommon understanding of Hafiz at the time, but it was very different from the severe rebuke that admirers of Hafiz would receive from Iqbal some years later:

Beware of Hafiz the drinker
His cup is full of the poison of death. . . .
There is nothing in his market except wine
With two cups his turban has been spoiled.
He is a Muslim but his belief is girdled with the unbeliever's belt
His faith is fractured by the beloved's eyelashes.
He gives weakness the name of strength
His musical instrument leads the nation astray. . . .
The sound of his music betokens decline
The voice he hears from on high is the Gabriel of decline.[13]

When it came to theosophical Sufism, Thanawi and some of his disciples made serious efforts to show that the doctrines of controversial Sufis like Ibn al-ʿArabi (d. 1240) could in fact frequently be shown to conform to proper Islamic norms. Yet, he also believed that Sufi metaphysics was not the kind of thing that people ought to worry much about. That mystics like Ibn al-ʿArabi had thought and written a great deal about such matters was incontestable, but ultimately it was irrelevant to the quality of one's religious life. And even

Thanawi acknowledged a certain "alienation" with some of Ibn al-ʿArabi's doctrines.[14]

For their part, Islamists like Mawdudi were much closer to the modernists in their critique of the Sufis than they were to many among the ʿulama. Asked by a leader of the Jamaʿat-i Islami to explain his opposition to that organization, Husayn Ahmad Madani had listed criticism of revered Sufis and Sufi practices as one of the grounds for it. With biting sarcasm, Madani had concluded,

> I am an old-style Muslim, a strict adherent of the Hanafi norms, a servant of the Sufi guides. You [on the other hand] are the bright lamps of a new Islam. I seek to help Muslims tread the path of the pious forbears and see their salvation in it. You gentlemen wish to have Muslims follow Mawdudi's new Islam. You consider his revivalism—which even the likes of the Renewer of the Second Millennium (*Mujaddid-i alf-i thani* [that is, Shaykh Ahmad Sirhindi, d. 1624]), Shah Wali Allah, and Sayyid Ahmad [of Rae Bareli, d. 1831] were not fated to accomplish— as the means of salvation for Muslims; and you seek to rid Muslims of the thirteen centuries-long ignorance ([or pagan materialism] Arabic: *jahiliyya*; Urdu: *jahiliyyat*), that has continued from the time of the first generations till today and that has afflicted all but a few leaders and imams. With such principled disagreement, there is no hope that you can exert any influence on me or that I can have any on you.[15]

This was no mere polemic. As Mawdudi saw it, Sufism's concern with the "purification of the soul" (*tazkiya-i nafs*) was not quite in line with proper Islamic teachings, and that divergence had had several results. Sufi institutions and practices had failed to produce individuals who could challenge the forces of jahiliyya or who could resist its inroads into the realm of Islam. The Sufis tended to see the purification of the soul as a means to attaining a vision of God in this world and the privileged knowledge that supposedly came with it, but there was no Qur'anic sanction for such aspirations and no reason why human beings would need that kind of knowledge. Nor did the other forms of spiritual advancement that the Sufis spoke of ever result, Mawdudi said, in the kind of individuals that the Prophet had shaped through *his* teachings. The closest that the purification of the soul came to the purposes of Islam was in fostering piety—*taqwa*—among people. But such taqwa tended to remain limited to outward comportment. And where it did shape one's life more deeply, it did so only at the individual level.

> This limited conception [of taqwa, and of the purification of the soul] has no place in it for the understanding of larger social issues. Thus the benefit of what even the best of our pious people do in purifying their souls is nothing more than to provide observant subjects and religiously

devout servants to governments that themselves are in rebellion [against God]. The subjects and servants that the public education provided by these governments produces may have other qualities, but what they do not have is honesty and righteousness; and that is a cause of considerable harm to these governments. This deficiency is remedied by those of our institutions that exist for the purification of the soul.[16]

This remarkable analysis was first published in Mawdudi's monthly journal, *Tarjuman al-Qur'an*, in 1953, though a similar view found expression in many others of his earlier and later writings. It is as uncompromising in its castigation of Sufism as anything that Fazlur Rahman or Parwez would ever write on the subject.

Sufi practices have been the object of considerable attention from the state, too, and a good deal of it has been unfavorable. One illustrative example comes from 1942, when the Punjab legislative assembly passed the Music in Muslim Shrines Bill to curb women's singing and dancing in the precincts of Sufi shrines. As the statement of the bill's objectives had put it, "To celebrate the anniversaries of such saints with all that is immoral, disgraceful, and vexatious to the noble mind, despicable and repugnant to the law of Shariat, is highly inconsistent not only with the spirit underlying the occasions but is a travesty of the faithfulness and esteem that is shown to the holy saint by his followers and affords a positive slur on the holy name of Islam."[17] The debate on the bill made clear that the "slur" in question came from the fact that many of those singing at the shrines of "recognized Muslim saints"[18] were courtesans and professional dancers. A few years earlier, the Shi`a Young Men's Association of Lahore had tried to prevent "bazaar women"—that is, prostitutes—from participating in Muharram processions.[19] But the reach of the 1942 bill was broader in seeking to make all female singing to the accompaniment of music and all female dancing a punishable offense. Some members of the assembly wanted, unsuccessfully as it turned out, to make it wider still by branding singing even without musical instruments as a cognizable offense.

There were, however, weighty arguments against the bill. Among the most notable of those to articulate them was one Pir Akbar Ali, whose association with the world of devotional, shrine-based Sufism is underlined by his honorific ("pir"). He was also an Ahmadi.[20] If singing was wrong, he said, then it was wrong irrespective of whether men or women did it, and yet the bill singled out only the women.[21] Further, "even a female singer adheres to some sort of belief and faith for her salvation and according to that belief she wants to go and sing at a shrine."[22] Some of his other objections raised larger questions, and they are worth quoting together with the recorded interjections of some of the other members of the house:

> By whom is the "Muslim saint" to be recognized? (An honourable member: "By the Muslim community.") ... [W]hat is meant by recog-

nized? Further, who is a saint? In the whole of Islamic literature, there is no reference to any saint.... Moreover a "Muslim shrine" is nowhere defined. (An honourable member: How do you define Muslim?)[23]

The last question, in parentheses, from an unnamed member of the house, would arise forcefully in Pakistan with reference to the Ahmadis, and it may have already been an allusion to Akbar Ali's faith. In any case, in opposing the bill, Akbar Ali also argued that it constituted government interference in religious matters and, more specifically, that it contravened the authority of the shrine's guardian to manage it in accordance with the terms of the pious endowments (*awqaf*; singular: *waqf*) attached to it. Such objections cut little ice with the supporters of the bill. Instead, there were indications that some members of the house had begun to look forward to a postcolonial era when there would be new and greater opportunities to reshape the religious landscape in more sweeping ways. One legislator cited Q 22.41 ("Those who, when We establish them in the land, keep up the prayer, pay the prescribed alms, command what is right, and forbid what is wrong ...") and continued: "If this is a fact that the Muslims have been enjoined by the Holy Quran to do all these things when they get political power, how does it become him [that is, Pir Akbar Ali] to oppose such bills."[24]

In Pakistan, the most significant form that state intervention would take vis-à-vis Sufi shrines was the bringing of waqf endowments under its direct control. Sufi shrines were not the only establishments supported by waqfs, but they were by far the most prominent of them. Given that many visitors to the shrines leave donations at them, they are also the most lucrative.[25] In 1938, the North-West Frontier Province had already seen the enactment of the Muslim Waqfs Act. The idea of government regulation of waqfs had been opposed, however, by leading Deobandi scholars, notably Husayn Ahmad Madani and Mufti Kifayat Allah (d. 1953), the president of the Jam`iyyat al-`Ulama-i Hind, and the bill that was enacted in the Frontier was a much watered down version of what had been proposed by way of government oversight.[26] Around the same time, in late colonial Punjab, the Unionist-led government of Sir Sikandar Hyat Khan (d. 1942) that would later support the enactment of the Music in Muslim Shrines Bill had also attempted to bring the waqfs under its control. In that instance, many of those associated with influential shrines had successfully blocked the initiative.[27] Roughly two decades later, the martial law regime of General Ayub Khan was not willing to brook any such opposition. Accordingly, the West Pakistan Waqf Properties Ordinance of 1959 created the position of a chief administrator with the authority to bring waqf endowments under the direct control of the government and to require the custodians of properties not taken over by the government to administer them in accordance with governmental stipulations.[28] An ordinance issued in 1961 reaffirmed the provisions of the earlier legislation.[29] In

1962, another ordinance was promulgated to regulate waqf properties in East Pakistan.[30] These ordinances, and other legislation enacted in the Ayub Khan, Zulfikar Ali Bhutto, and Zia al-Haqq years, gave wide powers to the government in regulating the waqf, made it a punishable offense not to register an endowment with the office of the waqf administrator,[31] and imposed a tax on the endowment's income.[32]

Pakistani governments have also taken measures to inscribe the saints into a narrative of nation-building and social uplift.[33] Visiting the shrine-rich town of Uch in southern Punjab in November 1952, governor-general Ghulam Muhammad had harangued the shrine keepers thus:

> Your ancestors played a great part in spreading Islam and its ideals of service and in spreading learning. But it appears that all these foun- tainheads of culture and spiritualism have been converted into small jagirs [fiefdoms]—living on grants and offerings.... It is the duty of all of us to work for the revival of Islamic learning and to pull out from the sloth and stagnation of jagirdars [feudal lords] who trade in the name of their illustrious predecessors and thrive on gifts ... and do not fulfill adequately the corresponding obligations imposed on them.[34]

Such admonishment, though helping justify official oversight, has seldom been accompanied by notable government success in social uplift *through* shrines. In any case, the degree to which Pakistani governments have been able to reach into Sufi institutions to regulate their waqfs and attendant af- fairs has had little parallel when it comes to the regulation of madrasas. I will return to this point later in this chapter.

Finally, though some prominent pirs have been part of anti-Ahmadi agita- tions,[35] controversies surrounding Ahmadism have ironically added to the already considerable vulnerabilities of Sufism in Pakistan. This owes itself to the fact that it is through strongly mystical interpretations that the followers of Mirza Ghulam Ahmad have tended to explain his claims. Mirza Nasir Ahmad, the head of the Rabwah-based Ahmadi community, invoked the Sufi tradition several times while being cross-examined about his beliefs in the National Assembly of Pakistan in the summer of 1974. At one point, he ob- served, for instance, that the Ahmadis viewed the prophetical claims of Ghu- lam Ahmad in metaphorical (*majazi*) terms, much like the Sufis spoke of cer- tain things as having a metaphorical rather than real (*haqiqi*) existence.[36] Some of Ghulam Ahmad's statements were, moreover, attributable to a mys- tical "unveiling" (*kashf*).[37] Mirza Nasir Ahmad also used the key Sufi term *fana*—annihilation of the self—in speaking of how Ghulam Ahmad viewed himself in relation to the Prophet Muhammad.[38] And he referred to Ghulam Ahmad as "the founder of the Ahmadi order" (*bani-yi silsila-i Ahmadiyya*),[39] which is exactly how one might refer to the founder of a Sufi order.

Significantly, some of the debate in the assembly between the representatives of the Ahmadi community and the attorney-general of Pakistan who was leading the proceedings had turned on the legitimacy of Sufi claims to receiving "revelations" from God. The Ahmadis told the house that such revelations could sometimes take the form of a Sufi believing that, in his particular circumstances, a passage that had once being revealed to Muhammad was again being sent down to him. It was in these terms that the *Lahore-based* Ahmadis tried to explain Ghulam Ahmad's claims to being the recipient of revelations from God. From the perspective of this Ahmadi group, even his claim to receive revelations did not make Ghulam Ahmad a prophet—which, to them, he was not. The point was, of course, that Ghulam Ahmad's claim should be unobjectionable if some such claim was granted for, say, `Abd al-Qadir Jilani (d. 1166), the putative founder of the Qadiri Sufi order whose followers are especially numerous among the Barelawis of South Asia, or for Shaykh Ahmad Sirhindi.[40] `Abd al-Mannan `Umar, the representative of the Lahore-based Ahmadis, observed further that the Sufis had sometimes referred to their masters as "prophets"; Rumi, for instance, had done so. But this was only in a metaphorical sense, intended only to underscore the Sufi master's authority.[41] The attorney-general seemed never to have heard of such Sufi discourses and he was appropriately baffled by them. As he admonished the representative of the Lahore-based Ahmadis at one point during the in-camera session: "Talk about God, the Qur'an, and hadith. Leave Rumi, leave him alone! For only the former [sources] are binding upon us; nothing else is binding."[42]

For many of those, too, who *had* heard of such things, these were potentially embarrassing, even incendiary, topics to discuss in a milieu in which the image of the Sufi masters had come to be purveyed to people in a highly sanitized manner. As Shah Ahmad Nurani (d. 2003), the leader of the Barelawi-oriented Jam`iyyat `Ulama-i Pakistan said at one point while Ghulam Ahmad's mystical unveilings were under discussion, "the explanation [*sic*, using the English word] should be brief, and should be in light of the Qur'an and the hadith."[43] This was a remarkable position to take for the leader of a doctrinal orientation most closely associated in Pakistan with mystical Islam and often most vulnerable to attack precisely on grounds that many of their Sufi-inflected beliefs and practices lacked sufficient warrant in the Islamic foundational texts.[44]

It is worth noting, incidentally, that embarrassing topics like these could be, and sometimes were, treated with more nuance by contemporaries. In a learned discussion of some of Ibn Taymiyya's philosophical and theological writings, the modernist `alim Hanif Nadwi had briefly commented on the Damascene scholar's critique of Ibn al-`Arabi. Nadwi noted in this context that Ibn al-`Arabi had spoken of "sainthood" (*wilaya*) as a *continuing* form of "nonlegislative prophethood," a rank reserved to people of great spiritual achievement and one that Ibn al-ʿArabi took to be higher than that of prophets because the appearance of such figures, unlike the prophets', was potentially open-ended.[45] Without any hint of being scandalized by this, Nadwi observed straightforwardly that Ibn al-ʿArabi's reference to the saint's "prophethood" was entirely metaphorical, though it was still wrong; and that Ibn Taymiyya, for one, had been highly critical of such conceptions of sainthood. On Nadwi's showing, there was no ambiguity in Ibn Taymiyya's mind about the limits of the Sufi master's authority, and he had sought to correct Ibn al-ʿArabi on that score.[46] Yet, in highlighting Ibn Taymiyya's sustained engagement with the Islamic rational sciences, Nadwi also showed that Ibn Taymiyya was far from being the "reactionary" and the "literalist" that he has been portrayed to be by Orientalist scholars (*mustashriqin*)[47] What makes Nadwi's commentary especially noteworthy is the fact that he was a scholar of the Ahl-i Hadith or Salafi persuasion, often viewed as the least compromising of modern Sunni orientations in their adherence to the foundational texts and their rejection of things lacking a clear warrant in them. By his own acknowledgment, Nadwi's understanding even of the Qur'an owed something to Sufi interpretations.[48] At the same time, Nadwi, too, could take stringent positions: he is said to be among the first people to have argued in print that the Ahmadis be declared a non-Muslim minority in the then newly founded Pakistan.[49] Though a gifted scholar like Hanif Nadwi could apparently hold these different views in a tense balance, the ability to do so and the space in which to attempt it were in increasingly short supply by the 1970s. This had consequences not only for modernism and for the minorities, but also for Sufism.

Appealing to Sufism

The many challenges Sufi thought and practice have faced in recent times have not, however, erased their deep mark on modern and contemporary Islam. Iqbal is not the only modernist whose religious thought is imbued with a Sufi ethos. Khalifa Abdul Hakim, for instance, had written his PhD dissertation on the metaphysics of Rumi. Intellectuals from a wide spectrum shared this engagement with the great poet. Iqbal, of course, took Rumi as his muse, but Ashraf ʿAli Thanawi, too, had discoursed extensively on the *Masnawi* of Rumi at his hospice in Thana Bhawan. Thanawi's spiritual master, Imdad Allah, who had immigrated to Mecca in the aftermath of the Mutiny of 1857, used to dilate on the *Masnawi* for the benefit of his Indian visitors.[50] As observed earlier, Muhsin al-Mulk, a close associate of Sir Sayyid Ahmad Khan, had made extensive use of Rumi in some of his early writings.[51] The point is not, of course, that these intellectuals would have put such classics to similar use. They often did not. It is rather that there was a shared body of texts—mystically inflected texts among others—that they engaged with even as many of them were highly critical of particular aspects of Sufi thought. And the modernists were not necessarily different from the others in this regard.

The modernists have not shied away from the *practice* of Sufism either. Iqbal, for instance, had been initiated into the Qadiri Sufi order.[52] And governor-general Ghulam Muhammad was a devotee of the teachings of Waris 'Ali Shah (d. 1905), a modern-day saint buried in the town of Dewa in UP.[53] The latter was a very different kind of Sufi master than, say, the Deobandi Ashraf 'Ali Thanawi. While Thanawi was known for hewing close to the Islamic legal norms, Waris 'Ali wanted to see religious and other divides among people transcended. His disciples included Muslims of varied orientations as well as non-Muslims, and he liked to participate in Hindu religious festivals.[54] He was not known for a punctilious performance of ritual prayers,[55] and his willingness to allow unveiled women into his presence could scandalize people.[56] It is hard to know what precisely had attracted the anglicized bureaucrat Ghulam Muhammad to him, though the Sufi master's universalism, which included an attentiveness to the products of a Westernized education, as well as the absence of the kind of legal formalism that figures so prominently in modernist caricatures of the 'ulama, surely had something to do with it. The modernists have long held that Islam, suitably expressed in the idiom of the contemporary world, could appeal not just to educated Muslims—precisely the sort of people most at risk, from this vantage, of being turned off by the 'ulama's lifeless creed and rituals—but also to non-Muslims. Ghulam Muhammad would have seen Waris 'Ali Shah to be an example of such ecumenical appeal.

General Ayub Khan, while keeping company with some harsh critics of Sufism, was reputed to have a pir of his own—in this instance, the keeper of the shrine of Dewal Sharif near Rawalpindi.[57] Several subsequent heads of government and of the state, including Benazir Bhutto, Asif 'Ali Zardari (Bhutto's widower and the country's president, 2008–13), and Raja Pervaiz Ashraf (prime minister in 2012–13), are known to have had their pirs.[58] Yusuf Reza Gilani, who served as prime minister between 2008 and 2012, is a member of a prominent family of pirs from Multan in the Punjab. And the Cambridge-educated politician Shah Mehmood Qureshi, who served as foreign minister under Gilani, is the keeper of the shrine of Baha al-din Zakariyya (d. 1267) in Multan. This hereditary position was previously occupied by his father, Sajjad Hussein Qureshi (d. 1997), who was the governor of the Punjab during Zia al-Haqq's last years.

Lived Sufism is nonetheless viewed with considerable ambivalence in many Western-educated circles.[59] Even as the death anniversaries of revered saints buried in Pakistan are commemorated with high-ranking government functionaries in attendance, and more than one head of the state or government has visited the shrines of saints buried in India,[60] a politician's association with a living pir is typically a matter of rumor, of innuendo, and, on the politician's part, of some embarrassment. This is not the case for such other aspects of religious practice as, say, the performance of ritual prayers, the pilgrimage to Mecca, even noninstitutional forms of Sufi-inflected piety.

The strong yet frequently concealed presence of mystical sensibilities in the life of some among the modernist elite is best illustrated, perhaps, with reference to a high-ranking bureaucrat, Qudratullah Shahab (d. 1986). Shahab had begun his career in colonial India as a member of the much coveted Indian Civil Service and later rose to the position of principal secretary to the governors-general Ghulam Muhammad and Iskandar Mirza and to President Ayub Khan. He served subsequently as the secretary of information and education and, for some years during the Ayub Khan era, as Pakistan's ambassador to the Netherlands.[61] Besides an illustrious career that kept him for many years in extraordinarily close proximity to the centers of power, Shahab was a noted man of letters. His autobiography, published posthumously, is a notable literary achievement as well as an intimate record of hitherto unknown facets of his life. His mystical sensibilities are foremost among those facets.

Shahab's encounters with the paranormal had begun while he was a young member of the colonial civil service posted in the eastern Indian state of Orissa. The house he inhabited there was reputed to be haunted, and he began to experience strange occurrences in it: stones, rocks, and sometimes bones would rain down on his rooms, windows and doors would open and shut by themselves, the dining table would begin floating in the air, an old gramophone would produce the sounds of a woman sobbing and of someone being strangled to death. In due course, Shahab discovered that a former member of the civil service had had a relationship with a Hindu woman, had murdered her after she became pregnant, and had buried her body in the living room of the house. Once the body had been recovered and cremated according to Hindu rites, the commotion ceased. Instead, on three occasions, Shahab now heard the melodious sound of someone reciting "There is no god but Allah"—the Islamic profession of the faith. Everything was to remain peaceful afterward.[62] These experiences gave him, Shahab later wrote, an insight into matters relating to the spirit (*ruh*). What he learned about Western writings on parapsychology did not offer much satisfaction, however, and he felt that Eastern—presumably Indian—spiritualists were not much more than mere tricksters. Instead, it was in Islam that the highest forms of this knowledge were to be found.[63] This recognition brought him to Sufism. The mystical path (*tariqa*) he chose for himself was that of the Uwaysis.[64]

The Uwaysis take their name from Uways al-Qarani, a "companion" of Muhammad who, unlike the rest, had never actually met the Prophet. In contrast with members of the other orders, who are formally initiated into them at the hands of a Sufi master, the Uwaysis, true to their forbear, undergo no formal induction and there is no recognizable structure to this "order." Already as a schoolboy, Shahab reports having seen the Prophet Muhammad in a dream. Later, after entering government service, he had once listened to a village mosque preacher speak of the affectionate relationship between Muhammad and his daughter Fatima and had prayed to God to let Fatima intercede for him in order to be guided by God to the Uwaysi order. That prayer was answered, and Shahab began receiving written communications, in English, from someone who called himself "a ninety-years-young fakir" and subsequently just "Ninety." Shahab did not say when those communications began, though they would continue for a good quarter century.[65] One of the people to whom Shahab would dedicate his autobiography is Ninety. His autobiography ends with reflections on the mystical path and some prayers that he had found to be efficacious. As would befit an Uwaysi, the discoveries on the Sufi path were his own, though the language in which he described them was indebted to the Islamic mystical lexicon, and he did acknowledge his debt to several Sufi luminaries of the remote and recent past—among them `Abd al-Qadir Jilani (d. 1166), Shihab al-din Abu Hafs `Umar al-Suhrawardi (d. 1234), Qutb al-din Bakhtiyar Kaki (d. 1235), Rumi (1273), Imdad Allah (d. 1899), and Ashraf `Ali Thanawi (d. 1943).

Shahab had the education and the intellectual sophistication to compare his experiences to modern reflections on parapsychology and to articulate the results of his mystical experimentation in the language of Sufism. At least some of what he thought he had heard and seen in the haunted house in Orissa would not, however, have surprised the unlettered people whose lives he governed as a bureaucrat. It is not a little ironic that there should have been so little distance between the beliefs of ordinary people and those of a top bureaucrat working for regimes bent upon eradicating such "superstition."[66]

Interests such as Shahab's have been explored in fiction, too. A notable example is a novel *Raja Gidh* ("Vulture King"), by the respected playwright and novelist Bano Qudsiyya (d. 2017). First published in 1981, it follows the rootless career of a university student in Lahore. It describes his unfulfilling relationship with several women—a fellow student who is in love with another man, a married woman desperate to have a child, an aging prostitute from the city's red light district—and it chronicles his equally unsatisfying efforts to find spiritual solace. He gets no peace at Sufi shrines and even a seemingly powerful mystic's promise to put him in touch with the spirit of a dead lover remains unrealized. He does come to understand, however, that there is no distinct line separating the "abnormal" from the "supernormal." In the end, it is personal spiritual experience rather than institutional Sufism that has guided him to this recognition. This widely read novel is dedicated to Shahab.[67]

Sufism has also shaped modernism in ways other than the belief and practice of particular individuals, of course. Two of these are worth noting. First, as seen earlier, modernism has had strong ethical sensibilities and these are indebted, in no small measure, to Sufi ethics. For all his criticism of Sufism, Iqbal derived his core ethical commitments from the world of the Sufis. As he put it in his *Reconstruction of Religious Thought in Islam*, "the world of today needs a Rumi to create an attitude of hope and to kindle the fire of enthusiasm for life."[68] Khalifa Abdul Hakim's *Islamic Ideology*, published in the early years of Pakistan to acquaint Western-educated Muslims with their religious tradition but also to demonstrate how Islam was the best hope for a universal brotherhood, is another case in point. The book amply reflects Abdul Hakim's background in Western Idealist philosophy, but Sufi motifs are unmistakable in his treatment of Islamic ethics. Abdul Hakim wrote:

> Islam says that the human soul is the Spirit of God Himself and man is created to assimilate more and more the attributes of God. Truth, Beauty, Love, Peace and Happiness are intrinsic values because they are rooted in Ultimate Reality; we conceive them in their relativity but they are absolute as attributes of God. They have to be preserved by man and morality consists in the effort to preserve them.[69]

He went on: "The being of God, notwithstanding complete transcendence, is by knowledge and power immanent in entire Nature and in the soul of man. All the three are an integral whole.... Men had cut asunder what God had joined and the main service of Islam was to reunite the sundered parts again."[70] This integrationist ethics envisaged the unity of the human race, though with the pointed exclusion of the polytheists.[71] It is rare in this book for Abdul Hakim to adduce anything other than passages from the Qur'an and the traditions of the Prophet, though Sufis make an occasional appearance. In any case, Sufis from ʿAttar (d. ca. 1220) to Ibn al-ʿArabi to Rumi to the Indian mystic and poet Sarmad (d. 1661) would have recognized a good deal of Abdul Hakim's ethics as their own.[72] Many others would have seen his sharp attacks on the hidebound formalism of the mulla as expressing their own sentiment.

In a brief, undated essay titled "Mullaism," which was first delivered as a talk on Radio Pakistan sometime probably in the early 1950s (and which is not to be confused with his "Iqbal and the Mulla"), Abdul Hakim took what for the Muslim modernists is a remarkably favorable view of the Sufis.[73] Unlike the mullas, who have historically done nothing toward the spread of Islam, the Sufis, he said, have been the agents of proselytism in India. Whereas the mulla worships mere externals, the "true Sufi" seeks that which is inside: "acquainted with the spirit of the religion, he looks at core principles and is not disputatious about subsidiary issues."[74] Given that a key modernist concern has always been to reinterpret and reform what are taken to be subsidiary legal norms in light of the core values of the Islamic foundational texts, there is a remarkable accord here between the true Sufis and their ethical values, on the one hand, and those of the modernists, on the other. Abdul Hakim did not make this last point explicitly, but it is hard not to see it as animating this analysis.[75]

Abdul Hakim's idealized portrait of the Sufi also points to a second facet of modernism's indebtedness to Sufism, and this concerns the very distinction between the inner and the outer, the true spirit and external form. Beginning at least with Syed Ameer Ali, Muslim modernists have often spoken in terms of the spirit of Islam, which they have taken to be in accord with their own religious sensibilities. If the Islam of the `ulama does not agree with that of the modernists, it is, on this view, because the `ulama's formulaic and hidebound interpretations of the foundational texts contravene the true spirit of the religion. The *Civil and Military Gazette*, a newspaper well-known for its hard-hitting criticism of the `ulama, had put it this way in August 1952, as the anti-Ahmadi sentiment was heating up in the Punjab: "Liberation of the soul from the alien bondage of arrogant disdain and fanatical hatred is the sine qua non for the realization of self. Neither the hypocritical cant of self-righteous pietists nor the antics of dogmatic factionists have [*sic*] any place in a large-minded devotion to religion. Those who preen themselves on the possession of a prerogative to proclaim judgments on the validity of experience not conforming to theirs are the deadliest intruders in the realm of the spirit and must be banished therefrom to save the same from sacrilege."[76] It is not just that such characterizations of the `ulama would resonate with many Sufis; their key terms and categories are themselves indebted to the Sufi lexicon. As Yohanan Friedmann has observed, this is a vocabulary that is pervasive, for instance, in the writings of Shaykh Ahmad Sirhindi, among the most influential of premodern Indian Sufis. To Sirhindi, the religion of the common people was given over to mere form and externalities, whereas the Sufis were able to penetrate to the essence of things, their true nature. At another level of analysis, particular things could have their own outer and inner—that is, more real and truer—dimensions.[77] Such views are standard fare in Sufi discourses, of course, but they are also influential in modernist conceptualizations of an ethically centered Islam. Indeed, they have come to inform the work of the modernists *irrespective* of the specificities of their attitude toward Sufism itself.

Yet, if Sufi ethics could help rescue Islam from its unenlightened spokesmen, they also had the potential to undermine, when in the wrong hands, the grand narratives of Pakistani nationalism. No one illustrates this danger better, perhaps, than G. M. Syed (d. 1995), a Sindhi politician and Sufi who had once occupied a position of leadership in the Muslim League but had then broken with Jinnah to spend the rest of his long life promoting the cause of Sindhi ethnic nationalism. Unsurprisingly, the Pakistani governing elite saw him as representing the most sinister of threats to the existence of the country. What merits attention in the present context is the fact, however, that Syed's Sindhi nationalism was firmly anchored in his understanding of Sufism. This

Sufism was a blend of Ibn al-ʿArabi's "unity of being" (*wahdat al-wujud*)—which Syed took to mean that artificial distinctions resting on race, class, and religion should be abolished, though he did not quite explain what the implications of doing so would be for a specifically *Sindhi* nationalism—and the ideas of Shah ʿAbd al-Latif (d. 1752), Sindh's most revered poet. He combined this with an evolutionary outlook, indebted to modern science, with the implication that religion was in need of constant adaptation to change.[78] Calls for social justice were also a prominent part of his thought.[79] Syed's invocation of Sufism could not but be anathematic to the country's rulers: as if a socioeconomically laced appeal to regional sentiment in the name of a particular understanding of Islam was not threatening enough, there also were disconcerting similarities between some of Syed's ideas and those of the mainstream modernists. It is true that most of the latter would not have gone so far as to characterize, as Syed did, core Islamic rituals as merely a holdover from a tribal past. Yet, they, too, shared a suspicion of "mere" ritualism. Social justice had had a place in their discourses, too—from Iqbal to the Objectives Resolution to Abdul Hakim to Fazlur Rahman. And the Sufi saint to whose teachings Ghulam Muhammad, the governor-general, was so devoted would probably have warmed to the sight of G. M. Syed's funeral, at which "[p]assages from the Quran, the Bhagavad Gita, the Bible, the Torah, and the *Shah-jo-risalo* (the collection of verses of Shah Abdul Latif) were read."[80] Then there was the fact that both Syed and the modernists governing the state wanted to enlist Sufism and the saints of old in the nationalist cause.[81] Syed's just happened to be the wrong cause, and his brand of Sufism was the more perverse for it.

If the modernists' suspicion of Sufi thought and practice sits uncomfortably beside their appeal to it, the Deobandi ʿulama, too, despite particular misgivings, have long drawn on Sufi language and thought in many of their own formulations. A striking example is offered by the way Shabbir Ahmad ʿUsmani, the most prominent of the Deobandis to support the movement for Pakistan, justified that support to a baffled interlocutor. Asked how he could side with the Westernized leadership of the Muslim League after having opposed it for many years, ʿUsmani responded by quoting a statement attributed to the tenth-century Baghdadi mystic al-Junayd (d. 910): "the truthful person changes a hundred times in a day [in his quest for the truth] whereas the hypocrite [concerned with keeping appearances] sticks to the same position for a hundred years."[82] The ambivalence of this statement hardly needs underscoring. Though the Muslim League leaders were grateful for any support they could muster, such expressions of it would not have put to rest questions about how much to rely on the ʿulama. The statement also points to the pains the likes of ʿUsmani had to take, the lengths they had to go to, in explaining their support for Pakistan. The relevant point here is nonetheless that it was in terms of a Sufi idea that he did so on some at least of such occasions.

Perhaps an even more telling moment, so far as Sufism is concerned, had come two decades earlier. On a visit to the Hijaz to participate in an international conference convened by Ibn Sa`ud in 1926, `Usmani took the opportunity to urge the newly installed Wahhabi king to show forbearance toward those engaging in devotional practices at revered shrines. At a time when the Wahhabis were busy destroying such shrines in the name of a pristine Islam, `Usmani argued that the king ought to chart a careful path between strictness and leniency, as the Prophet had in his time. Ibn Sa`ud responded that his government was tolerant in matters on which the various schools of Sunni law had long had disagreements, but that there could be no leniency in upholding monotheism in all its purity. To this, `Usmani retorted that what was in question was not whether God alone was to be worshipped but what "worship" (`ibada) itself meant. Bowing or prostrating before something other than God was, he argued, not necessarily to worship it. People prostrating themselves before the graves of holy men could well be punished by the king, `Usmani said, but they could not legitimately be treated as polytheists. As `Usmani reported it, Ibn Sa`ud listened politely and then referred the matter to the `ulama in his entourage.[83]

This remarkable exchange did not go anywhere, but it serves to illustrate the significant gulf between the Wahhabis and the Deobandis. Despite the Deobandi criticism of Sufi excesses, `Usmani's position here was unmistakably entrenched in a Sufi worldview. And it had strong similarities with the views of Sufis of a different doctrinal ilk. For instance, Khwaja Hasan Nizami (d. 1955), a journalist and Sufi of the Chishti order, had written a short tract in 1920 in which he had vigorously defended the practice of prostration before one's Sufi master or his shrine—he was associated with the much-frequented shrine of Nizam al-din Awliya (d. 1325) in Delhi.[84] Nizami, too, made a distinction here between an act of prostration that amounted to worship and one that was merely a matter of showing respect to another human being. He argued that God himself had set the precedent for the latter practice by commanding the angels to prostrate themselves to Adam; and that it was the *refusal* to do so that had led to the damnation of Iblis, who would henceforth be Satan. At his moment of triumph, as the Qur'an describes it, the brothers of Joseph, too, "fell down prostrate before him."[85] This would be inconceivable for Joseph and Jacob to allow—both recognized as prophets by Muslims— if God did not approve of it. The objection that this practice related to pre-Islamic prophets was disposed of by Nizami on the grounds that any such practice remained allowable to Muslims unless it had specifically been abrogated by Islam. Nizami then went on to provide impressive evidence that a long succession of venerated Sufis had allowed their devotees to prostrate to them—some explicitly on grounds that they had seen their own masters allow it. To disallow it, Nizami concluded in quoting Nizam al-din Awliya, was to either consider such Sufi masters as ignorant of the teachings of Islam or as violating them. Neither option was tolerable for anyone who wished to maintain a relationship with these Sufi masters.[86]

Hasan Nizami was not the sort of Sufi that the Deobandis would have wanted to associate themselves with. His stance on devotional practices was often at considerable remove from the effort of the Deobandis to promote a scripturalist Islam anchored in hadith and the legal tradition. Yet, as `Usmani's exchange with the Saudi king shows, the Deobandis shared more with their Sufi and Barelawi rivals than they would have liked to admit. It was certainly more than what they shared with the Wahhabis of Arabia.[87]

The question of venerating tombs is not the only thing that highlights a long-standing Deobandi tolerance of what the Wahhabi-Salafis, on the one hand, and many modernists, on the other, would dismiss as polytheism or, at best, as rank superstition. The use and dispensation of amulets provides another important illustration. Sufi pirs have often been castigated by their critics for dealing in amulets (ta `wiz), and for milking an illiterate and gullible clientele in so doing. Yet, even as he distinguished himself from shopkeepers masquerading as pirs, Ashraf `Ali Thanawi, too, gave out amulets when requested, and it was not only Muslims but also Hindus that he catered to in this respect. Nor was it only illiterate villagers who sought these amulets. So, too, did `Abd al-Majid Daryabadi, the aforementioned journalist who went on to produce important commentaries on the Qur'an in both Urdu and English.[88] For his part, Mufti Muhammad Shafi`, Deoband's last mufti before the partition of India, did not see anything to be apologetic about when it came to amulets. In a small book he published toward the end of his life, Shafi` collected the tried and tested supplicatory prayers he had learnt from his father—who, like Shafi`, had once been a teacher at the madrasa in Deoband—as well as others his father had passed on to him from Deobandi stalwarts. Also included in this collection were templates for amulets to be used for different purposes—for subduing enemies, overcoming illness, treating someone who had ingested a poison, curing those possessed or afflicted with disturbing thoughts, helping a woman conceive.[89] If anyone thought that Deobandi reformism led to a disenchanted world, this little book would have served as a useful corrective to that impression. It is not its purpose to do so, however. Rather, it is an altogether unselfconscious work, concerned simply with providing to people what Shafi` took to be effective prayers and amulets. It does not seek to defend the Deobandis against the charge that they disdained such things. Nor, by the same token, is it concerned with *justifying* the practice of dealing in amulets. Rather, it takes the legitimacy of such practices entirely for granted.[90]

A more recent work by Mas`ud Azhar (b. ca. 1968), a madrasa-trained Deobandi militant, is no less instructive in this regard. Azhar is the founder of the Jaish-i Muhammad, a much-feared militant organization active in Indian Kashmir. It was banned by General Pervez Musharraf in January 2002, though it has continued to be implicated in terrorism in India in subsequent years. Azhar was in an Indian jail when an Indian passenger airliner was hijacked in December 1999 to Kabul, then under Taliban rule, and the captors demanded Azhar's freedom as part of their demands.[91] I will return to him in the next chapter. What bears mentioning in the present context is a short book that Azhar published in November 2001, weeks after the beginning of the American attack on Afghanistan in the aftermath of September 11.[92] The book focuses on God's "beautiful names," often reckoned to be ninety-nine and highlighting one or another of God's attributes—the Merciful, the All-Powerful, the Creator, the Forgiver, the Controller, the Provider, the Guardian, and so forth. The invocation and recitation of these names (*zikr*) has long had a place in Sufi devotionalism and, though Azhar is highly critical elsewhere of pirs and their practices, this work fits into that devotional genre.[93] What he tells his readers about the efficacy of reciting a particular name of God a certain number of times over a particular period of time also serves a function similar to that of amulets. Reciting certain names of God helps, he says, to restore health,[94] benefit crops,[95] provide for one's material and financial needs,[96] improve relations between spouses, protect against miscarriages,[97] and so forth. The names of God are useful in one's dealings with those in power, too. Some help gain freedom from imprisonment,[98] others are good in relation to the oppressors[99] or in helping avoid the harshness of a ruler.[100] But the ruler, too, can invoke them to good effect—for example, by way of making people subservient to himself.[101] Then there are the names of God whose efficacy is geared to the battlefield, which is what would have made this work relevant for Pakistanis going to Afghanistan to fight alongside the Taliban. Some help defeat the enemy,[102] others protect the family in one's absence,[103] yet others have the effect of making one fearless against the enemy[104] or fearsome *to* the enemy[105] and of warding off the enemy's evil in other ways.[106] This is zikr at its most efficacious, though it can also have the effect of making one privy, as has been the case with many Sufi masters, to hidden forms of knowledge.[107]

Mas'ud Azhar straddles the boundary between the 'ulama and Islamism. Other Islamists, too, have appealed to Sufism, again notwithstanding their severe criticism of it. In an early autobiographical account, first published in 1932, Mawdudi had noted that he belonged to a family with a long and prestigious lineage in the Chishti Sufi order and indeed that he was named after a Sufi progenitor—Abul-A'la Mawdudi (d. 1528)—who was the first of the family to have settled in India.[108] Mawdudi's father, too, though he had studied for some time at Aligarh College, had become a devout Sufi, with deleterious results for his legal practice.[109] Mawdudi himself was never a practicing Sufi but, as he wrote in 1951, he had frequented the company of those who were and his critical view of Sufism was not to be dismissed as based on mere ignorance of this phenomenon.[110]

The criticism itself had needed to be toned down, however. A book published in 1972 by the quasi-official press of the Jama'at-i Islami presented a collection of Mawdudi's writings on the subject of Sufism. Some of these were, indeed, critical of Sufi practice, but, as a whole, the anthology made the point that true Sufism was a legitimate facet of Islam and that insinuations about Mawdudi's opposition to it were false.[111] The book reproduced the early autobiography that had highlighted Mawdudi's Sufi lineage. For the benefit of those who may not have gotten the point even then, the book provided a full Chishti Sufi genealogy for Mawdudi, complete with the revered luminaries of this influential order.[112]

Some years earlier, in 1966, Mian Tufail Muhammad (d. 2009), the general-secretary of the Jama'at-i Islami and subsequently its head (amir), had published an abridged Urdu translation of 'Ali Hujwiri's (d. ca. 1071) *Kashf al-mahjub*, one of the early classics of Persian Sufism.[113] Hujwiri—commonly known as Data Ganj Bakhsh, "the lord who bestows treasures"—is buried in Lahore, and his shrine is probably the most frequently visited of all in Pakistan.[114] Tufail Muhammad's volume is based on an earlier translation of the *Kashf al-mahjub*, but the decision to produce it is suggestive both of the enduring appeal of Sufism and of the Islamists' desire to tap into some of that appeal. It suggests as well that, unlike many other Islamists, in both South Asia and in the Middle East, at least some of those associated with the Jama'at-i Islami of Pakistan have sought not only to base their norms in the foundational texts and the practices of the earliest Muslims but also to maintain a sense of continuity with the subsequent history of Islam. In his preface to this book, Tufail Muhammad lamented the fact that the products of an English education had come to see even "the clowns and singers and tricksters" of Europe as worth emulating while being altogether unfamiliar with their own saints like 'Ali Hujwiri, Ahmad Sirhindi, and Shah Wali Allah.[115] It was in order to make such figures familiar to people once again and to show them that Muslim societies had continued to produce such luminaries even in their age of decline that Tufail Muhammad had undertaken this work.[116] Incidentally, the project also suggests that the Jama'at-i Islami has drawn its following, and even some of its leadership, not only from people with a strongly scripturalist or even just a Deobandi orientation—to which Mawdudi was personally close—but also from those with a more devotional bent, in the manner of the Barelawis. He had great affection, Tufail Muhammad noted in his preface to this book, for Abul-Hasanat Muhammad Ahmad Qadiri (d. 1961), a prominent Barelawi scholar who had produced an Urdu translation of the *Kashf al-mahjub*, and he had wanted to publish that work from the Jama'at-i Islami's press. In the end, however, the translation that Tufail Muhammad relied on in producing his own edition was a different one, for that is what was available to him in prison while he was working on it.[117] `Abd al-Ghafur Ahmad, a later vice president of the Jama`at, also belonged to the Barelawi orientation.[118] This again shows that at least some in the Jama`at have had deeper roots in Sufi devotional piety than may have been required simply by the imperatives of broadening their religio-political appeal. Such imperatives, too, cannot be discounted, however. They did have something to do, for instance, with the decision of Qazi Husayn Ahmad (d. 2013), who became the head of the Jama`at in 1987, to begin his mass-mobilization campaign that year with a visit to the shrine of `Ali Hujwiri.[119]

Even as the modernists, the `ulama, and the Islamists have drawn upon Sufism in their particular ways, those recognizable primarily as Sufis have continued, as might be expected, to cultivate their devotional practices. And they have sought to find resources in their hallowed tradition to also bolster their authority and their public presence. Perhaps the most important contemporary illustration of how they have done so is Muhammad Tahir al-Qadiri.

Born in Jhang in 1951, Tahir al-Qadiri received substantial Islamic education though apparently not a formal degree from a madrasa. Instead, he earned a master's degree in Islamic studies from the University of the Punjab and subsequently a bachelor's degree in law and a PhD from the same university.[120] A scholar and preacher of the Barelawi orientation with strong Sufi leanings, he was a protégé of the Zia al-Haqq regime and of the politically ascendant Nawaz Sharif and his family: he gave sermons at a mosque built by Sharif's father in Lahore and came subsequently to make well-received appearances discussing Qur'anic themes on what in the 1980s was the sole channel of the national television.[121] His doctoral dissertation, defended in 1984, reflected the sensibilities guiding state-sponsored Islamization at the time. It offered a spirited defense of Islamic criminal law in comparison with "the Western penal system [which] has totally collapsed to check [sic] and curtail effectively the rising graph of crime."[122] With some help from Sharif, he also founded in the early 1980s his educational and religious movement, the Minhaj al-Qur'an. Not long after the end of the Zia al-Haqq era, Tahir al-Qadiri had a falling out with Sharif, whereupon he established a political party of his own, the Pakistan Awami Tahrik. He later moved to Toronto, Canada, from where he has directed what now professes to be a global Minhaj al-Qur'an while seeking to bring about "revolutionary" change in Pakistani politics. The latter effort has resulted in some high-profile appearances in Pakistan, most notably in the summer of 2014. In concert with the former cricket star turned politician Imran Khan, a sit-in by Tahir al-Qadiri and his followers in the federal capital brought Islamabad to a standstill for several days that summer. Although the core demand of the sit-in—the resignation of Prime Minister Nawaz Sharif—remained unmet and Tahir al-Qadiri soon flew back to Canada, he had shown an impressive ability to challenge the government.[123]

Some of that challenge was covertly enabled by a military leadership keen to cut the prime minister down to size.[124] It surely also had to do with the failure even of popularly elected leaders to address the chronic problems of ordinary people: according to one survey in 2014, "the cumulative inflation since 2007–08 has led to real increase in price of flour (58 p[er]c[ent]); potatoes (241 pc), pulses (93 pc), sugar (27 pc), and milk (60 pc)." Nearly a third of the total population, or sixty-five million people, fell below the poverty line.[125] But Tahir al-Qadiri also drew on a reservoir of devotional Sufi and Barelawi sentiment, which he has cultivated dexterously over many years and in terms of which he has articulated a good deal of his appeal. For instance, he has published a collection of no less than 2,500 of his short benedictions (*durud o salam*) in honor of the Prophet. He had composed them in Arabic, and they are said to have been "very well received by the shaykhs, researchers, and `ulama of the Arab world." One of Tahir al-Qadiri's disciples subsequently translated the work into Urdu.[126] Another of his books, a compilation of hadith on a variety of topics (including faith, rituals, supplicatory prayers, the virtues of the Prophet and his companions, ethical teachings, and so on), carries separate chains of transmission that link him to the eponymous founders of the four schools of Sunni law; to Bukhari and Muslim—the compilers of the most authoritative of the Sunni collections of hadith; and to the Sufi masters `Abd al-Qadir Jilani and Ibn al-`Arabi.[127] For all the criticism long directed at him by many `ulama, Ibn al-`Arabi remains an immensely influential figure in Sufi circles. So is `Abd al-Qadir Jilani. Tahir al-Qadiri's effort to show that he is an authentic and authorized legatee of religious knowledge from revered Sufi masters, among others, makes him a holy personage in his own right. It was on such veneration that he drew in bringing many thousands—including a large number of women—to his sit-in in Islamabad in the summer of 2014.[128]

A Changing Landscape?

This overview has left us with a rather ambiguous understanding of the place of Sufism in the religious sphere in Pakistan and, before that, in colonial South Asia. On the one hand, the Sufis and their institutions have faced severe challenges from many sides. On the other, Sufism has also exerted a major influence on a variety of religious orientations and their adherents have continued to appeal to it. Large numbers of people still visit Sufi shrines, and not only on the occasion of the saint's death anniversary.[129] Sufi sensibilities have never been limited, however, to contact with shrines, which is to say that the incidence of such visits does not give us the full picture of how Sufi thought and practice continue to inform the lives of countless people in local contexts.[130]

And yet Sufism in Pakistan may be rather less vibrant today than it was in colonial India a century ago. Two caveats are in order before proceeding to illustrate this point. One of these is that my observations relate not to devotional practice at local levels, but rather to the intellectual and religio-political dimensions of Sufism—writings by and discourses of Sufis, questions of reform, the impact of politics and the state on Sufi piety, and so forth. The other caveat is that any discussion of decline in case of Sufism—and of other facets of Islam, for that matter—carries with it the interpretive danger of reaffirming the decline narratives commonly encountered in Western histories of Sufism *as well as* in the Sufis' own telling of their past, not to mention modernist renderings of that past.[131] My interest here is not, however, in asking how contemporary Sufism in Pakistan, or in the Muslim world at large, compares with a putative golden age of Sufism in medieval Islam but rather in how contemporary Sufism compares with some facets of it in colonial India, which itself is usually seen as part of a tradition in decline.[132] While recognizing that the decline of Sufism in contemporary Muslim societies remains a matter of scholarly disagreement,[133] some indications of what I take to be key indicators of a diminished presence that Sufism has in contemporary Pakistan are worth examining.

First, a significant contrast is to be noticed between the production of Sufi works in colonial India and those that have been published in Pakistan over the past half century or so. For instance, Ahmad Riza Khan (d. 1921), a Sufi of the Qadiri order and the founder of the Barelawi orientation, was a prolific writer with an output that included not only polemical works against rival orientations and countless fatwas but also Sufi devotional works. Barelawis in Pakistan, and in India, have done much to reprint such works, but comparable works have not been produced by later Barelawis, and certainly not on the master's scale. To a Barelawi, this fact would serve only to underscore the incomparable stature of Ahmad Riza, and one would not wish to be seen as competing with the master in this or any other respect. Yet, the fact remains that the intellectual output of the later Barelawis, on Sufi as on other topics, has been significantly smaller than what the founder of their doctrinal orientation had produced in British India.

Much the same could be said about the Deobandis, so far as Sufism is concerned. The figure who looms largest in this regard is of course Ashraf `Ali Thanawi, who died in the last years of colonial rule. Over the course of a long career, Thanawi had published numerous legal and exegetical works. But he and his immediate disciples had also produced a large corpus of Sufi writing, including the aforementioned work on Hafiz, a multivolume commentary on the *Masnawi* of Rumi, works on the tenth-century Sufi martyr Hallaj and on Ibn al-`Arabi, books providing guidance to those seeking the Sufi path and, not least, a substantial collection of the master's own spiritual discourses. Deobandis of a Sufi bent have spent considerable energy and financial resources on reprinting and, by way of anthologies, of repackaging these writings, but no Deobandi of either India or Pakistan has produced anything on Thanawi's scale when it comes to Sufism. Later Deobandis *have* produced a great deal by way of commentaries on the Qur'an and hadith as well as varied works on law, but this serves only to highlight the contrast with the meager output on explicitly Sufi themes.[134]

This is not just a question of intellectual productivity, however. The past hundred years or so have also seen a significant shift in the cultural orientation of South Asian Islam. Irrespective of what Iqbal thought of Hafiz, he was entirely at home in the cultural idiom of the medieval Persian poet, just as he was in the rich tradition of Persian Sufi poetry in general. Similarly, it made sense for Thanawi to discourse on Rumi and Hafiz because there was an audience for it. Three generations later, most educated Muslims in South Asia are no longer literate in Persian.[135] Ideas traceable to the classics of Persian Sufism still remain part of local discourse in particular contexts.[136] Even so, the sort of direct access to the mystical heritage that had once been taken for granted is no longer available to most people; and this has had implications for how Sufi thought has fared in contemporary Pakistan.

Second, even as Sufism has benefited much from modern technologies and the unprecedented means of travel, communication, and the dissemination of knowledge made possible by them, modern scientific sensibilities have also undermined the presuppositions of an earlier era. For instance, it was possible for Thanawi to argue that a child born to a woman whose husband had been away for years was legitimate, for it was conceivable that the husband had visited his wife without having been seen by anyone or that he had been transported miraculously to his wife by a saint or a jinn.[137] As a Sufi master, for whom miraculous deeds were uncontroversial matters, Thanawi would not have had to give excessively free rein to his imagination to make such a supposition. Already in his lifetime, some people were sufficiently perplexed by his views on this score to ask if he had been misunderstood;[138] and the master himself acknowledged that such occurrences were improbable.[139] In any case, such fatwas, intended as they were to provide a legal cover to women accused of sexual impropriety, are likely to be accepted less willingly by those seeking them today than they were in an earlier age.[140] Put another way, legal rulings are often significantly less rooted in, or tempered by, a quasi-Sufi perspective on things than they were some generations ago.

Third, though one does not notice much defensiveness on Sufi matters in the writings of an Ahmad Riza Khan or a Thanawi, it is unmistakable in some more recent works. The Qur'an commentary of Pir Karam Shah (d. 1998), a Chishti Sufi of Barelawi leanings who, in the Zia al-Haqq era, served on the Federal Shari'at Court and subsequently the Shari'at Appellate Bench of the Supreme Court, provides a telling instance. The commentary, first published in the 1960s, makes a point of defending Barelawi beliefs and practices against the charge that they verge on polytheism, arguing, for instance, that seeing saints and holy men as necessary means to reach God the more effectively is not tantamount to taking them as partners with God.[141] This strategy is not well-designed, however, to put nagging doubts to rest about whether Sufi practices do indeed conform to scriptural norms. Leaving aside the quality of the defense a Sufi is able to mount against critics, the range of issues on which such defense has had to be offered has continued to grow, and Barelawi Sufis have been rather more vulnerable on this score than others. Conversely, it would be far more unusual for a Deobandi today to defend the practice of prostration to shrines than it was in the 1920s. A greater distance now separates the Barelawi from the Deobandi views on particular devotional practices than it did a century ago. This has meant, to return to my previous point, a certain narrowing of the space for Sufism *within* Deobandi circles. Thanawi is often credited with enhancing the alignment of Sufi practice with juridical norms, and there is little doubt that this was a concern that animated his reformist vision. Yet, he tended to allow much wider scope for flexibility of interpretation, more room for controversial views, in the realm of Sufism than he did in legal matters. By the same token, he cautioned his disciples and readers against any excessive effort to bring the one into accord with the other.[142] About three-quarters of a century after his death, the logic of this realignment has gone in a decidedly legalistic direction. Deobandi muftis have arguably come to define the Islam of ordinary believers more often, and with fewer gray areas, than do any competing Sufis of this orientation.

Fourth, as the example of the Pakistani bureaucrat Qudratullah Shahab suggests, some of the vulnerabilities of Sufism may lie, paradoxically, in the very expressions of its appeal. It is significant that Shahab had adopted the Sufi way not by affiliating himself with any of the institutional orders that one might have expected him to, but rather by choosing the Uwaysi path, which lacks any organized structure, any accredited chain of masters and disciples. When embarking upon his spiritual quest, he had prayed to God to let him be inducted into this order for he was "a seeker of God's way and lacked the ability to traverse on the straightforward paths."[143] The appeal of true Sufism went hand in hand for him with a deep suspicion of institutional Sufism and of what he took to be fake claims to mystical prowess. A much publicized case in 1968 had been that of the so-called Box Pir (*dabba pir*), who had the reputation for miraculously adding money to the boxes his devotees brought to him with some money already in them.[144] Shahab's own experiences on the Sufi path had made it clear to him that

> there are no hidden secrets involved in Sufism or in traversing the path. Sufi practices (*azkar, ashghal awr muraqabat*) ... are not esoteric things but rather practices that are well-known and altogether clear in their own way in each order. As for what the wayfarer experiences

during such practices, discussing them [with others] is meaningless. They are like a marriage. A marriage is not a secret. Everyone understands the purposes, practices, and results of a marriage, but no one talks about what goes on in the bridal chamber. . . . The Sufi path is a "kindergarten" that helps incline people towards the shari`a, but it is also full of delight and of extremely enjoyable discoveries. A large number of the wayfarers is so engrossed in this delight as to become immobilized and to lose their way towards the true goal, viz, the shari`a. Such unfortunate people sometimes emerge as the Box Pir and sometimes they engage, through their fake shops, in the black marketing of Sufism. . . . The reward of those who escape from falling headlong into such alluring pits is that they are eventually able to start walking on the high road of the shari`a. Sufism and its path have no goal or meaning other than [being able to do] this.[145]

Sufis like Thanawi would have concurred with Shahab's insistence on the shared goals of Sufism and the shari`a, though with the caveats noted earlier. Shahab, however, sought an altogether *independent* path to Sufi practice. This fit well, though he does not say so, into the life of a high-ranking government official wary of being seen as submitting to anything other than a governmental hierarchy. It does not, however, fit well with conventional conceptions of authoritative guidance in Sufism. Thanawi, for one, would have seen Shahab's mystical orientation as another expression of modernist hubris.

The Sufi orders from which Shahab had wanted to keep his distance are hardly static, and some have made impressive efforts to adjust themselves to changing times. Though the Sabiri Chishtis of Pakistan—a suborder in the Chishti spiritual lineage—have sought to maintain a sense of continuity in their teachings and practices, as Robert Rozehnal has argued, it is noteworthy that a succession of their Sufi masters was educated exclusively in Western or Westernized institutions of learning. Muhammad Zauqi Shah (d. 1951), whom we met in chapter 4, had studied at Aligarh College. His successor, Shahidullah Faridi (d. 1978), was an Englishman—born John Gilbert Lennard—who had briefly studied at Oxford before coming to live in late colonial India and subsequently in Pakistan. Another master, Wahid Bakhsh Sial (d. 1995), had been an army officer educated at the Dehra Dun military academy in colonial India. The next Chishti Sabiri master, Siraj `Ali Muhammad, graduated from the Air Force Academy of Pakistan.[146] Such profiles are far closer to those of many modernists and Islamists than they are to the Pakistani `ulama's; and they are certainly very different from those of the Chishti masters of the late nineteenth and the early twentieth centuries. For all the attraction the recent Sufi masters may hold for a segment of middle-class Pakistanis in showing how Sufi ethics can give meaning to one's life in a changing world, there remain questions about whether a coherent Sufi tradition can, in fact, be maintained outside the framework of a more traditional educational and religious formation.[147] In the first half of the twentieth century, Ashraf `Ali Thanawi, also a Sabiri Chishti, could tap simultaneously into the scholarly and Sufi traditions to attract large numbers of disciples. It is difficult to say the same of the latter-day Sabiri Chishti masters.

The case of a contemporary pir, Zulfiqar Ahmad (b. 1953) of the Naqshbandi order, has parallels with the Sabiri Chishtis while also revealing some differences. By training an electrical engineer with no formal religious education, he draws liberally in his discourses on the language of modern science in explaining Islam, the Qur'an, and Sufism to his audiences. A good part of his appeal clearly rests on that language. Yet, he is also a staunch Deobandi who regales his listeners with edifying anecdotes about the luminaries of that orientation, and he has devoted much energy to establishing and running Deobandi madrasas.[148] His efforts suggest some recognition of the need to rest Sufi piety on more traditional grounds, though they remain uncertain in their long-term effects.

Fifth, Sufi shrines in Pakistan have been far more vulnerable to governmental regulation than have the madrasas. Despite major governmental initiatives in the early 1960s, the late 1970s, and then in the aftermath of September 11, 2001, to regulate them, most madrasas—and all of the leading ones—have remained autonomous and independent of the government for all practical purposes. Though the `ulama have not been averse to benefiting from the largesse of the rich or from government assistance, the organizational model of many among them has been anchored since the late nineteenth century in an informal economy that includes a large number of small financial contributions from ordinary believers.[149] Almost by definition, such contributions lie outside government control. Many shrines, on the other hand, have historically depended on charitable endowments, typically in the form of land grants. Their scale may be gleaned from the fact that nearly a third of the total revenue of Sindh at the time of its annexation by the British in 1843 had accrued to "ecclesiastical establishments,"[150] which primarily meant Sufi shrines. Government takeover of such properties was not only financially lucrative, it was also the most effective way of checking the influence of those associated with them. As observed earlier, a succession of waqf regulations has subsequently brought them under government regulation in Pakistan. Significantly, many of the madrasas that the government did succeed in bringing under its control from the 1960s were also those associated with *shrines*, and bureaucratic officials have often had wide leeway in determining the curriculum of such schools.[151] By contrast, even as many Pakistani madrasas have come to accept the public school curriculum as part of their education, the `ulama have maintained firm control of their institutions and of just how the public school curriculum would be combined with a more traditional religious education.

The political influence enjoyed by large shrine-holders in the Punjab and Sindh could have conceivably enabled them to prevent governmental control of waqf endowments. It occasionally did so, as in late colonial Punjab. Much of that influence has tended, however, to be focused on preserving *local* political and economic interests rather than the independence of the shrines as a category of institutions.[152] Once again, there is an instructive contrast with the madrasas. Since the early 1960s, the ʿulama have mobilized their considerable energies to organize madrasa "boards" along doctrinal lines to oversee the affairs of these institutions, to standardize the education imparted at them and, above all, through a closing of their ranks, to resist perceived government encroachment. Caretakers of Pakistani shrines have also made occasional effort to close their ranks; but such efforts have been desultory and notably ineffective.[153]

Finally, while the attack on Sufi practices and institutions has often taken the form of polemics against them or, as the case may be, of government regulation, recent years have witnessed such attacks in a more literal sense, too. They are usually attributable to the Pakistani Taliban and allied groups, and they have targeted Sufi shrines across the country. The much revered shrine of ʿAli Hujwiri was attacked by a suicide bomber in July 2010, with a death toll of around forty-five people.[154] That same year, an attack on the shrine of Sakhi Sarwar in southern Punjab killed another fifty people.[155] Other attacks have targeted the Bari Imam shrine outside Islamabad in 2005 and the shrines of Baba Farid Ganjshakar in Pakpattan, Punjab, and ʿAbdallah Shah Ghazi in Karachi, both in 2010.[156] Unsurprisingly, Khyber Pakhthunkhwa, the Frontier province that is home to the Taliban, has borne the brunt of such attacks, the most notable of them being on the shrine of the revered Sufi poet Rahman Baba in March 2009.[157] ISIS, too—the Islamic State in Iraq and Syria—has claimed some bombings, notably the one carried out at the shrine of Lal Shahbaz Qalandar in Sehwan, Sindh, in February 2017.[158]

Such attacks can be viewed from several distinct but overlapping perspectives. As observed earlier, sectarian Sunni and Shiʿi militants have targeted their rivals in a variety of locations, including mosques and in Twelver Shiʿi imambargahs. How does the targeting of shrines compare with those attacks? An obvious similarity is, of course, that both are clearly marked religious spaces. A significant difference is, however, that the mosques and imambargahs have not usually been attacked in their own right but rather to target the people gathered there; the shrines, on the other hand, are targets of attack for what they stand for in themselves.[159] In this sense, the shrines are rather more like the public schools that the Taliban have attacked in the Frontier province than they are like the mosques at which they and others have also targeted their rivals. Though in some cases, notably the school massacre in Peshawar in December 2014, the Taliban have, indeed, attacked those studying at schools,[160] they have mostly sought to destroy school buildings for what they represent—government authority and the perceived encroachment of an alien, un-Islamic culture.

An attack on shrines challenges that authority in some other, related ways, too. In the aftermath of September 11, 2001, Pakistani governments have made some half-hearted but not inconspicuous efforts to promote Sufi devotionalism as an antidote to religio-political militancy in the country. For instance, in 2009, the government of Prime Minister Yusuf Riza Gilani established the Sufi Advisory Council "with [the] aim [of] combating extremism and fanaticism." Some years earlier, President Pervez Musharraf had set up a National Sufi Council with similar goals.[161] Representatives of Western governments have sometimes also let themselves be seen as patrons of Sufi devotionalism. For instance, in July 2009, the British foreign secretary David Miliband paid visits to the tombs of several Sufis in Multan in what some saw as an effort to "charm ... moderate Muslims."[162] And in April 2010, it was reported that the US ambassador to Pakistan, Anne W. Patterson, had allocated $149,000 for conservation work on three Sufi shrines in the Punjab.[163] Insomuch as venerated Sufi shrines have become associated with the War on Terror, it is not surprising that some of that terror has come to visit these shrines.

Taliban attacks on shrines also represent none too subtle efforts to remake the religious landscape. Sufi shrines have long been sites of practices frowned upon by those of a scripturalist bent, and it is some of those practices that the Music in Muslim Shrines Act of 1942 had sought to outlaw in late colonial Punjab. There is little to suggest that that act was effective in curbing them, however. On the contrary, it remains common for important Pakistani shrines to host what are billed as "cultural" events on the occasion of the saint's death anniversary, the `urs. For instance, a fair held in conjunction with the `urs of Sayyid Wilayat Shah in Chakwal, in the Punjab, in September 2013, featured sporting competitions, bullfighting, and music.[164] And at the `urs of Sachchal Sarmast in Sindh, the chief minister of the province was reported in 2014 to have given out awards to the best male and female singers.[165] Pakistani Taliban and allied groups do not take a benign view of such practices. The shrine of Sakhi Sarwar in southern Punjab was attacked by a suicide bomber while "devotees were performing devotional dance at the main entrance."[166] This subsequently led the local government to ban the use of musical instruments at the saint's `urs on grounds that it was "a security threat."[167] In the case of the shrine of Rahman Baba near Peshawar, the president of the association looking after it reported that "some 'Taliban-like people' having long hair and beards used to come there and ask the caretaker why he had not barred women from visiting the shrine." Some Taliban had reportedly also said that praying in the adjacent mosque was forbidden, presumably given its proximity to the shrine.[168]

Though relatively new to Pakistan, the targeting of shrines is hardly unheard of in other contexts. In late medieval Iran, Central Asia, and South Asia, rulers and invaders had desecrated the shrines with which their defeated rivals were associated.[169] For instance, Zahir al-din Babur, who went on to found the Mughal dynasty in India, had commanded the destruction of the tomb of "a heretic wandering dervish" while campaigning in the Bajaur region in the winter of 1519. Coincidentally, this region now forms part of Pakistan's North-West Frontier and it has been a stronghold of the Pakistani Taliban.[170] In more recent times, it is worth recalling the Wahhabi destruction of venerated tombs in the Hijaz in the 1920s, which had caused widespread consternation in India and was the immediate backdrop against which Shabbir Ahmad `Usmani had addressed the Saudi king on the question of prostration at shrines.[171] In the mid-1930s, as relations between the Shi`is and Sunnis of Lucknow deteriorated, some had warned that it was a matter of time before Sunni extremists, then attacking Shi`i rituals, began targeting *Sunni* devotional practices and tombs as well.[172] In our own times, shrines have been attacked and destroyed in several Muslim societies—for instance, Mali, in West Africa; Mosul, in Iraq; and elsewhere.[173] Like many of those agitating in the Madh-i sahaba cause in late colonial Lucknow, the Taliban are classifiable as Deobandis rather than as Wahhabis or Salafis. Yet, their targeting of shrines remains atypical for the Deobandis.[174] As if to underscore this, the Taliban have not spared the Deobandis associated with particular shrines either.[175] Practitioners of Sufi devotional music have also been targeted on occasion. In June 2016, Amjad Sabiri, a noted *qawwali* singer, was assassinated in Karachi; a Taliban group claimed responsibility for it while vaguely accusing Sabiri of blasphemy.[176]

Dramatic as it is, we should not, however, exaggerate the impact of the Taliban attack on Sufi shrines. Though some are predictably dissuaded by such attacks from visiting the shrines, others have continued to do so. A peasant woman seeking a saint's help to ward off the financial disaster of a failed crop will still come to his shrine, as would those fleeing their land after failing to pay their debts.[177] Those attracted to a saint's teachings, or to his poetry, would do so too,[178] and so would homeless women looking for shelter.[179] At the same time, and though the Taliban have sought to change things in a hurry and in the bluntest possible form, their actions are not always discontinuous with earlier, less violent efforts to refashion the religious landscape. And this gives to them a greater significance, so far as their impact on Pakistani Sufism is concerned, than merely the blowing up of particular shrines in the years following September 2001. Many things separate the proponents of the Music in Muslim Shrines Bill, or their modernist successors in Pakistan, from the Taliban. But the desire to see a particular religious worldview forcibly imposed upon others is not among them.

Yet, if modernism, despite some indebtedness to Sufism, has not been good for it, the decline of modernism has, paradoxically, not been good for it either. The debilitation of Pakistani modernism has meant its ceding a great deal of the initiative in the articulation of Islamic discourses to some highly conservative circles, heightening in turn the vulnerability as well as the defensiveness of the Sufis.[180] For its part, the declining fortunes of Sufism have made modernist Islam more vulnerable to its challengers. Iqbal had observed long ago that Sufism's otherworldly attitudes had made young Muslims receptive to modern European ideologies.[181] The noted British orientalist Sir Hamilton Gibb echoed this worry in an influential work of his own.[182] In the 1960s, Fazlur Rahman, too, made a similar point in cautioning in his book, *Islam*, against the modern "one-sided legacy of anti-Sufism."[183] Sufism met many more needs of people than only the religious, Rahman wrote, and if it was made to vacate the space it had traditionally occupied in people's lives without a proper "social reconstruction programme," that space could be vulnerable to Communist movements.[184] This was a powerful warning at the height of the Cold War. But in good modernist fashion, Rahman was disdainful of what was on offer in the free world, too. His own, unforgiving, view of Sufism notwithstanding, he concluded his book with the plea that "the genuine inner life of the 'heart'—the basic élan of Sufism—must be reintegrated in the Shari`a and can be neglected only on pain, in the long run, of succumbing to the devastating onslaughts of modern secularism."[185] In the early twenty-first century, it was neither communism nor secularism but radical Islamism whose onslaughts had come to be the most devastating.[186] It is to them and to an explication of the context in which they have been experienced in Pakistan that we now turn.

CHAPTER SEVEN

Religion, Violence, and the State

SINCE THE TERRORIST ATTACKS of September 11, 2001, no topic has been debated more often in the international media, policy circles, and among observers of Muslim societies than the question of Islam's relationship with violence and war.[1] As a state professing to be an Islamic Republic and one that was closely allied with the Taliban—hosts to Usama bin Laden and many of his associates—Pakistan, too, has received extensive scrutiny in varied circles for its ties with Islamist militant organizations and its role in enabling them to operate within and outside its borders as instruments of strategic policy. Though an examination of developments in the aftermath of those attacks is among the purposes of this chapter, the concerns here are broader. Taking a number of key illustrations from the entire span of Pakistan's history, this chapter seeks to shed some further light on how we might try to understand the fraught relationship between Islam, the state, and religiously inflected justifications for violence. How have the Pakistani political and military establishments shaped the context in which appeals to jihad have been framed or in which particular groups have taken to violent agitation on what they profess to be religious grounds? What "Islamic" resources have been utilized by such groups? And what difficulties have the modernizing governing elite faced in taking or keeping charge of the narratives whereby the resort to arms has been justified at various points in the country's history? These are among our questions here.

Kashmir, 1947–48

Any discussion of religion, violence, and the Pakistani state must necessarily begin with Kashmir. The denial to the new state of a predominantly Muslim region contiguous with it has always remained high on the list of the injustices done to Pakistan by the departing British and by the government of independent India. The Pakistani political and military leadership has repeatedly sought to right this wrong. The first such effort was made already in Jinnah's lifetime in the form of covert operations in Kashmir. With the active encouragement of the government and logistical support from the military, tribal militias and other volunteers had begun pouring into Kashmir almost immediately after the birth of Pakistan. This was in response to widely publicized reports of atrocities against local Muslims by the Hindu ruler of the state. In turn, this infiltration precipitated the formal accession of Kashmir to India, the dispatch of Indian troops there, and the threat of a full-fledged war between India and Pakistan. By the time a ceasefire took effect in Kashmir in January 1949 through the intervention of the United Nations, about a third of the erstwhile princely state had been "liberated" by the irregular forces fighting on Pakistan's behalf. A plebiscite was promised by the UN to allow the people of Kashmir to decide their future. It never took place, ensuring that Kashmir would remain at the forefront of the disputes between India and Pakistan. What concerns us here is not the political and military history of the conflict in Kashmir, however, but rather some of the ways in which invocations of Islam have featured in this conflict.

The years 1947–48 were not the first time armed bands had entered Kashmir to take on the local government. In 1931, Muslims in the Punjab and elsewhere in British India had begun sending groups of volunteers to aid Kashmiri Muslims in their effort to end what they saw as the oppressive and anti-Muslim policies of the state's ruler. The Deobandi luminary Ashraf ʿAli Thanawi was asked at the time about the legitimacy of such operations and, true to his quietist politics, he had strongly discouraged them. If Muslims had the means to offer effective resistance, he said, they should do so. If not, they ought to bear their hardship patiently, for sporadic agitation or mere shows of force tended to exacerbate rather than relieve the problems they were trying to remedy.[2] Mawdudi, too, was asked in 1948 about the legitimacy of irregular military operations in Kashmir and whether it constituted a jihad. Startling many people, he had demurred, arguing that they could qualify as jihad only if the government of Pakistan openly declared it to be such—covertly supporting warfare while maintaining diplomatic and trade relations with the enemy, India, was no way to conduct jihad.[3] With his history of sharp denunciations of the Muslim League leadership and of its credentials to steward the demand for a separate Muslim homeland, Mawdudi was not a popular figure in government circles in Pakistan. His views on Kashmir confirmed them in their grim view of him. Some prominent religious voices were also heard in opposition to Mawdudi, of which two deserve notice.

In early July 1948, Shabbir Ahmad ʿUsmani wrote to Mawdudi to correct his "gravely erroneous" position on the Kashmir war.[4] ʿUsmani argued that India's actions in violating its earlier understandings with Pakistan—for instance, by forcibly annexing the territory of Junagadh, whose ruler had acceded to Pakistan, or condoning the massacre of Muslims in India—meant that it had

already acted in bad faith and that Pakistan was therefore under no obligation to maintain its part of any agreements with it.[5] He argued further that
an agreement between two countries did not necessarily prevent volunteers
from each country from engaging, in their *individual* capacity, in military
operations.[6] In a subsequent fatwa, `Usmani also made it clear that a jihad
remained valid even if the Muslim government calling for it—in this instance,
covertly—was not committed to proper Islamic norms.[7]

In his response to `Usmani, Mawdudi continued to insist that a Muslim
government could not engage in jihad against a country with which it maintained treaty relations.[8] He also showed a rather surer grasp of international
law than had `Usmani. A treaty between two countries was not automatically
nullified if the private citizens of one attacked those of the other, he said, but
that hardly meant that the terms of an interstate treaty had no implications
for the behavior of putatively private individuals. Such individuals, too, bore
"moral responsibility" to abide by the treaty to which their country was a sig-
natory.[9] In a biting challenge, Mawdudi asked `Usmani to declare in a fatwa
that that was not the case.[10] Remarkably for men who had spent all of their
lives until that point in regions that were now part of India, neither `Usmani
nor Mawdudi seems to have worried much—at least not publicly—about how
the jihad in Kashmir might complicate the lives of the Muslims still living in
India.[11]

Before this exchange between `Usmani and Mawdudi had concluded, a
veteran of anti-colonial struggle in the Frontier had busied himself in writing
a treatise in refutation of some of Mawdudi's views. Unlike `Usmani, Fazl-i
Ilahi Wazirabadi (d. 1951) was not a trained religious scholar, and not even,
like Mawdudi, a well-educated religious intellectual. Instead, he owed his credentials to long years of exile in the tribal areas of the Frontier, where he had
been part of a militant, puritanical movement—the Jama`at al-mujahidin—
that traced its origins to Sayyid Ahmad of Rae Bareli in the early nineteenth
century.[12] Shortly after his return from exile in July 1948, an aged Wazirabadi
was asked about the burning question of the day, the legitimacy of military
operations in Kashmir. He responded in detail, pointedly refuting Mawdudi's
views without however referring to him by name.[13] Though he shared the gist
of his views with `Usmani, Wazirabadi was considerably more emphatic in
underscoring the obligatoriness of the jihad in Kashmir. Lacking `Usmani's
juridical learning, he was also significantly less constrained by any rules of war
on which the Islamic legal tradition has long insisted.[14] Jihad became obligatory, he said, if any one of the following seven reasons for it were to be found
in a particular situation: the need to work toward the dominance of Islam;
self-preservation; guarding helpless Muslims against unbelievers; avenging
oneself against the unbelievers; waging war on account of the unbelievers'
breach of contract; fighting for national liberation; and rescuing Muslims from
godless rule. He adduced Qur'anic passages and hadith reports in support of

each of these grounds and asserted that all seven were fully operative in case of Kashmir.[15] Where `Usmani had been content simply to cite the enemy's bad faith as a justification for a Muslim state to consider existing agreements with it void without having to publicly renounce them, Wazirabadi held that the enemy needed to be *punished* for its bad faith. And he argued that this punishment should take the form of "such general massacre that successive generations, till the Day of Judgment, would remember the consequences of violating agreements."[16]

Wazirabadi was also of the view that no taint of mundane—as opposed to religious—considerations could compromise the quality of jihad. Fighting in defense of such "worldly" (*dunyawi*) interests as life, property, and progeny qualified as jihad;[17] and those who branded a war fueled by nationalist sentiment as something other than jihad, he said in a transparent allusion to Mawdudi's well-known views on the incompatibility of Islam and nationalism, were only aiding the enemy.[18] Conversely, if the government was unable to openly engage in jihad, it should not be pressed to do so, though people ought to continue engaging in the war effort in their individual capacities.[19] Finally, it was not necessary that those leading a jihad be the most virtuous of people;[20] indeed, he said, people were obligated to submit even to a leader who was guilty of "major sins."[21]

The significance of Wazirabadi's treatise lies in the spirited case it makes for the jihad in Kashmir. It consists as well in its enthusiastic embrace of the governing elite, and in this respect it stands in marked contrast with the suspicions and ambiguities that we have observed in earlier chapters in the relationship between the `ulama and the Islamists, on the one hand, and the modernists, on the other. It also serves as an important early illustration of the shared interests of religious militants—in whose circles this book has remained influential[22]—and the Pakistani military. Over the course of the country's history, the military has often sought to employ religio-political groups to destabilize the Indian hold over Kashmir. Works like Wazirabadi's have provided the ideological underpinnings for such action, showing in the process how a long-standing religious tradition can be invoked to give weight and authenticity to it.

Mawdudi realized soon enough that his views on the jihad in Kashmir could prove very costly to his Jama`at-i Islami. No nonstate actors then engaged in the fighting in Kashmir would have wanted their actions to be counted as anything less than jihad. The public opinion was decidedly hostile to India and to what everyone saw as the forced accession of Muslim-majority Kashmir to a Hindu-dominated nation. And the political elite were almost as one in seeing Mawdudi in sinister colors. Already by mid-September 1948, less than a week after Jinnah's death, Mawdudi had reversed his position. Writing to `Usmani, Mawdudi said that the government of Pakistan had come to acknowledge the presence of its forces in Kashmir, which amounted in effect to giving clear notice of its intentions to the enemy. It was now justified for the people of Pakistan to take part in the jihad in Kashmir. Indeed, he said, the Jama`at-i Islami itself intended to do so.[23]

This volte face did not help Mawdudi very much, not least because he had continued to take uncompromising positions on other issues. His commitment to the idea of the sovereignty of God entailed, for instance, that one could owe allegiance only to God, not to a state that did not recognize His sovereignty. As has been seen, that recognition would come a little later, in the form of the Objectives Resolution of March 1949. In the meanwhile, in the fall of 1948, Mawdudi saw himself and some of his close associates incarcerated and his party's publications proscribed.[24]

The undeclared war in Kashmir was an easy sell to the country as jihad. Yet, the government had run a significant risk in mobilizing Islam for it. It was never quite in control of the incursions into Kashmir and the fury of the tribesmen on both sides of the porous Pakistan-Afghanistan border at reports about the desecration of Sufi shrines in India—itself a prelude to the tribal infiltration—could easily turn against the Pakistani government itself. One tribal leader was reported in September 1947 to have characterized the Muslim leadership "as a body of infidels for favouring Hindus and Sikhs," referring unfavorably to its efforts to protect non-Muslims living in the Frontier region.[25] Wazirabadi's seemingly full alignment with the government on the jihad in Kashmir also carried a potentially steep price, and not simply in terms of what the religious groups in the country would expect in return for their support. It was also that, with so unambiguous a case for everyman's jihad, the government might not be able to rein in the nonstate actors, or to calibrate the religious appeals that had helped galvanize them, when it needed to do so.

Punjab, 1953

Although we have already examined several key facets of the anti-Ahmadi agitation of 1953 in the previous chapters, I briefly return to it here to highlight two additional things: first, some of the complexity of the relationship between latent religious sentiment and its cultivation from outside, and second, the unexpected forms that that brew could take.

For many Muslims, few issues can come close to the rallying power of defending the honor of the Prophet Muhammad. Yet, even in such delicate matters, it was not without considerable help from forces external to the religious sentiment in question that a full-blown agitation could take shape in 1953. It was easy to characterize this agitation as "madness," as Daultana, the Punjab chief minister, later did, or, again in his words, as "religious hysteria [that] demanded nothing short of martyrdom."[26] Yet, Daultana had an ax to grind against the central government, as has been seen. And the proceedings of the

Court of Inquiry investigating the 1953 agitation leave little doubt that he had helped manufacture some of the hysteria in question. Newspapers that his government subsidized were found, for instance, to be feeding the frenzy.[27] For his part, the prime minister, Nazimuddin, tended to have a more favorable view of the `ulama than did most other modernists in the government, but he, too, wanted to put their goodwill to political uses of his own: in mollifying them on the Ahmadi question, he had hoped to secure their support on the shape of the future constitution.[28] The military had its own interests to promote in handling the agitation. As matters slipped out of government control in the provincial capital, the military had pointedly failed to come to the aid of the civil law-enforcement authorities or to act while those authorities remained in charge.[29] When it did finally step in, there was no mistaking the message that the military had succeeded where the civilians had failed. At the other end, the Ahrar needed to rehabilitate themselves in Pakistani society and politics, and fueling the anti-Ahmadi sentiment in the name of the Prophet's sullied honor, and of Islam itself, was a most effective way to do so. None of this is to reduce the agitation to the machinations of particular quarters. There *was* a strong religious sentiment to be mobilized, a deeply felt religious issue to appeal to. But it was not a new issue, and it would not have become the basis of significant unrest without interested parties working on it, albeit in nonconcerted ways.

To turn to my second point here, if those engaging in jihad in Kashmir *could* turn against the Pakistani government itself, as they sometimes would in the following decades, it was not long before the anti-Ahmadi agitation did in fact acquire a distinctly anti-government aspect. As the inspector-general of the Punjab police wrote after it had been crushed, "The agitation was very widespread. I don't think that all these persons had sympathy with the objects of the agitation. What was apparent was that they had no sympathy with the Government."[30] The rhetoric of jihad was invoked as well, except that its target was not just the Ahmadis but, shockingly, also what some referred to as the "satanic government."[31] A mosque preacher in Okara was reported to have threatened that people "won't defend country [*sic*] if it was attac[k]ed by enemy under present circumstances."[32] And a ring leader of the agitation had taunted the government that it should be fighting India rather than its own citizens.[33]

Islam and War: 1965 and 1971

Religious motifs were freely invoked when Pakistan did go to war with India, in 1965 and again in 1971. In 1965, the government of President Ayub Khan had begun covert operations in Indian-held Kashmir with the calculation that the conflict with India would remain limited to this contested territory and that, in this circumscribed war-theater, Pakistan would have a military advantage. India saw no reason to limit its counteroperations to Kashmir, however, and on September 6 it attacked West Pakistan along the international borders.

The war was presented to the nation as the result of Indian aggression and as a jihad. The `ulama fully supported the war effort, as did the Islamists. In the weeks preceding September 6, Barelawi and Deobandi organizations had declared the Kashmiris' struggle against Indian occupation to be a jihad.[34] So did Mawdudi this time around, observing after the ceasefire that while the actual fighting (*qital*) had ceased, the broader struggle (jihad) would have to continue until the goal of Kashmiri self-determination had been achieved.[35] Support for the war was not limited to any one segment of society. It was a moment of patriotic fervor, and almost everyone seemed to be on board.[36] Though many Bengalis had resented the prominence that Kashmir was given in determining the state's military priorities and expenditures, just as they were "mortified at the suggestion that ... [East Pakistan's] defence lay in West Pakistan,"[37] there was much outpouring of patriotic sentiment in the eastern wing, too. The valor of the Pakistani troops was celebrated by poets of all political leanings, and some made a point of also highlighting the contribution of Bengali troops.[38]

The seventeen-day war had ended in a stalemate, though the state's propaganda machine led people to believe, as many still do, that Pakistan was the victor. Triumph against a much bigger, more powerful aggressor, which had never reconciled itself to the creation of a Muslim homeland, was often explained not just in terms of the gallantry of the Pakistani troops, of which there was impressive evidence, but also of God's special favor on Pakistan. Much myth-making went into the narratives of the war. Evoking Qur'anic allusions to divine help during some of the Prophet Muhammad's military engagements,[39] stories circulated of white- or green-robed beings coming to the assistance of Pakistani troops on the battlefield, and of deeds that could only be understood as miraculous. Holy men were reported to have seen the Prophet in dreams with the assurance that the victory belonged to Pakistan; the Prophet's cousin `Ali, a famed warrior and the first Shi`i imam, was likewise seen expressing his intention to assist the country in the war effort.[40] A religious aura surrounded the war even for those at the highest levels of government. As Qudratullah Shahab, the principal secretary to the president, later recounted it, Ayub Khan was once allowed by the Saudi government to go inside the Ka`ba and to pray there. "He had prayed there to God to not let our head bow down to India." Shahab commented: "A prayer inside the house of God is never futile—the war of 1965 is clear proof of this."[41] That this view should have been expressed in a posthumous autobiography that is far from being uncritical of Ayub Khan is an indication of the depth and reach of the religious feeling that the war of 1965 had aroused.

In his writings on the war, the modernist intellectual Ghulam Ahmad Parwez was as eager as anyone Ayub Khan could find to highlight its religious
dimensions. To Parwez, not only did the troops embody the sort of virtues
that the Qur'an extolls, some even exemplified God-like qualities. God's at-
tribute of not being overtaken by slumber or sleep (Q 2.255) was manifested
in them, too;[42] their officers had emulated the Prophet's "excellent example"
on the battlefield;[43] and their valor reminded Parwez that they were the children of a being—Adam—to whom the angels had once prostrated.[44] As Parwez toured some of these famed battlefields in the Punjab, they constantly
brought to mind yet other Qur'anic motifs, which he dutifully passed on to his
readers.

Parwez was not content, however, simply to endorse this holy war. He also
wanted to correct misconceptions about it. Though the idea of supernatural
forces coming to the aid of the soldiers had probably helped the war effort
and its legitimacy in certain quarters, it did not accord with Parwez's modernist sensibilities. As he reported it, some soldiers were themselves perturbed
by such stories for their implication that all "credit" belonged to the supernatural forces, not to those who had actually laid down their lives in battle.[45]
Parwez assured such soldiers that God did His work in the world not through
unseen forces but rather by way of human beings.[46] "God's succor" likewise
meant that to act in accordance with the laws and principles He had established for human conduct was what paved the way to success.[47] If there was
any spiritual power, it lay in the holy warrior's own strength.[48] Coming upon
a shrine that had somehow escaped cannon-fire despite its proximity to a
battlefield, Parwez ridiculed the belief that this had had something to do
with the saintliness of the person buried there.[49] The title of this article—
"Pakistan's New Pilgrimage Sites"—suggested that people should be revering
the locations of celebrated military encounters and the soldiers who had seen
action there, not decaying Sufi tombs.

Like many others of Parwez's ventures in the service of Ayub Khan, this
extraordinary desire to foster a civil religion for Pakistan did not come to anything. A government's interests are seldom adequately served, after all, by
aligning itself exclusively with any single constituency. Though the Ayub
Khan regime marked the apogee of Islamic modernism, it needed also to benefit from the "superstitions" of those who could be persuaded that spiritual
beings had in fact fought side by side with Pakistani troops in 1965. In such
instances, the interests of a Parwez were not in full accord with those of the
regime. That did not prevent him from adding his veneer of religious legitimacy to the war effort.

Mawdudi, too, contributed to the effort and he portrayed the war's successful outcome as a mark of God's special favor on the country. In a speech on
Radio Pakistan less than two weeks after the cease fire, Mawdudi commented

on how the war had impacted people and what lessons were to be drawn from it:

> In just a matter of days, a great revolution has taken place among the people, leading one to suppose that the nation that now lives in this country is not the one that was here during the past eighteen years [since independence].... Reports from the battlefront tell us that twenty men of ours defeated two hundred, a hundred of ours defeated a thousand enemy soldiers. Our nation ... stood like an iron wall in backing the troops.... In a very short while, the moral condition of the people has been rectified. Crime and sinful actions have come to an end.... Such events show that just as Pakistan had come into existence purely by the grace of God, so too is the grace of God its guardian. This country came about on account of Islam. Islam has made it triumphant [in the war]. It would be gross ingratitude if, with the passage of time, we began to forget the Benefactor who has enriched us with such blessings.[50]

Though the government was willing to give airtime to Mawdudi on national radio, as it did many others, he too had his ax to grind. Mawdudi and the Ayub Khan regime were not friends. Reviving memories of the Jama`at-i Islami's opposition to the movement for Pakistan and of Mawdudi's refusal in 1947 to recognize the operations in Kashmir as a jihad, and alleging that the Jama`at sought to establish a "fascist regime," the government had banned the party in January 1964.[51] After the ban was overturned by the Supreme Court later that year,[52] Mawdudi threw in his weight in the presidential elections in early 1965 on the side of Jinnah's sister, Fatima, who was challenging Ayub Khan for the nation's highest office. Mawdudi's patently exaggerated sense of wonder at how the nation seemed to have abandoned its waywardness of the past eighteen years was a none too subtle reminder to people that seven of those years had been passed under Ayub Khan. By the same token, the Jama`at wanted to put pressure on the regime to roll back some of what the religious groups saw as its anti-Islamic measures. The government was not receptive to any such pressure, and it did not help improve relations between the two camps.

The war in 1971 posed challenges of a different order so far as the mobilization of Islam was concerned. Religious motifs could be deployed effortlessly when it came to the war with India, but that war was itself precipitated by the civil war in East Pakistan. It was one thing for the Awami League to be a secessionist party, and for India to have an interest in providing it with all manner of support. It was quite another for the military of a Muslim state to wage war against its own people. Nonetheless, Islam was invoked in this instance, too, to provide some public justification for what turned out to be a horrendous military action in East Pakistan. Muslim Bengalis had long been seen by north Indian observers as continuing Hindu practices, as too anchored in a Hindu culture, too close to their Hindu neighbors. Such views had continued to find resonance in both political and religious circles in West Pakistan. From this vantage, the Bengalis always seemed to be out of step with policies the government wanted to pursue for the greater good of the country and its culture or, for that matter, with demands emanating from the religious groups. For instance, they had bitterly opposed making Urdu the sole national language of Pakistan, though it was the language in which much of modern South Asia's Islamic literature had been produced. Jinnah had already rebuked the Bengalis for it in March 1948:

> [L]et me make it very clear to you that the State Language of Pakistan is going to be Urdu and no other language. Anyone who tries to mislead you is really the enemy of Pakistan. Without one State language, no nation can remain tied up solidly together and function.... [D]o not fall into the trap of those who are the enemies of Pakistan. Unfortunately, you have fifth-columnists—and I am sorry to say they are Muslims—who are financed by outsiders. But they are making a great mistake. We tolerate the enemies of Pakistan; we are not going to tolerate quislings and fifth-columnists in our State.[53]

The anti-Ahmadi agitation of 1953, too, had made little impression on East Bengal.[54] It did not take much attentiveness to see, however, that there was no lack of Islamic sentiment in the eastern wing. Rural East Bengal at the time of Pakistan's birth was reportedly "saturated" with `ulama and madrasas.[55] Nazimuddin, a prime minister with a distinctly pro-`ulama attitude, was a Bengali. British consular officials had noted during the Suez Crisis of 1956 that pan-Islamic sentiment was especially strong in East Pakistan.[56] And of the 113 `ulama who had signed a fatwa in early 1970 declaring socialism to be unbelief, 78 were from East Pakistan and 35 from the western wing.[57] Caricatures about the lack or the inauthenticity of Islam in the region would persist nonetheless. Years later, some of those associated with the muhajir organization, the MQM, would refer to their Sindhi opponents in similar terms: "Sindhis are non-Muslims, like Bengalis."[58]

General A.A.K. Niazi, who commanded the troops in East Pakistan from April 1971 until the fall of Dhaka in December that year, treated it as "enemy territory,"[59] with all that that meant in terms of slaughter, plunder, and rape. Given the aforementioned stereotypes about the inhabitants of the province, which were exacerbated by the Indian involvement in bolstering the secessionist insurgency, the distinction between Bengali and Hindu was easily blurred. As reported by the Hamoodur Rehman Commission that the government had established to look into Pakistan's defeat in the 1971 war, "During his visit to formations in East Pakistan Gen. Gull Hassan used to ask his soldiers 'how many Bengalis you have shot.'"[60] An officer remembered General Niazi asking members of a military unit "how many Hindus we had killed."[61] General Niazi's appeals to Islam sound jarring in this context, but they were not infrequent. "Islam preaches peace under normal circumstances," he is reported to have told the troops in August 1971. "But being a realistic way of life it realizes that constant maintenance of peace depends on the ability to repel force.... As Muslims we have always fought against an enemy who is numerically and materially superior. The enemy never deterred us. It was [with] the spirit of jihad and dedication to Islam that the strongest adversaries were mauled and defeated by a handful of Muslims. The battles of Uhad, Badar, Khyber and Damascus are the proof of what the Muslims could do."[62] The poetry he recited to them also had strong religious overtones: "What remarkable distinction have the holy warriors received from God / If they die, they are martyrs, and if they live, they are war heroes (*ghazi*). / They seek only the pleasure of the Lord, not material gain / A Self-sufficient Being has surely endowed them with this manner of self-sufficiency!"[63] Even as he subsequently denied the allegations against him, General Niazi had himself highlighted his religious turn. Asked by the Hamoodur Rehman commission about what it elsewhere called his "notorious reputation for sexual immorality,"[64] he responded: "I became very religious during the East Pakistan trouble. I was not so before. I thought more of death than these things."[65]

Among the religio-political parties, the Jama`at-i Islami in particular lent crucial support to the military operation in East Pakistan. Mawdudi did not have very much to say about the havoc wreaked by the army's action, but he was categorical in denouncing reports of atrocities against non-Bengalis "by Bengali nationalists with Muslim-sounding names." Most Muslims in East Pakistan had stayed away from such brutal acts, he said. "But those who have joined hands with the unbelievers in oppressing Muslims do not deserve to be considered Muslims or to be given any concession on account of being Muslim."[66] In June 1971, Mawdudi also published a "memorandum to the Muslim world," in which he defended the conduct of the Pakistani troops in the eastern wing.[67] The Jama`at, however, went beyond giving moral support to the Yahya Khan regime. Its associates established paramilitary groups that worked in tandem with the military in countering the insurgency. In response, the martial law authorities rewarded the Jama`at in various ways. Notably, the party was given a substantial portion of the parliamentary seats from which members of the Awami League had been disqualified, in the aftermath of the 1970 elections, on account of their secessionism.[68] Even by the standards of a marriage of convenience, this was a very peculiar union of an Islamist party whose ideological influence radiated across the Muslim world and a regime whose head—Yahya Khan—was notorious for flouting recognizable Islamic norms. If invocations of Islam did not help the regime in its handling of East

Pakistan, it was not for lack of trying. The failure may well have confirmed the governing elite and their newfound Islamist allies in their conviction that the East Pakistani soil was infertile for the cultivation of Islam.

The Afghan Jihad and Kashmir: The 1980s and the 1990s

If East Pakistan in 1971 was treacherous territory for jihad, Afghanistan after the Soviet invasion in December 1979 was ideally suited for it. Relations between Pakistan and Afghanistan had never been happy and, already in the 1950s, the Pakistani defense establishment had sought to secure British (and American) military aid by raising the specter of a Soviet advance through Afghanistan.[69] That threat came closest to realization when Soviet troops entered Afghanistan at the "invitation" of its government, putting Pakistan at the frontline of the Cold War. Afghans had begun streaming into the North-West Frontier Province (NWFP) and Baluchistan, the two provinces bordering Afghanistan, since the socialist overthrow of the government of President Muhammad Daud Khan in April 1978 (the "Saur Revolution"), and their numbers would eventually exceed three million. The Afghan political organizations that soon came to play a prominent role in the anti-Soviet war also set up their base in Pakistan; some of these were being supported by Pakistan as a way of countering Afghanistan's unfriendly policies toward it already from Zulfiqar Ali Bhutto's early days in office.[70] And it was through Pakistan that much of the financial and military assistance from the United States and elsewhere would pass to the Afghan fighters. The idea of jihad provided the central narrative to this anti-Soviet struggle.

Some of the resonance of the idea owed itself to a wider context. As would be recalled, General Zia al-Haqq had come to power in the wake of a popular agitation calling for the implementation of the Nizam-i Mustafa, "the Prophet's system." Less than two years later, on the occasion of the Prophet's birth anniversary, Zia al-Haqq had inaugurated what purported to be the beginnings of such a system. Islamization in Pakistan was one part of the context in which the narrative of jihad found meaning. Another was a change, one that had preceded Zia al-Haqq's coup, toward greater space for Islam within the military. Quite apart from its willingness to deploy religious symbols as needed, there were signs under Bhutto of a more conspicuous religiosity in the military's officer ranks. This may have been assisted by changing trends in the recruitment patterns. As Shuja Nawaz has observed, "data from ... the Pakistan Army indicate that since the 1970s recruitment moved from the traditional districts to new cities.... The expansion of cities, particularly in the Punjab, created a new base for recruitment to the volunteer army: the children of the lower-middle class, akin to Zia's own background, who chose the military because of its economic and social advantages rather than military traditions."[71] Zia al-Haqq, appointed chief of the army staff (COAS) in early

1976, was a noticeably observant officer, with some affinity for the Jama'at-i Islami. The scope for Islamic symbolism in the military would grow under him, both as COAS and as the head of the state, though without noticeably compromising the military's much vaunted professionalism.[72]

The immediate, and most directly pertinent, context for the articulation of a narrative of jihad was provided, of course, by the Soviet invasion of Afghanistan. From the perspective of a people as jealous of their faith as of their freedom, it was bad enough to be ruled by a communist regime. That it was the puppet of an occupying Soviet force made things much worse. If there was an unambiguous and globally resonant argument to be made for jihad, Afghanistan under Soviet occupation had furnished it. Apart from numerous Afghans, religio-political groups in Pakistan—notably the Jama'at-i Islami and many Deobandis and Salafis—rallied to the cause. So did people from the Arab Middle East and elsewhere.

Mosques had often played a crucial role in mobilizing religio-political movements in Pakistan, notably during the 1953 and 1974 anti-Ahmadi agitations and in the Nizam-i Mustafa movement that had helped topple Bhutto in 1977. They came to have an active role in shaping public support for the Afghan struggle as well. In Friday sermons, imams expounded at length on jihad and pointed to Afghanistan as the very embodiment of Muslim suffering and of opportunities for Muslims everywhere to pay their dues to a long neglected obligation. Given that madrasas, unlike mosques, often are residential institutions, which meant that—in the Frontier province—they could house male refugees and actual or prospective participants in the jihad, they too acquired an unprecedented importance during the years of the anti-Soviet struggle. None among them matched the aforementioned Dar al-'Ulum Haqqaniyya in Akora Khattak, near Peshawar, in this respect. In 1985, an estimated 60 percent of its 680 students were Afghan.[73] As Sami' al-Haqq, the president of this madrasa and a leader of the Jam'iyyat al-'Ulama-i Islam, put it around the same time, "[s]ince the beginning of the Jihad the Dar al-'Ulum Haqqaniyyah has lifted any rule concerning attendance, coming and going for the Afghan students and for those who ... participate in the Jihad. Groups of students leave to participate in the Holy War for a month or two or more and when they come back, others leave."[74]

Jihad by then had become part of the dominant discourse in Pakistan. In a speech in December 1987 marking eight years of the Soviet occupation of Afghanistan, 'Abdul Qayyum Haqqani, a respected teacher at the Haqqaniyya madrasa, observed as much: "If you look at your country these days, you will see that conferences and seminars on jihad are being held, processions are being taken out, statements are being issued and resolutions [on jihad] are being adopted." His point was not, however, to express satisfaction at this state of affairs. It was rather that mere conferences and resolutions were not enough; what would guarantee the success of jihad, he said, was "complete faith and trust in God" as well as Muslim unity.[75] General Zia al-Haqq would have concurred. As one of his closest associates, General K. M. Arif, the vice chief of army staff, later said of him: "[h]e was convinced of the rightness of the [Afghan] cause and he followed the course relentlessly.... In the process, the [Afghan] Mujahideen developed implicit faith in Pakistan, and they felt assured that the Zia administration would neither waver in its determination to support their cause nor compromise their interests for reasons of expediency."[76] It had taken much more, of course, than faith—in God, in the justness of the cause, in Pakistan's commitment to it—to win the war in Afghanistan. The concerted efforts of the CIA and the Pakistani military intelligence, the Inter-Services Intelligence (ISI); the supply of large quantities of American arms and of American and Arab monetary resources; fighters from across the Muslim world, including Pakistan; and the long unraveling of the Soviet Union itself, which the Afghan war served to hasten, had all contributed to the outcome. The fact remains nonetheless that no event in twentieth-century Islam matches the symbolic power of the Afghan jihad. And its effects continue to reverberate today.

Afghanistan has proved to be fertile soil for jihad in Indian Kashmir, too. Indeed, there was a seamless web between the warfare in Afghanistan and the insurgency in Kashmir in the 1990s—and this both from the Pakistani military angle and from that of the nonstate actors. For the ISI, the anti-Soviet struggle provided opportunities to train fighters for operations in Kashmir, some of whom would rise to prominence in the years following the end of the Soviet occupation of Afghanistan. It is not an accident that violence in Kashmir began to flare up just when the jihad against the Soviet Union was winding down.[77] The advantages of having a friendly regime that could provide Pakistan with "strategic depth" on its western frontier in confronting the enemy on the *eastern* front, not to mention training camps for militants intended for Indian Kashmir, were important considerations in Pakistan's interest in the rise of the Taliban, too. After the fall of the Taliban in the wake of September 11, 2001, the military would continue to provide covert support to the insurgency led by those claiming that regime's mantle in Afghanistan. This was a way of countering a US-supported Afghan government that was markedly less friendly toward Pakistan, and on better terms with India, than many among the Pakistani ruling elite thought they could tolerate.

The case of the Markaz al-Da`wa wal-Irshad, founded in 1986 by Hafiz Muhammad Sa`id, a Salafi (that is, Ahl-i Hadith) lecturer at the University of Engineering in Lahore, offers us a useful illustration of continuities between Afghanistan and Kashmir at nonstate levels as well. Subsequently called the Jama`at al-Da`wa, it has come to adopt a political, charitable, and missionary persona. Its militant wing, focused on India, is the much feared and better known Lashkar-i Tayba, which gained international notoriety for an attack on the historic Red Fort in Delhi in December 2000. Banned by Pakistan in early 2002, it has continued to operate, with its most dramatic terrorist operation taking place in Mumbai in the fall of 2008. For its part, the Jama`at al-Da`wa, though indistinguishable in terms of leadership and goals from the Lashkar-i Tayba, has managed to elude proscription.[78]

Before returning to Hafiz Sa`id, another instance of the continuities in question merits notice. This relates to Mas`ud Azhar, whom we met in the previous chapter, and who came of age as the anti-Soviet Afghan struggle was entering its final phases. Born in Bahawalpur in southern Punjab, an arid and poverty-stricken part of the province, Azhar received his advanced religious education at the Jami`at al-`Ulum al-Islamiyya madrasa in Karachi. Those associated with the madrasa, founded in 1955 by Muhammad Yusuf Bannuri, have often been at the forefront of religio-political activism, including the anti-Ahmadi agitation of 1974 and sectarian militancy in the 1980s and the 1990s. Its graduates participated in the Afghan jihad as well, and Mas`ud Azhar, who had begun teaching at the madrasa after completing his education there, was among them. It was not in actual combat, however, but rather as an ideologue propagating the cause of jihad and a leader of militant organizations that he was to come to public—indeed, international—attention. His lecture tours on jihad took him not only to various parts of Pakistan but also to Bangladesh, Central Asia, the Arab Middle East, Kenya, Somalia, Sudan, and Britain. He has published a number of magazines to disseminate his message and to mobilize a support network for it: the *Sada-i mujahid*, *Zarb-i mu'min*, and, for a primarily female readership, *Banat-i `A'isha*. Azhar is also the founder of Jaish-i Muhammad, a militant organization best known for its activities in Indian Kashmir; he had previously been associated with Harkat al-mujahidin, a Deobandi organization active in Afghanistan since the mid-1980s.[79] In 1994, as noted earlier, he had been captured and jailed by the Indian government and was released some years later as part of a hostage settlement brokered by the Taliban. Azhar's activities in relation to both Afghanistan and Indian Kashmir were in consonance with the strategic goals of the Pakistani military establishment, and it is not surprising that Azhar has lived in the open, for the most part, even after the state had branded his organization a terrorist group.

A brief sampling of themes, drawn here from a two-volume collection of speeches that date prior to September 11, 2001, help illustrate Mas`ud Azhar's worldview. The jihad in Afghanistan receives extensive coverage, of course, and within it there is much that has to do with the miraculous and the otherworldly: a handful defeat large contingents; tanks are destroyed with mere stones;[80] people see a strangely holy light (*nur*) emanating from the graves of martyrs;[81] those about to be martyred see visions of the heavenly maidens (*hur*) awaiting them.[82] On a *this*-worldly plane, jihad is the means of restoring a long-lost dignity to Muslims, of protecting the honor of women, of defending the Qur'an against sacrilege.[83] It is also a means for the `ulama to regain their social standing, to reassert their leadership roles. The lack of respect for their vocation that the `ulama have long suffered in society can be remedied by their entering the fray of jihad. As Azhar told his audience at the Bury madrasa in Britain in 1993, it was not just the religious realm that properly belonged to the `ulama, and to them alone; they ought to assume leadership roles in the arena of active combat as well.[84] Another theme relates to Azhar's conviction that no great piety is required to embark upon jihad.[85] This point need not be seen as contradicting the previous one about the need for the `ulama's leadership. It is meant simply to refute objections that jihad becomes binding only on those who have first attained a certain level of personal piety. Azhar, of course, sees such objections as bad excuses for not undertaking jihad at all. His position here is also a way of trying to safeguard the reputation of jihad from the notoriously bad behavior of many mujahidin warlords, especially after the Soviet withdrawal.[86] On another note, though the Deobandi Azhar would not have wanted to show any affinity with Mawdudi, he does seem on occasion to echo the latter. Much like Mawdudi had argued that the moral formation people needed in order to transform the political realm could happen only *within* the political realm rather than outside it or prior to entering it, so Azhar insists that the ability to wage successful jihad would come only after entering the arena of jihad: one cannot expect to develop that ability prior to entering the fray any more than one could learn to swim without being in a body of water.[87]

Hafiz Muhammad Sa`id is no less emphatic than Azhar in the exhortation to jihad. As a Salafi, his is a more austere and markedly less colorful discourse, however.[88] Nor is Sa`id a traditionally trained `alim; instead, he has master's degrees in Arabic and Islamic studies from the University of the Punjab, and, as noted, it was at the University of Engineering in Lahore that he taught Islamic studies for many years.[89] What he says about the `ulama is not by way of affirming their authority, as the Deobandi Azhar does, but rather to point to how they have often been busy turning people *away* from jihad. As he puts it in a searing rebuke to unnamed doctrinal rivals, presumably the Deobandis and the Barelawis, many `ulama refrain from giving jihad its due for fear that people would divert all their donations to its cause and leave mosques and madrasas unfunded.[90] He also castigates the `ulama for playing into the hands of the Western powers by fanning intra-Muslim sectarian conflict and thereby diverting the Muslim focus away from jihad against the infidel.[91] Sa`id's targets in jihad—Kashmir, India more broadly, and the West—are the same as Azhar's. But there is also a strong sense that the Muslim society itself needs to be cleansed of the quasi-polytheistic beliefs and practices that pervade it. As a Salafi, he is more perturbed by such practices than is Azhar, but not so much, as will be seen, as to want to take up arms against putatively Muslim societies. Though ordinary people gravitating to a militant organization in the name of jihad have not necessarily done so *because of* its doctrinal orientation,[92] the dictates of his own orientation and the need to school people in it are never far from Sa'id's thinking. Jihad is, he says, "the best university for an understanding of religion."[93] His specific point here is that, contrary to the views of many 'ulama, there is no division of labor between those who study religion and those who fight; jihad itself is a means to imbibing proper Islam.[94] Yet, the Islam that people are expected to internalize at the Lashkar-i Tayba's camps carries an emphatically Salafi shape.[95]

There are significant differences between Sa'id and Azhar on the proper attitude that is to be adopted toward the government as well. Azhar's mobilization for jihad would come to suit the interests of the Pakistani military and political establishments less well in the aftermath of September 11, 2001, than it had before that momentous day. Following daring attacks by the Jaish-i Muhammad in Srinagar in October 2001 and on the Indian parliament in December that year, Pakistan banned this organization, among many others.[96] This signaled a continuation of some of the realignment away from jihad that General Musharraf had initiated under intense American pressure immediately after September 11. The Jaish obviously saw it as a betrayal of Pakistan's long-standing commitment to Kashmir, and it responded in kind. In an effort to reorient the country's priorities and commitments back to a more familiar direction, it masterminded an assassination attempt against General Musharraf in December 2003. The attempt failed, though investigations into it revealed that some within the Pakistan Air Force itself had helped with the plot.[97] The danger that the military's allies among the militants could turn against it had lurked around this relationship since Pakistan's first forays into Kashmir. It was never closer to taking concrete shape than in the early years of the twenty-first century.

Azhar's expressions of anti-Americanism also became more strident once the United States went about dislodging his ideological allies, the Taliban, from power in Afghanistan. His editorial for *Banat-i 'A'isha*, the journal for women, from November 2001 offers an illustration:

> [Like Mullah Muhammad 'Umar and the Taliban], the Jaish-i Muhammad is an organization of God's friends and America's enemies; and hundreds of thousands of Muslim men and women are always ready for its service. As for the friends of America, they are people who have emancipated cinema houses [from any restraint] and have made mosques desolate. They are those who have compelled the daughters of Mother 'A'isha to abandon their veils and dance on stage with men.... They are those who, in the name of enlightenment and modern education, have spread shamelessness (*be-haya'i*), nationalism, and the love of wealth among Muslims. They are those who, in viewing the poor as worse than dogs, have made them contemptible in society—in

the process darkening their own face and their prospects for salvation on the Day of Judgment.... The friends of America are people who, after reading a few Urdu books, give weight in matters of religion to their own opinions [rather than to those of the `ulama] and try to harm Islam by talking ill of the `ulama.... They are the cowards who do not go out for jihad and who consider fighting America as [self-] destructive. Such people give out the appearance of being peace-loving; in reality, they want to impose America upon Muslims.[98]

Jihad, anti-Americanism, social justice, and a strident critique of what are taken to be the fruits of Westernized modernism are all intertwined here. These themes are well-represented in Azhar's pre-2011 discourses as well. The military establishment's putative break with the militants was new, however, and so was the stridency of Azhar's reaction to it.

Hafiz Sa`id, too, has nursed that anger, and he has not been reticent in his criticism of modernizing, pro-American Muslim regimes or of the moral waywardness of Muslim societies under their watch.[99] Indeed, he has gone so far as to characterize those "prostrating" before America to be guilty of *shirk*— associating partners with the omnipotent God.[100] Yet, it is a telling indication of what divides those engaged in jihad from one another that Sa`id has not drawn the same conclusions from a putatively Muslim regime's lapses as have some others. As Sa`id reports it, people objecting to the Lashkar-i Tayba's activities in Indian Kashmir argue that it should target the "idolatrous" (*taghuti*) government and the "dens of polytheism" at home before engaging in jihad against non-Muslims abroad.[101] He returns to this and related ideas often,[102] which suggests that they have some purchase even in his own circles. But Sa`id considers such views misguided. While the Prophet Muhammad was engaged in military hostilities with the Meccan polytheists, Sa`id notes in justifying his own stance, he had been willing to enter into an alliance even with the polytheists and the Jews of Medina.[103] Bad Muslim rulers might be hypocrites (*munafiqin*)—a resonant Qur'anic term for members of the Prophet's community in Medina who were busy collaborating with his enemies— but, Sa`id insists, they are not unbelievers. That is to say that though they ought to be reprimanded for their misconduct, it is impermissible to wage war against them.[104] There is also a pragmatic reason, he says, for showing restraint. Taking on bad Muslim rulers would lead to further repression on their part and a civil war, with adverse effects for jihad against non-Muslims and for the growth of Islamic movements.[105]

Although some Pakistani Salafis remain highly critical of Sa`id for his single-minded advocacy of jihad to the exclusion of almost everything else,[106] he clearly belongs to the strain of Salafism that believes in keeping its peace with the government at home.[107] Sa`id claims to have met Usama bin Laden in Afghanistan,[108] but this is not Bin Laden's Salafism; it is the Salafism of

`Abd al-`Aziz bin Baz (d. 1999), the grand mufti of Saudi Arabia, who was an avid supporter of the jihad in Afghanistan *and* a pillar of the Saudi establishment. Given the Lashkar-i Tayba's religious convictions, it has remained much more amenable to a continuing alignment with the Pakistani military, despite the latter's professed *re*alignments, than have Mas`ud Azhar and his associates.

The Pakistani *Taliban*

General Musharraf's decision, in the wake of September 11, 2001, to provide logistical support to the United States in its military operations against the Taliban created much resentment in the country, and not just in militant circles. Those comprising the Taliban regime were adherents of the Deobandi orientation and many Deobandi `ulama—even those embarrassed by the Taliban's stringent policies regarding women and their education—had tended to view them as well-intentioned and devout Muslims who were on their way to establishing a properly Islamic polity.[109] Hafiz Sa`id, too, despite the difference in doctrinal orientation, has had no bad things to say about them. The Deobandis were understandably among those most vexed by Pakistan's collusion in the destruction of the Islamic emirate next door. A number of scholars had traveled to Kabul under the Taliban regime and had been honored as state guests; this was in accord with how these Deobandi `ulama thought they ought to be treated, but very different from their official standing in Pakistan.[110] Many others, too, saw the visiting of American reprisals on the Taliban to be unjust, given that they had not been proven to be complicit in the September 11 attacks. As the American air campaign began in October 2001, thousands of volunteers from the tribal areas of the Frontier province and elsewhere crossed into Afghanistan to help defend the Taliban regime.[111] In a reverse movement over the following months and years, remnants of the Taliban regime as well as Arab, Central Asian, and other fighters who had lived in Afghanistan under the Taliban sought refuge in the Pakistani tribal areas. Usama bin Laden, too, was suspected of hiding in that region. Once again, there was intense US pressure on the Pakistani military to capture these fleeing foreign militants; the new US-backed government that had come to power in Kabul also clamored for action against Pakistan-based Taliban and allied groups that had slowly begun to regroup to launch an insurgency inside Afghanistan. Operations against such individuals and groups were unpopular in Pakistan because they were seen by many as conducted entirely at the bidding of the United States. They also involved the military's going deep into tribal territory whose governance even the colonial-era British had left to local notables, the tribal *malik*s and *khan*s. The fiercely independent-minded inhabitants of the region proved to be less than understanding of such forays. Further, as became clear repeatedly, such operations often caused considerable collateral damage. Madrasas suspected of being used by militants—as they had previously been, with the *encouragement* of the government and the military, by the mujahidin—were sometimes targeted by the Pakistani army. In one of the earliest and most notable of such instances, in October 2006, a military airstrike destroyed a madrasa in Bajaur, killing more than eighty-two people; a number of the victims were young boys, some eleven and twelve years old.[112] In a country where the *regulation* of madrasas has remained a highly controversial matter, a military attack of this kind could only create deep anxiety about where the country was heading.

It was in this broad context that, from around 2004, groups claiming affinity with the Taliban began to emerge in the tribal areas of the Frontier province. By late 2007, an umbrella organization called the Movement of the Pakistani Taliban (Tahrik-i Taliban-i Pakistan, or TTP) had established itself, under the leadership of Baitullah Mehsud (d. 2009), as a terrifying network of these groups; many others unaffiliated with it operated along similar lines in the province.[113] Like the Afghan Taliban of the mid-1990s, the Pakistani Taliban stood for the implementation of the shari`a. As in the Afghan case, this too was often a mix of recognizable shari`a norms, notably the hudud punishments, and Pashtun tribal custom. The admixture with other things notwithstanding, the rhetoric of implementing the shari`a was powerful, and it resonated, as had the practices of the Afghan Taliban, well beyond their own territory. Before Pakistani military operations came to disrupt the functioning of the Taliban's judicial system in the tribal areas, the national press had reported with some frequency on incidents in which men and women accused of adultery were stoned to death and severe punishments were meted out for other offenses.[114] The killing of women accused of sullying tribal honor is nothing new, of course, in the Frontier province or in other parts of the country. News items appear regularly on such incidents. The most egregious cases are often accompanied by expressions of resolve by members of the government to do something about them. In 2016, a Pakistani documentary filmmaker, Sharmeen Obaid-Chinoy, won an Academy Award for a powerful depiction of "honor crimes"; the film had been screened at the prime minister's house following its nomination for an Oscar.[115] What was different about the Pakistani Taliban's administering of their punishments, compared to the incidents that take place in, say, rural Sindh or the Punjab, was not just the language of the shari`a that was employed but also the attendant contrast with the state's failure to implement Islamic law: as would be recalled, no such punishments had ever been carried out under the Hudood Ordinances of General Zia al-Haqq. And at precisely the time that the Pakistani Taliban were setting up their shari`a courts, the government of General Pervez Musharraf was busy *dismantling* Zia al-Haqq's Hudood laws.

There were other contrasts, too. In a country where the formal judicial system is widely perceived by ordinary people to be chronically inefficient, unresponsive to their needs, and favoring the rich and the well-connected, even the brutality of Taliban-style justice was not enough to offset the appeal of its swiftness, and not just in the tribal areas. The very admixture of Taliban-style shari`a with tribal custom would have made it intelligible to local people, and the language in which this law was administered was the natural language of those people. The same could not be said of the country's judicial system, whose official language continues to be English. As a survey of civil case litigants at the district courts in Lahore found in 2010–11, "over half of the overall respondents (55.5%) fac[ed] the predicament of not being able to comprehend the laws and regulations pertaining to their cases at all due to the language used."[116]

The Pakistani Taliban also represented rough and ready, Robin Hood-like forms of social justice, though that imagery is not peculiar to them in contemporary Pakistan.[117] Pamphlets circulated in September 2006 in Miramshah, North Waziristan, inviting people to alert the Taliban "if any incident of robbery, dacoity [banditry] or any other criminal act took place in the area."[118] Petty traders and peasants with their particular grievances against a corrupt and indifferent government tended also to gravitate toward the Taliban.[119] Journalists and other observers have disagreed about whether Taliban initiatives in this regard are better seen as remedying social ills, as facets of organized crime, or some combination of both.[120] The appeal to social justice was, in any case, a powerful one, and it certainly helped that many of those occupying leadership positions in the Taliban movement had come from humble backgrounds: Baitullah Mehsud was the son of a small-time imam at mosques in the tribal areas.[121] In an effort to remake the social and political structure in the tribal areas and, of course, to punish those seen as collaborating with the enemy, the Taliban and allied groups had begun, from about 2004, to target the local landed elite deemed to be oppressive and insufficiently Islamic. A 2008 estimate put the number of such notables, the maliks and khans, killed at the hands of the Taliban in the tribal areas at more than 500.[122]

The Taliban targeted military personnel as well and sought, indeed, to make an example of them. A suicide bomber killed more than forty soldiers just over a week after the attack on the madrasa in Bajaur;[123] on occasion, they have beheaded captured soldiers and uploaded videos of their execution on the Internet.[124] It would have taken great restraint on the part of the Taliban to limit their operations to areas under their immediate influence in the tribal areas. They showed no such restraint. Repeatedly, they struck elsewhere in the country, attacking mosques, public gatherings, markets, and military installations. The assassination of Benazir Bhutto in December 2006 was widely believed to be the doing of the Taliban, though they denied responsibility for it.[125] They did claim responsibility for trying, in 2012, to kill Malala Yusufzai, the courageous teenager from the Swat district of the Frontier province who had come to international attention for her public criticism of the Taliban, and especially their closure of schools for girls. Yusufzai survived the attempt on her life and went on to win the Nobel peace prize in 2014.[126] Among the most horrendous of the Taliban's actions was the attack in December 2014 on a military-run public school in Peshawar in which more than 130 schoolchildren were killed.

Despite repeated professions to the contrary, and long after the fall of the Taliban regime in Afghanistan, the Pakistani military would maintain a relationship with Taliban groups on both sides of the Pakistan-Afghanistan border. Many in the military and the political establishments, *and* in religious circles, made a distinction between the "good" and the "bad" Taliban: the former served the interests of Pakistan by undermining unfriendly Afghan governments, notably that of President Hamid Karzai (2004–14); the latter challenged the Pakistani state. From a slightly different perspective, the good Taliban were waging war against the US and NATO presence in Afghanistan, while the bad Taliban were attacking innocent Pakistanis. In the immediate aftermath of the school massacre of December 2014, Prime Minister Nawaz Sharif declared that "there will be no distinction between good and bad Taliban. The nation will continue this war [against them] with full resolve till [the] elimination of the last terrorist."[127] Even as military operations against the Pakistani Taliban and allied groups continued, however, it was difficult to be convinced that government and military support for *all* Taliban groups had in fact ceased. When Mulla Akhtar Mansur, the successor of Mulla Muhammad ʿUmar as the head of the Afghan Taliban, was killed by a US drone in Balochistan in May 2016, he was found to be in possession of a Pakistani passport. Using an alias, he had traveled between Karachi and Dubai on no fewer than eighteen occasions between 2006 and 2015.[128] This caused much embarrassment to the government, but it did not surprise many people. In June 2016, it was reported that the Khyber Pakhtunkhwa government, led by the Pakistan Tahrik-i Insaf of Imran Khan, had earmarked $2.8 million for the Dar alʿUlum Haqqaniyya in the province's budget.[129] This, of course, is the madrasa more closely associated with the Taliban than any other in either Pakistan or Afghanistan.

It is important, however, to keep such patronage in perspective. In Pakistan, it has tended to be available not just to religio-political groups and religious institutions but to "secular" organizations as well. For instance, the vast influence that the MQM has wielded in Karachi since the mid-1980s, indeed, the very continuation of the party in existence, has owed a good deal to various forms of state support. While some of it can take Machiavellian forms— for instance, a government's desire to mobilize the MQM as a counterweight to political challengers—the support in question can also come from the fact that state functionaries at local levels belong to the linguistic community this party represents, sympathize with its cause, and have been willing to divert state resources to it. The MQM's ties with and dependence on the state have not stopped it from challenging successive Pakistani governments. Nor have they prevented the law enforcement agencies and even the military from launching periodic "clean-up operations" against it.[130] From this perspective at least, the Pakistani Taliban and the state's inconsistencies toward them are less anomalous than might appear otherwise.

The ʿulama, too, have wavered in their attitudes regarding the Taliban and their excesses. Given the Deobandi orientation of the Taliban, it is unsurprising that the Barelawis have been consistent in their hostility toward them from the Taliban's very inception. They have long derided the Deobandis in general as "Wahhabis" or "Najdis"—in reference to Ibn ʿAbd al-Wahhab's place of origin—and the instances in which Arab and Pakistani Salafis, on the one hand, and the Taliban and other Deobandi militants, on the other, have seemed to pursue shared goals have only confirmed the Barelawis in their worst fears of them all.[131] For their part, the Deobandi ʿulama have found it difficult to take a clear position on the actions of the Pakistani Taliban. Suicide bombing would seem to be a fairly clear candidate for the ʿulama's condemnation both because suicide is widely believed to be forbidden by Islamic law and because civilians tend to be the overwhelming victims of such attacks. There is, however, no consensus on whether or how to condemn even this practice, and some have endorsed it without reservation. This is a point that merits a brief detour before proceeding further.

In a four-volume commentary devoted to explicating verses of the Qur'an that bear on the topic of jihad, the aforementioned Masʿud Azhar comments several times on the question of suicide bombing, often characterized as "self-sacrificing (*fida'i*) jihad." The most explicit of such discussions occurs with reference to Q 8.60, which reads: "Prepare whatever forces you can muster, including warhorses, to frighten off God's enemies and yours, and warn others unknown to you but known to God." The word translated here as "frighten off" (*turhibun*) is commonly used for terrorism (*irhab*) in modern Arabic, though it is obviously anachronistic to read its modern connotations into Qur'anic usage. Many Muslim commentators have struggled with the proper rendering of this term, but not Masʿud Azhar. He writes:

> The infinitive form of turhibun is irhab, which is called terrorism these days. The word irhabi, in the sense of terrorist, has been turned into a term of abuse. Muslims need to be very careful in this regard. God has Himself commanded that the enemies of religion should be terrorized (*dahshat-zada*). Consequently, those who undertake irhab, that is, who terrorize the enemy, are acting according to a Qur'anic commandment. To criticize such people or to condemn the blessed practice of irhab is a grievous mistake and a clear sin.[132]

Asking what serves the purpose of terrorizing the enemy, he answers:

> The enemies of Islam will not be terrorized much if Muslims continue to use [literally: make] only conventional weapons, for the enemy has more powerful weapons of that kind. Consequently, there are three excellent ways of following this Qur'anic command in the present age. First, readying self-sacrificing fighters and finding ever new ways to carry out such jihad. There is no antidote that the enemies of Islam have to this form of preparation for waging war. The self-sacrificing fighters of this age are to be congratulated that their terror (dahshat) has caused tremors in the lofty halls of unbelief. These people of God are undoubtedly the ones to have acted properly in accordance with this verse. Second, efforts should be made to render bomb-making materials (literally: gunpowder [*barud*]) more effective. Praise be to God, Muslims have sharp and fertile minds in their midst. If people are introduced to this Qur'anic commandment and they are told that preparing for jihad is an obligation and that terrorizing God's enemies amounts to worship, those capable of making more effective and powerful bombs are sure to step up. This is a weapon that turns the tables in battle and gives strength to self-sacrificing attacks. Third, under all circumstances, Muslims should build nuclear weapons and they should invest their abilities and their [material] means into this effort.[133]

Mas'ud Azhar's is an extreme position among the 'ulama, though he is scarcely the only one espousing it. Many others have sought to curb the practice of suicide bombing and other forms of terrorism, though the very effort to forge a consensus on this matter has sometimes revealed the fault lines within their ranks. A statement issued by a group of prominent 'ulama in 2008 is instructive in this regard. Even as it affirmed the Islamic prohibition of suicide, it acknowledged the belief of "some people" that

> in the case of genuine need in a legitimate war, it is permissible to resort to a suicide attack provided non-culpable people are not a target. This would be akin to the well-known stories of Pakistani soldiers who had strapped bombs to their bodies when facing Indian aggression at the battlefront of Chawinda in 1965. They had thrown themselves before Indian tanks and thereby stopped their advance. Since this is a matter of juridical disagreement (*ijtihadi mas'ala*), if a person resorts to such action in defense of his country and community against the enemy in a just war (*ja'iz awr bar-haqq jang*), it is to be hoped that God will accept his sacrifice on the basis of the purity of his intentions. But all this has to do with a just war against a clear and open enemy. It has nothing to do with a situation in which believing Muslims

(*kalima-go musalman*), or such non-Muslims whose lives and property have been made inviolable by God, are being targeted. A Muslim who professes the faith, however sinful he might be in practice, enjoys the inviolability given to him by God. And the Qur'an and the hadith have characterized the murder of such a person as an unforgivable sin.... A suicide attack that targets Muslims or peaceful citizens of a Muslim state comprises a double sin: that of willfully killing a person ... and that of suicide, on whose prohibition there is no disagreement.[134]

Though the language of good and bad Taliban is not used in this statement, it does serve to bring it to mind through the distinction between a just war on behalf of country and community (the good Taliban in Afghanistan) and attacks on fellow Muslims (the bad Taliban). But even as regards the latter, it leaves unresolved the key question of whether the Pakistani Taliban or other militants consider those they target for attack as Muslims at all: the Pakistani Taliban have sometimes characterized the military personnel engaged in operations against them as "apostates," punishable by death according to Islamic law.[135] In the same vein, if the government they are fighting is deemed to be doing the bidding of a Western, non-Muslim power, then it is the Taliban, not the military personnel, that are really fighting on behalf of country and community; it is the *military* that is fighting fellow Muslims, not the Taliban. Such interpretive niceties are not spelled out in the 2008 statement. But it does not take any great imagination to detect them there. Also worth noting, incidentally, is this statement's none too subtle reminder that it is soldiers of the Pakistan army who had first used a tactic akin to suicide bombing.[136]

How the distinction between the good and the bad Taliban serves to undergird that between good and bad suicide bombing is sometimes more explicit. In late 2013, a delegation of the Afghan Taliban's shadow government visited various Pakistani ʿulama to put forth their viewpoints and to help cultivate a favorable public opinion in the country. On the matter of suicide bombing (*fida'i hamla*), the delegation explained that the success of the Taliban insurgency in Afghanistan had depended on this "greatest of the weapons of the oppressed" and that any fatwa seeking to unequivocally condemn this practice would weaken their struggle. The response to this by Abu ʿAmmar Zahid al-Rashidi, a prominent Deobandi religious scholar and the head of an important madrasa in Gujranwala, is instructive. He recognized, Zahid al-Rashidi told them, that this was a weapon of the weak: "Therefore, we have no objection to its use in a legitimate war or jihad. However, we do not consider legitimate the destruction that is being wrought through it in different parts of Pakistan on residential areas, mosques, imambargahs, churches, and marketplaces. This is in no way acceptable to us.... We have clear reservations about such attacks and we consider it essential to maintain and clarify the difference between legitimate self-sacrificing attacks and illegitimate suicide operations."[137] What is significant about this statement is not the distinction itself between good and bad suicide bombing, for that, as noted, is a mere corollary of the distinction between the good and the bad Taliban. Rather, it is the fact that Zahid al-Rashidi is not a radical; he would normally pass for a relatively moderate member of the Pakistani `ulama. He has repeatedly opened the pages of *al-Shari`a*, his madrasa's monthly journal, to viewpoints from different religio-political camps and has thereby contributed toward shaping an informed public opinion on religious and political matters in the country. In this instance, his position resonates with many Deobandi scholars, and others beyond their ranks. And there is little reason to think that it is in any obvious conflict with the policies of the military establishment either, so far as the Taliban are concerned.

Changing the Narrative?

In an important book on strategic thinking about war in a world transformed by information technologies, Emile Simpson has argued that war can no longer be viewed in polarized terms as an exclusively military confrontation between two sides. Wars in the contemporary world, of which his prime example is the warfare in Afghanistan after the terrorist attacks of 2001, are best seen in "kaleidoscopic" terms, with many different audiences whose members bring their own perspectives on how to interpret the events of the war and what judgments to make upon them. It is not just that one side's claims to victory in battle are disputed by the other side; that has frequently been the case for as long as people have gone to war. It is also that many others, who are not direct parties to the conflict in question, are able to draw their own conclusions about victory and defeat, about justice and injustice, and about the moral underpinnings of particular actions. As Simpson puts it, "The proliferation of strategic audiences beyond the enemy means that force no longer has a clear target: one cannot 'force' an outcome on a strategic audience that is not the enemy; they may well be free to ignore the war's military outcome."[138] War, he argues, is a language, one that is understood and interpreted differently by different people.

Speaking specifically of the Taliban of post-2001 Afghanistan, Simpson suggests that they are best seen not as a unified movement but rather as a "franchise": while some groups are motivated by a religious cause, others, guided by self-interest, jockey for power and for a redressal of grievances in local contexts. Much the same could be said, though Simpson does not, of the umbrella movement that purports to represent the Pakistani Taliban. That insurgent groups become part of this franchise for their particular reasons means that those who speak in the name of the Taliban must continually struggle to project an image of an overarching unity of purpose. It also means that any effort to counter the putative appeal of the Taliban would not necessarily carry equal conviction in *all* relevant circles, for the simple reason that that appeal rests on different grounds for different people. A key challenge facing a government and a military that seeks to counter insurgencies such as the Taliban's, Simpson says, is to frame a narrative that provides audiences with "a structure through which to interpret action."[139] This structure must be sufficiently polyvalent to allow different audiences the space in which to understand the actions in question from their particular perspective. Yet, it must have some coherence to it if it is to remain a "strategic narrative" at all: "the strategist has to consider how a narrative can gain purchase on audiences whose political persuasions vary widely, without coming apart."[140]

For all the difficulties inherent in being able to speak for the franchise, the Pakistani Taliban have been remarkably successful in articulating a broadly coherent narrative. Its shape and content, already alluded to, are summarized easily. This is a war in which simple and devout Muslims are pitted against an arrogant, materialistic superpower and the mercenary troops that illegitimate and godless "Muslim" rulers have provided to that superpower for short-term material gain. Those on the good side of this war seek the implementation of the shari`a. Successive Pakistani governments have promised it, too, but they have never been sincere in such pledges. The Taliban who had come to power in Afghanistan in the mid-1990s had shown to the world that a shari`a-based polity could in fact be created even with the most meager of resources; the latter-day Taliban intend to follow that model, which ultimately is none other than that of the Rashidun caliphs of early Islam. There might be excesses in how the Taliban have gone about their business, but they are so "inflamed" by the circumstances in which they find themselves that one can understand those excesses without having to condone them.[141] Finally, this is a war of the little man—the oppressed, the weak, the dispossessed—against the big man and all those who stand behind him, whether it is the local landlord, the corrupt political establishment of Pakistan, a military deeply implicated in lucrative businesses, or the United States and "the West."[142]

The necessity of a narrative against militant Islamists has come to be widely acknowledged at the highest levels in Pakistan.[143] Why has it been so difficult, however, for the government and the military to give coherent expression to it, in response, say, to the Taliban's? The answer most commonly given to this question is that the military has had a strong interest in nurturing the Taliban—as well as other militant groups—and that even as military action has been undertaken, with considerable success, against the bad Taliban, the good Taliban remain important to the pursuit of its strategic interests.[144] There is much truth to this view, as has been seen. Yet, we need to look deeper to account for the absence or at least the tenuousness of a strategic narrative in response to such challenges.

For one thing, and even perhaps with the best intentions, it is not easy to reorient or undo a long-standing, state-supported discourse on jihad. Whether it was the insurgency in Kashmir at the time of Pakistan's birth or in the 1990s, the wars with India in 1965 and 1971, or the Afghan war in the 1980s, the idea of jihad figured prominently in nationalist rhetoric. The notion that a Mawdudi could see the covert actions of the Pakistani military in Kashmir as anything other than jihad was damning for him in this context. Questioning the head of the Ahmadi community during the in-camera session of the National Assembly in 1974, the attorney-general was likewise incredulous that the community's founder could have gone quite so far as to outlaw jihad altogether. That he had allegedly done so in abject submission to the interests of a foreign, colonial, power rankled even more at a time when, in the early 1970s, anti-imperialist and Third Worldist sentiments were in the ascendant in Bhutto's Pakistan.[145] The identification of the military, and of the state itself, with jihad would only grow in subsequent decades. Militant Islamists and many among the `ulama may never have put much stock in the sincerity of that identification, but its long history would give them enough grounds for moral outrage at any suggestion that the investment in jihad might need to be scaled back.

The difficulties of forging a counternarrative are also exacerbated in a milieu in which Islamist militants have tended to be significantly more successful than their opponents in aligning themselves with the religious tradition. This rhetorical alignment posits that to be opposed to the militants is to oppose jihad, which is to dispute a key Islamic imperative and to question the words and actions of some of Islam's most revered figures; one could scarcely hold such positions and still be a Muslim. Mas`ud Azhar's commentary on the Qur'anic teachings on jihad provides a useful illustration of how traditional resources are put to use in making this case. Azhar casts a remarkably wide net in the exegetical writings he adduces in this book. From among premodern scholars, his sources include commentaries by Razi (d. 1210), Qurtubi (d. 1273), Nasafi (d. 1310), Abu Hayyan (d. 1344), and Ibn Kathir (d. 1373). Early modern and modern commentators he quotes include Shah `Abd al-Qadir (d. 1827, a son of Shah Wali Allah), Alusi (d. 1853), Rashid Rida (d. 1935), Ashraf `Ali Thanawi (d. 1943), Shabbir Ahmad `Usmani (d. 1949), Abul-Kalam Azad (d. 1958), Ahmad `Ali Lahori (d. 1962), Mufti Muhammad Shafi` (d. 1976), and `Abd al-Majid Daryabadi (d. 1977).[146] Commending some of the writings that he considers to have been most helpful to his own work, he notes that Thanawi "has explicated topics relating to jihad with marvelous learning."[147] That may well be so, but it should be recalled that Thanawi had the reputation of being one of most politically quiescent of the colonial `ulama. He was a bitter opponent of the Khilafat movement and he had expressed himself in opposition to the infiltration of armed Muslim bands into Kashmir in the 1930s. Azhar acknowledges none of this. Nor does he need to actually cite Thanawi in support of some of his most violent prescriptions. It is enough for Azhar to make the implicit but rhetorically powerful point that his views on jihad are not just his; they carry the full weight of Deobandi thought, which, in turn, is presented as altogether continuous with the Islamic exegetical tradition.

There *are* contemporary Deobandi scholars who have counseled reason and moderation in response to the actions of the militants. Here is one example, from November 2009. It comes from Mufti Muhammad Zahid, a professor of hadith at a madrasa in Faisalabad:

> The present time has imposed a great responsibility on the Deobandi leadership.... This responsibility is not best fulfilled by condemning America, the present [Pakistani] government, or the current system (nizam). As commendable as such [criticism] might be, it is considerably less demanding than the task of providing patient and determined leadership to those of our own folk who might be committing errors.... The truth is that the Deobandi leadership will have to come out of its interest-based shell and provide this leadership.... In my estimation, if we were to speak in a proper and reasoned manner, it would not be ineffective. The necessary condition for this is that policy matters should not be given the status of sacred doctrine; they should be open to general debate, and we ought to foster the ability to listen to things that diverge from an established point of view. Today, the setbacks that the US, Britain, and their allies suffer in Afghanistan are the subject of public debate in the West; policies are criticized, discussions take place, and failures are debated. The truth is: I fear that such openness might well prove to be the biggest strength of the West.[148]

These are bold words, considering that the militants do not take kindly to criticism of their ways.[149] A combination of the instinct for self-preservation, misgivings about the US-led War on Terror, and the desire not to be seen as allied with corrupt regimes cravenly submissive to the will of Western powers has meant, however, that much of the initiative in the articulation of discourses on jihad has rested with the likes of Mas`ud Azhar.[150] The fact that a notorious militant can publish an attractively produced four-volume work on jihad and go largely unchallenged by fellow `ulama is also a revealing indication of the difficulties the *governing elite* face in fashioning, should they so desire, a counternarrative. I will return to this point later.

Counternarratives did not, of course, need to rest on *Islamic* grounds. In 1959, Qurrat al-`Ayn Haydar (d. 2007), an emigrant from the United Provinces (UP) and the scion of a distinguished literary family, published a novel that is considered by many to be among the greatest works of Urdu fiction to be produced in the twentieth century. At nearly 800 pages, this monumental text— *Ag kar darya* (*The River of Fire*)—encompasses two millennia of Indian history, from ancient times to the decade after the partition of the subcontinent.

The characters are indigenous and foreign-born; Buddhist, Hindu, Muslim, Christian, and Jewish; Indian and Pakistani. They often shade into one another over the course of time, revealing the shallowness of identities but also the great cruelty such identities can inflict upon people. One of these characters is Abul-Mansur Kamaluddin, an expatriate from Baghdad serving as a courtier to a regional Muslim king in sixteenth-century India. While wandering in Bengal after his patron has lost his throne, Kamaluddin ruminates: "Human beings are not really human beings. They are blood-thirsty wolves.... Should I kill that man ahead because he maintains a tuft of hair on his head and worships the cow? If I didn't kill him first, would he finish me off because I don't have that tuft of hair? I should destroy the beautiful Shivpuri because millions of statues adorn the temples there. But what harm do those statues do to me? Would I cease to be a Muslim if I tolerated those statues? What is Islam?"[151] Kamaluddin eventually marries an "untouchable" Bengali woman and takes up farming as a profession. Before being killed by the soldiers of a conquering Muslim army, he had come to believe that his adopted home was not, as many jurists would have it, "the land of war (*dar al-harb*) but rather the abode of peace (*dar al-salam*). There is no difference between the land of war and the land of peace. It is only a difference of attitude: the wars are not between two religions but rather between two political powers."[152] Centuries later, Kamal Riza, a leftist Muslim who emigrates to Pakistan after spending several years in England and failing to find a decent means of livelihood in post-partition India, offers a blistering critique of how Islam was being invoked in the new Muslim homeland:

> Islam—the mistreatment to which this word has been subjected! If the Pakistani team loses a cricket match, Islam itself is thought to be in danger. Every last problem in the world gets examined with reference to it.... The irony is that those who invoke Islam have no truck with the philosophy of religion. All they know is that Muslims ruled over Christian Spain for 800 years, over Hindu India for 1000 years, and that the Ottomans dominated eastern Europe for centuries. Besides imperialism, no one mentions anything, such as Islam's great humanistic traditions; no one feels the need to talk about the cosmopolitanism of the Arab philosophers, of the Iranian poets, of the Indian Sufis. No one pays attention to the philosophy of `Ali and Husayn. Islam is being presented as an extremely aggressive religion and way of life.[153]

Qurrat al-`Ayn Haydar's was a genuine counternarrative, but it was obviously ill-suited to the needs of the new state, for her critique of religious violence was predicated on a questioning of the very foundations on which the ideological state had come to base itself. To compound things further, the novel was published at a very unpropitious time, the year after the rise to power of General Ayub Khan. Though Haydar was well-connected with the

Pakistani political and literary elite and worked, ironically, for the federal government's ministry of information, her novel seems to have made her stay in
Pakistan untenable. In early 1961, she decided to leave the country, going
first to England and not long after to India, where she lived for the rest of her
life.[154]

Unlike Qurrat al-`Ayn Haydar, modernist intellectuals in Pakistan did
make some effort from time to time to address jihad on Islamic grounds. A
notable example is Khalifa Abdul Hakim, whose discussion of jihad in his *Islamic Ideology*, first published in 1951, represents a useful articulation of the
modernist narrative on the subject. Simply put, "Islam, the Religion of Peace,
had to wage war to protect and establish itself."[155] Given that it is a "rational"
religion, Islam's teachings on war strike an ideal balance. It does not renounce
the resort to arms, for to do so would make it impossible for it to realize its
goals—"to reestablish social order, to prevent persecution and to create conditions of the Reign of Law instead of a Reign of Terror."[156] But it does rule
out the use of force for territorial, political, or economic gain, and even to
spread the faith.[157] Wars waged by Muslims for such ends were not properly
Islamic.[158] The only ones that qualified were those undertaken against oppression, in pursuit of liberty, and for social justice. Indeed, the Qur'anic injunction to "fight . . . in the way of the Lord means fighting for social justice; it
does not mean fighting to spread a certain dogma. . . . Fight for social justice
only is enjoined by Islam; a war for any other purpose would be un-Islamic."[159]

Jihad as social justice was a powerful idea, one that Abdul Hakim saw as
potentially resonating with the world at large. However, so far as its immediate audience in Pakistan was concerned, it would have had to be accompanied by some concrete efforts to ameliorate the socioeconomic condition of
ordinary people. Such efforts would remain in short supply. Sir Firoz Khan
Noon, the governor of East Bengal who had wanted to distribute copies of
Abdul Hakim's *Islamic Ideology* to the `ulama,[160] was, for one, among the
major landholders of the Punjab; he would actively work to undo the land
reforms attempted by his predecessor in the Punjab when he became the chief
minister of that province in 1953.[161] Published not long after the war in Kashmir, Abdul Hakim's work did have the merit, though, of helping the state explain and justify its militaristic ventures in the name of fighting oppression
and injustice. It also represented an attempt, as one would expect from Abdul
Hakim, to wrest control of the discourses on jihad from the traditionalist
`ulama. Nearly three decades later, Fazlur Rahman also spoke of jihad as the
means to a just social order, but with a rather different inflection:

> Jihad . . . is a total endeavor, an all-out effort—"with your wealth and
> lives," as the Qur'an frequently puts it—to "make God's cause succeed"
> (9:40). . . . [T]he concept of the ultimate end of this endeavor (*al-
> akhira*) is pivotal to the whole system of Qur'anic thought. The concept

of *akhira* implies that man needs not *just* economic justice; economic justice itself is for a higher end, for man does not live from hour to hour and from day to day like animals but his vision must see through the consequences of his actions and aim at the end which constitutes the meaning of positive human effort. This is the end which cannot be achieved without jihad, for it is God's unalterable law that He will not bring about results without human endeavor.[162]

Well before the War on Terror gave new urgency to such matters, but already in cognizance of the nonstate actors operating in Afghanistan and elsewhere, Javed Ahmad Ghamidi had argued for his part that the Qur'anic teachings on warfare were addressed not to Muslims qua individuals but rather to the collectivity—that is, to the state.[163] Ghamidi further posited that jihad in the Prophet's time could take two basic forms: it was a way of countering oppression and injustice and it was God's instrument for punishing those against whom all effort at persuasion had been exhausted. The latter kind of jihad, he argued, was limited only to the prophets, so that the sole surviving form of jihad in the post-prophetical era was the one that fought injustice.[164]

Such arguments would continue to be made in the years following 2001. In a book of essays on jihad and related matters first published in 2005, Dr. Muhammad Faruq Khan—a psychiatrist by training, an autodidact scholar of Islam, and a close associate of Ghamidi—vigorously defended views similar to his mentor's. He argued that jihad could be declared and prosecuted only by established political authority, and that nonstate actors were therefore illegitimate on Islamic grounds. He also argued that the Qur'an's injunction to "fight [the unbelievers] until there is no more persecution and the religion is God's alone" (Q 8.39) referred to the Arabian peninsula of Muhammad's time rather than to the world at large. For to interpret it to mean the latter would entail not only divesting people of the freedom of religion that the Qur'an had promised them, it would also confirm non-Muslims in their worst suspicions of Islam as a war-mongering faith.[165] Elsewhere in the book, Faruq Khan offered a vigorous critique of the Afghan Taliban's effort to impose their "village culture" on all of Afghanistan[166] and he held them responsible for bringing destruction upon the country in the wake of September 11.[167] He was also critical of the Pakistani policy toward Afghanistan, notably its cynically keeping the Afghan opposition divided during the anti-Soviet struggle in order to ensure that it remained subservient to Pakistani interests.[168] Faruq Khan had been a member of the committee headed by Justice Majida Rizvi that had recommended the repeal of General Zia al-Haqq's Hudood ordinances.[169] Before he was assassinated in October 2010, he was slated to become the vice chancellor of a university the government was in the process of establishing in Swat, until recently a stronghold of the Taliban. It was not his views on the

Hudood Ordinances, however, but rather those on jihad that were singled out by the Taliban group that claimed responsibility for his murder.[170]

The Taliban were not alone in objecting to the views on jihad held by Ghamidi and his associates. Already before the events of September 11, the Deobandi scholar Zahid al-Rashidi had taken issue with Ghamidi's understanding of the relevant teachings of the Qur'an and his reading of the Prophet's career as well as the practical implications of those views. In that regard, he had made the none-too-subtle point that they amounted to delegitimizing warfare in defense of the homeland.[171] On Zahid al-Rashidi's showing, Ghamidi and his associates were defeatists; their counsel to people whose country—India under the British, Algeria under the French, Afghanistan under the Soviets—had been taken over by an oppressive non-Muslim minority was to never fight back but rather to bow their heads in submission or leave for other havens.[172]

This sort of criticism, unlike the Taliban's, steers clear of any threat of violence against those holding the wrong kind of views. It can be damning nonetheless. Yet, even without its discouragement, or of messages delivered through targeted assassinations, writings on jihad by Pakistani modernists have not amounted to a sustained discourse. In this, they contrast not only with recent militant writings on the subject but, remarkably, even with the work of early colonial-era modernists such as Chiragh Ali, Sayyid Ahmad Khan, and Ameer Ali. Consequently, when forced by circumstances to deal with a crisis, Pakistani governments have often found precious little resources at hand, and those mustered have not necessarily made the case for them. Already in 1953, the more perceptive of the government officials who had helped quell the anti-Ahmadi agitation recognized, as the district magistrate of Rawalpindi had observed, that "such a movement cannot be eliminated by repressive methods alone. A vigorous drive must be launched to inculcate sound doctrine and sense into the people's mind."[173] Yet, he had also noted that "it was almost impossible for us to find anybody to join us in the work of publicity."[174] A half century later, in the immediate aftermath of the terrorist attacks of September 11, 2001, the government of General Pervez Musharraf was not notably more successful in finding religious scholars who would argue on its behalf. While several others were lukewarm to it, one of the most prominent of the `ulama the government had sent to Kabul to negotiate with the Taliban on the question of surrendering Usama bin Laden to the United States was decidedly hostile to any realignment in Pakistani policy. This was Mufti Nizam al-din Shamzai, a professor of hadith at the Jami`at al-Ulum al-Islamiyya in Karachi. In late October 2001, he was quoted as saying: "Musharraf openly supports the US and its allies against the Taliban. And under Islamic laws if any Muslim cooperates with infidels against Muslims, he must be excommunicated from the religion."[175] His son even fought in Afghanistan on the Taliban's side.[176]

My final example in this regard deserves a slightly fuller account. In early 2007, in the very heart of the nation's capital, two brothers in charge of the Lal Masjid ("Red Mosque") and the Hafsa madrasa for women attached to it began engaging in vigilante action to uphold what they regarded as the demands of the shari`a.[177] Madrasa students took over a children's public library to protest the demolition of mosques built on public property without government authorization; the city's video and DVD stores were threatened with dire consequences if they did not remove objectionable items; massage parlors, alleged to be brothels, were raided and, in one instance, several Chinese men and women working there were kidnapped, causing serious embarrassment to the government; a local shari`a court was established in the city; and there were incessant demands that the government commit itself to implementing the shari`a throughout the country and that it repeal the Protection of Women Act of 2006. The Lal Masjid was said to have large amounts of ammunition, and, on one occasion, the mosque's imam went so far as to threaten "suicide attacks if the government impedes the enforcement of the Sharia and attacks Lal Masjid and its sister seminaries."[178] The government once again summoned a team of religious scholars to help defuse the crisis, among them, Mufti Muhammad Rafi` `Usmani, the president of the Dar al-`Ulum madrasa in Karachi and the elder brother of Taqi `Usmani. Efforts at mediation came to nothing, however, and the mosque was stormed by the military, resulting in the death of more than a hundred people holed up inside. Not unlike Taqi `Usmani's adverse public commentary on the Protection of Women Act, Rafi` `Usmani's verdict on the government's handling of the Lal Masjid crisis was severe. He was critical of the Lal Masjid brothers for their vigilantism, but he reserved the most unsparing diatribe for the Musharraf regime, and not just with reference to the Lal Masjid operation:

> The people of Pakistan have nurtured the military with their taxes and with great financial sacrifice. [The military] is our trust, our savings, our power, the guardian of our borders—and we are proud of it. But you are misusing it in cowardly, unjust, and foolish campaigns.... You are using this military according to the dictates of [our] enemies.... Your courage no longer works in Kashmir. You have withdrawn your troops from Kargil. Nor does your courage help defend the western borders in preventing NATO forces from violating Pakistan's sacred frontiers. Your "courage" is now directed instead against the madrasa in Bajaur and in killing its wronged students. Your bravery is now focused on the boys and girls of the Hafsa madrasa. Such are your cowardly, unjust, brutal acts. Yet you say that peace and security should be established. You do everything to destroy peace and security, and then you tell us that the `ulama should play their part in restoring peace.[179]

The Lal Masjid episode added much fuel to the activities of the Pakistani Taliban and it was followed by a spate of suicide bombings. There were rumors that many more madrasa students, young men *and* women, had been killed in this episode than the government had acknowledged, which exacerbated the outrage against the government response to the crisis. But the relevant point here has to do with Rafi` `Usmani. The harshness of his criticism was striking precisely because he was not one of the "inflamed" people who had burned all bridges to the government. He belonged instead to a family of `ulama, and headed a madrasa, that had enjoyed official patronage for much of Pakistan's history; they would not break with the government even after the Lal Masjid operation. It was not just the need to maintain some popular credibility that had prompted a reaction like Rafi` `Usmani's, however. Rather, it expressed a deep-seated anxiety at what the `ulama and the Islamists saw as a foreign-inspired hostility to Islam itself. With scholars like Rafi` `Usmani and Taqi `Usmani to rely on, or Shamzai for that matter, there were severe limitations to what the government could do to fashion a new narrative on jihad.

Even if the government had received robust support from the likes of the `Usmani brothers, no strategic counternarrative has much hope of appealing to people at a doctrinal level if, as observed earlier, some of the basic needs of those people at the socioeconomic level remain unaddressed. The Taliban may have ties to organized crime, but their appeals to social justice are meaningful in disenfranchised circles. Unsurprisingly, support for the Taliban, both in Pakistan and in Afghanistan, is far more likely to be found among landless peasants than it is among the more affluent.[180] And to the extent that Mas`ud Azhar's exegetical arguments carry a sense of authenticity and weight in particular circles, it is not unrelated to the fact that he has also given expression to the economic woes of the poverty-stricken.

I conclude with three points. First, in light of the landscape and trends this chapter has reviewed, it seems necessary to chart a middle path between two commonly encountered positions. One of these—seen frequently in the international media, many Western policy analyses, and some academic circles—takes Islam to be the key factor in shaping particular instances of the Muslim resort to violence. The other, rather more in vogue among foreign and indigenous observers specifically of Pakistan affairs, takes Islamist and other forms of militancy to be the result of the machinations of the state. To revisit the second position first, the state elite have indeed had an important role in defining the context in which appeals to Islam have been articulated. This was so in the Kashmir war in 1947–48, in the wars between Pakistan and India in 1965 and 1971, during Pakistan's involvement in the Afghan jihad in the 1980s, and in its involvement in the insurgency in Indian Kashmir in the 1990s and later. Yet—and this relates to the first of the aforementioned positions—

nonstate religio-political forces have had their own interests and commitments as well. They have had considerable Islamic resources with which to shape the wider context and to make their case in it, even if these resources are not always drawn upon in a manner that others would recognize as above board.[181] And it is not just pragmatic political considerations but doctrinal constraints, too, that have shaped their stance. Hafiz Muhammad Sa`id and his Lashkar-i Tayba, for instance, have been guided by their considered religious view that one is to wage war not against a Muslim government but only against out-right infidels. This may be small comfort for a regime that *could* eventually find itself branded infidel, with all that it entails.[182] Yet, the point is that even when religious convictions are open to interpretation, they are scarcely irrele-vant to how particular courses of action are adopted, vis-à-vis the government or toward doctrinal rivals. Even the militant groups allied with the ruling establishment are seldom its puppets. Indeed, they are as likely to use such government patronage as has been available to them, and at least as adroit at doing so, as the government and the military have been in putting such non-state actors to use for their own ends. A certain convergence between the in-terests of these groups and particular governmental policies does help explain why these groups have been able to operate at particular times rather than at others, but their action is not reducible exclusively to the policies in ques-tion any more than it is to the religious resources they have drawn upon.

Second, even as the relationship between particular religio-political groups and the government has sometimes undergone quite significant change over the years, core disagreements have often continued to simmer just below the surface of particular alliances. Mawdudi and the Jama`at-i Islami were viewed by the government as dangerous opponents in Pakistan's early years, and, in 1953, the martial law authorities in the Punjab went so far as to sentence Mawdudi to death for his alleged role in inciting the anti-Ahmadi distur-bances. By the time of the civil war in East Pakistan in 1971, however, the Jama`at-i Islami had emerged as a key ally of the government and the mili-tary. That alliance would find another major expression during the anti-Soviet Afghan struggle and in its aftermath. Yet, it is hard to imagine that the concord between the Jama`at and the Yahya Khan regime could have been very durable; even the rapport with the Islamizing regime of General Zia al-Haqq had begun to fray after some years. Similarly, the strategic congruence in the 1990s between the Pakistani military and the likes of Mas`ud Azhar did not do much to resolve the contradictions underlying that relationship: Azhar's understanding of Islam, and of the `ulama's leadership roles, is decid-edly not the government's or the military's. Such examples add to those en-countered earlier regarding the fraught relationship between the modernists and their religious rivals. They also serve to further illustrate the point that particular religio-political groups have an agency that is not reducible to mo-mentary convergences of interest between them and the government.[183]

Finally, throughout the history of Pakistan, the state and its institutions have usually been able to meet the challenges that militant groups and other agitators have posed to them in the name of Islam. The agitation of 1953 had brought the provincial capital to a standstill, but that challenge was crushed as soon as the government and the military decided that it was time to do so. In more recent years, despite dire predictions of a creeping "Talibanization," even of the state falling to Taliban-like groups, the military has been able to make significant inroads into territory controlled by the militants and to restore government writ in many of those areas. Alarmist predictions in some international quarters about the collapse of the state are clearly much exaggerated. Yet, as noted, a resort to force without a counternarrative in terms of which particular constituencies might reasonably be expected to make sense of a governmental response does not add to the legitimacy either of the government or of the measures in question.[184] As the anti-Ahmadi agitation of 1953 came to a boil, Mawdudi had offered a severe indictment of the government's failure to explain or justify its position on the issue: "We have given our arguments with full clarity. If anyone has an argument that is opposed to it, he should bring it forth. To insist on something without supporting argument or proof is what the 'mulla' is accused of, but now the ones guilty of it will be those who are proud of *not* being mullas. They should know that the combined power of public opinion and of reasoned argument will eventually defeat them."[185] I will return to some related issues in the epilogue. In the meanwhile, a parallel with modernist legislation is worth considering here. From the Muslim Family Laws Ordinance of 1961 to the Protection of Women Act of 2006, the Pakistani governing elite have been able not merely to enact modernist laws unpopular in conservative circles but also, through the courts, to uphold them.[186] Yet, the very success of such legislation has tended to exact a not insignificant cost in terms of religious legitimacy—of the laws and of those backing them. That legitimacy deficit is broad in its effects. It has constrained successive Pakistani governments in efforts toward regulating the country's ever growing madrasas, too, and it underlies the inability of those governments to muster any widespread support in religious circles for countering Islamist militancy. Given how hard this militancy has hit the country— "from 2001 to November 2013, 48,994 people were killed ... including 5,272 personnel of the law-enforcement agencies," with all that that means for their families and extended kin—this is an extraordinary deficit.[187]

Epilogue

HOW SIGNIFICANTLY HAS ISLAM in Pakistan changed over the course of the country's history? More broadly, how different does the religious landscape look in the early twenty-first century in relation to how it had appeared a hundred or so years earlier? These are the questions with which I conclude this book. I begin, however, with some illustrations of what has *not* changed very much.

In mid-1960, with Ayub Khan at the apex of his power, his Ministry of the Interior produced a candidly titled memo outlining a "scheme for supervision and control of religious institutions and religious activity."[1] The scheme was more or less equally divided between a rationale for such control and the means toward it. The rationale was that religion had come to be regulated by the state from the time of the early `Abbasids and that the Mughals in India were among the dynasties that had continued that practice with notable success. So did the princely states of India, Hyderabad being an especially successful instance. "The complete absence till the day of the Indian occupation [of Hyderabad in 1948] of sectarian controversy or communal rioting which were everyday features of life in British India was in a great measure due to Government control of religious activity.... Maulana Maudoodi during the best part of his life in Hyderabad was no more than a religious thinker and writer. His rise as a politicoreligious figure in Pakistan can be directly attributed to the lack of those inhibitive institutions which prevented exploitation of religion for selfish and political ends."[2] Put differently, British colonial India—as opposed even to the princely states—was an anomaly in the history of Islam so far as the failure to regulate religion was concerned, and Pakistan was paying the price of having inherited that anomaly.

The rationale also had to do with the modernist vision of promoting, under government control, an Islam that was "progressive," anchored in the "fundamentals" rather than in empty ritualism, and concerned with "the virtues of truthfulness, honesty, courage, forbearance and perseverance."[3] These would have been important goals for a modernizing regime at any other time, too. What made them especially pressing, from the viewpoint of the Ministry of the Interior, was its sense that the religious groups were coming together not just in their own right but potentially also in opposition to the government. In a foreboding reference to the formation of boards to oversee the affairs of madrasas belonging to various doctrinal orientations, the memorandum noted that "the Deobandis [were] ... clubbing together and consolidating themselves" and so were the Barelawis.[4] The Shi`a and the Ahmadis were already well-organized communities. And the Ahl-i Hadith, too, seemed to be united in their "reactionary" ways.[5] No evidence was offered that these rival orientations were about to join hands against the government, but the perception that they were all disgruntled did raise that possibility.

What the ministry proposed on this occasion was the formation of a department of religious affairs at both the central and provincial levels. The central office would provide broad guidelines for the regulation of the religious sphere, while the provincial and local administrations would register and oversee Islamic institutions, credential preachers, administer waqf properties, and take charge both of Islamic research as well as of proselytism abroad.[6] The idea, much favored by the `ulama, that such matters ought to be left to those representing particular doctrinal orientations was dismissed out of hand: "It sounded alright in alien, non-Muslim rule, [but] it has no significance in present conditions."[7]

This was not the first time since independence, as the authors of the scheme were aware,[8] that such proposals had been taken up by the government. Nor would it be the last. The government made a serious effort to reform madrasa education in 1962; there was a secret governmental initiative toward the end of the Ayub Khan era to tackle the "fundamental conflict" between the conservatives and the progressive forces; the Ministry of Religious Affairs was established by prime minister Zulfikar Ali Bhutto in 1974; and more efforts to reform and regulate madrasas were to come under Zia al-Haqq and Musharraf. Such efforts have not been without results. Yet, as has been seen, the results in question have not necessarily been what successive regimes had intended. The government's checkered and often undistinguished record of regulating Islam is one key area in which things have not changed very much over the course of the country's history.

Throughout this book, we have encountered many instances of suspicion, recrimination, polemic, and caricature in the relationship between the modernists and the religious conservatives. That, too, has remained a constant—in this instance, from well before the birth of Pakistan. The difficulties of that relationship did not prevent the modernists and the `ulama from joining hands at critical moments, be it during the Khilafat movement in the 1920s or the movement for a separate Muslim homeland in the 1940s; nor did they prevent the Islamists from lending their support to the modernizing governing elite and the military during the wars of 1965 and 1971, the Afghan war in the 1980s, and the insurgency in Indian Kashmir from the end of that decade. Yet, in all of those instances, and in many others, the long history of mutual suspicion and, indeed, hostility has never receded very far into the background and it has resurfaced at every opportunity. The obstacles Pakistani governments have faced in regulating the religious sphere have a direct correlation with this history.

In terms of its key signposts at least, that religious sphere also represents considerable stability. South Asia is a region that has seen enormous upheaval since the mid-nineteenth century: subjection to colonial rule; the massive impact of the two world wars on society and economy; famines and other disasters; the partition of India, with its unprecedented levels of violence and dislocation; the subsequent break-up of Pakistan; the impact of the Iranian revolution, of the Soviet occupation of Afghanistan and, in more recent years, of global terrorism. It is remarkable, however, that none of the Islamic orientations that existed or were in the process of emerging at the turn of the twentieth century had ceased to exist a hundred years later. Even the Ahmadis, for all the state-sanctioned and other persecution directed at them, survive, and not just abroad but also within Pakistan. The staying power of these orientations is especially impressive when we remind ourselves that several of them are of relatively recent vintage. By the same token, the `ulama representing the various Sunni and Shi`i orientations have not merely continued to exist in society but have also, in many cases, extended the range of their activities and their reach in the public and religious spheres. This institutional and sociopolitical prominence of the `ulama undergirds a good deal of the continuity that is to be observed in Islam in South Asia from the mid-nineteenth century onward. And it is not to be taken for granted, since the `ulama have not fared equally well in all modern Muslim societies.

What then *has* changed in this landscape? Just as the advent of colonialism had begun to usher in major transformations in Muslim religious life from the mid-nineteenth century, including the emergence of new doctrinal orientations, the end of colonial rule and, in particular, the establishment of a Muslim homeland has continued to shape Islam in ways both obvious and subtle. The birth of Pakistan was an opportunity for the modernists to put their ideals into practice—to not only rid Islam of the sectarian squabbles that had rent its fabric and made Muslims weak and petty, but also to demonstrate to everyone that a properly understood Islam had much to contribute to the world at large. To Islamists like Mawdudi, the new state represented the imperative to proclaim the sovereignty of God in all its legal and political implications and thereby to fulfill the terms of the contract that Muslims were party to by virtue of being Muslims.[9] To the `ulama, for their part, the birth of Pakistan was an occasion to assume leadership roles that had eluded them for much of Islam's history, to reorient people's belief and practice not just through time-tested activities at the grassroots and by way of teaching and writing, but also through state legislation and public policy. There is much that is new in the ensuing competition among rival trends, but also in their continuing engagement with one another, and it would be inconceivable without the framework provided by what professes to be an Islamic state.

Within it, though building on prior developments, the aforementioned fixtures of the religious landscape have continued to undergo changes of their own. The ʿulama are a case in point here. Where most religious scholars of the late nineteenth and the early twentieth centuries had been entirely lacking in any formal exposure to Western learning (and even pioneering modernists like Sayyid Ahmad Khan spoke no English), it is not unusual for leading figures among the contemporary ʿulama to have had some schooling in the Western sciences. Indeed, some of their success in reaching broader audiences rests precisely on an ability to demonstrate a familiarity with modern forms of knowledge, including the English language. It is no exaggeration to say that the contemporary ʿulama have done better at acquiring Western learning, and at benefiting from so doing, than the modernists have in developing a credible grounding in the Islamic tradition and in enhancing the religious credentials that go with any such accomplishment. Some contemporary Sufi groups are equally instructive in this regard. The shaykhs of the Chishti Sabiri order in Pakistan have tended to have a modern, Western education—from Aligarh, Oxford, the Dehra Dun Military Academy, the Pakistan Air Force Academy. Zulfiqar Ahmad, a prominent Naqshbandi pir who belongs to the Deobandi orientation, is an electrical engineer by training and vocation. If anything, the Sufis have gone further in this regard than have the ʿulama, which is owing in part at least to the fact that the ʿulama are products of what remains a well-structured system of Islamic education while the Sufis are not.

Given that the doctrinal orientations that dot the religious landscape of Pakistan are not abstract entities but are defined rather by the *people* who adhere to and represent them, we should not be surprised to see that they, too, have undergone significant change while retaining the lineaments of a broad continuity.[10] Some of the changes in question are internal to these orientations, whereas others relate to their position vis-à-vis one another. An example of the former is the space Sufism now occupies among the Deobandis. As seen in chapter 6, Sufi piety retains its appeal in many circles, and even the militant Deobandi leader of the Jaish-i Muhammad recommends practices with an unmistakable Sufi resonance to his audiences. Nonetheless, devotional piety has less room in contemporary Deobandi thought and practice than it did a hundred or even fifty years ago. And though efforts to revive Sufi practice, as with the aforementioned Zulfiqar Ahmad, are not reducible to an extension of specifically Deobandi influence, they do have an unmistakable aspect of the latter.[11]

As for the relative standing of particular religious orientations vis-à-vis one another, the most significant change has to do with the leading presence of the Deobandis in the public and religious spheres. This is a development that has long been in the making, but it has been consolidated in Pakistan, with help from the modernists. Their suspicion of the `ulama notwithstanding, the modernists have tended to view the textually anchored Deobandi approach to Islam as closer to their own than, say, the Islam of the Barelawis, let alone that of the Shi`a. The modernists might be thought to have an even greater affinity with the scripturalism of the Ahl-i Hadith, except that stereotypes about the latter's "reactionary" ways have long persisted, and the small numbers they command make them less useful for purposes of government patronage. For their part, the Islamists of the Jama`at-i Islami have often been able to accommodate people of varying doctrinal orientations within their ranks. That, incidentally, has itself been a cause of some suspicion among their rivals, who have taken it to suggest that the Jama`at is lacking in religious scruples.[12] For all that, Mawdudi's understanding of Islam tends to reveal greater affinity with that of the Deobandis than it does with any other doctrinal orientation. And Qazi Husayn Ahmad, a subsequent amir of the Jama`at-i Islami (1987–2009), was the son of a leader of the Jam`iyyat al-`Ulama-i Hind in the late colonial North-West Frontier Province, and he had, in fact, been named after Husayn Ahmad Madani.[13] More than others, the Deobandis have been able to combine scripturalism with a continuing fidelity to the Hanafi legal tradition, religio-political activism with Sufi piety, scholarly productivity with populism, and this has paid dividends in terms of a greater reach and influence in state and society. The Deobandis were also the first to develop the model of loosely affiliated madrasas supported by small-time local contributions, and their madrasas have been the greatest beneficiaries of it without yet forswearing more lucrative sources of patronage at home or abroad.

The hardening of boundaries between and among key doctrinal orientations represents another significant change over the course of the past hundred years. It is scarcely unexpected for some such delineation of boundaries to have taken place, of course, as an expression of the very survival and development of the orientations in question. What *is* worth remarking on is when and how its effects have come to be felt. Though difficult to demonstrate in the absence of large-scale empirical studies, it seems to be far less common in Pakistan today for Sunnis of different doctrinal persuasions to participate in Shi`i rituals commemorating the martyrdom of their imam, Husayn, than it was a hundred years ago. Initiatives toward the development of a distinctly Sunni symbolism to compete with that of the Shi`a had already been witnessed in late colonial India, and they came to find new expressions at the hands of the virulently anti-Shi`i Sipah-i Sahaba in the 1980s. The context in which this latter-day development has taken place is characterized not merely by a long history of sectarian squabbles or local politics, however, but also by events of a global significance, such as the Iranian revolution and Islamic revivalism more broadly. This new phase in the history of Shi`i-Sunni relations has been accompanied by sectarian violence on a scale that had little parallel in colonial India or in the first decades of Pakistan. In 1929, to take another example, a prominent Barelawi scholar had written a book extolling Husayn alongside a number of other pre-Islamic and Islamic holy figures. Though he took occasional issue with Shi`i interpretations of particular events, this book, by Abul-Hasanat Muhammad Ahmad Qadiri, could have passed for the work of a Shi`i preacher. It is difficult to imagine a contemporary Barelawi scholar producing such a work.[14]

The starkest example of hardening attitudes relates, of course, to the Ahmadis. Their exclusion through the constitutional amendment of 1974 had built on earlier developments, not just those of 1953 but also in colonial India. As would be recalled, Iqbal had felt offended by the Ahmadi refusal to see other Muslims *as* Muslims and, on this and other grounds, he had urged the colonial government to declare the Ahmadis a separate religious community. Yet, several of Iqbal's contemporaries had not viewed the Ahmadis as non-Muslim, and attitudes toward the Lahore-based Ahmadis, who did not consider Mirza Ghulam Ahmad to be a prophet, were considerably less strident. Though the decision of Zafrulla Khan to speak at a public meeting of the Rabwa-based Ahmadis had helped galvanize the agitation of 1953, it was still possible in 1965 for the Lahore-based Ahmadis to publish front-page advertisements in the national press to announce their events.[15] The Rabwah-based Ahmadis were not outcastes either. Justice M. R. Kayani, one of the two judges investigating the 1953 Punjab disturbances, had visited the Ta`lim al-Islam College in Rabwah as a guest of honor and applauded the fact that about 45 percent of its students were non-Ahmadis.[16] Students of the college competed in intercollegiate competitions; in March 1970, they were reported to have won the rowing championship hosted by the University of the Punjab.[17] Things would look decidedly different by the fall of 1974 and different still a decade later, when it was made a criminal offense for the Ahmadis to pass off as Muslims.

The apparent suddenness of the agitation in 1974 should not obscure the deep roots of the anxieties the Ahmadis had provoked among those hostile to them. The government's capitulation to the demands was nonetheless a turning point: it ratified the impulse toward sharper boundaries between what did or did not count as Islam, and it fostered the hope, already expressed by some in Pakistan's first years, that more of such boundaries would be drawn.[18] On the face of it, the government had acted very differently in 1953 from how it responded in 1974. What the two occasions shared, however, was the government's unwillingness or inability to offer a reasoned defense of its position. As has been seen, that inability would characterize its dealings with the post-September 2001 Taliban and their supporters, too.

In Pakistan's early decades, there existed some promising intellectuals who could not only explain and bolster modernist positions but also help cultivate something of a middle ground between the modernists and the conservatives. From among the `ulama, we met two such figures, Hanif Nadwi and Ja`far Phulwarwi, in chapter 3. Khalifa Abdul Hakim's Institute of Islamic Culture, where they were both employed, was a semi-official site for the articulation of modernist viewpoints, and it produced a good deal of Islamic literature in the 1950s and the 1960s. Not all of the positions of a Nadwi or a Phulwarwi suited government policy or interests. As observed earlier, Nadwi had been among the first in Pakistan to call for the exclusion of the Ahmadis from the Muslim community.[19] Yet, he was anything but the "reactionary" that the Ministry of Interior's memorandum of 1960 had led policy makers to expect when dealing with members of the Ahl-i Hadith. Nor did he embody the uncompromising zealotry that "would rest content only if Governmental action supports reversion to conditions obtaining in Arabia 1300 years ago."[20] The space such intellectuals occupied between rival camps—the modernists, the `ulama, the Islamists—was nonetheless ambiguous, and this may be further illustrated by a brief look at another figure, Murtaza Ahmad Khan Maikash (d. 1959). A significant contrast between present-day Pakistan and its religious landscape in the 1950s and the 1960s is marked precisely by the absence of such intermediate intellectuals from the contemporary scene.

Maikash was educated at prominent colonial-era institutions, the Government College and the Islamia College of Lahore. A poet—*maikash*, "winedrinker," was his literary name—and a journalist, he worked for about ten newspapers, including the Persian-language *Afghanistan*, over the course of his life. He also served for some time as a lecturer in journalism at the University of the Punjab and as a member of the editorial board of the Urdu *Encyclopedia of Islam*, which, too, was housed at the university. Maikash wrote several books, of which two are broad-ranging historical surveys: a world history, "from the flint stone to the atom bomb," completed in 1945 but first published in 1950, and a history of Islam, which was completed in 1947 and first published shortly thereafter. Both works, for which he drew on sources in Persian, Arabic, Urdu, and English, shed some light on his thinking.

His rationale for writing the world history—dedicated to the Afghans for maintaining their neutrality during World War II—was that people had come to inhabit a globalized world, with events in one part of it affecting lives in another: "in these circumstances, studying the history of just one nation, one group, or one country cannot produce that breadth of thought and vision that

is essential to lead one's life in the present age." Nor could one properly evalu-
ate contemporary trends and movements of a worldwide reach without view-
ing them from a global perspective. Such histories existed aplenty in European languages, but none in Urdu, which is why he had proceeded to write
one.[21] He hoped, too, that historical information about the founding figures
of the major religions would "save people from that narrow-mindedness of
religious prejudice that has afflicted them in the past and does still."[22]

Maikash was not reticent about injecting commentary into his survey. Following an account of historical and cultural developments until the time of the
Mongol invasions of the Middle East in the thirteenth century, he observed:

> The Muslims of this age can claim credit for the development of many
> areas of knowledge. It is surprising, however, that they did not turn
> their attention to developing or improving the science of politics....
> Coming out of their desert and becoming the rulers of other countries,
> Arab Muslims rapidly fell victim to the old ways of Roman and Persian
> kingship; only the democratic sensibilities of Islam were able to keep
> the bitterness of those ways from acquiring intolerable proportions.
> The establishment of personal [that is, authoritarian] rule among Mus-
> lims meant that Muslim intellectuals would fail to develop a science of
> politics or a form of government that they could have called their own
> and which would have saved them from recurring rebellions, strife,
> civil wars, and courtly intrigues.[23]

Another example relates to his derision of Muslim intellectual sterility at the
end of the nineteenth century, which he took to stand in sharp contrast to
the intellectual and technological advances in the West, even as it evoked for
him the condition of Europe in the Dark Ages:

> Muslim debates in their age of decline had to do with such things as
> whether it was permissible or impermissible to raise one's hands as
> part of the prayer ritual, should the *Fatiha* [the opening chapter of the
> Qur'an] be recited at graves, was it legitimate to feed the poor for the
> spiritual benefit of deceased holy people, was it allowed or forbidden
> to eat [the meat of] an owl.... The Christians of the age of ignorance
> characterized every new product of scientific research as reprehensible
> innovation and heresy. Muslims living in *their* age of decline, too, had
> adopted the practice of viewing every invention as reprehensible inno-
> vation and heresy simply because the wealth of knowledge had now
> passed into the hands of the Western Christians.[24]

Maikash was harsh in his criticism of his contemporary West, too. He saw
it as materialistic, promiscuous, and increasingly devoid of moral values.[25] In
the aftermath of World War II and the establishment of the United Nations,
the world stood in a balance: the great powers—the United States, Britain,

and the Soviet Union—could come together to reenslave the world or they could help usher in an era of justice and equality.[26] A globally shared system of education could, he said in concluding his book, promote a better life for everyone, but he was skeptical of the prospects of any such system being instituted.[27]

The two-volume history of Islam is also an illuminating work. Maikash wrote the preface to the first edition in early 1947, though a subsequent edition took account of developments up to around 1950. He gave his Islamic sentiments somewhat freer rein in this book than he had in his world history. A notable example occurs in his concluding lines:

> In all non-Muslim states, whether socialist or capitalist and democratic, modern civilization is rebelling against those ethical and social limits that religion and morality seek to impose upon people for their own good. The nations that call themselves Muslim are also being swept away like straws by this raging flood.... The conservative (*muhafiz-kār*) groups working in Muslim countries toward the preservation of religious norms are being dismissed as past-oriented (*qadamat pas-and*) by the enlightened (*rawshan khayal*) votaries of modern civilization. In these storms of transgression and iniquity erupting from one end of the world to the other, there seems to be no escape for those calling themselves Muslims. Yet the truths and virtues of the religion of Islam are so real and so concrete that they are bound to draw some section or the other of the human race to themselves. From within the storms of insolence represented by current trends, there would arise those righteous movements whose flagbearers will again bring glory to Islam and thereby succeed in ridding humanity of its troubles.... The manifest lesson of Islam's history is that those calling themselves Muslim have succeeded and progressed [in the world] only to the degree that they have been guided by the desire to seek God's favor and success in the hereafter.[28]

This romantic vision of an eventual Islamic restoration was not, however, characteristic of the book as a whole, which was marked rather by a sober analysis of historical developments. In his survey of early twentieth-century history, he did speak of the "fever of modernism" when referring to Mustafa Kemal in Turkey (1923–38) and Reza Shah in Iran (r. 1925–41), and he showed how the efforts of King Amanullah of Afghanistan (r. 1919–29) to pursue similar policies had led to the undoing of his once promising reign.[29] Yet, his tone in this context, to take just this one example, was unsentimental. He observed that, in emulating Turkey and Iran, the Afghan king had failed to realize that his subjects were considerably more traditional than were the citizens of those two countries. Further, British intrigue had helped fan the flames of religious resentment against the king's policies while also turning the products of *modern* education against him. Nor did Maikash gloss over the opportunism of the alliance Amanullah's successors had forged with the religious opposition in the country. He even referred to the religious groups as "past-oriented" and, more strikingly, to the king's unseating with their co-operation as a *"reactionary* revolution" (*irtija`i inqilab*).[30]

This is the language of a modernist, but Maikash, who lamented such language elsewhere,[31] was not a modernist. In 1953, he was a member of the Majlis-i `amal—the Committee of Action—spearheading the anti-Ahmadi agitation.[32] This fact would seem to be enough to inspire modernist misgivings. The inspector-general of the Punjab police was asked by the Court of Inquiry looking into that agitation, after he had defined a mulla as "a semi-educated person who misleads people in the name of religion and opposes all progress [but also] ... an educated person [who] ... uses religion for an ulterior object," if Maikash fit that definition. The inspector-general's response: "Some of the articles written by him were written in the strain of Mullaism."[33] Maikash's testimony before the Court of Inquiry would have confirmed that view. Asked by the court if he had read Jinnah's famous speech of August 11, 1947 ("in course of time all these angularities of the majority and minority communities, the Hindu community and the Muslim community ... will vanish"), Maikash said, incredulously, that he had not. Having read it at the court's instance, he told the judges that Jinnah's idea of the state, as articulated in that speech, was "fundamentally opposed" to his own.[34] Representing the agitation's Committee of Action before the court, Maikash also asked some uncomfortable questions about why the sympathizers of the anti-Ahmadi camp did not enjoy the much touted freedom of religious expression to express *their* core Islamic beliefs.[35]

For its part, in a backhanded compliment to his historical interests and with reference to his literary name, the court quizzed Maikash on the caliph from early Islam "who used to drink every Friday after divine service," and whether Maikash knew that "some of the most difficult philosophical questions were discussed by the fuqaha [jurists] in Baghdad and Damascus when they were drunk."[36] Though Maikash showed little inclination to play along, such questioning went beyond the court's entertainment.[37] Quite apart from showing that intellectuals like Maikash were either not knowledgeable enough about the history of Islam or not honest enough to admit to its seamier sides, the key point being made was the futility of looking up to a romanticized version of that history for present and future models.[38]

A religious honorific, "mawlana," accompanied his name, but Maikash was no mere camp follower of the traditionalist `ulama. The idea, for instance, that Muslims living under European colonialism were like the Europeans of the Dark Ages in their meaningless religious squabbles sounds extraordinary when one recognizes that some of these issues were precisely what differentiated one doctrinal orientation of colonial India from another. To the Barelawis, the Deobandis, and the Ahl-i Hadith, these were anything but small, ridiculous questions. Maikash himself has been claimed by the Barelawis as one of their own. It is under the auspices of a Barelawi publishing house that his history of Islam was reprinted in 2006.[39] This should not, however, obscure the critical distance from these orientations to which the remarks under discussion point. As for the anti-Ahmadi agitation of 1953, it is not far-fetched to think that he would have seen it as an illustration precisely of the kind of revivalist movements that the concluding lines of his history of Islam had envisioned some years earlier.[40] It was not as "religious hysteria," which is what it was to the chief minister of the Punjab,[41] but in terms of a historical analysis that Maikash would have wanted to make sense of such events.

Maikash's analysis had its limits, and these go beyond an occasional romanticism.[42] The desire he had expressed in his world history to help rid people of "the narrow-mindedness of religious prejudice" had clearly done little to lessen his own prejudices. Yet, for all their unsavory ways, such intellectuals did have the potential to serve as a bridge between the modernists and the more conservative segments of society.[43] The 1953–54 Court of Inquiry grudgingly recognized this to a degree by allowing Maikash to represent the anti-Ahmadi agitation's Committee of Action at the court. This was no mean assignment considering that Husain Shaheed Suhrawardy, the secular Bengali politician who would go on to serve as the prime minister of Pakistan (1956–57), had preceded Maikash as the counsel for the Committee.[44] However, it would have taken sustained effort to tame intellectuals like Maikash and to put them to use in the service of modernism. Some rethinking of modernist convictions was needed, too, but there has seldom been much appetite for it among the governing elite.[45]

In a remarkable contrast with some other Muslim countries, notably Indonesia, few modernist institutions were established in Pakistan's early (or, for that matter, later) decades with the aim of producing Islamic scholarship or of educating people in new understandings of Islam.[46] There was a Department of Islamiat (Islamic Studies) that existed in the early years under the auspices of the Punjab government's Directorate of Public Relations. But given that it functioned essentially as part of the official bureaucracy, the department had little space within which to formulate credible viewpoints, and it was always subject to the day-to-day interests of the government.[47] Officials at this department were later found to be feeding articles to the press and patronizing some virulently anti-Ahmadi newspapers, presumably as a way of helping the provincial government in its ongoing tussle with the center.[48] Further, at least some of those on the payroll of the department had no clear qualifications for the job: as the Court of Inquiry discovered, one of them was an illiterate wrestler from Lahore who had been hired to instruct children living in prison (presumably with their inmate parents) not only in physical education but also in the basics of Islam.[49] The Islamic Research Institute and the Council of Islamic Ideology, for their part, were high-profile bodies, but they, too, were, and remain, instruments of government policy rather than sites of modernist thought with any measure of independence.[50] While he was its director, Fazlur Rahman had brought international scholarly attention to the institute, but that had owed largely to his own stature and pains rather than to any particular governmental investment in it. The Institute of Islamic Culture in Lahore had initially shown greater promise, but it too now stands as a shadow of its earlier self.[51] None of these, moreover, was designed as teaching institutions. Unlike the traditionalist `ulama, the likes of Hanif Nadwi and Ja`far Phulwarwi produced no successors. Fazlur Rahman, the towering figure of the 1960s and the most gifted modernist intellectual to have been associated with *any* Pakistani government, was no bridge-builder. And though he had considerable influence on intellectual trends in Turkey and Indonesia, his legacy in Pakistan itself was small.[52] Colleges and universities would seem to have been the most promising sites for modernist initiatives to put down roots and find distinctive expressions. But the long-standing weakness of public education, including higher education, made that difficult. Further, in an apparent paradox for a state that has always foregrounded its Islamic commitments, the study of Islam has tended to be seen at universities as suited only to the least gifted. Perhaps the greatest beneficiaries of Islamic studies in the university system are the graduates of madrasas, who have been able to add degrees from Westernized institutions to their credentials as `ulama. This has enabled them to break down some of the long-standing barriers between the products of the college and the madrasa and to reach broader audiences. But it has done little for the modernists.

What all this amounts to is, of course, a further illustration of the decline of Islamic modernism in Pakistan. That, in turn, is among the starkest contrasts between the religious landscape of Pakistan's first two decades and the present. The sort of self-confidence that Liaquat Ali Khan had exuded in March 1949 in envisioning Pakistan as a "laboratory" for progressive Islamic ideals in the service of all humankind [53] has had few parallels in more recent years. It has little in common, for instance, with General Pervez Musharraf's elusive desire to chart a path of "enlightened moderation" between Islamist radicalism and the failings of particular policies adopted by Western powers. Nor does it have much in common with Benazir Bhutto's vision, set out in a posthumous book, of tolerant interpretations of Islam that would steer the Muslim world and the West away from a collision course. Democracy, she argued in that book, is the panacea for religious radicalism. It is "dictatorships [that have] tended to favor hardline traditionalist interpretations of religion in return for the theocrats' providing a fig leaf of religious legitimacy to autocracy."[54] While her desire to see the growth of a robust middle class, economic opportunity, the empowerment of women, and a strong civil society was commendable, of course, she gave little sense in this book of how this would be brought about in Pakistan. There was scant acknowledgment, too, of the failures of her two governments in contributing much in those directions. Some of her proposals would have struck even sympathetic readers as odd. She suggested, for instance, that "the [Persian] Gulf states ... jump-start economic and intellectual development in the rest of the Islamic world. This is what my father tried to do for Pakistan, and this is what I tried to do as prime minister in my two terms in office."[55] Such suggestions take little account of the fact, however, that the oil-rich authoritarian Arab states of the region are not well-known for fostering intellectual growth, except in tightly delimited spheres, and there is some irony in looking to them as a way of promoting Bhutto's central concern—institutionalizing democratic norms. Also lost is the further irony that it was under the elder Bhutto, and partly through closer ties with Saudi Arabia and the influx of Pakistani labor in the Middle East during his time, that a new foundation had come to be laid for conservative socioreligious change in the 1980s.

A related contrast between Pakistan's first decades and today has to do with the modernist elite's moral authority. As a British consular official saw it in 1951, "[t]o the Prime Minister [Liaquat Ali Khan] and to 'Islamic Socialists' of his way of thinking, the authority of Mr. Jinnah or, indeed, of common sense, is enough to justify a particular interpretation of Islam."[56] The `ulama and the Islamists would not have gone so far in recognizing that authority, though they, too, could not quite defy it. For his part, Liaquat Ali Khan had the backing of the preeminent `alim Shabbir Ahmad `Usmani even when the two were not quite on the same page. That sort of authority would soon evaporate. This was not only because subsequent members of the modernizing elite could not point to the kind of accomplishments as the founding fathers or because they often lacked political legitimacy. It also had to do with their failure to put in much effort into providing credible alternatives to the positions espoused by the `ulama and the Islamists. For their part, the latter have poured great energy into making *their* case. Mawdudi's extensive writings made him the most influential Islamist ideologue in twentieth-century South Asia and one of the most visible of them in the wider Muslim world. Even some of those with a history of hostility toward him drew approvingly on his commentary on the Qur'an.[57] In more recent years, the Jaish-i Muhammad's Mas`ud Azhar has presented his reading of the jihad-related verses of the Qur'an in the form of a very substantial commentary. The Islamists and the `ulama have also been adept at actively *weakening* the moral authority of the modernists, as seen earlier with reference to Mufti Taqi `Usmani, and they have done so while benefiting from the patronage of the governing elite.

Though a good deal of the responsibility for the enervation of modernism rests, then, with the Pakistani governing elite and their intellectual associates, religio-political trends in the wider Muslim world have not been friendly to modernism either.[58] The defeat of the Arab states in the 1967 war with Israel was a significant contributor to the declining appeal of secular Arab nationalism and the growing prominence of Islamist trends in the Middle East and elsewhere. More or less in tandem with it, the vast financial resources that had become available to Middle Eastern petroleum-exporting countries enabled them to invest in religious causes as never before. Under Saudi patronage, this meant the growth of Salafi mosques and schools, though the beneficiaries were not all Salafis. Mawdudi, who was not a Salafi, had advised the Saudi government on plans for the establishment of the Islamic University of Medina; he was the first recipient of the Faisal Prize for services to Islam (instituted by the Saudi government in memory of King Faisal, r. 1964–75); and some of his followers would later have prominent positions at the Saudi-supported International Islamic University in Islamabad.[59] The prospects of Saudi patronage had also helped reorient the government of Zulfikar Bhutto away from the harder edges of its leftist leanings. The unprecedented opportunities that the oil wealth had created in the Middle East for labor from countries like Pakistan fostered as well the growth of a petite bourgeoisie that would become the bulwark of conservative religious change in the 1980s. By the beginning of that decade, the impact of the Islamic revolution in Iran and of the mobilization for the anti-Soviet jihad in Afghanistan had begun to have ripple effects of their own across the Muslim world. This was no longer a time when scholars and policy analysts could confidently predict the sweeping march of westernization and secularization.

It was not inevitable that such transregional trends should strengthen anti-modernist currents in Pakistan, but they did, especially because the ground had long been prepared for them within the country. Though the Bhutto regime would have probably capitulated anyway to the anti-Ahmadi agitation of 1974, it did matter that the Saudi-sponsored Muslim World League had taken the lead in declaring the Ahmadis non-Muslim. Two other illustrations are also in order here. Rethinking the hudud in a manner Fazlur Rahman had tried to in the mid-1960s was a significantly more arduous exercise in the Pakistan of the 1980s not only because it was Zia al-Haqq rather than Ayub Khan who was in power but also because revolutionary Iran was flaunting its commitment to Qur'anic law next door. The winds, internationally, were not blowing in the direction of explaining away the hudud, but rather of implementing them. Islamization could be lucrative, too, and not just in terms of a regime's image. Though Islamists and the ʿulama have long called for the elimination of financial interest from the economy, it was more tempting for a government to heed such demands, even if superficially, at a time when petroleum-rich Muslim countries were helping to underwrite Islamic banking. In this instance, too, the 1980s and the 1990s were not propitious decades for Islamic arguments in *favor* of financial interest—arguments Fazlur Rahman had made with much learning in the 1960s. In 2002, General Pervez

Musharraf did manage to have an impending ban on interest-based transactions overturned by a stacked Shari`at Appellate Bench of the Supreme Court, but the rushed decision was little more than the affirmation of a military ruler's wishes. There was barely a mention of Rahman's work by *any* side on that occasion.[60]

By the 1980s and the 1990s, the `ulama and the Islamists had come to substantially encroach upon the terrain inhabited by Islamic modernism in colonial India and in the first decades of Pakistan.[61] Two concluding points are worth noting in this regard. First, despite modernist stereotypes, the `ulama are not necessarily averse to accommodating themselves and their norms to changing needs. As seen in chapter 3, they and the Islamists of Pakistan's early years had articulated maximalist Islamic positions for the country's constitution, yet they were not unwilling to accept modernist views that diverged significantly from their own. Nor were the `ulama uniformly opposed to sidestepping stringent rules laid out in works of great antiquity and authority, as the judges of the 1953–54 Court of Inquiry discovered with some discomfort.[62] So far as the Islamists are concerned, even the powerful idea of the sovereignty of God could be deployed not only to delegitimize modernist legal initiatives but also to *legitimize* Islamist participation in democratic politics. None of this is to deny that many among the `ulama and the Islamists are fully capable of living up to modernist caricatures of them. It is merely to note that among the blind spots most damaging to the modernists' own cause has been their unwillingness to see much nuance or internal differentiation among their conservative rivals. The need to recognize such nuance and to build on it is not a matter of intellectual generosity; it is pragmatic politics.[63] Second, though tempting to see its decline as the passing of an era, Islamic modernism is not necessarily a thing only of the past. The Pakistani governing elite retain their modernist impulses. And modernism lives on, among other things, in the impact it has had on rival trends over the course of the past hundred years. In not a few cases, that impact has, ironically, strengthened those trends vis-à-vis modernism. For its part, modernism's control of or proximity to the levers of political power has not required a concomitant investment in the bolstering of its intellectual defenses. This need not have been the outcome, of course, and it might yet be different as a result of decisions still to be made. A change in modernist intellectual fortunes would depend, however, upon serious, not wishful, thinking about Islam and on engaging with it as something more than as a tool of political legitimation. It would also depend upon the social, economic, and political conditions in which such thinking takes place.

NOTES

Introduction

1. Writing in the early 1940s, Wilfred Cantwell Smith reckoned the Indian modernist Syed Ameer Ali's *Spirit of Islam* to be "the most widely quoted modern book on the religion" in Egypt. Wilfred Cantwell Smith, *Modern Islam in India: A Social Analysis* (London: Victor Gollancz, 1946), 55. Ameer Ali's *Critical Examination of the Life and Teachings of Mohammed* (London: Williams & Norgate, 1873) had developed some two decades after its first appearance into *The Life and Teachings of Mohammed, or the Spirit of Islam* (London: W. H. Allen, 1891), and later still into *The Spirit of Islam* (London: Methuen, 1967; first published under this as the main title in 1896). On Ameer Ali (d. 1928), see Smith, *Modern Islam*, 49–55; Aziz Ahmad, *Islamic Modernism in India and Pakistan, 1857–1964* (London: Oxford University Press, 1967), 86–97.

2. Political histories of Pakistan are, however, more readily available. For some notable examples, see Mohammad Waseem, *Politics and the State in Pakistan* (Islamabad: National Institute of Historical and Cultural Research, 1994); M. Rafique Afzal, *Pakistan: History and Politics, 1947–1971* (Karachi: Oxford University Press, 2001); Ayesha Jalal, *The Struggle for Pakistan: A Muslim Homeland and Global Politics* (Cambridge, MA: Harvard University Press, 2014); and Christophe Jaffrelot, *The Pakistan Paradox: Instability and Resilience*, trans. Cynthia Schoch (New York: Oxford University Press, 2015).

3. For a penetrating critique of such distinctions, see Shahab Ahmed, *What Is Islam? The Importance of Being Islamic* (Princeton, NJ: Princeton University Press, 2016). An important ethnographic study that demonstrates how ordinary villagers in a remote region of Pakistan's Khyber Pakhtunkhwa province (previously the North-West Frontier Province) bordering Afghanistan sometimes engage in serious debate on religious and related matters, see Magnus Marsden, *Living Islam: Muslim Religious Experience in Pakistan's North-West Frontier* (Cambridge, UK: Cambridge University Press, 2005).

4. Proceedings of the Court of Inquiry, 1953–54, the Punjab Archives, Lahore (hereafter, Court of Inquiry Proceedings). These records were the basis of the *Report of the Court of Inquiry Constituted under Punjab Act II of 1954 to Enquire into the Punjab Disturbances of 1953* (Lahore: Superintendent, Government Printing, 1954). Apart from this report, and with one important exception, these records have not been utilized in any study so far. The exception is Ali Usman Qasmi, *The Ahmadis and the Politics of Religious Exclusion in Pakistan* (London: Anthem Press, 2014), though this work draws on them only with reference to the anti-Ahmadi agitation.

5. For an overview of British colonial constructions of India, the contrasts it was seen as representing with the world of the colonizers, and the liberal assumptions guiding or, as the case may be, mitigating such contrasts, see Thomas R. Metcalf, *Ideologies of the Raj* (Cambridge, UK: Cambridge University Press, 1995), especially 28–43. Also see Karuna Mantena, *Alibis of Empire: Henry Maine and the Ends of Liberal Imperialism* (Princeton, NJ: Princeton University Press, 2010).

6. Earl of Cromer, *Modern Egypt*, 2 vols. (London: Macmillan, 1908), 2: 184, speaking of Muhammad Bayram (d. 1889) of Tunisia. Quoted in Albert Hourani, *Arabic Thought in the Liberal Age, 1798–1939* (Cambridge, UK: Cambridge University Press, 1983), 251.

7. Sayyid Ahmad Khan, "Islam," in idem, *Khutbat-i Sir Sayyid*, ed. Muhammad Isma`il Panipati, 2 vols. (Lahore: Majlis-i taraqqi-i adab, 1972–73), 1: 508–9; for the full text

of the lecture, see ibid., 500–533. For an English translation, see Christian W. Troll, *Sayyid Ahmad Khan: A Reinterpretation of Muslim Theology* (Delhi: Vikas Publishing House, 1978), 307–32; quotation at 314. I use Troll's translation with some modifications.

8. Fazlur Rahman, "Some Islamic Issues in the Ayyub Khan Era," in Donald P. Little, ed., *Essays on Islamic Civilization Presented to Niyazi Berkes* (Leiden: E. J. Brill, 1976), 301–2.

9. Cf. Smith, *Modern Islam in India*, 293.

10. Classic early statements of Islamic modernism include, besides Ameer Ali's work, Khayr al-din al-Tunisi, *Aqwam al-masalik fi ma `rifat ahwal al-mamalik* (Tunis: Matba`at al-dawla, 1867); Syed Ahmed Khan, *A Series of Essays on the Life of Mohammed and Subjects Subsidiary Thereto* (London: Trübner & Co., 1870); Cheragh Ali, *The Proposed Political, Legal, and Social Reforms in the Ottoman Empire and Other Mohammadan States* (Bombay: Education Society's Press, 1888); Muhammad `Abduh, *Risalat al-tawhid* (Bulaq: al-Matba`a al-kubra al-amiriyya, 1897); Mohammad Iqbal, *The Reconstruction of Religious Thought in Islam* (London: Oxford University Press, 1934); and Muhammad Rashid Rida, *Tafsir al-Qur'an al-hakim, al-shahir bi-Tafsir al-manar*, 12 vols., 3rd ed. (Cairo: Dar al-manar, 1947–54; first serialized in Rida's Cairo-based journal *al-Manar*). For a notable articulation of the modernist position from Pakistan's first years, see Khalifa Abdul Hakim, *Islamic Ideology*, 2nd ed. (Lahore: Institute of Islamic Culture, 1953; first published in 1951); all references are to this edition, unless indicated otherwise.

11. *The Constituent Assembly of Pakistan Debates*, 16 vols. (Karachi: Manager of Publications, Government of Pakistan, 1947–54 [hereafter, *CAPD*]), 5/1: 5.

12. There are not insignificant commonalities between Muslim modernist aspirations and those of what James Scott characterizes as the Western "high modernists" of the late nineteenth and the early to mid-twentieth centuries. "At [high modernism's] ... center was a supreme self-confidence about continued linear progress, the development of scientific and technical knowledge, the expansion of production, the rational design of social order, the growing satisfaction of human needs, and, not least, an increasing control over nature (including human nature) commensurate with scientific understanding of natural laws. *High* modernism is thus a particularly sweeping vision of how the benefits of technical and scientific progress might be applied—usually through the state—in every field of human activity." James C. Scott, *Seeing Like a State* (New Haven, CT: Yale University Press, 1998), 89–90. Emphasis in the original. The scientific, technological, and developmentalist aspects of the modernist enterprise fall largely outside the purview of the present work, however.

13. The most influential instance of this view is Albert Hourani, *Arabic Thought in the Liberal Age, 1798–1939* (Cambridge, UK: Cambridge University Press, 1983; first published in 1962). Also see Malcolm H. Kerr, *Islamic Reform: The Political and Legal Theories of Muhammad `Abduh and Rashid Rida* (Berkeley: University of California Press, 1966), esp. 221–23; and Charles Kurzman, *Modernist Islam, 1840–1940: A Sourcebook* (New York: Oxford University Press, 2002), 26.

14. A handful of the writings of some prominent contemporary or near contemporary figures are worth mentioning here by way of illustration. (Unless they wrote in English, I mention, where possible, a sampling of their writings available in English.) Fazlur Rahman, *Major Themes of the Qur'an* (Minneapolis: Bibleotheca Islamica, 1980); idem, *Islam and Modernity: Transformation of an Intellectual Tradition* (Chicago: University of Chicago Press, 1982); Mahmoud Sadri and Ahmad Sadri, *Reason, Freedom, and Democracy in Islam: The Essential Writings of Abdolkarim Soroush* (New York: Oxford University Press, 2000); Abdolkarim Soroush, *The Expansion of Prophetic Experience*, trans. Nilou Mobasser, ed. Forough Jahanbakhsh (Leiden: Brill, 2009); Tariq Ramadan, *Radical Reform: Is-*

lamic Ethics and Liberalism (New York: Oxford University Press, 2009); Muhammad Khalid Masud, *Shariʿa Today: Essays on Contemporary Issues and Debates in Muslim Societies* (Islamabad: National Book Foundation, 2013); Andreas Christmann, *The Qurʾan, Morality and Critical Reason: The Essential Muhammad Shahrur* (Leiden: Brill, 2009); Mohammed Abed Jabri, *Democracy, Human Rights, and Law in Islamic Thought* (London: I. B. Tauris, 2009); idem, *The Formation of Arab Reason: Text, Tradition, and the Construction of Modernity in the Arab World* (London: I. B. Tauris, 2011); Nasr Hamid Abu Zayd, *Mafhum al-nass: Dirasa fi ʿulum al-Qurʾan* (Cairo: al-Hayʾa al-Misriyya lil-kitab, 1990); idem, *Naqd al-khitab al-dini* (Cairo: Sina lil-nashr, 1992). A posthumously published book by a former Pakistani prime minister, Benazir Bhutto, also merits inclusion in this list: *Reconciliation: Islam, Democracy, and the West* (New York: Harper, 2008). See, finally, the useful anthology of contemporary modernist writings in Mehran Kamrava, ed., *The New Voices of Islam: Rethinking Politics and Modernity* (Berkeley: University of California Press, 2006).

15. On some of the constitutive elements of Islamic liberalism, see Bruce K. Rutherford, *Egypt after Mubarak: Liberalism, Islam, and Democracy in the Arab World* (Princeton, NJ: Princeton University Press, 2008), 77–130, especially 121–22. Rutherford characterizes this trend as "Islamic constitutionalism" while noting its affinity with liberalism (ibid., 121–22, n. 204). Also see Leonard Binder, *Islamic Liberalism: A Critique of Development Ideologies* (Chicago: University of Chicago Press, 1988), 4–5; Muhammad Khalid Masud, "Islamic Modernism," in Muhammad Khalid Masud, Armando Salvatore, and Martin van Bruinessen, eds., *Islam and Modernity: Key Issues and Debates* (Edinburgh, UK: Edinburgh University Press, 2009), 255. The transition from modernism to liberalism is suggested, for instance, by the titles of two anthologies edited by Charles Kurzman: *Liberal Islam: A Sourcebook* (New York: Oxford University Press, 1998) and the aforementioned *Modernist Islam, 1840–1940.* Kurzman's *Liberal Islam* is not, however, temporally circumscribed, and includes not just contemporary public intellectuals but also earlier figures such as Muhammad Iqbal.

16. Hourani, for instance, occasionally refers to some of the intellectuals and activists of his "liberal age" as modernists or as Islamic modernists. See *Arabic Thought*, 193, 267, 353. In an influential work on constitutional developments in Pakistan's early years, Binder had spoken of Islamic modernism to refer to things many of which he would later characterize as Islamic liberalism in a study on the Middle East. See Leonard Binder, *Religion and Politics in Pakistan* (Berkeley: University of California Press, 1961); cf. idem, *Islamic Liberalism.*

17. On the tension in the Indian context between the statist and "communitarian" proclivities of liberalism, on the one hand, and its concern with the individual, on the other, see C. A. Bayly, *Recovering Liberties: Indian Thought in the Age of Liberalism and Empire* (Cambridge, UK: Cambridge University Press, 2012). Rutherford, too, stresses the central position of the state in the thinking of those he refers to as the Islamic constitutionalists. See *Egypt after Mubarak*, 121–28. On the authoritarian dimensions of Islamic modernism, see chapter 2, later.

18. On the relationship between modernism and Islamism, see Roxanne L. Euben and Muhammad Qasim Zaman, eds., *Princeton Readings in Islamist Thought: Texts and Contexts from al-Banna to Bin Laden* (Princeton, NJ: Princeton University Press, 2009), 9–10; Michael Cook, *Ancient Religions, Modern Politics: The Islamic Case in Comparative Perspective* (Princeton, NJ: Princeton University Press, 2014), 393–98; Binder, *Islamic Liberalism*, 357; Charles J. Adams, "The Ideology of Mawlana Mawdudi," in D. E. Smith, ed., *South Asian Politics and Religion* (Princeton, NJ: Princeton University Press, 1966), 371–97.

19. Sayyid Abul-A`la Mawdudi, *Islam ka nazariyya-i siyasi* (Lahore: Markazi maktaba-i Jama`at-i Islami, 1955; first published in 1939), 34–35. The English words "negative" and "positive" are Mawdudi's own. For another rendering of this passage, see Sayyid Abul A`la Maududi, *The Islamic Law and Constitution*, trans. Khurshid Ahmad, 2nd ed. (Lahore: Islamic Publications, 1960), 154.

20. Mawdudi acknowledges that his Islamic state may also have something in common with communist and fascist states but immediately adds that his state, unlike those others, is not dictatorial. Mawdudi, *Islam ka nazariyya-i siyasi*, 35.

21. For a useful overview of the scholarship on the `ulama in medieval Islam, see R. Stephen Humphreys, *Islamic History: A Framework for Inquiry* (Princeton, NJ: Princeton University Press, 1991), 187–208.

22. On the transformations the `ulama have undergone in modern times and the claims to authority they have articulated in conditions of momentous change, see Muhammad Qasim Zaman, *The Ulama in Contemporary Islam: Custodians of Change* (Princeton, NJ: Princeton University Press, 2002).

23. By contrast, Muslim modernists would occupy a much smaller space in any broad-ranging study of Islam in post-colonial India. Such a study remains a desideratum. It would be illuminating, too, to compare the development of Islam in Pakistan with how it has evolved in post-colonial India, but this book is not the place for it.

24. For an influential example for the Middle East, see Daniel Lerner, *The Passing of Traditional Society: Modernizing the Middle East* (Glencoe, IL: Free Press, 1958); for South Asia, see Smith, *Modern Islam in India*, especially 293–98.

25. For a classic expression of this binary from the first years of Pakistan, see the 1954 *Report of the Court of Inquiry*. For a discussion of this binary, see Qasmi, *The Ahmadis*, 22–29.

26. The modernists would not find much fault, for instance, with Smith's characterization of late colonial Deobandi `ulama: *Modern Islam*, 295–96. It is telling that Deobandi traditionalists did not find fault with it either. It is favorably quoted, though with some license in translation, in the official history of the Deoband madrasa. See Sayyid Mahbub Rizwi, *Ta'rikh-i Dar al-`Ulum Deoband*, 2 vols. (Deoband: Idara-i ihtimam-i Dar al-`Ulum Deoband, 1977–8), 1: 462–63.

27. Michael Levenson, "Introduction," in idem, ed., *The Cambridge Companion to Modernism*, 2nd ed. (Cambridge, UK: Cambridge University Press, 2011), 3.

28. On such underpinnings, see Michael Bell, "The Metaphysics of Modernism," in ibid., 9–32. Also see note 12, earlier.

29. Nils Gilman, *Mandarins of the Future: Modernization Theory in Cold War America* (Baltimore, MD: Johns Hopkins University Press, 2003), 7.

30. One notable example is Rahman, *Islam and Modernity*. He speaks in it of "classical Islamic modernism" and "contemporary modernism."

Chapter One. Islamic Identities in Colonial India

1. For the early history of Deoband, to which I am indebted here, see Barbara D. Metcalf, *Islamic Revival in British India: Deoband, 1860–1900* (Princeton, NJ: Princeton University Press, 1982).

2. See, for instance, the statement in Deoband's monthly magazine on the occasion of the imperial *darbar*, the celebrations in India marking the coronation of King George V: *al-Qasim* (Deoband), 2/4 (November 1911): "Darbar-i tajposhi" (unnumbered first page), at http://eap.bl.uk/database/results.a4d?projID=EAP566;r=18467 (accessed September 26, 2017).

3. On the financial patronage received by some Deobandis from the princely states of Hyderabad and Bhopal, see R/1/1/2006: Anti-Government Propaganda by Maulana Husain Ahmad Madani, 3–4, 17, 20, 34 (British Library; hereafter, BL). Also see *al-Qasim*, 6/2 (August 1915): 16–17. The support of the Afghan king Zahir Shah (r. 1933–73) for the Deoband madrasa was acknowledged by its administrators with the building of a monumental gate in his honor, the Bab al-Zahir, which still exists.

4. On his life and thought, see Usha Sanyal, *Devotional Islam and Politics in British India: Ahmad Riza Khan Barelwi and His Movement, 1870–1920* (Delhi: Oxford University Press, 1996).

5. See Muhammad Siddiq Najibabadi, *Anwar al-mahmud `ala sunan Abi Dawud*, 2 vols. (Karachi: Idarat al-Qur'an wal-`ulum al-Islamiyya, 1986; first published in 1937), 35–36. For the chains of transmissions through which Wali Allah himself was authorized to transmit classic works of hadith onward, see Shah `Abd al-`Aziz, *al-`Ujala al-nafi`a* (Khanewal: al-Maktaba al-sa`idiyya, 1975), 53–97. On the centrality of chains of transmission (*isnad*s) in Islamic religious culture, see William A Graham, "Traditionalism in Islam: An Essay in Interpretation," *Journal of Interdisciplinary History* 23 (1993): 495–522.

6. On Siddiq Hasan Khan's networks and the misgivings they created in British circles, see R/1/1/40: "Wahabi Agents Dispatched by Sadik Hassan, Husband of the Begum of Bhopal, to the Soudan, Hodeida, Yemen and Mecca" (BL). Also see Seema Alavi, *Muslim Cosmopolitanism in the Age of Empire* (Cambridge, MA: Harvard University Press, 2015), 267–330. On the writing of hadith commentaries by scholars belonging to this orientation, see Zaman, *The Ulama*, 40–41.

7. See Justin Jones, *Shi`a Islam in Colonial India: Religion, Community and Sectarianism* (Cambridge, UK: Cambridge University Press, 2012).

8. See, for instance, *Rudad-i ijlas-i panjum, All India Shi`a Conference, mun`aqida ... 30 September ta 2 October 1911 ba-maqam Banaras* (Lucknow: Mi`yar Press, n.d. [1912]), 31–58; *Rudad-i ijlas-i shashum, All India Shi`a Conference, mun`aqida ... 18-19-20 October, 1912 ba-maqam Patna* (Lucknow: Mi`yar Press, n.d. [1913]), 142–96. For these and other published reports, see Annual Proceedings of the All India Shia Conference, 1907–40, Nehru Memorial Museum and Library, microfilm R-12261–8. Cited hereafter as AISC, *Rudad*, with the relevant bibliographic information.

9. Ibid., AISC, *Rudad-i ijlas-i panjum* (1911), 49.

10. Jones, *Shi`a Islam*, 117–20, though he seems to exaggerate the extent of the `ulama's continuing influence on this body.

11. Muhammad Rashid Rida, "al-Khutba al-ra'isiyya fi Nadwat al-`ulama li-sahib *al-Manar*," *al-Manar* (Cairo), 15 (1912): 334–35.

12. For Deoband, see note 2, earlier. For the Shi`a, see the presidential address by Sayyid Najm al-Hasan at the inaugural session of the All India Shi`a Conference: in AISC, *Rudad-i ijlas-i awwal ... 6-8 October 1907 ba-maqam Lucknow* (Lucknow [name of publisher illegible], n.d. [1908]), 58; also see ibid., 89–90. For the Barelawis, see Sanyal, *Devotional Islam*, 268–301. And for the Ahmadis, see Yohanan Friedmann, *Prophecy Continuous: Aspects of Ahmadi Religious Thought and Its Medieval Background* (Berkeley: University of California Press, 1989), 34–36.

13. `Abd al-Qadir Badayuni, *Muntakhab al-tawarikh*, ed. Ahmad `Ali and W. N. Lees, 3 vols. (Calcutta, 1864–69; reprint, Osnabrük: Biblio Verlag, 1983), 2: 246; quoted from A. Azfar Moin, *The Millennial Sovereign: Sacred Kingship and Sainthood in Islam* (New York: Columbia University Press, 2012), 165.

14. Akbar Ilahabadi, *Kulliyyat-i Akbar* (Lahore: Sang-i mil Publications, 2008), 238–39.

15. Mohammad Iqbal, "Qadianis and Orthodox Muslims," in *Speeches and Statements of Iqbal*, compiled by "Shamloo" (Lahore: Al-Manar Academy, 1948), 97. Iqbal goes on to

quote the verse from Akbar Ilahabadi. Ibid., 98. Iqbal's statement was published in a news-paper, the *Statesman*, in May 1935 (ibid., 107).

16. John Hurd and Ian J. Kerr, *India's Railway History: A Research Handbook* (Leiden: Brill, 2012), 2. For the growth of route miles between 1861 and 1946–47, see ibid., 3.

17. Ibid., 148.

18. Arthur F. Buehler, *Sufi Heirs of the Prophet: The Indian Naqshbandiyya and the Rise of the Mediating Sufi Shaykh* (Columbia: University of South Carolina Press, 1998), 195–96.

19. See ʿAbd al-Majid Daryabadi, *Hakim al-ummat: Nuqush wa taʾassurat* (Delhi: Saʿdi Book Depot, 1990), for extensive examples of the master's correspondence. Dary-abadi, a journalist and a translator of the Qurʾan into English, was in correspondence with Thanawi over the last fifteen years of the latter's life. See ibid., 599. On Thanawi's letter writing habits, see ibid., 85, 243. By Daryabadi's reckoning, Thanawi received thirty to forty letters every day (ibid., 85).

20. Ashraf ʿAli Thanawi, *Tahrib-i tarbiyat al-salik*, 2 vols., 2nd ed. (Thana Bhawan: Maktaba-i taʾlifat-i Ashrafiyya, n.d.); Muhammad Qasim Zaman, *Ashraf ʿAli Thanawi: Islam in Modern South Asia* (Oxford: Oneworld, 2008), 91–92.

21. Muhammad Rashid Rida, "Muqaddimat al-kitab," in A. J. Wensinck, *Miftah kunuz al-sunna*, trans. Muhammad Fuʾad ʿAbd al-Baqi (Lahore: Suhayl Academy, 1987; first published Cairo: Matbaʿat Misr, 1934), p. "waw" (front matter pagination in Arabic letters).

22. Jones, *Shiʿa Islam*, 37.

23. See Sajida Sultana Alvi, "Renewal of the Čišti Order in Eighteenth-Century Pun-jab," in Denis Hermann and Fabrizio Speziale, eds., *Muslim Cultures in the Indo-Iranian World during the Early Modern and Modern Periods* (Berlin: Klaus Schwarz Verlag, 2010), 216–46.

24. Christian W. Troll, *Sayyid Ahmad Khan: A Reinterpretation of Muslim Theology* (Delhi: Vikas, 1978), 28–34; David Lelyveld, "Young Man Sayyid: Dreams and Biographi-cal Texts," in Usha Sanyal, David Gilmartin, and Sandria B. Freitag, eds., *Muslim Voices: Community and the Self in South Asia* (Delhi: Yoda Press, 2013), 253–72, at 267–69.

25. For the fragment that he translated from this book, see Muhammad Ismaʿil Pani-pati, ed., *Maqalat-i Sir Sayyid* (Lahore: Majlis-i taraqqi-i adab, 1962–), 5: 430–44.

26. Altaf Husayn Hali, *Hayat-i javid* (Aligarh: Muslim University Institute, 1922; first published in 1901), 379–81, 387–92.

27. Muhsin al-Mulk, *Ayat-i bayyinat* (Karachi: Dar al-ishaʿat, 1960). This work was translated from Urdu into Persian by a noted anti-Shiʿi polemicist of colonial India. For this translation, see Muhammad ʿAbd al-Shakur Laknawi, *Baqiyyat-i salihat, tarjama-i Ayat-i bayyinat* (Lahore: Suhayl Academy, 1976).

28. Muhsin al-Mulk, *Kitab al-mahabbat wal-shawq* (Agra: Matba-i mufid-i ʿamm, 1905). Cf. Muhammad Amin Zubayri, *Hayat-i Muhsin* (Aligarh: Muslim University Press, 1934), 235–36.

29. For an overview of some of Muhsin al-Mulk's religious ideas, see Ahmad, *Islamic Modernism*, 64–71.

30. Altaf Husayn Hali, *Hayat-i Saʿdi* (Lahore: Majlis-i taraqqi-i adab, 1961). This book was first published in 1886. The view that Hali's biography of Saʿdi was superior to his book on Sayyid Ahmad Khan was Abul-Kalam Azad's: ʿAbd al-Razzaq Malihabadi, *Azad ki kahani khud Azad ki zabani* (Delhi: Iʿtiqad Publishing House, 2008), 192–93.

31. Nazir Ahmad, *al-Huquq wal-faraʾiz*, 3 vols. (Delhi: Matbaʿ-i Qasimi, 1905–6), 1: 6. On Nazir Ahmad, see the studies collected in M. Ikram Chaghatai, ed., *Deputy Nazir Ahmad: A Biographical and Critical Appreciation* (Lahore: Pakistan Writers Cooperative

Society, 2013). Also see Margrit Pernau, *Ashraf into Middle Class: Muslims in Nineteenth Century Delhi* (Delhi: Oxford University Press, 2013), 257–63, 356–61.

32. On his life and career, see Sayyid Sulayman Nadwi, *Hayat-i Shibli* (A`zamgarh: Dar al-musannifin, 1943).

33. Mirza Muhammad Hadi, trans., *Hikmat al-Ishraq* (Hyderabad: Dar al-tab`, Jami`a `Usmaniyya, 1925). This is a commentary by Qutb al-din al-Shirazi (d. 1310) on a work by Yahya al-Suhrawardi (d. 1191). The ancient Greek works he translated include the *Republic* of Plato and Aristotle's *Nicomachean Ethics*. His translations of contemporary writings included George Frederick Stout's *Groundwork of Psychology* (1903) and William McDougall's *Introduction to Social Psychology* (1908). These translations were published under the auspices of the Osmania University in Hyderabad, with which he was associated for some years. His novel, *Umrao Jan Ada*, published ca. 1899, has in turn been translated into English: Khushwant Singh and M. A. Husaini, *Umrao Jan Ada* (Bombay: Orient Longman, 1961); it has also been made into films in both Pakistan (1972) and India (1981). On Hadi's life and career, see Maymuna Ansari, *Mirza Muhammad Hadi, Mirza o Ruswa: sawanih hayat awr adabi karname* (Lahore: Majlis-i taraqqi-i adab, 1963).

34. AISC, *Rudad-i ijlas-i awwal . . . 6–8 October 1907*, 133–34.

35. Ibid., 146–53.

36. This view, no doubt shared by many, is expressed by Sulayman Nadwi: *Hayat-i Shibli*, 290.

37. David Lelyveld, "Disenchantment at Aligarh: Islam and the Realm of the Secular in Late Nineteenth Century India," *Die Welt des Islams* 22 (1982): 85–102.

38. Hali, *Hayat-i javid*, 196–99, 389; David Lelyveld, *Aligarh's First Generation: Muslim Solidarity in British India* (Princeton, NJ: Princeton University Press, 1978), 141–42.

39. Cf. Hali, *Hayat-i javid*, 155, 381.

40. Sulayman Nadwi, *Hayat-i Shibli*, 319.

41. Lelyveld, "Disenchantment."

42. Cf. Lelyveld, *Aligarh's First Generation*, 134–42.

43. Hali, *Hayat-i javid*, 309; Lelyveld, *Aligarh's First Generation*, 105. Muir's biography of the Prophet, *The Life of Mahomet*, was published in two volumes in 1858 and in four volumes in 1861. Among other high-ranking positions in India, he served as the lieutenant governor of the North-Western Provinces from 1868 to 1874. On him, see Avril A. Powell, *Scottish Orientalists and India: The Muir Brothers, Religion, Education and Empire* (Woodbridge, UK: Boydell Press, 2010).

44. Hali, *Hayat-i javid*, 300–320. For his attitudes toward the Bengalis, see ibid., 307–8.

45. Cf. Sulayman Nadwi, *Hayat-i Shibli*, 295.

46. For an overview of the events described here, see Muhammad Qasim Zaman, *Modern Islamic Thought in a Radical Age: Religious Authority and Internal Criticism* (Cambridge, UK: Cambridge University Press, 2012), 11–14.

47. Aligarh's Old Boys Association was established in 1899, a year after the death of Sayyid Ahmad Khan. See Lelyveld, *Aligarh's First Generation*, 332.

48. M. Naeem Qureshi, *Pan-Islam in British Indian Politics: A Study of the Khilafat Movement 1918-1924* (Leiden: Brill, 1999), 25, 30, 47–49.

49. See Shibli Nu`mani, *Safarnama-i Rum o Misr o Sham* (Lucknow: Anwar al-matabi`, n.d.), 100–104.

50. Zaman, *Modern Islamic Thought*, 4–5.

51. Abul Kalam Azad, *Mas'ala-i khilafat o jazira-i `Arab* (Calcutta: All India Khilafat Committee, 1920), 140–41. Part of this work was delivered as a speech in Calcutta in February 1920.

52. Ibid., 109–19, esp. 115.

53. Ibid., 144. Azad was not alone in such criticism; and Deoband was sensitive to it. For a detailed response from Deoband, see Shabbir Ahmad `Usmani, "Tashrih-i waqi`a-i Deoband: `Ata-i i`zaz ki haqiqat," al-Qasim 6/2 (August 1915): 1–17.

54. FO 686/149: Silk Letters Case, Statement by Matlub-ur-Rahman, September 24, 1916, 210. The National Archives, UK (hereafter, TNA).

55. Mohamed [Muhammad] Ali, My Life: A Fragment, ed. Afzal Iqbal (Lahore: Sh. Muhammad Ashraf, 1942; reprint, 1946), 108–33.

56. Azad, Mas'ala-i khilafat, 141–43.

57. M. Şükrü Hanioğlu, Atatürk: An Intellectual Biography (Princeton, NJ: Princeton University Press, 2011), 104.

58. For the text of this fatwa in English translation, see P. C. Bamford, Histories of the Non-Cooperation and Khilafat Movements (Delhi: Government of India Press, 1925; reprint, Delhi: Deep Publications, 1974), 251–55.

59. For this fatwa, see Ghulam Rasul Mihr, ed., Tabarrukat-i Azad (Hyderabad: `Usmaniyya Book Depot, 1959), 203–6. On the public response to the fatwa and its aftermath, see Qureshi, Pan-Islam, 174–232.

60. Syed Jamaluddin, "The Barelvis and the Khilafat Movement," in Mushirul Hasan, ed., Communal and Pan-Islamic Trends in Colonial India (Delhi: Manohar, 1985), 403–4.

61. Ashraf `Ali Thanawi, al-Ifadat al-yawmiyya min al-ifadat al-qawmiyya, 10 vols. (Lahore: Idara-i ta'lifat-i Ashrafiyya, 1984–86), 9: 109; Zaman, Ashraf `Ali Thanawi, 40.

62. For `Abd al-Bari's views on this matter, see Qureshi, Pan-Islam, 104, 125. For Thanawi's criticism of such concessions, see Thanawi, al-Ifadat, 2: 54. Also see Daryabadi, Hakim al-ummat, 130–34.

63. Zaman, Ashraf `Ali Thanawi, 44.

64. Bamford, Histories, 253.

65. Mohamed Ali, My Life, 61. Emphasis added. Muhammad `Ali did not, however, limit his disdain to the `ulama on the wrong side of the political divide. He was equally unsparing of the English-educated Muslims opposed to the Khilafat movement. Ibid., 61.

66. Gail Minault, The Khilafat Movement: Religious Symbolism and Political Mobilization in India (New York: Columbia University Press, 1982), 206–7.

67. Census of India 1911, vol. 14: Punjab, part 1, report by Pandit Hari Kishan Kaul (Lahore: Civil and Military Gazette Press, 1912), 163, quoting an undated lecture by Iqbal on the "Muslim Community."

68. See Zaman, Modern Islamic Thought, 14–17.

69. Afzal Iqbal, Life and Times of Mohamed Ali (Delhi: Idarah-i Adabiyat-i Delhi, 1978), 381.

70. This is from an undated but pre-1905 poem titled "Naya shiwala," included in Iqbal's first poetic collection, Bang-i dara (1924). Unless otherwise noted, all references are to Iqbal's verse as gathered in his Urdu and Persian collected works of poetry. For this line, see Muhammad Iqbal, Kulliyyat-i Iqbal (Urdu) (Lahore: Iqbal Academy, 1997), 115.

71. Muhammad Iqbal, Rumuz-i bikhudi, in idem, Kulliyyat-i Iqbal (Persian) (Lahore: Shaykh Ghulam `Ali & Sons, n.d.), 112. The translation is by A. J. Arberry, The Mysteries of Selflessness: A Philosophical Poem (London: John Murray, 1953), 29. Iqbal himself dated his turn to the kind of themes articulated in this work to 1907. See his letter to Sayyid Sulayman Nadwi, November 10, 1919, in Shaykh `Ata Allah, ed., Iqbal nama, 2 vols. (Lahore: Shaykh Muhammad Ashraf, n.d.), 1: 110.

72. Iqbal, Javid nama, in idem, Kulliyyat-i Iqbal, Farsi, 650. Translation by A. J. Arberry, Javid Nama (London: George Allen & Unwin, 1966), 55 (with some change in punctuation).

73. For the text of this address, see S. S. Pirzada, ed., *Foundations of Pakistan*, 2 vols. (Karachi: National Publishing House, 1970), 2: 153–71; quotation at 2: 154.

74. Ibid., 2: 169.

75. Iqbal to Niyaz al-din Khan, December 3, 1920, in *Makatib-i Iqbal banam-i Khan Niyaz al-din Khan* (Lahore: Iqbal Academy, 1986), 55; Qureshi, *Pan-Islam*, 197, 256–58.

76. Mohammad Iqbal, *The Reconstruction of Religious Thought in Islam* (London: Oxford University Press, 1934), 149. The book was first published in 1930 as *Six Lectures on the Reconstruction of Religious Thought in Islam* (Lahore: Kapur Art Printing Works, 1930). My references are to the 1934 edition.

77. Iqbal, *Reconstruction*, 149.

78. Ibid., 154.

79. For instance, Iqbal, *Javid nama*, in idem, *Kulliyyat-i Iqbal* (Persian), 654; trans. Arberry, *Javid Nama*, 58 (speaking in the voice of the Ottoman grand vizier Sa`id Halim Pasha [d. 1921]).

80. For an overview of this controversy, see Barbara D. Metcalf, *Husain Ahmad Madani: The Jihad for Islam and India's Freedom* (Oxford, UK: Oneworld, 2009), 112–16.

81. See Husayn Ahmad Madani, *Muttahida qawmiyyat awr Islam* (Delhi: Qawmi ekta trust, n.d. [1972; first published ca. 1938]), 29–30; cf. 64–68; Metcalf, *Husain Ahmad Madani*, 116.

82. Muhammad Iqbal, "Statement on Islam and Nationalism in Reply to a Statement of Maulana Hussain Ahmed Published in 'Ehsan' on the 9th March 1938," in "Shamloo," ed., *Speeches and Statements*, 223–39, at 227.

83. Ibid., 228. This is a rare instance of modernist suspicion of ethical ideals. For the ethical commitments of Islamic modernism, see chapter 2.

84. "Shamloo," ed., *Speeches and Statements*, 233.

85. Ibid., 239.

86. Rizwi, *Ta'rikh*, 1: 446; Metcalf, *Islamic Revival*, 111.

87. Francis Robinson, *The `Ulama of Farangi Mahall and Islamic Culture in South Asia* (London: Hurst & Company, 2001), 71, 106.

88. FO 686/149: Silk Letters Case, Statement by Matlub-ur-Rahman, September 25, 1916, 221–22 (TNA).

89. Mahmud Hasan, *Hama'il sharif mutarjam* (Bijnor: Madina Press, n.d.). On the indebtedness to the translation of Shah `Abd al-Qadir, Wali Allah's son, see ibid., 1–7.

90. Ashraf `Ali Thanawi, *Ahkam-i talaq wa nizam-i shar`i `adalat, ya`ni al-hila al-najiza-i jadid*, ed. Khurshid Hasan Qasimi (Lahore: al-Faysal, 1996). This is a new and retitled edition of the original 1933 work.

91. As one member of the house from east Punjab had noted during the debate on the bill, "*Al Hilatul Najiza* was prepared by Maulana Ashraf Ali of Thana Bhawan, who is one of the greatest divines of the present age in India.... [T]his book is most authoritative, being written by that great Mufti ... and endorsed by the Ulema of Deoband and Saharanpur." L/PJ/7/1065: Muslim Dissolution of Marriages Act 1939, extracts from the legislative assembly debates, 5/11: 23 (Ghulam Bhik Nairang) (BL). Saharanpur was the town housing a Deobandi madrasa second in importance to the one at Deoband itself. The mover of the bill, Muhammad Ahmad Kazmi, was also from Saharanpur.

92. L/PJ/7/1065: Muslim Dissolution of Marriages Act 1939, 76 (BL).

93. For instance, ibid., 69 (A.A.A. Fyzee [Bombay]); ibid., 1/9: 2–3 (extracts from the legislative assembly debates [Abdul Qaiyum, NWFP]); ibid. 5/1: 17 (M. Asaf Ali, Delhi).

94. Ibid., 1/9: 12 (extracts from the legislative assembly debates).

95. Ibid., 5/11: 17–21 (extracts from the legislative assembly debates).

96. L/PJ/7/943: Muslim Personal Law (Shariat) Application Act, 1937, and amending acts: 7 (BL).

97. Ibid., 76.

98. Ibid., 76 (statement of objects and reasons).

99. David Gilmartin, *Empire and Islam: Punjab and the Making of Pakistan* (Berkeley: University of California Press, 1988), 171–74.

100. Hussain Ahmed Madani, *An Open Letter to the Moslem League* (Lahore: Dewan Publications, 1946), 62; Gilmartin, *Empire and Islam*, 173.

101. L/PJ/7/943: Muslim Personal Law (Shariat) Application Act, 1937: 98.

102. Venkat Dhulipala, *Creating a New Medina: State Power, Islam, and the Quest for Pakistan in Late Colonial North India* (Delhi: Cambridge University Press, 2015), 48, 51.

103. See William Gould, *Hindu Nationalism and the Language of Politics in Late Colonial India* (Cambridge, UK: Cambridge University Press, 2004), 201–33.

104. For the full text of Jinnah's speech, see Pirzada, ed., *Foundations*, 2: 327–39; quotation at 337–38.

105. Ibid., 2: 341 (resolution 1).

106. "Taqrir ba`that al-Hind," *Majallat al-Azhar* (Cairo), 8/5 (1937): 380–81.

107. See Rahmat Ali et al., "Now or Never: Are We to Live or Perish Forever?" in K. K. Aziz, ed., *Complete Works of Rahmat Ali* (Islamabad: National Commission on Historical and Cultural Research, 1978), 1: 5–10. Though signed by several others, Rahmat Ali is believed to be the tract's author (ibid., xx–xxi).

108. See Ayesha Jalal, *The Sole Spokesman: Jinnah, the Muslim League and the Demand for Pakistan* (Cambridge, UK: Cambridge University Press, 1985).

109. For a critique of Jalal along these lines, see Dhulipala, *Creating a New Medina*. The phrase "bargaining counter" is Jalal's, *Sole Spokesman*, 187.

110. Madani, *Muttahida qawmiyyat*, 30–31, 38.

111. Ibid., 63, 68, 70, 75–76.

112. Cf. Peter Hardy, *The Muslims of British India* (Cambridge, UK: Cambridge University Press, 1972), 242–46.

113. Iqbal, "Statement on Islam and Nationalism," in "Shamloo," ed., *Speeches and Statements of Iqbal*, esp. 228–39.

114. For the text of Azad's speech, delivered at Ramgarh on March 19, 1940, see Malik Ram, ed., *Khutbat-i Azad* (Delhi: Sahitiya Academy, 1974), 269–300; quotation at 299.

115. Pirzada, ed., *Foundations*, 2: 338. Azad's speech was delivered in Urdu, whereas Jinnah's was in English.

116. Z. H. Zaidi et al., eds., *Quaid-i-Azam Mohammad Ali Jinnah Papers* (Islamabad: Quaid-i-Azam Papers Project, 1993–2009 [hereafter, *JP*]), 3rd ser., 15: 583. On the reaction to this telegram, which was soon made public, see ibid., 593, 594, 611, 635, 637, 650–51.

117. Jinnah to Raghib Ahsan, April 2, 1941 in *JP*, 3rd ser., 16: 393. This was in response to a religious scholar's offer to stay with Jinnah to give him instruction in Islam and the Qur'an. See Raghib Ahsan to Jinnah, *JP*, 3rd ser., 16: 382–83.

118. Cf. Jalal, *Sole Spokesman*, 5.

119. Jamil-ud-din Ahmad, ed., *Some Recent Speeches and Writings of Mr. Jinnah* (Lahore: Sh. Muhammad Ashraf, 1943), 230.

120. Ibid., 454 (presidential address to the League's 30th session, Delhi, April 24, 1943).

121. Jamil-ud-din Ahmad, ed., *Speeches and Writings of Mr. Jinnah*, 2 vols. (Lahore: Shaikh Muhammad Ashraf, 1960–64 [hereafter, *Speeches*]), 1: 575.

122. Ibid., 2: 208–9. For the quotation from Gibbon, reproduced with some minor inaccuracies, see Edward Gibbon, *The History of the Decline and Fall of the Roman Empire*, ed. J. B. Bury, 7 vols., 4th ed. (London: Methuen & Co., 1911), 5: 395.

123. Jinnah was hardly the first to put it this way. Ameer Ali, for one, had said something similar in his classic *Spirit of Islam*, 165: "The Islam of Mohammed recognises no caste of priesthood.... Each human being is his own priest."

124. Muhammad Ishaq Sandelawi, *Islam ka siyasi nizam* (A`zamgarh: Matba`-i Ma`arif, 1957). While the title page gives the author's name as Muhammad Ishaq Sandelawi and introduces him as a professor at the Nadwat al-`Ulama in Lucknow, the author's prefatory note is signed as "Muhammad Ishaq Siddiqi." I draw here on an earlier discussion of this book in Muhammad Qasim Zaman, "South Asian Islam and the Idea of the Caliphate," in Madawi al-Rasheed, Carool Kersten, and Marat Shterin, eds., *Demystifying the Caliphate: Historical Memory and Contemporary Contexts* (London: Hurst, 2013), 57–79, at 65–67. For another discussion, see Dhulipala, *Creating a New Medina*, 232–43.

125. Ishaq Nadwi, *Islam ka siyasi nizam*, 11.

126. Ibid., 12.

127. Ibid., 11–13.

128. Ibid., 58–68.

129. Ibid., 67.

130. Ibid., 202.

131. Ibid., 198.

132. Ibid., 186–87.

133. We do know, however, that the views put forth by some leading religious scholars in 1950 to guide the constitution-making process in Pakistan were quite similar to Ishaq Nadwi's on a veritable veto that the `ulama were to have on the decisions of the head of the state. Mawdudi, on the other hand, clearly favored a head of state who would enjoy decisive authority in the manner of the classical caliph. See Binder, *Religion and Politics*, 175–76. In his detailed account of the `ulama's recommendations, Binder makes no reference to the work of Ishaq Nadwi.

134. Muhammad Manzur Nu`mani to Shabbir Ahmad `Usmani, November 26, 1945, in Sherkoti, ed., *Anwar*, 146–55, quotations at 149–51 and 152.

135. Ahmad, *Some Recent Speeches*, 233.

136. See Bernard Weiss, *The Spirit of Islamic Law* (Athens: University of Georgia Press, 1998), 145–71, especially 151–54.

137. Dhulipala, *Creating a New Medina*, 311.

138. Anwar al-Hasan Sherkoti, ed., *Khutbat-i `Usmani* (Lahore: Nazar Sons, 1972), 73–80, at 77–78. Also see "Mukalamat al-sadrayn," in ibid., 89–109, at 101–2. This is a summary of a conversation between the pro-Muslim League scholar Shabbir Ahmad `Usmani and several pro-Congress Deobandi `ulama. And see Shabbir Ahmad `Usmani, *Hamara Pakistan* (Hyderabad, Deccan: Nafis Academy, n.d. [1946]), 63–65.

139. For a review of Barelawi positions on the question of Pakistan, see Sanyal, *Devotional Islam*, 302–27.

140. Simon Wolfgang Fuchs, "Relocating the Centers of Shi`i Islam: Religious Authority, Sectarianism, and the Limits of the Transnational in Colonial India and Pakistan," PhD dissertation, Near Eastern Studies, Princeton University, 2015, 72–88.

141. The most sophisticated study to date of Jinnah's elite politics is Jalal, *The Sole Spokesman*.

142. For an analysis of the religious rhetoric of the election campaign in the Punjab in 1945–46, on which I draw here, see David Gilmartin, "A Magnificent Gift: Muslim Nationalism and the Election Process in Colonial Punjab," *Comparative Studies in Society and History* 40/3 (1998): 415–36.

143. Husayn Ahmad Madani, *Mr. Jinnah ka purasrar mu`amma awr uska hall* (Delhi: Jam`iyyat al-`Ulama-i Hind, 1945), 35–37.

144. Diwan Sayyid Al-i Rasul to Nawab Ismail Khan, September 6, 1946, Archives of the Freedom Movement, 439: 19–20a (National Archives of Pakistan [hereafter, NAP]).

145. The statement was quoted in a letter from one Hamid Hasan Qadri to Jinnah, July 22, 1946. See David Gilmartin, "Religious Leadership and the Pakistan Movement in the Punjab," *Modern Asian Studies*, 13 (1979), 510. On the support of the Punjab pirs for the Muslim League during the election campaign of 1945–46, see ibid; and Gilmartin, *Empire and Islam*, 213–22.

146. For the election results, see Jalal, *Sole Spokesman*, 150, 161, 167, 170–71. On Jinnah's political maneuverings that made for this success, see ibid., 126–73.

147. Cf. Pirzada, ed., *Foundations*, 2: 170–71.

148. "Draft Extracts from the Speeches of Maulana Shabbir Ahmad Usmani Regarding the Policy and Progress of Jamiat-ul-Ulema-i-Hind," Archives of the Freedom Movement, 439: 48a (NAP). The last sentence ("religion and political authority are twins") is an ancient Persian adage that `Usmani quoted in its familiar Arabic translation.

149. On the support of influential pirs for the anti-Ahmadi agitation of 1953, see Court of Inquiry Proceedings, 1: 352, 354. Even the sajjada nishin of the famed Shaykh Ahmad Sirhindi's (d. 1624) tomb in the *Indian* Punjab had presided over an anti-Ahmadi rally in the Pakistani city of Okara; ibid., 3: 235. The mosque adjoining the tomb of the revered Chishti saint Baba Farid (d. 1266) in Pakpattan had posters announcing "the last hiccups of the Yazidi government"; ibid., 3: 367. The resonance of this slogan cannot be appreciated without recognizing that the Umayyad caliph Yazid I (r. 680–83) is an especially reviled figure not just in Shi`i Islam but also to many Sunnis. It was during his rule that Husayn, the Prophet's grandson and the third Shi`i imam, was martyred.

150. Habib [*sic*] to K. H. Khurshid, February 3, 1946, *JP*, 2nd ser., 12: 545.

151. Muhammad Iqbal, "Islam as a Moral and Political Ideal," in Latif Ahmad Sherwani, ed., *Speeches, Writings, and Statements of Iqbal* (Lahore: Iqbal Academy, 1977), 103. First published in the *Hindustan Review* (Allahabad), July 1909.

Chapter Two. Modernism and Its Ethical Commitments

1. As Wilfred Cantwell Smith observed in 1951, drawing on his discussions with Pakistani intellectuals, the widespread "demand that Pakistan should be an Islamic state is a Muslim way of saying that Pakistan should build for itself a good society. Not merely an independent or a strong or a wealthy or a modern society; all those things, perhaps, but also a good society." Wilfred Cantwell Smith, *Pakistan as an Islamic State: Preliminary Draft* (Lahore: Shaikh Muhammad Ashraf, 1951), 68; cf. idem, *Islam in Modern History* (Princeton, NJ: Princeton University Press, 1957), 239.

2. Many of the authoritarian dimensions that James Scott highlights for the "high modernism" of the late nineteenth and the twentieth centuries are relevant to Pakistan's modernist governing elite, too. Cf. Scott, *Seeing Like a State*, 93–97. Also see Markus Daechsel, *Islamabad and the Politics of International Development in Pakistan* (Cambridge, UK: Cambridge University Press, 2015); and Tabinda M. Khan, "Institutions not Intentions: Rethinking Islamist Participation in Muslim Democracies," PhD dissertation, Department of Political Science, Columbia University, 2014. On "traditional authoritarianism," as a leading modernist characterized it, see Fazlur Rahman, *Islam*, 2nd ed. (Chicago: University of Chicago Press, 1979; first published in 1966), 78. For *traditionalist* anxieties about modernist authoritarianism, see Thanawi, *al-Ifadat*, 5: 154–55 (#178).

3. *Life*, January 5, 1948; enclosed with Altaf Husain to F. Amin, January 29, 1948 in *JP*, 1st ser., 7: 68.

4. *JP*, 1st ser., 7: 116.

5. Jinnah's presidential address, August 11, 1947, in *CAPD*, 1/2 (August 11, 1947), 18–21, at 19–20; Ahmad, ed., *Speeches*, 2: 399–405, at 402–3.

6. See Yasmin Khan, *The Great Partition: The Making of India and Pakistan* (New Haven, CT: Yale University Press, 2007), 155, 210 n. 12.

7. *JP*, 1st ser., 6: 220 (speech at a public rally on October 30, 1947).

8. The speech, delivered on January 25, 1948, is paraphrased in *JP*, 1st ser., 7: 57–58. It was delivered to mark the birthday of the Prophet Muhammad. The `ulama had a very different and specific view of what it meant to be guided by the shari`a. For an example, cf. the Jam`iyyat al-`Ulama-i Islam's "address of welcome" to Jinnah, Bannu, April 16, 1948, in *JP*, 1st ser., 7: 419 (citing Q 5.4, 5.52–53, 2.124).

9. For the text of the resolution as moved by the prime minister, see *CAPD*, 5/1: 1–2 (March 7, 1949). Emphasis mine. The text of the resolution as eventually adopted by the house was identical to the proposed text. See ibid., 100–101 (March 12, 1949).

10. On the incoherence of the Objectives Resolution, see Binder, *Religion and Politics*, especially 147, 149; Ayesha Jalal, *The State of Martial Rule: The Origins of Pakistan's Political Economy of Defence* (Cambridge, UK: Cambridge University Press, 1990), 284–85.

11. Speaking to the Karachi High Court Bar Association in August 1952, the governor-general Ghulam Muhammed would put it this way: "You have to unearth Islam from under the debris where the dust of despots and corrupt people have buried it during the centuries and you will find that its message is simple and clear in democracy and equality of men and in harmony with the highest ideals known to anybody in the world." For the text of this speech, see Press Information Department, Government of Pakistan, August 28, 1952, p. 5, in DO 35/3185: Pakistan Internal Affairs (TNA).

12. See introduction, note 11.

13. *Census of Pakistan: Population According to Religion (Table 6)* (Karachi: Ministry of the Interior, Government of Pakistan, 1951), 1.

14. *CAPD*, 5/1, 90–91 (speech by Sris Chandra Chattopadhyaya, East Bengal, March 12, 1949).

15. *CAPD*, 5/1, 93.

16. *Report of the Basic Principles Committee* (Karachi: Manager of Publication, Government of Pakistan Press, 1952), 7. The Basic Principles Committee had submitted its initial recommendations in September 1950, but these had been quickly withdrawn in the face of opposition to them. See Afzal, *Pakistan*, 64–70; also see chapter 5. All references to the BPC report are to its 1952 recommendations.

17. *CAPD*, 15/13, 420, 425 (Chattopadhyaya, October 24, 1953).

18. *Report of the Basic Principles Committee*, 4–6.

19. *CAPD*, 15/17, 589 (Chakraverty, October 29, 1953).

20. *Report of the Basic Principles Committee*, 2.

21. *CAPD*, 15/19, 640, 644 (Seth Sukhdev, a Hindu member from Sindh, October 31, 1953).

22. Abdur Rahman, governor of East Bengal, to Khawaja Nazimuddin, the prime minister, August 18, 1952, with enclosed lists of Hindu members of the constituent assembly and the East Bengal legislative assembly allegedly maintaining residences in India. 2 (1)-PMS/52: Correspondence with HE the Governor of East Bengal: 163–69 (NDC). A subsequent letter from the governor to the prime minister tried to disqualify these Hindu parliamentarians on the much more serious charge of being complicit in blaspheming the Prophet. Abdur Rahman to Nazimuddin, August 23, 1952, in ibid., 177–78. Nothing came of the governor's efforts on this occasion.

23. See chapter 1, note 122.

24. Khalifa Abdul Hakim, *Islamic Ideology*, 227–28, quotation at 228. Hegel is not explicitly invoked here, but he could not have been far from the author's mind.

25. *Report of the Basic Principles Committee*, 4–6.

26. On its characterization as a "mullah board," see *CAPD*, 15/6, 129 (Sardar Shaukat Hyat Khan, October 13, 1953). For rebuttals, ibid., 129, 166.

27. The dissertation was published as a book under the same title. See Khalifa Abdul Hakim, *The Metaphysics of Rumi* (Lahore: Institute of Islamic Culture, 1959; first published, by a different press, in 1933).

28. Khalifa Abdul Hakim, *Shrimad Bhagavat Gita* (Mumbai: Bharatiya Vidya Bhawan, 2001). As far as I am aware, this Urdu translation has never been published in Pakistan. Incidentally, Iqbal, too, had once expressed his wish to render the *Gita* into Urdu. See his letter to Maharaja Kishan Prashad, October 11, 1921, in Muhammad ʿAbdallah Qurayshi, ed., *Ruh-i makatib-i Iqbal* (Lahore: Iqbal Academy, 1977), 268; also quoted in the introduction by Rafiq Zakariyya to Abdul Hakim, *Shrimad Bhagavat Gita*, 10.

29. Ghulam Muhammed to the prime minister, Khwaja Nazimuddin, May 31, 1952, with an extract from a note in Urdu by Khalifa Abdul Hakim. File 1(1)-PMS/52 (Correspondence with the Governor-General of Pakistan): 84–85 (NDC). The situation as Abdul Hakim had described it was grim. The educated Bengalis "say that the West Pakistanis have now become our rulers in place of the English. Their feeling is that the [West] Pakistanis consider them contemptible (*zalil*) and treat them with contempt" (ibid., 85).

30. Telegram from Firoz Khan Noon, the governor of East Bengal, to the governor-general, February 16, 1952. File 2 (1)-PMS/52 (Correspondence with HE the Governor of East Bengal): 16 (NDC).

31. Abdul Hakim, *Islamic Ideology*, 296.

32. Iqbal, *Reconstruction*, 120.

33. Khalifa Abdul Hakim, *Iqbal awr mulla*, 8th printing (Lahore: Bazm-i Iqbal, 1952).

34. *Dawn*, December 12, 1952, reproduced in Court of Inquiry Proceedings, Appendices, 86–87.

35. M. Anwar Ali, "Note on the Situation as It Developed from the 5th March 1953," Court of Inquiry Proceedings, 1: 240–41 (pp. 20–21 of the "Note").

36. *CAPD*, 15/14, 471 (Nishtar, Punjab, October 26, 1953).

37. *CAPD*, 15/17, 590–91 (Chakraverty, East Bengal, October 29, 1953).

38. *The Constitution of the Islamic Republic of Pakistan* (Karachi: Department of Advertising, Films and Publications, Government of Pakistan, 1956 [hereafter, *1956 Constitution*]), article 23, clause 1.

39. Ibid., article 32, clause 2.

40. Ibid., article 198.

41. Ibid., article 197.

42. Cf. Afzal, *Pakistan*, 129–30, 136–37. On other developments mentioned in this and the following paragraphs, ibid., 117–219.

43. "Islam—A Dynamic and Progressive Movement," in *Speeches and Statements by Field Marshal Mohammad Ayub Khan, President of Pakistan*, vol. 1: October 1958–June 1959 (Karachi: Pakistan Publications, n.d.), 110–14, at 110–11.

44. Ibid., 111.

45. Ibid., 112–14; quotation at 113. On this speech, cf. Muhammad Munir, *From Jinnah to Zia*, 2nd ed. (Lahore: Vanguard Books, 1980; first published in 1979), xvii, 81–83.

46. Ayub Khan's visit to the madrasa was apparently an effort to conciliate the ʿulama after some unfavorable comments on them, and on the place of Islam in the forthcoming constitution, by his law minister. See L. B. Walsh Atkins, UK High Commission, Karachi, to H. A. Twist, Commonwealth Relations Office (CRO), May 25, 1959, in DO 35/8962: In-

fluence of Islam on Pakistan Internal Situation. There is not much that was conciliatory in the president's speech, however, as Walsh Atkins too observed.

47. Afzal, *Pakistan*, 228; cf. Qudrat Allah Shahab, *Shahab nama* (Lahore: Sang-i mil Publications, 1987), 713–19.

48. Mohammad Ayub Khan, *Friends Not Masters: A Political Autobiography* (New York: Oxford University Press, 1967), 188, quoting a note titled "A Short Appreciation of Present and Future Problems of Pakistan" that he had written in October 1954 while in London en route to the United States. For the full text, see ibid., 186–89.

49. Ibid., 207–10; Afzal, *Pakistan*, 231–33.

50. *The Constitution of the Republic of Pakistan* (Washington, DC: Embassy of Pakistan, 1962 [hereafter, *1962 Constitution*]), articles 155–65.

51. Ayub Khan, *Friends*, 205. Cf. Fazlur Rahman, "Implementation of the Islamic Concept of State in the Pakistani Milieu," *Islamic Studies* 6 (1967), 207: "the Parliamentary system is obviously unsuitable for such a strong executive as is envisaged by the Qur'an."

52. *1962 Constitution*, article 6 (under "Principles of Law-making").

53. Ibid., chapter 2, article 8 (under "Islamic Way of Life").

54. Ibid., articles 199–206.

55. Ibid., article 207.

56. Compare the respective preambles to the 1956 and 1962 constitutions. Also compare the *1956 Constitution*, article 25, clause 1 with the *1962 Constitution*, "Principles of Policy," no. 1.

57. *1962 Constitution*, article 1, clause 1.

58. *Report of the Constitution Commission, Pakistan, 1961* (Karachi: Manager of Publications, 1962), 72.

59. Fazlur Rahman, "Some Islamic Issues in the Ayyub Khan Era," in *Essays on Islamic Civilization Presented to Niyazi Berkes*, ed. Donald P. Little (Leiden: E. J. Brill, 1976), 286.

60. On Parwez and this movement, see Ali Usman Qasmi, *Questioning the Authority of the Past: The Ahl al-Qur'an Movements in the Punjab* (Karachi: Oxford University Press, 2011), 216–86.

61. Government of Pakistan, Ministry of Information and Broadcasting, "Minutes of the Committee of [*sic*] Fundamental Conflict held on Monday the 17th April 1967 . . . ," 2, Ghulam Ahmad Parwez Papers (hereafter, GAPP), Parwez Memorial Research Scholars Library, Lahore. For Parwez's membership of the committee, see Cabinet Secretariat, Cabinet Division, Government of Pakistan, no. 95/CF/67, April 15, 1967, in file titled "Conference on Fundamental Conflict" (GAPP).

62. Qasmi, *Questioning the Authority*, 260–69, makes a case for a direct influence of Parwez on Ayub Khan's religious views and policy.

63. See, for instance, Parwez to Ayub Khan, June 18, 1960, 4–5: "The fundamental problem is how to translate effectively Quranic Ideology into constitution without bringing in the reactionary Ulema. . . . The so-called Ulema would oppose every move to establish a truly Quranic order. They opposed the creation of Pakistan and would now oppose the establishment of a truly Islamic constitution. They exist by turning the clear commands of Quran into an esoteric system of knowledge. . . . The development of Muslim Law in Pakistan has been in spite of them. . . . [The] adoption of Quran as the basis of Law will not only provide with [*sic*] a basic working code and freely given loyalty of the nation, but will also take the wind out of the conspiracies that are afoot to misguide the nation" (GAPP).

64. For some instances, see Ghulam Ahmad Parwez, *Lughat al-Qur'an*, 4 vols. (Lahore: Idara-i tulu`-i Islam, 1960–61), 1: 214–15 (the Qur'anic "Adam" as a prototypical not

a historical person, let alone the first prophet of God); 1: 241–45 (angels as natural and psychological forces, following the Egyptian reformer Muhammad ʿAbduh); 1: 343–46 (Iblis, the Qurʾanic Satan, as a psychological propensity rather than an actual being); 1: 444–47 (jinn as a reference to the nomads of Arabia); 3: 1123–24 ("worship of God" as government according to God's law; cf. ibid., 3: 1041).

65. Ayub Khan to Parwez, July 2, 1960 (GAPP).

66. Parwez to Ayub Khan, July 16, 1960, 8 (GAPP). Cf. Ghulam Ahmad Parwez, *Qurʾani qawanin* (Lahore: Idara-i tuluʿ-i Islam, 1967), 21–22; Qasmi, *Questioning the Authority*, 251. Yet, Parwez also held that the punishments prescribed in the Qurʾan should be implemented only in conditions similar to those for which they had been devised (Parwez, 49). In effect, this would allow a government to put them in abeyance without denying their "inalterable" character.

67. Note Parwez's complaint that the press had largely ignored his responses to the questionnaire of the constitution commission of 1960. Parwez to Ayub Khan, June 18, 1960, 2–3; Parwez to Ayub Khan, July 16, 1960, 1 (GAPP). Parwez attributed some of this ostracism to the "mulla": "In my literature he sees his own political and economic death. He has therefore made my literature a taboo and myself a wet paint, with the result that the press, public platform, broadcasting, educational institutions, in short every avenue of expression is closed on me. So much so that even in the Army my literature is treated as 'out of bounds.'" Parwez to Ayub Khan, February 6, 1965, 4 (GAPP).

68. For the text of the fatwa and the names of its signatories, see *Parwez key bare main ʿulama ka muttafiqa fatwa* (Karachi: Madrasa-i ʿArabiyya Islamiyya, n.d.). Writing to Ayub Khan about it, Parwez objected to its self-characterization as "the unanimous verdict of the Ulema of the umma," but he did not mention anyone among the ʿulama who had been opposed to it. Parwez to Ayub Khan, March 15, 1962 (GAPP).

69. On this initiative, its background, and the conservative opposition to it, see chapter 3.

70. Khursheed-ul-Hasan, "Fundamental Rights Bill Passed by N.A.," *Dawn*, December 25, 1963. For the text of the first amendment, see "Text of Fundamental Rights Bill," *Dawn*, December 28–29, 1963.

71. Ayub Khan, *Friends*, 210; cf. *1962 Constitution*, 2.

72. "Ayub Elected League President," *Dawn*, December 25, 1963.

73. Even the president's basic democrats took their guidance from the ʿulama rather than Ayub Khan when it came to Islamic matters. As Parwez observed with much frustration in commenting on the proceedings of the basic democrats' convention in January 1962, they "opposed the Family Laws on the ground that they did not enjoy the favor of the Ulema. The plea is indicative of the extent to which the Democrats are influenced by the Ulema." Parwez to Qudrat Ullah Shahab, February 12, 1962 (GAPP).

74. These biographical details are based, in part, on Rahman's curriculum vitae included with the revised proposal for a project on Islam and Social Change submitted to the Ford Foundation in 1972. See enclosures with L. Binder to R. Frodin, July 21, 1972, Ford Foundation grant # 74–141: Islam and Social Change, reel #3087, Rockefeller Archives Center (hereafter, FF 74–141, RAC). Rahman and Leonard Binder of the University of Chicago were the principal investigators of this project. On Rahman's father, the Deobandi scholar, cf. "Thanvi, Rahman State Their Case," *Dawn*, October 9, 1963.

75. Quoted in the mission statement of the institute's journal: "Introducing the Journal," *Islamic Studies* 1/1 (March 1962): 1–4, at 1.

76. Fazlur Rahman, "Concepts Sunnah, Ijtihad and Ijmaʿ in the Early Period," *Islamic Studies* 1 (1962): 5–21. These and subsequent articles in the series were republished

as his *Islamic Methodology in History* (Karachi: Central Institute of Islamic Research, 1965). My references here are to this book.

77. Rahman, *Islamic Methodology*, 80.

78. See ibid., 75: "what resulted from *Hadith* eventually was not *some* formalization but a total fixation. The present need undoubtedly is to re-loosen this formalism and to resume the threads from the point where the living *Sunnah* had voluntarily emptied itself into the *Hadith* dam" (italics in the original). Also ibid., 188–90.

79. For a critique of Parwez, though without naming him, see ibid., 69–71.

80. Cf. ibid., 139–44. Incidentally, there is a strong echo of the idealist British philosopher and historian R. G. Collingwood (d. 1943) in some of Rahman's formulations—for example, when critiquing the aspiration of modern Islamic reformist movements to return to the ways of the first Muslims. "But the big question is: how can a piece of history be literally repeated? The only sense [in which this idea can be properly understood] . . . is that Muslims must perform and enact in the twentieth century that whose [*sic*] moral and spiritual dimensions match those of the Muslims' performance in the seventh and eighth centuries. But this means not just a simple 'return' to the Qur'an and the *Sunnah* as they were acted in the past but a true *understanding* of them that would give us guidance *today*." Rahman, *Islamic Methodology*, 143. Emphasis in the original. I have seen no indication that Rahman was directly acquainted with Collingwood's work. But it is worth noting that Collingwood's *Idea of History* was posthumously published in 1946, not long before Rahman arrived at Oxford for his DPhil. Collingwood, who was the university's Waynflete Professor of Metaphysical Philosophy until his resignation in 1941, would have been much talked about at Oxford during those years.

81. Rahman, *Islamic Methodology*, 181. Rahman here acknowledges his agreement, at least in part, with Joseph Schacht, *The Origins of Muhammadan Jurisprudence* (Oxford, UK: Clarendon Press, 1950), 224.

82. Rahman, *Islamic Methodology*, esp. 1–24.

83. Ibid., 189.

84. Fazlur Rahman, "Riba and Interest," *Islamic Studies* 3 (1964): 1–43. The Urdu original was published in *Fikr o nazar* 1/5 (November 1963). My references here are to the English version. For a brief discussion, see Muhammad Qasim Zaman, "Religious Discourse and the Public Sphere in Contemporary Pakistan," *Revue des mondes musulmans et de la Méditerranée* 123 (2008), 60–62.

85. Rahman, "Riba," 7.

86. Ibid., 12–30.

87. Ibid., 21–22.

88. Ibid., 21–24.

89. "Thanvi, Rahman State Their Case"; Rahman, "Some Islamic Issues," 292–95.

90. "Thanvi, Rahman State Their Case." The book in question was Fazlur Rahman, *Prophecy in Islam: Philosophy and Orthodoxy* (London: George Allen & Unwin, 1958).

91. "Thanvi, Rahman State Their Case." For a detailed discussion of Rahman and Smith with particular reference to McGill, see Megan Brankley Abbas, "Knowing Islam: The Entangled History of Western Academia and Modern Islamic Thought," PhD dissertation, Department of History, Princeton University, 2015, chapter 2. On Rahman more generally, including the controversy with Thanawi, see idem, "Between Western Academia and Pakistan: Fazlur Rahman and the Fight for Fusionism," *Modern Asian Studies* 51 (2017): 736–68.

92. "Thanvi, Rahman State Their Case"; "Questions and Answers," *Dawn*, October 9, 1963.

93. "Thanvi, Rahman State Their Case"; Abbas, "Between Western Academia and Pakistan," 755.

94. Cf. Rahman, "Some Islamic Issues," 292.

95. For Rahman's views on this matter, see *Islamic Methodology*, 190; idem, "Religion and Planned Parenthood in Pakistan," in Olivia Schieffelin, ed., *Muslim Attitudes toward Family Planning* (New York: Population Council, 1967), 94–97.

96. "Meetings of the Governors' Conference held on ... the 23rd, 24th, and 25th of February, 1967 at Rawalpindi," case no. GC8/1/67: The Fundamental Conflict, Minutes: 5 (GAPP). The committee is sometimes referred to as the Committee on Islamic Ideology. Part of its mandate was to examine the matter of the fundamental conflict. It was also to "define the ideology of Islam and to make [the] Mulla useful in the process of nation-building." See note dated September 2, 1967, by M. Muqaddas, section officer, Cabinet Division, in 97/CF/67: Ruat-i-Hilal Committee and the Moon Controversy: 14 (NDC).

97. Cf. Craig Baxter, ed., *Diaries of Field Marshal Mohammad Ayub Khan, 1966–1972* (Karachi: Oxford University Press, 2007), 90 (entry for April 30, 1967). Ayub Khan did not mention that he had commissioned this book, but this is noted by Rahman in the curriculum vitae submitted to the Ford Foundation in 1972 (see enclosures with L. Binder to R. Frodin, July 21, 1972, FF 74–141 (RAC). There, the book is called "Pakistan as an Islamic State."

98. See Fazlur Rahman, "The Qur'anic Concept of God, the Universe and Man," *Islamic Studies* 6/1 (March 1967): 1–19; idem, "Some Reflections on the Reconstruction of Muslim Society in Pakistan," *Islamic Studies* 6/2 (1967): 103–20; idem, "Implementation." Ayub Khan did not mention the title of the article he read, but it is likely to have been the first one, not only because he calls it the "first chapter" of the book (Baxter, ed., *Diaries*, 90) but also because that was the only article from this series that was in print when Rahman met the president to discuss the project.

99. Rahman, "Implementation," 205 and 222 n. 22.

100. Rahman, "Some Reflections," 117–18.

101. Rahman, "Implementation," 212.

102. Ibid., 206; idem, "Some Reflections," 118. Parwez had a similar view: *Qur'ani qawanin*, 31–32. Also Parwez to Ayub Khan, June 18, 1960, 5, characterizing the "establishment of parties [as] *shirk*"—associating partners with the one God.

103. Rahman, "Some Reflections," 107. In support, Rahman adduced Q 22.41 as well as Q 3.104, 110, 114 and Q 9.72.

104. Rahman, "Some Reflections," 112, adducing Q 4.82. Cf. Rahman, "Implementation," 215.

105. Rahman, "Qur'anic Concept of God," 17–18, citing Aristotle, *Metaphysics*, trans. Hugh Tredennick (Cambridge, MA: Harvard University Press [Loeb Classical Library], 1947), 2: 167. Parwez had been no less effusive. Writing to request an audience with the president, he had observed in September 1961: "It seems that your coming to power has been for completion of some Divine scheme and therefore there is no doubt that the enforcement of Quranic principles is bound to materialize through you.... I rejoice to visualize the scene when on the Day of Judgment Islam will advance to greet and bless you for reviving it in Pakistan after a thirteen century long exile from the Muslim world." Parwez to Ayub Khan, September 15, 1961 (GAPP). The reification of Islam is complete here with Parwez underlining the word.

106. Fazlur Rahman, *Major Themes of the Qur'an* (Minneapolis: Bibliotheca Islamica, 1980), 43.

107. Afzal, *Pakistan*, 323.

108. N. J. Barrington to R. M. Purcell, January 24, 1967, FCO 37/182: Internal Political Affairs in West Pakistan, 1967–68: 1 (Foreign Office Files for India, Pakistan, and Afghan-

istan, 1972–80, electronic resource, at www.archivesdirect.amdigital.co.uk/Introduction /FO_India/default.aspx [hereafter, TNA; Electronic Resource]). Already in early 1965, Parwez, too, had warned the president about the "pitiable" economic condition of the people: "The majority of them cannot get two square meals a day. Wealth is accumulating in fewer hands and the majority of the population is driven to penury. Our economists say that inflation is the natural consequence of the various developments undertaken in the country and, therefore, poor man will have to suffer till the country has fully developed. I beg to differ from this conclusion." Parwez to Ayub Khan, February 6, 1965 (GAPP).

109. "The Arrest of the Mullahs," note by M.F.H. Beg enclosed with R. G. Beer, British High Commission, Karachi, to N. J. Barrington, February 2, 1967, DO 134/32: Correspondence between Rawalpindi, Lahore, Karachi, Dacca on Pakistan General Politics, 1966–67, folder 2: 264 (TNA; Electronic Resource).

110. "Minutes of the Meeting of the Committee of Fundamental Conflict," April 17, 1967, 1 (GAPP).

111. "Hilal Body Meeting," *Dawn*, January 11, 1967.

112. N. J. Barrington, British High Commission, Rawalpindi, to R. M. Purcell, January 24, 1967, in DO 134/32: Correspondence between Rawalpindi, Lahore, Karachi, Dacca . . . , folder 2: 257 (TNA; Electronic Resource).

113. "The Arrest of the Mullahs," citing Altaf Gauhar, who was then secretary of the Ministry of Information and Broadcasting and a confidant of the president. A copy of the order issued to the press not to report on these matters is included in a note from N. J. Barrington to R. M. Purcell, February 16, 1967: DO 134/32: Correspondence between Rawalpindi, Lahore, Karachi, Dacca . . . , folder 2: 271 (TNA; Electronic Resource).

114. Samuel P. Huntington, *Political Order in Changing Societies* (New Haven, CT: Yale University Press, 1968), 251.

115. Ayub Khan to Parwez, July 2, 1960 (GAPP).

116. Rahman, *Islam*, 31. For the Urdu translation of this chapter, see Fazlur Rahman, "Qur'an-i majid," trans. Muhammad Sarwar, *Fikr o nazar* 5/4 (October 1967): 249–68; for the quoted passage, ibid., 251.

117. Fazlur Rahman, "Divine Revelation and the Prophet," *Dawn*, August 25, 1968.

118. See Zaman, *Modern Islamic Thought*, 237, 316–17.

119. File 331/CF/68-2620: Controversy on Dr. Fazlur Rahman's book "Islam"; minutes and decisions of the cabinet meeting on September 4, 1968 (NDC). The cabinet clearly did not know that Urdu translations of the book's individual chapters had been appearing in the journal of the Islamic Research Institute for more than a year by that time. (See note 116, earlier.) Those translations had probably contributed to the opposition of the `ulama, most of whom did not read English at that time. That publicizing those translations would help clear the air was a curious observation.

120. Baxter, *Diaries*, 253 (entry for September 5, 1968).

121. *Imroz* (Lahore), September 6, 1968: "Idara-i tahqiqat-i Islami ke director Fazlur Rahman musta`fi hogae."

122. See chapter 7, note 53.

123. For these events, see Afzal, *Pakistan*, 337–49.

124. On him, see Peter Custers, "Maulana Bhashani and the Transition to Secular Politics in East Bengal," *Indian Economic and Social History Review* 47 (2010): 231–59, esp. 249–52.

125. "2.5 Million Strike in West Pakistan," *New York Times*, March 18, 1969.

126. Afzal, *Pakistan*, 376.

127. Willem van Schendel, *A History of Bangladesh* (Cambridge, UK: Cambridge University Press, 2009), 124–25.

128. For the election results, see Afzal, *Pakistan*, 394–99.

129. Around 1.5 million people were said to be in India as refugees in May 1971, perhaps as many as 10 million by the end of the year. Schendel, *History of Bangladesh*, 163–64.

130. *The Report of the Hamoodur Rehman Commission of Inquiry into the 1971 War* (Lahore: Vanguard, n.d. [2000]), 317; Schendel, *History of Bangladesh*, 173. There was extensive sexual violence, too, on which see Nayanika Mookherjee, *The Spectral Wound: Sexual Violence, Public Memories, and the Bangladesh War of 1971* (Durham, NC: Duke University Press, 2015). Needless to say, the violence perpetrated by the opposing side—notably, the Bengali militia Mukti Bahini—was no less atrocious or extensive.

131. Muhammad Umar Memon, "Pakistani Urdu Creative Writing on National Disintegration: The Case of Bangladesh," *Journal of Asian Studies* 43 (1983): 105–27; Kamran Asdar Ali, *Communism in Pakistan: Politics and Class Activism 1947–1972* (London: I. B. Tauris, 2015), 200–205; Gary J. Bass, *The Blood Telegram: Nixon, Kissinger, and a Forgotten Genocide* (New York: Vintage Books, 2014), 328–30.

132. "Mulk ke liye sab se bara khatra socialism hai," *Nawa-i waqt*, February 25, 1970. For the fatwa (in English translation) and its signatories, see *New Times* (Rawalpindi), February 27, 1970, enclosed with R. E. Escritt, British High Commission, Rawalpindi, to P. J. Priestley, Foreign and Commonwealth Office, March 10, 1970, FCO37/681: Political Parties in Pakistan (TNA; Electronic Resource).

133. On the event, see *Report on Islamic Summit 1974 Pakistan, Lahore February 22–24, 1974* (Islamabad: Department of Films and Publications, Ministry of Information and Broadcasting, Government of Pakistan, n.d. [1974]). Almost immediately after coming to power, Bhutto had proceeded on a tour of a number of Muslim countries, including Iran, Turkey, Egypt, Syria, Libya, Algeria, Tunisia, and Morocco. This January 1972 tour was followed by a second tour in May that year, which took him to the United Arab Emirates, Kuwait, Iraq, Saudi Arabia, Jordan, Lebanon, Sudan, Ethiopia, Somalia, Mauritania, Guinea, and Nigeria. See ibid., 5.

134. Syeda Abida Hussain, *Power Failure: The Political Odyssey of a Pakistani Woman* (Karachi: Oxford University Press, 2015), 96.

135. Ali, *Communism in Pakistan*, 167–94.

136. See Ghafir Shahzad, *Data Darbar Complex: Ta`mir se takmil tak* (Lahore: Idrak Publications, 2004), 32, 41. The door was made in Iran.

137. Fazlur Rahman to Zulfikar Ali Bhutto, December 2, 1974, FF 74–141 (RAC). Emphasis in the original; the words underlined here are added to the typed letter in pen.

138. Zulfikar Ali Bhutto to Fazlur Rahman, January 5, 1975, FF 74–141 (RAC). Emphasis in the original. For the speech to which this exchange refers, see *National Assembly of Pakistan Debates*, 5/39 (Karachi: Manager of Publications, n.d. [1974]; hereafter, *NAPD*), 565–70.

139. Fazlur Rahman, "A Note on the Task before the Ministry of Religious Affairs," enclosure, as Annexure B, with "Report of Professor Fazlur Rahman's Visit to Pakistan in Summer, 1975, in Connection with the 'Islamic Education' Project of the University of Chicago," FF 74–141, 1. The note was written at the request of Kausar Niazi, the minister of religious affairs. See "Report of Professor Fazlur Rahman's Visit to Pakistan," 4 (RAC).

140. "A Note on the Task before the Ministry of Religious Affairs," 1–2. Emphasis in the original.

141. Ibid., 2–4; Abbas, "Between Western Academia and Pakistan," 762.

142. Fazlur Rahman, "Suggestions for the PPP Election Manifesto (1976) on the Subject of Islam," enclosed, as Annexure A, with "Report of Professor Fazlur Rahman's Visit to Pakistan in Summer 1975," 1–2, FF 74–141 (RAC). Emphasis in the original.

143. The manifesto did, however, echo Rahman's recommendation to the Ministry of Religious Affairs to set up an institution to train imams and preachers. See *Pakistan People's Party Manifesto, January 1977* (Rawalpindi: Pakistan People's Party Central Secretariat, n.d.), 40.

144. Ibid., 40.

145. Cf. Mir Zohair Hussain, "Islam in Pakistan under Bhutto and Zia-ul-Haq," in Hussin Mutalib and Taj ul-Islam Hashmi, eds., *Islam, Muslims and the Modern State* (New York: St. Martin's Press, 1994), 47–79, especially 57. Also see Jaffrelot, *The Pakistan Paradox*, 463–67.

146. "Report of Professor Fazlur Rahman's Visit to Pakistan in Summer 1975," 5, FF 74–141 (RAC).

147. Quoted, from a May 1946 article, in Aftab Ahmad, *Muhammad Hasan `Askari, aik mutala`a: Zati khutut ki rawshani main* (Lahore: Sang-i mil Publications, 1994), 37.

148. Ibid., 17–55. I base my account of `Askari's intellectual transformation on Aftab Ahmad's interpretation. On `Askari, see also Mehr Afshan Farooqi, *Urdu Literary Culture: Vernacular Modernity in the Writing of Muhammad Hasan Askari* (New York: Palgrave Macmillan, 2012); Aamir R. Mufti, *Enlightenment in the Colony: The Jewish Question and the Crisis of Postcolonial Culture* (Princeton, NJ: Princeton University Press, 2007), 14–21; Ali, *Communism*, 103–13. `Askari had translated only the first 400 or so pages of Shafi`'s multivolume commentary till the time of his death: see the foreword by Muhammad Taqi Usmani to Mufti Muhammad Shafi`, *Ma`ariful Qur'an*, vol. 1, translated by Muhammad Hasan Askari and Muhammad Shamim (Karachi: Maktaba-i Dar al-`Ulum, 1996), xvii–xviii. The entire set was published in eight volumes between 1996 and 2005.

149. On this, see Mark Sedgwick, *Against the Modern World: Traditionalism and the Secret Intellectual History of the Twentieth Century* (New York: Oxford University Press, 2004).

150. As observed in the introduction, my usage of the term "modernism" is not concerned with what it means in a European and American literary and cultural context. `Askari's work is, however, an example of a critique directed simultaneously at modernism in that sense as well as at Islamic modernism.

151. Muhammad Hasan `Askari, *Jadidiyyat* (Rawalpindi: `Iffat Hasan, 1979). On the date of the composition of this work (ca. 1969) and its intended audience, see Ahmad, *Muhammad Hasan `Askari*, 43.

152. `Askari, *Jadidiyyat*, 41.

153. Ibid., 28.

154. Ibid., 59–60, quotation at 60. Cf. ibid., 101.

155. Cf. Ahmad, *Muhammad Hasan `Askari*, 40–43. Even as he moved toward the `ulama during the Ayub Khan era, `Askari had maintained some of his literary pursuits. For instance, in 1968, he had published an Urdu translation of Herman Melville's *Moby Dick*. See the advertisement of the book in *Nawa-i waqt*, February 12, 1968.

156. For a recent example, see Muhammad Taqi `Usmani, *Islam awr hamari zindagi*, 10 vols. (Lahore, Pakistan: Idara-i Islamiyyat, 2010). This work, whose title may be rendered *Islam and Our Life*, is a collection of a number of `Usmani's writings and sermons. The volumes deal with matters of belief, ritual, and other religious practices (vols. 1, 2, 10), good and bad morals and etiquette (vols. 7–9), Sufi ethics (vol. 6), the family (vol. 5), the teachings of Islam on economic matters (vol. 3), and the norms of social comportment (vol. 4). Although this is a work on ethics, `Usmani's interest is overwhelmingly in personal ethics rather than in the ethical dimensions of public and political life. Indeed, as he

argues in commenting on Q 5.105, the best path to the reform of society is through reforming the self. See `Usmani (2010, 6:45–62).

157. All four books—*Khushbu, Sad barg, Khud kalami,* and *Inkar*—are part of her
collected works: Parvin Shakir, *Mah-i tamam: Kulliyyat* (Delhi: Educational Publishing
House, 1995). The first of these was published in November 1977, in the early months of
Zia al-Haqq's martial law, though the preface to it is dated September 1976. Another col-
lection of Shakir's poetry was published posthumously: *Kaf-i a'ina* (Islamabad: Murad
Publications, n.d.).

158. C. M. Naim, "Parveen Shakir: A Note and Twelve Poems," *Annual of Urdu Studies* 8 (1993): 181–91, at 184, 185.

159. This is contained in the last of the collections of poetry published in her lifetime:
Inkar (1990), now part of her collected works, *Mah-i tamam.* For a useful discussion of
Shakir's work, see Imran Hameed Khan, "A Room of Her Own: Romance, Resistance, and
Feminist Thought in Modern Urdu Poetry," PhD dissertation, Department of Asian Stud-
ies, University of Texas, Austin, 2015, 185–234.

160. For a survey of political developments since the death of General Zia al-Haqq,
see Jalal, *The Struggle for Pakistan,* 259–396.

161. See, for instance, two tracts on this question by a noted Deobandi religious scholar:
Muhammad Yusuf Ludhianawi, `Awrat ki sarbarahi* (Karachi: Maktaba-i bayyinat, n.d.).
The first was written shortly after Benazir Bhutto's assumption of office as prime minister
in 1988, the second in 1993.

162. Mawdudi explained this as an instance of having to opt for the lesser evil. See
Seyyed Vali Reza Nasr, *The Vanguard of the Islamic Revolution: The Jama`at-i Islami of
Pakistan* (Berkeley: University of California Press, 1994), 41–42.

163. I refer to him as Mawlana Fazlur Rahman not only to highlight his credentials
as one of the `ulama but also to distinguish him from the modernist intellectual of that
name.

164. My discussion here of legal developments in the late 1980s and the 1990s draws
on Zaman, *The Ulama,* 89–91.

165. "Enforcement of Shariah Ordinance, 1988, June 15, 1988," in All Pakistan Legal
Decisions, Central Statutes 29, quoted in Charles H. Kennedy, "Repugnancy to Islam—
Who Decides?" *International and Comparative Law Quarterly* 41 (1992): 769–88, at 777.

166. Kennedy, "Repugnancy," 778–79.

167. This was the view of Ghulam Hyder Wyne, then the chief minister of the Punjab.
Quoted in Kennedy, "Repugnancy," 779, n. 44.

168. The fullest account of the rise of the Taliban and its background is by Ahmad
Rashid: *Taliban: Militant Islam, Oil and Fundamentalism in Central Asia* (New Haven,
CT: Yale University Press, 2000). Also see Zaman, *The Ulama,* 136–43; David B. Edwards,
Before Taliban: Genealogies of the Afghan Jihad (Berkeley: University of California Press,
2002); Gilles Dorronsoro, *Revolution Unending: Afghanistan, 1979 to the Present,* trans.
John King (London: Hurst, 2005); and Thomas Barfield, *Afghanistan: A Cultural and
Political History* (Princeton, NJ: Princeton University Press, 2010), 225–350.

169. Rahimullah Yusufzai, "Taliban Enforce Islamic Justice," *News,* March 1, 1996.

170. "Pak Agencies Not Backing Taliban: PM," *News,* February 19, 1995.

171. Bhutto, *Reconciliation,* 115.

172. Cf. Husain Haqqani, *Pakistan: Between Mosque and Military* (Washington, DC:
Carnegie Endowment for International Peace, 2005), 236.

173. Rashid, *Taliban,* 90. On the role of Bhutto's interior minister, Naseerullah Babar,
see ibid., 27–29, 184–85.

174. "Text of Fifteenth Constitutional Amendment Bill," *Dawn,* August 29, 1998.

175. For estimates of terrorism and Taliban insurgency-related deaths in Pakistan, see chapter 7, note 187. On the financial cost, a military spokesman stated in September 2016 that the country "had suffered a cumulative loss of $106.98 billion in the war on terror between 2001 and 2015." Iftikhar A. Khan, "IS Footprints Eliminated from Pakistan: Army," *Dawn*, September 4, 2016.

176. On the 2002 ruling of the Shari`at Appellate Bench and its context, see Zaman, "Religious Discourse," 55–73.

177. Pervez Musharraf, "A Plea for Enlightened Moderation," *Washington Post*, June 1, 2004. Cf. idem, *In the Line of Fire: A Memoir* (New York: Free Press, 2006), 297–99.

178. Qudssia Akhlaque, "OIC to Discuss Challenges Faced by Muslim World," *Dawn*, June 1, 2004.

179. Khawar Ghumman, "Oct 12 Takeover Made Part of SSC Curriculum," *Dawn*, December 30, 2006.

180. For an overview of Ghamidi's thought, see Muhammad Khalid Masud, "Rethinking Shari`a: Javed Ahmad Ghamidi on Hudud," *Die Welt des Islams* 47 (2007): 356–75.

181. Ibid., 368.

182. Ibid., 370.

183. Javed Ahmad Ghamidi, *Mizan*, 3rd ed. (Lahore: al-Mawrid, 2008), 491–92.

184. Sadaf Aziz, "Making a Sovereign State: Javed Ghamidi and 'Enlightened Moderation,'" *Modern Asian Studies* 45 (2011): 598–99.

185. Ghamidi, *Mizan*, 511.

186. Ibid., 490–92. He adduces Q 9.5, 9.11 and a hadith report that has the Prophet say: "I have been commanded to fight people until they testify that there is no god but Allah and Muhammad is His messenger, establish prayer and pay the zakat."

187. See Ghamidi, *Mizan*, 610–30, esp. 611, 614, 626. Following his mentor, Amin Ahsan Islahi, and the latter's teacher, Hamid al-din Farahi, Ghamidi argues against stoning to death as the punishment for adultery. See Javed Ahmad Ghamidi, *Burhan*, 3rd ed. (Lahore: Dar al-ishraq, 2001), 34–124, esp. 81–84.

188. Ghamidi, *Mizan*, 615, 628–30; idem, *Burhan*, 81–84.

189. Fazlur Rahman, "The Concept of Hadd in Islamic Law," *Islamic Studies* 4 (1965): 237–51.

190. Declan Walsh, "Islamic Scholar Attacks Pakistan's Blasphemy Laws," *Guardian*, January 20, 2011. On the associate, Muhammad Faruq Khan, who was assassinated, see chapter 7, note 170.

191. See, for example, Muhammad Shakil Auj, *Ta`birat* (Karachi: Kulliyya-i ma`arif-i Islamiyya, 2013), 215.

192. Ibid., 315.

193. Ibid., 201–18.

194. Ibid., 135–48. The word "coexistence" is his, in English. Ibid., 147. For the argument that the Qur'anic "believers" includes many non-Muslims, see Fred M. Donner, *Muhammad and the Believers: At the Origins of Islam* (Cambridge, MA: Harvard University Press, 2010). Auj was, however, not acquainted with Donner's work.

195. Muhammad Shakil Auj, *Nisa'iyyat: Chand fikri o nazari mabahis* (Karachi: Kulliyya-i ma`arif-i Islamiyya, Jami`a Karachi, 2012), 37–48.

196. Ibid., 95–107.

197. Ibid., 243–64, 301–4.

198. Ibid., 227–42.

199. Ibid., 61–71.

200. Ibid., 62.

201. Ibid., 19–36.

202. Ibid., 129–43. Oddly, he does not refer to Thanawi in this discussion.

203. Ibid., 297–99.

204. Imtiaz Ali, "KU Dean Shakeel Auj Shot Dead," *Dawn*, September 19, 2014.

205. Ibid.

206. For the text of this petition, see Haya Fatima Iqbal, "Remembering Dr. Shakeel Auj: The Man Who Wasn't Afraid," blogpost, September 18, 2015, at www.dawn.com/news /1207553 (accessed January 25, 2016).

207. Ziaur Rehman, "A Pakistani Scholar Accused of Blasphemy Is Shot Dead," *New York Times*, September 18, 2014.

208. For the text of the fatwa and of the letter stating that it was fake, see Iqbal, "Remembering Dr. Shakeel Auj." The alleged fatwa and the letter are from Mufti Muhammad Rafi `Usmani, the president of the Dar al-`Ulum of Karachi. Cf. Ali, "KU Dean."

209. On the seeming ubiquity of different kinds of violence in contemporary Karachi, see Laurent Gayer, *Karachi: Ordered Disorder and the Struggle for the City* (New York: Oxford University Press, 2014).

210. Muhammad Khalid Masud, *Islamic Legal Philosophy: A Study of Abu Ishaq al-Shatibi's Life and Thought* (Islamabad: Islamic Research Institute, 1977). This book, reprinted several times, is based on Masud's PhD dissertation.

211. For a useful summary of Shatibi's views, see Wael B. Hallaq, *A History of Islamic Legal Theories: An Introduction to Sunni Usul al-fiqh* (Cambridge, UK: Cambridge University Press, 1997), 164–74.

212. Muhammad Khalid Masud, *Shari`a Today: Essays on Contemporary Issues and Debates in Muslim Societies* (Islamabad: National Book Foundation, 2013), 67–68. Masud has also drawn on Wali Allah to make the point that the normative authority of the shari`a rests in good measure on its ability to accord with social mores, which is to say—though Masud does not say it in so many words—that efforts to impose the shari`a from the top down would be oppressive and counterproductive. Masud also suggests that shari`a rulings need to remain receptive to changing needs and to *become* receptive to the input of those who have traditionally been excluded from thinking about the law. See ibid., 107–8, 113–16.

213. Ibid., 67–68.

214. Ibid., 212. See also ibid., 247.

215. Auj, *Nisa'iyyat*, 19–36.

216. Sa`id Ahmad Jalalpuri, "Kiya Islam mukammal zabita-i hayat nahin?" *Bayyinat* 70/11 (January 2008): 3–14, at 6–7. Masud's remarks had first appeared in *Nawa-i waqt*, November 7, 2007. They are quoted in Jalalpuri, 5.

217. Kalbe Ali, "Muslim Women Cannot Object to Husbands' Marriages: CII Chief," *Dawn*, October 22, 2014; Kalbe Ali, "CII Justifies 'Light Beatings' for Errant Wives," *Dawn*, May 27, 2016. For a brief profile of Shirani, see http://cii.gov.pk/aboutcii/Chairmansprofile .aspx (accessed August 10, 2016). The council had taken some highly conservative positions in the Zia al-Haqq era, too. See, for instance, chapter 5, note 86.

218. "Senator Seeks Increased Women's Role in CII," *Dawn*, November 21, 2016.

219. Rahman, *Major Themes*; cf. idem, "The Qur'anic Concept of God, the Universe and Man," *Islamic Studies* 6 (1967): 1–19.

220. Richard G. Hovannisian, ed., *Ethics in Islam* (Malibu, CA: Undena Publications, 1985).

221. Auj, *Ta`birat*, front matter.

222. See the affectionate obituary of Ghulam Muhammad by Abdul Hakim: "Sabiq Governor-General Ghulam Muhammad nawwar Allah marqadahu," *Saqafat* 3/6 (December 1956): 7–18.

223. Significantly, once his formal association with the government had ended, some of the same ʿulama who had opposed him most vociferously became, by his own account, considerably more accommodating. Reporting on his visit to the prominent Deobandi scholar Muhammad Yusuf Bannuri in the summer of 1974, both to seek his cooperation for the Islam and Social Change project and to sound him out on the Ahmadi issue then engulfing the country (see chapter 5), Rahman observed that "he did me the honour of welcoming me and making me sit immediately on his right side!" Mufti Muhammad Shafiʿ of the Dar al-ʿUlum madrasa, whom Rahman met separately, also "welcomed me with kindness, even warmth.... [Ilis] son (Muhammad Taqi [ʿUsmani]) was also very kind and, in fact, paid me a visit the next day and again assured me of help." Fazlur Rahman, "A Report of My Visit to Pakistan," enclosed with Rahman to Reuben Frodin, October 7, 1974: 6–7, FF 74–141 (RAC).

224. "Enlightened Moderation Threat to Country: Qazi," *Dawn*, March 23, 2005.

225. Khalifa Abdul Hakim, *Islamic Ideology* (Lahore: Publishers United, 1951), chapter 14. The second edition, published in 1953, had already replaced it with a different chapter ("Reconstruction and Renaissance").

226. In an effort, perhaps, to salvage his socialist leanings and to distinguish them from the threat of communism, Khalifa Abdul Hakim had written a book in which he had sought to show that Islam met the material needs of people better than did communism. See his *Islam and Communism*, 3rd ed. (Lahore: Institute of Islamic Culture, 1962; first published in 1951).

227. Ali, *Communism*, 167–94, esp. 171.

228. *Status of Labour Rights in Pakistan: The Year 2014* (Karachi: Pakistan Institute of Labour Education and Research, 2015), 23. On the effects of privatization, see ibid., 23. Ali, *Communism*, 61, notes that about one-third of nonagricultural labor was unionized in 1947. He reminds us, however, that "[l]ess than 1 percent of [Pakistan's] ... population were involved in wage labour" at the time. Also see Shazia Hasan, "Only One Percent of Pakistan's Labour Is Unionized," *Dawn*, May 1, 2015.

229. *Report of the Constitution Commission*, 75–76.

230. Even Abdul Hakim, with his noted interest in Hindu scriptures, had a view of polytheism that raised questions about whether the Hindus could be good Pakistani citizens. "Islam considers only polytheism as the root of all evil which degrades Man and God and disrupts humanity by numerous hostile objects of worship. Polytheism is not a mere metaphysical belief, harmless to hold as a speculative hypothesis; it cuts into the lives of those who hold it. It makes them superstitious and lowers their morality and stands in the way of personal and social unity and well-being." *Islamic Ideology*, 157. Though he allowed elsewhere that "reformed Hinduism is becoming more and more monotheistic" (ibid., 45), the extent to which Pakistan's Hindu population was not yet monotheistic was clearly the degree to which it represented a challenge to morality and to national integration.

231. An important influence on Abdul Hakim's thought was the work of the Danish philosopher and theologian Harald Höffding (d. 1931), who had argued that "the essence of religion is not contained in the dogmas which have been formulated once and for ever. These may be set aside." Harald Höffding, *Philosophy of Religion*, trans. from the German by B. E. Meyer (London: Macmillan, 1906), 352. Instead, religion was concerned with the "conservation of values" seen by its adherents as "the highest." Ibid., 217–44, especially 218. This was in line with Muslim modernist sensibilities. As Abdul Hakim would put it, "To me it appears that religious belief could not be characterized in better terms." *Islamic Ideology*, 50. Yet, Höffding had also highlighted the importance of "[t]he Church as the bearer of a great tradition, of a group of figures in which countless generations ... have deposited their deepest experiences of life—everything that they have felt, thought and suffered under the

buffetings of fate in small things as well as in great." Höffding, *Philosophy of Religion*, 352–53. This did not go well with modernist attitudes toward the millennium-old Islamic tradition, but Abdul Hakim's initiative to foster a new space for the `ulama may well have owed something to it.

Chapter Three. The `Ulama and the State

1. "Maulana Usmani Passes Away," *Dawn*, December 14, 1949.

2. *CAPD*, 5/5, 94–95 (Liaquat Ali Khan, March 12, 1949).

3. For the original Urdu text, which I follow here, see Sherkoti, ed., *Anwar*, 231–39. For the official English translation, see *CAPD*, 5/3, March 9, 1949, 43–48. The English translation diverges in some respects from the Urdu text.

4. In his address to the Karachi High Court Bar Association in August 1952, the governor-general, Ghulam Muhammad, too, had steered clear of any suggestion that the implementation of Islamic law might be expected of public officials professing Islamic commitments. Instead, he had limited himself to calling upon "the educated classes ... to inspire people and to inculcate in them those moral and spiritual values conferred by the Quran without which no leadership can achieve moral and spiritual progress." Press Information Department, Government of Pakistan, August 28, 1952, 5, in DO 35/3185: Pakistan Internal Affairs (TNA). A lack of reference to Islamic law is especially remarkable in that the governor-general was addressing lawyers and jurists.

5. Sherkoti, ed., *Anwar*, 237–38; *CAPD*, 5/3, March 9, 1949, 47.

6. Sherkoti, ed., *Anwar*, 235, 237; *CAPD*, 5/3, March 9, 1949, 45, 46.

7. *CAPD*, 5/1, March 7, 1949, 3.

8. Sherkoti, ed., *Anwar*, 235; *CAPD*, 5/3, March 9, 1949, 45.

9. *CAPD*, 5/1 (March 7, 1949), 3.

10. Ahmad, ed., *Speeches*, 2: 208–9. For this passage, see chapter 1, note 122.

11. Sherkoti, ed., *Anwar*, 234; *CAPD*, 5/3, March 9, 1949, 44.

12. See "The Views of the Board of Talimmat-e-Islamia [*sic*] on certain items referred to them by the sub-committee on federal and provincial constitutions and distribution of powers" (April 1950) and "Views of the Board of Talimat-e-Islamia" (August 1950), in Binder, *Religion and Politics*, appendixes A and B, 383–429. I will refer to the two documents, the second a supplement to the first, as Views I and II, and will follow Binder's pagination for them. For Binder's discussion of these recommendations, see *Religion and Politics*, 155–82.

13. "Views" I, in Binder, *Religion and Politics*, 394.

14. Ibid., 385.

15. Ibid., 387–88; "Views" II, ibid., 417–25.

16. Ibid., 409–10.

17. Ibid., 410–12.

18. "Views" I, ibid., 388.

19. Ibid., 386.

20. Cf. "Views" II, ibid., 406–7.

21. The best instance of this is Binder, *Religion and Politics*, who points as well to the incoherence of the Board's views: 154–82.

22. "Views" I, ibid., 389–91.

23. "Views" II, ibid., 427–29; cf. ibid., 407–8.

24. Ibid., 409–10.

25. Binder, *Religion and Politics*, 172. Cf. ibid., 343, referring to the *Report of the Court of Inquiry* into the anti-Ahmadi agitation of 1953 to make the point that the `ulama

did not accept the idea of human legislation. See *Report of the Court of Inquiry*, 211–12. Also Qasmi, *The Ahmadis*, 152.

26. "Views" I, in Binder, *Religion and Politics*, 396.

27. Binder, *Religion and Politics*, 178–82.

28. *Fundamental Principles of an Islamic State, Formulated at a Gathering of Ulama of Various Muslim Schools of Law under the Presidentship of Allama Syed Suleiman Sahib Nadvi* (Karachi: N.p., n.d. [1951]), 2.

29. Binder, *Religion and Politics*, 336–37. The modernist Ghulam Ahmad Parwez believed, for his part, that the constitution of 1956 was "un-Islamic." This was his way of justifying the 1958 military coup. He also thought that political parties, taken for granted by the 1956 constitution, had as little basis in Islam as did "religious sects." Parwez to Ayub Khan, June 18, 1960, pp. 1 and 4 of the letter (GAPP).

30. See the anguished letter of Muhammad Manzur Nu`mani, November 26, 1945, and `Usmani's response to it, December 29, 1945, in Sherkoti, ed., *Anwar*, 146–55. Nu`mani was then a member of the Deoband madrasa's advisory council and the editor of an Urdu monthly. On him, see Rizwi, *Ta'rikh*, 2: 155–56. Also see `Usmani's exchange, November–December 1945, with Habib al-Rahman Ludhianawi, a Deobandi scholar and politician: Sherkoti, ed., *Anwar*, 155–65.

31. Court of Inquiry Proceedings, part 2: 886–87. Mosque preachers, too, had sometimes "accused the high government officials of moral depredations." "Extracts from Confidential Weekly Diaries, Sialkot," March 14, 1953, in ibid., vol. 2: 217. On the two judges of the court, see Qasmi, *The Ahmadis*, 25–29.

32. For a biographical sketch of Hanif Nadwi by a former colleague and fellow member of the Ahl-i Hadith, see Muhammad Ishaq Bhatti, *Qafila-i Hadith* (Lahore: Maktaba-i Quddusiyya, 2003), 272–379. Also see the collection of essays in Hanif Nadwi's honor: Muhammad Ishaq Bhatti, ed., *Armughan-i Hanif* (Lahore: Idara-i saqafat-i Islamiyya, 1980).

33. Muhammad Hanif Nadwi, *Mas'ala-i ijtihad* (Lahore: Idara-i saqafat-i Islamiyya, 1952).

34. Ibid., 2, 5–6. Cf. Wali Allah, *Hujjat Allah al-baligha*, 2 vols. (Cairo: Dar al-turath, 1936), 1: 4–5; Marcia Hermansen, *The Conclusive Argument from God: Shah Wali Allah of Delhi's Hujjat Allah al-Baligha* (Leiden: Brill, 1996), 11.

35. Nadwi, *Mas'ala-i ijtihad*, 163–64.

36. Ibid., 109, following (slightly inaccurately) Muhammad b. `Ali al-Shawkani, *Irshad al-fuhul ila tahqiq al-haqq min `ilm al-usul* (Cairo: Muhammad `Ali Subayh, 1930), 220.

37. Nadwi, *Mas'ala-i ijtihad*, 109–10.

38. Ibid., 117.

39. Ibid., 117.

40. Cf. ibid., 127. Wali Allah, too, had spoken of the Prophet's ijtihad. See *Hujja*, 1: 123–24; Hermansen, *Conclusive Argument*, 357–60.

41. Nadwi, *Mas'ala-i ijtihad*, 128–29.

42. Ibid., 129.

43. Ibid., 172.

44. Ibid., 172.

45. Ibid., 114–16. For the relevant passage in Shatibi, though Nadwi does not give a reference to it, see Abu Ishaq al-Shatibi, *al-Muwafaqat fi usul al-shari`a*, ed. `Abdallah Daraz, 4 vols. (Cairo: al-Matba`a al-Rahmaniyya, n.d.), 4: 111. Also see Muhammad Khalid Masud, *Muslim Jurists' Quest for the Normative Basis of Shari`a* (Leiden: ISIM Occasional Papers, 2001), 13.

46. Nadwi, *Mas'ala-i ijtihad*, 180–82.

47. Ibid., 180.

48. Weiss, *Spirit*, 158–63.

49. Nadwi, *Mas'ala-i ijtihad*, 181.

50. See Zaman, *Modern Islamic Thought*, 221–60.

51. Muhammad Ja`far Nadwi Phulwarwi, *al-Din yusr* (Lahore: Idara-i saqafat-i Is-lamiyya, 1955). For a brief discussion, see Zaman, *Modern Islamic Thought*, 207–9. For a biographical sketch, see Muhammad Ishaq Bhatti, *Bazm-i arjumandan* (Delhi: al-Kitab International, 2005), 351–99.

52. Phulwarwi, *al-Din yusr*, 170–71. For the other examples, see ibid., 168–70.

53. Ibid., 8–9. This part of the discussion also occurs in Phulwarwi's *Izdiwaji zindagi ke-liye ahamm qanuni tajawiz* (Lahore: Idara-i saqafat-i Islamiyya, 1955), 96–109, at 96–97. A similar point was made much earlier, in 1884, by Sayyid Ahmad Khan: see "Islam," in his *Khutbat*, 1: 530–31.

54. Phulwarwi, *al-Din yusr*, 9. For a fuller discussion of ritual prayer, and elements of "ease" that the later tradition has obscured, see ibid., 295–315. Husayn Ahmad Madani, too, had once invoked the example of ritual prayer to make the point that shari`a stipulations can vary in light of circumstances. See Najm al-din Islahi, ed., *Maktubat-i Shaykh al-Islam*, 4 vols. (Deoband: Maktaba-i diniyya, 1963), 1: 399–400 (letter to `Abd al-Wahhab Gumthallawi, January 18, 1942).

55. Phulwarwi, *al-Din yusr*, 350. For the full discussion of hudud, see ibid., 347–68.

56. Ibid., 352–55.

57. Ibid., 356–59. For the pains medieval jurists often took to arrive at an understanding of Qur'anic teachings on such matters, which could lead to avoiding the infliction of the harsher penalties, see Weiss, *Spirit*, 101–12. Also see Intisar A. Rabb, *Doubt in Islamic Law* (Cambridge, UK: Cambridge University Press, 2015).

58. Phulwarwi, *al-Din yusr*, 358.

59. Ibid., 366, citing Ibn Qayyim al-Jawziyya, *I`lam al-muwaqqi`in `an Rabb al-`alamin*, ed. Muhammad Muhyi al-din `Abd al-Hamid, 4 vols. (Cairo: Matba`at al-sa`ada, 1955), 3: 16. Also see Nawir Yuslem Nurbain, "Ibn Qayyim's Reformulation of the Fatwa," unpublished MA thesis, Institute of Islamic Studies, McGill University, 1995, 89.

60. Phulwarwi, *al-Din yusr*, 367–68. For a poetic expression of a similar idea, see Parvin Shakir, "Aik buri `awrat" ("A Bad Woman"), in idem, *Khushbu*, the first of the four books (each with independent pagination) in her *Mah-i tamam*, 351–57.

61. In a letter to Ghulam Ahmad Parwez, who had urged him not to write on "religious" (as distinguished from literary and historical) topics while employed at the institute, Phulwarwi had denied that he was constrained in his work by this employment. Parwez's point was not, of course, that Phulwarwi had to take undesirable modernist positions by virtue of his affiliation with the institute but rather that he presumably had to water down some of his positions because this government-supported institute did not want to ruffle too many conservative feathers. The letter is undated but seems to have been written in 1957–58, like several others of Phulwarwi's letters in this collection. In another undated letter, Phulwarwi did concede that he said certain things in the interest of expediency—again, presumably not to excessively agitate the conservative sentiment in society—but insisted that he did not do so at anyone's bidding. Also see Phulwarwi to Parwez, April 23, 1957 (GAPP).

62. Hanif Nadwi, *Mas'ala-i ijtihad*, 112–13.

63. Ibid., 99, 140.

64. For a discussion of the report, the note of dissent, and the Muslim Family Laws Ordinance promulgated on the basis of the report, see Khan, "Institutions not Intentions," chapter 4.

65. "Report of the Commission on Marriage and Family Laws," *Gazette of Pakistan (Extraordinary)*, June 20, 1956, 1197–1232, at 1200; Iqbal, *Reconstruction*, 141. The other two kinds of ijtihad that Iqbal had identified had to do with the authority to arrive at legal rulings within the parameters of a school of law but without the constraint of earlier views, and the authority to rule on specific issues left unaddressed by the school's founding fathers. Ibid., 141.

66. "Report of the Commission on Marriage," 1200–1201.

67. Ibid., 1202. A similar vision is set forth in elaborate detail in Abdul Hakim, *Islamic Ideology*, especially 214–45.

68. "Report of the Commission on Marriage," 1203.

69. Ibid., 1203.

70. For the commission's recommendations, which in part were based on the results of a questionnaire to which responses had been elicited from the public, see ibid., 1207–32.

71. Ibid., 1216.

72. Ihtisham al-Haqq Thanawi, "Shadi commission ki report ka ikhtilafi note," *Gazette of Pakistan (Extraordinary)*, August 30, 1956, 1505–1604. This note was published both in Urdu and in an English translation. My references here are to the Urdu original (1505–60). On Thanawi, see Abu Salman Shahjahanpuri, ed., *Mawlana Ihtisham al-Haqq Thanawi ki ap biti* (Karachi: Mawlana Ihtisham al-Haqq Thanawi Academy, 1993).

73. Thanawi, "Shadi commission," 1505–25.

74. Ibid., 1527.

75. Ibid., 1527, 1529, 1530.

76. Ibid., 1529.

77. Ibid., 1532–40.

78. Ibid., 1544–46.

79. "Report of the Commission on Marriage," 1232.

80. Thanawi, "Shadi commission," 1549.

81. Ibid., 1528, 1547, 1550, 1557.

82. The Deobandis, as represented by Ihtisham al-Haqq Thanawi, were not alone in their criticism of the marriage commission's report. The Barelawis, too, condemned it. See Mujeeb Ahmad, *Jam`iyyat `Ulama-i-Pakistan 1948–1979* (Islamabad: National Institute of Historical and Cultural Research, 1993), 19. So did the Jama`at-i Islami. See Khurshid Ahmad, ed., *Marriage Commission Report X-Rayed* (Karachi: Chiragh-e-Rah Publications, 1959).

83. Phulwarwi, *Izdiwaji zindagi*, 96–109, esp. 96.

84. Ibid., 28–29. Also see ibid., 103: "It has come to be asserted in our times that human beings have no right to make the law. If what is meant by this law relates to the limits set down by God (*hudud-i Ilahiyya*), then this view can be accepted, though only to a certain degree. By if it means 'by-laws' [*sic*], then this view is altogether incorrect. In our view, it would be better to put it this way: The human being has the authority to make law but not to make up religion."

85. Ibid., 66.

86. Court of Inquiry Proceedings, part 2: 658–59. Also see ibid., 660. The judges' reference here is to the English translation, which the British had commissioned in the late eighteenth century for use in their courts in India. See Charles Hamilton, trans., *The Hedaya, or Guide: A Commentary on the Mussulman Laws*, 4 vols. (London: T. Bensley, 1791). Qasimi was educated at two premier Deobandi madrasas, the parent institution in the town of Deoband and the Mazahir al-`Ulum in Saharanpur (Court of Inquiry Proceedings, part 2: 658; on his teaching the *Hidaya*, see ibid., 659. Among his works is a compilation of some of the discourses of the Deobandi Sufi master Ashraf `Ali Thanawi.

See Muhammad `Abd al-Halim Qasimi, ed., *Ashraf al-malfuzat* (Lahore: Wifaq Press, n.d. [1976]).

87. Cf. Joseph Schacht, *An Introduction to Islamic Law* (Oxford, UK: Clarendon Press, 1964), 105.

88. For both quotations, see "Thanvi, Rahman State Their Case," *Dawn*, October 9, 1963.

89. "Notification: Establishment of Central Institute of Islamic Research: Nomination of the Board of Governors," March 11, 1960, in 324/CF/1959–2274: Creation of an Islamic Research Centre (NDC).

90. I borrow this phrase from Charles L. Glenn, *The Ambiguous Embrace: Government and Faith-based Schools and Social Agencies* (Princeton, NJ: Princeton University Press, 2000).

91. Khursheed-ul-Hasan, "Men's Right of Divorce Restricted," *Dawn*, March 3, 1961. For the text of the law, see ibid., "Ordinance on Family Laws: Text."

92. "A Great Step Forward," *Dawn*, March 5, 1961. Emphasis in the original. Ghulam Ahmad Parwez wrote to the newspaper's editor to commend him for "projecting so successfully Quranic principles against dogma and blind orthodoxy." Parwez to Altaf Husain, March 12, 1961 (GAPP).

93. Muhammad Shafi` to Ayub Khan, April 1, 1961 (GAPP). The letter, typed in Urdu, is three pages long; an annexure, commenting on specific provisions of the Muslim Family Laws Ordinance, comprises another seven pages. Also see Khan, "Institutions not Intentions," 297–98.

94. Shafi` to Ayub Khan, April 1, 1961, p. 5 of the annexure.

95. Ibid., p. 1 of the annexure.

96. Ibid., p. 1 of the annexure.

97. Ibid., p. 2 of the letter.

98. Ibid., p. 7 of the annexure.

99. Muhammad Rafi` `Usmani, *Hayat-i mufti-i a`zam* (Karachi: Idarat al-ma`arif, 1994), 166.

100. Nazr Ahmad, *Ja'iza-i madaris-i `arabiyya-i Maghribi Pakistan* (Lyallpur: Jami`a Chishtiyya Trust, 1960), 294. The 56-acre gift had come from a South African Muslim. See Muhammad Rafi Usmani's preface to Azizur Rahman, *Introducing Darul `Uloom Karachi*, trans. Muhammad Shameem (Karachi: Public Information Department, Darul `Uloom Karachi, n.d.), 7.

101. Note by S. Hashim Raza, joint secretary, Ministry of Information and Broadcasting, appended to Raza's letter to A. A. Hamid, joint secretary, Cabinet Secretariat, July 29, 1955, 207-CF-54-2147: Orders of the Egyptian Government Controlling Sermons in Mosques; Preparation of Khutbas (NDC). Cf. *Report of the Court of Inquiry*, 214–18.

102. Memo from S. M. Jamil Wasti, Ministry of Information and Broadcasting, January 5, 1956, with an appended note by S. Hashim Raza. The quotation is from Raza's note on "the action taken in the matter for completion of the record," 207-CF-54-2147 (NDC).

103. Mufti Muhammad Shafi`, *Ma`arif al-Qur'an*, 8 vols. (Karachi: Idarat al-ma`arif, 1969–73). In his preface to the first volume of this work, Shafi` does mention its origins in a radio program but not the background to it, of which he may not have been aware. See ibid., 1: 9–10. The preface is dated July 1963. Shafi`'s radio program was discontinued in June 1964, though he had reached only the end of chapter 14 of the Qur'an by that time (see ibid., 9 n. 1).

104. See chapter 2, note 148.

105. The copy of Shafi`'s letter in the Parwez Papers has a notation from one M. Ali in the President's Secretariat asking "Can you produce an answer to this?" (Shafi` to Ayub

Khan, April 1, 1961, p. 7 of the annexure). Also see Qudratullah Shahab to Parwez, April 28, 1961, asking Parwez to draft a response, presumably to Shafi`'s letter (GAPP).

106. *A'ili qawanin Qur'an-i karim ki rawshani main* (Lahore: Ittihad Printing Press, n.d.). Parwez's name does not appear on the title page, but the tract was issued under the auspices of his *Tulu`-i Islam* and is unmistakably by him. It was written shortly after the first session of the National Assembly convened under the new constitution in June–July 1962 (see ibid., 19). I am grateful to Steve Millier for making this text available to me.

107. Mufti Muhammad Shafi`, "A'ili qanun par mukhtasar tabsira," *Bayyinat* (Karachi), 1/6–7 (March–April 1963): 9–48, at 13–14. Cited in Khan, "Institutions not Intentions," 297–98. I am grateful to Dr. Khan for sharing a copy of Shafi`'s article with me. In a move to embarrass the government, this article proceeds to publish not just Shafi`'s letter to the president but also his full indictment of the 1961 ordinance.

108. For instance, see the statements in support of these ordinances by Mufti Mahmud and Shah Ahmad Nurani, the leaders of the Deobandi Jam`iyyat al-`Ulama-i Islam and the Barelawi Jam`iyyat al-`Ulama-i Pakistan, respectively. *Nawa-i waqt*, February 13, 1979. For expressions of the support for them by Ihsan Ilahi Zahir of the Ahl-i Hadith and the Jama`at-i Islami leader `Abdul Ghafur Ahmad (who was then a member of Zia al-Haqq's cabinet), see *Nawa-i waqt*, February 11, 1979.

109. Asma Jahangir, "What the Protection of Women Act Does and What Is Left Undone," Human Rights Commission of Pakistan, *State of Human Rights in 2006* (Lahore: Human Rights Commission of Pakistan), 11, at www.hrcp-web.org/hrcpDetail_pub3.cfm?proID=374 (accessed September 28, 2008).

110. Charles Kennedy, "Implementation of the Hudood Ordinances," in idem, *Islamization of Laws and Economy: Case Studies on Pakistan* (Islamabad: Institute of Policy Studies), 64. Cf. Jahangir, "What the Protection of Women Act Does," 9; Moeen H. Cheema and Abdul-Rahman Mustafa, "From the Hudood Ordinances to the Protection of Women Act: Islamic Critiques of the Hudood Laws of Pakistan," *UCLA Journal of Islamic and Near Eastern Law* 8/1 (2009): 15–16.

111. "Text of Federal Shariat Court Judgment in Zafran Bibi Case," *Dawn*, August 21, 2002. This is the text of the court's detailed judgment. It had released her on the basis of an earlier decision in June 2002. On this case, see also Waseem Ahmad Shah, "Zafran Case Sent to Shariat Court," *Dawn*, May 8, 2002; Abdul Sami Paracha, "Mother Narrates Zafran's Ordeal," ibid., May 13, 2002; Seth Mydans, "In Pakistan, Rape Victims Are the 'Criminals,'" *New York Times*, May 17, 2002; idem, "Sentenced to Death, Rape Victim Is Freed by Pakistani Court," *New York Times*, June 8, 2002; Hina Azam, *Sexual Violation in Islamic Law: Substance, Evidence, and Procedure* (Cambridge, UK: Cambridge University Press, 2015), 3–4.

112. National Commission on the Status of Women, Government of Pakistan, *Report on Hudood Ordinances 1979* (Islamabad: National Commission on the Status of Women, 2003). On Justice Majida Rizvi, the first woman to be appointed as a judge of a higher court, see "Interview: Truth and Justice," *Dawn*, February 2, 2013.

113. *Report on Hudood Ordinances* (2003), 39.

114. For a discussion of the Hudood ordinances, the debate on it, the work of Justice Rizvi's committee, and the Protection of Women Act of 2006, see Khan, "Institutions not Intentions," chapter 5. For an earlier account of some of these matters, see Muhammad Qasim Zaman, "Pakistan: Shari`a and the State," in Robert W. Hefner, ed., *Shari`a Politics: Islamic Law and Society in the Modern World* (Bloomington: Indiana University Press, 2011), 220–26.

115. Ahmed Hassan, "NA Committee to Review Amended Draft," *Dawn*, September 16, 2006; cf. idem, "Govt Yields to MMA on Hudood Laws," ibid., September 12, 2006.

116. Others included Sarfaraz Naʿimi and Munib al-Rahman, both of whom belonged to the Barelawi orientation. See Ahmad Hassan, "Govt Yields to MMA on Hudood Laws," *Dawn*, September 12, 2006. Naʿimi was then the president of the Jamiʿa Naʿimiyya of Lahore; Munib al-Rahman was the president of the board of Barelawi madrasas as well as chairman of the Ruʾyat al-Hilal Committee, the official body that certifies the sighting of the moon in determining the beginning and the end of the month of Ramadan.

117. Muhammad Taqi ʿUsmani, *The Text of the Historic Judgment on Riba (Interest), Given by the Supreme Court of Pakistan, 23rd December 1999 ... Section Written by Maulana Justice Muhammad Taqi Usmani* (Petaling Jaya: Other Press, 2001).

118. "Usmani Monetary Interest Led to His Removal," *Dawn*, June 12, 2002.

119. Ibid.

120. For example, "Govt's Ulema Team," *Dawn*, September 10, 2006.

121. Amir Wasim, "MMA Rejects 'Agreed' Draft. Impasse on Hudood Bill Persists," *Dawn*, September 15, 2006.

122. Cf. Jahangir "What the Protection of Women Act Does," 5–6. For the full text of the act, see www.pakistani.org/legislation/2006/wpb.html (accessed April 21, 2010).

123. Raja Asghar, "Some Respite for Women, at Last: Protection of Rights Bill Gets through NA," *Dawn*, November 16, 2006.

124. Iftikhar A. Khan, "Musharraf Finds Kind Words for PPP," *Dawn*, November 16, 2006.

125. Ahmed Hassan, "MMA to 'Resign' in December," *Dawn*, November 17, 2006.

126. Muhammad Taqi ʿUsmani, *Amendments in Hudood Laws: The Protection of Women's Rights Bill—An Appraisal* (Islamabad: Institute of Policy Studies, 2006); idem, *Hudud qawanin: Mawjuda bahth awr aʾinda laʾiha-i ʿamal* (Islamabad: Institute of Policy Studies, 2006); idem, *Hudud qawanin main tarmim: Tahaffuz-i huquq-i niswan bill kiya hai? Aik mutalaʿa* (Islamabad: Institute of Policy Studies, 2006); idem, "The Real Contents," *Dawn*, December 24, 2006; idem, "The Reality of 'Women Protection Bills,'" at www.hudoodordinance.com (accessed October 29, 2007; the site is no longer available); idem, "Making Pakistan Safe for Rapists," at www.albalagh.net/women/0096.shtml (accessed October 29, 2007).

127. Taqi ʿUsmani, "Reality."

128. ʿUsmani, "Reality," citing Charles Kennedy, "The Status of Women in Pakistan," in Kennedy, *Islamization*, 74.

129. Taqi ʿUsmani, "Making Pakistan Safe for Rapists." This article draws on an essay by Taqi ʿUsmani in the Urdu language as well as on the text of an interview with him. It is not clear if he chose its title himself. But given that it appears on a website associated with his madrasa and in view of his knowledge of the English language, it seems reasonable to assume, at the very least, his approval of how the article was titled.

130. Taqi ʿUsmani, "Making Pakistan Safe for Rapists"; cf. Cheema and Mustafa, "From the Hudood Ordinances," 41–44.

131. "Interview: Truth and Justice."

132. Council of Islamic Ideology, *Hudood Ordinance 1979: A Critical Report* (Islamabad: Council of Islamic Ideology, 2007). Also see Muhammad Tufayl Hashimi, *Hudud Ordinance: Kitab o sunnat ki rawshani main* (N.p.: ʿAwrat Foundation, 2004).

133. On the membership of the committee, see *Report on the Hudood Ordinances* (2003), 2. On Taqi ʿUsmani's declining to be part of the committee's work, ibid., 2, 39, 108.

134. Nasir Iqbal, "CII Objects to Having Been Sidelined on Hudood Laws," *Dawn*, September 22, 2006.

135. Cf. Zaman, *The Ulama*, 78–83.

136. *Report of the Committee Set Up by the Governor of West Pakistan for Recommending Improved Syllabus for the Various Darul Ulooms and Arabic Madrasas in West Pakistan* (Lahore: Superintendent of Government Printing, 1962 [hereafter, *Report*, 1962]), appendix I, esp. p. xxiii.

137. Ibid., 14–23; quotation at 14.

138. Ibid., 14.

139. Ibid., 19.

140. Ibid., 25 and 1.

141. *Report qawmi committee barai dini madaris Pakistan* (Islamabad: Ministry of Religious Affairs, 1979), 65–77, esp. 66–67.

142. "Provinces Views on Madaris Ordinance Ignored," *News*, June 22, 2002.

143. "Wafaqul Madaris May Get Varsity Status," *Dawn*, February 23, 2005.

144. See Muhammad Qasim Zaman, "Pluralism, Democracy, and the `Ulama," in Robert W. Hefner, ed., *Remaking Muslim Politics* (Princeton, NJ: Princeton University Press, 2005), 80–81.

145. For the text of the National Action Plan, see http://nacta.gov.pk/NAPPoints20.htm (accessed June 11, 2017). On the Taliban's killing of the schoolchildren, see Ismail Khan, "Taliban Massacre 131 Schoolchildren," *Dawn*, December 17, 2014.

146. For Ludhianawi's critique, see *Bayyinat* (Karachi) 38/2 (January 1981): 2–28; also see *Bayyinat* 47/1 (1985): 35–63. For a summary of its contents, see Zaman, *The Ulama*, 78–81.

147. *Bayyinat* 38/2 (January 1981): 12–13; quoted in Zaman, *The Ulama*, 79.

148. *Bayyinat* 38/2 (January 1981), 16; Zaman, *The Ulama*, 79.

149. *Bayyinat* 38/2 (January 1981), 27; Zaman, *The Ulama*, 79.

150. Kashif Abbasi, "Five Seminary Boards to Adopt FBISE Syllabus," *Dawn*, July 14, 2016.

151. See the statement by the head of the madrasa board alliance in ibid.

152. Mukhtar Allah Haqqani, *Fatawa Haqqaniyya*, 6 vols. (Akora Khattak: Jami`a Dar al-`Ulum Haqqaniyya, 2002), 1: 124–25.

153. "Mufti Shamzai Shot Dead near Jamia Binoria," *News*, May 31, 2004; Rahimullah Yusufzai, "A Swati Boy Who Became Mufti," ibid., May 31, 2004.

154. "Cleric, Trader and Activist Shot Dead in 'Sectarian Attacks' across City," *Dawn*, September 11, 2014.

155. Muhammad `Imran Ashraf `Usmani, *Shirkat wa muzarabat `asr-i hazir men* (Karachi: Idarat al-ma`arif, 2001); Muhammad Zubayr Ashraf `Usmani, *Jadid ma`ashi nizam men Islami qanun-i ijara* (Karachi: Idarat al-ma`arif, 2005). The former is Taqi `Usmani's son, the latter, his nephew.

156. Matthew J. Nelson, "Dealing with Difference: Religious Education and the Challenge of Democracy in Pakistan," *Modern Asian Studies* 43 (2009): 591–618, at 595.

157. See Khan, "Institutions not Intentions," 30–31, n. 44.

158. See chapter 1, note 151.

159. Abdul Hakim, *Islamic Ideology*, xxiv.

160. This finding is based on a survey carried out by Nelson between 2003 and 2005, in which he interviewed nearly 800 people, mostly urban and educated, from across Pakistan regarding schooling preferences for their children. See Nelson, "Dealing with Difference," 594, 600–613.

161. In 2004–5, the Jama`at-i Islami had 454 madrasas, with 2,749 teachers and a reported enrollment of 52,774. See Pervez A. Shami and Imtiaz Khan, *Report on Deeni Madaris of Pakistan: Base-line Information, 2003–2004 and 2004–2005* (Islamabad:

Academy of Education Planning and Management, Ministry of Education, Government of Pakistan, 2006), 20.

162. Muhammad Khan Qadiri and Muhammad Siddiq Qamar, *Tahrik-i minhaj al-Qur'an awr a'inda qiyadat* (Lahore: Idara-i minhaj al-Qur'an, 1988), 26. For the other goals and achievements of the movement, see ibid., 24–33.

163. On this movement, see Sadaf Ahmad, *Transforming Faith: The Story of al-Huda and Islamic Revivalism among Urban Pakistani Women* (Syracuse, NY: Syracuse University Press, 2009). On its presentation of Islam as modern and rational, ibid., 71–77. Also see the important study by Faiza Mushtaq, "New Claimants to Religious Authority: A Movement for Women's Islamic Education, Moral Reform and Innovative Traditionalism," PhD dissertation, Department of Sociology, Northwestern University, 2010.

164. See Mushtaq, "New Claimants," chapter 6.

165. For a discussion of the `ulama's criticism of Hashmi and al-Huda, see ibid., chapter 4. Also see Muhammad Taqi `Usmani, *Fatawa-i `Usmani*, ed. Muhammad Zubayr Haqq Nawaz, 3 vols. (Karachi: Maktaba-i ma`arif al-Qur'an, 2006–12), 1: 86–90.

166. The characterization is Mushtaq's: "New Claimants."

167. *Report*, 1962, 4.

168. "Bring Students into Mainstream, Madaris Told," *News*, January 1, 2005.

169. *Pakistan Education Statistics, 2013-2014* (Islamabad: Ministry of Federal Education and Professional Training, 2015), 42, at www.aepam.edu.pk/Files/EducationStatistics/PakistanEducationStatistics2013-14.pdf (accessed June 23, 2015).

170. Ibid., 75; Kashif Abbasi, "New Report Reveals One-tenth of All Children Enrolled in Madressahs," *Dawn*, April 22, 2015.

171. *Pakistan Education Statistics, 2013-2014*, 75. The primary school student numbers grew from 17,567,581 in 2011–12 to 17,869,859 in 2013–14. The number of high school students declined during those years from 2,691,595 to 2,318,840. The number of madrasa students increased during this period from 1,759,141 to 1,836,143. Ibid., 75. Also see Abbasi, "New Report."

172. International Crisis Group, *Education Reform in Pakistan* (Brussels: International Crisis Group, 2014), 14.

173. The statement went on to claim that the number of students enrolled with madrasas had grown by 40 percent during 2008–9. See Khawar Ghumman, "Enrolment in Seminaries Rises by 40pc," *Dawn*, October 28, 2009. This dramatic assertion remains unverified.

174. On the collection and disbursement of zakat under Zia al-Haqq, see Jamal Malik, *Colonialization of Islam: Dissolution of Traditional Institutions in Pakistan* (Delhi: Manohar, 1996), 85–119; on their proceeds going to madrasas, ibid., 143–53. Of the more than 2,500 madrasas that existed in the Punjab ca. 1995, about 800 were reportedly recipients of zakat funds from the government. See "Punjab ke dini madaris: Zakat fund se kis ko kitna milta hai?" *Zindagi* (Lahore), February 17–23, 1995, 38.

175. Malik, *Colonialization*, 206–7.

176. Rashid, *Taliban*, 90–92.

177. 3 (3)-PMS/48: Correspondence with the Hon'ble Minister for Finance, 145–49, at 147–48 (NDC). The memo was prepared by one Abdul Matin Chaudhry. In forwarding it to the prime minister, the finance minister had signaled his concurrence with its contents.

178. Ibid., 149.

179. Khwaja Shahabuddin, minister of the interior, to the premiers of North-West Frontier, East Punjab, Sind et al., March 24, 1949. 108/CF/48–1888: Minutes, cabinet meetings (NDC).

180. Gilles Kepel, *Jihad: The Trail of Political Islam* (Cambridge, MA: Harvard University Press, 2002), 64–65.

181. Kalbe Ali, "Seminaries Boom in Absence of Govt Checks," *Dawn*, April 29, 2016, quoting Mufti Munib al-Rahman, the head of the five-board madrasa consortium.

182. Kepel, *Jihad*, 384, citing Ian Skeet, *OPEC: Twenty-Five Years of Prices and Politics* (Cambridge, UK: Cambridge University Press, 1988), 240–44.

183. See chapter 2, notes 133 and 146. Also see Zulfikar Ali Bhutto to Edward Heath, the British prime minister, January 25, 1974, FCO 37/1504: Second Islamic Summit Conference, Lahore, 20–24 February 1974: 7–8 (TNA; Electronic Resource).

184. Omar Noman, "The Impact of Migration on Pakistan's Economy and Society," in H. Donnan and P. Werbner, eds., *Economy and Culture in Pakistan: Migrants and Cities in a Muslim Society* (London: Macmillan, 1991), 83.

185. Ibid., 90.

186. See, for instance, Court of Inquiry Proceedings, 3: 86, 108, 111, 191, 270, 282–83.

187. Hints of changing religious attitudes as a possible effect of work in the Arab Middle East have continued to occasionally come to light. Tashfeen Malik, who, together with her US-born husband, was involved in a deadly shooting rampage in San Bernardino, California, in December 2015, had grown up in Saudi Arabia, where her father had moved with his family a quarter century earlier. The father had once been a mail carrier in southern Punjab. As his brother was reported to have observed, he was "a normal Barelvi Muslim, but might have taken interest in Salafi Islam in Saudi Arabia." Shakeel Ahmed and Fareedullah Chaudhry, "Tashfeen Malik Was Like Normal Students at BZU," *Dawn*, December 8, 2015. Also see Declan Walsh, "In Conservative Pakistani City, a 'Saudi Girl' Who Stood Out," *New York Times*, December 7, 2015. Incidentally, Malik had also been briefly associated with al-Huda, the aforementioned women's piety movement, though that does not appear to have had any direct bearing on her radical views.

188. Zia al-Haqq had come to power in July 1977. The last results of the survey conducted by the reform committee were received in May 1979 (*Report*, 1979, 14). There was clearly not enough time for the madrasas to grow so dramatically in less than two years.

189. See Abu `Ammar Zahid al-Rashidi, "Dini madaris ke nisab o nizam main islah ki zarurat," *al-Shari`a* 22/1 (January 2013): 6. On the attempted takeover of the madrasa, also see Mufti Mahmud's speech in the National Assembly, *NAPD* 5/16 (June 17, 1976): 486.

190. Jonathan Addleton, *Undermining the Centre: The Gulf Migration and Pakistan* (Karachi: Oxford University Press, 1992), 88–98.

191. See *Fihrist-i madaris-i mulhiqa-i tanzim al-madaris (Ahl-i sunnat) Pakistan* (Lahore: Markazi daftar tanzim al-madaris Pakistan, 1990), 3.

192. Ali, "Seminaries Boom."

193. Finance minister Ghulam Muhammad to the prime minister, Liaquat Ali Khan, December 16, 1949, 3 (1)-PMS/49: Correspondence with Hon'ble Minister for Finance (NDC).

194. Mahmud Hasan, trans., *al-Qur'an al-karim wa tarjamat ma`anihi wa tafsiruhu ilal-lugha al-Urdiyya* (Medina: Majma` khadim al-haramayn al-sharifayn al-malik Fahd li-tiba`at al-mushaf al-sharif, 1993). This new edition was published for free distribution in association with the Saudi-sponsored Muslim World League.

195. Shabbir Ahmad `Usmani, *Tafsir-i `Usmani*, 2 vols. (Lahore: Maktaba-i Rahmaniyya, n.d.). The commentary was completed in 1932.

196. Muhammad Taqi `Usmani, *Hindustan ka taza safar* (Deoband: Dar al-kitab, 2010). For the text of his speeches, see Muhammad Taqi `Usmani, *Khutbat-i dawra-i Hind*, ed. Sa`adat Allah Khan Qasimi (Karachi: Maktaba-i ma`arif al-Qur'an, 2012).

197. Taqi `Usmani, *Hindustan*, 63.

198. Ibid., 11, 41, 56.

199. Ibid., 17–38.

200. Cf. ibid., 37, 60–61.

201. Ibid., 34, quoting the words of one Riyasat ʿAli Bijnori.

202. Middle Eastern businesses have continued to advertise in the monthly journal of Taqi ʿUsmani's madrasa. See, for instance, the advertisement of Pak-Qatar General Takaful, an Islamic insurance company, in *al-Balagh*, January 2016 (back matter).

203. See, for example, Taqi ʿUsmani, *Khutbat*, 46, 48, 50, 54, 56, 90–93, 103–6, 112, 196, 204, 227, 233–34, 297, 309, 318–19.

204. See Graham, "Traditionalism," especially 522.

205. *Khutbat*, 312. The lecture, delivered at a madrasa in Bangalore, is titled "Two Means of Guidance: The Book of God and the Men of God." Ibid., 305–20.

206. Ibid., 312–13, referring to Q 1.7.

Chapter Four. Islamism and the Sovereignty of God

1. The term "authority" is broad and evocative enough to serve as a convenient rendering of both Arabic terms here.

2. Marmaduke Pickthall, *The Meaning of the Glorious Koran: An Explanatory Translation* (New York: Alfred A. Knopf, 1930), 598 (rendering the title of Q 67 as "The Sovereignty"). The translation was dedicated to the Nizam.

3. Needless to say, Bodin and Hobbes had quite different conceptions of sovereignty, and both differed from other early modern theorists writing on this matter. For a brief survey, see Quentin Skinner, "The Sovereign State: A Genealogy," in Hent Kalmo and Quentin Skinner, eds., *Sovereignty in Fragments: The Past, Present and Future of a Contested Concept* (Cambridge, UK: Cambridge University Press, 2010), 26–46.

4. On the idea of the "Artificiall person," see Thomas Hobbes, *Leviathan*, ed. Richard Tuck (Cambridge, UK: Cambridge University Press, 1996), chapter 16, 111–15; Skinner, "The Sovereign State," 35–37.

5. The premodern exegetical tradition is of course vast, as is the corpus of the modern commentaries. The examples I adduce here are illustrative of some broad trends in this literature on the questions under consideration, though no such sample can claim to represent the full range of the relevant opinions.

6. Abu Jaʿfar Muhammad b. Jarir al-Tabari, *Jamiʿ al-bayan ʿan taʾwil ay al-Qurʾan*, 30 vols. (Cairo: Mustafa al-Babi al-Halabi, 1954–68), 3: 222; Abu ʿAbdallah Muhammad b. Ahmad al-Qurtubi, *al-Jamiʿ li-ahkam al-Qurʾan*, 20 vols. (Cairo: Dar al-katib al-ʿArabi, 1967), 4: 52, 54; Fakhr al-din al-Razi, *al-Tafsir al-kabir*, 32 vols. (Tehran, n.p., n.d.), 8: 4.

7. Tabari, *Jamiʿ*, 3: 222; Razi, *al-Tafsir*, 8: 5–6; Qurtubi, *al-Jamiʿ*, 4: 55; Ibn Kathir, *Tafsir al-Qurʾan al-ʿazim*, ed. Mustafa al-Sayyid Muhammad, Muhammad al-Sayyid Rashad, Muhammad Fadl al-ʿAjamawi, ʿAli Ahmad ʿAbd al-Baqi, and Hasan ʿAbbas Qutb, 15 vols. (Giza: Muʾassasat Qurtuba, 2000), 3: 42.

8. Qurtubi, *al-Jamiʿ*, 18: 206 (commentary on Q 67.1).

9. Ibn Kathir, *Tafsir*, 3: 42 (commentary on Q 3.26).

10. al-Husayn b. Masʿud al-Baghawi, *Tafsir al-Baghawi, Maʿalim al-tanzil*, ed. Muhammad ʿAbdallah al-Nimr et al., 8 vols. (Riyadh: Dar tayba, 1993), 2: 23.

11. Razi, *al-Tafsir*, 8: 7 (commentary on Q 3.26).

12. Ruzbihan al-Baqli, *Araʾis al-bayan*, ed. Ahmad Farid al-Mizyadi, 3 vols. (Beirut: Dar al-kutub al-ʿilmiyya, 2008), 1: 75.

13. Tabari, *Jami*`, 12: 220. Also see Sana Allah Panipati (d. 1810), *Tafsir-i mazhari*, trans. from Persian into Urdu by Sayyid `Abd al-Da'im al-Jalali, 6 vols. (Delhi: Nadwat al-musannifin, 1962), 6: 154.

14. Qurtubi, *al-Jami*`, 9: 192. Cf. ibid., 6: 439 (commenting on Q 6.57—where the phrase occurs again—he explained that God alone decides whether to delay or hasten punishment for the wrongdoers).

15. Tabari, *Jami*`, 13: 14; Qurtubi, *al-Jami*`, 9: 228.

16. Ibn Kathir, *Tafsir*, 8: 43 (commentary on Q 12.40).

17. Razi, *al-Tafsir*, 18: 175 (commentary on Q 12.67).

18. Razi, *al-Tafsir*, 8: 7–8 (commentary on Q 3.26). This was also the view of the proponents of the divine right of kings in English constitutional history. See Skinner, "The Sovereign State," 30 (citing Sir John Hayward, *An Answer to the First Part of a Certaine Conference, Concerning Succession* [1603]).

19. For the dictum and the gloss on it, see Sayf al-din al-Amidi, *al-Ihkam fi usul al-ahkam*, 2 vols. (Cairo: Matba`at Muhammad `Ali Subayh, 1929), 1: 41; quoted in Urdu translation in Sayyid Sulayman Nadwi, "Hakim-i haqiqi sirf Allah ta`ala hai," in idem, *Maqalat-i Sulayman*, ed. Shah Mu`in al-din Nadwi (A`zamgarh: Matba`-i ma`arif, 1971), 3: 366–88, at 381. Mawdudi also quoted Amidi, whom he took to say that "Allah is the Sovereign and no command is worthy of obedience except that which is given by Him." Sayyid Abul A`la Maududi, *The Islamic Law and Constitution*, trans. Khurshid Ahmad, 2nd ed. (Lahore: Islamic Publications, 1960), 275.

20. Muhibb Allah al-Bihari, *Musallam al-thubut*, 2 vols. (Cairo: al-Matba`a al-Husayniyya, n.d.), 1: 16–17. My translation is based on Sulayman Nadwi's in his "Hakim-i haqiqi," 383–84. The Ash`aris, Maturidis, and Mu`tazila are schools of theology.

21. Amir `Ali Malihabadi, *Tafsir mawahib al-Rahman*, 30 vols. (Lucknow: Nawal Kishore, 1926–31), 3: 146–51. (This Amir `Ali, an Ahl-i Hadith scholar, is not to be confused—as he is sometimes—with the modernist Syed Ameer Ali.) For some other examples, see Panipati, *Tafsir*, 2: 208–12; Shihab al-din al-Alusi, *Ruh al-ma`ani*, 30 vols. (Beirut: Dar ihya al-turath al-`Arabi, 1970), 3: 112–14; Siddiq Hasan Khan (d. 1890), *Fath al-bayan fi maqasid al-Qur'an*, ed. `Abdallah ibn Ibrahim al-Ansari, 15 vols. (Beirut: al-Maktaba al-`asriyya, 1992), 2: 211.

22. Muhammad Rashid Rida, *Tafsir al-Qur'an al-hakim, al-shahir bi-Tafsir al-manar*, 12 vols., 3rd ed. (Cairo: Dar al-manar, 1947–54), 3: 270 (commenting on Q 3.26).

23. Ibid., 270–71.

24. Ibid., 270; cf. ibid., 271. Rida here follows his mentor, the modernist scholar Muhammad `Abduh, whose influence pervades this commentary.

25. Ibid., 271, again following `Abduh.

26. Olivier Carré, *Mysticism and Politics: A Critical Reading of Fi Zilal al-Qur'an by Sayyid Qutb (1906–1966)*, trans. Carol Artigues (Leiden: Brill, 2003), 202.

27. A noteworthy earlier discussion of the idea of the sovereignty of God in the context of Pakistani constitutional debates is Manzooruddin Ahmed, *Pakistan: The Emerging Islamic State* (Karachi: Allies Book Corporation, 1966). This book is based on the author's PhD dissertation, "The Concept of Divine Sovereignty in Pakistan," Columbia University, Department of Political Science, 1960. The study, written from a Muslim liberal perspective, is useful in showing how the idea of divine sovereignty figured in the early constitutional history of Pakistan, but it does not do much toward putting the development of this idea in an historical context. Instead, it examines it as a way of showing how Pakistan's first constitution, of 1956, "was successful in bringing about the synthesis between Islamic principles and the Western institutions" (Ahmed, *Pakistan*, 244). For other discussions

of divine sovereignty, see Mahmud Ahmad Ghazi, "Islam ke siyasi nizam main iqtidar-i a`la ka tasawwur," *al-Balagh* (Karachi), 5/10 (December 1971): 21–28; Carré, *Mysticism,* esp. 192–94; Sayed Khatab, *The Power of Sovereignty: The Political and Ideological Philosophy of Sayyid Qutb* (London: Routledge, 2006), esp. 7–46; Andrew F. March, "Genealogies of Sovereignty in Islamic Political Theology," *Social Research* 80 (2013): 293–321; and Jan-Peter Hartung, *A System of Life: Mawdudi and the Ideologisation of Islam* (New York: Oxford University Press, 2014), 100–110, 205–9.

28. Sayyid Qutb, *Fi zilal al-Qur'an,* 6 vols. (Beirut: Dar al-shuruq, 1974), 4: 1990 (commentary on Q 12.40). On his sense of the significance of this passage, see ibid., 1989, 1991.

29. Though of relatively recent coinage, the term *hakimiyet* was in use in the sense of sovereignty in the late Ottoman and early Republican Turkish circles in the late nineteenth and the early twentieth centuries. See Banu Turnaoğlu, *The Formation of Turkish Republicanism* (Princeton, NJ: Princeton University Press, 2017), 73–74, 229–30

30. See *al-Manar* (Cairo), 7 (1904): 577–80; reprinted in Rida, *Tafsir al-manar,* 6: 405–9 (commenting on Q 5.44–47). The request for the fatwa had come from Mawlawi Nur al-din of the Punjab, whom I take to be the person leading the Ahmadi community after the death of its founder, Mirza Ghulam Ahmad (d. 1908). On Nur al-din (d. 1914), see Friedmann, *Prophecy Continuous,* 13–14.

31. Cf. Qutb, *Zilal,* 2: 898 (commenting on Q 5.44).

32. For instance, Binder, *Islamic Liberalism,* 174–77; Carré, *Mysticism,* 25; Hartung, *A System of Life,* 100–105, 205–9. Also see Hasan al-Hudaybi, *Du`at la qudat* (Cairo: Dar al-tiba`a wal-nashr al-Islamiyya, n.d. [1977]), 16–19, 63–65, 72–73. Putatively written by the leader of the Egyptian Muslim Brotherhood (1951–73), this work is highly critical of Qutb (who is not mentioned by name), though rather less so of Mawdudi, who *is* mentioned and some of whose ideas Hudaybi takes to have been misinterpreted by others (ibid., 72–73). On Hudaybi and this work, see Barbara Zollner, *The Muslim Brotherhood: Hasan al-Hudaybi and Ideology* (London: Routledge, 2009).

33. Mawdudi, *Islam ka nazariyya-i siyasi,* 22–23. In his translation of the Qur'an and the commentary on it, Mawdudi renders the relevant part of Q 12.40 as follows: "The authority of rulership (*farmanrawa'i ka iqtidar*) belongs to none other than God." He does not however use the term *hakimiyyat* in discussing this verse. See Sayyid Abul-A`la Mawdudi, *Tafhim al-Qur'an,* vol. 2, 2nd ed. (Lahore: Maktaba-i ta`mir-i insaniyyat, 1958), 402–4.

34. Abul-A`la Mawdudi, *Qur'an ki char bunyadi istilahen* (Delhi: Markazi maktaba-i Jama`at-i Islami,1981; first published in 1941), 20.

35. Ibid., 27.

36. Ibid., 28.

37. Ibid., 28.

38. Ibid., 28–29. Mawdudi evoked the Qur'anic phrase *malik al-mulk* (Q 3.26) often in his discourses. It also occurs in the constitution of the Jama`at-i Islami. For the original version, see "Dustur-i Jama`at-i Islami," in Mawdudi, *Musalman awr mawjuda siyasi kashmakash* (Pathankot: Maktaba-i Jama`at-i Islami, n.d.), 3: 208–20, at 209. For a later iteration of the constitution, see *Dustur-i Jama`at-i Islami Pakistan* (Lahore: Markazi maktaba-i Jama`at-i Islami Pakistan, 1952), 11 (article 3).

39. Ali Suavi, "al-Hakim huwa Allah," *Ulum Gazetesi,* Rebiülahir 1286/August 1, 1869, 18–31. I am grateful to M. Şükrü Hanioğlu for drawing my attention to this article and for translating portions of it for me. On Suavi, see Şerif Mardin, *The Genesis of Young Ottoman Thought: A Study in the Modernization of Turkish Political Ideas* (Princeton, NJ: Princeton University Press, 1962), 360–84; on the question of sovereignty, ibid., 366–67, 373–74. See also Turnaoğlu, *Formation of Turkish Republicanism,* 73–79.

40. Suavi refers, inter alia, to Muhammad A`la ibn `Ali al-Tahanawi's (fl. 1745) ency-clopedic work on the meaning of theological, juridical, and other technical terms. For the relevant passage, see al-Tahanawi, *Mawsu`at istilahat al-`ulum al-Islamiyya*, 6 vols. (Beirut: Khayyat, 1966), 2: 380, s.v. "al-hakim."

41. "Inil-hukm illa lillah," *al-Hilal* (July 1, 1913), 5–8, at 7.

42. Ibid., 7.

43. See *Qur'an-i majid mutarjam bil-tarajim al-thalath* (Delhi: al-Matba` al-Mujtaba'i, 1872), 263.

44. Nazir Ahmad, *Chiragh-i hidayat*, ed. Muhammad Isma`il Afzal (Lahore: Shaykh Ghulam `Ali, n.d.), 288; idem, *Matalib al-Qur'an* (Lucknow: Nazir Press, n.d.), 130.

45. John Richardson, *A Dictionary of Persian, Arabic and English* (London: William Bulmer, 1806), 379–80. The work was first published in 1777.

46. In his Persian translation of the Qur'an, Wali Allah had rendered *al-hukm* in Q 12.40 as *farmanrawa'i. Qur'an-i majid mutarjam bil-tarajim al-thalath*, 263. The 1829 edition of Richardson's *Dictionary* translates a cognate term, *farmanguzari*, as sover-eignty (and empire). *A Dictionary of Persian, Arabic and English* (London: Parbury, Allen & Co., 1829), 1084. That Persian term does not occur in the 1806 edition.

47. Powell, *Scottish Orientalists and India*, 277, n. 101. Also see ibid., 230–31.

48. Mohamed Ali, *My Life: A Fragment*, ed. Afzal Iqbal (Lahore: Shaikh Muhammad Ashraf, 1946), 108.

49. Ibid., 205.

50. Maulana Muhammad Ali, *The Holy Qur'an: Arabic Text, English Translation and Commentary* (Lahore: Ahmadiyyah Anjuman Isha`at Islam, 1973), 136 and n. 406.

51. Ibid., 1079–80. Also see his preface to this chapter (ibid., 1079) and n. 2526.

52. Mohamed Ali, *My Life*, 165–69.

53. Ibid., 168–69; quotation at 168.

54. H. G. Wells, *Mr. Britling Sees It Through* (New York: Macmillan, 1916), 439, 442. The words in quotation marks are from a letter Mr. Britling was trying to write to the fa-ther of the slain German youth. Part of this text is also quoted in Mohamed Ali, *My Life*, 149.

55. H. G. Wells, *God the Invisible King* (New York: Macmillan, 1917), xiii. This, too, was a book Muhammad `Ali had read during his confinement, along with Wells's *The Soul of a Bishop* (1917). See Mohamed Ali, *My Life*, 148–53.

56. Mohamed Ali, *My Life*, 153.

57. Minault, *The Khilafat Movement*, 139–40, 169–72.

58. For the full proceedings of the two trials, see R. V. Thadani, ed., *The Historic State Trial of the Ali Brothers and Five Others* (Karachi: R. V. Thadani, 1921). For a contem-porary Urdu version of Muhammad `Ali's statement at the city magistrate's court, see *Bayan-i Mawlana Muhammad `Ali sahib . . . jo ra'is al-ahrar Mawlana Muhammad `Ali sahib . . . ne Karachi ke magistrate ki `adalat main diya*, compiled by Munshi Mushtaq Ahmad (Delhi: Swaraj Printing Works, 1921). For brief comments on this trial, see Mi-nault, *Khilafat Movement*, 172–74.

59. Thadani, ed., *Historic State Trial*, 69–70. In the Urdu version of the statement, it is the term *shahanshahi* ("monarchy") that is used for what the original English version characterizes as "sovereignty." See Muhammad `Ali, *Bayan*, 11. The translator of the Urdu version is not specified. It may have been the compiler, Munshi Mushtaq Ahmad.

60. For his part, Maulana Muhammad Ali had translated the key sentence as "Judg-ment is only Allah's." The Qur'anic quotations in the Urdu version of the statement given at the city magistrate's court seem to be based on Nazir Ahmad's translation, though they depart from it in some ways. Cf. Muhammad `Ali, *Bayan*, 11.

61. Thadani, ed., *Historic State Trial*, 283.

62. Ibid., 314–15.

63. Ibid., 324, citing Matthew 6.10. The "k" in king George is in lowercase in the original. The reference is to King George V (r. 1910–36).

64. On the proposed title of the book, see the introduction by Afzal Iqbal to Mohamed Ali, *My Life*, vii–viii. A section of that incomplete book was published by the editor under the title *My Life: A Fragment*. See ibid., viii–ix.

65. See Abul-A`la Mawdudi, "Khud niwisht," in Muhammad Yusuf Bhutta, ed., *Mawlana Mawdudi apni and dusron ki nazar main*, 2nd ed. (Lahore: Idara-i ma`arif-i Islami, 1984), 23–39, at 32–35. This is a brief autobiographical essay that Mawdudi had written in 1932.

66. Ibid., 32–33.

67. Ibid., 33.

68. Cf. Maududi, *Islamic Law and Constitution*, 233: "the acceptance and admission of the *de jure* sovereignty of God is *Islam* and its denial is *Kufr*" (unbelief; italics in the original).

69. See John Calvin, *Institutes of the Christian Religion* in *John Calvin: Works and Correspondence* (Charlottesville, VA: InteLex Corporation, 1995), electronic edition, note 1 to book 1, chapter 13, at http://libwebprod.princeton.edu/resolve/lookup?url=http://pm.nlx.com/xtf/view?docId=calvin/calvin.01.xml (accessed March 23, 2014).

70. Mawdudi, *Tahrik-i azadi-i Hind awr Musalman*, vol. 2, 2nd ed. (Lahore: Islamic Publications, 1973): 190–99, at 191–92. Cf. idem, *Tafhim al-Qur'an*, 6 vols. (Lahore: Idara-i tarjuman al-Qur'an, 2008), 1: 254–55, n. 48 (commenting on Q 3.51). Qutb, too, spoke of the Kingdom of God (*mamlakat Allah*), though without invoking the Bible. See *Zilal*, 3: 1433–34 (introduction to Q 8).

71. Thadani, ed., *Historic State Trial*, 283. For Mawdudi's insistence that God alone is the source of law, see *Islam ka nazariyya-i siyasi*, 21–24.

72. This language appears, for instance, in a letter the Prophet Muhammad is said to have written to the Christians of Najran. See Ahmad b. Abi Ya`qub al-Ya`qubi, *Ta'rikh*, ed. M. T. Houtsma, 2 vols. (Leiden: Brill, 1883), 2: 89. Quoted in Michael Cook, "Is Political Freedom an Islamic Value?" in Quentin Skinner and Martin van Gelderen, eds., *Freedom and the Construction of Europe*, 2 vols. (Cambridge, UK: Cambridge University Press, 2013), 2: 289–90, n. 26. The letter also has Muhammad call the Christians "to the authority (*wilaya*) of God and away from that of [His] slaves." Ya`qubi, *Ta'rikh*, 2: 89.

73. Mawdudi, "Pakistan main Islami qanun kyun nahin nafidh ho-sakta?" in idem, *Tahrik-i azadi-i Hind*, 2: 335–64, at 360. This was a speech Mawdudi had delivered at the Lahore Law College in January 1948. For an English translation, see Maududi, *Islamic Law and Constitution*, 39–72, at 67.

74. For a cautious discussion of the relationship of Iqbal and Mawdudi, see Seyyed Vali Reza Nasr, *Mawdudi and the Making of Islamic Revivalism* (New York: Oxford University Press, 1996), 34–39.

75. Mawdudi, *Islam ka nazariyya-i siyasi*, 38–39; Cook, "Political Freedom," 302.

76. Mawdudi, *Islam ka nazariyya-i siyasi*, 38.

77. Iqbal, *Asrar-i khudi*, in *Kulliyyat-i Iqbal* (Persian), 44–46; R. A. Nicholson, trans., *The Secrets of the Self (Asrar-i-Khudi): A Philosophical Poem* (Lahore: Sh. Muhammad Ashraf, 1944), 78–84.

78. Mohammad Iqbal, "Muslim Democracy," *The New Age* (1916), 251, quoted in Nicholson, "Introduction," *Secrets of the Self*, xxix n. 1.

79. Iqbal did, however, speak of "the Kingdom of God on earth," which, as he explained in a letter to R. A. Nicholson, "means the democracy of more or less unique individuals,

presided over by the most unique individual possible on this earth." Nicholson, "Introduction," *Secrets of the Self*, xxviii–xxix. Compare Mawdudi, *Islam ka nazariyya-i siyasi*, 43–44: "The position of the imam, amir, or head of the government in an Islamic state consists in this alone: that ordinary Muslims, to whom the caliphate belongs, choose the best amongst them and entrust the powers [of their caliphate] to him. That the term caliph is used for him does not mean that he alone is the caliph; it means rather that the caliphate of ordinary Muslims has become concentrated in his person." (The term "concentrate[d]" is Mawdudi's own.)

80. Sayyid Abul-A`la Mawdudi, *Dawlat-i Asafiyya awr hukumat-i Britaniyya ke siyasi ta`alluqat ki ta'rikh par aik nazar* (Haydarabad: N.p., 1928).

81. For a study of Hyderabad's "minor sovereignty" in a comparative framework, see Eric Lewis Beverley, *Hyderabad, British India, and the World: Muslim Networks and Minor Sovereignty, c. 1850–1950* (Cambridge, UK: Cambridge University Press, 2015). Beverley does not, however, discuss Mawdudi or his work. On the protest to the United Nations, see ibid., 54–56, 286–87.

82. Mawdudi, *Dawlat-i Asafiyya*, 3, paraphrasing, without disapproval, Sir John Malcolm's characterization of Hyderabad. Ibid., 188, quoting the Viceroy, Lord Reading, who had made clear to the Nizam that his "internal sovereignty" came from the British, to whom the likes of him were accountable in the final analysis. For the text of Reading's letter in Urdu translation, see ibid., 186–90.

83. Abul-Mahasin Sajjad, *Hukumat-i Ilahiyya*, ed. Mujahid al-Islam Qasimi (Phulwari Sharif: Imarat-i shar`iyya Bihar wa Orissa, 1999), 42–53.

84. Ibid., 134.

85. Wells, too, was anything but friendly to clerical authority, which makes it ironic that *Mr. Britling* was read at a school for chaplains during World War I. See David C. Smith, *H. G. Wells: Desperately Mortal* (New Haven, CT: Yale University Press, 1986), 224.

86. Hifz al-Rahman Seoharwi, "Muqaddima," in Sajjad, *Hukumat-i Ilahiyya*, 17–32, esp. 22–24, 26–30.

87. Seoharwi, "Muqaddima," 19–20.

88. Hifz al-Rahman Seoharwi, *Islam ka iqtisadi nizam* (Delhi: Nadwat al-musannifin, 1942), 110–11 and n. 1. For a discussion of Seoharwi and of this book, see Zaman, *Modern Islamic Thought*, 234–39.

89. Hifz al-Rahman Seoharwi, *Islam ka iqtisadi nizam* (Lahore: Mushtaq Book Corner, n.d.), 126 n. 1. This fourth and final edition of the book was published in 1951. As Seoharwi noted in his preface to this edition, it represented no change over the previous edition, which was published in 1946 (ibid., 17–18). The Kharijis refer to a religio-political orientation in early Islam whose most famous slogan, "There is no judgment other than God's," has become synonymous with anarchic challenges to constituted authority.

90. See Sayyid Abul-A`la Mawdudi, *Tahrik-i azadi-i Hind awr musalman* (Lahore: Islamic Publications, 1964), 1: 304–25.

91. *Dustur-i Jama`at-i Islami Pakistan* (Lahore: Markazi maktaba-i Jama`at-i Islami Pakistan, 1952), 11–12.

92. Ibid., 15.

93. S. M. Zauqi to M. A. Jinnah, January 12, 1940, *JP*, 3rd ser., 15: 41–45; quotations at 42–43.

94. On the life and career of Zauqi Shah, see Robert Rozehnal, *Islamic Sufism Unbound: Politics and Piety in Twenty-first Century Pakistan* (New York: Palgrave Macmillan, 2007), 46–59.

95. See Muhammad Zauqi Shah, "Tahrik-i Abul-A`la," in Wahid Bakhsh, ed., *Mazamin-i Zauqi* (Karachi: Mahfil-i zawqiyya, n.d.), 279–302; for a criticism of Mawdudi's

goal of establishing a "divine government" (*hukumat-i Ilahi*), see ibid., 292–94. For other direct and indirect criticism of Mawdudi, see ibid., 303–5. An English collection of Zauqi Shah's articles (see the following note) also bears the same title as the Urdu collection.

96. This correspondence is reproduced in Wahid Bakhsh, ed., *Mazamin-e-Zauqi* (English) (Karachi: J. G. Lennard and Co., 1948), 47–64. The letters are undated, but one of Zauqi Shah's letters gives December 26, 1932, as the date of his previous letter to Pickthall (ibid., 59).

97. Ibid., 61. Emphasis in the original.

98. Ibid., 63.

99. Ibid., 51.

100. Ibid., 61.

101. *CAPD*, 5/1 (March 7, 1949): 7.

102. See Rafi` `Usmani, *Hayat-i mufti-i a`zam*, 153–54, for a facsimile of what purports to be an early draft of the Objectives Resolution in the handwriting of Shabbir Ahmad `Usmani and with further annotations on it by Mufti Muhammad Shafi`.

103. Jama`at-i Islami, *Rudad-i Jama`at-i Islami*, 7 vols., 7th ed. (Lahore: Shu`ba-i nashr o isha`at, Jama`at-i Islami Pakistan, 1989), 6: 102–7.

104. Abdul Hakim, *Islamic Ideology*, 210.

105. Cf. ibid., 154.

106. Sulayman Nadwi, "Hakim-i haqiqi." The article was first published in *Ma`arif* (A`zamgarh), a monthly journal of which Sulayman Nadwi was the long-time editor.

107. Ibid., 386–87.

108. Ibid., 368.

109. Ibid., 387–88.

110. Syed Sulaiman Nadvi, *Sovereignty of Allah*, trans. Syed Abu Asim (Karachi: Maktabat al-sharq, 1953).

111. *Fundamental Principles of an Islamic State*, 3.

112. Muhammad Shafi`, *Dustur-i Qur'ani* (Karachi: Dar al-Ulum, 1953), 6, 12. Twelve thousand copies of this tract, in both Urdu and English, were distributed free of charge (see ibid., front matter).

113. Ghulam Ahmad Parwez, *Qur'an ka siyasi nizam* (Lahore: Idara-i tulu`-i Islam, n.d.), 37–38. This booklet is based on an article first published in Parwez's monthly, *Tulu`-i Islam*, in March 1960. My references here are to the booklet.

114. Ibid., 29.

115. Ibid., 34.

116. Ibid., 29; cf. 27.

117. Ibid., 31–34.

118. Ibid., 28.

119. For this metaphorical image, see ibid., 28.

120. Mawdudi, "Islam main qanun-sazi ka da'ira-i `amal," in idem, *Tafhimat*, 3 vols. (Lahore: Islamic Publications, 1965), 3: 7–14, at 7. This is the text of a paper Mawdudi had read at the International Islamic Colloquium, held in Lahore in December–January, 1957–58. Also see Mawdudi, *Tafhim al-Qur'an*, 2 (1958 ed.), 37 n. 41 (commenting on Q 7.54).

121. Rahman, "Implementation," 208–9. Emphasis in the original.

122. Ibid., 209.

123. Ibid., 209.

124. See, for instance, Mawdudi, "Majalis-i qanun-saz ki rukniyyat shar`i haythiyyat se," in idem, *Tahrik-i azadi-i Hind*, 2: 233–35 (this piece is dated December 1945).

125. Sayyid Abul-A`la Mawdudi, *Aik nihayat ahamm istifta* (Lahore: Maktaba-i Jama`at-i Islami, n.d.).

126. Ibid., 6, n. 1. For the quotation from the opening address of the advocate-general, see Moti Ram, ed., *Two Historic Trials in the Red Fort* (Delhi: n.p., n.d. [1946]), p. 19. On the Indian National Army and the movement associated with it, see Sugata Bose, *His Majesty's Opponent: Subhas Chandra Bose and India's Struggle against Empire* (Cambridge, MA: Harvard University Press, 2011). For an echo of Mawdudi's view in the work of an erstwhile associate, see Amin Ahsan Islahi, *Islami riyasat* (Lahore: Maktaba-i markazi anjuman-i khuddam al-Qur'an, 1977), 228.

127. Mawdudi, "Pakistan main Islami qanun," in idem, *Tahrik-i azadi-i Hind awr Musalman*, 2: 354–57.

128. Irfan Ahmad, *Islamism and Democracy in India: The Transformation of the Jamaat-e-Islami* (Princeton, NJ: Princeton University Press, 2009).

129. Nasr, *Vanguard*, 127–31.

130. M. Ikramullah, Ministry of Foreign Affairs and Commonwealth Relations, to Habib I. Rahimtoola, Pakistan's high commissioner in the UK, October 2, 1948. 26 (4)-PMS/48: Misc. Correspondence during HPM's Visit to the UK, vol. 3: 32 (NDC).

131. Resolutions passed at the March 17 and April 6–8, 1949, sessions of the consultative assembly in Jama`at-i Islami, *Rudad*, 6: 106–7. Also see Mawdudi, *Tahrik-i azadi-i Hind*, 2: 228 n. 1; Court of Inquiry Proceedings, part 2, 915–16 (statement by Amin Ahsan Islahi). Cf. Nasr, *Vanguard*, 124–25.

132. See Muhammad Sarwar, *Jama`at-i Islami awr Islami dustur* (Lahore: Sindh Sagar, 1956), 120–21, 128 (quoting Mawdudi's statement in support of the constitution).

133. For a hard-hitting criticism of Mawdudi and his Jama`at for their acceptance of the Objectives Resolution and the 1956 constitution, see ibid., esp. 38–138. Sarwar's concern in this book is not to show the inadequacy of these foundational documents, of course, but rather to argue that Mawdudi's acceptance of them was hypocritical. They represented not a victory for him but rather a humiliating defeat, Sarwar said, since many of his demands regarding the place of Islam in Pakistan's public life were rejected by the modernist framers of those documents.

134. Nasr, *Vanguard*, 162.

135. *Report of the Hamoodur Rehman Commission*, 289.

136. The question has received rather different assessments from observers of the Jama`at. See, for instance, Nasr, *Vanguard*, 40–41; Hartung, *System of Life*, 232.

137. Sayyid Abul-A`la Mawdudi, *Tahrik-i Islami ka a'inda la'iha-i `amal*, 3rd ed. (Lahore: Islamic Publications, 1966), 178–79. For a useful account of the crisis the Jama`at faced in 1957, see Nasr, *Vanguard*, 31–43.

138. Mawdudi, *Tahrik-i Islami*, 195. For the reference to the career of the Prophet Muhammad, see ibid., 194–95.

139. Ibid., 194.

140. What he did say in his famous 1957 speech was that the whole party could not be judged by the ethical lapses of some of its members, that the party's moral fiber was stronger than that of its competitors in the political arena, and that the right response to a corrupt political field was not to flee it but rather to enter it with the resolve to change things for the better. See Mawdudi, *Tahrik-i Islami*, 222–24; also 219–21 for Mawdudi's response to worries that the party would go "morally bankrupt" in the existing political arena. The point about the working of the shari`a is more unambiguously his. See Mawdudi, "Pakistan main Islami qanun," in idem, *Tahrik-i azadi-i Hind*, 2: 348–51; Maududi, *Islamic Law and Constitution*, 53–57.

141. See Sarwar, *Jama`at-i Islami*.

142. In an important study, Markus Daechsel has argued that the "discourse of development," as it found expression in the Pakistan of the 1950s and the 1960s, was a means for

a "sovereignty-obsessed" governing elite to put that sovereignty on display. Paradoxically, however, the imperatives of development, as understood by Western experts advising the government, were also in significant conflict with postcolonial aspirations to sovereignty, and this conflict remained unresolved. Daechsel, *Islamabad*. Mawdudi's sovereignty *of God* served, for its part, to simultaneously delegitimize the development discourse *and* postcolonial claims to sovereignty. Such challenges could not but be anathematic to the Ayub Khan regime.

143. Ishaq Nadwi, *Islam ka siyasi nizam*, 12–14 (God as *muqtadir-i aʿla*, which is glossed in English as "sovereign"). Mawdudi's influence is palpable on what Ishaq Nadwi said about God's sovereignty and on the "political polytheism" (*siyasi shirk*) involved in failing to recognize it (14–15). This work does not really count therefore as a case of the ʿulamaʾs *independent* articulation of such matters.

144. Muhammad Taqi ʿUsmani, *Islam awr siyasi nazariyyat* (Karachi: Maktaba-i maʿarif, 2010), 173–77. By this point, it was possible for Taqi ʿUsmani to straightforwardly translate *al-hukm* in Q 6.57 and 12.40 as sovereignty (*hakimiyyat*). Thus, his Urdu rendering of the relevant portion of these verses translates as "sovereignty belongs to God alone."

145. For the Urdu text (*asl hakim, tashriʿi awr takwini haysiyyat se*), see Muhammad Taqi ʿUsmani, *Nifaz-i shariʿat awr us-ke masaʾil* (Karachi: Maktaba-i Dar al-ʿUlum, 1992), 19. For the Arabic version ("al-hakim al-haqiqi . . ."), produced and published by the Jamaʿat-i Islami, see *al-Mabadi al-asasiyya lil-dawla al-Islamiyya* (Karachi: al-Jamaʿa al-Islamiyya, n. d.), 3.

146. For the Urdu version, see *Pakistan ka manshur-i azadi* (Karachi: Manager, Governor General Press, n.d. [1950]), unpaginated front matter. The difference between the connotations of the English and the Urdu versions was noted long ago by Smith, *Pakistan as an Islamic State*, 78–79.

147. In his *System of Life*, Hartung has provided the most detailed investigation so far of how some modern Western intellectual trends shaped Mawdudi's thought. He does not, however, explore the provenance of the sovereignty of God in that study.

148. Besides examples already noted (see note 33, earlier), see Mawdudi, *Tafhim al-Qurʾan*, 2 (1958 ed.): 37 n. 41 (commenting on Q 7.54).

149. I draw here on the account of the early activities of this office—the Dar al-ʿuruba lil-daʿwa al-Islamiyya—in Jamaʿat-i Islami, *Rudad*, 7: 163–78.

150. See William E. Shepard, *Sayyid Qutb and Islamic Activism: A Translation and Critical Analysis of Social Justice in Islam* (Leiden: E. J. Brill, 1996), xx, 8, 43, 105–6. On the various editions of this book, see ibid., 357.

151. For instance, see Khalil Ahmad Hamidi, *Tahrik-i Islami ke asarat* (Lahore: Mansura Book Center, 1976), 13.

152. Ghulam Ahmad Parwez to Ayub Khan, January 12, 1968 (GAPP).

153. Mawdudi, "Islam main qanun-sazi ka daʾira-i ʿamal," in idem, *Tafhimat*, 3: 7–14, at 7–8. Also published in *International Islamic Colloquium Papers, December 29, 1957–January 8, 1958* (Lahore: Punjab University Press, 1960), 21–28 (of the Urdu section of this volume). What may have irritated Parwez even more about Mawdudi's prominence at this event (he was on its organizing committee) is that a number of leading Western scholars of Islam were also in attendance at it. These included Alessandro Bausani, G. E. von Grunebaum, A.K.S. Lambton, Bernard Lewis, Louis Massignon, Steven Runciman, and W. C. Smith. Some among them may well have been sympathetic to Mawdudi's view of what the sovereignty of God meant in an Islamic context.

154. Mawdudi, "Islam main qanun-sazi," in idem, *Tafhimat*, 3: 9–14. Mawdudi had taken a similar position in his statement to the Court of Inquiry investigating the anti-Ahmadi riots of 1953. See *Report of the Court of Inquiry*, 211–12.

155. "Even if an ijtihad undertaken without the various precautions [that Mawdudi had elucidated] and according to one's capricious interpretations is given the force of law on the basis of political power, it would not be accepted by the collective conscience of Muslims. Nor can it properly become part of an Islamic legal system. The moment the political power that has enforced it leaves the scene, its law would be tossed into the trash bin." Mawdudi, *Tafhimat*, 3: 13–14.

156. Rahman, "Implementation," 208.

157. *CAPD*, 5/5 (March 12, 1949 [Zafrulla Khan]): 71.

158. Ibid., 65–72, especially 66.

159. Shabbir Ahmad `Usmani, *al-Shahab, ya`ni Mirza'iyyon ke irtidad ka thubut awr qatl-i murtadd ke shar`i dala'il* (Karachi: Dar al-isha`at, 1974); Friedmann, *Prophecy Continuous*, 29.

Chapter Five. Religious Minorities and the Anxieties of an Islamic Identity

1. See chapter 2, note 5.

2. Jawaharlal Nehru to B. C. Roy, April 4, 1950, in Jawaharlal Nehru, *Selected Works of Jawaharlal Nehru*, 2nd ser. (New Delhi: Jawaharlal Nehru Memorial Fund, 1984–), 14/1: 170–73, at 171.

3. The figures from the 1998 census are available at www.census.gov.pk/Religion.htm (accessed January 2, 2014). For the figures from the 2017 census, which were provisional and incomplete at the time of this writing, see Khaleeq Kiani, "Country's Population Surges to Nearly 208m," *Dawn*, August 26, 2017.

4. *Report of the Court of Inquiry*, 10. Cf. Court of Inquiry Proceedings, part 5: 2351 (Mirza Bashiruddin Mahmud Ahmad, the head of the Ahmadi community). Two decades later, in hearings at a closed session of the National Assembly, Mirza Nasir Ahmad, the then head of the Ahmadis, gave a significantly higher figure, 3.5 to 4 million, as the size of his community in Pakistan at that time. National Assembly of Pakistan, *Proceedings of the Special Committee of the Whole House Held in Camera to Consider the Qadiani Issue*, 21 parts, August 5–September 7, 1974 (Islamabad: National Book Foundation, n.d. [2011]), no. 1 August 5, 1974, 29, at http://archive.org/details/1974-na-committee-ahmadiyya (accessed October 8, 2013; hereafter, Proceedings of the Special Committee). Also see *Nawa-i waqt*, August 1, 1974.

5. On the size of the Shi`i population in Pakistan, see Andreas Rieck, *The Shias of Pakistan: An Assertive and Beleaguered Minority* (New York: Oxford University Press, 2015), xi. The best study to date on Shi`i religious thought in Pakistan is Fuchs, "Relocating the Centers." The question of the anxieties generated by the Shi`a among the Sunnis is not, however, among those Fuchs examines in his work. In an important study of religion and the state in Pakistan with reference to the Ahmadis, sociologist Sadia Saeed does address the question of "why the Ahmadiyya community provokes unique anxieties for political and religious actors in Pakistan," but the focus of her study is on the state rather than on the `ulama and the Islamists, as is the case in this chapter. See Sadia Saeed, *Politics of Desecularization: Law and the Minority Question in Pakistan* (Cambridge, UK: Cambridge University Press, 2016), quotation at 3.

6. Friedmann, *Prophecy Continuous*, 183; cf. Smith, *Modern Islam in India*, 65.

7. Unless otherwise indicated, my discussion here is primarily concerned with those who consider Mirza Ghulam Ahmad as a prophet. On Ahmadi doctrines, see Friedmann, *Prophecy Continuous*.

8. "Shamloo," ed., *Speeches and Statements*, 120–21 (responding to Jawaharlal Nehru's criticism of his anti-Ahmadi stance); ibid., 239 (castigating the nationalist views of Husayn Ahmad Madani and likening them to those of the Ahmadis).

9. Ibid., 94.

10. Ibid., 100.

11. Also see chapter 4, note 159 (with reference to Shabbir Ahmad `Usmani).

12. For the `ulama's testimony in this case, which was presided over by the district magistrate of the princely state of Bahawalpur (now in the Pakistani Punjab), see *Bayanat-i `ulama-i rabbani bar irtidad-i firqa-i qadiyyani* (Deoband: Maktaba-i rashad, 1989). The case was decided in favor of the plaintiff.

13. "Shamloo," ed., *Speeches and Statements*, 103.

14. Mohammad Iqbal, "The Doctrine of Absolute Unity as Expounded by Abdul Karim al-Jilani," *Indian Antiquary* (Bombay), 29 (1900), reprinted in Syed Abdul Vahid, ed., *Thoughts and Reflections of Iqbal* (Lahore: Sh. Muhammad Ashraf, 1964), 3–27, at 9. That this essay by Iqbal could still be reprinted in Pakistan in the 1960s is a telling indication that attitudes toward the Ahmadis were not uniformly hostile even by that late date.

15. "Kiya Mirza Ghulam Ahmad Sahib Qadiyyani ke pairaw kafir hain? Imam al-Hind Mawlana Abul-Kalam Azad ka fatwa," *Zamindar*, November 18, 1923. I am grateful to Rajarshi Ghose for drawing my attention to this fatwa.

16. Cf. Daryabadi, *Hakim al-ummat*, 260.

17. S. Zainulabadin to Liaquat Ali Khan, May 19, 1940, *JP*, 3rd ser., 15: 340. Zainulabadin was an office holder in an Ahmadi organization.

18. See Ayesha Jalal, *Self and Sovereignty: Individual and Community in South Asian Islam since 1850* (London: Routledge, 2000), 375, 442, 447. On Iqbal, ibid., 294–97, 364–69.

19. Jinnah to S. Zainulabadin, May 5, 1944, *JP*, 2nd ser., 10: 338–39. For the query to which this was a response, see Zainulabadin to Jinnah, April 30, 1944, ibid., 329. In an earlier meeting with Pir Akbar Ali, an Ahmadi member of the Punjab legislative assembly, Jinnah had told him that "according to the latest constitution of the All India Muslim League there was no bar to members of the Ahmadiyya community joining the Muslim League, and that as members of the League they would be entitled to such privileges as are enjoyed by members of other various sects of Muslims." See enclosure with Zainalabadin to Jinnah, April 30, 1944, *JP*, 2nd ser., 10: 329.

20. For overviews of this history, see Afzal, *Pakistan*, 64–70, 102–9; Binder, *Religion and Politics*, 183–296.

21. That there could be significant differences among the modernists in their attitude toward the `ulama is well illustrated by the case of Nazimuddin, who had wanted to go as far as he could in negotiating with them. His own brother, Khawaja Shahabuddin, the governor of the North-West Frontier Province at the time, was among those who had advocated crushing "Mullaism." To such suggestions, Nazimuddin had responded at one point by equating Islam and the `ulama's Islam in a manner quite uncharacteristic of other modernists. As summarized later by an observer, the prime minister had remarked at a cabinet meeting in late February 1953: "There were persons in this meeting who were for crushing mullaism and Peerism and, as a matter of fact, Islam itself [but] ... that he in all conscience could not be a party to this and that he would resign." Court of Inquiry Proceedings, Appendices, 132 (Chaudhry Muhammad Hussain). It is telling, however, that he did not resign, choosing instead to stand with his colleagues in government.

22. See the inspector-general of police's "Note on the Situation as it Developed from the 5th March 1953," Court of Inquiry Proceedings, 1: 223–24.

23. Ibid., 2: 110–11.

24. Ibid., 2: 285, 293.

25. See the statement by the deputy inspector-general of police, Punjab, in ibid., 1: 249 (7–8 of the statement).

26. Ibid., 216, 231; 2: 464.

27. Ibid., part 4: 1596; *Report of the Court of Inquiry*, 347.

28. The preacher in question was Muhammad Ishaq Mansehrawi (d. 1962). For his role in helping bring the agitation to an end in Rawalpindi, see Court of Inquiry Proceedings, 2: 488; cf. *Report of the Court of Inquiry*, 179. For a brief biographical sketch (which does not mention this role), see Fuyuz al-Rahman, *Mashahir `Ulama*, 3 vols. (Lahore: Frontier Publishing Company, n.d.), 2: 467–53. It was Zafar `Ali Khan, the proprietor and editor of the *Zamindar* and an influential poet and bête noire of the Ahmadis in colonial India, who in 1936 had characterized Mansehrawi's mosque as "the laborer's." See Zafar `Ali Khan, "Masjid-i angur, Rawalpindi," in idem, *Kulliyyat-i Mawlana Zafar `Ali Khan*, ed. Zahid `Ali Khan (Lahore: al-Faysal, 2011), 197 (in the collection titled *Nigaristan*). Also quoted in Fuyuz al-Rahman, *Mashahir*, 2: 653.

29. Court of Inquiry Proceedings, 1: 187.

30. Ibid., 1: 106. This may just have been by way of punishing anyone not cooperating with the effort to shut down the city, but it probably also had a class dimension to it.

31. The British high commissioner and the American ambassador in Karachi were unwilling to see Zafrulla Khan resign in the face of the pressure on him. Gilbert Laithwaite, the UK high commissioner, to Percivale Liesching, CRO, London, July 23, 1952. DO 35/3185. Also see the UK high commissioner's telegram to CRO, April 11, 1953, DO 35/5370: 65 (TNA). For his part, the prime minister had told a group of leading figures representing the anti-Ahmadi movement in January 1953 that "if he removed Ch. Muhammad Zafarullah Khan from the Cabinet, Pakistan would not get a grain of wheat from the United States of America." Court of Inquiry Proceedings, part 1: 132 (testimony by Abul Hasnat Muhammad Ahmad Qadri). In his own testimony, the former prime minister denied that he had "said anything of the kind. What I said to them was that the removal of . . . Zafarullah Khan would create difficulties for us in obtaining wheat quickly because even India had to face great difficulties in that behalf. . . . I was confident that ultimately we would get wheat from America whether or not . . . Zafrullah Khan remained as our Foreign Minister. We, however, wanted it urgently and a quick decision was necessary." Ibid., part 3: 1353.

32. Mandal resigned in September 1950. He had already left Pakistan for India, and his resignation was a cause of severe embarrassment to the government of Pakistan. On this episode and Mandal's vilification by some members of the government, see 3 (18)- PMS/50: Resignation of Mr. J. N. Mandal, Minister for Law and Labor, Government of Pakistan (NDC). Mandal's grievances had to do with the government's inattention to the plight of the scheduled castes in East Bengal. See Mandal to the Prime Minister, January 19, 1950, detailing instances of police brutality against the minority community. 3 (3)- PMS/50: Correspondence with Hon'ble Minister for Law and Labour (NDC).

33. Sayyid Abul A`la Mawdudi, *Qadiyyani mas'ala*, 2nd ed. (Lahore: Islamic Publications, 1963). The tract was first published on March 5, 1953, at the height of the anti-Ahmadi agitation. It was soon translated into English, Sindhi, and Bengali. Some months after the agitation had been extinguished, the superintendent of police, Lahore, told the Court of Inquiry that the Urdu version had been disseminated in 35,000 copies. Court of Inquiry Proceedings, 1: 364.

34. Court of Inquiry Proceedings, part 5: 2412.

35. *Report of the Court of Inquiry*, 75.

36. Muhammad Zafrulla Khan, *Islam: Its Meaning for Modern Man* (London: Routledge and Kegan Paul, 1962), 14. Also see his statement in response to a government directive, obliquely referring to him, that no federal or provincial minister "use his official

position in propagation [of] any sectarian creed." Court of Inquiry Proceedings, 1: 77–78. For the official communique, see ibid., 1: 76. Zafrulla Khan's response was published in *Dawn*, August 17, 1952.

37. Court of Inquiry Proceedings, part 3: 1405. Also see ibid., part 3: 1455–56.

38. In the early years of Pakistan, some Ahmadi bureaucrats were also suspected of using their office to proselytize. See Court of Inquiry Proceedings, part 3: 1283, 1294 (testimony of Sardar Abdur Rabb Nishtar, a former governor of the Punjab).

39. *CAPD*, 5/5 (March 12, 1949): 69.

40. A. K. Brohi, "Thoughts on the Future Constitution of Pakistan," *Dawn*, August 24, 1952 (italics mine). Brohi was not an Ahmadi. Cf. the response of Mian Mumtaz Daultana, the chief minister of the Punjab during the 1953 agitation, when asked by the Court of Inquiry about how he would have responded to the anti-Ahmadi demands if he were, as the court had put it, "the dictator of Pakistan." "If it depended entirely on my will, I would have done my best to see that these demands were not raised. The demands in themselves were not fundamental or immediately necessary in any way for Pakistan." Court of Inquiry Proceedings, part 6: 2691–92.

41. See, for instance, *CAPD*, 5/5 (March 12, 1949): 65–66, 68–69.

42. Ahmadi modernism, it is worth noting, has had its limits. Unlike other modernists, the Ahmadis have tended to defend polygyny rather than reinterpret the Qur'an in such a way as, in effect, to do away with this institution. See Friedmann, *Prophecy Continuous*, 184. Zafrulla Khan, too, had some very conservative views regarding veiling and women working outside the home. See Qurrat al-ʿAyn Haydar, *Kar-i jahan daraz hai*, 3 vols. (Delhi: Educational Publishing House, 2003), 2: 468, 537.

43. Cf. Mawdudi, *Qadiyyani masʾala*, 38–40. There were hints of this in government circles, too. In a wide-ranging "Scheme for Supervision and Control of Religious Institutions and Religious Activity," prepared by the Ministry of the Interior in 1960, it was noted that the Ahmadi community had established "an organization which copies institutions which are typical of a Government." 54/CF/60–2293: Administration of Mosques; Training of Imams; Scheme for Supervision and Control of Religious Institutions and Religious Activity; Employment of Itinerant Preachers; Streamlining of Auqaf Properties in East Pakistan: 33 (NDC).

44. *Report of the Court of Inquiry*, 47–48.

45. See *Nawa-i waqt*, May 14, 1974, and news reports for the days that followed.

46. See *Jang*, June 2, 1974.

47. *Nawa-i waqt*, May 31, 1974.

48. Ibid., May 19, 1974.

49. Ibid., May 23, 1974.

50. *Dawn*, May 19, 1974, and press coverage of this event on the following days.

51. See, for instance, *Nawa-i waqt*, May 30, 1974; *Dawn*, May 30, 1974.

52. Alan Mitchell, Commissioner, Lahore Division, to C. C. Garrett, Chief Secretary to Government of the Punjab, January 27, 1935, L/PJ/7/751: Ahrar-Ahmadiya Dispute at Qadian, Punjab: 206 (BL).

53. Ibid., 203.

54. Copy of D.O. Letter no. C16(1), S.B., from the Government of the Punjab to the Government of India, Home Department, January 21–23, 1935, L/PJ/7/751: 241 (BL).

55. Court of Inquiry Proceedings, part 3: 1367. On Ahmadi provocations, see also the statement of Fida Hassan, the commissioner of Rawalpindi division, ibid., 2: 376–77.

56. *Nawa-i waqt*, May 31, 1974; June 1, 1974; June 15, 1974; August 17, 1974.

57. Justice Samdani later complained about this: "The government should know that it is wrong not to publish the report of an enquiry ordered for the benefit of the public. At

the same time it is also interesting to note that there was no demand from the public, either, that the report be published." K.M.A. Samdani, *Reminiscence* (N.p., n.d. [ca. 2005]), 90.

58. See the statement by the head of the Ahmadi community before the Samdani commission: *Nawa-i waqt*, August 1, 1974. Cf. ibid., July 16, 1974.

59. For the text of this resolution, see *Proceedings of the Special Committee*, no. 15 (August 30, 1974), 1971–74. Earlier, in spring 1973, the legislative assembly of Pakistani ("Azad") Kashmir had called for the Ahmadis to be declared non-Muslims, thereby helping bring the issue back into the limelight and putting some pressure on the Bhutto government. See Muhammad Taqi `Usmani, "Qadiyani—ghayr Muslim kiyon?" *al-Balagh* 7/5 (July 1973): 3–11.

60. Laurence Pumphrey, "The Ahmadiya Issue," dated September 24, 1974 (p. 3 of the note). FCO 37/1501: Issue of Atrocities Committed against Ahmadiyya Muslim Community in Pakistan (TNA; Electronic Resource). Ahmadi contributions to Bhutto's election campaign are mentioned in the confidential note by A. A. Halliday, British Embassy Islamabad, February 15, 1973. Ibid., 28.

61. Demands to have the Ahmadis removed from key positions followed the Rabwah incident almost immediately. See, for instance, *Nawa-i waqt*, May 31, 1974; ibid., June 15, 1974; ibid., June 18, 1974; *Jang*, June 22, 1974.

62. On the Ahmadis' alleged military ambitions, see also *Nawa-i waqt*, June 22, 1974. For other statements to this effect, see ibid., June 25, 1974.

63. Ibid., June 28, 1974.

64. Ibid., June 18, 1974. The leader of the Ahmadi community was also questioned about the Ahmadi mission in Israel during the in-camera session of the National Assembly. See *Proceedings of the Special Committee*, no. 8 (August 21, 1974), 1007–15. Also see ibid., no. 15 (August 30, 1974), 2048–56.

65. *Jang*, June 28, 1974.

66. *Nawa-i waqt*, July 11, 1974.

67. See Vazira Zamindar, *The Long Partition and the Making of Modern South Asia* (New York: Columbia University Press, 2007).

68. For these advertisements, see *Jang*, July 5, 7, 8, 1974; ibid., July 8, 1974, for a defense on Bannuri's behalf. Also see *Dawn*, July 4, 6, 8, 1974. The idea that religious conflicts in Pakistan are stoked by outsiders has had its purchase in the highest circles of government, too. For instance, in 1963, following Shi`i-Sunni riots in Muharram, Ayub Khan had ordered an investigation into whether `ulama and Shi`i preachers visiting Pakistan from India had been involved. No evidence of their involvement was found. "Note for the President," by Habibullah Khan, Minister of Home and Kashmir Affairs, March 15, 1965, in 390/CF/63: Shia-Sunni Incidents; Influence of Religious Leaders from India (NDC).

69. *Nawa-i waqt*, July 11, 1974.

70. *Jang*, June 1, 1974 (speech by Kausar Niazi, the minister of information and of religious endowments).

71. *Nawa-i waqt*, June 27, 1974.

72. *Jang*, August 27, 1974. Mir also took the opportunity in this statement to deny that he was an Ahmadi.

73. That the Bhutto era would prove to be a time of considerable growth for religious institutions is ironic in hindsight, but fostering such growth was no part of government policy and it was, in any case, not perceptible to most people living through those years.

74. *Jang*, June 20, 1974; *Nawa-i waqt*, July 18, 1974.

75. *Nawa-i waqt*, July 11, 1974.

76. Ibid., June 26, 1974.

77. Ibid., June 29, 1974. Also see ibid., July 4, 1974; *Jang*, June 30, 1974.

78. Muhammad Manzur Nu`mani to Shabbir Ahmad `Usmani, November 26, 1945, in Sherkoti, ed., *Anwar*, 149–51.

79. It was only in late 2011 that the proceedings of this in-camera session were quietly released to the public. The proceedings comprise a little over 3,000 pages in print.

80. For the text of this ordinance, see *Promulgation of New Ordinance: Qadianis' Anti-Islamic Activities* (Islamabad: Directorate of Films and Publications, Ministry of Information and Broadcasting, Government of Pakistan, n.d. [1984]); quotation at 3 (introduction).

81. For the full range of blasphemy laws, many of which had originated in the colonial era, see M. Mahmood, *The Pakistan Penal Code, 1860, as Amended Up to Date* (Lahore: al-Qanoon Publishers, 2009), 867–92. Sections 295-B, 295-C, 298-A, 298-B, and 298-C were added in the Zia al-Haqq years. For an ethnographic account of these laws and their colonial origins, see Asad Ali Ahmed, "Specters of Macaulay: Blasphemy, the Indian Penal Code, and Pakistan's Postcolonial Predicament," in Raminder Kaur and William Mazzarella, eds., *Censorship in South Asia: Cultural Regulation from Sedition to Seduction* (Bloomington: Indiana University Press, 2009), 172–205.

82. Din Mohammad, governor of Sindh, to Khwaja Nazimuddin, the prime minister, August 10, 1952, enclosing an untitled note marked "top secret." File 3(20)-PMS/52 (Correspondence with the Hon'ble Minister for Refugees and Rehabilitation): 87–91; the quotation is at 89. (NDC). Cf. Qasmi, *The Ahmadis*, 133; the tension between the state's Islamic and liberal aspirations is a key theme of Qasmi's study.

83. *NAPD*, 5/39, 565–70.

84. See *Jang*, January 6, 1984 (speech by Justice Tanzil al-Rahman, the chairman of the Council of Islamic Ideology, at a convention of the `ulama). For a discussion of the jurisprudence on the Ahmadi issue in subsequent years, see Naveeda Khan, *Muslim Becoming: Aspiration and Skepticism in Pakistan* (Durham, NC: Duke University Press, 2012), 111–16; Saeed, *Politics of Desecularization*, 178–208.

85. This time around, the movement that the `ulama and allied groups launched to press for their demands had, as Saadia Saeed has observed, "a very narrow base." Saeed, *Politics of Desecularization*, 159–61; quotation at 161. In contrast with Saeed, ibid., 164, I see the 1984 ordinance less as a matter of the government "caving in to the demands of the religious establishment" than its helping to generate them. The strongest indication of this is provided by the fact that it was the recommendation of the Council of Islamic Ideology that the religious groups wanted to see implemented. See, for instance, *Jang*, April 18, 1984; ibid., April 20, 1984.

86. *Jang*, January 6, 1984.

87. Nasr, *Vanguard*, 195–96.

88. Karam Haydari, ed., *Taqarir o tajawiz-i `ulama convention* (Islamabad: Wizarat-i madhhabi umur wa aqalliyyati umur, n.d. [1980]), 31. The scholar quoted here is Sayyid Mahmud Ahmad Rizwi, a Sunni belonging to the Barelawi orientation. The reference to "the pure members of the Prophet's household" (*ahl-i bayt*) is worth clarifying here. To the Twelver Shi`a, the phrase refers to Muhammad, his daughter Fatima, her husband `Ali, and their children and descendants. This pointedly excludes other members of Muhammad's family, such as his wife, `A'isha, or Muhammad's uncle, al-`Abbas, whose descendants would later go on to found the `Abbasid dynasty (r. 750–1258), under which several of the Shi`i imams lived difficult lives. To the Sunnis, the Prophet's household carries an expansive meaning. And Mahmud Ahmad Rizwi's invocation of it was intended as an appeal to defend the honor of those the Shi`a typically leave out of their reckoning. Allegations that the honor of an official was more important to the government than the Prophet's had been heard during the 1953 anti-Ahmadi agitation as well. See, for instance,

"Extracts from Weekly Confidential Diaries, Sialkot District, January 24, 1953," in Court of Inquiry Proceedings, 2: 207.

89. Cf. A. P. Fabian to R. D. Lavers, British Embassy, Islamabad, September 15, 1980, FCO 37/2358: Internal Political Situation in Pakistan, 1980: 89 (TNA; Electronic Resource).

90. Born an Isma`ili, Jinnah had later converted to Twelver Shi`ism. See Faisal Devji, *Muslim Zion: Pakistan as a Political Idea* (Cambridge, MA: Harvard University Press, 2013), 215–19.

91. AISC, *Rudad-i ijlas-i bist o nuhum ba-maqam Patna ... mun`aqida 29, 30, 31 December, 1938* (Lucknow: Sarfaraz Qawmi Press, n.d. [1939]), 8–9 (the published proceedings do not have continuous page numbers; the reference here is to the independently paginated report on the conference proceedings by Sayyid Muntakhab Husayn). Also see ibid., 19–20, for a denial, against newspaper reports, that Jinnah had intended to speak at the conference.

92. *The Leader* (Allahabad), May 10, 1939, quoted in Jones, *Shi`a Islam*, 201.

93. Sir Harry Haig to Lord Linlithgow, May 9, 1939, L/PJ/5/267: 86 (United Provinces Governor's Reports [BL]).

94. On Madani's leadership role in the Madh-i sahaba controversy, see Haig to Linlithgow, April 18, 1939, with Haig's note on "The Lucknow Madhe Sahaba Controversy," L/PJ/7/2587: 38 (BL). Also Haig to Linlithgow, October 24, 1938, Eur. Mss. F125/101: 95 (Correspondence with the Governor of the United Provinces and His Secretary, vol. 2, 1938 [BL]).

95. Madani to Muhammad `Abd al-Rahman, September 8, 1947, in Islahi, ed., *Maktubat-i Shaykh al-Islam*, 2: 288.

96. Ibid., 2: 288, quoting *Madina* (Bijnor), December 1, 1945.

97. Musa belonged to the predominantly Shi`i Hazara ethnicity. In recent years, members of this community have borne the brunt of Sunni militancy in the Balochistan province.

98. I. I. Chundrigar, prime minister of Pakistan for a mere two months in late 1957, was also a Shi`i. Rieck, *Shias of Pakistan*, 73.

99. A. P. Fabian to Graham Archer, September 7, 1980, British Embassy, Islamabad, FCO 37/2358: 85 (TNA; Electronic Resource). As this report makes clear, British diplomats in Islamabad were skeptical that the figure was quite so high, and so were the Indian consular officials.

100. These motifs are examined in Oskar Verkaaik, *Migrants and Militants: Fun and Urban Violence in Pakistan* (Princeton, NJ: Princeton University Press, 2004), 100–101, 145–49, 159–60. The MQM is not, however, a Shi`i organization but one based on linguistic ties among the Urdu-speaking emigrants to Pakistan. Initially called the Muhajir Qawmi Movement (the "national movement of the migrants"), it changed its name to Muttahida Qawmi Movement (the "united national movement") in 1997. This did not do much, though, to expand its support base beyond its core constituency. Ibid., 57.

101. On the size of her father's initial landholdings, see Hussain, *Power Failure*, 81.

102. Andreas Rieck, "The Struggle for Equal Rights as a Minority: Shia Communal Organizations in Pakistan, 1948–1968," in Rainer Brunner and Werner Ende, eds., *The Twelver Shia in Modern Times* (Leiden: Brill, 2001), 274, 276, and n. 38.

103. Zaman, *The Ulama*, 117 and 233–34 n. 37. Also see Sayyid Muhammad Saqalayn Kazimi, *Imamiyya dini madaris-i Pakistan: Ta'rikh o ta`aruf* (Lahore: Wifaq al-madaris al-Shi`a Pakistan, 2004), 5, 53, 99, 128, 198, 205, 226, 246, 395, 439, 441, 451, 458, 466, 555, 581, 583, 613, 625, and 629.

104. There has been considerable contestation *within* the ranks of the Shi`a, too, on the reform of particular beliefs and practices. For some aspects of this contestation, which

falls outside the purview of the discussion here, see Syed Hussain Arif Naqvi, "The Controversy about the Shaikhiyya Tendency among Shia `Ulama in Pakistan," in Brunner and Ende, eds., *The Twelver Shia*, 135–49; Fuchs, "Relocating the Centers," chapter 2.

105. Jones, *Shi`a Islam*, 100–105.

106. Written statement by superintendent of police, Gujranwala, July 12, 1953, in Court of Inquiry Proceedings, 2: 372. Emphasis added.

107. Shibli Nu`mani, *Muwazana-i Anis o Dabir* (Lahore: Maktaba-i din o dunya, n.d.) At its 1912 session in Patna, the All India Shi`a Conference had adopted a resolution calling on the governments of Bengal and Madras to remove two of Shibli's books, on the Rashidun caliph `Umar and the `Abbasid caliph al-Ma'mun, from the curriculum of the educational institutions under their jurisdiction. Both books were deemed to be unfavorable to Shi`i views. The Bengal government accepted the request, but the Madras government turned it down. See AISC, *Rudad-i ijlas-i shashum*, 5, 158–61; AISC, *Rudad-i ijlas-i hashtum, All India Shi`a Conference, mun`aqida ... 18-19-20 October, 1914 ba-maqam Lucknow* (Lucknow: Muhammadi Press, n.d. [1915]), 87.

108. Syed Akbar Hyder, *Reliving Karbala: Martyrdom in South Asian Memory* (New York: Oxford University Press, 2006), 137–59. On Mawlana Muhammad Ali, see ibid., 149–50.

109. Faiz Ahmad Faiz, "Marsiya-i imam," in idem, *Sham-i shahr-i yaran*. This poetic collection is part of Faiz's collected works, *Nuskha-ha'i wafa* (Lahore: Maktaba-i karawan, n.d.), 551–56. The poem was composed in 1964.

110. Shakir, "Idrikni," in *Sad barg*, one of the four books (with independent pagination) in her *Mah-i tamam*, 131–32. For a brief discussion, and for the translation, which I have used with modifications, see Hyder, *Reliving Karbala*, 194–95.

111. Advertisement in *Jang*, January 1, 1977.

112. Rieck, *Shias of Pakistan*, 75–78, 138–42, 162–71. Also see Mohammad Musa, *Jawan to General: Recollections of a Pakistani Soldier* (Karachi: East & West Publishing Company, 1984), 198–204.

113. Rieck, *Shias of Pakistan*, 199.

114. *Sawad-i a`zam ke mulki o milli huquq ke tahaffuz ke-liye ahamm Sunni mutalabat* (Lahore: Khuddam-i ahl-i sunnat wal-jama`at, n.d. [1973]. Microfiche. New Delhi: Library of Congress Office, 1995), 7, 9.

115. See, for instance, Maududi, *Islamic Law and Constitution*, 68–70.

116. Haydari, ed., *Taqarir*, 163–64; quotation at 163.

117. On the TNFJ, see Zaman, *The Ulama*, 114–18. For its leaders' opposition to the "shari`at bills" of the late 1980s, consider the following sampling of banner headlines in the party newspaper, *Rizakar*: "Passage of the Shari`at Bill Would Strengthen Sectarianism" (July 16, 1986: 1); "Shari`at Bill a Conspiracy to Deprive Muslims of Their Fundamental Rights" (July 24, 1986: 1); "We Are Opposed Not to the Implementation of the Shari`at but Rather to a Particular Way of Thinking [about It]" (November 8–16, 1986: 1); "Shari`at Bill Opposed to Popular Aspirations" (December 16, 1986: 1); "We Will Not Accept the Shari`at Bill at Any Cost" (May 8, 1987: 1); "Proposed Shari`at Bill Not Acceptable to All Schools of Thought" (March 24, 1987: 1); "We Will Not Permit a Controversial Shari`at Bill to Be Implemented" (August 1–8, 1989: 1); "Realities Not Taken into Consideration in Preparing the Shari`at Bill" (September 24–30, 1989: 1); "Shari`at Bill Undermines the Stability of Pakistan (January 24, 1990: 1).

118. Rieck, *Shias of Pakistan*, 133–45.

119. A. P. Fabian to R. D. Lavers, March 5, 1979: 3, British Embassy, Islamabad, FCO 37/2188: Internal Political Situation in Pakistan, 1979: 11 (TNA; Electronic Resource). The Shi`i leader quoted in this document is not named.

120. Sayyid Safdar Husayn Najafi, "Har sadi ke mujaddid `ulama," in idem, *Mabadi-yyat-i hukumat-i Islami* (Lahore: Imamiyya publications, 1981), 35–42, at 41.

121. *Jang*, February 2, 1984.

122. Haydari, ed., *Taqarir*, 50–51; quotation at 51. Ansari was referring to article 12 of the Iranian constitution. See *Qanun-i asasi-i jumhuri-i Islami-i Iran* (Tehran: Wizarat-i farhang wa irshad-i Islami, 1989), 31.

123. Rudolph Peters, *Crime and Punishment in Islamic Law* (Cambridge, UK: Cambridge University Press, 2005), 162–63.

124. Ibid., 163.

125. *Nawa-i waqt*, February 11, 1979.

126. Haydari, ed., *Taqarir*, 113–14. For Zahir's full speech on this occasion, see ibid., 108–21.

127. On Zahir, see Jawid Jamal Daskawi, *Ihsan Ilahi Zahir* (Lahore: Jang Publishers, 1990).

128. Najafi, "Islami tarz-i hukumat Shi`a [sic] nuqta-i nazar se," in idem, *Mabadi-yyat-i hukumat-i Islami*, 43–65, esp. 62–65, quotation at 65. The article is undated, but internal evidence suggests that it was written in late 1979. On Najafi, see Sayyid Husayn `Arif Naqwi, *Tazkira-i `ulama-i Imamiyya-i Pakistan* (Islamabad: Markaz-i tahqiqat-i Farsi-i Iran wa Pakistan, 1984), 140–44. Among Najafi's translations is his Urdu rendering of Khomeini's *Tawzih al-masa'il* (Tehran: Sazman-i tablighat-i Islami, 1983). The print run for this edition was 50,000 (ibid., front matter), a substantial number by Pakistani standards.

129. Hussain, *Power Failure*, 550–51.

130. On these organizations and their leaders, see Zaman, *The Ulama*, 111–43. For a candid acknowledgment of the fear that anti-Shi`i rioting following Jhangawi's assassination had inspired in Abida Hussain, see Hussain, *Power Failure*, 357–65.

131. See Abu Rayhan Zia al-Rahman Faruqi, *Sipah-i Sahaba kiya hai, kiya chahati hai?* (n.p., n.d.); idem, *Sipah-i sahaba ka nasb al-`ayn awr taqaze* (Faisalabad: Idara-i isha`at al-ma`arif, 1994). The author is a former head of the organization.

132. See Abu Rayhan Zia al-Rahman Faruqi, *Khilafat World Order* (Faisalabad: Idara-i isha`at al-ma`arif, 2003).

133. Ihtasham ul Haque, "Lashkar, Jaish, TJP, TNSM & SSP Banned," *Dawn*, January 13, 2002.

134. Jawaharlal Nehru, "His Highness the Aga Khan," in S. Gopal, general ed., *Selected Works of Jawaharlal Nehru* (Delhi: Orient Longman, 1972–82), 7: 470–74 (first published in *Modern Review*, November 1935).

135. Ibid., 7: 472.

136. Abdul Hakim, *Iqbal awr mulla*, 19. The first sect mentioned in this passage is the Twelvers, while the one with "many millionaires" refers to the affluent Isma`ilis. Those mentioned last are of course the Ahmadis. For the view that "most of the Pakistani Shi`a are unbelievers," straightforwardly expressed by Muhammad Farid (d. 2005), the leading mufti of the Dar al-`Ulum Haqqaniyya, Akora Khattak, see Mufti Muhammad Farid, *Fatawa-i Faridiyya*, ed. Muhammad Wahhab Manglori, 7 vols. (Zarobi: Dar al-`Ulum Siddiqiyya, 2013), 1: 133. He had the same view of the Iranian Shi`a (ibid., 3: 561–62) and of the Isma`ilis (ibid., 1: 138–40).

137. How the response of Shi`i religious scholars and activists toward the Ahmadis has differed from that of the Sunnis is a question also worth exploring. I leave it aside here, except to note that, in taking a position against the Ahmadis, the Shi`is have not lost sight of the possibility that some such fate could be visited upon them as well. In 1953, the deputy commissioner of Gujranwala had noted that though the Majlis-i `amal leading the

charge against the Ahmadis had two Shi`i members, they had kept aloof, "presumably afraid of becoming the next target, after the Ahmadis, to be declared a minority." Court of Inquiry Proceedings, 2: 263. In the summer of 1974, a group of fifty Shi`i `ulama had affirmed their commitment to the doctrine of the finality of Muhammad's prophethood even as they had distanced themselves from the social boycott of the Ahmadis then being practiced in some circles. See *Jang*, August 2, 1974. Shi`i concerns were not misplaced. Some of those active in the anti-Ahmadi agitation in 1974 would emerge as the leaders of anti-Shi`i sectarianism in the 1980s (Zaman, *Ulama*, 114), and a social boycott of the Shi`is has also been attempted on occasion. See *Rizakar*, October 8, 1986: 2; ibid., February 24, 1989: 4.

138. In his testimony before the Court of Inquiry in January 1954, Mirza Bashiruddin Mahmud, the head of the Ahmadi community, had stated that "what the Qur'an calls a purely Islamic Government is now an impossibility," though he thought that such a government had, indeed, existed under the first successors of the Prophet, the Rashidun caliphs. Court of Inquiry Proceedings, part 5: 2334–35.

139. The year 1984 might seem to be an exception, but, as noted, there was no countrywide agitation on this issue then, only a regime's effort to shore up its credentials.

140. "A Report of My Visit to Pakistan," 7, enclosure with Rahman to Frodin, October 7, 1974, FF 74–141 (RAC).

141. My interpretation here differs from Qasmi's, who sees putative similarities between the Pakistani Sunnis and the Ahmadis, beyond the question of the finality of Muhammad's prophethood, as fueling Sunni anxieties toward them. The Shi`a, for their part, are seen, as some Shi`is do themselves, as more clearly distinguishable from both communities. See Qasmi, *The Ahmadis*, 224–26.

142. "Mob Kills 3 Members of Ahmadi Community," *Dawn*, July 29, 2014; Nabeel Anwar Dhakku, "Ahmedis in a Chakwal Village Fear for Their Lives," ibid., June 9, 2015; Wasim Ashraf Butt, "Factory Torched in Jhelum over Blasphemy Allegation," ibid., November 22, 2015. Also see ibid., August 6, 2009: "Is There an End?"

143. *Zaheeruddin v. the State, The Supreme Court Monthly Review*, 26/8 (1993): 1718–80, at 1777. The Blasphemy Act dates from 1697, not 1679.

144. On the Christian community of Pakistan and how the blasphemy laws have affected it, see Linda S. Walbridge, *The Christians of Pakistan: The Passion of Bishop John Joseph* (London: RoutledgeCurzon, 2003).

145. See, for instance, `Aziz al-Rahman, "Qanun-i tahaffuz-i namus-i risalat awr masihiyyon ka na-rawa tarz-i `amal," *al-Balagh* 33/2 (June 1998): 3–9.

146. The fourteen-year-old was one of three Christians brought to court for blasphemy. One of them was assassinated before the case went to trial in the lower court, another after the Lahore High Court overturned that verdict. The minor was whisked out of the country soon thereafter. On this case, see "PM Offers Meaningful Dialogue to Opposition," *News*, February 4, 1995; "Blasphemy Case: Rehmat, Salamat to the Gallows," ibid., February 10, 1995; "Countrywide Rallies Reject Change in Blasphemy Law," ibid., May 28, 1995.

147. Asim Hussain, "Apostasy Decree Issued against Taseer," *News*, November 25, 2010.

148. "Taseer Falls to Security Guard's Bullets," *Dawn*, January 5, 2011; Carlotta Gall, "Governor's Assassination Deepens the Divide in Pakistan," *New York Times*, January 6, 2011; idem, "Pakistan Faces a Divide of Age on Muslim Law," *New York Times*, January 11, 2011.

149. For a somewhat similar argument, made with reference to the Ahmadis rather than the Shi`a, see Saeed, *Politics of Desecularization*. Saeed posits that the failure of the

governing elite to "settle" the relationship between religion and the state has given repeated opportunities to religious groups to assert themselves on sites such as that provided to them by the question of the Ahmadis' status. See, for instance, ibid., 106, 218–19.

Chapter Six. The Contested Terrain of Sufism

1. Zia al-Rahman Faruqi, *Sipah-i sahaba ka nasb al-`ayn*, 41, quoting the revered saint `Abd al-Qadir Jilani. Also see `Ali Sher Haydari, *Jawahirat-i Haydari*, ed. Muhammad Nadim Qasimi (Lahore: Maktabat al-sahaba, 2010), 157, for the characterization of the Prophet's companions as the medium (*wasita*) through which his effulgence (*fayz*) reaches ordinary believers. This is strongly evocative of the Sufi masters serving as such intermediaries. Haydari, who was assassinated in August 2009, had once been the Sipah-i Sahaba's patron-in-chief.

2. Muhammad Iqbal, *The Development of Metaphysics in Persia* (Lahore: Bazm-i Iqbal, 1959; first published London, 1908), 82–83. Emphasis in the original.

3. Iqbal, *Reconstruction*, 177–78.

4. Ibid., 143.

5. Iqbal, "Baghi murid," in *Kulliyyat-i Iqbal* (Urdu), 496. This poem is part of Iqbal's collection *Bal-i Jibril*. On Iqbal's critique of Sufism, see also Carl W. Ernst, *The Shambhala Guide to Sufism* (Boston: Shambhala, 1997), 200–203. In discussing the modernists, the Islamists, and the state, among others, in their relationship with Sufism (ibid., 199–228), Ernst covers some of the same ground as I do in this chapter.

6. Rahman, *Islam*, 140. Also ibid., 143, 144.

7. Rahman, *Islamic Methodology*, 109–12.

8. Rahman, *Islam*, 144.

9. Ibid., 153. Cf. Rahman, *Islamic Methodology*, 117, where he dates this development to the twelfth century.

10. Ghulam Ahmad Parwez, *Ae kushta-i sultani o mulla'i o piri* (Lahore: Idara-i tulu`-i Islam, n.d.), 14. Parwez gives no reference for the quoted statement of Iqbal.

11. Thanawi, *al-Ifadat*, 4: 179.

12. Ashraf `Ali Thanawi, *`Irfan-i Hafiz: Hafiz-i Shirazi ke mashhur wa maqbul Farsi diwan ki sufiyana wa `arifana Urdu sharh* (Karachi: Nafis Academy, 1976).

13. Muhammad Iqbal, *Masnawi-i asrar-i khudi* (Lahore: Union Steam Press, n.d. [1915]), 66–72. Translation based, in part and with modifications, on Abu Sayeed Nur-ud-Din, "Attitude towards Sufism," in Hafeez Malik, ed., *Iqbal: Poet Philosopher of Pakistan* (New York: Columbia University Press, 1971), 287–300, at 294. When the work was first published in 1915, these lines caused enough consternation in influential circles for the modernist poet to omit them from later editions of that book. The original 1915 edition I use here is at the British Library, with Iqbal's autograph.

14. See Zaman, *Ashraf `Ali Thanawi*, 85–88.

15. Islahi, ed., *Maktubat*, 2: 403–28, at 427–28. The letter is addressed to Abul-Lays Nadwi, the first leader of the Jama`at-i Islami of India following the end of colonial rule. It does not carry a date, but internal evidence suggests that it was written ca. 1951. For Abu'l-Lays's letter, in which he had complained of Deobandi propaganda, as well as a fatwa, against Mawdudi and had invited Madani to the annual session of the Jama`at-i Islami, see ibid., 2: 403–5. The two people Madani refers to in this quotation, besides Wali Allah, are the famed sixteenth- to seventeenth-century Naqshbandi Sufi, Ahmad Sirhindi, and the early nineteenth-century reformer, Sayyid Ahmad of Rae Bareli, who had led an abortive effort to establish a polity on the northwest frontier of India.

16. Mawdudi, "Sa`y-i la hasil," in `Asim Nu`mani, *Tasawwuf awr ta`mir-i sirat: Mawlana Mawdudi ki tahriron ki rawshani main* (Lahore: Islamic Publications, 1972), 102–7; quotation at 106. Though the advent of Islam was supposed to have brought the age of jahiliyya to an end, Mawdudi argued that Muslims had come to be afflicted by a new malaise of quasi-pagan ignorance and materialism. In the letter quoted earlier, Madani alluded to this view of Mawdudi and what it meant for how the history of Islam itself was to be judged. Like the idea of the sovereignty of God, Mawdudi's formulation of the notion of jahiliyya also came to acquire a prominent place in the writings of Sayyid Qutb.

17. L/PJ/7/5297: The Music in Muslim Shrines Act 1942: 6 (BL).

18. Ibid., 5.

19. AISC, *Rudad-i ijlas-i bist o shashum ... mun`aqida 26, 27, 28 October, 1935 ba-maqam Rae Bareli* (Lucknow: Sarfaraz Qawmi Press, n.d. [1936]), 12–13. Despite the opposition of some members, who could not see why the women in question should be excluded from the processions, the AISC passed a resolution in support of the Shi`a Young Men's action. Ibid., 62–63.

20. See chapter 5, note 19.

21. L/PJ/7/5297: The Music in Muslim Shrines Act: 16–17.

22. Ibid., 12.

23. Ibid., 17.

24. Ibid., 18. This was stated by Raja Fateh Khan, a legislator from Rawalpindi.

25. According to an estimate from 2007, donations at the shrine of Shaykh `Ali Hujwiri in Lahore amounted to nearly 160 million rupees per year (approximately $2.6 million). Altogether, the 320 or so shrines under the control of the Awqaf Department in the Punjab generated revenue of 590 million rupees in 2006–7 (around $9.7 million). The department's expenses on these shrines amounted to 400 million rupees (roughly $6.6 million) that year. See Abdul Manan, "Auqaf Meets Its Expenses with Income from Shrines," *Daily Times*, August 27, 2007. On the number of shrines in the Punjab, see "Blast at Baba Farid's Shrine Kills Six," *Express Tribune*, October 26, 2010. This article gives the figure of 800 million rupees (around $9.3 million, according to the exchange rate then) as the revenue of the awqaf shrines in the Punjab, of which about 80 percent took the form of pious donations. The Awqaf Department of Sindh has approximately 250 shrines and mosques under its control. See "250 Shrines and Mosques under Auqaf Dept, Tells Sharmila," *Daily Times*, February 12, 2013.

26. See L/PJ/7/2413: "NWFP Muslim Waqfs Act 1938" (BL). On the opposition to it of Madani and Kifayat Allah, see ibid., 72.

27. The abortive initiative had taken the form of the Muslim Auqaf Bill, moved in the Punjab legislative assembly in 1937. See Gilmartin, *Empire and Islam*, 160–64.

28. Syed H. M. Naqvi and Syed Mahmudunnasir, *The Law of Waqfs* (Lahore: All Pakistan Legal Decisions, 1968), 115, 117.

29. The 1962 constitution gave the provisions of the 1961 waqf ordinance legal protection to preempt the possibility of its being deemed by the courts to be in contravention of fundamental rights. See M. Farani, *Law of Auqaf and Evacuee Trusts* (Lahore: Lahore Law Times Publications, n.d. [1967]), 4.

30. Naqvi and Mahmudunnasir, *Law of Waqfs*, appendix: "The East Pakistan Waqfs Ordinance, 1962," with independent pagination.

31. Ibid., appendix, 21–22.

32. Ibid., appendix, 24.

33. See Katherine Ewing, "The Politics of Sufism: Redefining the Saints of Pakistan," *Journal of Asian Studies* 42/2 (1983): 251–68.

34. "G-G Pleads for Revival of Islamic Learning," *Dawn*, November 28, 1952.

35. See chapter 1, note 149.

36. *Proceedings of the Special Committee*, no. 2: 338–39. Cf. ibid., no. 12: 1542–43, 1655, 1663–64, 1675, 1681 (the views of the Lahore-based Ahmadis on this matter).

37. Ibid., no. 4: 537–45. Cf. ibid., no. 12: 1543 (the views of the Lahore-based Ahmadis).

38. Ibid., no. 3: 361.

39. Ibid., no. 3: 471.

40. Ibid., no. 12: 1685–87. For an early refutation of such arguments, see Murtaza Ahmad Khan (Maikash), *Alburz shikan gurz `urf mirza'i nama* (Lahore: Taj Company, 1938 [hereafter, *Mirza'i nama*]), 201–116.

41. *Proceedings of the Special Committee*, no. 12: 1680–81, 1726. For one of the verses he cited from Rumi, see *Masnawi-i ma`nawi*, ed. Tawfiq Subhani (Tehran: Wizarat-i far-hang wa irshad-i Islami, 1995), part 5: 702 (verse 742): "O disciple, he [the pir] is the prophet (*nabi*) of his time / For the light of the prophet is manifest in him." Also see Court of Inquiry Proceedings, 6: 65 (statement of the Ahmadiya Anjuman Ishaat-i-Islam, Lahore). The beliefs of the Lahore-based group, though notably less extravagant than those of the Rabwa-based Ahmadis, may have been more threatening in that they tended to accentuate the similarity between the claims of Mirza Ghulam Ahmad and those of some medieval Sufi saints. For a passing recognition of this point, see Murtaza Ahmad Khan (Maikash), *Mirza'i nama*, 201.

42. *Proceedings of the Special Committee*, no. 13: 1735.

43. Ibid., no. 4: 547.

44. For other efforts by the `ulama to refute the Ahmadi invocation of the Sufi tradition, see ibid., no. 15: 2006–14; no. 16: 2577–81.

45. Muhammad Hanif Nadwi, `Aqliyyat-i Ibn Taymiyya* (Lahore: Idara-i saqafat-i Islamiyya, n.d.), 331–38 The book has no date of publication, but the Library of Congress catalogue gives it as 1965.

46. Ibid., 351–52 and, more generally, 349–56.

47. Ibid., preface, v–vi. The words "reactionary" and "literalist" are given in English.

48. See Muhammad Hanif Nadwi, *Lisan al-Qur'an*, 2 vols. (Lahore: Idara-i saqafat-i Islamiyya, 1983), 1: 33. This is a posthumous and incomplete work on the lexicon of the Qur'an.

49. Muhammad Hanif Nadwi, *Mirza'iyyat nae zawiyon se*, ed. Muhammad Sarwar Tariq (Faisalabad: Tariq Academy, 2003; first published in 1952). On this book, see Bhatti, *Qafila-i hadith*, 333.

50. Ashraf `Ali Thanawi, *Imdad al-mushtaq* (Delhi: Maktaba-i Burhan, 1981; first published in 1925), 32–33. For Thanawi's own discourses on the *Masnawi*, see idem, *Kelid-i masnawi*, 24 vols. (Multan: Idara-i ta'lifat-i ashrafiyya, 2005; first published 1924–33).

51. See chapter 1, note 28.

52. Iqbal to Sayyid Sulayman Nadwi, November 13, 1917, in `Ata Allah, *Iqbal nama*, 1: 79.

53. Shahab, *Shahab nama*, 455. For a detailed hagiography of Waris `Ali Shah by a contemporary who had received an English education and subsequently became a disciple, see Fazl Husayn Siddiqi Warisi, *Mishkat-i haqqaniyya* (Karachi: H. M. Sa`id, 1982). This book was first published in 1919. Also see Claudia Liebeskind, *Piety on Its Knees: Three Sufi Traditions in South Asia in Modern Times* (Delhi: Oxford University Press, 1998), esp. 177–223.

54. Fazl Husayn Warisi, *Mishkat*, 128.

55. Ibid., 69.

56. Ibid., 66.

57. The president, however, had a rather mixed view of the pir. "This type of people are more relaxed and broad-minded," he wrote in his diary after a meeting with him in April 1967, "unlike the mullahs whose minds are grooved and narrowed. One can talk philosophy with them at the same time." *Diaries of Field Marshal Mohammad Ayub Khan*, 84 (entry for April 19, 1967). For a more sour view after he had left office, see ibid., 366: "I am told that Pir of Dewal, having exploited my name for so long and amassing so much wealth by skillfully duping people, now talks against me in an attempt to rehabilitate himself. For some time past he had been losing ground as people discovered that he was a skillful fraud" (entry for February 24, 1970). Speaking with a British consular official, Mawdudi, for his part, characterized the pir of Dewal Sharif as "the Rasputin of Pakistan." DO 134/34: Correspondence between Rawalpindi, Lahore, Karachi, Dacca on Pakistan General Politics, 1967–68 (N. J. Barrington's interview with Mawdudi, September 13, 1967, item #83) (TNA; Electronic Resource).

58. Anjum Niaz, "The Pir in the Palace," *Dawn*, July 14, 2013; Imran Ali Teepu, "PM into Spiritual Healers," ibid., September 19, 2012.

59. For an illustration, see Daechsel, *Islamabad*, 239–42.

60. "Asif Ali Zardari Offers Prayers at Ajmer Sharif, Announces $1 Million," *Times of India*, April 8, 2012; Sagnik Dutta, "Ajmer Hasn't Helped Pak VIPs," *Sunday Guardian*, April 8, 2012, at www.sunday-guardian.com/new/ajmer-hasnt-helped-pat-vips (accessed July 24, 2016).

61. A "secretary" is the head, in the federal government structure, of the secretariat that administers a ministry. See Charles H. Kennedy, *Bureaucracy in Pakistan* (Karachi: Oxford University Press, 1987), 6–8. The principal secretary to the governor-general and, after 1956, to the president and the prime minister is the highest bureaucratic official in the secretariat attached to that office.

62. Shahab, *Shahab nama*, 161–69.

63. Ibid., 169–71.

64. On this Sufi path, see *The Encyclopedia of Islam*, 2nd ed. (Leiden: Brill, 1960–2002), s.v. "Uwaysiyya" (by J. Baldick).

65. Shahab, *Shahab nama*, 797.

66. Cf. Daechsel, *Islamabad*, 241.

67. Bano Qudsiyya, *Raja gidh* (Lahore: Sang-i mil publications, 1981). The words "abnormal" and "paranormal" are from the last line of the novel: ibid., 564.

68. Iqbal, *Reconstruction*, 115. As he stated elsewhere in these lectures, "Humanity needs three things today—a spiritual interpretation of the universe, spiritual emancipation of the individual, and basic principles of a universal import directing the evolution of human society on a spiritual basis. Modern Europe has, no doubt, built idealistic systems on these lines, but experience shows that truth revealed through pure reason is incapable of bringing that fire of living conviction which personal revelation alone can bring. . . . The idealism of Europe never became a living factor in her life, and the result is a perverted ego seeking itself through mutually intolerant democracies whose sole function is to exploit the poor in the interest of the rich. Believe me, Europe today is the greatest hindrance in the way of man's ethical advancement." Ibid., 170. Though Sufism was hardly the only source or instance of the "spirituality" that Iqbal spoke of, his repeated invocation of Sufi thinkers and poets shows that he took it to be a major instance of it, just as it represented to him a "religious psychology" (ibid., 125) far superior to the psychology then developing in his contemporary West. The ethical dimensions of this Sufi-inflected spirituality are also clear in Iqbal's thought, not least in the preceding passage. It is difficult therefore to agree with the sweeping view of Hamilton Gibb that "what lies behind his thought is a Sufi

theology, not the Sufi ethic. It was the Sufi ethic that Iqbal hated, because to him it was the symbol and source of passivity and resignation. And it is just here that his chief weakness as a religious thinker lies, for Sufism, without its ethical and ascetic disciplines, runs to seed and becomes—as Iqbal himself expressed it—'the pursuit of a nameless thing.'" H.A.R. Gibb, *Modern Trends in Islam* (Chicago: University of Chicago Press, 1947), 82. The equation between passivity and "the Sufi ethic" was Gibb's, not Iqbal's.

69. Abdul Hakim, *Islamic Ideology*, 133. Here and elsewhere, Abdul Hakim's understanding of religion and morality is also influenced by the Danish theologian Höffding's idea of the "conservation of values," as he acknowledges. Ibid., 50.

70. Ibid., 158–59.

71. Ibid., 157. On the exclusion of the polytheists, which would have included Pakistani Hindus, see ibid., 157.

72. `Attar and Ibn al-`Arabi are not mentioned in this book, but Rumi and Sarmad are. See ibid., 138.

73. Khalifa Abdul Hakim, "Mullaiyyat," in Shahid Husayn Razzaqi, ed., *Maqalat-i Hakim*, 3 vols. (Lahore: Idara-i saqafat-i Islamiyya, 1969), 3: 183–91.

74. Ibid., 187.

75. The sharp contrast between Sufi-inspired ethical values and the lifeless formalism of the mulla's Islam is repeatedly evoked as well in Abdul Hakim's extended meditation on the Urdu and Persian verse of the great nineteenth-century poet Ghalib: Khalifa Abdul Hakim, *Afkar-i Ghalib* (Lahore: Maktaba-i mu`in al-adab, 1973; first published in 1954). See, for instance, ibid., 454–56.

76. "Soul of Pakistan," editorial, *Civil and Military Gazette*, August 20, 1952. Cutting in DO 35/3185 (Pakistan Internal Affairs) (TNA). It is worth noting that an Ahmadi, Khawaja Nazir Ahmad, was a "controlling shareholder" of the newspaper at the time. Court of Inquiry Proceedings, part 2: 923.

77. Yohanan Friedmann, *Shaykh Ahmad Sirhindi* (Delhi: Oxford University Press, 2000), 113. For the point that the putative conflict in the work of many Sufis and poets between unbelief and belief "is rather, in most cases, that between outward form and inner meaning," see Abdul Hakim, *Afkar-i Ghalib*, 29.

78. See, in particular, G. M. Sayyid [Syed], *Jaysa main ne dekha* (Karachi: Idara-i furugh-i insaniyyat, 1972). This book was first published in Sindhi in 1968. The English translation is titled *Religion and Reality* (Lahore: Fiction House, 2012; first published in 1986).

79. For a useful study, see Oskar Verkaaik, "Reforming Mysticism: Sindhi Separatist Intellectuals in Pakistan," in Magnus Marsden, ed., *Islam and Society in Pakistan: Anthropological Perspectives* (Karachi: Oxford University Press, 2010), 111–31.

80. Ibid., 119–20.

81. With some difference of interpretation, I am indebted here to Verkaaik, ibid., especially 128–30.

82. Sherkoti, *Anwar*, 165 (`Usmani to Habib al-Rahman Ludhianawi, December 29, 1945).

83. Ibid., 68–70. For another speech by `Usmani in which he returned to the question of the veneration of tombs and urged Ibn Sa`ud not to destroy such tombs, see ibid., 71–75. Summaries of these speeches come from a diary `Usmani kept during his visit to the Hijaz. The contents of this diary are reproduced in Sherkoti, *Anwar*, 68–80.

84. Khwaja Hasan Nizami, *Murshid ko sajda-i ta`zim*, 11th ed. (Delhi: Khwaja Awlad Kitab Ghar, 1970; first published in 1920).

85. Q 12.100 (following Arberry, *The Koran Interpreted*).

86. Nizami, *Murshid ko sajda-i ta`zim*, 53–61.

87. Nizami himself had made the point that the Deobandis had no grounds to disagree with his position on prostration. See ibid., 5–6. This is an exaggerated claim. For another Deobandi view on the question of prostration to anyone other than God, see Mufti Muhammad Shafi`, *Mazarat-i awliya Allah par `urs ki shar`i haysiyyat*, collected in idem, *Sunnat o bid`at* (Karachi: Idarat al-ma`arif, n.d.), 81–83. Shafi` roundly condemned the practice but did not characterize it as unbelief (*kufr*)—that is, as long as the intention was not to worship the being in question. This legal opinion was first issued ca. 1931. About two centuries earlier, Wali Allah as well had noted that excessive veneration of shrines was a grave sin but that it did not amount to unbelief. Shah Wali Allah, *al-Tafhimat al-Ilahiyya*, ed. Ghulam Mustafa al-Qasimi, 2 vols. (Hyderabad: Shah Wali Allah Academy, 1967–70), 2: 49–50 (#34).

88. Zaman, *Ashraf `Ali Thanawi*, 98, 100.

89. Mufti Muhammad Shafi`, *Mere walid-i majid awr unke mujarrab `amaliyyat* (Karachi: Dar al-isha`at, 1975), 72–73, 76, 78, 82, 84, 86.

90. On the making of amulets by Deobandi `ulama in Chitral, in the Frontier province, see Marsden, *Living Islam*, 157–92. Even as it shows that reform-minded Deobandi `ulama, too, can deal in amulets, this otherwise admirable ethnographic account is premised on the counterintuitiveness of this being the case.

91. For brief accounts of Azhar's career on which I draw here and later, see Sultan Mahmud Ziya, "A'ina-i kirdar," in Muhammad Mas`ud Azhar, *Khutbat-i jihad*, ed. Sultan Mahmud Ziya, 2 vols. (Karachi: Maktaba-i Hasan, 2001), 1: 7–15. (Vol. 1 was first published in August 1994 and vol. 2 in May 1996. The edition of the two volumes used here was published in April 2001.) On Azhar's career and his Jaish-i Muhammad, see also Muhammad `Amir Rana, *Jihad-i Kashmir o Afghanistan: Jihadi tanzimon awr mazhabi jama`aton ka aik ja'iza* (Lahore: Mash`al Books, 2002), 140–65; Zahid Hussain, *Frontline Pakistan: The Struggle with Militant Islam* (London: I. B. Tauris, 2007), 61–70.

92. Muhammad Mas`ud Azhar, *Tuhfa-i sa`adat* (Karachi: Idarat al-khayr, 2001). On the publication date, see front matter and 5–6.

93. Azhar himself makes no effort, however, to connect it to any larger framework of Sufi thought and practice.

94. Ibid., 17, 25, 158–62.

95. Ibid., 21, 61.

96. Ibid., 48, 58, 71, 153–57.

97. Ibid., 92.

98. Ibid., 83, 149.

99. Ibid., 85, 95, 105.

100. Ibid., 19, 20, 27, 30, 32, 51, 61, 138, 174–75.

101. Ibid., 22, 32, 62, 69, 114, 122, 133, 176–77.

102. Ibid., 31, 34, 47, 50, 107, 134.

103. Ibid., 75.

104. Ibid., 25.

105. Ibid., 52.

106. Ibid., 163–66.

107. Ibid., 17, 29, 45–46, 56, 112, 185.

108. Mawdudi, "Khud-niwisht," in Bhutta, ed., *Mawlana Mawdudi apni and dusron ki nazar main*, 25.

109. Ibid., 26–29.

110. Mawdudi in his monthly journal, *Tarjuman al-Qur'an* (August 1951), quoted in Nu`mani, *Tasawwuf*, 39–40.

111. See, for instance, Nu`mani, *Tasawwuf*, 33.

112. Ibid., 30–32.

113. `Ali Hujwiri, *Kashf al-mahjub*, translated and abridged by Mian Tufail Muham-mad, 2nd ed. (Lahore: Islamic Publications, 1968; the first edition, not available to me, was published in 1966). The work was completed while Tufail Muhammad was in jail in 1961–62. See ibid., 21, 30.

114. According to an estimate from 2004, 28,000 to 32,000 people visited the shrine every day, and 55,000 to 60,000 did so on Thursdays and Fridays. Ghafir Shahzad, *Data Darbar Complex: Ta`mir se takmil tak* (Lahore: Idrak Publications, 2004), 12. The source of this estimate is an employee of the Awqaf Department of the Punjab province.

115. Tufail Muhammad, trans., *Kashf al-mahjub*, 23.

116. Ibid., 24.

117. Ibid., 26–29. This is the translation by Muhammad Husayn Gondlawala (Lahore: Malik Muhammad Din, n.d.). See ibid., 29. This work was not available to me.

118. See interview with `Abd al-Ghafur Ahmad in *Jang*, April 25, 1984.

119. Nasr, *Mawdudi*, 124.

120. For the official biography of Tahir al-Qadiri, see "A Profile of Shaykh-ul-Islam Dr. Muhammad Tahir-ul-Qadri," at www.minhaj.org/english/tid/8718/A-Profile-of-Shaykh -ul-Islam-Dr-Muhammad-Tahir-ul-Qadri.html (accessed June 22, 2016). The profile does not mention any madrasa from which he had graduated—a significant liability from the perspective of many Pakistani `ulama. Other hagiographic works do claim, however, that he had completed the full madrasa curriculum—again without naming a madrasa where he did so. See Qadiri and Qamar, *Tahrik-i minhaj al-Qur'an*, 110–11.

121. See Sher Ali Khan, "Tahirul Qadri: The Odd Man Out," *Herald*, September 2014, at http://www.dawn.com/news/1135526 (accessed June 27, 2016).

122. Muhammad Tahir-ul-Qadri, "Punishments in Islam: Their Classification and Philosophy," PhD dissertation, University of the Punjab, Lahore, 1984, 495, at http://eprints .hec.gov.pk/1475/1/1359.htm (accessed June 22, 2016).

123. On these events and his career more generally, see Jaffrelot, *The Pakistan Para-dox*, 282–94; Ayesha Siddiqa, "Tahir-ul-Qadri: Revolutionary or Stooge?" *Newsline*, July 2014, at http://newslinemagazine.com/magazine/tahir-ul-qadri-revolutionary-or-stooge (accessed June 22, 2016); Khan, "Tahirul Qadri: The Odd Man Out."

124. The Nawaz Sharif government wanted to bring General Musharraf to trial for treason on account of a state of emergency he had decreed in late 2007 to stave off a show-down with the Supreme Court. The military establishment was averse to seeing its former head humiliated in this manner. See Jaffrelot, *The Pakistan Paradox*, 282–94, 352–56.

125. "Sit-ins Show Deep-rooted Discontent," *Dawn*, September 14, 2015, quoting data provided by the Institute for Policy Reforms, a Lahore-based think tank.

126. Muhammad Tahir al-Qadiri, *Dala'il al-barakat fil-tahiyyat wal-salawat*, trans. Zuhur Allah al-Azhari (Lahore: Minhaj al-Qur'an Publications, 2009), 49. The quotation is from the introduction by the translator.

127. Muhammad Tahir al-Qadiri, *al-Minhaj al-sawiyy min al-hadith al-nabawiyy*, 13th printing (Lahore: Minhaj al-Qur'an Publications, 2008; first published in 2005), 1–25.

128. On the women in his sit-in and the contrast between his protest and that of Imran Khan's rallies, at which, "with the blare of song and music ... the atmosphere was more festive than charged with revolutionary zeal," see Zahid Hussain, "The Last Episode," *Dawn*, August 20, 2014.

129. For instance, the local government in Sindh expected no fewer than 1.5 million people to attend the `urs of Lal Shahbaz Qalandar in Sehwan in June 2013. "Lal Shahbaz Qalandar's 761st Urs," *Express Tribune*, June 29, 2013. In his study of *mulids*—the saints' birth anniversaries—in Egypt, Samuli Schielke argues that their appeal to people belonging

(or aspiring to belong) to the middle class, the "festivity" with which they have long been associated, and probably also the number of people attending them have all diminished over the course of the twentieth century. See Samuli Schielke, *The Perils of Joy: Contesting Mulid Festivals in Contemporary Egypt* (Syracuse, NY: Syracuse University Press, 2012), esp. 197. Whether this is also the case so far as popular attendance at major Sufi shrines in Pakistan is concerned awaits systematic study.

130. See Marsden, *Living Islam*, especially 33, 241–42 (with reference to Chitral in Khyber Pakhtunkhwa).

131. See Ernst, *Shambhala Guide*, 24–45, 199–215.

132. A useful criticism of such approaches is offered by Carl W. Ernst and Bruce B. Lawrence, *Sufi Martyrs of Love: The Chishti Order in South Asia and Beyond* (New York: Palgrave Macmillan, 2002).

133. For two different views on Egypt, see Valerie J. Hoffman, *Sufism, Mystics, and Saints in Modern Egypt* (Columbia: University of South Carolina Press, 1995), arguing against decline; Schielke, *Perils of Joy*, arguing for it. On West Africa, strongly arguing against any decline, see Rüdiger Seesemann, *The Divine Flood: Ibrahim Niasse and the Roots of a Twentieth-century Sufi Revival* (New York: Oxford University Press, 2011). For Sufism in Bangladesh, see Hans Harder, *Sufism and Saint Veneration in Contemporary Bangladesh: The Maijbhandaris of Chittagong* (London: Routledge, 2011), arguing for the continuing vitality of shrine-based devotionalism; and Katy Gardner, *Global Migrants, Local Lives: Travel and Transformation in Rural Bangladesh* (Oxford, UK: Clarendon Press, 1995), for the argument that, while shrines have continued to thrive, the "purists" have coopted some shrines into a framework of reformed Islam, leaving many others to the poor and the uneducated and often causing some decline in attendance at them (see, for instance, Gardner, *Global Migrants*, 263). On institutional Sufism's declining fortunes in contemporary Afghanistan, see David B. Edwards, *Caravan of Martyrs: Sacrifice and Suicide Bombing in Afghanistan* (Berkeley: University of California Press, 2017), 65–66, 96, 99–100, 127–28, 134, 139. On Pakistan itself, the indicators I note in what follows may be compared with the upbeat assessment in Rozehnal, *Islamic Sufism Unbound*.

134. My point here is hardly to dispute that "[a] movement like Sufism ... should not necessarily be judged by the literature it produces." Fritz Meier, "The Mystic Path," in Bernard Lewis, ed., *The World of Islam* (New York: Thames and Hudson, 1976), 127; quoted in Seesemann, *Divine Flood*, 6. It is only that Sufi intellectual output has fallen markedly in Pakistan in comparison with the intellectual productivity of colonial-era Sufi masters. One partial exception is the discourses of Zulfiqar Ahmad Naqshbandi, a contemporary Deobandi pir belonging to the Naqshbandi Sufi order. But his publications do not match Thanawi's in quantity and certainly not in their range. On him, see note 148, later.

135. For a similar point for a wider cultural zone, "the Balkans-to-Bengal complex," see Ahmed, *What Is Islam?*, 524–26. There are exceptions, of course. Jawwad S. Khawaja, a former judge of the Lahore High Court and of the Supreme Court, and briefly, in 2015, the latter's chief justice, was well-known for his Sufi proclivities and for drawing inspiration from the likes of Hafiz. See Asad Rahim Khan, "Jawwad S. Khawaja: Poetic Justice," *Herald*, April 2016, at http://herald.dawn.com/news/1153394 (accessed November 6, 2016). Such exceptions serve only to prove the rule, however.

136. See Marsden, *Living Islam*, 240–44.

137. Thanawi, *Imdad al-fatawa*, 2: 516–20 (#617–18).

138. Ibid., 2: 516, 518.

139. Cf. ibid., 2: 519.

140. In a fatwa on a related question, Mufti Muhammad Farid of the Dar al-ʿUlum Haqqaniyya had noted in 1974 that a child born within two years of the husband's absence

from home was legitimate, since that was the extreme outer limit of gestation. He made no reference, however, to the role of any supernatural forces in transporting the husband to her wife during those two years. Farid, *Fatawa-i Faridiyya*, 6: 132. In another case, a husband working abroad had invoked modern science to dispute his paternity of a child born six months after he had left for work in Qatar. He had told his wife: "No medical history anywhere in the world accepts that a child can be born within this time period." The mufti responded, however, that a child born in this time frame was in fact legitimate. Ibid., 6: 125–26 (the question or the answer is not dated).

141. Pir Muhammad Karam Shah, *Ziya al-Qur'an*. 5 vols. (Lahore: Ziya al-Qur'an Publications, 1978), 1: 24–25 (commenting on Q 1.4). Also see ibid., 2: 667 (commenting on Q 17.57). For other instances of his defense of Barelawi beliefs and practices, see ibid., 1: 172 (commenting on Q 2.248 to justify the veneration of relics); 2: 609–14 (commenting on Q 16.115 to argue that sacrificing animals in honor of holy men is not a polytheistic practice). The first edition of this work was published in two volumes in 1965–70; my references are to the 1978 edition.

142. For a fuller discussion of this point, see Zaman, *Ashraf ʿAli Thanawi*, 84–90.

143. Shahab, *Shahab nama*, 795.

144. On the saga of Dabba Pir, who was the subject of much ridicule by investigative journalists and was eventually arrested, see *Imroz*, August 27, 1968. Also see the coverage in the newspaper on the following days and the editorial on "fake pirs and holy men" ("Jaʿli pir faqir") (ibid., August 30, 1968). Most of the boxes the police recovered from his residence belonged to women (ibid., August 27, 1968). In self-defense, the pir had claimed that he was helping people develop habits of thrift, presumably by way of putting away money in the said boxes (ibid., August 31, 1968). That he should have tried to appeal to such developmentalist sensibilities in justifying his practices as a pir, at a time when development was the leitmotif of the regime, is noteworthy here. On the discourse of development in this era, see Daechsel, *Islamabad*.

145. Shahab, *Shahab nama*, 799–800.

146. See Rozehnal, *Islamic Sufism Unbound*, especially 46–87. On Siraj ʿAli Muhammad, ibid., 132–34. On the sense of continuity with the past, see ibid., especially 9.

147. According to Rozehnal, members of the Chishti Sabiri order in Pakistan "number in the thousands." Ibid., 132. While allowing for Rozehnal's caution against gauging a Sufi order's significance simply on the basis of the numbers it can muster (ibid.), "thousands" in what is the world's sixth most populous country obviously suggest a miniscule figure.

148. On his educational and professional background, see Muhammad Aslam Naqshbandi, *Halat-i faqir: Sawanih hayat-i mahbub al-ʿulama wal-sulaha hazrat mawlana hafiz pir Zulfiqar Ahmad Naqshbandi Mujaddidi* (Faisalabad: Maktabat al-faqir, 2013), 30–41; on the madrasas he has established or patronizes, ibid., 245–60. For a useful illustration of his style of discourse, see Zulfiqar Ahmad Naqshbandi, *Khutbat-i Hind*, compiled by Khalil al-Rahman Sajjad Nuʿmani Naqshbandi, 2 vols. (Mamdapur, Maharashtra, n.p., 2011).

149. *Black* economy, too, "calculated at three times the size of the official economy" in 2000, is a contributor to religious causes. (On this estimate, see Ayesha Siddiqa, *Military Inc.: Inside Pakistan's Military Economy* [London: Pluto Press, 2007], 153.) Asked in December 1980 if black marketing was permissible, Mufti Muhammad Farid of the Dar al-ʿUlum Haqqaniyya responded: "In the present age, black [marketing] is only a legal crime [as distinguished from one according to the shariʿa], since it harms the administrative system (*intizam*). In countries where the doors to apostasy are wide open and where opposing and combating the Islamic system is not outlawed, on what basis are their rulers to be considered worthy of obedience?" Farid, *Fatawa-i Faridiyya*, 7: 48–49. Also see ibid., 86–87.

150. Sarah F. D. Ansari, *Sufi Saints and State Power: The Pirs of Sind, 1843-1947* (Cambridge, UK: Cambridge University Press, 1992), 34.

151. Malik, *Colonialization*, 62.

152. For a similar point, though not with reference to charitable endowments, see Muhammad Amir Rana, "Dilemma of Barelvi Politics," *Dawn*, August 24, 2014.

153. Malik, *Colonialization*, 64-65.

154. "Death Toll Rises to 45," *Dawn*, July 2, 2010.

155. "DG Khan Shrine Bombing: Death Toll Reaches 50," *Express Tribune*, April 4, 2001. One of the attackers was a teenage schoolboy from the Frontier province.

156. Somini Sengupta and Salman Masood, "Blast Kills 19 at Pakistani Shrine during Muslim Festival," *New York Times*, May 28, 2005; "Sixth Shrine Hit," *Dawn*, April 4, 2011.

157. Ali Hazrat Bacha, "Terrorists Turn on Sufi Saint's Shrine," *Dawn*, March 6, 2009 (the shrine of Rahman Baba, in Hazarkhwani, near Peshawar). For other instances, see "Mazarat par hamlon ki tafsil, *Express*, July 3, 2010 (the shrine of `Abd al-Ra'uf Malang Baba, in December 2007; Abu Sayd Baba's shrine in the Khyber Agency of the tribal areas, in March 2008; the tomb of Bahadur Baba in Nowshera, near Peshawar, in March 2009; the tomb of the poet Amir Hamza Shinwari, in Landi Kotal, in May 2009); Ibrahim Shinwari, "Shrine Blown Up in Khyber," *Dawn*, July 16, 2010 (the shrine of Baba ji and three others, located in the tribal area of Landi Kotal); "Ten Killed in Terror Attack on Mosque-shrine," *Dawn*, March 5, 2011 (the shrine of Akhun Panju Baba, near Peshawar; on him, see Muhammad Amir Shah Qadiri, *Tazkira-i `ulama wa mashayikh-i Sarhad* [Peshawar: `Azim Publishing House, n.d.], 16-24); "Shrines Destroyed, Two Killed in Khyber," *Dawn*, December 11, 2011 (the shrines of Shaykh Nissa Baba and Shaykh Bahadur Bara, both in Landi Kotal); Ali Hazrat Bacha, "Peshawar Panj Pir Shrine Blast Kills Three," *Dawn*, June 22, 2012 (the Panjpir shrine in Hazarkhwani, near Peshawar); "Shrine Damaged in Peshawar Blast," *Dawn*, June 29, 2012 (the Mian Neka shrine, in Surizai, near Peshawar); "Blast Damages Shrine in Peshawar," *Dawn*, November 4, 2012 (the Phandu Baba shrine near Peshawar).

158. Qurban Ali Khushik, "Bloodbath at Sehwan Shrine; Over 75 Perish, 250 Injured," *Dawn*, February 17, 2017. It is worth noting that ISIS characterized the people targeted as a "Shia gathering." Ibid. In late 2016, ISIS had also carried out a bombing at a shrine in Khuzdar, Balochistan. Saleem Shahid and Abdul Wahid Shahwani, "52 Killed in Suicide Attack on Balochistan Shrine," *Dawn*, November 13, 2016.

159. The case of Ahmadi mosques is different, however. They have been attacked, as they were on several occasions in 1953, for what they represent rather than only to terrorize and kill those present there. For such attacks, see Court of Inquiry Proceedings, 1: 140; ibid., 2: 383.

160. Khan, "Taliban Massacre 131 Schoolchildren."

161. "Government to Set Up Sufi Advisory Council," *Dawn*, June 7, 2009. On the National Sufi Council, see Alix Philippon, "A Sublime, yet Disputed, Object of Political Ideology? Sufism in Pakistan at the Crossroads," *Commonwealth and Comparative Politics* 52 (2014): 271-92, at 283-86.

162. Baqir Sajjad Syed, "Miliband's Visit Seen as Bid to Back Moderates," *Dawn*, July 10, 2009.

163. "US Ambassador Announces Grants to Conserve Shrines," *News*, April 22, 2010.

164. Nabeel Anwar Dhakku, "Kabaddi, Bullfights Mark Annual Urs of Sufi Saint," *Dawn*, September 23, 2013.

165. Mansoor Mirani, "Thousands Attend Sachal Urs at Daraza Sharif," *Dawn*, July 14, 2014.

166. "DG Khan Shrine Bombing: Death Toll Reaches 50," *Express Tribune*, April 4, 2011.

167. Tariq Saeed Birmani, "Devotees Miss Drum Beat and Dance at Sakhi's Urs," *Dawn*, April 6, 2015. Portions of the shrine and the adjoining areas are subject to two jurisdictions, urban and rural (or "tribal"). The use of musical instruments was prohibited only on the urban side. Ibid. At the shrine of Lal Shahbaz Qalandar in Sehwan, too, the suicide bombing took place in February 2017 as a Sufi dance was being performed. Khushik, "Bloodbath at Sehwan Shrine." Defiant devotees returned the day after the blast for their ritual dance. "Devotees Resume Dhamal at Lal Shahbaz Qalandar Shrine," *Dawn*, February 18, 2017.

168. Ali Hazrat Bacha, "Terrorists Turn on Sufi Saint's Shrine," *Dawn*, March 6, 2009. Till recent times, women in the Frontier province have had considerable freedom to go into the inner sanctum of many shrines—more so than is the case at some major shrines in the Punjab. See Rozehnal, *Islamic Sufism Unbound*, 211.

169. A. Azfar Moin, "Sovereign Violence: Temple Destruction in India and Shrine Desecration in Iran and Central Asia," *Comparative Studies in Society and History* 57 (2015): 467–96.

170. Wheeler M. Thackston, trans., *The Baburnama: Memoirs of Babur, Prince and Emperor* (New York: Modern Library, 2002), 269; cited in Moin, "Sovereign Violence," 493.

171. Between 1926 and early 1932, the All India Shi`a Conference alone issued 93,100 appeals in protest against the Wahhabi desecration of tombs in Medina and elsewhere: AISC, *Rudad-i ijlas-i bist o chaharum ... ba-maqam Lahore, mun`aqida 24, 25, 26 March 1932* (publication data not available [ca. 1933]), 2 (report on the safeguarding of the holy sites; independently paginated).

172. AISC, *Rudad-i ijlas-i bist o haftum ... ba-maqam Lucknow, mun`aqida 25, 26, 27 December 1936* (Lucknow: Sarfaraz Qawmi Press, n.d. [1937]), 135.

173. "Militants Seek to Destroy Mali Shrines," *New York Times*, June 30, 2012; Tim Arango, "Tears, and Anger, as Militants Destroy Iraq City's Relics," *New York Times*, July 30, 2014.

174. Mufti Muhammad Farid, the leading Deobandi jurisconsult of the Dar al-`Ulum Haqqaniyya, Akora Khattak, was asked in February 1989 whether it was permissible to kill the custodian of a shrine where "un-Islamic" practices took place and whether the custodian's residence, too, could be set on fire. In response, the mufti had cautioned against any such action even as he suggested rectifying the custodian's sinful practices by nonviolent means. Farid, *Fatawa-i Faridiyya*, 1: 307. For another instance, see ibid., 3: 325 (a fatwa from July 1975, characterizing the destruction of tombs associated with un-Islamic ways as a *Salafi* ["Najdi"] practice).

175. Ibrahim Shinwari, "Shrine Blown Up in Khyber," *Dawn*, July 16, 2010.

176. Imtiaz Ali, "Qawwali Star Sabri Gunned Down in Karachi," *Dawn*, June 24, 2016. The funeral prayer for the singer was performed by the custodian of the revered shrine of Baba Farid al-din Ganj Shakar, which is located in Pakpattan, Punjab. See "Amjad Sabiri ke janaze main shahr umadd aya," *Jang*, June 24, 2016.

177. For such instances, see Muhammad Hussain Khan, "No Barriers to Bhittai," *Dawn*, July 20, 2014.

178. "Devotees Throng Rahman Baba Shrine," *Dawn*, April 6, 2014. The shrine was destroyed by the Taliban in March 2009 but subsequently rebuilt. Also see *Dawn*, April 4, 2015: "Rahman Baba's Urs Begins in Peshawar."

179. Shiza Malik, "For Some a Shrine, for Others a Refuge," *Dawn*, November 30, 2014. This is the tomb of a woman named Nur al-Nisa or Mai Sahiba near Dina in the Punjab. It is overseen by women.

180. The fact that Sufi motifs are sometimes encountered in the discourses of contemporary militant leaders has not done much toward improving the fortunes of institutional

Sufism. Conversely, a superior court judge's drawing on Sufi ethics in support of social justice—as evidenced by the recently retired Jawwad Khawaja—has done more to highlight his idiosyncrasy than it has to rejuvenate the relevant areas of Sufi or modernist thought. Also see his speech as the outgoing chief justice of the Supreme Court, an office he occupied for a mere twenty-three days: "Farewell Address by Hon'ble the Chief Justice of Pakistan Mr. Justice Jawwad S. Khawaja," at www.supremecourt.gov.pk/web/page.asp ?id=2028 (accessed November 6, 2016). On his tenure, curtailed from the beginning by an impending retirement, see Nasir Iqbal, "Justice Khawaja's 23-day Tenure as CJP Begins Tomorrow," *Dawn*, August 16, 2015.

181. See note 3, earlier.

182. H.A.R. Gibb, *Mohammedanism* (London: Oxford University Press, 1949), 188–89.

183. Rahman, *Islam*, 254.

184. Ibid., 248. Rahman acknowledges his debt to Gibb's observations here: ibid., 247. Ernst, *Shambhala Guide*, 202–3, has remarked on the indebtedness of modernist assessments of Sufism to the work of European orientalists. That influence was not unidirectional, however.

185. Rahman, *Islam*, 254.

186. In a much publicized 2010 fatwa against militancy, Tahir al-Qadiri also highlights the historical role of Sufism in dealing with the crises facing Muslims, and he, too, quotes Gibb (without indicating his source) to make that point. He laments that militant attacks on the Sufi hospices (*khanaqahs*) had imperiled their very existence, but his criticism is also directed against those associated with these institutions. The khanaqah was once "an all-encompassing welfare institution," he says, catering as much to people's spiritual as to their material needs. Such practices are now in abeyance; the guardians of the khanaqahs have relocated to luxurious urban abodes, with the result that poor people have been forced to turn to madrasas, which indoctrinate their children at will. Muhammad Tahir al-Qadiri, *Dahshat gardi awr fitna-i Khawarij* (Lahore: Minhaj al-Qur'an Publications, 2010), 584–86. Tahir al-Qadiri's fatwa has also been published in Arabic and English versions. The final chapter in which this discussion occurs is not part of the English version: Muhammad Tahir-ul-Qadri, *Fatwa on Terrorism and Suicide Bombing* (Lahore and London: Minhaj-ul-Quran International, 2010); the Arabic version was not available to me. There is some irony in Tahir al-Qadiri's complaint that the custodians of the Sufi hospices had moved away from them since he does not live in close proximity to his Pakistani disciples either.

Chapter Seven. Religion, Violence, and the State

1. For a sophisticated treatment of this question in a broad historical and comparative framework, see Cook, *Ancient Religions, Modern Politics*, especially 215–48.

2. Thanawi, *al-Ifadat*, 1: 73–96.

3. These views are summarized in Mawdudi's letter to Shabbir Ahmad `Usmani, July 13, 1948, in Sherkoti, ed., *Anwar*, 211–14.

4. `Usmani to Mawdudi, July 7, 1948, in Sherkoti, ed., *Anwar*, 206. For the full correspondence, see ibid., 206–20.

5. Ibid., 207–10 (July 7, 1948).

6. Ibid., 209. Also `Usmani to Mawdudi, August 8, 1948, in ibid., 215.

7. Ibid., 222–24, at 223. The fatwa was published in *Zamindar*, on June 17, 1949.

8. Mawdudi to `Usmani, July 13, 1948, in Sherkoti, ed., *Anwar*, 211–14. A key passage Mawdudi invokes in support of his position is Qur'an 8.58.

9. Sherkoti, ed., *Anwar*, 213–14. Ibid., 217–18 (September 6, 1948).

10. Ibid., 214, 218.

11. That question was at the center of Indian Muslim concerns. See the "Indian Muslim Leaders' Memorandum to Dr. Graham," in DO 35/3005: Position of Muslims in the Indian Union: 17–20 (August 17, 1951) (TNA). Frank Graham was the United Nations' representative on Kashmir. The memorandum was signed by fourteen prominent Indian Muslim public figures, including Zakir Hussain, the vice chancellor of Aligarh Muslim University and a future president of India, and Hifz al-Rahman Seoharwi, a member of the Indian parliament and a leader of the Jam`iyyat al-`Ulama-i Hind.

12. On this movement, see Ayesha Jalal, *Partisans of Allah: Jihad in South Asia* (Cambridge, MA: Harvard University Press, 2008), 58–113; Lal Baha, "The Activities of the Mujahidin 1900–1936," *Islamic Studies* 18 (1979): 97–168.

13. Fazl-i Ilahi Wazirabadi, *Mas'ala-i jihad-i Kashmir awr uski mukhtasar ta'rikh* (Rawalpindi: Tanzim al-da`wa ilal-Qur'an wal-sunna, 1997; first published in 1948). For a brief account of Wazirabadi's life, see the introduction by `Abd al-Rashid Azhar, ibid., 37–40. All references are to this edition unless otherwise noted.

14. For an overview of the rules of war, see Hallaq, *Shari`a*, 324–34.

15. Wazirabadi, *Mas'ala-i jihad*, 50–90. For another discussion of Wazirabadi's book, see Jalal, *Partisans*, 292–94.

16. Wazirabadi, *Mas'ala-i jihad*, 57. Also see ibid., 59–60, adducing Qur'an 8.55–57.

17. Wazirabadi, *Mas'ala-i jihad*, 67, referring to Qur'an 2.246. Wazirabadi made extensive use in this context of what he took to be the relevant lessons from the Qur'an's retelling of the story of Saul, David, and Goliath (Q 2.246–51). For the very different use to which this story was put by Ashraf `Ali Thanawi, see Zaman, *Ashraf `Ali Thanawi*, 52–54. On another note, though Wazirabadi did not say so, life, property, and progeny are well-recognized elements of what the medieval jurists called the purposes of the shari`a.

18. Wazirabadi, *Mas'ala-i jihad*, 67–68.

19. Ibid., 235–40.

20. Ibid., 175–80.

21. Ibid., 177–78, citing `Ala al-din `Ali b. Muhammad al-Khazin (d. 1341), *Tafsir al-Khazin, al-musamma Lubab al-ta'wil fi ma`ani al-tanzil*, 7 vols. (Cairo: al-Maktaba al-tijariyya al-kubra, 1961), 1: 221, regarding Saul's killing of many "`ulama and the pious (*al-`ubbad*)" on account of their upbraiding him for trying to murder David. Wazirabadi, however, was misleading here. He gave the impression that David and others had been willing to fight under Saul's banner despite the latter's reprehensible ways. Yet, Saul had shown his true colors *after* the battle that the Qur'an speaks of, not before it. See al-Khazin, *Tafsir*, 1: 220–22.

22. The 2004 edition of this book carries a preface by Hafiz Muhammad Sa`id, the leader of the Lashkar-i tayba. Fazl-i Ilahi Wazirabadi, *Jihad-i Kashmir: Farziyyat, fazilat awr ta'rikh* (Lahore: Dar al-Andalus, 2004), 19–22.

23. Mawdudi to `Usmani, September 16, 1948, in Sherkoti, ed., *Anwar*, 219–20.

24. Nasr, *Vanguard*, 121–22.

25. "Intelligence Reports Concerning the Tribal Repercussions to the Events in the Punjab, Kashmir, and India" (for week ending September 20, 1947), Mss. Eur. F164/48: 10. Mudie Papers (BL). On the strong reaction among Afghans at the reported desecration of shrines, notably that of Shaykh Ahmad Sirhindi, see ibid., 9–10.

26. Court of Inquiry Proceedings, 9: 85.

27. Memo from the home secretary, Government of the Punjab, to the chief minister, July 4, 1952, annexure H-1, ibid., 1: 74. In February 1953, around the time the anti-Ahmadi

agitation was coming to a boiling point, the provincial government had given the *Zamindar*, the most strident of the anti-Ahmadi newspapers, a large share of otherwise scarce newsprint. Ibid., 9: 40.

28. This, at least, is what Daultana thought. Ibid., part 6: 2483.

29. Ibid., part 4: 1751, 1781–82 (Mian Anwar Ali, inspector-general of Police, Punjab); ibid., part 5: 2089 (Ghias-ud-Din Ahmad, home secretary, Government of the Punjab); ibid., 1: 6 (Hafiz Abdul Majid, chief secretary, Punjab).

30. M. Anwar Ali, "Report on the Disturbances," July 18, 1953, ibid., 1: 209 (p. 53 of the report). Cf. the assessment of the district magistrate of Gunranwala, characterizing it as "a large-scale anti-Government agitation" (ibid., 2: 295, memo dated April 19, 1953).

31. On calls for jihad against the Ahmadis, see the police report from Pakpattan, March 12, 1953, in ibid., 3: 155. For the motif of the "satanic government," see M. Anwar Ali, Inspector-general Punjab Police, to G. Ahmad, Secretary to the Government of Pakistan, Ministry of the Interior, March 10, 1953, in ibid., 1: 244.

32. Daily situation report relating to Montgomery district, March 21, 1953, ibid., 3: 313.

33. Ibid., part 5: 2157 (quoting `Abd al-Sattar Niazi).

34. *Nawa-i waqt*, August 23, 1965 (Barelawis); ibid., August 30, 1965 (Deobandis).

35. Ibid., October 11, 1965. The distinction between qital and jihad is premised on the idea that while the former refers specifically to warfare, the latter—jihad—signifies struggling in God's cause in a variety of possible ways, of which taking up arms is only one. Mawdudi's point was that all such ways of reaching the desired goal could count as jihad.

36. Public figures who had failed to support it were mercilessly criticized. See, for instance, Shorish Kashmiri, "Faiz Ahmad Faiz ke nam," *Nawa-i waqt*, November 14, 1965. This is a poem in which Kashmiri, a journalist associated with the Majlis-i Ahrar, asks Faiz Ahmad Faiz, the great Urdu poet with markedly leftist leanings, why he had not written anything in support of the war.

37. "Constitution Bill Passed," *Dawn*, March 1, 1956, quoting the Bengali leader of the opposition, H. S. Suhrawardy.

38. Shorish Kashmiri, "Mashriqi Pakistan ko salam," *Nawa-i waqt*, October 6, 1965. Reprinted in Shorish Kashmiri, *al-Jihad o al-jihad* (Lahore: Matbu`at-i chatan, n.d.), 65–66. This is a collection of Kashmiri's poems on the 1965 war.

39. Q 3.124–27.

40. *Nawa-i waqt*, October 11, 1965: "Muta`addid buzurgon ko Pakistan ki fath o nusrat ki basharatain."

41. Shahab, *Shahab nama*, 500.

42. Ghulam Ahmad Parwez, *Pakistan ki na'i 'ziyarat gahen'* (Lahore: Idara-i tulu`-i Islam, n.d.), 12. This short piece was first published in Parwez's monthly journal, *Tulu`-i Islam*, in January 1966. For the date of publication, see Khadim `Ali Javed, *Ishariyya-i majalla-i Tulu`-i Islam* (Lahore: al-Nur Publishers, 1991), 315. My references here are to the self-standing reprint (quotation marks around *ziyarat gahen* in the original; I will omit them in the following references).

43. Ibid., 13–14, adducing Q 33.21.

44. Parwez, *Ziyarat gahen*, 8, with reference to Q 2.34.

45. Parwez, *Ziyarat gahen*, 14–15, using the English word "credit." Also see Parwez to Lt. Col. A. R. Siddiqi, Director, Public Relations, General Headquarters, Rawalpindi, January 31, 1968 (GAPP).

46. Parwez, *Ziyarat gahen*, 16–17.

47. Ibid., 17–18, with reference to Q 22.40.

48. Parwez, *Ziyarat gahen*, 19.

49. Ibid., 23.

50. *Nawa-i waqt*, October 5, 1965. Also see ibid., October 8, 1965. Cf. Q 8.65: "Prophet, urge the believers to fight: if there are twenty of you who are steadfast, they will overcome two hundred, and a hundred of you, if steadfast, will overcome a thousand of the disbelievers."

51. "Press Note on Jamaat," *Dawn*, January 7, 1964.

52. A petition against the banning of the party had been turned down by the West Pakistan High Court but accepted by the High Court in East Pakistan. It then went to the Supreme Court, whose chief justice at the time was the noted Christian jurist A. R. Cornelius. See O. R. Blair, UK High Commission, Karachi, to G. L. Simmons, CRO, July 29, 1964. DO 196/418: Banning of Fundamentalist Muslim Movement Jamaat-i-Islami in Pakistan (TNA).

53. See Jinnah's speech in Dacca, March 21, 1948, in *JP*, 1st ser., 7: 227–35; quotation at 234.

54. As Khwaja Nazimuddin told the Court of Inquiry, while the chief ministers and governors of the other provinces were part of the deliberations on the anti-Ahmadi agitation, those of East Bengal were not, "because it is practically not a problem in East Pakistan." Court of Inquiry Proceedings, part 3: 1325. Also ibid., part 3: 1345, 1371–72.

55. File 3 (3)-PMS/48: Correspondence with the Hon'ble Minister for Finance, 145–49 (NDC). See chapter 3, note 177.

56. UK High Commissioner in Pakistan to the CRO, November 21, 1956, in DO 35/6340: Pakistan Attitude to Arab-Israeli Crisis, October 1956: 131. Also UK High Commissioner to the Secretary of State for Commonwealth Relations, December 6, 1956, ibid., 3 (TNA).

57. See "Mulk ke liye sab se bara khatra," *Nawa-i waqt*, February 25, 1970.

58. Quoted in Verkaaik, *Migrants and Militants*, 155 (from the *Frontier Post* [Peshawar], July 25, 1990). Though a small minority, there are more Hindus in Sindh than in any other province of post-1971 Pakistan (about 7.5 percent of the province's population according to the 1998 census, at www.pbs.gov.pk/sites/default/files//tables/POPULATION%20BY%20RELIGION.pdf [accessed October 20, 2016]). Some among them had allied themselves with the Sindhis in opposition to the muhajirs. As Verkaaik notes, this view of the Sindhi as non-Muslim was opposed by other members of the MQM. Verkaaik, *Migrants and Militants*, 155, 158–59.

59. This is what he is reported to have said the day he assumed the Eastern Command: "What have I been hearing about shortage of rations? . . . This is enemy territory. Get what you want. This is what we used to do in Burma." *Report of the Hamoodur Rehman Commission*, 503.

60. Ibid., 510.

61. Ibid., 510. Racism played a part, too. As one army general from West Pakistan is reported to have said in Dhaka in December 1970 with reference to the Awami League, "Don't worry . . . we will not allow these black bastards to rule over us." Siddiq Salik, *Witness to Surrender* (Karachi: Oxford University Press, 1977), 29; quoted in Siddiqa, *Military Inc.*, 77. Also see Bass, *The Blood Telegram*, 81–83.

62. A. R. Siddiqi, *The Military in Pakistan: Image and Reality* (Lahore: Vanguard, 1996), 204–6, quoted in Husain Haqqani, *Pakistan: Between Mosque and Military* (Washington, DC: Carnegie Endowment for International Peace, 2005), 76–77. Badr, Uhud, and Khaybar refer to some of the Prophet Muhammad's battles; Damascus was captured by Muslim troops in 636, during the reign of the caliph `Umar.

63. Siddiqi, *The Military in Pakistan*, 205. My translation of these verses differs somewhat from Siddiqi's. The "self-sufficient one" (*be-niyaz*) is a common Urdu translation of the Qur'anic *al-samad* (Q 112.2).

64. *Report of the Hamoodur Rehman Commission*, 520.

65. *Report of the Hamoodur Rehman Commission*, 504. Upon assuming his charge in East Pakistan in April 1971, General Niazi is reported to have asked the officer transferring the command to him, "When are you going to hand over your concubines to me?" See Salik, *Witness*, 92; quoted in Mookherjee, *The Spectral Wound*, 132.

66. Text of the statement issued by Mawdudi on April 30, 1971 in Hafiz al-Rahman Ahsan, *Jama`at-i Islami awr Mashriqi Pakistan* (Lahore: Tasnim Academy, 1971), 118–19.

67. Sayyid Abul-A`la Mawdudi, "Afwaj-i Pakistan ki karawai ke khilaf propaganda ka jawab: Mawlana Mawdudi ka memorandum dunya-i Islam ke nam," *Tarjuman al-Qur'an*, 75/4 (June 1971): 9–23.

68. Haqqani, *Pakistan*, 77–78. Decades later, some of those allegedly involved in these war crimes were prosecuted in Bangladesh by the government of prime minister Sheikh Hasina, the daughter of the country's founder, Sheikh Mujibur Rahman. See Ellen Barry, "Bangladesh Hangs 2 Leaders Convicted of War Crimes," *New York Times*, November 22, 2015: A14; "Pakistan Condemns BD JI Chief's Execution," *Dawn*, May 12, 2016.

69. See, for instance, R.W.D. Fowler, UK High Commission, Karachi, to J.M.C. James, CRO, May 3, 1957, DO 35/6349: Threats to Defense of West Pakistan (TNA). British officials dismissed Pakistani warnings of this threat, voiced by Ayub Khan, as self-interested and exaggerated.

70. K. M. Arif, *Working with Zia: Pakistan's Power Politics, 1977–1988* (Karachi: Oxford University Press, 1995), 306.

71. Shuja Nawaz, *Crossed Swords: Pakistan, Its Army, and the Wars Within* (Karachi: Oxford University Press, 2008), 385.

72. For a balanced assessment on this score, see Stephen P. Cohen, *The Pakistan Army* (Berkeley: University of California Press, 1984), 86–104. Also see Aqil Shah, *The Army and Democracy: Military Politics in Pakistan* (Cambridge, MA: Harvard University Press, 2014), 162–65.

73. Malik, *Colonialization*, 207.

74. Quoted in ibid., 207.

75. `Abd al-Qayyum Haqqani, *Khutbat-i Haqqani*, ed., Muhammad Ramazan, 3rd ed. (Akora Khattak: Mu'tamar al-musannifin, 1991; first published in 1988), 93 (first quotation) and 95 (second quotation).

76. Arif, *Working with Zia*, 321–23.

77. On the connection between Afghanistan and Kashmir, see Vahid Brown and Don Rassler, *Fountainhead of Jihad: The Haqqani Nexus, 1973–2012* (London: Hurst, 2013), 69–70.

78. For an overview, see Rana, *Jihad-i Kashmir o Afghanistan*, 235–58; idem, *Jihad awr jihadi: Pakistan awr Kashmir ke ahamm jihadi rahnumaon ka ta`aruf* (Lahore: Mash`al Books, 2003), 19–30. The Lashkar-i Tayba long continued to maintain a visible presence in remote regions of Afghanistan. See Mujib Mashal, "Rugged Afghan Region Lies beyond Reach of Aid and Time," *New York Times*, December 26, 2015.

79. On the Harkat al-mujahidin, see Rana, *Jihad-i Kashmir*, 166–82.

80. Azhar, *Khutbat*, 1: 39.

81. Ibid., 1: 188.

82. Ibid., 1: 188; cf. 1: 91. As might be expected, such narratives appear in other works relating to Afghanistan, too—notably in the writings of `Abdallah `Azzam (d. 1989), a Palestinian who exercised a significant influence on Bin Laden. See Edwards, *Caravan of Martyrs*, 95–105.

83. On the lack of resort to jihad as imperiling women's honor, a familiar motif in the context of Kashmir, see Azhar, *Khutbat*, 1: 41–42, 44, 62, 160. On the otherwise unexplained sacrilege toward the Qur'an, ibid., 1: 62, 135, 206. On Muslim humiliation resulting from an abandonment of jihad, ibid., 1: 206–8.

84. Ibid., 1: 56–57.

85. Ibid., 1: 36–38.

86. Ibid., 2: 101.

87. Ibid., 1: 109.

88. I draw here primarily on two exegetical works by Hafiz Muhammad Sa`id: *Tafsir surat al-tawba*, compiled by `Ubayd al-Rahman Muhammadi (Lahore: Dar al-Andalus, n.d. [2006]) and *Tafsir surat Yusuf*, compiled by Hafiz Muhammad Siraj (Lahore: Dar al-Andalus, n.d. [2009]). The former is a commentary on chapter 9 of the Qur'an and the latter on chapter 12.

89. Rana, *Jihad awr jihadi*, 20.

90. Sa`id, *Tafsir surat al-tawba*, 85.

91. This is a key theme in a series of Friday sermons he delivered in Lahore between December 2014 and March 2015: Muhammad Sa`id, *Khutbat-i Qadisiyya: Fitna-i takfir— asbab, nuqsanat, awr us se bachao ke tariqe* (Lahore: Dar al-Andalus, n.d. [2015]).

92. For this point, see Cabeiri deBergh Robinson, *Body of Victim, Body of Warrior: Refugee Families and the Making of Kashmiri Jihadists* (Berkeley: University of California Press, 2013), 181.

93. Sa`id, *Tafsir surat al-tawba*, 415.

94. Ibid., 415–22, commenting on Q 9.122.

95. Rana, *Jihad-i Kashmir o Afghanistan*, 251–53.

96. The organization soon denied, allegedly on instructions from unnamed intelligence agencies in Pakistan, that it had been responsible for the attack on the Indian parliament. See Rana, *Jihad-i Kashmir*, 157.

97. Musharraf, *In the Line of Fire*, 245–48. Also see Hussain, *Frontline Pakistan*, 67–70. A second attempt on Musharraf's life was made by a different group later that month.

98. Muhammad Mas`ud Azhar, *Ae Musalman behen* (Karachi: Maktaba-i Hasan, 2004; first published in 2003), 104–5. For the date of this editorial (November 10, 2001), see ibid., 101. "Mother `A'isha" is, of course, one of the wives of the Prophet Muhammad. Militant Sunni organizations have often referred to her in this familiar way.

99. Sa`id, *Tafsir surat al-tawba*, 79, 281 (Muslim rulers afraid of the United States and acting as its instruments); ibid., 281 (moral waywardness). Also see Sa`id, *Tafsir surat Yusuf*, 196 (one cannot buy even a packet of soap or a matchbox without a woman's picture on it: "Evil is dancing naked today and it is as though goodness is hiding its face in shame …").

100. Hafiz Muhammad Sa`id, *Khutbat-i Qadisiyya* (Lahore: Dar al-Andalus, n.d. [2014]), 101–2. The title of this collection of Sa`id's sermons is the same as the main title of another work of his. I distinguish between the two by also giving the subtitle of the latter (*Khutbat-i Qadisiyya: Fitna-i takfir*).

101. Sa`id, *Tafsir surat al-tawba*, 42.

102. Ibid., 181–82, 193; idem, *Tafsir surat Yusuf*, 211, 275–78.

103. Sa`id, *Tafsir surat tawba*, 42–44.

104. Ibid., 48, 280–83. Also see idem, *Khutbat-i Qadisiyya: Fitna-i takfir*, 70, 72–73, 90–91, 140, 99–100, 105–10.

105. Sa`id, *Tafsir surat tawba*, 283.

106. Rana, *Jihad-i Kashmir o Afghanistan*, 236; idem, *Jihad awr jihadi*, 23.

107. Sa`id has also been critical of movements like ISIS (the Islamic State in Iraq and Syria), arguing that "rather than armed jihad against Muslim rulers, it is necessary to urge them to act according to the teachings of Islam and to reform their ways." He considers ISIS to be a Western conspiracy against Muslims. "Da`ish jaisi tanzimen Musalmanon ke-liye bara khatra hain," *Nawa-i waqt*, January 1, 2016.

108. Rana, *Jihad awr jihadi*, 21.

109. See Zaman, *The Ulama*, 139–41.

110. Ibid., 140.

111. See, for instance, Abdullah Jan, "Thousands to Enter Afghanistan Today," *News*, October 28, 2001; Anwarullah and Haleem Asad, "TNSM Supporters Head for Kabul," *Dawn*, October 28, 2001.

112. Anwarullah Khan, "82 Die as Missiles Rain on Bajaur," *Dawn*, October 31, 2006; ibid., "The Dargai Carnage" (editorial), November 10, 2006.

113. The TTP was banned in August 2008, prompting a spokesman to scoff: "Tehrik-i-Taliban is not a political organization that can be barred from parliament by imposing a ban." "Tehrik-i-Taliban Banned," *Dawn*, August 26, 2008.

114. "Woman, Two Men Stoned, Publicly Executed," *Dawn*, March 15, 2007; Ibrahim Shinwari, "Woman and Three Men Publicly Executed," ibid., June 5, 2007; "Couple Stoned to Death in Fata," ibid., April 2, 2008; Ali Hazrat Bacha, "Two Women of 'Loose Character' Executed," *Dawn*, August 21, 2008; "Video Shows Killing of Man and Woman," April 18, 2009, at www.dawn.com/news/846839/video-shows-killing-of-man-and-woman (accessed April 18, 2009); Syed Hassan Mahmood, "Militants Cut Off Hands of Alleged Thieves," May 16, 2010, at www.dawn.com/news/851951/militants-cut-off-hands-of-alleged-thieves (accessed May 16, 2010).

115. The film, *A Girl in the River: The Price of Forgiveness*, is a production of HBO Documentary Films and was released in 2015. See also "No Honour in Honour Killing: PM," *Dawn*, February 23, 2016.

116. Osama Siddique, *Pakistan's Experience with Formal Law: An Alien Justice* (Cambridge, UK: Cambridge University Press, 2013), 135–42; quotation at 138. As part of the survey, 440 people were interviewed (ibid., 107). On the inefficiency of the judicial system, as perceived by the respondents, see ibid., 116–35. Part of the reason for the rise and growth of a Taliban-affiliated movement in the Swat region of the Khyber Pakhtunkhwa province was widespread resentment at the working of the judicial system. In an effort to mollify local sentiment, the government instituted a legal regime in 2009 with a shari`a-laden nomenclature (the Nizam-i Adl Regulation) and with an emphasis on a quick disposal of cases. In other respects, however, there was little to differentiate it from the legal system elsewhere in the country. See ibid., 385–98.

117. Urban dacoits in Karachi have sometimes projected a similar image. See Gayer, *Karachi*, 123–62, especially 159.

118. Pazir Gul, "Miramshah Taliban Open Office," *Dawn*, September 28, 2006.

119. Jane Perlez, "Militants Draw New Front Line inside Pakistan," *New York Times*, November 2, 2007: A1, 6.

120. See Zaman, *Modern Islamic Thought*, 221–23.

121. "Pesh-Imam's Son Became Pakistan's Most Wanted Militant," *Dawn*, August 8, 2009.

122. Jane Perlez and Pir Zubair Shah, "Pakistan Uses Tribal Militias in Tribal War," *New York Times*, October 24, 2008. As one might expect, not all maliks have been on the Taliban's wrong side. When Baitullah Mehsud married a second time not long before his death, it was to the daughter of a notable from South Waziristan. See "Pesh-Imam's Son."

123. Ismail Khan, "Suicide Attack on Army Base: 40 Troops Dead," *Dawn*, November 9, 2006.

124. Sailab Mehsud, "Kidnapped Security Personnel Butchered," June 22, 2012, at www.dawn.com/news/728684/kidnapped-security-personnel-butchered (accessed June 23, 2012); Salman Masood, "Video from Taliban Shows the Killing of 16 Pakistanis," *New York Times*, July 16, 2011.

125. "Baitullah Denies Role in Attack," *Dawn*, December 30, 2007.

126. Khalilur Rehman Bacha, "14-Year Old Activist Shot and Critically Wounded," *Dawn*, October 10, 2012; Declan Walsh, "Taliban Gun Down a Girl Who Spoke Up for Rights," *New York Times*, October 10, 2012; Declan Walsh, "Two Champions of Children Are Given Nobel Peace Prize," *New York Times*, October 11, 2014.

127. Zulfiqar Ali, "Distinction between Good, Bad Taliban No More: PM," *Dawn*, December 18, 2014. For his part, Hafiz Muhammad Sa`id has criticized efforts to erase the distinction between the good and the bad Taliban: see *Khutbat-i Qadisiyya: Fitna-i takfir*, 134.

128. Saleem Shahid, "Frequent Flyer 'Mansour' Used Pakistan Airports," *Dawn*, May 24, 2016.

129. Khalid Kheshgi, "RS 300 m Allocated for Madrassa in KP Budget, Assembly Told," *News*, June 17, 2016. Explaining the allocation, Imran Khan observed that it would "help seminary students assimilate in our society, bring them into the mainstream and keep them away from radicalization." Amir Wasim, "Zardari Questions Allocation for Haqqania Seminary," *Dawn*, June 27, 2016.

130. My observations here are based on Gayer, *Karachi*, especially 101–9. "Operation Clean-up" was the name of a major military crackdown on the MQM in 1992–94. See ibid., 75.

131. Barelawi polemics apart, there remains a sharp doctrinal divergence between the Hanafi Deobandis and the Salafis. For some illustrations, see Farid, *Fatawa-i Faridiyya*, 1: 117, 153–60.

132. Muhammad Mas`ud Azhar, *Fath al-Jawwad fi ma `arif ayat al-jihad*, 4 vols. (Lahore: Maktaba-i `irfan, 2007–9), 2: 279.

133. Ibid., 2: 279–80. For another explicit commendation of suicide bombing, see Muhammad Mas`ud Azhar, *Faza'il-i jihad* (Karachi: Maktaba-i Hasan, 2001), 354 and, more generally, 329–54. This book is an Urdu abridgement of and commentary on a work by a medieval scholar, Ibn al-Nahhas (d. 1411), *Mashari` al-ashwaq ila masari` al-`ushshaq*.

134. "Mawjuda buhran—asbab awr `ilaj: Mulki surat-i hal par mulk ke mumtaz `ulama-i kiram ka mushtaraka mawqif," *al-Faruq* 24/4 (May 2008): 5–10, quotation at 6. *al-Faruq* is the monthly journal of Jami`a Faruqiyya, a prominent Deobandi madrasa of Karachi known for its militant ties. Qari Husayn, "the Pakistani Taliban's chief suicide bomb instructor," was reportedly a graduate of this madrasa. See Jane Perlez and Pir Zubair Shah, "In Violent Karachi, Pakistani Insurgency Finds a Haven and a Forge," *New York Times*, May 22, 2010: A4.

135. Masood, "Video from Pakistan." They have also referred to Pakistan as an "infidel" state, justifying attacks against government offices. Ismail Khan, "Suicide Blast Hits Pakistan, Killing 22," *New York Times*, December 30, 2015. In this latter instance, the bombing was carried out by a breakaway Taliban group called the Jama`at al-Ahrar. For what it is worth, it should be noted that leading Pakistani newspapers did not mention that the group in question had referred to the state as infidel. For instance, see the reporting in *Nawa-i waqt*, December 30, 2015 ("Mardan: Nadra office ke gate par khudkush dhamaka"); Mohammad Riaz Mayar, "26 Killed in Blast outside Nadra Office in Mardan,"

News, December 30, 2015. In 1953, too, the anti-Ahmadi agitators had occasionally characterized the police and the military taking action against them as apostates (*murtadd*). See Superintendent Police, Sialkot to Deputy Inspector-General, CID, Lahore, March 10, 1953, in Court of Inquiry Proceedings, 2: 37.

136. In May 2017, a number of prominent `ulama, among them Mufti Rafi` `Usmani of the Dar al-`Ulum of Karachi, issued a much clearer denunciation of terrorism and suicide bombing in the form of a fatwa. The fatwa was unveiled at a conference in Islamabad at which the president of Pakistan, Mamnoon Hussain, also spoke. This public association of the signatories with the government could not have gone down well with other `ulama and Islamists, however. Indeed, Sami al-Haqq of the Dar al-`Ulum Haqqaniyya, the madrasa most closely associated with the Taliban before and after 9/11, was reported to have distanced himself from it. It is also worth noting that the original draft on which the fatwa was based had had some biting criticism of government policies, all of which was excised from the publicized fatwa. For the text of the fatwa, see "Jihad Jurisdiction of State, Suicide Attackers Are Traitors, Declares Fatwa," May 29, 2017, at www.dawn.com/news /1335797 (accessed June 1, 2017); for the original draft, see Munib al-Rahman, "Qawmi bayaniyya awr ahl-i madaris," *al-Shari`a* 28/4 (April 2017): 33–38. For Sami al-Haqq's opposition, see the editorial in *Dawn*, June 1, 2017: "Fatwa against Terrorism."

137. Zahid al-Rashidi, "Mawjuda surat-i hal awr Afghan Taliban ka mawqif," *al-Shari`a* 25/2 (February 2014): 2–5, at 3. A "book of rules" issued in 2010 by the Taliban leadership to guide and regulate the conduct of their followers allows for suicide bombing, but with certain conditions, viz that the person undertaking it is properly trained for the act, the target is worthwhile, efforts are made to avoid the killing of common people, and the act has been authorized by the leadership. See "Taliban's Code of Conduct," in Yoshinobu Nagamine, *The Legitimization Strategy of the Taliban's Code of Conduct: Through the One Way Mirror* (New York: Palgrave Macmillan, 2015), 157–58 (article #57).

138. Emile Simpson, *War from the Ground Up: Twenty-first Century Combat as Politics* (London: Hurst, 2012), 84.

139. Ibid., 181.

140. Ibid., 181.

141. For the imagery of moderate versus inflamed voices among notables and `ulama in the tribal areas, see "Mawjuda buhran," *al-Faruq* 24/4 (May 2008): 8.

142. On the business interests of the Pakistani military, see Siddiqa, *Military Inc.*

143. See Intikhab Hanif, "Ulema Must Undo Extremist Narrative of Religion: PM," *Dawn*, March 12, 2017; "Jihad Jurisdiction of State," quoting remarks by the president, Mamnoon Hussain.

144. A good deal of the journalistic and policy-oriented literature on the Pakistani Taliban and allied groups takes this view. For one example, see Brown and Rassler, *Fountainhead*.

145. See the illuminating exchange between Yahya Bakhtiar, the attorney-general, and Mirza Nasir Ahmad, the head of the Ahmadi community, in *Proceedings of the Special Committee*, part 9: 1205–6. Bhutto's Third Worldism had been heightened by the Western powers' failure to come to the aid of Pakistan in its moment of need in 1971 and by Britain's decision soon afterward to recognize Bangladesh as a sovereign state. It was in that context that Pakistan noisily quit the British Commonwealth in January 1972.

146. For some of the key works Azhar uses, see his introduction to the book in *Fath al-Jawwad*, 1: 529–31.

147. Ibid., 1: 530.

148. Mufti Muhammad Zahid, "Mawjuda pur-tashaddud tahriken awr Deobandi fikr o mizaj," *al-Shari`a* 20/11–12 (November–December 2009), 79.

149. A number of scholars and preachers have, in fact, been killed by the Taliban and allied groups for expressing opposition to them. See, for instance: Ashfaq Yusufzai, "Wafaqul Madaris VP Shot Dead," *Dawn*, September 16, 2007; Muhammad Faisal Ali, "Suicide Bomber Kills Anti-Taliban Cleric Allama Naeemi," *Dawn*, June 13, 2009; "Ex-MNA among 32 Killed: Terrorists Attack Wana Seminary, Kurram Jirga," *Dawn*, August 24, 2010; "Pro-Govt Cleric Shot Dead in Lakki Marwat," *Dawn*, May 14, 2012.

150. As noted earlier, the Barelawis have been more forthcoming than many others in condemning religious militancy. The most illustrative example is Muhammad Tahir al-Qadiri, *Dahshat gardi awr fitna-i Khawarij*. The fatwa's impact within Pakistan is unclear, however. And doctrinal rivals are likely to see it as better suited to currying favor with Western governments and policy circles than to addressing the views of the contemporary militants, with whom it does not engage directly. Tahir al-Qadiri is a Canadian citizen, and the English version of the fatwa has a foreword by John L. Esposito of Georgetown University and a blurb by Fareed Zakaria of CNN.

151. Qurrat al-`Ayn Haydar, *Ag ka darya* (Lahore: Maktaba-i jadid, 1959), 165–66.

152. Ibid., 201. The domains of war/unbelief and of peace/Islam are familiar legal categories in Islamic juristic thought. The domain referred to here as dar al-salam is commonly called the *dar al-Islam* (the abode of Islam or submission).

153. Ibid., 692–93.

154. The best account of Qurrat al-`Ayn Haydar's life is her three-volume autobiography: *Kar-i jahan daraz hai*. The second volume is devoted to her years in Pakistan. On her anxiety about what the imposition of martial law meant for freedom of literary expression, see Shahab, *Shahab nama*, 513.

155. Abdul Hakim, *Islamic Ideology*, 178.

156. Ibid., 183.

157. Ibid., 181, 183.

158. Ibid., 181.

159. Ibid., 190.

160. See chapter 2, note 30.

161. "Fortnightly Report from the Deputy High Commissioner for the United Kingdom in Lahore for the Fortnight ending 16th June 1953": 2, in DO 35/5296: Fortnightly Deputy High Commissioner's Reports from Lahore (TNA); Ayub Khan, *Friends not Masters*, 87; Afzal, *Pakistan*, 58.

162. Rahman, *Major Themes*, 64. Emphasis in the original.

163. Ghamidi, *Mizan*, 581 and n. 4 on the same page.

164. Ibid., 579–80, 601.

165. Muhammad Faruq Khan, *Jihad, qital, awr `alam-i Islam* (Lahore: Dar al-tazkir, 2005), 72–74.

166. Ibid., 187–88.

167. Ibid., 191–96.

168. Ibid., 183–84.

169. *Report on Hudood Ordinances* (2003), 2.

170. See Jane Perlez, "Killing of Pakistan Doctor Part of Taliban War on Educated," *New York Times*, October 9, 2010; Jamal Hoti, "Moderate Scholar Dr Farooq Killed in Mardan, *Dawn*, October 3, 2010; "VC of Swat Varsity Shot Dead in Mardan," *News*, October 3, 2010.

171. Abu `Ammar Zahid al-Rashidi, Mu`izz Amjad, Khurshid Nadim, and Faruq Khan, *Janab Javed Ahmad Ghamidi ke halqa-i fikr ke sath aik `ilmi awr fikri mukalama* (Gujranwala: al-Shari`a Academy, 2007). This is the record of a debate between Zahid al-Rashidi and some of Ghamidi's students on a variety of questions, including jihad. Faruq Khan was among Zahid al-Rashidi's interlocutors.

172. Ibid., 80.

173. The district magistrate, Rawalpindi, to the home secretary, Punjab, March 31, 1953 in Court of Inquiry Proceedings, 2: 411.

174. Ibid., 2: 411.

175. *Dawn*, October 29, 2001. On the delegation to the Taliban of which Shamzai was a member, see ibid., September 28–29, 2001. Taqi `Usmani, too, was a member of the delegation.

176. Hussain, *Frontline Pakistan*, 43.

177. The mosque's name had to do with the color in which it had originally been painted rather than with any leftist predilections. I draw here on an earlier discussion: Zaman, "Pakistan: Shari`a and the State," 227–28.

178. Syed Irfan Raza, "Lal Masjid Threatens Suicide Attacks," *Dawn*, April 7, 2007.

179. Muhammad Rafi` `Usmani, "Lal masjid intizamiyya awr hukumat ke darmiyan muzakarat kiyun nakam huwe?" *al-Balagh*, 42/7 (August 2007): 3–14, at 9. For his criticism of the Lal Masjid brothers, see ibid., 5.

180. Jane Perlez and Pir Zubair Shah, "Taliban Enlist an Army of Pakistan's Have-nots," *New York Times*, April 17, 2009. Cf. Simpson, *War from the Ground Up*, 81.

181. The question of what counts as "Islamic" is, of course, a vexed matter. The point here is not, however, that particular invocations of Islam are recognized as credible or persuasive by all others—which would hardly ever be the case—but only that some sustained effort to invoke Islam is made at all.

182. As should be clear from the foregoing, Sa`id has continued to maintain a thin line between, on the one hand, condemning Muslim regimes for seeking to "deceive God and His servants" with their lip service to Islam (Sa`id, *Khutbat-i Qadisiyya*, 119) and, on the other, arguing against branding such regimes as infidel (a central theme of his *Khutbat-i Qadisiyya: Fitna-i takfir*). That line might be less distinct to his listeners and readers, but *he* defends it on doctrinal grounds.

183. For a similar argument with reference to the criminal gangs of Karachi, see Gayer, *Karachi*, 134–38; and with reference to religio-political groups pressing for their anti-Ahmadi demands in a political context in which the relationship between religion and the state remains unsettled, see Saeed, *Politics of Desecularization*, especially 143, 146, 218.

184. See also Zaman, "Pluralism, Democracy, and the `Ulama"; Khan, "Institutions not Intentions."

185. Mawdudi, *Qadiyyani mas'ala*, 52–53. Quotation marks around "mulla" in the original. The tract was published on March 5, 1953, the day, as the Punjab chief minister later observed, "[m]ore firing had taken place ... than probably ever before in the history of Lahore in the course of a popular agitation." Court of Inquiry Proceedings, 9: 81. The incitement this tract was believed to have provided to the agitators was a key reason why a military court sentenced Mawdudi to death, though that sentence was soon commuted to imprisonment.

186. Martin Lau, "Pakistan," *Yearbook of Islamic and Middle Eastern Law* 9 (2002): 372–78, at 375–76.

187. Ismail Khan, "Pakistan Most Terror-hit Nation," *Dawn*, February 23, 2014.

Epilogue

1. Ministry of the Interior, "Scheme for Supervision and Control of Religious Institutions and Religious Activity," July 13, 1960, 54/CF/60–2293: Administration of Mosques, etc., 29–42 (NDC).

2. Ibid., 31. There is little historical merit in the claim that the ʿAbbasids and the Mughals had had any notable success in regulating religious life in their realm. As for Hyderabad, the rulers of this state did make efforts in the early twentieth century to foster an inclusive, cosmopolitan culture that would allow different religious and intellectual traditions to coexist, but that is not quite the same thing as the public regulation of religion. On Hyderabad, see Kavita Saraswathi Datla, *The Language of Secular Islam: Urdu Nationalism and Colonial India* (Honolulu: University of Hawaiʾi Press, 2013).

3. "Scheme for Supervision," 36–37.

4. Ibid., 33.

5. Ibid., 33.

6. Ibid, 37.

7. Ibid., 40.

8. Ibid., 31–32.

9. On this idea of a contract, see Maududi, *Islamic Law and Constitution*, 48–50.

10. See Mark Bevir, *The Logic of the History of Ideas* (Cambridge, UK: Cambridge University Press, 1999), 203–4, for a useful warning against "hypostatizing" traditions, which in our case would apply well to the doctrinal orientations in question.

11. On his madrasas, see chapter 6, note 148. Though polemics against rival doctrinal orientations are not a prominent part of his discourses, they are scarcely absent from them. For some examples, see Aslam Naqshbandi, *Halat-i faqir*, 308, 314–15 (contra Barelawis); Zulfiqar Ahmad Naqshbandi, *Khutbat-i Hind*, 2: 169–70 (against the Shiʿa); idem, *Maʿarif al-suluk*, ed. Mustafa Kamal Naqshbandi (Faisalabad: Maktabat al-faqir, 2012), 54–56 (against the Ahl-i Hadith; ibid., 56–57, on the Barelawis). It is worth noting, too, that the first female madrasa Zulfiqar Ahmad had established, in his native Jhang in 1986, was the Jamiʿa ʿAʾisha Siddiqa (named after the Prophet's wife) and located in the very neighborhood (Mahalla Pipliyanwala) in which Haqq Nawaz Jhangawi had founded the Sipah-i Sahaba in 1984. On this madrasa and its location, see Aslam Naqshbandi, *Halat-i faqir*, 41, 247–48; cf. Muhammad Ilyas Balakoti, *Amir-i ʿazimat: Hazrat Mawlana Nawaz Jhangawi* (Jhang: Jamiʿa ʿUsmaniyya, n.d.), 137. No source I have come across mentions any connection between Zulfiqar Naqshbandi and Haqq Nawaz.

12. See Shahjahanpuri, *Mawlana Ihtisham al-Haqq Thanawi*, 13–16.

13. Nasr, *Vanguard*, 55.

14. Abul-Hasanat Sayyid Muhammad Ahmad Qadiri, *Awraq-i ghamm* (Lahore: Rizwi kutubkhana, 1972). On 1929 as the date of the book's completion, see ibid., 538. Qadiri, it is worth noting, was a long-serving imam of the historic Wazir Khan mosque, which would serve as the nerve center of the anti-Ahmadi agitation in Lahore in 1953. See Court of Inquiry Proceedings, 1: 173.

15. *Nawa-i waqt*, December 17, 1965.

16. See M. R. Kayani, *Afkar-i parishan* (Lahore: Pakistan Writers Cooperative Society, 1965), 183–94, at 194. The text of the speech he had delivered on the occasion is undated. Also see Qasmi, *The Ahmadis*, 26.

17. *Nawa-i waqt*, March 16, 1970. Cf. Kayani, *Afkar*, 194.

18. See chapter 5, note 136.

19. See chapter 6, note 49.

20. "Scheme for Supervision," 33, again speaking with reference to the Ahl-i Hadith.

21. Murtaza Ahmad Khan Maikash, *Tarikh-i aqwam-i ʿalam*, 2nd ed. (Lahore: Majlis-i taraqqi-i adab, 1958), 7; quotation at 7. For the dedication, ibid., 5.

22. Ibid., 8.

23. Ibid., 370–71.

24. Ibid., 661–62. Emphasis added.

25. Ibid., 766–67.

26. Ibid., 769–70.

27. Ibid., 781.

28. Murtaza Ahmad Khan Maikash, *Tarikh-i Islam*, 2 vols., 2nd ed. (Lahore: Makta-ba-i A`la Hazrat, 2006), 2: 432.

29. Ibid., 2: 365–77.

30. Ibid., 2: 374.

31. Cf. ibid., 2: 432.

32. Court of Inquiry Proceedings, 1: 352–53.

33. Ibid., part 4: 1701–2 (Mian Anwar Ali).

34. Ibid., part 2: 503.

35. Ibid., part 4: 2003.

36. Ibid., part 2: 501–2.

37. The two judges of the Court of Inquiry were sensitive, however, to the public impact of such lines of questioning. Though the proceedings of the court were regularly reported in the national press, this was among the portions specifically marked as "not to be published." Ibid., part 2: 501–3.

38. For a concise statement to this effect, see *Report of the Court of Inquiry*, 231–32.

39. The publisher's name, Maktaba-i A`la Hazrat, evokes a common honorific for Ahmad Riza Khan, the founding figure of the Barelawi orientation. During his lifetime, however, Maikash may have been less clearly affiliated with the Barelawis than he would later appear to be. In his *Mirza'i nama*, 199–200, he thanked *both* Barelawi and Deobandi `ulama for assistance with the book, though without identifying their doctrinal orientations.

40. See note 28, earlier.

41. See chapter 7, note 26.

42. For instance, in line with many other contemporary and later observers, he repeated stereotypes about the materialism of the modern West. Some of his contemporaries, however, had taken a significantly more nuanced view of this matter. See Zaman, *Modern Islamic Thought*, 159–60.

43. Looking for people with a "clean" record could mean that the government might find no one to rely on. In the aftermath of the 1953 agitation in the Punjab, the government wanted to know the names of the religious scholars and imams who had taken no part in the agitation. The district magistrate of Rawalpindi responded: "If the Government desired only the names of the mullahs who have taken <u>absolutely no part</u>, I fear that the answer will be nil." Secret memo to the home secretary, Punjab, March 31, 1953, Court of Inquiry Proceedings, 2: 412–13 (words underlined in the original; also see chapter 7, notes 173–74). This was disheartening. Yet, it did not mean that the `ulama and the Sufi pirs were necessarily unwilling to work with the government, even on an issue as sensitive as this one. Thus, several prominent religious figures were mentioned among those "secretly cooperating" with the government during the 1953 agitation. Among these were Mawlana Ghulam Allah Khan, who presided over a mosque that had played a central role in the agitation in Rawalpindi (ibid., 2: 431); Mawlana `Abd al-Hannan, a respected scholar who officiated at another Rawalpindi mosque and whom the city's superintendent of police credited not just with "whole-hearted" cooperation but also with "keeping the female volunteers out of this agitation" (ibid., 2: 440); and the influential pir of Golra Sharif (ibid., 2: 455).

44. As the anti-Ahmadi movement gained momentum, Suhrawardy had come out in support of its demands. See Court of Inquiry Proceedings, 1: 216, 230–31.

45. For a somewhat similar point in the context of French secularism and its relationship with the Muslim inhabitants of the Republic, see John R. Bowen, *Why the French*

Don't Like Headscarves: Islam, the State, and Public Space (Princeton, NJ: Princeton University Press, 2007), especially 247–49.

46. On modernist institutions and associations in Indonesia, see Robert W. Hefner, *Civil Islam: Muslims and Democratization in Indonesia* (Princeton, NJ: Princeton University Press, 2000); R. Michael Feener, *Muslim Legal Thought in Modern Indonesia* (Cambridge, UK: Cambridge University Press, 2007); Abbas, "Knowing Islam."

47. The head of the Directorate of Public Relations was also the secretary of the Department of Islamiat. On the work of the department, see Court of Inquiry Proceedings, 3: 1265–67.

48. See chapter 7, note 27.

49. Court of Inquiry Proceedings, part 4: 1496. This person, one Amir Bakhsh, was also active in converting rural folk to Islam: ibid., 1496–97. Ironically, the wrestler himself was an Ahmadi, though he noted that those overseeing the final act of conversion were non-Ahmadi ʿulama. Two figures he named in this connection (ibid., 1497—Ahmad ʿAli and Ghulam Murshid—were reputable Deobandis. Ahmad ʿAli was the adopted son of the noted Deobandi scholar ʿUbayd Allah Sindhi; Ghulam Murshid was a long-serving imam at Lahore's largest mosque, the Badshahi Masjid. The fact that an Ahmadi was converting people to Islam with the formal assistance of Deobandi ʿulama suggests that it was then possible to work across these boundaries. Yet, the wrestler-proselyte was conscious that there *were* boundaries to be minded. Asked by the court why he had not employed an Ahmadi ʿalim to oversee the conversion, he responded: "I went to Maulvi Muhammad Hussain Qureshi, who is an Ahmadi, but he said that if he went to perform the ceremony, not only he but I myself and the person who had to be converted would be brick-batted." Ibid., 1497.

My point in adducing the wrestler's case is not that someone like him was necessarily unsuited for the job he was assigned. It is only that the department's choice of particular people had less to do with their credentials and much more with considerations of patronage. This much emerged clearly from the relevant proceedings of the Court of Inquiry.

50. This is not limited to Islamic institutions. As a recent study of the judicial system in Pakistan has shown, the federal and provincial academies that exist to train judges are also characterized by excessive control "by the top judicial leadership—a fact which is palpably resented within the academies and believed to hinder operational autonomy, flexibility, and initiative." Such overregulation is often accompanied by chronic inattention to the academies by those responsible for them, with their administration left in practice to "skeletal staffs . . . [that] have little capacity, training, time, and most importantly, autonomy, to focus on the training program structure, pedagogy, curricula, syllabi, and quality evaluation." Siddique, *Pakistan's Experience with Formal Law*, 398–409, quotations at 403–4.

51. See, for instance, Karamat Bhatty, "Institute of Islamic Culture Desperate for Funding," *Express Tribune*, October 25, 2011.

52. On Rahman's influence on Indonesian intellectuals, see Abbas, "Knowing Islam." For his reception in Turkish divinity schools, see Felix Körner, *Revisionist Koran Hermeneutics in Contemporary Turkish University Theology: Rethinking Islam* (Würzburg: Ergon, 2005).

53. *CAPD*, 5/1, 5.

54. Bhutto, *Reconciliation*, 273, 284; quotation at 284.

55. Ibid., 295–96.

56. J. McCormick, "The Mullahs and Their Influence in Pakistan," memo enclosed with L. B. Grafftey Smith, UK High Commissioner, Karachi, to C. R. Attlee, CRO, February 14, 1951 in DO 35/3185: Pakistan Internal Affairs (p. 4 of the memo [TNA]). Cf. Daultana's

statement to the 1953–54 Court of Inquiry: "Unquestioned leadership of the nation died with the Qai[d]-i-Azam. It became increasingly difficult for those who followed to resist the temptation of stabilising their popularity by calling to their assistance an appeal which had overwhelming emotional support of the people—namely the appeal of Islam and of the march toward an Islamic State. Unfortunately, the conception was never given precise content." Court of Inquiry Proceedings, 9: 7.

57. See Altaf Gauhar, *Translations from the Qur'an* (London: Islamic Information Services, 1977; first published in 1975). The translations in this book are based on "the exquisite Urdu Translation and valuable explanatory notes" of Mawdudi's *Tafhim al-Qur'an*. Ibid., 1. In the late 1960s, Gauhar (d. 2000) was the information secretary of President Ayub Khan. Mawdudi was arrested in January 1967 after "the Government," as Gauhar described it to some journalists, "were just fed up with the Mullahs." R. G. Beer to N. J. Barrington, British High Commission, February 2, 1967, with enclosed note titled "The Arrest of the Mullahs." DO 134/32: Correspondence between Rawalpindi, Lahore, Karachi, Dacca, item #264 (TNA; Electronic Resource).

58. For a useful overview, on which I draw here, see Kepel, *Jihad*, 61–80.

59. For his blueprint of an Islamic university, see Sayyid Abu'l-A`la Mawdudi, "Aik Islami university ka naqsha," in idem, *Ta`limat* (Lahore: Islamic Publications, 1963), 155–65. On the prize, see the official website of the King Faisal International Prize, http://kfip .org/service-to-Islam (accessed February 26, 2016).

60. See Zaman, "Religious Discourse," 60–71. The decision in 1999 against financial interest by the Shari`at Appellate Bench of the Supreme Court did, however, discuss Fazlur Rahman in an attempt to refute his arguments. The court was presided over by Justice Khalil-ur-Rehman Khan. For the full text of that decision, see Khalil-ur-Rehman Khan, *The Supreme Court's Judgement on Riba* (Islamabad: Shari`ah Academy, 2008); on Fazlur Rahman, ibid., 111–14.

61. See Saeed, *Politics of Desecularization*, especially 178–208 and 221–22, for the argument that the Pakistani higher judiciary had come to be increasingly subject from the mid-1980s to religio-political forces in the country—pressures it had often been able to resist until then.

62. See chapter 3, note 86.

63. See also Zaman, "Pluralism, Democracy, and the `Ulama"; Khan, "Institutions not Intentions."

GLOSSARY

`alim—Traditionally educated religious scholar.

amir—Leader or head.

dar al-`ulum—Institution of Islamic learning; see also madrasa.

din—Faith; religion.

fatwa—Legal opinion issued by a jurisconsult; see also mufti.

fiqh—Islamic law and jurisprudence.

fitna—Disorder; chaos. The term is also used for the first civil war in the history of Islam (656–61 CE), with which began the division of the Muslim community into hostile factions and later into distinct sects.

fuqaha (singular: faqih)—Scholars of Islamic law.

hadith—Traditions attributed to the Prophet Muhammad, regarded by Muslims as second to the Qur'an as a source of religious guidance and law.

hakimiyya—Sovereignty.

hudud (sometimes spelled as hudood; singular, hadd)—Punishments expressly sanctioned in the Qur'an and the sunna and, unlike many other punishments, not subject to being mitigated by the ruler or the aggrieved party.

hukm—Authority; a legal ruling; judgment.

ijma`—Consensus; considered to be a source of legal norms in Sunni jurisprudence.

ijtihad—Systematic reflection on the foundational sources of the law to arrive at legal rulings on matters not already or explicitly determined by the sacred law.

imam—Leader or head of the community; the person leading the ritual prayers; those descendants of `Ali (d. 661) who are regarded by the Shi`a as their infallible guides.

imambargah—Sites dedicated to Shi`i devotional practices.

jahiliyya–The "age of ignorance" prior to the advent of Islam; pagan materialism.

jihad—"Struggle" in God's cause, which may or may not involve taking up arms.

madh—Praise.

madhhab—School of law.

madrasa—Institution of traditional Islamic learning.

mawlana—Honorific used to designate a religious scholar.

mawlawi—A religious scholar or religious functionary.

millat (Arabic: milla)—A community as defined by ties of faith.

mufti—A jurisconsult; one who issues legal opinions; see also fatwa.

mujahidin—Those waging jihad. The term has often also been used to refer to those participating in the armed struggle against the Soviet occupation of Afghanistan.

mujtahid—A practitioner of ijtihad.

mulk—Authority.

mulla—A religious scholar. The term has pejorative connotations in modern South Asian usage.

pir—A Sufi master.

qawm—Nation as defined by ties of ethnicity, shared territory, and language.

qital—Warfare.

Rashidun—The first four caliphs—Abu Bakr (r. 632–34); `Umar (r. 634–44); `Usman (r. 644–56); `Ali (r. 656–61)—to succeed the Prophet Muhammad. They are viewed by the Sunnis as "rightly guided" (*rashidun*), with a religious stature second only to that of the Prophet.

riba—Financial interest; usury.

sahaba—The companions of the Prophet Muhammad.

sajjada nishin—"The occupier of the [Sufi master's] prayer rug"; the guardian of a Sufi shrine.

shari`a—The totality of Islamic legal and ethical norms; the sacred law of Islam.

shaykh—A Sufi master; a religious scholar.

Sufi—Muslim mystic.

sunna (or Sunnah)—The normative example of the Prophet Muhammad, typically expressed in the form of reports relating his teachings and conduct; see also hadith.

taqlid—"Investing with authority"; following the legal rulings of earlier scholars, or of the school of law to which one professes adherence.

tasawwuf—Sufism.

`ulama (singular: `alim)—"People of knowledge"; traditionally educated religious scholars.

umma—The worldwide community of Muslims.

`urs—The death anniversary of a saint, commemorated at his or her shrine.

wali—"Friend [of God]"; a saint.

waqf (plural: awqaf)—Charitable endowments.

zakat—Islamic alms tax paid annually on one's accumulated wealth; one of the five "pillars" of the faith.

zina—Unlawful sexual intercourse.

THE ARABIC DEFINITE article *al-* is ignored in listing proper names and book titles. Thus, al-Tabari would be found under "T" rather than under "A." Newspaper articles are listed in the bibliography only when they carry a byline.

Archival Sources

PAKISTAN

National Documentation Center, Cabinet Division, Islamabad

Prime Minister's Secretariat Files

3 (3)-PMS/48: Correspondence with the Hon'ble Minister for Finance.

26 (4)-PMS/48: Miscellaneous Correspondence during HPM's Visit to the UK.

3 (1)-PMS/49: Correspondence with Hon'ble Minister for Finance.

2 (1)-PMS/50: Correspondence with the Governor, East Bengal.

3 (3)-PMS/50: Correspondence with Hon'ble Minister for Law and Labour.

3 (18)-PMS/50: Resignation of Mr. J. N. Mandal, Minister for Law and Labour, Government of Pakistan.

1 (1)-PMS/52: Correspondence with the Governor-General of Pakistan.

2 (1)-PMS/52: Correspondence with HE the Governor of East Bengal.

3 (20)-PMS/52: Correspondence with the Hon'ble Minister for Refugees and Rehabilitation.

Cabinet Files

108/CF/48–1888: Minutes, Cabinet Meetings.

207/CF/54–2147: Orders of the Egyptian Government Controlling Sermons in Mosques; Preparation of Khutbas.

324/CF/1959–2274: Creation of an Islamic Research Centre.

54/CF/60–2293: Administration of Mosques; Training of Imams; Scheme for Supervision and Control of Religious Institutions and Religious Activity; Employment of Itinerant Preachers; Streamlining of Auqaf Properties in East Pakistan.

390/CF/63: Shia-Sunni Incidents; Influence of Religious Leaders from India.

97/CF/67: Ruat-i-Hilal Committee and the Moon Controversy.

331/CF/68–2620: Controversy on Dr. Fazlur Rahman's Book "Islam."

The Punjab Archives, Lahore

Proceedings of the Court of Inquiry, 1953–54 (following, with some modification, the contents as listed in Ali Usman Qasmi, *The Ahmadis and the Politics of Religious Exclusion in Pakistan* [London: Anthem Press, 2014], 259)

Vol. 1: Written Statements of Officers Stationed in Lahore.

Vol. 2: Written Statements of Officers Stationed in Sialkot, Gujranwala, and Rawalpindi.

Vol. 3: Written Statements of Officers Stationed in Multan, Lyallpur, and Montgomery.

Vol. 6: Written Statements of the Muslim League; Jamaat-i-Islami; Ahmadya Anjuman-i Ishaat-i Islam, Lahore; Ghazi Siraj-ud-Din Munir; Mutawalli Wazir Khan Mosque, Lahore.

Vol. 9: Written Statement of Mian Mumtaz Muhammad Khan Daultana, Ex-Chief Minister, on Behalf of the Previous Ministry.

Unnumbered volume: Appendices with the Statement of Mian Mumtaz Muhammad Khan Daultana, Ex-Chief Minister, Punjab.

Part 1: Statements and Cross-examination of Witnesses, #1–42.

Part 2: Statements and Cross-examination of Witnesses, #43–106.

Part 3: Statements and Cross-examination of Witnesses, #107–23.

Part 4: Statements and Cross-examination of Witnesses, # 124–31.

Part 5: Statements and Cross-examination of Witnesses, #132–37.

Part 6: Statement and Cross-examination of Witness #138: Mian Mumtaz Muhammad Khan Daultana.

National Archives of Pakistan, Islamabad

Archives of the Freedom Movement (AFM)

Vol. 437: Jamiat-ul-Ulema-i-Hind/Islam, part ii (Deoband file), 1945.

Vol. 438: Jamiat-ul-Ulema-i-Hind/Islam, part iii, 1946.

Vol. 439: Jamiat-ul-Ulema-i-Hind/Islam, part iv (Ulema and Mashaikh Conference, Lahore), 1946–47.

Parwez Memorial Research Scholars Library, Lahore

Ghulam Ahmad Parwez Papers

INDIA

Nehru Memorial Museum and Library, Delhi

Annual Proceedings of the All India Shia Conference, 1907–40; Microfilm: R-12261-68

A copy of this microfilm is also held by Princeton University Libraries, Princeton, NJ.

UNITED KINGDOM

The National Archives, Kew

Dominion Office Papers

DO 35/3005: Position of Muslims in the Indian Union.

DO 35/3185: Pakistan Internal Affairs.

DO 35/5296: Fortnightly Deputy High Commissioner's Reports from Lahore.

DO 35/5370: Religious Disturbances in Pakistan; Anti-Ahmadiyya Riots, March 1953.

DO 35/6349: Threats to the Defense of West Pakistan.

DO 35/8962: Influence of Islam on Pakistan Internal Situation.

DO 35/6340: Pakistan Attitudes to Arab/Israeli Crisis, October 1956.

DO 196/418: Banning of Fundamentalist Muslim Movement Jamaat-i-Islami in Pakistan.

Foreign Office

FO 686/149: Silk Letters Case.

British Library, London

Private Papers and Manuscripts

Linlithgow Collection.
    Mss. Eur. F.125/101.
Mudie Collection.
    Mss. Eur. F 164/12–19.

India Office Records

L/PJ/7/2587: The Sunni-Shia Controversy in Lucknow (Madhe Sahaba).
L/PJ/5/267: United Provinces Governor's Reports.
L/PJ/7/751: Ahrar-Ahmadiya Dispute at Qadian, Punjab.
L/PJ/7/943: Muslim Personal Law (Shariat) Application Act, 1937, and Amending
    Acts.
L/PJ/7/1065: Muslim Dissolution of Marriages Act 1939.
L/PJ/7/5297: The Music in Muslim Shrines Act 1942.
L/PJ/7/2413: NWFP Muslim Waqfs Act 1938; NWFP Muslim Waqf (Amendment)
    Act 1939; NWFP Muslim Waqfs Act 1947. Microfilm: IOR Neg 15918.
R/1/1/40: Wahabi Agents Dispatched by Sadik Hassan, Husband of the Begum of
    Bhopal, to the Soudan, Hodeida, Yemen and Mecca.
R/1/1/2006: Anti-Government Propaganda by Maulana Husain Ahmad Madani.

UNITED STATES

Rockefeller Archive Center, Sleepy Hollow, New York

Ford Foundation Grant # 74–141: Islam and Social Change (reel # 3087).

Government Publications

Bamford, P. C. *Histories of the Non-Co-operation and Khilafat Movements*. Delhi: Government of India Press, 1925; reprint, Delhi: Deep Publications, 1974.
Census of India 1911. Vol. 14: Punjab, Part 1. Report by Pandit Hari Kishan Kaul. Lahore: Civil and Military Gazette Press, 1912.
Census of Pakistan: Population According to Religion (Table 6). Karachi: Ministry of the Interior, Government of Pakistan, 1951.
Census of Pakistan 1961. Vol. 1: Pakistan. Karachi: Ministry of Home and Kashmir Affairs, n.d.
The Constituent Assembly of Pakistan. *Debates, 1947–1954*. 16 vols. Karachi: Manager of Publications, Government of Pakistan, 1947–54.
The Constitution of the Islamic Republic of Pakistan. Karachi: Department of Advertising, Films and Publications, Government of Pakistan, 1956.
The Constitution of the Republic of Pakistan. Washington, DC: Embassy of Pakistan, 1962.
Council of Islamic Ideology. *Hudood Ordinance 1979: A Critical Report*. Islamabad: Council of Islamic Ideology, 2007.
Kaul, Harikishan. *Census of India, 1911. Vol. 14: Punjab, Part 1 (Report)*. Lahore: Civil and Military Gazette Press, 1912.

Latimer, C. *Census of India, 1911. Vol. 13: North-West Frontier Province.* Peshawar: D. C. Anand & Sons, Government Printers, 1912.

The National Assembly of Pakistan. *Debates.* Karachi: Manager of Publications, 1972–76.

———. *Proceedings of the Special Committee of the Whole House Held in Camera to Consider the Qadiani Issue.* Published in 21 parts, August 5–September 7, 1974. At http://archive.org/details/1974-na-committee-ahmadiyya (accessed October 8, 2013).

National Commission on the Status of Women, Government of Pakistan. *Report on Hudood Ordinances 1979.* Islamabad: National Commission on the Status of Women, 2003.

Pakistan Education Statistics, 2013–2014. Islamabad: Ministry of Federal Education and Professional Training, 2015. At www.aepam.edu.pk/Files/EducationStatistics/Pakistan EducationStatistics2013-14.pdf (accessed June 23, 2015).

Pakistan ka manshur-i azadi. Karachi: Manager, Governor General Press, n.d. (1950).

Promulgation of New Ordinance: Qadianis' Anti-Islamic Activities. Islamabad: Directorate of Films and Publications, Ministry of Information and Broadcasting, Government of Pakistan, n.d. (1984).

Qanun-i asasi-i jumhuri-i Islami-i Iran. Tehran: Wizarat-i farhang wa irshad-i Islami, 1989.

Report of the Basic Principles Committee. Karachi: Manager of Publications, Government of Pakistan Press, 1952.

"Report of the Commission on Marriage and Family Laws." *Gazette of Pakistan (Extraordinary),* June 20, 1956: 1197–1232.

Report of the Committee Set Up by the Governor of West Pakistan for Recommending Improved Syllabus for the Various Darul Ulooms and Arabic Madrasas in West Pakistan. Lahore: Superintendent, Government Printing West Pakistan, 1962.

Report of the Constitution Commission, Pakistan, 1961. Karachi: Manager of Publications, Government of Pakistan Press, 1962.

Report of the Court of Inquiry Constituted under Punjab Act II of 1954 to Enquire into the Punjab Disturbances of 1953. Lahore: Superintendent, Government Printing, 1954.

Report on Islamic Summit 1974 Pakistan, Lahore February 22–24, 1974. Islamabad: Department of Films and Publications, Ministry of Information and Broadcasting, Government of Pakistan, n.d. (1974).

Report qawmi committee bara'i dini madaris-i Pakistan. Islamabad: Ministry of Religious Affairs, 1979.

Published Documents

Baxter, Craig. Ed. *Diaries of Field Marshal Mohammad Ayub Khan, 1966–1972.* Karachi: Oxford University Press, 2007.

Pirzada, Syed Sharifuddin. Ed. *Foundations of Pakistan. All-India Muslim League Documents, 1906–1947.* 2 vols. Karachi: National Publishing House, 1970.

Qadiri, Muhammad Jalal al-din. *Khutbat-i All India Sunni Conference, 1925–1947.* Gujarat: Maktaba-i Rizwiyya, 1978.

The Report of the Hamoodur Rehman Commission of Inquiry into the 1971 War. Lahore: Vanguard, n.d. (2000).

Rozina, Parvin. Ed. *Jam `iyyat al-`Ulama-i Hind: Dastawizat-i markazi ijlasha-i `amm.* 2 vols. Islamabad: National Institute of Historical and Cultural Research, 1980–81.

Zaheeruddin v. the State. The Supreme Court Monthly Review (Lahore), 26/8 (1993): 1718–80.

Zaidi, Z. H. Ed. *Quaid-i-Azam Mohammad Ali Jinnah Papers.* Islamabad: Quaid-i-Azam Papers Project, 1993–2009.

Other Published Works

Abbas, Megan Brankley. "Between Western Academia and Pakistan: Fazlur Rahman and the Fight for Fusionism." *Modern Asian Studies* 51 (2017): 736–68.

Abbasi, Kashif. "Five Seminary Boards to Adopt FBISE Syllabus." *Dawn*, July 14, 2016.

——. "New Report Reveals One-tenth of All Children Enrolled in Madressahs." *Dawn*, April 22, 2015.

`Abd al-`Aziz, Shah. *al-`Ujala al-nafi`a*. Khanewal: al-Maktaba al-sa`idiyya, 1975.

`Abduh, Muhammad. *Risalat al-tawhid*. Bulaq: al-Matba`a al-kubra al-amiriyya, 1897.

Abdul Hakim, Khalifa. *Afkar-i Ghalib*. Lahore: Maktaba-i mu`in al-adab, 1973.

——. *Iqbal awr mulla*. 8th printing. Lahore: Bazm-i Iqbal, 1952.

——. *Islam and Communism*. 3rd ed. Lahore: Institute of Islamic Culture, 1962; first published in 1951.

——. *Islamic Ideology*. Lahore: Publishers United, 1951.

——. *Islamic Ideology*. 2nd ed. Lahore: Institute of Islamic Culture, 1953.

——. *The Metaphysics of Rumi*. Lahore: Institute of Islamic Culture, 1959.

——. "Mullaiyyat." In *Maqalat-i Hakim*, 3 vols., ed. Shahid Husayn Razzaqi, 3: 183–91. Lahore: Idara-i saqafat-i Islamiyya, 1969.

——. "Sabiq Governor-General Ghulam Muhammad nawwar Allah marqadahu." *Saqafat* 3/6 (December 1956): 7–18.

Abdul Hakim, Khalifa. Trans. *Shrimad Bhagavat Gita*. Mumbai: Bharatiya Vidya Bhawan, 2001.

Abdul Vahid, Syed. *Thoughts and Reflections of Iqbal*. Lahore: Sh. Muhammad Ashraf, 1964.

Abu Zayd, Nasr Hamid. *Mafhum al-nass: Dirasa fi `ulum al-Qur'an*. Cairo: al-Hay'a al-Misriyya lil-kitab, 1990.

——. *Naqd al-khitab al-dini*. Cairo: Sina lil-nashr, 1992.

Adams, Charles J. "The Ideology of Mawlana Mawdudi." In *South Asian Politics and Religion*, ed. D. E. Smith, 371–97. Princeton, NJ: Princeton University Press, 1966.

Addleton, Jonathan. *Undermining the Centre: The Gulf Migration and Pakistan*. Karachi: Oxford University Press, 1992.

Afzal, M. Rafique. *Pakistan: History and Politics, 1947–1971*. Karachi: Oxford University Press, 2001.

Ahmad, Aftab. *Muhammad Hasan `Askari, aik mutala`a: Zati khutut ki rawshani main*. Lahore: Sang-i mil, 1994.

Ahmad, Aziz. *Islamic Modernism in India and Pakistan, 1857–1964*. London: Oxford University Press, 1967.

Ahmad, Irfan. *Islamism and Democracy in India: The Transformation of the Jamaat-e-Islami*. Princeton, NJ: Princeton University Press, 2009.

Ahmad, Jamil-ud-din. Ed. *Speeches and Writings of Mr. Jinnah*. 2 vols. Lahore: Shaikh Muhammad Ashraf, 1960–64.

——. Ed. *Some Recent Speeches and Writings of Mr. Jinnah*. Lahore: Sh. Muhammad Ashraf, 1943.

Ahmad, Khurshid. Ed. *Marriage Commission Report X-Rayed*. Karachi: Chiragh-e-Rah Publications, 1959.

Ahmad, Mujeeb. *Jam`iyyat `Ulama-i-Pakistan 1948–1979*. Islamabad: National Institute of Historical and Cultural Research, 1993.

Ahmad, Nazir. *Chiragh-i hidayat*. Ed. Muhammad Isma`il Afzal. Lahore: Shaykh Ghulam `Ali, n.d.

——. *al-Huquq wal-fara'iz*. 3 vols. Delhi: Matba`-i Qasimi, 1905–6.

——. *Matalib al-Qur'an*. Lucknow: Nazir Press, n.d.

Ahmad, Nazr. *Ja'iza-i madaris-i `arabiyya-i Maghribi Pakistan*. Lyallpur: Jami`a Chish-tiyya Trust, 1960.

———. *Ja'iza-i madaris-i `arabiyya-i Maghribi Pakistan*. Lahore: Muslim Academy, 1972.

Ahmad, Sadaf. *Transforming Faith: The Story of al-Huda and Islamic Revivalism among Urban Pakistani Women*. Syracuse, NY: Syracuse University Press, 2009.

Ahmed, Asad Ali. "Specters of Macaulay: Blasphemy, the Indian Penal Code, and Paki-stan's Postcolonial Predicament." In *Censorship in South Asia: Cultural Regulation from Sedition to Seduction*, ed. Raminder Kaur and William Mazzarella, 172–205. Bloomington: Indiana University Press, 2009.

Ahmed, Manzooruddin. *Pakistan: The Emerging Islamic State*. Karachi: Allies Book Cor-poration, 1966.

Ahmed, Shahab. *What Is Islam? The Importance of Being Islamic*. Princeton, NJ: Prince-ton University Press, 2016.

Ahmed, Shakeel, and Fareedullah Chaudhry. "Tashfeen Malik Was Like Normal Students at BZU." *Dawn*, December 8, 2015.

Ahsan, Hafiz al-Rahman. *Jama`at-i Islami awr Mashriqi Pakistan*. Lahore: Tasnim Academy, 1971.

Akhlaque, Qudssia. "OIC to Discuss Challenges Faced by Muslim World." *Dawn*, June 1, 2004.

Alavi, Seema. *Muslim Cosmopolitanism in the Age of Empire*. Cambridge, MA: Harvard University Press, 2015.

Ali, Imtiaz. "Qawwali Star Sabri Gunned Down in Karachi." *Dawn*, June 24, 2016.

Ali, Kalbe. "CII Justifies 'Light Beatings' for Errant Wives." *Dawn*, May 27, 2016.

———. "Muslim Women Cannot Object to Husbands' Marriages: CII Chief." *Dawn*, Octo-ber 22, 2014.

———. "Seminaries Boom in Absence of Govt Checks." *Dawn*, April 29, 2016.

Ali, Kamran Asdar. *Communism in Pakistan: Politics and Class Activism 1947–1972*. Lon-don: I. B. Tauris, 2015.

Ali, Maulana Muhammad. *The Holy Qur'an: Arabic Text, English Translation and Com-mentary*. Lahore: Ahmadiyyah Anjuman Isha`at Islam, 1973.

Ali, Mohamed (Muhammad `Ali). *Bayan-i Mawlana Muhammad `Ali sahib … jo ra'is al-ahrar Mawlana Muhammad `Ali sahib … ne Karachi ke magistrate ki `adalat main diya*. Compiled by Munshi Mushtaq Ahmad. Delhi: Swaraj Printing Works, 1921.

———. *My Life. A Fragment*. Ed. Afzal Iqbal. Lahore: Sh. Muhammad Ashraf, 1942; re-print, 1946.

Ali, Muhammad Faisal. "Suicide Bomber Kills Anti-Taliban Cleric Allama Naeemi." *Dawn*, June 13, 2009.

Ali, Rahmat, Mohammad Aslam Khan, Sheikh Mohammad Sadiq, and Inayat Ullah Khan. "Now or Never: Are We to Live or Perish Forever?" In *Complete Works of Rah-mat Ali*, vol. 1, ed. K. K. Aziz, 5–10. Islamabad: National Commission on Historical and Cultural Research, 1978.

Ali, Syed Ameer. *A Critical Examination of the Life and Teachings of Mohammed*. Lon-don: Williams & Norgate, 1873.

———. *The Life and Teachings of Mohammed, or the Spirit of Islam*. London: W. H. Allen, 1891.

———. *The Spirit of Islam*. London: Christophers, 1922.

Ali, Zulfiqar. "Distinction between Good, Bad Taliban No More: PM." *Dawn*, December 18, 2014.

al-Alusi, Shihab al-din. *Ruh al-ma`ani*. 30 vols. Beirut: Dar ihya al-turath al-`Arabi, 1970.

Alvi, Sajida Sultana. "Renewal of the Čišti Order in Eighteenth-Century Punjab." In *Muslim Cultures in the Indo-Iranian World during the Early Modern and Modern Periods*, ed. Denis Hermann and Fabrizio Speziale, 216–46. Berlin: Klaus Schwarz Verlag, 2010.

al-Amidi, Sayf al-din. *al-Ihkam fi usul al-ahkam*. 2 vols. Cairo: Matba`at Muhammad `Ali Subayh, 1929.

Ansari, Maymuna. *Mirza Muhammad Hadi, Mirza o Ruswa: sawanih hayat awr adabi karname*. Lahore: Majlis-i taraqqi-i adab, 1963.

Ansari, Sarah F. D. *Sufi Saints and State Power: The Pirs of Sind, 1843–1947*. Cambridge, UK: Cambridge University Press, 1992.

Anwarullah and Haleem Asad. "TNSM Supporters Head for Kabul." *Dawn*, October 28, 2001.

Arango, Tim. "Tears, and Anger, as Militants Destroy Iraq City's Relics." *New York Times*, July 30, 2014.

Arberry, A. J. Trans. *Javid Nama*. London: George Allen & Unwin, 1966.

———. Trans. *The Koran Interpreted*. 2 vols. New York: Simon & Schuster, 1996.

Arif, K. M. *Working with Zia: Pakistan's Power Politics, 1977–1988*. Karachi: Oxford University Press, 1995.

Aristotle. *Metaphysics*. Trans. Hugh Tredennick. 2 vols. Cambridge, MA: Harvard University Press (Loeb Classical Library), 1947.

`Askari, Muhammad Hasan. *Jadidiyyat*. Rawalpindi: `Iffat Hasan, 1979.

`Ata Allah, Shaykh. Ed. *Iqbal nama*. 2 vols. Lahore: Shaykh Muhammad Ashraf, n.d. (1950–51).

Auj, Muhammad Shakil. *Nisa'iyyat: Chand fikri o nazari mabahis*. Karachi: Kulliyya-i ma`arif-i Islamiyya, Jami`a Karachi, 2012.

———. *Ta`birat*. Karachi: Kulliyya-i ma`arif-i Islamiyya, 2013.

Azad, Abu'l-Kalam. *Khutbat-i Azad*. Ed. Malik Ram. Delhi: Sahitiya Academy, 1974.

———. *Mas'ala-i khilafat wa jazira-i `Arab*. Calcutta: All India Khilafat Committee, 1920.

Azam, Hina. *Sexual Violation in Islamic Law: Substance, Evidence, and Procedure*. Cambridge, UK: Cambridge University Press, 2015.

Azhar, Muhammad Mas`ud. *Ae Musalman behen*. Karachi: Maktaba-i Hasan, 2004.

———. *Fath al-Jawwad fi ma`arif ayat al-jihad*. 4 vols. Lahore: Maktaba-i `irfan, 2007–9.

———. *Faza'il-i jihad*. Karachi: Maktaba-i Hasan, 2001.

———. *Khutbat-i jihad*. Ed. Sultan Mahmud Ziya. 2 vols. Karachi: Maktaba-i Hasan, 2001.

———. *Tuhfa-i sa`adat*. Karachi: Idarat al-khayr, 2001.

Aziz, Sadaf. "Making a Sovereign State: Javed Ghamidi and 'Enlightened Moderation.'" *Modern Asian Studies* 45 (2011): 597–629.

Bacha, Ali Hazrat. "Peshawar Panj Pir Shrine Blast Kills Three." *Dawn*, June 22, 2012.

———. "Terrorists Turn on Sufi Saint's Shrine." *Dawn*, March 6, 2009.

———. "Two Women of 'Loose Character' Executed." *Dawn*, August 21, 2008.

Bacha, Khalilur Rehman. "14-Year Old Activist Shot and Critically Wounded." *Dawn*, October 10, 2012.

Badayuni, `Abd al-Qadir. *Muntakhab al-tawarikh*. Ed. Ahmad `Ali and W. N. Lees, 3 vols. Calcutta, 1864–69; reprint, Osnabrük: Biblio Verlag, 1983.

al-Baghawi, al-Husayn b. Mas`ud. *Tafsir al-Baghawi, Ma`alim al-tanzil*. Ed. Muhammad `Abdallah al-Nimr et al., 8 vols. Riyadh: Dar tayba, 1993.

Baha, Lal. "The Activities of the Mujahidin 1900–1936." *Islamic Studies* 18 (1979): 97–168.

Bakhsh, Wahid. Ed. *Mazamin-e-Zauqi* (English). Karachi: J. G. Lennard and Co., 1948.

———. Ed. *Mazamin-i Zauqi* (Urdu). Karachi: Mahfil-i zawqiyya, n.d. (1977).

Balakoti, Muhammad Ilyas. *Amir-i `azimat: Hazrat Mawlana Haqq Nawaz Jhangawi*. Jhang: Jami`a `Usmaniyya, n.d. (1990).

al-Baqli, Ruzbihan. *Ara'is al-bayan.* Ed. Ahmad Farid al-Mizyadi, 3 vols. Beirut: Dar al-kutub al-`ilmiyya, 2008.

Barfield, Thomas. *Afghanistan: A Cultural and Political History.* Princeton, NJ: Princeton University Press, 2010.

Barry, Ellen. "Bangladesh Hangs 2 Leaders Convicted of War Crimes." *New York Times,* November 22, 2015.

Bass, Gary J. *The Blood Telegram: Nixon, Kissinger, and a Forgotten Genocide.* New York: Vintage Books, 2014.

Bayanat-i `ulama-i rabbani bar irtidad-i firqa-i qadiyyani. Deoband: Maktaba-i rashad, 1989.

Bayly, C. A. *Recovering Liberties: Indian Thought in the Age of Liberalism and Empire.* Cambridge, UK: Cambridge University Press, 2012.

Bell, Michael. "The Metaphysics of Modernism." In *The Cambridge Companion to Modernism,* 2nd ed., ed. Michael Levenson, 9–32. Cambridge, UK: Cambridge University Press, 2011.

Beverley, Eric Lewis. *Hyderabad, British India, and the World: Muslim Networks and Minor Sovereignty, c. 1850–1950.* Cambridge, UK: Cambridge University Press, 2015.

Bevir, Mark. *The Logic of the History of Ideas.* Cambridge, UK: Cambridge University Press, 1999.

Bhatti, Muhammad Ishaq. *Bazm-i arjumandan.* Delhi: al-Kitab International, 2005.

———. *Qafila-i hadis.* Lahore: Maktaba-i Quddusiyya, 2003.

Bhatti, Muhammad Ishaq. Ed. *Armughan-i Hanif.* Lahore: Idara-i saqafat-i Islamiyya, 1980.

Bhatty, Karamat. "Institute of Islamic Culture Desperate for Funding." *Express Tribune,* October 25, 2011.

Bhutta, Muhammad Yusuf. Ed. *Mawlana Mawdudi apni and dusron ki nazar main.* 2nd ed. Lahore: Idara-i ma`arif-i Islami, 1984.

Bhutto, Benazir. *Reconciliation: Islam, Democracy, and the West.* New York: Harper, 2008.

al-Bihari, Muhibb Allah. *Musallam al-thubut.* 2 vols. Cairo: al-Matba`a al-Husayniyya, n.d. (1908).

Binder, Leonard. *Islamic Liberalism: A Critique of Development Ideologies.* Chicago: University of Chicago Press, 1988.

———. *Religion and Politics in Pakistan.* Berkeley: University of California Press, 1961.

Birmani, Tariq Saeed. "Devotees Miss Drum Beat and Dance at Sakhi's Urs." *Dawn,* April 6, 2015.

Bose, Sugata. *His Majesty's Opponent: Subhas Chandra Bose and India's Struggle against Empire.* Cambridge, MA: Harvard University Press, 2011.

Bowen, John R. *Why the French Don't Like Headscarves: Islam, the State, and Public Space.* Princeton, NJ: Princeton University Press, 2007.

Brohi, A. K. "Thoughts on the Future Constitution of Pakistan." *Dawn,* August 24, 1952.

Brown, Vahid, and Don Rassler. *Fountainhead of Jihad: The Haqqani Nexus, 1973–2012.* London: Hurst, 2013.

Brunner, Rainer, and Werner Ende. Eds. *The Twelver Shia in Modern Times.* Leiden: Brill, 2001.

Buehler, Arthur F. *Sufi Heirs of the Prophet: The Indian Naqshbandiyya and the Rise of the Mediating Sufi Shaykh.* Columbia: University of South Carolina Press, 1998.

Butt, Sajjad Shafiq. "441,565 Students Are Enrolled in Punjab Madraris," *News,* January 2, 2006. At www.accessmylibrary.com/article-1G1-140436575/pakistan-over-400000-stu dents.html (accessed June 29, 2013).

Butt, Wasim Ashraf. "Factory Torched in Jhelum over Blasphemy Allegation." *Dawn*, November 22, 2015.

Calvin, John. *Institutes of the Christian Religion*, in *John Calvin: Works and Correspondence*. Charlottesville, VA: InteLex Corporation, 1995. At http://libwebprod.princeton.edu/resolve/lookup?url=http://pm.nlx.com/xtf/view?docId=calvin/calvin.01.xml (accessed March 23, 2014).

Carré, Olivier. *Mysticism and Politics: A Critical Reading of Fi Zilal al-Qur'an by Sayyid Qutb (1906-1966)*. Trans. Carol Artigues. Leiden: Brill, 2003.

Chaghatai, M. Ikram. Ed. *Deputy Nazir Ahmad: A Biographical and Critical Appreciation*. Lahore: Pakistan Writers Cooperative Society, 2013.

Cheema, Moeen H., and Abdul-Rahman Mustafa. "From the Hudood Ordinances to the Protection of Women Act: Islamic Critiques of the Hudood Laws of Pakistan." *UCLA Journal of Islamic and Near Eastern Law* 8 (2009): 1–48.

Christmann, Andreas. *The Qur'an, Morality and Critical Reason: The Essential Muhammad Shahrur*. Leiden: Brill, 2009.

Cohen, Stephen P. *The Pakistan Army*. Berkeley: University of California Press, 1984.

Cook, Michael. *Ancient Religions, Modern Politics: The Islamic Case in Comparative Perspective*. Princeton, NJ: Princeton University Press, 2014.

——. "Is Political Freedom an Islamic Value?" In *Freedom and the Construction of Europe*, 2 vols., ed. Quentin Skinner and Martin van Gelderen, 2: 283–310. Cambridge, UK: Cambridge University Press, 2013.

Cromer, Earl of. *Modern Egypt*. 2 vols. London: Macmillan, 1908.

Custers, Peter. "Maulana Bhashani and the Transition to Secular Politics in East Bengal." *Indian Economic and Social History Review* 47 (2010): 231–59.

Daechsel, Markus. *Islamabad and the Politics of International Development in Pakistan*. Cambridge, UK: Cambridge University Press, 2015.

Daryabadi, `Abd al-Majid. *Hakim al-ummat*: *Nuqush wa ta'assurat*. Delhi: Sa`di Book Depot, 1990.

Daskawi, Javid Jamal. *Ihsan Ilahi Zahir*. Lahore: Jang Publishers, 1990.

Datla, Kavita Saraswathi. *The Language of Secular Islam: Urdu Nationalism and Colonial India*. Honolulu: University of Hawai'i Press, 2013.

Devji, Faisal. *Muslim Zion: Pakistan as a Political Idea*. Cambridge, MA: Harvard University Press, 2013.

Dhakku, Nabeel Anwar. "Ahmedis in a Chakwal Village Fear for Their Lives." *Dawn*, June 9, 2015.

——. "Kabaddi, Bullfights Mark Annual Urs of Sufi Saint." *Dawn*, September 23, 2013.

Dhulipala, Venkat. *Creating a New Medina: State Power, Islam, and the Quest for Pakistan in Late Colonial North India*. Delhi: Cambridge University Press, 2015.

Donner, Fred M. *Muhammad and the Believers: At the Origins of Islam*. Cambridge, MA: Harvard University Press, 2010.

Dorronsoro, Gilles. *Revolution Unending: Afghanistan, 1979 to the Present*. Trans. John King. London: Hurst, 2005.

Dutta, Sagnik. "Ajmer Hasn't Helped Pak VIPs." *Sunday Guardian*, April 8, 2012.

Edwards, David B. *Before Taliban: Genealogies of the Afghan Jihad*. Berkeley: University of California Press, 2002.

——. *Caravan of Martyrs: Sacrifice and Suicide Bombing in Afghanistan*. Berkeley: University of California Press, 2017.

The Encyclopedia of Islam. 2nd ed. Leiden: Brill, 1960–2002.

Ernst, Carl W. *The Shambhala Guide to Sufism*. Boston: Shambhala, 1997.

Ernst, Carl W., and Bruce B. Lawrence. *Sufi Martyrs of Love: The Chishti Order in South Asia and Beyond.* New York: Palgrave Macmillan, 2002.

Ewing, Katherine. "The Politics of Sufism: Redefining the Saints of Pakistan." *Journal of Asian Studies* 42 (1983): 251–68.

Faiz, Faiz Ahmad. *Nuskha-ha'i wafa.* Lahore: Maktaba-i karawan, n.d. (1984).

Farani, M. *Law of Auqaf and Evacuee Trusts.* Lahore: Lahore Law Times Publications, n.d. (ca. 1967).

Farid, Muhammad. *Fatawa-i Faridiyya.* 7 vols. Ed. Muhammad Wahhab Manglori. Zarobi: Dar al-`Ulum Siddiqiyya, 2013.

Farooqi, Mehr Afshan. *Urdu Literary Culture: Vernacular Modernity in the Writing of Muhammad Hasan Askari.* New York: Palgrave Macmillan, 2012.

Faruqi, Zia al-Rahman. *Khilafat World Order.* Faisalabad: Idara-i isha`at al-ma`arif, 2003.

———. *Sipah-i sahaba ka nasb al-`ayn awr taqaze.* Faisalabad: Idara-i isha`at al-ma`arif, 1994.

———. *Sipah-i Sahaba kiya hai, kiya chahati hai?* N.p., n.d.

Feener, R. Michael. *Muslim Legal Thought in Modern Indonesia.* Cambridge, UK: Cambridge University Press, 2007.

Fihrist madaris-i mulhiqa-i tanzim al-madaris (Ahl-i sunnat) Pakistan. Lahore: Markazi daftar tanzim al-madaris Pakistan, 1990.

Friedmann, Yohanan. *Prophecy Continuous: Aspects of Ahmadi Religious Thought and Its Medieval Background.* Berkeley: University of California Press, 1989.

———. *Shaykh Ahmad Sirhindi.* Delhi: Oxford University Press, 2000.

Fundamental Principles of an Islamic State, Formulated at a Gathering of Ulama of Various Muslim Schools of Law under the Presidentship of Allama Syed Suleiman sahib Nadvi. Karachi: N.p., n.d. (1951).

Gall, Carlotta. "Governor's Assassination Deepens the Divide in Pakistan." *New York Times,* January 6, 2011.

———. "Pakistan Faces a Divide of Age on Muslim Law." *New York Times,* January 11, 2011.

Gardner, Katy. *Global Migrants, Local Lives: Travel and Transformation in Rural Bangladesh.* Oxford, UK: Clarendon Press, 1995.

Gauhar, Altaf. *Translations from the Qur'an.* London: Islamic Information Services, 1977.

Gayer, Laurent. *Karachi: Ordered Disorder and the Struggle for the City.* New York: Oxford University Press, 2014.

Ghamidi, Javed Ahmad. *Burhan.* 3rd ed. Lahore: Dar al-ishraq, 2001.

———. *Mizan.* 3rd ed. Lahore: al-Mawrid, 2008.

Ghazi, Mahmud Ahmad. "Islam ke siyasi nizam main iqtidar-i a`la ka tasawwur." *al-Balagh* 5/10 (December 1971): 21–28.

Ghumman, Khawar. "Enrolment in Seminaries Rises by 40pc." *Dawn,* October 28, 2009.

———. "Oct 12 Takeover Made Part of SSC Curriculum." *Dawn,* December 30, 2006.

Gibb, H.A.R. *Modern Trends in Islam.* Chicago: University of Chicago Press, 1947.

———. *Mohammedanism: An Historical Survey.* London: Oxford University Press, 1949.

Gibbon, Edward. *The History of the Decline and Fall of the Roman Empire.* Ed. J. B. Bury. 7 vols. 4th ed. London: Methuen & Co., 1911.

Gilman, Nils. *Mandarins of the Future: Modernization Theory in Cold War America.* Baltimore, MD: Johns Hopkins University Press, 2003.

Gilmartin, David. *Empire and Islam: Punjab and the Making of Pakistan.* Berkeley: University of California Press, 1988.

———. "A Magnificent Gift: Muslim Nationalism and the Election Process in Colonial Punjab." *Comparative Studies in Society and History* 40/3 (1998): 415–36.

——. "Religious Leadership and the Pakistan Movement in the Punjab." *Modern Asian Studies* 13 (1979): 485–517.

Giustozzi, Antonio. *Koran, Kalashnikov, and Laptop: The Neo-Taliban Insurgency in Afghanistan.* New York: Columbia University Press, 2008.

Glenn, Charles L. *The Ambiguous Embrace: Government and Faith-based Schools and Social Agencies.* Princeton, NJ: Princeton University Press, 2000.

Gopal, S. General ed. *Selected Works of Jawaharlal Nehru.* 15 vols. Delhi: Orient Longman, 1972–82.

Gould, William. *Hindu Nationalism and the Language of Politics in Late Colonial India.* Cambridge, UK: Cambridge University Press, 2004.

Graham, William A. "Traditionalism in Islam: An Essay in Interpretation." *Journal of Interdisciplinary History* 23 (1993): 495–522.

Gul, Pazir. "Miramshah Taliban Open Office." *Dawn,* September 28, 2006.

Hadi, Mirza Muhammad. *Umrao Jan Ada.* Trans. Khushwant Singh and M. A. Husaini. Bombay: Orient Longman, 1961.

Hadi, Mirza Muhammad. Trans. *Hikmat al-Ishraq.* Hyderabad: Dar al-tab`, Jami`a Uthmaniyya, 1925.

Hali, Altaf Husayn. *Hayat-i javid.* Aligarh: Muslim University Institute, 1922; first published in 1901.

——. *Hayat-i Sa`di.* Lahore: Majlis-i taraqqi-i adab, 1961.

Hallaq, Wael B. *A History of Islamic Legal Theories: An Introduction to Sunni Usul al-fiqh.* Cambridge, UK: Cambridge University Press, 1997.

——. *Shari`a: Theory, Practice, Transformations.* Cambridge, UK: Cambridge University Press, 2009.

Hamidi, Khalil Ahmad. *Tahrik-i Islami ke asarat.* Lahore: Mansura Book Center, 1976.

Hamilton, Charles. Trans. *The Hedaya, or Guide: A Commentary on the Mussulman Laws.* 4 vols. London: T. Bensley, 1791.

Hanif, Intikhab. "Ulema Must Undo Extremist Narrative of Religion: PM." *Dawn,* March 12, 2017.

Hanioğlu, M. Şükrü. *Atatürk: An Intellectual Biography.* Princeton, NJ: Princeton University Press, 2011.

Haqqani, `Abd al-Qayyum. *Khutbat-i Haqqani.* Ed. Muhammad Ramazan. 3rd ed. Akora Khattak: Mu'tamar al-musannifin, 1991.

Haqqani, Husain. *Pakistan: Between Mosque and Military.* Washington, DC: Carnegie Endowment for International Peace, 2005.

Haroon, Sana. *Frontier of Faith: Islam in the Indo-Afghan Borderland.* London: Hurst, 2007.

Harder, Hans. *Sufism and Saint Veneration in Contemporary Bangladesh: The Maijbhandaris of Chittagong.* London: Routledge, 2011.

Hardy, Peter. *The Muslims of British India.* Cambridge, UK: Cambridge University Press, 1972.

Hartung, Jan-Peter. *A System of Life: Mawdudi and the Ideologisation of Islam.* New York: Oxford University Press, 2014.

Hasan, Mahmud. Trans. *Hama'il sharif mutarjam.* Bijnor: Madina Press, n.d.

——. Trans. *al-Qur'an al-karim wa tarjamat ma`anihi wa tafsiruhu ilal-lughat al-Urdiyya.* Medina: Majma` khadim al-haramayn al-sharifayn al-malik Fahd li-tiba`at al-mushaf al-sharif, 1993.

Hasan, Shazia. "Only One Percent of Pakistan's Labour Is Unionized." *Dawn,* May 1, 2015.

Hashimi, Muhammad Tufayl. *Hudud Ordinance: Kitab o sunnat ki rawshani main.* N.p.: `Awrat Foundation, 2004.

Hassan, Ahmed. "Govt Yields to MMA on Hudood Laws." *Dawn*, September 12, 2006.

———. "NA Committee to Review Amended Draft." *Dawn*, September 16, 2006.

Haydar, Qurrat al-`Ayn. *Ag ka darya*. Lahore: Maktaba-i jadid, 1959.

———. *Kar-i jahan daraz hai*. 3 vols. Delhi: Educational Publishing House, 2003.

Haydari, `Ali Sher. *Jawahirat-i Haydari*. Ed. Muhammad Nadim Qasimi. Lahore: Maktabat al-sahaba, 2010.

Haydari, Karam. Ed. *Taqarir o tajawiz `ulama convention*. Islamabad: Wizarat-i madhhabi umur wa aqalliyyati umur, n.d. (1980).

Hefner, Robert W. *Civil Islam: Muslims and Democratization in Indonesia*. Princeton, NJ: Princeton University Press, 2000.

Hermansen, Marcia. Trans. *The Conclusive Argument from God: Shah Wali Allah of Delhi's Hujjat Allah al-Baligha*. Leiden: Brill, 1996.

Hobbes, Thomas. *Leviathan*. Ed. Richard Tuck. Cambridge, UK: Cambridge University Press, 1996.

Höffding, Harald. *The Philosophy of Religion*. Trans. from the German by B. E. Meyer. London: Macmillan, 1906.

Hoffman, Valerie J. *Sufism, Mystics, and Saints in Modern Egypt*. Columbia: University of South Carolina Press, 1995.

Hoti, Jamal. "Moderate Scholar Dr Farooq Killed in Mardan." *Dawn*, October 3, 2010.

Hourani, Albert. *Arabic Thought in the Liberal Age, 1798–1939*. Cambridge, UK: Cambridge University Press, 1983.

Hovannisian, Richard G. Ed. *Ethics in Islam*. Malibu, CA: Undena Publications, 1985.

al-Hudaybi, Hasan. *Du`at la qudat*. Cairo: Dar al-tiba`a wal-nashr al-Islamiyya, n.d. (1977).

Hujwiri, `Ali. *Kashf al-mahjub*. Trans. and abridged by Mian Tufail Muhammad. 2nd ed. Lahore: Islamic Publications, 1968.

Humphreys, R. Stephen. *Islamic History: A Framework for Inquiry*. Princeton, NJ: Princeton University Press, 1991.

Huntington, Samuel P. *Political Order in Changing Societies*. New Haven, CT: Yale University Press, 1968.

Hurd, John, and Ian J. Kerr. *India's Railway History: A Research Handbook*. Leiden: Brill, 2012.

Hussain, Asim. "Apostasy Decree Issued against Taseer." *News*, November 25, 2010.

Hussain, Mir Zohair. "Islam in Pakistan under Bhutto and Zia-ul-Haq." In *Islam, Muslims and the Modern State*, ed. Hussin Mutalib and Taj ul-Islam Hashmi, 47–79. New York: St. Martin's Press, 1994.

Hussain, Syeda Abida. *Power Failure: The Political Odyssey of a Pakistani Woman*. Karachi: Oxford University Press, 2015.

Hussain, Zahid. *Frontline Pakistan: The Struggle with Militant Islam*. London: I. B. Tauris, 2007.

———. "The Last Episode." *Dawn*, August 20, 2014.

Hyder, Syed Akbar. *Reliving Karbala: Martyrdom in South Asian Memory*. New York: Oxford University Press, 2006.

Ibn Kathir. *Tafsir al-Qur'an al-`azim*. Ed. Mustafa al-Sayyid Muhammad, Muhammad al-Sayyid Rashad, Muhammad Fadl al-`Ajamawi, `Ali Ahmad `Abd al-Baqi, and Hasan `Abbas Qutb. 15 vols. Giza: Mu'assasat Qurtuba, 2000.

Ibn Qayyim al-Jawziyya. *I`lam al-muwaqqi`in `an Rabb al-`alamin*. Ed. Muhammad Muhyi al-din `Abd al-Hamid. 4 vols. Cairo: Matba`at al-sa`ada, 1955.

Ihtasham ul Haque. "Lashkar, Jaish, TJP, TNSM & SSP Banned." *Dawn*, January 13, 2002.

Ilahabadi, Akbar. *Kulliyyat-i Akbar*. Lahore: Sang-i mil Publications, 2008.

International Crisis Group. *Education Reform in Pakistan*. Brussels: International Crisis Group, 2014.

International Islamic Colloquium Papers, December 29, 1957–January 8, 1958. Lahore: Punjab University Press, 1960.

Iqbal, Afzal. *Life and Times of Mohamed Ali*. Delhi: Idarah-i Adabiyat-i Delhi, 1978.

Iqbal, Haya Fatima. "Remembering Dr. Shakeel Auj: The Man Who Wasn't Afraid." *Dawn*, September 18, 2015. At www.dawn.com/news/1207553 (accessed January 25, 2016).

Iqbal, Muhammad. *The Development of Metaphysics in Persia: A Contribution to the History of Muslim Philosophy*. London: Luzac & Co., 1908.

———. "Islam as a Moral and Political Ideal." In *Speeches, Writings, and Statements of Iqbal*, ed. Latif Ahmad Sherwani, 85–103. Lahore: Iqbal Academy, 1977.

———. *Kulliyyat-i Iqbal* (Urdu). Lahore: Iqbal Academy, 1990.

———. *Makatib-i Iqbal banam-i Khan Niyaz al-din Khan*. Lahore: Iqbal Academy, 1986.

———. *Masnawi-i asrar-i khudi*. Lahore: Union Steam Press, n.d. (1915).

———. "Qadianis and Orthodox Muslims." In *Speeches and Statements of Iqbal*, compiled by "Shamloo," 93–100. Lahore: al-Manar Academy, 1948.

———. *The Reconstruction of Religious Thought in Islam*. London: Oxford University Press, 1934.

———. *Six Lectures on the Reconstruction of Religious Thought in Islam*. Lahore: Kapur Art Printing Works, 1930.

———. *Speeches and Statements of Iqbal*. Compiled by "Shamloo." Lahore: al-Manar Academy, 1948.

———. "Statement on Islam and Nationalism in Reply to a Statement of Maulana Hussain Ahmed Published in 'Ehsan' on the 9th March 1938." In *Speeches and Statements of Iqbal*, compiled by "Shamloo," 223–39. Lahore: al-Manar Academy, 1948.

Iqbal, Nasir. "Justice Khawaja's 23-day Tenure as CJP Begins Tomorrow." *Dawn*, August 16, 2015.

Islahi, Amin Ahsan. *Islami riyasat*. Lahore: Maktaba-i markazi anuman-i khuddam al-Qur'an, 1977.

Islahi, Najm al-din. Ed. *Maktubat-i Shaykh al-Islam*. 4 vols. Deoband: Maktaba-i diniyya, 1963.

Jabri, Mohammed Abed. *Democracy, Human Rights, and Law in Islamic Thought*. London: I. B. Tauris, 2009.

———. *The Formation of Arab Reason: Text, Tradition, and the Construction of Modernity in the Arab World*. London: I. B. Tauris, 2011.

Jaffrelot, Christophe. *The Pakistan Paradox: Instability and Resilience*. Trans. Cynthia Schoch. New York: Oxford University Press, 2015.

Jahangir, Asma. "What the Protection of Women Act Does and What Is Left Undone." In *The Human Rights Commission of Pakistan, State of Human Rights in 2006*, 5–15. Lahore: Human Rights Commission of Pakistan. At www.hrcp-web.org/hrcpDetail_pub3.cfm?proID=374 (accessed September 28, 2008).

Jalal, Ayesha. *Partisans of Allah: Jihad in South Asia*. Cambridge, MA: Harvard University Press, 2008.

———. *Self and Sovereignty: Individual and Community in South Asian Islam since 1850*. London: Routledge, 2000.

———. *The Sole Spokesman: Jinnah, the Muslim League, and the Demand for Pakistan*. Cambridge, UK: Cambridge University Press, 1985.

———. *The State of Martial Rule: The Origins of Pakistan's Political Economy of Defence*. Cambridge, UK: Cambridge University Press, 1990.

Jalal, Ayesha. *The Struggle for Pakistan: A Muslim Homeland and Global Politics*. Cambridge, MA: Harvard University Press, 2014.

Jalalpuri, Sa`id Ahmad. "Kiya Islam mukammal zabita-i hayat nahin?" *Bayyinat* 70/11 (January 2008): 3–14.

[Jama`at-i Islami Pakistan]. *Dustur-i Jama`at-i Islami Pakistan*. Lahore: Markazi maktaba-i Jama`at-i Islami Pakistan, 1952.

———. *al-Mabadi al-asasiyya lil-dawla al-Islamiyya*. Karachi: al-Jama`a al-Islamiyya, n.d.

———. *Rudad-i Jama`at-i Islami*. 7 vols. 7th ed. Lahore: Shu`ba-i nashr o isha`at, Jama`at-i Islami Pakistan, 1989.

Jamaluddin, Syed. "The Barelvis and the Khilafat Movement." In *Communal and Pan-Islamic Trends in Colonial India*, ed. Mushirul Hasan, 400–413. Delhi: Manohar, 1985.

Jan, Abdullah. "Thousands to Enter Afghanistan Today." *News*, October 28, 2001.

Javed, Khadim `Ali. *Ishariyya-i majalla-i Tulu`-i Islam*. Lahore: al-Nur Publishers, 1991.

Jones, Justin. *Shi`a Islam in Colonial India: Religion, Community and Sectarianism*. Cambridge, UK: Cambridge University Press, 2012.

Kamrava, Mehran. Ed. *The New Voices of Islam: Rethinking Politics and Modernity*. Berkeley: University of California Press, 2006.

Karam Shah, Pir Muhammad. *Ziya al-Qur'an*. 5 vols. Lahore: Ziya al-Qur'an Publications, 1978.

Kashmiri, Shorish. "Faiz Ahmad Faiz ke nam." *Nawa-i waqt*. November 14, 1965.

———. *al-Jihad o al-jihad*. Lahore: Matbu`at-i chatan, n.d. (1966).

———. "Mashriqi Pakistan ko salam." *Nawa-i waqt*, October 6, 1965.

Kayani, M. R. *Afkar-i parishan*. Lahore: Pakistan Writers Cooperative Society, 1965.

Kazimi, Sayyid Muhammad Saqalayn. *Imamiyya dini madaris-i Pakistan: Ta'rikh wa ta`aruf*. Lahore: Wifaq al-madaris al-Shi`a Pakistan, 2004.

Kennedy, Charles. *Bureaucracy in Pakistan*. Karachi: Oxford University Press, 1987.

———. *Islamization of Laws and Economy: Case Studies on Pakistan*. Islamabad: Institute of Policy Studies, 1996.

———. "Repugnancy to Islam—Who Decides?" *International and Comparative Law Quarterly* 41 (1992): 769–88.

Kepel, Gilles. *Jihad: The Trail of Political Islam*. Cambridge, MA: Harvard University Press, 2002.

Kerr, Malcolm H. *Islamic Reform: The Political and Legal Theories of Muhammad `Abduh and Rashid Rida*. Berkeley: University of California Press, 1966.

Khan, Anwarullah. "82 Die as Missiles Rain on Bajaur." *Dawn*, October 31, 2006.

Khan, Asad Rahim. "Jawwad S. Khawaja: Poetic Justice." *Herald*, April 2016. At http://herald.dawn.com/news/1153394 (accessed November 6, 2016).

Khan, Iftikhar A. "IS Footprints Eliminated from Pakistan: Army." *Dawn*, September 4, 2016.

Khan, Ismail. "Pakistan Most Terror-hit Nation." *Dawn*, February 23, 2014.

———. "Suicide Attack on Army Base: 40 Troops Dead." *Dawn*, November 9, 2006.

———. "Suicide Blast Hits Pakistan, Killing 22." *New York Times*, December 30, 2015.

———. "Taliban Massacre 131 Schoolchildren." *Dawn*, December 17, 2014.

Khan, Khalil-ur-Rehman. *The Supreme Court's Judgement on Riba*. Islamabad: Shari`ah Academy, 2008.

Khan, Mohammad Ayub. *Friends Not Masters: A Political Autobiography*. New York: Oxford University Press, 1967.

———. *Speeches and Statements by Field Marshal Mohammad Ayub Khan, President of Pakistan*. Vol. 1: October 1958–June 1959. Karachi: Pakistan Publications, n.d. (1959).

Khan, Muhammad Faruq. *Jihad, qital, awr `alam-i Islam*. Lahore: Dar al-tazkir, 2005.

Khan, Muhammad Hussain. "No Barriers to Bhittai." *Dawn*, July 20, 2014.

Khan, Muhammad Zafrulla. *Islam: Its Meaning for Modern Man*. London: Routledge and Kegan Paul, 1962.

Khan, Naveeda. *Muslim Becoming: Aspiration and Skepticism in Pakistan*. Durham, NC: Duke University Press, 2012.

Khan, Sayyid Ahmad (Syed Ahmed Khan). *Khutbat-i Sir Sayyid*. Ed. Muhammad Isma`il Panipati. 2 vols. Lahore: Majlis-i taraqqi-i adab, 1972–73.

———. *Maqalat-i Sir Sayyid*. Ed. Muhammad Isma`il Panipati. Lahore: Majlis-i taraqqi-i adab, 1962–.

———. *A Series of Essays on the Life of Mohammed and Subjects Subsidiary Thereto*. London: Trübner & Co., 1870.

Khan, Sher Ali. "Tahirul Qadri: The Odd Man Out." *Herald*, September 2014. At www.dawn.com/news/1135526 (accessed June 27, 2016).

Khan, Siddiq Hasan. *Fath al-bayan fi maqasid al-Qur'an*. Ed. `Abdallah ibn Ibrahim al-Ansari. 15 vols. Beirut: al-Maktaba al-`asriyya, 1992.

Khan, Yasmin. *The Great Partition: The Making of India and Pakistan*. New Haven, CT: Yale University Press, 2007.

Khatab, Sayed. *The Power of Sovereignty: The Political and Ideological Philosophy of Sayyid Qutb*. London: Routledge, 2006.

Khawaja, Jawwad S. "Farewell Address by Hon'ble the Chief Justice of Pakistan Mr. Justice Jawwad S. Khawaja." At www.supremecourt.gov.pk/web/page.asp?id=2028 (accessed November 6, 2016).

al-Khazin, `Ala al-din `Ali b. Muhammad. *Tafsir al-Khazin, al-musamma Lubab al-ta'wil fi ma `ani al-tanzil*. 7 vols. Cairo: al-Maktaba al-tijariyya al-kubra, 1961.

Kheshgi, Khalid. "RS 300 m Allocated for Madrassa in KP Budget, Assembly Told." *News*, June 17, 2016.

Khomeini, Ruhollah. *Tawzih al-masa'il*. Trans. into Urdu by Safdar Husayn Najafi. Tehran: Sazman-i tablighat-i Islami, 1983.

Khursheed-ul-Hasan. "Fundamental Rights Bill Passed by N.A." *Dawn*, December 25, 1963.

———. "Men's Right of Divorce Restricted." *Dawn*, March 3, 1961.

Khushik, Qurban Ali. "Bloodbath at Sehwan Shrine; Over 75 Perish, 250 Injured." *Dawn*, February 17, 2017.

Kiani, Khaleeq. "Country's Population Surges to Nearly 208m." *Dawn*, August 26, 2017.

Körner, Felix. *Revisionist Koran Hermeneutics in Contemporary Turkish University Theology: Rethinking Islam*. Würzburg: Ergon, 2005.

Laknawi, `Abd al-Shakur. *Baqiyyat-i salihat, tarjama-i Ayat-i bayyinat*. Lahore: Suhayl Academy, 1976.

Lau, Martin. "Pakistan." *Yearbook of Islamic and Middle Eastern Law* 9 (2002): 372–78.

Lelyveld, David. *Aligarh's First Generation: Muslim Solidarity in British India*. Princeton, NJ: Princeton University Press, 1978.

———. "Disenchantment at Aligarh: Islam and the Realm of the Secular in Late Nineteenth Century India." *Die West des Islams* 22 (1982): 85–102.

———. "Young Man Sayyid: Dreams and Biographical Texts." In *Muslim Voices: Community and the Self in South Asia*, ed. Usha Sanyal, David Gilmartin, and Sandria B. Freitag, 253–72. Delhi: Yoda Press, 2013.

Lerner, Daniel. *The Passing of Traditional Society: Modernizing the Middle East*. Glencoe, IL: Free Press, 1958.

Levenson, Michael. "Introduction." In *The Cambridge Companion to Modernism*, 2nd ed., ed. Michael Levenson, 1–8. Cambridge, UK: Cambridge University Press, 2011.

Liebeskind, Claudia. *Piety on Its Knees: Three Sufi Traditions in South Asia in Modern Times*. Delhi: Oxford University Press, 1998.

Ludhianawi, Muhammad Yusuf. `Awrat ki sarbarahi*. 2 parts. Karachi: Maktaba-i bayyinat, n.d.

Madani, Husayn Ahmad. *Mr. Jinnah ka purasrar mu`amma awr uska hall*. Delhi: Jam`iyyat al-`Ulama-i Hind, 1945.

———. *Muttahida qawmiyyat awr Islam*. Delhi: Qawmi ekta trust, n.d. (1972; first published ca. 1938).

———. *An Open Letter to the Moslem League*. Lahore: Dewan Publications, 1946.

Mahmood, M. *The Pakistan Penal Code, 1860, as Amended up to Date*. Lahore: al-Qanoon Publishers, 2009.

Mahmood, Syed Hassan. "Militants Cut Off Hands of Alleged Thieves." *Dawn*, May 6, 2010. At www.dawn.com/news/851951/militants-cut-off-hands-of-alleged-thieves (accessed May 6, 2010).

Maikash, Murtaza Ahmad Khan. *Alburz shikan gurz `urf mirza'i nama*. Lahore: Taj Company, 1938.

———. *Tarikh-i aqwam-i `alam*. 2nd ed. Lahore: Majlis-i taraqqi-i adab, 1958. First published in 1950; subsequent editions published in 1962 and 2012.

———. *Tarikh-i Islam*. 2 vols. 2nd ed. Lahore: Maktaba-i A`la Hazrat, 2006.

Malihabadi, `Abd al-Razzaq. *Azad ki kahani khud Azad ki zabani*. Delhi: I`tiqad Publishing House, 2008.

Malihabadi, Amir `Ali. *Tafsir mawahib al-Rahman*. 30 vols. Lucknow: Nawal Kishore, 1926–31.

Malik, Jamal. *Colonialization of Islam: Dissolution of Traditional Institution in Pakistan*. Delhi: Manohar, 1996.

Malik, Shiza. "For Some a Shrine, for Others a Refuge." *Dawn*, November 30, 2014.

Manan, Abdul. "Auqaf Meets Its Expenses with Income from Shrines." *Daily Times*, August 27, 2007.

Mantena, Karuna. *Alibis of Empire: Henry Maine and the Ends of Liberal Imperialism*. Princeton, NJ: Princeton University Press, 2010.

March, Andrew F. "Genealogies of Sovereignty in Islamic Political Theology." *Social Research* 80 (2013): 293–321.

Mardin, Şerif. *The Genesis of Young Ottoman Thought: A Study in the Modernization of Turkish Political Ideas*. Princeton, NJ: Princeton University Press, 1962.

Marsden, Magnus. *Living Islam: Muslim Religious Experience in Pakistan's North-West Frontier*. Cambridge, UK: Cambridge University Press, 2005.

Mashal, Mujib. "Rugged Afghan Region Lies beyond Reach of Aid and Time." *New York Times*, December 26, 2015.

Masood, Salman. "Video from Taliban Shows the Killing of 16 Pakistanis." *New York Times*, July 16, 2011.

Masud, Muhammad Khalid. *Islamic Legal Philosophy: A Study of Abu Ishaq al-Shatibi's Life and Thought*. Islamabad: Islamic Research Institute, 1977.

———. "Islamic Modernism." In *Islam and Modernity: Key Issues and Debates*, ed. Muhammad Khalid Masud, Armando Salvatore, and Martin van Bruinessen, 237–60. Edinburgh, UK: Edinburgh University Press, 2009.

———. *Muslim Jurists' Quest for the Normative Basis of Shari`a*. Leiden: ISIM Occasional Papers, 2001.

———. "Rethinking Shari`a: Javed Ahmad Ghamidi on Hudud." *Die Welt des Islams* 47 (2007): 356–75.

——. *Shari`a Today: Essays on Contemporary Issues and Debates in Muslim Societies*. Islamabad: National Book Foundation, 2013.

Mawdudi [Maududi], Sayyid Abul-A`la. "Afwaj-i Pakistan ki karawai ke khilaf propaganda ka jawab: Mawlana Mawdudi ka memorandum dunya-i Islam ke nam." *Tarjuman al-Qur'an* 75/4 (June 1971): 9–23.

——. "Aik Islami university ka naqsha." In Sayyidi Abu'l-A`la Mawdudi, *Ta`limat*, 155–65. Lahore: Islamic Publications, 1963.

——. *Aik nihayat ahamm istifta*. Lahore: Maktaba-i Jama`at-i Islami n.d. (ca. 1946).

——. *Dawlat-i Asafiyya awr hukumat-i Britaniyya ke siyasi ta`alluqat ki ta'rikh par aik nazar*. Haydarabad: n.p., 1928.

——. *Islam ka nazariyya-i siyasi*. Lahore: Markazi maktaba-i Jama`at-i Islami, 1955.

——. *The Islamic Law and Constitution*. Trans. Khurshid Ahmad. 2nd ed. Lahore: Islamic Publications, 1960.

——. "Khud niwisht." In *Mawlana Mawdudi apni and dusron ki nazar main*, ed. Muhammad Yusuf Bhutta, 23–39. 2nd ed. Lahore: Idara-i ma`arif-i Islami, 1984.

——. *Musalman awr mawjuda siyasi kashmakash*, 3 vols. Pathankot: Maktaba-i Jama`at-i Islami, n.d.

——. *Qadiyyani mas'ala*. 2nd ed. Lahore: Islamic Publications, 1963.

——. *Qur'an ki char bunyadi istilahen*. Delhi: Markazi maktaba-i Jama`at-i Islami, 1981. First published in 1941.

——. *Tafhim al-Qur'an*. Vol. 2. 2nd ed. Lahore: Maktaba-i ta`mir-i insaniyyat, 1958.

——. *Tafhim al-Qur'an*. 6 vols. Lahore: Idara-i tarjuman al-Qur'an, 2008.

——. *Tafhimat*. 3 vols. Lahore: Islamic Publications, 1965.

——. *Tahrik-i azadi-i Hind awr Musalman*. Vol. 1: Lahore: Islamic Publications, 1964; vol. 2, 2nd ed.: Lahore: Islamic Publications, 1973.

——. *Tahrik-i Islami ka a'inda la'iha-i `amal*. 3rd ed. Lahore: Islamic Publications, 1966.

"Mawjuda buhran—asbab awr `ilaj: Mulki surat-i hal par mulk ke mumtaz `ulama-i kiram ka mushtaraka mawqif." *al-Faruq* 24/4 (May 2008): 5–10.

Mayar, Mohammad Riaz. "26 Killed in Blast outside Nadra Office in Mardan." *News*, December 30, 2015.

Mehsud, Sailab. "Kidnapped Security Personnel Butchered." *Dawn*, June 22, 2012. At www .dawn.com/news/728684/kidnapped-security-personnel-butchered (accessed June 23, 2012).

Mehsud, Sailab, and Pazir Gul. "Ruthless Fazlullah Is New Taliban Chief." *Dawn*, November 8, 2013.

Meier, Fritz. "The Mystic Path." In *The World of Islam*, ed. Bernard Lewis, 117–40. New York: Thames and Hudson, 1976.

Memon, Muhammad Umar. "Pakistani Urdu Creative Writing on National Disintegration: The Case of Bangladesh." *Journal of Asian Studies* 43 (1983): 105–27.

Metcalf, Barbara D. *Husain Ahmad Madani: The Jihad for Islam and India's Freedom*. Oxford, UK: Oneworld, 2009.

——. *Islamic Revival in British India: Deoband, 1860–1900*. Princeton, NJ: Princeton University Press, 1982.

Mihr, Ghulam Rasul. Ed. *Tabarrukat-i Azad*. Hyderabad: `Usmaniyya Book Depot, 1959.

Minault, Gail. *The Khilafat Movement: Religious Symbolism and Political Mobilization in India*. New York: Columbia University Press, 1982.

Mirani, Mansoor. "Thousands Attend Sachal Urs at Daraza Sharif." *Dawn*, July 14, 2014.

Moin, A. Azfar. *The Millennial Sovereign: Sacred Kingship and Sainthood in Islam*. New York: Columbia University Press, 2012.

Moin, A. Azfar. "Sovereign Violence: Temple Destruction in India and Shrine Desecration in Iran and Central Asia." *Comparative Studies in Society and History* 57 (2015): 467–96.

Mookherjee, Nayanika. *The Spectral Wound: Sexual Violence, Public Memories, and the Bangladesh War of 1971*. Durham, NC: Duke University Press, 2015.

Mufti, Aamir R. *Enlightenment in the Colony: The Jewish Question and the Crisis of Postcolonial Culture*. Princeton, NJ: Princeton University Press, 2007.

Muhsin al-Mulk (Mahdi `Ali Khan). *Ayat-i bayyinat*. Karachi: Dar al-isha`at, 1960.

——. *Kitab al-mahabbat wal-shawq*. Agra: Matba-i mufid-i `amm, 1905.

Munib al-Rahman. "Qawmi bayaniyya awr ahl-i madaris." *al-Shari`a* 28/4 (April 2017): 33–38.

Munir, Muhammad. *From Jinnah to Zia*. 2nd ed. Lahore: Vanguard Books, 1980.

Musa, Mohammad. *Jawan to General: Recollections of a Pakistani Soldier*. Karachi: East & West Publishing, 1984.

Musharraf, Pervez. *In the Line of Fire: A Memoir*. New York: Free Press, 2006.

——. "A Plea for Enlightened Moderation." *Washington Post*, June 1, 2004.

Mydans, Seth. "In Pakistan, Rape Victims Are the 'Criminals.'" *New York Times*, May 17, 2002.

——. "Sentenced to Death, Rape Victim Is Freed by Pakistani Court." *New York Times*, June 8, 2002.

Nadwi, Muhammad Hanif. `Aqliyyat-i Ibn Taymiyya*. Lahore: Idara-i saqafat-i Islamiyya, n.d. (1965).

——. *Lisan al-Qur'an*. 2 vols. Lahore: Idara-i saqafat-i Islamiyya, 1983.

——. *Mas'ala-i ijtihad*. Lahore: Idara-i thaqafat-i Islamiyya, 1952.

——. *Mirza'iyyat nae zawiyon se*. Ed. Muhammad Sarwar Tariq. Faisalabad: Tariq Academy, 2003. First published in 1952.

Nadwi, Sayyid Sulayman [Nadvi, Syed Sulaiman]. "Hakim-i haqiqi sirf Allah ta`ala hai." In Sayyid Sulayman Nadwi, *Maqalat-i Sulayman*, 3 vols., ed. Shah Mu`in al-din Nadwi, 3: 366–88. A`zamgarh: Matba`-i ma`arif, 1971.

——. *Hayat-i Shibli*. A`zamgarh: Dar al-musannifin, 1943.

——. *Sovereignty of Allah*. Trans. Syed Abu Asim. Karachi: Maktabat al-sharq, 1953.

Nagamine, Yoshinobu. *The Legitimization Strategy of the Taliban's Code of Conduct: Through the One Way Mirror*. New York: Palgrave Macmillan, 2015.

Naim, C. M. "Parveen Shakir: A Note and Twelve Poems." *Annual of Urdu Studies* 8 (1993): 181–91.

Najafi, Sayyid Safdar Husayn. *Mabadiyyat-i hukumat-i Islami*. Lahore: Imamiyya Publications, 1981.

Najibabadi, Muhammad Siddiq. *Anwar al-mahmud `ala sunan Abi Dawud*, 2 vols. Karachi: Idarat al-Qur'an wa'l-`ulum al-Islamiyya, 1986.

Naqshbandi, Muhammad Aslam. *Halat-i faqir: Sawanih hayat-i mahbub al-`ulama walsulaha hazrat mawlana hafiz pir Zulfiqar Ahmad Naqshbandi Mujaddidi*. Faisalabad: Maktabat al-faqir, 2013.

Naqshbandi, Zulfiqar Ahmad. *Khutbat-i Hind*. Compiled by Khalil al-Rahman Sajjad Nu`mani Naqshbandi. 2 vols. Mamdapur, Maharashtra, n.p., 2011.

——. *Ma`arif al-suluk*. Ed. Mustafa Kamal Naqshbandi. Faisalabad: Maktabat al-faqir, 2012.

Naqvi, Syed Hussain Arif [Sayyid Husayn `Arif Naqwi]. "The Controversy about the Shaikhiyya Tendency among Shia `Ulama in Pakistan" In *The Twelver Shia in Modern Times*, ed. Rainer Brunner and Werner Ende, 135–49. Leiden: Brill, 2001.

——. *Tazkira-i `ulama-i Imamiyya-i Pakistan*. Islamabad: Markaz-i tahqiqat-i Farsi-i Iran wa Pakistan, 1984.

Naqvi, Syed H. M., and Syed Mahmudunnasir. *The Law of Waqfs*. Lahore: All Pakistan Legal Decisions, 1968.

Nasr, Seyyed Vali Reza. *Islamic Leviathan: Islam and the Making of State Power*. New York: Oxford University Press, 2001.

———. *Mawdudi and the Making of Islamic Revivalism*. New York: Oxford University Press, 1996.

———. *The Vanguard of the Islamic Revolution: The Jama`at-i Islami of Pakistan*. Berkeley: University of California Press, 1994.

Nawaz, Shuja. *Crossed Swords: Pakistan, Its Army, and the Wars Within*. Karachi: Oxford University Press, 2008.

Nehru, Jawaharlal. *Selected Works of Jawaharlal Nehru*. 2nd ser. 46 vols. Delhi: Jawaharlal Nehru Memorial Fund, 1984–.

Nelson, Matthew J. "Dealing with Difference: Religious Education and the Challenge of Democracy in Pakistan." *Modern Asian Studies* 43 (2009): 591–618.

Niaz, Anjum. "The Pir in the Palace." *Dawn*, July 14, 2013.

Nicholson, R. A. Trans. *The Secrets of the Self (Asrar-i-Khudi): A Philosophical Poem*. Lahore: Sh. Muhammad Ashraf, 1944.

Nizami, Khwaja Hasan. *Murshid ko sajda-i ta`zim*. 11th ed. Delhi: Khwaja Awlad Kitab Ghar, 1970. First published in 1920.

Noman, Omar. "The Impact of Migration on Pakistan's Economy and Society." In *Economy and Culture in Pakistan: Migrants and Cities in a Muslim Society*, ed. H. Donnan and P. Werbner, 77–96. London: Macmillan, 1991.

Nu`mani, `Asim. *Tasawwuf awr ta`mir-i sirat: Mawlana Mawdudi ki tahriron ki rawshani main*. Lahore: Islamic Publications, 1972.

Nu`mani, Shibli. *Muwazana-i Anis o Dabir*. Lahore: Maktaba-i din o dunya, n.d.

———. *Safarnama-i Rum o Misr o Sham*. Lucknow: Anwar al-matabi`, n.d.

Nur-ud-Din, Abu Sayeed. "Attitude towards Sufism." In *Iqbal: Poet Philosopher of Pakistan*, ed. Hafeez Malik, 287–300. New York: Columbia University Press, 1971.

Pakistan People's Party Manifesto, January 1977. Rawalpindi: Pakistan People's Party Central Secretariat, n.d. (1977).

Panipati, Sana Allah. *Tafsir-i mazhari*. Trans. from Persian into Urdu by Sayyid `Abd al-Da'im al-Jalali. 6 vols. Delhi: Nadwat al-musannifin, 1962.

Paracha, Abdul Sami. "Mother Narrates Zafran's Ordeal." *Dawn*, May 13, 2002.

Parwez, Ghulam Ahmad. *Lughat al-Qur'an*, 4 vols. Lahore: Idara-i tulu`-i Islam, 1960–61.

———. *Pakistan ki na'i 'ziyarat gahen'*. Lahore: Idara-i tulu`-i Islam, n.d. (1966).

———. *Qur'ani qawanin*. Lahore: Idara-i tulu`-i Islam, 1967.

[Parwez, Ghulam Ahmad.] *A'ili qawanin Qur'an-i karim ki rawshani main*. Lahore: Ittihad Printing Press, n.d. (ca. 1962; issued under the auspices of Tulu`-i Islam).

*Parwez key bare main `ulama ka muttafiqa fatwa*. Karachi: Madrasa-i `Arabiyya Islamiyya, n.d. (1962).

Perlez, Jane. "Killing of Pakistan Doctor Part of Taliban War on Educated." *New York Times*, October 9, 2010.

———. "Militants Draw New Front Line inside Pakistan." *New York Times*, November 2, 2007.

Perlez, Jane, and Pir Zubair Shah. "Pakistan Uses Tribal Militias in Tribal War." *New York Times*, October 24, 2008.

———. "Taliban Enlist an Army of Pakistan's Have-nots." *New York Times*, April 17, 2009.

———. "In Violent Karachi, Pakistani Insurgency Finds a Haven and a Forge." *New York Times*, May 22, 2010.

Pernau, Margrit. *Ashraf into Middle Class: Muslims in Nineteenth Century Delhi*. Delhi: Oxford University Press, 2013.

Peters, Rudolph. *Crime and Punishment in Islamic Law.* Cambridge, UK: Cambridge University Press, 2005.

Philippon, Alix. "A Sublime, yet Disputed, Object of Political Ideology? Sufism in Pakistan at the Crossroads." *Commonwealth and Comparative Politics* 52 (2014): 271–92.

Phulwarwi, Shah Muhammad Ja`far. *al-Din yusr.* Idara-i thaqafat-i Islamiyya, 1955.

———. *Izdivaji zindagi ke-liye ahamm qanuni tajawiz.* Lahore: Idara-i thaqafat-i Islamiyya, 1955.

Pickthall, Marmaduke. *The Meaning of the Glorious Koran: An Explanatory Translation.* New York: Alfred A. Knopf, 1930.

Powell, Avril A. *Scottish Orientalists and India: The Muir Brothers, Religion, Education and Empire.* Woodbridge, UK: Boydell Press, 2010.

"Punjab ke dini madaris: Zakat fund se kis ko kitna milta hai?" *Zindagi,* February 17–23, 1995.

Qadiri, Abul-Hasanat Sayyid Muhammad Ahmad. *Awraq-i ghamm.* Lahore: Rizwi kutub-khana, 1972.

Qadiri, Muhammad Amir Shah. *Tazkira-i `ulama o mashayikh-i Sarhad,* vol. 1. Peshawar: `Azim Publishing House, n.d. (1964).

Qadiri, Muhammad Khan, and Muhammad Siddiq Qamar. *Tahrik-i minhaj al-Qur'an awr a'inda qiyadat.* Lahore: Idara-i minhaj al-Qur'an, 1988.

Qasimi, Muhammad `Abd al-Halim. Ed. *Ashraf al-malfuzat.* Lahore: Wifaq Press, n.d. (1976).

Qasmi, Ali Usman. *The Ahmadis and the Politics of Religious Exclusion in Pakistan.* London: Anthem Press, 2014.

———. *Questioning the Authority of the Past: The Ahl al-Qur'an Movements in the Punjab.* Karachi: Oxford University Press, 2011.

Qudsiyya, Bano. *Raja gidh.* Lahore: Sang-i mil publications, 1981.

Qur'an-i majid mutarjam bil-tarajim al-thalath. Delhi: al-Matba` al-Mujtaba'i, 1872.

Qurayshi, Muhammad `Abdallah. Ed. *Ruh-i makatib-i Iqbal.* Lahore: Iqbal Academy, 1977.

Qureshi, M. Naeem. *Pan-Islam in British Indian Politics: A Study of the Khilafat Movement, 1918–1924.* Leiden: Brill, 1999.

al-Qurtubi, Abu `Abdallah Muhammad b. Ahmad. *Al-Jami` li-ahkam al-Qur'an.* 20 vols. Cairo: Dar al-katib al-`arabi lil-tiba`a wa'l-nashr, 1967.

Qutb, Sayyid. *Fi zilal al-Qur'an,* 6 vols. Beirut: Dar al-shuruq, 1974.

Rabb, Intisar A. *Doubt in Islamic Law.* Cambridge, UK: Cambridge University Press, 2015.

Rahman, Azizur (Rahman, `Aziz al-) *Introducing Darul `Uloom Karachi.* Trans. Muhammad Shameem. Karachi: Public Information Department, Darul `Uloom Karachi, n.d.

———. "Qanun-i tahaffuz-i namus-i risalat awr masihiyon ka na-rawa tarz-i `amal." *al-Balagh* 33/2 (June 1998): 3–9.

Rahman, Fazlur. "The Concept of Hadd in Islamic Law." *Islamic Studies* 4 (1965): 237–51.

———. "Concepts Sunnah, Ijtihad and Ijma` in the Early Period." *Islamic Studies* 1 (1962): 5–21.

———. "Divine Revelation and the Prophet." *Dawn,* August 25, 1968.

———. "Implementation of the Islamic Concept of State in the Pakistani Milieu." *Islamic Studies* 6 (1967): 205–23.

———. *Islam.* 2nd ed. Chicago: University of Chicago Press, 1979.

———. *Islamic Methodology in History.* Karachi: Central Institute of Islamic Research, 1965.

———. *Major Themes of the Qur'an.* Minneapolis: Bibleotheca Islamica, 1980.

———. *Prophecy in Islam: Philosophy and Orthodoxy.* London: George Allen & Unwin, 1958.

———. "The Qur'anic Concept of God, the Universe and Man." *Islamic Studies* 6 (1967): 1–19.

———. "Qur'an-i majid." Trans. Muhammad Sarwar. *Fikr o nazar* 5/4 (1967): 249–68.

———. "Religion and Planned Parenthood in Pakistan." In *Muslim Attitudes toward Family Planning*, ed. Olivia Schieffelin, 94–97. New York: Population Council, 1967.

———. "Riba and Interest." *Islamic Studies* 3 (1964): 1–43.

———. "Some Islamic Issues in the Ayyub Khan Era." In *Essays on Islamic Civilization Presented to Niyazi Berkes*, ed. Donald P. Little, 284–302. Leiden: E. J. Brill, 1976.

———. "Some Reflections on the Reconstruction of Muslim Society in Pakistan." *Islamic Studies* 6 (1967): 103–20.

Ram, Malik. Ed. *Khutbat-i Azad*. Delhi: Sahitiya Academy, 1974.

Ram, Moti. Ed. *Two Historic Trials in the Red Fort*. Delhi: n.p., n.d. (1946).

Rana, Muhammad ʾAmir. "Dilemma of Barelvi Politics." *Dawn*, August 24, 2014.

———. *Jihad awr jihadi: Pakistan awr Kashmir ke ahamm jihadi rahnumaon ka taʾaruf*. Lahore: Mashʾal Books, 2003.

———. *Jihad-i Kashmir o Afghanistan: Jihadi tanzimon awr mazhabi jamaʾaton ka aik jaʾiza*. Lahore: Mashʾal Books, 2002.

Rashid, Ahmed. *Taliban: Militant Islam, Oil, and Fundamentalism in Central Asia*. New Haven, CT: Yale University Press, 2000.

Raza, Syed Irfan. "Lal Masjid Threatens Suicide Attacks." *Dawn*, April 7, 2007.

al-Razi, Fakhr al-din. *al-Tafsir al-kabir*. 32 vols. Tehran, n.p., n.d.

Rehman, Ziaur. "A Pakistani Scholar Accused of Blasphemy Is Shot Dead." *New York Times*, September 18, 2014.

Report of the Hamoodur Rehman Commission of Inquiry into the 1971 War (as Declassified by the Government of Pakistan). Lahore: Vanguard, 2000.

Richardson, John. *A Dictionary of Persian, Arabic and English*. London: William Bulmer, 1806.

———. *A Dictionary of Persian, Arabic and English*. London: Parbury, Allen & Co., 1829.

Rida, Muhammad Rashid. "al-Khutba al-raʾisiyya fi Nadwat al-ʾulama li-sahib *al-Manar*." *al-Manar* 15 (1912): 331–41.

———. "Muqaddimat al-kitab." In A. J. Wensinck, *Miftah kunuz al-sunna*, trans. Muhammad Fuʾad ʾAbd al-Baqi. Lahore: Suhayl Academy, 1987. First published Cairo: Matbaʾat Misr, 1934.

———. *Tafsir al-Qurʾan al-hakim, al-shahir bi-Tafsir al-manar*. 12 vols. 3rd ed. Cairo: Dar al-manar, 1947–54.

Rieck, Andreas. *The Shias of Pakistan: An Assertive and Beleaguered Minority*. New York: Oxford University Press, 2015.

———. "The Struggle for Equal Rights as a Minority: Shia Communal Organizations in Pakistan, 1948–1968." In *The Twelver Shia in Modern Times*, ed. Rainer Brunner and Werner Ende, 268–83. Leiden: Brill, 2001.

Rizwi, Sayyid Mahbub. *Taʾrikh-i Dar al-ʾUlum Deoband*. 2 vols. Deoband: Idara-i ihtimam-i Dar al-ʾUlum Deoband, 1977–78.

Robinson, Cabeiri deBergh. *Body of Victim, Body of Warrior: Refugee Families and the Making of Kashmiri Jihadists*. Berkeley: University of California Press, 2013.

Robinson, Francis. *The ʾUlama of Farangi Mahall and Islamic Culture in South Asia*. London: Hurst & Company, 2001.

Rozehnal, Robert. *Islamic Sufism Unbound: Politics and Piety in Twenty-first Century Pakistan*. New York: Palgrave Macmillan, 2007.

Rumi, Jalal al-din. *Masnawi-i maʾnawi*. Ed. Tawfiq Subhani. Tehran: Wizarat-i farhang wa irshad-i Islami, 1995.

Rutherford, Bruce K. *Egypt after Mubarak: Liberalism, Islam, and Democracy in the Arab World.* Princeton, NJ: Princeton University Press, 2008.

Sadri, Mahmoud, and Ahmad Sadri. Eds. and trans. *Reason, Freedom, and Democracy in Islam: The Essential Writings of Abdolkarim Soroush.* New York: Oxford University Press, 2000.

Saeed, Sadia. *Politics of Desecularization: Law and the Minority Question in Pakistan.* Cambridge, UK: Cambridge University Press, 2016.

Sa`id, Hafiz Muhammad. *Khutbat-i Qadisiyya.* Lahore: Dar al-Andalus, n.d. (2014).

———. *Khutbat-i Qadisiyya: Fitna-i takfir—asbab, nuqsanat, awr us se bachao ke tariqe.* Lahore: Dar al-Andalus, n.d. (2015).

———. *Tafsir surat al-tawba.* Compiled by `Ubayd al-Rahman Muhammadi. Lahore: Dar al-Andalus, n.d. (2006).

———. *Tafsir surat Yusuf.* Compiled by Hafiz Muhammad Siraj. Lahore: Dar al-Andalus, n.d. (2009).

Sajjad, Abul-Mahasin. *Hukumat-i Ilahiyya.* Ed. Mujahid al-Islam Qasimi. Phulwari Sharif: Imarat-i shar`iyya Bihar o Orissa, 1999.

Salik, Siddiq. *Witness to Surrender.* Karachi: Oxford University Press, 1977.

Samdani, K.M.A. *Reminiscence.* N.p., n.d. (ca. 2005).

Sandelawi, Muhammad Ishaq. *Islam ka siyasi nizam.* A`zamgarh: Matba`-i Ma`arif, 1957.

Sanyal, Usha. *Devotional Islam and Politics in British India: Ahmad Riza Khan Barelwi and His Movement, 1870–1920.* Delhi: Oxford University Press, 1996.

Sarwar, Muhammad. *Jama`at-i Islami awr Islami dustur.* Lahore: Sind Sagar, 1956.

*Sawad-i a`zam ke mulki wa milli huquq ke tahaffuz ke-li'e ahamm Sunni mutalabat.* Lahore: Khuddam-i Ahl-i Sunnat wal Jama`at, n.d. (1973). Microfiche. New Delhi: Library of Congress Office, 1995.

Sayyid [Syed], G. M. *Jaysa main ne dekha.* Karachi: Idara-i furugh-i insaniyyat, 1972.

———. *Religion and Reality.* Lahore: Fiction House, 2012.

Schacht, Joseph. *An Introduction to Islamic Law.* Oxford: Clarendon Press, 1964.

———. *The Origins of Muhammadan Jurisprudence.* Oxford: Clarendon Press, 1950.

Schendel, Willem van. *A History of Bangladesh.* Cambridge, UK: Cambridge University Press, 2009.

Schielke, Samuli. *The Perils of Joy: Contesting Mulid Festivals in Contemporary Egypt.* Syracuse, NY: Syracuse University Press, 2012.

Scott, James C. *Seeing Like a State.* New Haven, CT: Yale University Press, 1998.

Sedgwick, Mark. *Against the Modern World: Traditionalism and the Secret Intellectual History of the Twentieth Century.* New York: Oxford University Press, 2004.

Seesemann, Rüdiger. *The Divine Flood: Ibrahim Niasse and the Roots of a Twentieth-century Sufi Revival.* New York: Oxford University Press, 2011.

Sengupta, Somini, and Salman Masood. "Blast Kills 19 at Pakistani Shrine during Muslim Festival." *New York Times,* May 28, 2005.

Seoharwi, Hifz al-Rahman. *Islam ka iqtisadi nizam.* Delhi: Nadwat al-musannifin, 1942.

———. *Islam ka iqtisadi nizam.* Lahore: Mushtaq Book Corner, n.d. (2006).

———. "Muqaddima." In Abul Mahasin Sajjad, *Hukumat-i Ilahiyya,* ed. Mujahid al-Islam Qasimi, 17–32. Phulwari Sharif: Imarat-i shar`iyya Bihar o Orissa, 1999.

Shafi`, Muhammad Mufti. "`A'ili qanun par mukhtasar tabsira." *Bayyinat* 1/6–7 (March–April 1963): 9–48.

———. *Dustur-i Qur'ani.* Karachi: Dar al-`Ulum, 1953.

———. *Ma`arif al-Qur'an.* 8 vols. Karachi: Idarat al-ma`arif, 1969–73.

——. *Ma`ariful Qur'an.* 8 vols. Trans. into English by Muhammad Hasan Askari, Muhammad Shamim, Muhammad Wali Raazi, Ahmed Khalil Aziz, and Muhammad Ishrat Husain. Karachi: Maktaba-i Dar al-`Ulum, 1996–2005.

——. *Mazarat-i awliya Allah par `urs ki shar`i haysiyyat.* In Mufti Muhammad Shafi`, *Sunnat o bid`at,* 73–88. Karachi: Idarat al-ma`arif, n.d. (1963).

——. *Mere walid-i majid awr unke mujarrab `amaliyyat.* Karachi: Dar al-isha`at, 1975.

Shah, Aqil. *The Army and Democracy: Military Politics in Pakistan.* Cambridge, MA: Harvard University Press, 2014.

Shah, Waseem Ahmad. "Zafran Case Sent to Shariat Court." *Dawn,* May 8, 2002.

Shahab, Qudrat Allah. *Shahab nama.* Lahore: Sang-i mil Publications, 1987.

Shahid, Saleem. "Frequent Flyer 'Mansour' Used Pakistan Airports." *Dawn,* May 24, 2016.

Shahid, Saleem, and Abdul Wahid Shahwani. "52 Killed in Suicide Attack on Balochistan Shrine." *Dawn,* November 13, 2016.

Shahjahanpuri, Abu Salman. *Mawlana Ihtisham al-Haqq Thanawi ki ap biti.* Karachi: Mawlana Ihtisham al-Haqq Thanawi Academy, 1993.

Shahzad, Asif. "Over 250,000 Students in Punjab Seminaries." *Dawn,* January 22, 2002.

Shahzad, Ghafir. *Data Darbar Complex: Ta`mir se takmil tak.* Lahore: Idrak Publications, 2004.

Shakir, Parvin. *Kaf-i a'ina.* Islamabad: Murad Publications, n.d.

——. *Mah-i tamam: Kulliyyat.* Delhi: Educational Publishing House, 1995.

Shami, Pervez A., and Imtiaz Khan. *Report on Deeni Madaris of Pakistan: Base-line Information, 2003-2004 and 2004-2005.* Islamabad: Academy of Education Planning and Management, Ministry of Education, Government of Pakistan, 2006.

al-Shatibi, Abu Ishaq. *al-Muwafaqat fi usul al-shari`a.* 4 vols. Ed. `Abdallah Daraz. Cairo: al-Matba`a al-Rahmaniyya, n.d.

al-Shawkani, Muhammad b. `Ali. *Irshad al-fuhul ila tahqiq al-haqq min `ilm al-usul.* Cairo: Muhammad `Ali Subayh, 1930.

Shepard, William E. *Sayyid Qutb and Islamic Activism: A Translation and Critical Analysis of Social Justice in Islam.* Leiden: E. J. Brill, 1996.

Sherkoti, Anwar al-Hasan. Ed. *Anwar-i `Usmani.* Karachi: Maktaba-i Islamiyya, n.d. (1967).

——. *Khutbat-i `Usmani.* Lahore: Nazar Sons, 1972.

Sherwani, Latif Ahmad. Ed. *Speeches, Writings, and Statements of Iqbal.* Lahore: Iqbal Academy, 1977.

Shinwari, Ibrahim. "Shrine Blown Up in Khyber." *Dawn,* July 16, 2010.

——. "Woman and Three Men Publicly Executed." *Dawn,* June 5, 2007.

Siddiqa, Ayesha. *Military Inc.: Inside Pakistan's Military Economy.* London: Pluto Press, 2007.

——. "Tahir-ul-Qadri: Revolutionary or Stooge?" *Newsline,* July 2014. At http://newslinemagazine.com/magazine/tahir-ul-qadri-revolutionary-or-stooge (accessed June 22, 2016).

Siddiqi, A. R. *The Military in Pakistan: Image and Reality.* Lahore: Vanguard, 1996.

Siddique, Osama. *Pakistan's Experience with Formal Law: An Alien Justice.* Cambridge, UK: Cambridge University Press, 2013.

Simpson, Emile. *War from the Ground Up: Twenty-first Century Combat as Politics.* New York: Columbia University Press, 2012.

Skeet, Ian. *OPEC: Twenty-Five Years of Prices and Politics.* Cambridge, UK: Cambridge University Press, 1988.

Skinner, Quentin. "The Sovereign State: A Genealogy." In *Sovereignty in Fragments: The Past, Present and Future of a Contested Concept,* ed. Hent Kalmo and Quentin Skinner, 26–46. Cambridge, UK: Cambridge University Press, 2010.

Smith, David C. *H. G. Wells: Desperately Mortal*. New Haven, CT: Yale University Press, 1986.

Smith, Wilfred Cantwell. *Islam in Modern History*. Princeton, NJ: Princeton University Press, 1957.

———. *Modern Islam in India: A Social Analysis*. London: Victor Gollancz, 1946.

———. *Pakistan as an Islamic State: Preliminary Draft*. Lahore: Shaikh Muhammad Ashraf, 1951.

Soroush, Abdolkarim. *The Expansion of Prophetic Experience*. Trans. Nilou Mobasser. Ed. Forough Jahanbakhsh. Leiden: Brill, 2009.

Status of Labour Rights in Pakistan: The Year 2014. Karachi: Pakistan Institute of Labour Education and Research, 2015.

Suavi, Ali. "al-Hakim huwa Allah." *Ulum Gazetesi* Rebiülahir 1286/August 1, 1869: 18–31.

Syed, Baqir Sajjad. "Miliband's Visit Seen as Bid to Back Moderates." *Dawn*, July 10, 2009.

al-Tabari, Abu Ja`far Muhammad b. Jarir. *Jami` al-bayan `an ta'wil ay al-Qur'an*. 30 vols. Cairo: Matba`at Mustafa al-Babi al-Halabi, 1954.

al-Tahanawi, Muhammad A`la ibn `Ali. *Mawsu`at istilahat al-`ulum al-Islamiyya*. 6 vols. Beirut: Khayyat, 1966.

Tahir al-Qadiri, Muhammad. *Dahshat gardi awr fitna-i Khawarij*. Lahore: Minhaj al-Qur'an Publications, 2010.

———. *Dala'il al-barakat fil-tahiyyat wal-salawat*. Trans. Zuhur Allah al-Azhari. Lahore: Minhaj al-Qur'an Publications, 2009.

———. *Fatwa on Terrorism and Suicide Bombing*. Lahore: Minhaj-ul-Quran International, 2010.

———. *al-Minhaj al-sawiyy min al-hadith al-nabawiyy*. 13th printing. Lahore: Minhaj al-Qur'an Publications, 2008. First published in 2005.

"Taqrir ba`that al-Hind." *Majallat al-Azhar* 8/4–10 (1937): 302–11, 375–81, 444–51, 520–27, 586–98, 659–70, 732–42; 9/1 (1938): 60–70.

Teepu, Imran Ali. "PM into Spiritual Healers." *Dawn*, September 19, 2012.

Thackston, Wheeler M. Trans. *The Baburnama: Memoirs of Babur, Prince and Emperor*. New York: Modern Library, 2002.

Thadani, R. V. Ed. *The Historic State Trial of the Ali Brothers and Five Others*. Karachi: R. V. Thadani, 1921.

Thanawi, Ashraf `Ali. *Ahkam-i talaq wa nizam-i shar`i `adalat, ya`ni al-hila al-najiza-i jadid*, ed. Khurshid Hasan Qasimi. Lahore: al-Faysal, 1996.

———. *al-Ifadat al-yawmiyya min al-ifadat al-qawmiyya*. 10 vols. Lahore: Idara-i ta'lifat-i Ashrafiyya, 1984–46.

———. *Imdad al-fatawa*. Ed. Mufti Muhammad Shafi`. 6 vols. Karachi: Maktaba-i Dar al-`Ulum, 2004.

———. *Imdad al-mushtaq*. Delhi: Maktaba-i Burhan, 1981.

———. *`Irfan-i Hafiz: Hafiz-i Shirazi ke mashhur wa maqbul Farsi diwan ki sufiyana wa `arifana Urdu sharh*. Karachi: Nafis Academy, 1976.

———. *Kelid-i masnawi*. 24 vols. Multan: Idara-i ta'lifat-i ashrafiyya, 2005.

———. *Tabwib-i tarbiyat al-salik*. 2 vols. 2nd ed. Thana Bhawan: Maktaba-i ta'lifat-i Ashrafiyya, n.d.

Thanawi, Ihtisham al-Haqq. [Thanvi, Ihtisham-ul-Haq]. "Shadi commission ki report ka ikhtilafi note." *Gazette of Pakistan (Extraordinary)*, August 30, 1956: 1505–1604.

Troll, Christian W. *Sayyid Ahmad Khan: A Reinterpretation of Muslim Theology*. Delhi: Vikas Publishing House, 1978.

al-Tunisi, Khayr al-din. *Aqwam al-masalik fi ma`rifat ahwal al-mamalik*. Tunis: Matba`at al-dawla, 1867.

Turnaoğlu, Banu. *The Formation of Turkish Republicanism*. Princeton, NJ: Princeton University Press, 2017.

`Usmani, Muhammad `Imran Ashraf. *Shirkat wa muzarabat `asr-i hazir men*. Karachi: Idarat al-ma`arif, 2001.

`Usmani, Muhammad Rafi`. *Hayat-i mufti-i a`zam*. Karachi: Idarat al-ma`arif, 1994.

———. "Lal masjid intizamiyya awr hukumat ke darmiyan mudhakarat kiyun nakam huwe?" *al-Balagh* 42/7 (August 2007): 3–14.

`Usmani, Muhammad Taqi. *Amendments in Hudood Laws: The Protection of Women's Rights Bill—An Appraisal*. Islamabad: Institute of Policy Studies, 2006.

———. *Fatawa-i `Usmani*. Ed. Muhammad Zubayr Haqq Nawaz. 3 vols. Karachi: Maktaba-i ma`arif al-Qur'an, 2006–12.

———. *Hindustan ka taza safar*. Deoband: Dar al-kitab, 2010.

———. *Hudud qawanin main tarmim: Tahaffuz-i huquq-i niswan bill kiya hai? Aik mutala`a*. Islamabad: Institute of Policy Studies, 2006.

———. *Hudud qawanin: Mawjuda bahth awr a'inda la'iha-i `amal*. Islamabad: Institute of Policy Studies, 2006.

———. *Islam awr hamari zindagi*. 10 vols. Lahore: Idara-i Islamiyyat, 2010.

———. *Islam awr siyasi nazariyyat*. Karachi: Maktaba-i ma`arif, 2010.

———. *Khutbat-i dawra-i Hind*. Ed. Sa`adat Allah Khan Qasimi. Karachi: Maktaba-i ma`arif al-Qur'an, 2012.

———. "Making Pakistan Safe for Rapists." At www.albalagh.net/women/0096.shtml (accessed October 29, 2007).

———. *Nifaz-i shari`at awr us-ke masa'il*. Karachi: Maktaba-i Dar al-`Ulum, 1992.

———. "The Real Contents." *Dawn*, December 24, 2006.

———. "The Reality of 'Women Protection Bills.'" At www.hudoodordinance.com (accessed October 29, 2007).

———. "Qadiyyani—ghayr Muslim kiyon?" *al-Balagh* 7/5 (July 1973): 3–11.

———. *The Text of the Historic Judgment on Riba (Interest), Given by the Supreme Court of Pakistan, 23rd December 1999 ... Section Written by Maulana Justice Muhammad Taqi Usmani*. Petaling Jaya: Other Press, 2001.

`Usmani, Muhammad Zubayr Ashraf. *Jadid ma`ashi nizam men Islami qanun-i ijara*. Karachi: Idarat al-ma`arif, 2005.

`Usmani, Shabbir Ahmad. *Hamara Pakistan*. Hyderabad (Deccan): Nafis Academy, n.d. (1946).

———. *al-Shahab, ya`ni Mirza'iyyon ke irtidad ka thubut awr qatl-i murtadd ke shar`i dala'il*. Karachi: Dar al-isha`at, 1974.

———. *Tafsir-i `Usmani*, 2 vols. Lahore: Maktaba-i Rahmaniyya, n.d.

———. "Tashrih-i waqi`a-i Deoband: `Ata-i i`zaz ki haqiqat." *al-Qasim* 6/2 (August 1915): 1–17.

Verkaaik, Oskar. *Migrants and Militants: Fun and Urban Violence in Pakistan*. Princeton, NJ: Princeton University Press, 2004.

———. "Reforming Mysticism: Sindhi Separatist Intellectuals in Pakistan." In *Islam and Society in Pakistan: Anthropological Perspectives*, ed. Magnus Marsden, 111–31. Karachi: Oxford University Press, 2010.

Walbridge, Linda S. *The Christians of Pakistan: The Passion of Bishop John Joseph*. London: RoutledgeCurzon, 2003.

Wali Allah, Shah. *Hujjat Allah al-baligha*. 2 vols. Cairo: Dar al-turath, 1936.

———. *al-Tafhimat al-Ilahiyya*. Ed. Ghulam Mustafa al-Qasimi. 2 vols. Hyderabad: Shah Wali Allah Academy, 1967–70.

Walsh, Declan. "In Conservative Pakistani City, a 'Saudi Girl' Who Stood Out." *New York Times*, December 7, 2015.

Walsh, Declan. "Islamic Scholar Attacks Pakistan's Blasphemy Laws." *Guardian*, January 20, 2011.

———. "Taliban Gun Down a Girl Who Spoke Up for Rights." *New York Times*, October 10, 2012.

———. "Two Champions of Children Are Given Nobel Peace Prize." *New York Times*, October 11, 2014.

Warisi, Fazl Husayn Siddiqi. *Mishkat-i haqqaniyya*. Karachi: H. M. Sa`id, 1982.

Waseem, Mohammad. *Politics and the State in Pakistan*. Islamabad: National Institute of Historical and Cultural Research, 1994.

Wasim, Amir. "Zardari Questions Allocation for Haqqania Seminary." *Dawn*, June 27, 2016.

Wazirabadi, Fazl-i Ilahi. *Jihad-i Kashmir: Farziyyat, fazilat awr ta'rikh*. With a preface by Hafiz Muhammad Sa`id. Lahore: Dar al-Andalus, 2004.

———. *Mas'ala-i jihad-i Kashmir awr uski mukhtasar ta'rikh*. Rawalpindi: Tanzim al-da`wa ilal-Qur'an wal-sunna, 1997.

Weiss, Bernard. *The Spirit of Islamic Law*. Athens: University of Georgia Press, 1998.

Wells, H. G. *God the Invisible King*. New York: Macmillan, 1917.

———. *Mr. Britling Sees It Through*. New York: Macmillan, 1916.

al-Ya`qubi, Ahmad b. Abi Ya`qub. *Ta'rikh*. Ed. M. T. Houtsma. 2 vols. Leiden: Brill, 1883.

Yusufzai, Ashfaq. "Wafaqul Madaris VP Shot Dead." *Dawn*, September 16, 2007.

Yusufzai, Rahimullah. "A Swati Boy Who Became Mufti." *News*, May 31, 2004.

———. "Taliban Enforce Islamic Justice." *News*, March 1, 1996.

Zahid, Mufti Muhammad. "Mawjuda pur-tashaddud tahriken awr Deobandi fikr wa mizaj." *al-Shari`a* 20/11–12 (November–December 2009): 67–79.

Zahid al-Rashidi, Abu `Ammar. "Dini madaris ke nisab o nizam main islah ki zarurat." *al-Shari`a* 22/1 (January 2013): 2–9.

———. "Mawjuda surat-i hal awr Afghan Taliban ka mawqif." *al-Shari`a* 25/2 (February 2014): 2–5.

Zahid al-Rashidi, Abu `Ammar, Mu`izz Amjad, Khurshid Nadim, and Faruq Khan. *Janab Javed Ahmad Ghamidi ke halqa-i fikr ke sath aik `ilmi awr fikri mukalama*. Gujranwala: al-Shari`a Academy, 2007.

Zaman, Muhammad Qasim. *Ashraf `Ali Thanawi: Islam in Modern South Asia*. Oxford, UK: Oneworld Publications, 2008.

———. *Modern Islamic Thought in a Radical Age: Religious Authority and Internal Criticism*. Cambridge, UK: Cambridge University Press, 2012.

———. "Pakistan: Shari`a and the State." In *Shari`a Politics: Islamic Law and Society in the Modern World*, ed. Robert W. Hefner, 207–43. Bloomington: Indiana University Press, 2011.

———. "Pluralism, Democracy, and the `Ulama." In *Remaking Muslim Politics*, ed. Robert W. Hefner, 60–86. Princeton, NJ: Princeton University Press, 2005.

———. "Religious Discourse and the Public Sphere in Contemporary Pakistan." *Revue des mondes musulmans et de la Mediterranee* 123 (2008): 55–73.

———. "South Asian Islam and the Idea of the Caliphate." In *Demystifying the Caliphate: Historical Memory and Contemporary Contexts*, ed. Madawi al-Rasheed, Carool Kersten, and Marat Shterin, 57–79. London: Hurst, 2013.

———. *The Ulama in Contemporary Islam: Custodians of Change*. Princeton, NJ: Princeton University Press, 2002.

Zamindar, Vazira F. *The Long Partition and the Making of South Asia: Refugees, Boundaries, Histories*. New York: Columbia University Press, 2007.

Ziya, Sultan Mahmud. "A'ina-i kirdar." In Muhammad Mas`ud Azhar, *Khutbat-i jihad*, ed. Sultan Mahmud Ziya, 1: 7–15.

Zollner, Barbara. *The Muslim Brotherhood: Hasan al-Hudaybi and Ideology.* London: Routledge, 2009.

Zubayri, Muhammad Amin. *Hayat-i Muhsin.* Aligarh: Muslim University Press, 1934.

Newspapers and Magazines Cited

al-Balagh (Karachi)

Bayyinat (Karachi)

Civil and Military Gazette (Lahore)

Daily Times (Lahore)

Dawn (Karachi)

Express (Lahore)

Express Tribune (Islamabad)

Fikr o nazar (Karachi and Islamabad)

Imroz (Lahore)

Jang (Karachi)

al-Manar (Cairo)

Nawa-i waqt (Lahore)

News (Islamabad)

New Times (Rawalpindi)

New York Times (New York)

al-Qasim (Deoband)

Rizakar (Lahore)

Saqafat (Lahore)

al-Shari`a (Gujranwala)

Tarjuman al-Qur'an (Lahore)

Times of India (Delhi)

Washington Post (Washington, DC)

Zamindar (Lahore)

Zindagi (Lahore)

Unpublished Theses and Dissertations

Abbas, Megan Brankley. "Knowing Islam: The Entangled History of Western Academia and Modern Islamic Thought." PhD dissertation, Department of History, Princeton University, 2015.

Ahmed, Manzooruddin. "The Concept of Divine Sovereignty in Pakistan." PhD dissertation, Department of Political Science, Columbia University, 1960.

Fuchs, Simon Wolfgang. "Relocating the Centers of Shi`i Islam: Religious Authority, Sectarianism, and the Limits of the Transnational in Colonial India and Pakistan." PhD dissertation, Department of Near Eastern Studies, Princeton University, 2015.

Khan, Imran Hameed. "A Room of Her Own: Romance, Resistance, and Feminist Thought in Modern Urdu Poetry." PhD dissertation, Department of Asian Studies, University of Texas, Austin, 2015.

Khan, Tabinda M. "Institutions not Intentions: Rethinking Islamist Participation in Muslim Democracies." PhD dissertation, Department of Political Science, Columbia University, 2014.

Mushtaq, Faiza. "New Claimants to Religious Authority: A Movement for Women's Islamic Education, Moral Reform and Innovative Traditionalism." PhD dissertation, Department of Sociology, Northwestern University, 2010.

Nurbain, Nawir Yuslem. "Ibn Qayyim's Reformulation of the Fatwa." MA thesis, Institute of Islamic Studies, McGill University, 1995.

Tahir-ul-Qadri, Muhammad. "Punishments in Islam: Their Classification and Philosophy." PhD dissertation, University of the Punjab, Lahore, 1984. At http://eprints.hec.gov.pk /1475/1/1359.htm (accessed June 22, 2016).

Electronic Resources

www.aepam.edu.pk

www.albalagh.net

http://archive.org/details/1974-na-committee-ahmadiyya

www.census.gov.pk

http://cii.gov.pk

www.dawn.com

Endangered Urdu Periodicals: Preservation and Access for Vulnerable Scholarly Resources, British Library: EAP566; at http://eap.bl.uk/database/results.a4d ?projID=EAP566;r=18467

http://eprints.hec.gov.pk

Foreign Office Files for India, Pakistan, and Afghanistan, National Archives, UK (Electronic Resource); at www.archivesdirect.amdigital.co.uk/Introduction/FO _India/default.aspx

  DO 134/32: Correspondence between Rawalpindi, Lahore, Karachi, Dacca on Pakistan General Politics, 1966–67

  DO 134/34: Correspondence between Rawalpindi, Lahore, Karachi, Dacca on Pakistan General Politics, 1967–68

  FCO 37/182: Internal Political Affairs in West Pakistan, 1967–1968

  FCO 37/681: Political Parties in Pakistan

  FCO 37/1338: Internal Situation in Pakistan, 1973

  FCO 37/2188: Internal Political Situation in Pakistan, 1979

http://herald.dawn.com

www.hudoodordinance.com

http://kfip.org

http://libwebprod.princeton.edu

www.minhaj.org

http://nacta.gov.pk

http://newslinemagazine.com

www.pakistani.org

www.pbs.gov.pk

www.sunday-guardian.com

www.supremecourt.gov.pk

PRINCETON STUDIES IN MUSLIM POLITICS

A NOTE ON THE TYPE

{⁓⁓⁓⁓}

THIS BOOK has been composed in Miller, a Scotch Roman typeface designed by Matthew Carter and first released by Font Bureau in 1997. It resembles Monticello, the typeface developed for The Papers of Thomas Jefferson in the 1940s by C. H. Griffith and P. J. Conkwright and reinterpreted in digital form by Carter in 2003.

Pleasant Jefferson ("P. J.") Conkwright (1905–1986) was Typographer at Princeton University Press from 1939 to 1970. He was an acclaimed book designer and AIGA Medalist.

The ornament used throughout this book was designed by Pierre Simon Fournier (1712–1768) and was a favorite of Conkwright's, used in his design of the *Princeton University Library Chronicle.*